The OPTIMIST CREED

JEREMY P. TARCHER/PENGUIN
a member of Penguin Group (USA) Inc.
New York

The
OPTIMIST
CREED

CHRISTIAN D. LARSON

JEREMY P. TARCHER/PENGUIN
Published by the Penguin Group
Penguin Group (USA) Inc., 375 Hudson Street, New York,
New York 10014, USA ° Penguin Group (Canada), 90 Eglinton
Avenue East, Suite 700, Toronto, Ontario M4P 2Y3, Canada (a division of
Pearson Penguin Canada Inc.) ° Penguin Books Ltd, 80 Strand, London WC2R 0RL,
England ° Penguin Ireland, 25 St Stephen's Green, Dublin 2, Ireland (a division of
Penguin Books Ltd) ° Penguin Group (Australia), 250 Camberwell Road, Camberwell,
Victoria 3124, Australia (a division of Pearson Australia Group Pty Ltd) ° Penguin Books
India Pvt Ltd, 11 Community Centre, Panchsheel Park, New Delhi–110 017,
India ° Penguin Group (NZ), 67 Apollo Drive, Rosedale, North Shore 0632,
New Zealand (a division of Pearson New Zealand Ltd) ° Penguin Books
(South Africa) (Pty) Ltd, 24 Sturdee Avenue, Rosebank,
Johannesburg 2196, South Africa

Penguin Books Ltd, Registered Offices: 80 Strand, London WC2R 0RL, England

The Pathway of Roses was originally published in 1910
Your Forces and How to Use Them was originally published in 1910
Mastery of Self was originally published in 1907
The Ideal Made Real was originally published in 1909
Just Be Glad was originally published in 1912
First Jeremy P. Tarcher compilation of these works as The Optimist Creed 2012

Library of Congress Cataloging-in-Publication Data
Larson, Christian Daa, date.
The optimist creed / Christian D. Larson.
p.   cm.
ISBN 978-1-58542-993-6
1. New thought.   I. Title.
BF639.L356   2012   2012001359
289.9'8—dc23

While the author has made every effort to provide accurate telephone numbers and
Internet addresses at the time of publication, neither the publisher nor the author
assumes any responsibility for errors, or for changes that occur after publication.
Further, the publisher does not have any control over and does not assume
any responsibility for author or third-party websites or their content.

ALWAYS LEARNING   PEARSON

CONTENTS

PUBLISHER'S NOTE

This volume collects five of the most powerful books produced in the early twentieth century by inspirational writer Christian D. Larson: *The Pathway of Roses* (1910); *Your Forces and How to Use Them* (1910); *Mastery of Self* (1907); *The Ideal Made Real* (1909); and *Just Be Glad* (1912).

Larson is best known for the meditation called "The Optimist Creed." That short work originally appeared in his 1910 book *Your Forces and How to Use Them** under the title "Promise Yourself." In 1922, it was officially adopted as the manifesto of Optimist International, after which it became widely known as "The Optimist Creed." This anthology includes the meditation as it originally appeared in *Your Forces and How to Use Them*, and under its more popular title at the start of the volume.

---

*1912 is generally cited as the copyright date for this key work, but records show its earliest publication in 1910 by The Progress Company, Larson's own press.

THE OPTIMIST CREED

Promise Yourself . . .

To be so strong that nothing can disturb your peace of mind.

To talk health, happiness, and prosperity to every person you meet.

To make all your friends feel that there is something in them.

To look at the sunny side of everything and make your optimism come true.

To think only of the best, to work only for the best, and to expect only the best.

To be just as enthusiastic about the success of others as you are about your own.

To forget the mistakes of the past and press on to the greater achievements of the future.

To wear a cheerful countenance at all times and give every living creature you meet a smile.

To give so much time to the improvement of yourself that you have no time to criticize others.

To be too large for worry, too noble for anger, too strong for fear, and too happy to permit the presence of trouble.

To think well of yourself and to proclaim this fact to the world, not in loud words, but in great deeds.

To live in the faith that the whole world is on your side, so long as you are true to the best that is in you.

The
PATHWAY
of ROSES

CONTENTS

To live always in the Secret Places of the Most High,
To think only those thoughts that are inspired from above,
To do all things in the conviction that God is with us,
To give the best to all the world with no thought of reward,
To leave all recompense to Him who doeth all things well,
To love everybody as God loves us, and be Kind as He is Kind,
To ask God for everything and in faith expect everything,
To live in perpetual gratitude to Him who gives everything,
To love God so much that we can inwardly feel that My Father
    and I are one,
This is the prayer without ceasing, the true worship of the soul.

CHAPTER I

PATHS TO THE LIFE BEAUTIFUL

The thinking world of today is being filled with a phase of thought that has exceptional value. True, some of it is in a somewhat chaotic condition, but most of it is rich, containing within itself the very life of that truth that is making the world free. But in the finding of this truth, and in the application of its principles, where are we to begin? What are we to do first? And after we have begun, and find ourselves in the midst of a life so large, so immense and so marvelous that it will require eternity to live it all, what are the great essentials that we should ever remember and apply? What are the great centers of life about which we may build a greater and a greater life? These are questions that thousands are asking today, and the answer is simple.

First, recognize the great truth that every individual can live his own life exactly as he may desire to live. Man, himself, is the real master of his own existence, and he, himself, may determine how perfect and how beautiful that existence is to be.

Your life is in your own hands. You may live as you wish. You may secure from life whatever you desire, because there is no limit to life, and no limit to your capacity to live. The elements of life can be modified, changed, developed and perfected to comply with your own supreme demand; the increase of life can be realized in the exact measure of your largest need; you are in living touch with Infinite life, and there is neither limit nor end to the source of your supply.

To live in the constant recognition of this great truth, is to rise continually into higher and higher degrees of that mastery of life that gives man the power to live his life according to his most perfect ideals. To reach the goal that every ascending mind has in view, this truth, therefore, must ever be recognized and applied. It is one of those principles that we shall always require, no matter how high we may rise in the scale of divine being.

Second, desire that which you desire, and desire with all the power of mind and soul. We invariably receive what we desire, no more, no less. We get what we wish for if the power within that wish is as strong as we can make it.

The fact that we can have an ideal, proves that we have the power to secure it. The fact that we can formulate and appreciate a desire for something larger and better, proves that we can fulfill that desire. The great essential is to desire with the whole heart; that is, to give our desires all the life and power that we can possibly arouse from the depths of invincible being.

The true desire and the true prayer are synonymous. The true prayer is invariably some immensely strong desire expressed when the human mind feels the sublime touch of the Infinite mind; and the true desire must be in perfect touch with Infinite life in order to be filled with the invincible power of that life.

To cause every wish to come true, we must express all the power of mind and soul through every wish; but we cannot give expression to all the power within us until we awaken our spiritual natures, and we cannot awaken our spiritual natures until we begin to live with the Infinite. The largeness and immensity of the supreme spiritual life within us comes forth only as consciousness is spiritualized, and we gain spiritual consciousness by living and thinking constantly in the lofty state where we actually feel that God is closer than breathing, nearer than hands and feet.

We cannot desire too much, and when we desire with all the life and power that is within us, our desires shall positively be fulfilled. The wish must be whole-hearted, not half-hearted; it must contain all the power we have, not simply the limited actions of shallow thinking; and it must contain soul, not simply emotion, but that deep, spiritual feeling that touches the very spirit of limitless life and power.

Third, have faith in God, have faith in man, have faith in yourself, have faith in everything; and have faith in faith. When you have confidence in yourself you arouse everything that is stronger, greater and superior in yourself. In consequence, the more confidence you have in yourself, the more you will attain and accomplish. But the power of self-confidence is but an atom in comparison with the marvelous power of faith.

Faith takes mind and soul into the greater realms of life. It goes out upon the boundless, and awakens those interior spiritual forces that have the power to do anything. This is why all things become possible when we have faith.

It is the nature of faith to break bounds; to transcend limitations, and take life, thought and action into the universal. It is the nature of faith to unite the lesser with the greater, to unite the mind of man with the mind of God. Therefore, we shall always require faith; however far we may go into the greater, the superior and the boundless today, faith will take us farther still to-morrow. And that is our purpose; to realize our largest and dearest desires in the present, and then press on to the realization of other and far greater desires in the future.

Fourth, depend upon the superior man within for results, and give this greater man the credit for everything you accomplish. When you depend upon the personal self, you place yourself in touch only with the lesser forces on the surface; you therefore will accomplish but little; but when you depend upon the supreme spiritual self, you place yourself in touch with the greater powers within, and results will be greater in proportion.

When you give credit to the personal self, you ignore the interior spiritual man; you thereby fail to secure that greater wisdom and power that the spiritual man alone can supply. Instead of being led by that inner light that knows, you are led by the confusion of outer thought; you are turned away from the path that leads to truth, freedom and the perfect life, and your mistakes are many. Instead of being taken into the current of that invincible life that can carry you through to your very highest goal, you remain in the hands of mere physical energy, that energy that can do nothing more than simply keep your body alive.

Whenever you accomplish something worth while, and give the praise to your own outer personal self, you immediately lose your hold on those powers through which those results were gained; in consequence, failure will begin, and you will have to retrace all your former steps to again gain possession of that power that can do whatever you may wish to have done.

To constantly depend upon the greater self, to constantly expect the desired results from the greater self, and to always give credit to the greater self, is to constantly draw upon the limitless wisdom and power of the greater self—the supreme spiritual man within you. You thereby become larger and stronger in all the elements of your being, rising ever in the scale, gaining ground perpetually, and passing from victory to victory. What you desire you will receive because higher power is working through you, and as you ascend in the scale, there is nothing that you will not attain and accomplish.

The principal cause of failure among those who are trying to live in harmony with real truth, may be found in the general tendency to think of the outer person as the power that does things on the visible plane. But it is the interior man that gives the power, though the outer person is required to apply it. And the more thought we give to the interior man, the more life and power we bring forth from within.

The interior man is the man, created in the image and likeness of God; it is therefore evident that when you begin to live with the life and the power of the interior man, the expression of real greatness and real spirituality will begin. And from that moment you will not be limited to the power of the personal self; instead you will fill the personal self with that divine power from on high that is limitless, inexhaustible and invincible.

Fifth, live for a great purpose, and hold the central idea of that purpose constantly before mind. Do not live for the mere sake of prolonging existence; live for something that magnifies, on the largest possible scale, all the elements of existence. To live for a great purpose is to live a great life, and the greater your life, the greater the good that you will receive from life. The ruling desire of every living soul is to have life, and have it more abundantly; therefore, to fulfill that desire we must continue perpetually to live for that which produces more life. No matter how rich we may become in the real, spiritual life, here is a principle that we must ever remember and apply.

Do not work for yourself; work for the great idea that stands at the apex of your greatest purpose. The greater the idea for which you work, the greater will be your work; and it is he who does the greatest work that does the most for everybody, himself included. When your work is great you become a great power for good among thousands, and at the same time you do more for yourself than you could possibly do in any other manner.

When you begin to live and work for a great purpose, you get into the current of great forces, great minds and great souls. You gain from every source; all the powerful lives in the world will work with you; you become a living part of that movement in the world that determines the greater destiny of man; you become one of the chief elements upon which will depend the future of countless generations yet to be; you become one of the chosen of the Most High.

To live for a great purpose is to live in the world of great ideas, and great ideas awaken great thoughts. Man is as he thinks. Great thoughts produce great minds; from great minds proceed great works, and great works constitute the building material with which the kingdom upon earth is to be constructed.

When we begin to live for a great and good purpose, we place in action that law that causes all things to work together for good. Henceforth, nothing is in vain; every person, thing or event that comes into our world will add to the welfare, the richness and the beauty of that world. All things become ministers of the life that is real life, we have been giving our best everywhere, and we are receiving the best from every source in return.

To live for that which is high, lofty and sublime, is to walk with God; the love, the life, the power and the wisdom of the Infinite will ever be with us, and to have such companions is to be blessed indeed. Every moment will give us the peace that passeth understanding, every hour will be filled with the joy everlasting, and every day will be as a thousand years in celestial kingdoms on high.

To give the world emancipation is the ruling desire of all minds that are spiritually awakened; and these should remember that to overcome evil with good is the only way. Forget the wrong that may appear in the outer world of things, and give all your thought to the great good that is inherent in all things. You thereby place in action the greatest emancipating power that the human race will ever know.

We are in bondage because we have lived to please the person. Follow the soul and freedom shall come quickly. Then we shall please the person better than ever before. To follow the soul is to enter the greater domains of life, those domains from which we may secure everything that is rich and beautiful and superior in human existence. The soul leads, not only into the life more abundant, but also into the actual possession of all the spiritual riches that the greater life may contain. And when we find the kingdom that is within, all that we may desire in the without shall be added.

The soul that lives most perfectly in the present, creates most nobly for the future. Be yourself today, regardless of what happened yesterday. Be all that you are or can be today, and you will live in a fairer world tomorrow.

CHAPTER II

THE WAY TO FREEDOM

There is only one will in the universe just as there is only one mind. The one mind is the mind of God, the one will is the will of God. The mind of individual man is an individual or differentiated expression of the Infinite mind, and the largeness of this human mind depends upon how much of the one mind man may decide to appropriate. Man has the freedom to incorporate in his own individual consciousness as much of the Infinite mind as he may desire; and as the mind of the Infinite is limitless, the mind of man may continue to become larger and larger without any end.

The will of the individual mind is a partial expression of the will of God, just as the force of growth that is in each branch is a part of the same force that is in the vine, and the power of the individual will depends upon how perfectly the individual mind works in harmony with the Infinite mind.

There is no limit to the power of the will of God, the divine will; therefore, when the human will is as large a part of the divine will as the individual mind can appropriate and apply, the human will necessarily becomes immensely strong; and since the individual mind can appropriate a larger and a larger measure of the divine will, there is no limit to the power of will that can be developed in the mind of man.

To develop the true will, the first essential is to realize that there is but one will, and that we will with the one will just as we live the one life and think with the one mind, though in our thinking, living and willing, we do not, as a rule, do justice to that part of the whole which it is our privilege to use. We think, live and will too much as isolated entities instead of as divine beings eternally united with the Supreme.

The second essential is to realize that the divine will works only for better things and greater things. The path of the divine will is upward and onward forever, and its power is employed exclusively in building more lofty mansions for the soul. Therefore the will of God does not produce sickness, adversity or death; on the contrary, the will of God eternally wills to produce wholeness, harmony and life.

The ills of personal life are not produced by divine will; they are produced by man's inability to properly use that part of divine will that is being expressed in his mind, and his inability comes because man does not always apply his will in harmony with divine will.

When man uses his will as his own isolated power, he separates his mind more and more from the source of his power; in consequence, the power of his will becomes weaker, and he necessarily fails to accomplish what he has in view. He also falls apart from the one ascending current of life; he gets out of harmony with the true order of things, and sickness, trouble, adversity and want invariably follow.

The true use of the will is to apply the will in the full recognition of the oneness of the human will with the divine will. My will is as much of the divine will as I am using now, and it is my privilege to use as much of the divine will as I may desire. To constantly think of my will and the divine will as the same will, is to place my mind in such perfect harmony with limitless power of divine will that I can appropriate this power in larger and larger measure, and the more I appropriate, the stronger becomes the power of will in me.

When the individual mind is in such perfect harmony with the Supreme mind that the divine will can be given free and full expression, the will of the individual mind becomes invincible; the secret therefore of developing a powerful will is found here, and here alone.

The true will is never domineering nor antagonistic; neither does it ever apply the force of resistance. If you are antagonistic or have a tendency to resist everything that is not to your liking, it is proof conclusive that you are not in harmony with divine will. You are misdirecting your power, and are forming obstacles and pitfalls for yourself.

The divine will does not attempt to overcome evils and obstacles with antagonistic or domineering forces; the divine will does not fight wrong, it transforms wrong. It works in silence and serenity, but goes so deeply into the elements of things that it undermines the very first causes of all adverse or detrimental conditions. It does not resist the surface, but goes calmly beneath the surface and transforms those undercurrents from which surface conditions proceed.

The divine will, by going into the deeper life of all things, transforms all things into harmony with itself; and can transform all things because its power is supreme. Therefore when we are in the midst of adversity, we should not rail against fate nor antagonize those conditions that seem to work against us. We have within us the power of divine will, and this will can change everything for good.

But it not only can, it will. It is not the will of God to keep any person in adversity. It is the will of God to set every person free, and every person will be set free when he places his life completely in the hands of divine will.

When the individual mind can say, from the heart, Thy will be done, the individual life has been placed in the power of divine will and that life will at once begin to pass out of adversity, sickness, trouble and want, into the world of freedom.

However, we do not give up our individuality when we give our mind over to divine will; we do not become automatons in the hands of some superior power; on the contrary, we open our minds to that power that alone can produce individuality. The individuality we now possess has been formed by whatever measure of divine will that we have incorporated in our own conscious existence, and by opening our minds completely to divine will, we shall gain sufficient power to make our individuality infinitely stronger and superior to what it now is. Our purpose is not to be used by the Supreme, but to use the power of the Supreme.

To live the life of God, think the thought of God, and will with the will of God—that is the secret path to the highly developed individuality; and it is such an individuality that becomes a master mind, a Son of the Most High.

When the individual mind declares, Thy will be done, consciousness must fully recognize the presence of Supreme power, and must realize, with depth of thought and feeling, that Supreme power invariably leads to higher ground—the world of freedom and superior existence.

When the mind gives up to divine will in an indifferent, submissive, self-surrendering attitude, it is not giving up to divine will; it is simply giving up to the surrounding forces of fate. Such a mind will permit the forces of adversity to have their way, thinking that it is the will of God that much suffering must still be endured, and will consequently drift with circumstances, accepting whatever comes as a necessary chastisement.

This method, however, weakens the mind, and places the individual more out of harmony with God than ever before. We always place ourselves out of harmony with God when we accept evil as coming from Him, and we weaken our own ability to use divine will when we permit adversity to exist thinking that it was sent from God.

To give the mind over to divine will is not to give up at all, in the ordinary sense of that term; we simply place ourselves in that position where we can use the power of the one true will instead of a mere imitation. We blend our own desires and aims with that power that we **know** can see us through, and we work in the realization that whatever is detrimental in our plans will be eliminated as we press on toward the great goal in view.

The mind that is aimless, waiting for the will of God to take him where he belongs, will drift with fate. He is not in the hands of divine will, he is in the hands of circumstances because he has not given divine will something to do. God does not tell us what to do; He has given us the wisdom to know our own desires and our own tendencies, and He has given us the power to fulfil those desires, but we must take individual action; this is why we have individuality and free individual choice.

However, when we do take individual action, God will work with us if we enter into harmony with Him, and when He is with us, failure is impossible.

To use divine will, we must first have a lofty purpose in view; we must have something high and something definite that we wish to attain; we must have something upon which to apply the limitless power of divine will, and we must desire to reach that goal with the very deepest and strongest desires of heart and soul.

Then we must will to press on, knowing that we are using divine will, the Supreme will of the Most High, because this is the only will in the universe. It is the will that eternally wills the higher, the greater and the better—the will that is invincible, and always does what it wills to do.

To the minds of the many the true meaning of the will of God has not been made perfectly clear; therefore the majority, even among those who have strong spiritual tendencies, hesitate to give up to the absolute direction of higher power. There is a slight dread in the mind of the average person whenever he thinks of entering the uncertainty and the mysteriousness of the seeming void, and as long as things are reasonably well he does not care to give up to some power he knows nothing of. And as a true understanding of higher power can not be found among the many, there are, accordingly, but few who can actually declare, with the whole heart, "Thy will be done." We frequently pray for His will to guide us, nevertheless we inwardly expect to use our own wills in mostly everything we do. But such prayers are not true to the spirit, and therefore they prevent the soul from actually discerning the real meaning of God's will; and also prevent the mind from becoming a perfect channel for the expression of His will.

The universe is orderly from center to circumference, and everything is established upon the firm foundation of eternal right and universal good. There is a power that lives and moves throughout this vast immensity, and all those things that have a permanent place in the cosmos, or that are instrumental in any way, in promoting the purpose of life, have their source in this one power. All the laws and forces in existence spring originally from this power; it is therefore the center and source of all that lives and moves; and this power is the will of God. Accordingly, to do the will of the Father is to enter into harmony with the universal order and promote the great eternal plan.

The laws of life are all expressions of Supreme will. God wills eternally the right and the true, and the act of His willing originates and perpetuates the sublime plan of life that harmoniously thrills the entire cosmos during endless eternities. God's will is constant and changeless; therefore all the laws and principles in existence remain ever the same, as they are all the expression of the One Will. All that we see in the life of the universe is the eternal coming forth of Divine Will, and the perpetual returning to the One Source.

The true will in every soul is an individualization of Infinite Will, and the true use of the individual will means the doing of the will of God. The Infinite Will does not seek to control things, but seeks eternally to give itself to things. And here lies the secret in correctly using the human will, and in placing the human will in perfect harmony with God's will. When you can say with the whole heart, "Thy will be done," you are not giving up your own will, but you are placing your own will and the whole of your life in oneness with God and in harmony with the universal order. Therefore, when you do the will of God your own will becomes right, and becomes infinitely stronger than it ever was before.

When we act in perfect accord with the laws of life on all the planes of being, we are doing the will of God because what we call law in life is the will of God in expression in life. He who lives in perfect harmony with nature, who fully appreciates her grandeur and her beauty, and who daily seeks to be inspired by the loveliness of her presence is doing the will of God in the natural world. He who rightly employs all the elements of mind and body, and who furthers the purpose of his own being in constant growth and unfoldment is doing the will of God in the human world. He who searches the deep things of God and enters into that high state where God becomes "closer than breathing, nearer than hands and feet"; he who lives and moves and has his being in the infinite sea of divine light, and ever ascends higher and higher into the greater glories of God's kingdom, is doing the will of God in the spiritual world.

Whoever can say with his whole heart "Thy will be done," has placed the whole of his life in perfect accord with God; and henceforth he will seek to live in perfect harmony with all that is, because all is of God. To do the will of God is not only to place one's life in the hands of God, but to be at peace with all the world, and to give one's whole life to all the world. The will of God seeks eternally to give itself to things—all things; the will of man, to be in harmony with the will of God, must do the same.

However insignificant a law may seem to be, it is God working in that part of His universe; and as He is everywhere, manifesting His power everywhere, we must live and work with Him in all things, even the most trivial, if we would be in perfect accord with His life and always do His will. A law in life is a path to greater things; in truth, an open door through which we may pass more closely into His presence. We can meet God at every expression of life, and whenever we are in the highest state of harmony with our expression of life, we have met God in that place. And also, when we use that expression of life in entering into a larger measure of life, we do the will of God in that place. Therefore, whoever meets God everywhere, and does His will in every place, will realize the fullness of life at all times and under every circumstance. And to realize the fullness of life is to realize the allness of the good.

The incompleteness of human life, in general, is caused by our failure to enter into perfect accord with all the laws in our sphere of existence. We may be wholly right in some things while the very opposite in other things. We may be scrupulous in regard to the right use of some laws, and at the same time continually negligent in regard to others. There are many who take perfect care of their bodies, and comply most rigidly with all known physical laws, yet they violate the laws of mind nearly every hour of their existence. Others are very careful so as to think only the truth, and do their best to remain continually in the most beautiful states of mind; but while aiming to live in mental ideals they are wholly indifferent to the welfare of the body. Not infrequently we find people who live in perfect accord with intellectual laws but violate daily the moral laws. Also, too many who are the reverse. In brief, the majority do the will of God in some realms while living entirely at variance with His laws in other realms. And here we find the simple answer to many perplexing questions.

When some misfortune comes to you that you do not think you deserve, do not think that God is unjust or that fate is unkind. You have simply failed to do His will in all things. Do not blame others, do not blame fate, do not even blame yourself; simply proceed to readjust your life so that you may become one with Him in all things. Then all ills shall disappear, and you shall not only regain what you have lost but you shall, in addition, receive much more. Live in accord with all the laws of life physically, mentally and spiritually; do all things in the consciousness of God; do all things to the glory of God, and follow the light of His spirit in every thought and deed; then you will always do the will of God.

Though you may dwell upon the mountain tops of the spirit, though you may glory in the splendors of the cosmic realm, though your mind may go out upon the vastness of the limitless and your soul ascend to empyrean heights, still, do not for a moment deprive the body of anything that is rich and beautiful in physical existence. The great goal is the spiritual life, and in the spiritual life all the joys of sense, all the joys of intellect and all the joys of the highest heavens are divinely blended into one. The physical life is sacred. The earth is the foot-stool of the Most High. God lives in His heaven, but every atom in the visible universe thrills with the glory of His radiant presence.

CHAPTER III

THE SUPREME POINT OF VIEW

When we are upon the mountain top of life and look upon things from this lofty point of view, we discover that all is well. Wherever we may turn our vision we find the same—all is well. We can see all things and yet all is well with all things; the good alone is in evidence; everything is in the likeness of God, and we conclude that everything actually is as it was originally created by God—very good.

But when we descend to the valley we find many things quite different, and the problem is whether the scene on the mountain top was simply a beautiful vision, or the scene in the valley an unpleasant illusion.

To the mind in the valley the life of the valley alone seems real; to the mind on the heights the beauty and glory of sublime life alone seems real, while the regions below are but the undeveloped beginnings of some better day.

To decide which of these two minds is right is not necessary; we cannot know the truth by what seems to be true from a single point of view. It is results that demonstrate, therefore we must find what effect life in the valley has upon the whole of life, and what effect life on the heights has upon the whole of life.

To live in the valley alone, ignoring everything that may come from lofty realms, is to live in darkness, trouble and pain. This we know. To him who secludes himself in the lower regions of existence, nothing seems to be wholly well; there is usually something wrong or defective with everything with which he may come in contact, and life at best has but little to give.

How different, however, everything becomes when we begin to live on the heights. We not only find that all is well in these upper regions but all things become well in the lower realms the moment we begin to live in the upper. We must therefore conclude that all is well when **we** are well, but that we are not well unless we live on the heights.

We also conclude that the vision of the soul is true, that the ideal alone is real, and that man can see all things as they are only when entering sublime existence. And as all is well from the viewpoint of sublime existence, to think the truth man must always think that all is well.

To live in the lower realms is to live in pain; to live in the upper realms is to live in peace, freedom and joy. Then why should we continue to live in the lower, while wholly ignoring the upper? Why should we declare that the lower alone is real, and that the upper is but a pleasant dream? Is pain more real than joy? Is bondage more real than freedom, death more real than life?

True, daily experience sometimes seems to contradict the vision of the soul, but if darkness be present now, does that prove that light is always a mere dream? When we are wholly out of harmony we cannot understand, for the time being, how there can be any harmony; all seems to be discord; but the moment we fully recognize the absoluteness of universal harmony, discord is no more.

When all does not seem to be well in daily life, we may not feel that we can truthfully say that all is well, but there is a marked distinction between the outer appearance of discord and the inner reality of harmony; and it is the inner reality that we should live.

When discord appears on the surface, the cause may be found in the fact that we have descended from our true place; we have tried to go away from harmony and have thus produced discord. But the moment we return to harmony, the discord disappears, and all is well.

We must conclude therefore, that so long as we remain in the reality of harmony, all will be well, because all is always well in the world of harmony, and the world of harmony is the true world, the only true world—the world in which man was created to always live.

And we must remember the great truth that so long as man lives in the world of harmony there can be no discord anywhere; so long as he lives in the upper regions nothing can go wrong in the lower regions. The lower states of life are but effects of what man does, and when man is on the heights he will do only that which is well because all is always well on the heights; therefore, since like causes produce like effects, all will be well in the valley so long as man lives on the mountain top.

This being true, every person should always think that all is well, and should always live in that sublime life where all is absolutely well. Thus, that which is well, will manifest in every part of life, while that which did not seem to be well will pass away. Live in the true, and the whole of life becomes true.

Whoever discerns clearly the spiritual essence or divine substance which is the basis or soul of all reality, will manifest in the form, not only purity, but absolute immunity from all disease and from all adverse actions among physical elements and forces. His body will be spiritualized in proportion to this understanding, and will establish itself more and more firmly in that state of being where divine nature reigns supremely. To spiritualize the body is to give greater strength, more perfect health and more youthful vigor, as well as higher quality, to the body. To establish the body in the consciousness of the spirit is to give the body absolute protection from weakness or disease; in the spirit we find all the elements of perfect being for body, mind and soul, and we place the body in the spirit when we realize that every atom in the body is filled, through and through, with the real substance of spirit.

Make yourself a living example of the power of spirit. Do not permit a single weakness to continue for a moment. Do not say that you will be in the future; say that you are now; and you are, because you are the exact image of the Supreme.

CHAPTER IV

THE TRUE ORDER OF THINGS

What the individual life is to be, as a whole, or in any of its parts, depends upon where the consciousness of being is established, and there are three distinct planes in which this consciousness may be established; viz., the physical, the psychical and the spiritual.

To establish life in the physical is to become a materialist; there will be no consciousness of the finer things of existence, and the understanding of things in general will be one-sided; in consequence, the mind cannot see anything as it really is, and will make mistakes at every turn.

The materialist lives for the body alone, and depends upon the physical senses exclusively, both for knowledge and enjoyment; but the physical senses are never wholly reliable unless when employed by mental faculties that are above the physical; therefore the knowledge of the materialist is composed principally of illusions and half-truths, and his enjoyment is but an inferior imitation of real happiness.

The life of the materialist is necessarily full of troubles and ills because he cannot be in harmony with the true principle of life so long as he is living on the surface of life instead of in real life itself. In brief, all the ills of life can be traced to materialism, in one or more of its various forms; therefore, the materialist is not simply one who denies the existence of the soul; the materialist is any one who lives in the body, who has established his life in physical existence, and who employs objective senses and faculties only, regardless of what he may believe about God, the soul or the future.

Though a person may be thoroughly religious, as far as he knows, and may believe everything that sacred literature may say about things spiritual, if he cannot comprehend the spiritual except as it is expressed in physical acts, physical ideas, physical rites or physical symbols, he is still a materialist;

he is living in the world of tangible things, and has no consciousness of that higher power that produces things.

To be spiritual he must discern the spirit that is within things, back of things, above things; while his senses admire the outer symbol, his spiritual discernment must understand the interior significance of that symbol, otherwise he has not found real religion or real spirituality.

The mind that has not entered into real spirituality, is living in materiality, and to live in materiality is to be in bondage to the ills of this world; therefore true existence cannot be realized so long as life is established in the physical plane.

To establish life in the psychical plane is to be guided almost entirely by feeling and emotion; but no feeling is absolutely true unless it originates in the soul, and our feelings cannot originate in the soul unless we have established life in the spiritual plane. Therefore, the person who is living in the psychical plane, is living in a world of feelings, emotions, desires and sensations that are more or less abnormal. His mental world is artificial, composed principally of imaginations that are patterned after things from without instead of the understanding of absolute truth from within.

The imagination is always influenced a great deal by the play of the emotions; and when the emotions are the results of external suggestions, as they always are unless when we live in the spirit, the imagination will likewise be under the control of things, good and otherwise. This means that our thinking will be worldly, materialistic and more or less disordered, because as we imagine, so we think.

Therefore, to live in the psychical world is to live in a world of abnormal feeling and misdirected imagination; but true being cannot find its foundation in such a world. True being can be established only in the consciousness of truth, and the consciousness of truth can be gained only in the spirit.

When life is established in the spiritual state, the physical ceases to be materialistic, and the psychical ceases to be a troubled sea of conflicting emotions. Instead, the physical becomes an orderly expression of the pure, wholesome life of the soul, and the psychical becomes a world of the richest thought, the most sublime feeling and the highest mental enjoyment.

The spiritual state of being is the true foundation of being, because the spiritual alone has the necessary qualities. To establish life in any other state or upon any other plane is to act contrary to the true order of things, and trouble must necessarily follow. There is only one place for man to live, and that is in the soul. When he tries to live elsewhere, in mind or body, he separates himself from his great inheritance and does not receive what he has the right and the privilege to receive.

When there seems to be nothing in life, the fault lies with the man himself, not with the laws of his being. Instead of living in the spirit, where he could receive everything, he has gone to live in the emptiness of the material, where there is nothing to be had but the undesirable consequences of wrong-doing; and wrong-doing is the direct result of wrong-going, going away from the true state of being.

To live in the spiritual state is to give expression to everything that is in the spirit, because what we actually **live** we bring out into tangible existence; and the spirit contains everything that may be required to perfect the whole of existence—physical, mental and spiritual.

The belief that the spiritual life is apart from the mental and physical is not true; it is the spiritual alone that can make the physical and the mental complete; in brief, we do not begin to enjoy the body and the mind until we begin to live in the soul.

We cannot attain the most perfect physical health and the most perfect physical development until we can begin to draw upon the inexhaustible life of the spirit, nor can we attain the greatest intellectual power and the highest mental brilliancy until our minds are opened to real spiritual illumination.

To have health and wholeness of body, we must have an abundance of that life that is health and wholeness, and that life comes only from the soul. To gain that life we must live in the soul, and the life that we live we invariably bring forth into mind and body.

To perfect the beautiful in the physical form, we must, likewise, receive the necessary elements from the spiritual state. Beauty of form is produced by harmony in formation and **soul** in expression; but we can give forth neither harmony nor soul until we actually live in the soul.

The true development of mind, character and life, all depend upon our ever-increasing expression of the perfect qualities of the spiritual life; therefore the truest, the best and the greatest results from physical existence and mental existence can come only when we actually enter spiritual existence.

But to enter the spiritual is not simply to provide those essentials through which we may realize the ideal in the physical and the mental; to enter the spiritual is to enter another and a greater world—the transcendent kingdom of the soul—the sublime world of cosmic consciousness. It was into this world that Jesus entered when "his face did shine as the sun and his garment became white as the light." We can therefore imagine what is in store for those who open their eyes to its splendor and glory.

"Be not therefore anxious for the morrow. Sufficient unto the day is the evil thereof." The term "evil" signifies incompleteness, or that which needs perfecting, development and fulfillment now. The statement therefore means that we have sufficient to do to make the present moment full and complete, without giving any thought to what we are to be or do in the future. When the present moment is filled with the most perfect life that we can possibly realize, the seeming incompleteness of the present moment will simply become a perpetual growing process. Incompleteness will thus become a real step in growth; it will be like a growing bud, and will not be evil, only lesser good on the way to greater good. When the bud ceases to grow it decays, and becomes unwholesome, disagreeable. Likewise, when the buds in human life are checked in their growth they produce disagreeable conditions. And here is the cause of all the ills of the world. The remedy is to so live that all the power of life is centered upon the present moment. To give the whole of life to the present moment is to promote the growth of everything that exists in the life of the present moment. To live a full life now is to live more and more life now.

CHAPTER V

THE GOOD THAT IS IN YOU

The good that is inherent in everything is infinitely greater and more powerful than any imperfection or undeveloped condition that may exist in the outer world. And therefore when this good is recognized and brought out into real life, that which is not good must disappear. To apply this great truth to yourself, to others, to circumstances, is to place mind and soul in that attitude where conscious contact with the divine perfection in all things will be gained. In consequence, the good that is within will increase, while undesired conditions in the without will decrease. To recognize the greater good that is inherent in all things is to cause that good to become a greater and greater power in you, until it becomes just as strong in action as it previously was in realization.

Live in the conviction that "I am greater than all my ills or failures; that I am greater than the limitations of my circumstances, and greater than any condition that I can possibly meet." When you feel that you are greater than your ills, those ills cannot long remain, because what you inwardly feel, you realize, and what you realize, you bring forth into living expression. To open the mind to the great thought that the health that is within you is greater than any disease than you can ever know, is to open your life to the power of that health; and when the greater power of the health that is within you comes forth into the life of every atom in your being, the lesser power of disease, weakness or adverseness must vanish completely. No disease can long remain in your system after you begin to live in the constant conviction that the absolute health that is within you is infinitely greater and more powerful than all the sickness in the world. Nor can failure continue after you begin to realize that you, in the reality of your whole being, have the power to turn the tide of any circumstance that may ever appear in your world. The good that is within you is larger and more powerful than all the troubles, misfortunes or disappointments in existence; and this good, when fully recognized by you, will begin to work for you. It will work for your good, and will turn to good account everything that can happen.

When you know that you are greater than any undeveloped condition that may exist in mind or body, you gain the power to transcend limitations. Your consciousness begins to break bounds, and you find yourself in that larger, richer mental world that you so long have desired to reach. You are placed in touch with the universal and begin to draw upon the limitless for wisdom and power and joy. You no longer feel cramped, but realize that you are absolutely free to live the largest, the best and the most beautiful life that you can possibly picture. The ideals that you discover during the highest flights of mind and soul, are no longer considered impossibilities; you know that you can realize them all; to you there is no failure because the good that is within you is greater than all failure. You are above limitations; you are master of limitations, and have the power to transform every undeveloped condition into the highest form of completeness and superior worth. The lesser is passing away, and the greater is being realized in an ever increasing measure.

The good that is inherent in others is infinitely greater than all their faults, short-comings or imperfections; therefore we can readily forgive them for all these. There is more in man than the undeveloped surface, and it is this **more** that we will recognize, love and admire. When anyone goes wrong we will not criticize or complain; we cannot criticize anyone without harming everybody concerned, ourselves included; nor can we think well of anyone without helping everybody concerned, ourselves included. And everybody wants the best to happen to everybody. To live in constant recognition of the weaker side of human nature is to open the mind to weakness, discord, failure and unhappiness. We steadily grow into the likeness of that which we think of the most. But to live in constant spiritual touch with the great good that exists in everybody, is to open the mind to strength and happiness that cannot be measured. The most beautiful moments in life are realized when we feel that we are one with God and one with that something in man that is created in the image of God. And these moments may become eternal.

Whatever we may meet in life we should always remember that the good within all things is far greater than anything that may appear on the surface; and that this greater good will finally rule the day. When this good is to reign supremely in our world will depend upon us and us alone. The superior within us is always ready and will come forth into tangible expression whenever we are ready to receive it. But we are not ready until we give the greater good in all things the first thought, no matter what the circumstances may be. Whatever may come, meet it all with the thought that the good within is greater still. The good that is inherent in all things is always greater and more powerful. The greatest things in the without are insignificant in comparison. Therefore, we can readily understand how easily the circumstances and conditions in the external world could be changed for the better, provided the all-powerful good within us was called forth into tangible action. And now we smooth the pathway of life when we realize that there is a greater good in everything we meet. How kindly we feel toward all persons and all events; nothing seems adverse any more and what we previously looked upon as obstacles are now stepping stones in attainment. By recognizing the greater good in all things, we open our minds to the wisdom and the power that is contained in this greater good; and, in consequence, we are inspired by every circumstance and enriched by every experience. We gain something from everything we pass through, and every event, however adverse, simply tends to arouse more and more of the real greatness within. Even evil, in all of its forms, becomes a lifting power in our world, because we are in constant touch with the great good that is back of and above all evil. We are not crushed by the ills and the wrongs that may exist about us, but instead we are inspired to greater thoughts, greater deeds and a greater life. All things serve us because we have found that greater good in all things that is ever waiting to serve. We have become friendly with the best that is in the world, and the best is becoming friendly with us in return.

The great and good are many, but he who loves with such a love that with his love some other soul has scaled the heights and there beheld what life eternal holds in store for man, has wrought the noblest of them all. Then give me such a love in boundless measure. Give me the love of some inspired soul whose living presence, fair and strong, can spur me on and on to greater heights than human life has ever reached before—some pure and tender heart who knows the sacred longings of that life supreme within that must ascend and evermore ascend—some fair illumined soul whose spirit dwells within the vision of transcendent realms on high and knows that I am made for such a place. Then life shall be a life indeed to me; my sacred longings all shall be fulfilled, and every good that I can wish for shall be mine, for all the joys of earth and all of heaven's ecstasies sublime abide for evermore in such a love.

CHAPTER VI

GIVE YOUR BEST TO THE WORLD

We have looked far and wide for remedies, but in our search we have overlooked one of the greatest of all; and that is love. Not the love of the person; not mere sentiment or emotion, but that strong, spiritual feeling that makes every atom in your being thrill with the purest sympathy and the highest kindness; and that makes you feel that every creature in existence deserves your most tender care and attention.

When everything goes wrong with us, we blame fate, environment or the world; we forget that the world does to us what we have done to the world. When we blame the world for everything, the world will so act that it will be to blame; but when we love the entire world with the whole heart, the world will change toward us accordingly and be kind.

When you do not succeed, when no one seems to care for your service, or for your talents, there are two things to do; do your best and love much. Do not condemn the race because it is slow to appreciate your worth; when you do this you push the world further away from yourself, and its appreciation will decrease instead of increase. Love the world, the whole world, and love with all the power of heart and soul; this will bring the world nearer to you; you will enter into friendly relationship with the world; the race will thereby discover what you have to give and will come at once to receive your talent.

True achievement in any sphere of action depends upon real ability, and a strong, deep, whole-souled love. Real ability can be cultivated, and we can all learn to love much; therefore the future of any person may become far greater and more beautiful than the present.

When others speak wrongly against you, do not permit the slightest trace of ill-feeling; anger and indignation not only weaken your own system, but also cause you to attract disagreeable people and adverse conditions. Love those who have mistreated you; love them with the very deepest power of your soul and they will soon come to you to make everything right again. Love can change the worst hatred into the deepest love; and what is more, when you love everybody you attract only the best people and the best conditions.

Love much, and lovely souls will daily come into your life; and those people who are not as lovely as they might be, will become better because they have met you and felt the divine fires aflame in your soul.

When people are going wrong, just love them; not with the person, nor in a weak, sentimental sense, but with that strong, soul-love that comes from the very heart of the Infinite. Such love will lift anybody; and whoever is lifted up into the better becomes better. When we ascend in the scale of life we enter the truer and the higher; we enter the right and thereby become true and right.

When you have reason to think that others are trying to take advantage of you, have no fear. Do not condemn; do not think of the wrong they are planning to do; take God with you and love them; love as you never loved before, and the wrong they are holding against you will change and become a great power for your good instead. Love can change any condition or circumstance and every change that comes through love is a change for the better.

Love brings us into right relations with all persons and all things; love removes inharmony, perverted feelings, obstacles, barriers and all kinds of unnatural conditions, and produces that perfect oneness through which the beautiful life can come forth. He who has placed himself in oneness with man can easily find his unity with God; but no one can find God who does not love man. When we love the whole race with the whole heart, then we shall enter the presence of Him who is love.

It is the truth that "He is nearest to God who is nearest to man"; and the nearer we are to God, the more life and power we receive from above; in consequence, the more we can accomplish in the world, and the better off will the world be because we came here to live for a while.

To be at peace with everything is one of the greatest secrets to greatness, usefulness and high spiritual attainment; and he alone can find the peace that passeth understanding who loves everybody and loves much. But true spiritual love does not love because it expects to gain thereby; when we love in the spirit of gain our love is only material emotion, and does not come from the spiritual depths of the soul.

Pure soul-love loves because it **is** love, and must love. It loves because it is its very life to love, and could not cease loving without ceasing to be. And it cannot cease to be because the love that is love is eternal love. Therefore to awaken the love of the soul is to place in action one of the highest powers in the universe; a power that can do so much because it is so much.

To feel the interior presence of this love, with its high, strong, invincible power, perfectly blended with the sweetest tenderness, not only produces a joy that can not be measured but also lifts you into a universe that is fairer by far than we ever imagined heaven to be. And truly it is heaven we enter when we love with such a love, when we love as God loves.

Pure love sees no evil, no sin, no wrong; it does not live in the world of illusion or darkness; it is a child of the light and radiates its spiritual glory wherever it may be. Where love is, there will the light be also; and neither darkness, sickness nor sin can exist in the light.

There is nothing that will not be blessed by the presence of love; and the soul that loves with the spirit, that loves much and loves always, will meet the good alone. He has given his best to the world, and the world will open its heart to him and be kind. As the years pass by, the world will lavish upon him the richest treasures within its power to give, and nothing will be too good to place at his door. Blessings of all kinds from every direction will come in greater and greater abundance, and his life will be full with the best that God and man can give; because he has given his best to the world, and loved much.

The practical mind may think that this is only sentiment, and therefore has no value, neither for the physical life nor for the spiritual life. But too often the practical mind looks for his treasure in the realm of effect instead of in the realm of cause; in consequence, he finds but little of real value anywhere in life. The great things in life do not come through minds that dwell merely on the surface, that cannot rise above the world of tangible results. Everything that is beautiful and of real worth, whether it appeals to the eye, the ear, the intellect or the soul, has come through the mind that had visions, the mind that could soar to supreme heights, and behold the real splendor and glory of the world.

To be practical is well and necessary; but there is something else that comes first. This something else brings forth the substance, the material upon which practical efforts may be applied; therefore, the practical mind cannot act until the dreamer has had his vision.

The higher nature of man must act before the external mind can find anything of value to do; the soul must live and think before the person can attain and achieve, and the greater the love, the greater the life and the thought of the soul.

Whatever has added to the welfare of man in any age has been the product of the mind with the vision. All the good things of life have come from the world of visions and dreams. Someone entered the finer realms of life for a moment and brought back a treasure. The practical mind turned it to use, and the world was richer and better than it was before.

This being true, it is the very height of wisdom to train ourselves to enter consciously and frequently into those finer realms and thus bring forth more of its hidden treasures. It is the best we all seek, and since the best comes from the ideal world, the better we understand the ideal, the richer and greater life will become. To be practical in the largest sense of that term is to so live that we can touch the sublime on the one hand and turn every ideal into a living reality on the other.

The great mind is the dreamer, the prophet, the soul with visions; the mind that can soar to empyrean heights and reveal to the race some higher truth, some better way, and thereby elevate the whole of mankind. This is the mind that brings real values to the world, that makes life worth while; and one of his principal secrets is love.

When we love in this supreme, spiritual sense, we give a power to our practical efforts that we never gave before. We give life to our work; we do more and better work; results double and more; we do this through a power that many ignore as mere useless sentiment; and we thus demonstrate that love, the deep, strong, soul love, is as practical as any tangible force in the world.

There is nothing to lose but failure, and everything to gain, when we learn to love in this strong, high, universal sense. To begin, love as much as you can; be directly interested in the highest welfare of everybody; feel in the depths of the soul that we are all working together for the greatest good to all the race; and make this feeling so strong that it thrills every fiber in your being.

But do not love for effect; love because you feel love; and train yourself to feel love by loving with all the power of love, and in the highest, purest sense you know. He who tries to ascend will go up; he who tries to become strong will enter power; and he who tries to love everybody with the deepest, highest, strongest love of the soul will daily enter more and more deeply into the very spirit of that love that is love. And when you are awakened in the world of true spiritual love, real love takes possession of all your feelings and desires; and all your love will eternally love because it is love. From that moment you will constantly receive love from all the world and constantly give love to all the world. You will gain possession of one of the highest and one of the greatest powers in the universe, and the Infinite will always be with you. God is with every soul that loves much; because it is love, the deep, pure, spiritual love that gives man the power to know that My Father and I are One.

When there is anything you truly wish for, do not stand passively hoping that something may happen to make your wish come true; go out and make that wish come true; have the faith that you can; believe in the power that God has given you and God will give you more. Know that all the good in the universe lies in the path of him who has faith, and who will use the power of faith to make his own faith come true. He who only hopes, will see visions of good things, but will never reach them. But he who transforms his hope into faith and his faith into living works, will reach every lofty goal he has in view. To him nothing shall be impossible, for God is with him.

CHAPTER VII

GIVING MUCH AND RECEIVING MUCH

When you have attained or received something of exceptional worth, give God the glory. Do not praise yourself, or give your own personality the credit. All power comes from above, and the more we appreciate the source of this power the more we shall receive. The path to perpetual increase is to give God the glory for everything that comes, and when we realize that everything comes from God, everything that comes to us will have exceptional worth. Every moment will be a demonstration of the power of truth, every experience will be an open door to a larger, more beautiful world, and every person, thing or event that we may meet, will add to our welfare and joy. With God all things are possible, and when we give Him the glory for everything we are with Him in everything.

To live the life of the great eternal now in the consciousness of those spiritual elements in which the real man lives and moves and has his being, is to enter the new heaven and the new earth. In the spirit all things are forever new, and the life of the spirit is perpetual ascension into the newer, the larger, the more beautiful, the more sublime. When life seems barren and useless, we are not in the spirit, but the moment we enter the spirit, a million universes are revealed to mind, and the joy of existence becomes supreme. We are not required to search the world of things for happiness, worth, entertainment or events of interest; one moment in the spirit is far more interesting than a whole life of physical existence, and one hour in the cosmic world is a thousand ages of unbounded bliss.

Depend upon the Infinite and His power will see you through. We learn that the Lord fought for Israel in ages gone by, and he will do the same now, for He changeth never. The term "Israel" means one chosen of God, and every person who chooses to go with God will be chosen of God. Go **with**

God, live with God, walk with God, depend upon God in all things, and you will be chosen of God. When you choose God as your leader and your King, He will fight your battles; He will be with you always, and you will never see anything but victory. We fail only when we depend upon ourselves, ignoring the presence and the goodness of the Supreme. We go wrong only when we follow the light of our own darkness, forgetting that the guiding light of the Most High is at hand. This light knows what we ought to do, and when we follow this light we will always do that which is best.

The light of the spirit never leads into sickness, trouble or want. The light of the spirit invariably leads out of that which is evil, and into that which is good. To go with God is to go into freedom, into happiness and into everything that can add to the richness and beauty of life. God is rich and can give us everything we may need without depriving anyone of anything; and when God leads us on to victory no one will lose because we have gained. The best will happen to everybody, and the greatest good will come to all. The gain of one is the gain of the many, providing that gain was secured through higher power; and when the one ascends in the scale, millions will discover the light they so long have desired to see.

This is our purpose: To live the purest, the largest, the fairest, the most useful, the most beautiful and the most spiritual life possible, just for today. To be our very best here and now, with no desire to outshine some other being, but simply to be all that we are in divine being now. To fill the present moment with all the spiritual sunshine that we can possibly radiate through the crystal walls of love, peace, faith and joy; and to live so near to the Supreme that we may touch the hem of His garment whenever we so desire. This is life, and he who lives with such a purpose forever in view, shall never know an undesired moment.

To believe in the Christ is to enter into the Christ consciousness; not simply to believe something about what He was, but to realize what He is; to feel the sublime life that He felt, and to know that touch of the spirit that He knew. We believe in the Christ only when we can mentally feel the power of His life in our own divine nature, and we believe in His name, the name that is above all names, when we can inwardly discern the full spiritual significance of that name. Belief in the Christ is not of the letter, but of the spirit; not to be definitely expressed in words, but to be inwardly felt in the soul. To ask in the name of the Christ is to enter into the spiritual understanding of that name, into the very soul of the power of that name, and in that sublime state offer our prayer. When we enter into that realization where we know what the name of Christ signifies in the spirit, we can ask in His name; and what we ask in His name we invariably receive.

When we enter into the spirit of the name of the Christ we are in the supreme power of the Christ; we inwardly know what the Christ is and what He can do; and being in His power, we are in that power that can do and will do whatever we wish to have done. We fail to receive only when we are outside of that power that can give; but we invariably enter into the power of the Christ when we inwardly know the spiritual meaning of His name. To end a prayer by simply saying, "We ask it in Christ's name" is not sufficient; we ask in His name only when we can consciously feel that divinity that is defined by the name of the Christ. Words have no power unless they are spoken in the **feeling** of the spirit of that truth that the words are intended to convey. We speak to God only when we spiritually discern and inwardly feel what we say, and God answers only those prayers that are spoken to Him.

We should never try to eliminate evil. To resist evil, to give thought to evil, or to work against evil, is to give more life and power to the very thing you wish to remove. Overcome evil with good, but do not array the good against the evil, thinking that overcoming implies resistance or warfare. To overcome is to rise out of, forgetting the lesser by giving the whole of life to the greater. The purpose of life is to grow eternally into the greater good. Aim to fulfill this purpose and evil of every description will disappear. There is no wrong in the world that demands our attention. The good alone deserves our attention, and when the good receives all our attention, evil cannot exist any more. Build for the right; inspire every soul with an irresistible desire for the right, and everything you do will add to the power that makes for freedom. Think of the good, speak of the good, work for the good, live for the good, and the good only, and your life will be a light wherein darkness can never be.

The false prophet always predicts evil, trouble, misfortune and death. He can see only the weak side, the man made, the coming and going illusions. The true prophet can see that which lies behind the illusion, that which is possible, that which is in store, that which can be done and will be done. He keeps the eye single upon the high state, and thereby ascends into the reality of that vision which previously seemed but a dream. Every person who judges according to appearances is a false prophet; he forms conclusions that are not true to real life, and by following those conclusions causes that which is false and undesirable to come to pass. Every person who judges according to the divinity that is inherent in man is a true prophet; he brings truth into expression and thereby causes that which is true to prevail in tangible existence. The true prophet can see the greatness, the beauty and the perfection of the soul of man, and knowing that the soul is the master, predicts the coming of everything that is in the soul, or that the soul has the power to do; and all such predictions **will** come true.

God is sufficient. When you are in sickness, trouble, sorrow or want depend upon the Supreme. You need nothing else. Infinite power is greater than all power, and if you have perfect faith, this power will surely set you free, no matter what the condition of bondage may be. The ills of the world continue principally because we think that something else besides the Infinite is required. But to depend upon other things besides the one is idol worship. The true worship of God, the highest worship of God, is to live so near to God that we can, at all times, feel that power that can do everything, will do everything, is doing everything. When we worship God, in spirit and in truth, we do not seek help from things; we use things according to their nature, but we seek help from the Supreme alone.

There is no bondage in living according to the law; in brief, there is freedom only in that life that lives absolutely according to the law. A law is but a path to new realms, fairer than we have ever known before. To follow any law in life is to increase the greatness and the worth of life, and to follow all the laws of life is to grow perpetually into the highest good that body, mind and soul can possibly desire. And no one could wish for a greater freedom than this. To use the law is to gain our own; to misuse or ignore the law is to deprive ourselves of our own, and bring disorder, want and pain into life instead. The law never binds nor holds down; the power of all law moves eternally toward the heights, that supreme greatness that is waiting for man; and whoever follows the law will move with that power up unto those same heights.

Give God the glory for what you have and you will receive more. Be grateful for the measure that is coming to you and that measure will increase perpetually. This is the law and it will never fail unless you fail to do to others what God is doing to you. Giving and receiving must be equal in your life. We must give something for everything we receive; nothing is free; the universe is not built in that manner; but giving does not imply the gift of things. True giving and true being are one and the same in real life.

The act of giving produces just as much joy as the act of receiving, because both add to the richness of existence. When we give much we bring forth much from the depths of divine being, and what we bring forth becomes a permanent part of actual life. When we give much we add to life from the within; when we receive much we add to life from the without; and when the richness of the within is harmoniously blended with the richness of the without, then real living begins. But the two must be equal. When we give more than we receive, or receive more than we give, discord follows, and herein we find the cause of many troubles and ills. The lesser without cannot receive the greater within, nor can the greater without be appropriated and appreciated by the lesser within. The small, undeveloped mind cannot enjoy the sublime grandeur of nature, nor can the great, highly developed mind find contentment in crude, uncultivated surroundings. The without and the within must be in harmony if the highest happiness and the truest life is to be enjoyed, and this harmony is invariably secured when giving and receiving are equal. In truth, there is no other way; if we would have the real correspond with the ideal, and the capacity to enjoy be as large as the good things we have found to enjoy, we must give as much as we receive and receive as much as we give.

Before we can receive those things in the without that have worth, we must bring forth worth from the within. What we bring forth from the within we always give to the world, because no person can enrich his own spiritual life without enriching the whole world thereby. Before we can receive the best of all things in the without, we must bring forth the best of all things from the within. But to desire to give to the world from the richness of our own nature is not sufficient; many have done this and have found themselves in want, both physical and spiritual. To desire to receive is just as necessary as to desire to give. The two desires should be equally strong, and together should hourly grow in strength. The desire to receive is just as good as the desire to give, providing the two desires are equally dear to the heart. The more we receive the more we can give, and the more we give the greater our capacity to receive. Therefore, by placing ourselves in that position where we can constantly give more and more and constantly receive more and more, we not only add more and more to the richness and beauty and perfection of our own life, but we become a great power for good in the world. And this is our highest aim.

Before we can live a great life and receive from the external world those things that naturally belong to a great life, we must give forth into real life more and more of our own inherent greatness. Before we can receive as much from the world of things as our largest personal needs and desires may demand, we must unfold, develop and use those powers and talents that are necessary to the building of greater and greater things. Be of great use in the world and you give more and more to the world. In response the world will bring your own to you. He who actively is much, gives much; and he gives the most who serves the best.

To serve the human race in the largest and highest sense, we must bring forth into living expression the truest, the best and the greatest that we can possibly find in the depths of our own sublime being. And to this end we need all the inspiration we can receive from nature, all the love and friendship we can receive from man, and all the wisdom and power we can receive from God.

To become all that we are destined to become, we must receive the largest possible measure from every source, but we cannot receive the largest possible measure from any source unless we give all we have the power to give whenever we have the privilege to do so. And this privilege is ever present. Whatever our field of action may be we may give the very best that there is within us; and we will not do so in vain. Live a great life where you are; hide nothing that has worth; use every talent in full measure; bring forth into life and usefulness the highest powers that you know you possess, and you will enter into a greater and greater life, until you finally reach the supreme heights of exalted spiritual attainments. Awaken everything within you that can, in any manner, enrich, beautify and perfect the whole of life. Do not limit the giving of your greatest self to any one part or any one group of parts. Live for the universe and all that the vastness of the cosmos may contain.

The more we all give to the whole of life the more we all shall receive from the whole of life. We therefore have everything to gain by giving more and more everywhere, and by receiving more and more from every source in order that they may give again in still greater measure. And herein we find the secret to that beautiful life that God has prepared for them that love Him.

"Be not anxious for your life." Live your life according to the very highest light that is within you; use fully and well all the powers that you have received; give your best to the world at all times and under every circumstance, and depend upon the Infinite for every-thing that existence may need or desire. You will receive it. You need not be anxious about anything. God is greater than anything that can possibly happen. Have faith in Him and He will see you safely through. Things go wrong only when you fail to be your best and fail to take God with you in everything you do. It is therefore in your power to place yourself in that position where everything will go right. The lilies of the field are all that beautiful lilies can possibly be, and they depend wholly upon the powers divine that are within them. Accordingly, they are an inspiration to all the world.

CHAPTER VIII

AND ALL THINGS SHALL BE ADDED

But seek ye first his kingdom and his righteousness; and all these things shall be added unto you.—Mat. 6:33.

The kingdom of God is within, and manifests through man as the spiritual life. His righteousness is the right use of all that is contained in the elements of the spiritual life. The spiritual life being the complete life, the full expression of life in body, mind and soul, it is evident that the right use of the spiritual life will produce and bring everything that man may need or desire. The source of everything has the power to produce everything, providing the power within that source is used according to exact spiritual law.

The spiritual life being the source of all that is necessary to a full and perfect life, and the kingdom of God within being the source of the spiritual life, we can readily understand why the kingdom should be sought first; and also, why everything that we may require will be added when the first thought is given to spiritual living and righteous action. Righteous action, however, is not simply moral action, but the right use of the elements of life in all action.

To seek His kingdom first, it is not necessary to withdraw from the world, nor to deny oneself the good things that exist in the world; to seek the kingdom first, is to give one's strongest thought to the spiritual life, and to make spiritual thought the predominating thought in everything that one may do in life. In other words, go to God first for everything, place your greatest dependence upon His power to carry you through everything, and live so close to His kingdom within that you are fully conscious of that kingdom every moment.

To seek the kingdom first, the heart must be in the spirit; that is, to live the spiritual life must be the predominating desire; but the mental conception of the spiritual life must not be narrow; in brief, that conception must contain the perfection of everything that can possibly appear in life. To think of the spiritual life as being distinct from mind and body is to deter the spiritual life from being expressed in mind and body; but what is not expressed is not lived. To think about the spiritual, or to feel the emotional power of the spiritual, is not sufficient; but that is as far as the spiritual life has been taken by the average person; that the other things were not added is therefore no fault of the law.

The spiritual life must be thoroughly lived in mind and body; the power of the spirit must be made the soul of all power, and the law of spiritual action must be made the rule and guide in all action. When the spiritual is lived in all life, the richness, the quality and the worth of the spiritual will be produced in all life, and spiritual worth is the sum-total of all worth.

To enter the kingdom within is to enter health, harmony and happiness, because these three great principles reign supremely in the spiritual life of man. Therefore, by seeking the kingdom, health will be added, harmony will be added, happiness will be added. It is impossible to be sick in the spiritual life; and discord and unhappiness can no more exist in such a life than darkness can exist in the most brilliant light. But to seek the kingdom is not sufficient; we must also seek his righteousness. If we misuse any organ, faculty, function or power anywhere in body, mind or soul, we cannot remain in health no matter how spiritual we may try to be.

To seek his righteousness is to use everything in our world as God uses everything in His world; which means, in harmony with its own nature, in harmony with its sphere of action and in harmony with the law that tends upward and onward forever. Righteous action is that action that is always harmonious, and that always works for better things, greater things, higher things.

To enter the kingdom within is to enter more power, because there is no limit to the power of the spirit; and the more power we enter into or become conscious of, the more power we will give to mind and body. In consequence, the more spiritual we become the stronger we become, the more able we become, the more competent we become, and the more we can accomplish whatever our work may be. And he who can do good work in the world invariably receives the good things in the world. To his life will be added all those things that can make personal existence rich and beautiful.

To enter the kingdom is to enter the life of freedom. There is no bondage in the spirit, and as we grow in the spirit we grow out of all bondage; one adverse condition after another disappears until absolute freedom is gained. All bondage comes from incompleteness in living, and misuse of life in doing. But the spiritual life is full and complete, and it follows the law of righteous action in all doing; therefore, when we seek first His kingdom and His righteousness, perfect freedom in all things and at all times will invariably be added.

When we seek first the kingdom, all other things are not added in some mysterious manner; nor do they come of themselves regardless of our conscious effort to work in harmony with the law of life; that is, the law of being and doing all that lies within the power of life. We receive from the kingdom only what we are prepared to use in the living of a great life, and in the doing of great and noble things in the world. We receive only in proportion to what we give; and it is only as we work well that we produce results; but by entering the spiritual life we receive as much as we may require in order to give as much as we desire; and we gain the power to do everything that is necessary to give worth and superiority to our present state of existence.

When we enter the spiritual life we gain every quality that is required in making life full and complete in our own state of being; and we gain the power to produce and create in the external world whatever we may need or desire. In other words, we receive everything we want from the within, and we gain the power to produce everything we want in the without. We therefore need never take anxious thought about these "other things." By seeking first His kingdom and His righteousness, we shall positively receive them. The way will be opened, and we shall be abundantly supplied with the best that life can give.

Depend upon me. I will provide. This is the Word, eternally spoken from on high; and every awakened soul has learned the message, but the few alone have discerned its real interpretation.

God is rich, and nothing is too good for the children of God. The Spirit of the Infinite will provide; not bare necessities, but everything. Ask what thou wilt and I will answer thee.

It is the will of God that we should seek everything that is good, worthy and beautiful. The life of man should be full and complete; human existence should be rich in body, mind and soul, for this is the great divine purpose.

To think that we must live on bare necessities in order to be spiritual, is to limit our faith in the goodness and the power of God. The kingdom of

God is at hand now; we are expected to enter now, and this kingdom is abundantly supplied with everything that can enrich, perfect and beautify human life.

Seek ye first the kingdom, and all other things shall be added; not simply enough to live on, but **all** things. The love of God is infinite, and we cannot think of infinite love as wanting to give less than all. God has the power to give all. He also has the desire to give all, and therefore every soul may, at any time, receive all that present development can take possession of.

The more we ask of God the more we please God. To give is the highest pleasure of true love, and God is true love. To ask Him for everything, the most of everything and the best of everything is to enter into the life of the highest joy of heaven; and to live in such a life is to live indeed.

When we do not have what we want or what we need, we should remember that Spirit can provide, and that Spirit will provide if we only so desire. Depend upon me. I will not forsake thee nor leave thee. I am thy Redeemer, I will care for thee.

Take God at His word. Have faith in the message that comes from on high. Believe with all the power of mind and soul that God will do what love will do, because God is love. Open the heart to the influx of infinite love, and all that God can give will come with His love.

Do not hesitate to ask God for material things. God owns the universe. Everything is the product of His creative power; therefore it is all good, and what is good is good for man. What you can use to promote the welfare of everybody, including yourself, you may receive. Only remember this, that things spiritual must come first in your thought. You may have abundances of things material; there is more than enough to provide everybody with all the luxuries of life. You will not deprive anybody of anything by accepting from God all that His love can give. Others may receive as much from the same source; but seek first the things of the spirit, for this is the law.

Consider the lilies of the field. Why should not you be arrayed like one of these? It is the will of God that you should be, and you will give Him great pleasure by asking Him to clothe you even more gorgeously than they. But we must remember that we are not to take these things from others; we are to receive them from God. There is a great difference between the two methods, and there are few in the world that can see it.

To receive from God we must love the spiritual the best, though we must neither despise nor ignore the material. All is from God, and all will minister to the joy and beauty of life when used in harmony with a life that is lived in God. When we live in God, all things will be turned to good account, and when we work with God, all things will work together for greater good.

The world tries to get from man; the perfect way is to receive from God; and the moment we adopt the latter method, the way will be opened. Spirit will lead; we will know at each step what we are to do, and what step to take next will always be clear. Live close to God and have faith; no matter what may come or not, depend upon the spirit to lead and provide, and you will always do what is best.

However, we must never think that it is best for anyone to live in poverty, trouble and pain; no, this is never best, not even for a moment. The Infinite can provide something better here and now, and it is His will and good pleasure to do so.

When days of darkness are at hand, cling to the great truth, **spirit will provide**. Think of it constantly; live in the very soul of its presence; believe in it from the very depths of the heart. Things will take a turn. The door of opportunity will open. The desired change will come. There is nothing in the world that the Spirit cannot change for the better; therefore we may with perfect faith ask for any change desired. The best is intended for all of us. God is ever ready to give everything. Ask what thou wilt and I will answer thee.

To think of thee and feel thy presence near,
To rise above the world of doubt and fear,
To enter where the many mansions be,
To hold communion face to face with thee.

To find the secret place where all is still,
To feel thy joy and life my being thrill,
To know that health and wholeness now are mine,
To see thy light within forever shine,

To feel the peace that passeth thought and speech,
To know that I the endless heights shall reach,
That I thy Son for evermore shall be,
These are the sweetest thoughts of life to me.

CHAPTER IX

WHEN LIFE IS WORTH LIVING

To establish permanently the living of life in the spiritual state of being is the greatest need of man. But this is not possible so long as we live in that conception of spirituality that forgets the body. The body is the temple of the spirit, and must therefore receive just as much thought and attention as we give to the spirit. To neglect the body is to make real spirituality impossible, because real spirituality is a living thing, and must have a highly developed personality through which this **living** may be expressed. Spirituality is not simply in thought, feeling or abstract contemplation; there is no spirituality without the actual coming forth of real soul life; but the life of the soul does not come forth into tangible personal living unless the body is trained to respond to that life.

The spirituality that we seek is that full expression of the soul that fills every atom in the body and gives the sublime wholeness of divinity to the entire being of man. To be spiritual is to be complete in body, mind and soul; to live the fullness of real life in every element of life, and to bring forth the truest, the best and the most beautiful that exists within us. To become spiritual is to refine everything, perfect everything, beautify everything, and make the ideal real, not only in thought but in every part of physical life, mental life and spiritual life. To grow in spirituality is to continue perpetually to spiritualize the body, as well as mind and soul, until the visible man is as pure, as strong, as wholesome and as beautiful as the highest state of divine existence.

True spirituality will give health and vigor to the body, power and brilliancy to the mind, strength and perfection to the character, and sublime loveliness to the soul. The more spiritual you become the more beautiful you become in person, the more refined you become in all the elements of your nature, the more powerful you become in every thought and action, and the more comfort, happiness and real satisfaction you will receive from everything you may do in life. When spirituality is highly developed you live constantly on the heights; you see all things as they are in the real; you know that you are created in the image and likeness of God; you are in constant touch with the beauty and splendor of the cosmic world, and your joy is supreme. You are living in the light of the spirit, and your mind at times is so illumined by that light that your understanding of higher wisdom becomes extraordinary. You thus enter those lofty realms from which all true prophets have received their inspiration, and, accordingly, you become one of those who are chosen to be taught of God.

To enter real spirituality is to anchor the mind in that very power that holds and guides the universe; and such a mind is always safe. Such a mind will not go wrong; and even though it be strongly tempted, it will be removed from danger before it is too late. There is something in the higher world about us that can and does protect the soul; and those who are fixed on high in the spirit are ever in the care of this divine protection. Dangers, calamities or catastrophes will never touch them; they are invariably taken out safely, no matter what may happen; they are ever in the hands of God, and all is always well.

This higher guiding power, however, does not simply protect the chosen ones from that which is not desired; but those who have supreme faith in the spirit will be led on and on into the larger and larger realization of that which is desired. The spirit contains all, and to grow in the spirit is to receive all. Not simply that all that satisfies the demands of the intellect or the feelings of the soul, but that all that fully supplies every want, desire or need of the whole man. Spirituality is the highest good of all life realized in full living expression. In the spiritual life there is no need, neither is there any false desire. Every desire is true to the great purpose of eternal life, and every desire is fulfilled. In spiritual life every prayer is inspired by the wisdom of the spirit, and such prayers are always answered. Whatever God may lead us to do He will always give us the power to do.

The spiritual state of being is the great foundation of all being, and the source of everything that comes forth into perfect being; therefore, the more deeply we enter into the life and the power of the spirit the more fully conscious we become of those greater things that real life has in store; and whatever we become conscious of we invariably bring forth into tangible existence. The spiritual life contains real life, real power, real wisdom, real love, real harmony, real health, real purity, real peace, real joy, and to develop spirituality is to realize more and more of the real of these things until the perfection of divine being is unfolded and lived in the present personal form. In consequence, when we are in the spiritual life we need sacrifice nothing that has real value, while we gain more and more of everything that has greater value. When we begin to live the spiritual life we begin to feel that we are now upon the solid rock of eternal being, and we feel absolutely secure. We realize that we are in safety, in divinity, in the protecting care of higher power. We are becoming more and more conscious of the cosmic atmosphere, and this gives added assurance of complete protection, because this higher, sublimated atmosphere is so surcharged with living spirit that no ill from the world can possibly pass through. We are absolutely out of the ills of the world when we are in the spirit, just as we are absolutely out of darkness when we are in the light. And to grow in the spirit the first essential is to take what spiritual life we can now understand and give that life full, living expression in every atom of body, soul and mind.

There can be no real spirituality developed so long as we try to make such developments a matter of the soul alone; mind and body must be included or our efforts simply result in feelings and sentiments that are neither wholesome nor harmless. Spirituality is not a matter of sentiment, nor is it wholly concerned with a future state of existence. Spirituality is a full life just for to-day. It is a life that is all that it is now, and those who are in the spirit know that the time that now is, is eternal.

One touch of the spirit and all is well. Darkness and pain will vanish, sickness and sorrow take flight; weakness and bondage will pass away, and troubles can exist no more. To be touched by the spirit is to be filled through and through with the spirit, and where the spirit is there evil is not. What we have seen in our visions shall come to remain. What is revealed from on high shall come and abide with us always. Therefore let the soul dream on. Disturb not the peace of those sweet celestial slumbers, for what to us may appear to be spiritual sleep is but life in a greater world. And thus something from above comes to tell us, "dream on, fair soul, dream on."

To worship God in spirit and in truth, is to so live that we can always feel that He is with us no matter what we may think or say or do. To worship God is to take Him with us in everything, ask Him for everything, have faith that He will give us everything, and be grateful to Him because we inwardly know that we are receiving everything. To worship is not to believe and adore, but to live and love; not simply to accept the truth but to make the truth the living soul of every thought and word and deed. When we worship God in truth, we enter into His presence knowing that He is divine perfection and that we are created in His image and likeness. To believe that we are depraved beings, base sinners or imperfect human creatures, is not to be in the truth, because to be in the truth we are as God is. Therefore, while we have those beliefs we cannot worship God in truth. To worship God in truth we must enter the truth, and to enter the truth is to know that man is even now the perfect image of the Most High.

To worship God in the spirit, is to forget the letter and enter into the spiritual realization of His omnipresent life. When we are in the spirit we do not worship with audible words or visible attitudes, but with that exalted spiritual feeling that enters into the very soul of the Infinite and there awakens to the great eternal truth that "My Father and I are one." When we are in the spirit we inwardly know that "God is closer than breathing, nearer than hands and feet," and we can feel that sublime nearness thrill every atom in our being. We need nothing to prove to us that we are one with God, for we can feel that it is the truth. Nor do we question any more whether God be personal or not. We know that we are with Him and that He is with us; and that is sufficient. His personal presence is more real to us than our own existence; we therefore need not reason on that subject. We have seen Him in the spirit, but that which is in the spirit, form cannot measure, nor words define.

The word of God is the word of truth. All truth is Scripture wherever found or by whom presented; and all Scripture is written when the mind is in the spirit. Therefore, to understand the Scripture we must enter the spirit, and read while illumined by the spirit. We shall then find, upon every page, "the bread of heaven," "the waters of life," "the meat that ye know not of." The key to the Scriptures is not some system of symbolical interpretation, nor some special method of metaphysical or spiritual analysis. The key is simply to enter the spirit when you begin to read. The spirit reveals everything that is sacred and true.

To live exclusively in materiality, that is, in the lower story of being, is the cause of all weakness and weariness. The remedy for such conditions will therefore be found in spirituality, which means to live in the upper story. So long as the mind is "high" in the world of consciousness there can be no weakness or weariness in the person. We cannot be weary while we are filled with the strength of the Most High, and we are in perfect touch with this great strength while the mind is living in the "high places" of the spirit. When we come down to the earth earthy, we lose this superior power and become weak as mere men; we are limited in every respect and have to watch ourselves at every turn lest we overtax the system. But when we do all things in the realization that we are spiritual beings filled with supreme power from on high, there is no limit to what we can do. Our strength is eternally renewed because we are waiting upon the Lord; we are living with Him, doing all things for Him, and in return we receive all things from Him.

When the mind lives constantly in the higher states of being, more perfect oneness with the Infinite is attained. We come nearer and nearer to the Life and the Spirit of the Supreme, and, in consequence, we are supplied with new life and power every moment. We are going into the source of all power; we are beginning to live and move and have our being in the very essence of that power, and we are becoming stronger by far than all the weakness and the weariness in the world. We are no longer subject to the laws of material existence; what holds true in the life of mere man does not hold true for us any more; we have entered a new life and are ascending triumphantly to the supreme heights of that life. The seeming weakness of the flesh has given place to the limitless strength of the Spirit, for the very moment we begin to **live** in the spirit, the power of the spirit begins to **live** in us, and that which **lives** in us lives in every element of the body as well as in every attribute of mind and soul.

Spirituality is the perfect remedy for all the ills of life, and to live the spiritual life is the greatest thing that man can do. Therefore, to promote spiritual growth among all minds that are ready, is of more importance than all other objects and aims combined. Thousands realize this, and, in consequence, are ever in search for methods through which the life of the spirit may be found. Methods, however, are of secondary importance. When the heart begins to feel the need of the spirit, and all the powers of mind begin to desire the spirit, the perfect way will be opened. To promote spiritual growth we must live in the spiritual center of the divine that is within us, but that divine center is not found through methods. No system of mental gymnastics can open the gates to the kingdom within; nor can any system of logical reasoning in abstract truth cause the mind to be illumined with light from on high. Spiritual illumination does not come through a mere intellectual process, however exact; it comes only when the desires of the heart are spiritualized by a power that is infinitely greater than man.

To think the truth, even with absolute exactness, will not avail unless we think in the spirit of truth. The intellectual form of the truth has no power; it is the inner spirit of the truth that gives life, freedom and illumination to man. And when we begin to know this inner spirit of the truth our minds have entered into the very soul of the real. Then it is that we gain power that to many seems superhuman; then it is that we take full possession of our own life and our own destiny; then it is that we find the faith that moves

mountains, and through the life of this faith we press on and on to the great
goal we have in view, removing every barrier in the way, overcoming every
difficulty, surmounting every obstacle, rising higher than ever before every
time we fall, transforming every seeming defeat into a great and glorious
victory, passing through the fires of tribulation without even a hair being
scorched, and coming out of every trying experience with greater purity
and greater strength, realizing one ideal after another, ascending from one
pinnacle of attainment to one that is higher still, finding answer after answer
to the prayers we prayed in days gone by, until every desire is fulfilled and
every dream of the soul made true.

There is no reason whatever why anyone should become discouraged, or
be tempted to give up because the good things desired are not realized when
expected. That which is your own will positively come to you, and everything is your own that you can use in the building of a greater and more
beautiful life. Continue in the faith that you will now begin to realize the
fullness of life, and enter into the inner spirit of that faith. Some of the
greatest things in the world have been gained after many years of constant
faith and prayer—things that would not have been gained if those who
prayed had lived in discouragement and doubt. If there is anything that you
can use in the building of a great life, pray for it until you receive it no matter how many months or years may be required to cause your prayer to come
true. Pray in the inner spirit of faith and when the time is ripe, be it to-
morrow or twenty years from now, your prayer will be answered.

When your prayers are not answered at once, do not come to the conclusion that it is not best for you to have it; if that which you pray for will add
to the welfare of somebody's life, it is best for you to have it. Therefore,
continue to pray for it until you receive it. It is best that you should have
everything that is good and true and beautiful. All that is good is good for
man, and it is the will of God that man should receive it. But God gives us
only that which we desire. We have individual choice, and we must express
our desire in the true spirit of faith. What we ask for will come when our
faith is right and our life prepared to properly use the great good desired.

To promote spiritual growth the inner light must shine in the outer life,
and the inner world of divine truth must be expressed in every part of mind
and body. The expression of the divinity within is absolutely necessary, and
must be in every direction. Thousands to-day are expressing truth only for
the purpose of securing health of body and peace of mind, and though they
are having good results they will find ere long that in trying to perfect only
a part of the outer life they have failed to bring forth the whole of the inner

life. They will also find that the marvelous powers of the within have been permitted to sleep. After some years such minds will find that they have accomplished nothing more than being well and comfortable physically. But this is not all that we are living for. A genius is asleep in the subconscious of every mind; a spiritual giant is within us awaiting recognition; and in the soul is the Christ knocking at the door. These must not be kept waiting age after age while we are only concerned with being well and happy on the surface. It is not right to live a small life no matter how comfortable that life may be when we have received the gifts of the supreme life from on high.

The expression of the spirit should be universal in all the actions of man. The labor of the hands should be filled with the life of the spirit; the work of the mind should be animated with the one power of spirit, and every act of consciousness should feel the divine presence of the spirit. There are few, however, who think of expressing divine spirit in every day work, and consequently, the spiritual life becomes a thing apart. But when the personal life is separated from the spirit, darkness, confusion, sickness and trouble begin; existence becomes a burden, and though we may possess the wealth of the world, life has nothing of worth to give. There is no joy in things unless the power of the spirit is in the world of things. There is nothing to live for unless we live for the spirit, and when we begin to live for the spirit all things, from the least importance in the physical realm to the most precious elements in the highest spiritual realms—all become ministering angels, adding eternally to the worth, the beauty and the joy of personal life. To him who lives in the spirit, everything in life has much to give, and to him, the best alone is given.

When we think, the mind should be filled with the spirit, and our intellects will become brilliant in the true sense of that term. When we read, our eyes should be filled with the spirit, and our sight will ever become stronger and better. When we work, every muscle in the body should be filled with the spirit, and we should renew our strength from the source divine. We thus cause the outer life and the inner life to become one life, and it is such a life that we are here to live now. Say that life is beautiful, no matter how things may appear on the surface. Say that you are strong and well no matter how the body may feel. You will thus speak the truth about the true state of being; and what you say, you create. Say that you are well and you create health. Say that life is divinely beautiful and you create such a life. And what we create today, we shall realize tomorrow.

There are a number of methods through which the spiritual nature of man can be developed and brought into larger and larger expression, but

the majority of those methods are so complex that they lead more into intel-
lectuality than into spirituality. To develop the mind, with its many faculties, complex methods are, as a rule, necessary, but to develop the soul, the
simpler the methods are, the better. The secret is to keep the eye single upon
the sublime spiritual state, to form the highest possible conception of the
most perfect spiritual qualities imaginable, and to think of those things. The
power of concentration is truly extraordinary whenever it may be applied,
and its effectiveness is nowhere as thorough as in the world of the spirit. To
think constantly of things spiritual, with an effort to enter more and more
into the real life of the spirit, is to spiritualize all the elements of thought,
all the phases of consciousness, and all the active states of realization. In
consequence, everything in human life will become more spiritual.

What we think of we create; therefore the more we think of things spiritual the more spirituality we shall develop; and when the whole of thought
is concentrated constantly upon our highest spiritual ideal, we shall actually
move into the real spiritual state. There is a spiritual state of consciousness
immediately above the usual conscious state, and it is the lifting of mind and
thought up into this higher state that produces spirituality; therefore, spiritual development will necessarily require the ascending tendency in every
action in life. This requirement, however, is invariably supplied, when the
power of attention is constantly directed upon the spiritual state. When we
think of that which is spiritual, everything in life begins to ascend toward
the higher spiritual states; that is, when our thinking of the spiritual is inspired with a deep soul desire to rise and live on the heights.

Live with the beautiful side in human nature and your own life will grow more and more beautiful until you become an inspiration to all the world. Look for the greater good in all things and you will find God in all things. And when you find God in all things God will be with you in all things.

Say that life is beautiful, no matter how things may appear on the surface. Say that you are strong and well no matter how the body may feel. You will thus speak the truth about the true state of being; and what you say, you create. Say that you are well and you create health. Say that life is divinely beautiful and you create such a life. And what we create today, we shall realize tomorrow.

The pure in heart shall see God, and to be pure in heart is to think pure thoughts—the thought of sublime spiritual truth. The reason we do not see God is found in the fact that we have clouded our minds with impure thoughts—thought that is out of harmony with the divine order of things. Pure water is transparent; the same is true of a pure mind. The deep things of God are easily discerned through a pure mind, just as easily as the rocks of the river bed when the water is pure and still.

CHAPTER X

THE WAY, THE TRUTH AND THE LIFE

Jesus saith unto him, I am the way, and the truth, and the life; no one cometh unto the Father but by me.—John 14:6.

The great statements of Jesus Christ were never spoken from the personal, but always from the impersonal. No truth ever sprung from the personal mind because it is only the impersonal that can touch the universal, and it is only in the universal that absolute truth can be found. When the mind enters the impersonal state, consciousness comes in touch with the cosmic state of being, and in that state we realize the "I Am" of being. We discern what the "I Am" actually is, and we find that the consciousness of the "I Am" is the open door to the limitless vastness of the spiritual universe. "I am the door." Enter through the door of "I Am" and we pass into that immense world that is found on the upper side, or the divine side of sublime existence.

The "I Am" in every soul is the spirit of Christ within us, and when we become conscious of the Christ within us we can truthfully say that "the mind that was in Christ Jesus, the same mind is in me." The mind that was in Christ Jesus knew the "I Am" of eternal being; in brief, was the "I Am" of eternal being, and therefore could say that I am the way, and the truth, and the life. But this same "I Am" is in every soul and constitutes the real "me" of every soul, and as we grow in Christ we grow into the realization of that great truth that we are one with Christ, and that the same Christ that reigned supremely in the personality of Jesus shall reign supremely in us.

The Christ within us is the only begotten of the Father, and is created in the image and likeness of the Father. There is only one Son of God, but this one Son reigns in every soul, and constitutes the "I Am" in every soul. The "I Am" that occupies the throne of your spiritual being is the only begotten Son of God, and as this Son is like the Father you cannot grow into the likeness of the Father unless you do so through the Son. Nor can you enter into the presence of the Father without going through the Son, because it is the Son that unites the Father with you.

The Son of God is one with God, therefore if you wish to realize your oneness with God you must enter into the life and the spirit of the Son. In other words, you must become conscious of the "I Am" within you because it is this "I Am" that is created in the image of God, and we are not one with God unless we realize that we are created in the image of God. To be one with God is to know that we are in the Father and the Father in us, but we cannot enter into that consciousness wherein we know that we are in the Father until we are conscious of our exact likeness to the Father.

When Jesus declared, I am the way, he spoke in the consciousness of the Christ. It was the supreme "I Am" that made this great statement, and this "I Am" is the way. The supreme "I Am" is the way to everything that man may need or desire throughout eternity, for "I Am" in God, and in God we find the allness of all that is. The "I Am" is the way to God, because it is the "I Am" in man that is always one with God. "I am the door," and there is no other door; it is therefore evident that no one cometh unto the Father but by me.

To go to God you must go by way of the Christ; that is, you must enter into the inner consciousness of the Christ that reigns within us; you must enter so deeply into the spirit of your own sublime being that you can read-ily realize that "I Am," and know that "I Am" is not distinct from you but is the real and the eternal of you. "Where I am there ye shall be also." You shall some day enter that same exalted state where your consciousness of the "I Am" will be so perfect that you will know that you are "I Am." Then the supreme "I Am" will speak in you as he did in Jesus and will in like manner declare in you, "I am the way."

When we find the spirit of Christ within us we find the way; we then enter the path, the path that leads to the fullness of life and the perfection of being. To daily ascend higher and higher in the consciousness of this spirit of the Christ is to follow the Christ, and to follow the Christ is to enter the Kingdom.

The "I Am" is the truth because all truth has its source in the divine being of man. That the real man is created in the image of God is the one supreme truth, and the real man is the "I Am." To know the truth is to enter into the life and the spirit of the "I Am" within; that is, the Christ within, and to enter into the Christ is to enter into freedom because there can be no bondage or ill whatever in Him. This is how we gain freedom when we know the truth; not by forming intellectual concepts about truth, but by entering consciously into the spirit of the Christ within which is the truth.

To enter into the Christ consciousness is to become conscious of the real being of the Christ, and the real being of the Christ is identical with the real being of man. To become conscious of the real being of man is to know the truth concerning man, and when we know this truth we know that man is divine because man, in his eternal nature, is identical with the nature of the Christ. When we know that we are created in the likeness of truth we know that we are truth, and we can say, when speaking from the Christ consciousness, into which we have entered, "I am the truth." And when we know that we are truth we are conscious only of that which is truth. We cannot be out of the truth when we are in truth, and as there can be no ill or bondage in the truth we must necessarily be in absolute freedom while we are consciously in the truth.

The "I Am" is the life; all life comes from God, and the life that is in us is the life of the only begotten of God. The life eternal is the life of God in us, and it is the "I Am" in us that lives the life of God in us. To gain the life more abundant it is therefore necessary to enter more and more deeply into the consciousness of the "I Am" within. In brief, the more fully we realize the "I Am" or the Christ within us the more we live, and when we enter so perfectly into the Christ consciousness that we actually know that the real in us is identical with the "I Am" in us, then we begin to live the life eternal; then we actually enter eternity while still in personal form; then we know with positive conviction that we are immortal, and we need no further evidence for any other source whatever.

When we learn that "I am the door," and seek this door in the spiritual life within us, we shall find it; and as we pass through this door we enter the other side of life, the divine side, the eternal side. There we find the kingdom of God that is within us, and beyond is the shining shore. But we are not required to leave the personal form and the physical life in order to live on the other side of life. True being is to live on the spiritual side of life and to manifest the perfection of spiritual being in the personal side of life. Thus the Word becomes flesh and the glory of God is made visible in man.

For narrow is the gate, and straightened the way, that leadeth unto life. And those alone who are in the spirit can find it. Follow the light of the spirit in all things, choose the living Christ as the pattern in all things, and depend upon God in all things. Do not seek the truth; seek the spirit of truth. The spirit leads into all truth. To know the truth is to know the way. To be guided by the spirit into all truth is to walk in the light of the spirit all the way, and the way of light leads into the kingdom of eternal life. Follow the words of the Christ until the spirit is found; then follow the spirit into the greater life of the Christ. Keep the eye single upon that light that is revealed through the spiritual vision of the soul. Where that light is shining there is the gate; beyond is the way that leadeth unto life, and all who are in the spirit shall find it even now.

CHAPTER XI

TO KNOW AND THINK THE TRUTH

To mentally live in the spiritual understanding of truth, and to give constant expression, in thought, to the words of truth, is to train the mind to **know** the truth in a larger and larger measure; and to know the truth is to create and express true conditions, throughout the entire personality.

A statement of truth is the absolute truth expressed in words; that is, the mental or verbal expression of a certain state of perfect and divine being. Therefore, a statement of truth does not describe things as they are in the external, but describes man as he is in the spirit; and when the mind begins to think of man as he is in the spirit, the perfect qualities of the spirit will be unfolded and brought out into the personal life.

The life of the spirit is the true life of man because man is a spiritual being; the soul is the real man; the mind and the body are merely instruments. For this reason it is evident that when man thinks of himself he must necessarily think of himself as he is in the spirit. The conditions of the body do not describe the divine state of the soul; the soul is real, absolute, divine, perfect, complete, created in the image of God, while the personality is but a partial expression of the real, in many respects incomplete, and in a state of development.

When man thinks that the incomplete conditions of his personality constitute himself he is not thinking the truth about himself; his thought is false, and false thinking produces false or detrimental conditions in mind and body.

However, when he thinks of himself as he is in the divine perfection of his being, he is thinking the truth about himself; his thought is the truth, and the thinking of truth produces true or wholesome conditions in mind and body. Therefore, so long as man thinks of himself as being an imperfect personality he will cause his personality to be imperfect, weak, sickly and more or less in disorder; but when he constantly thinks of himself as he is in the perfect, wholesome, divine state of his real spiritual being, he will cause his personality to be wholesome, healthful, harmonious and in the most perfect state of order.

The truth gives freedom. To know the truth is to live in the perfect world of truth. When the mind discerns truth, all thought is created in the likeness of truth; all thought is truth; and man is as he thinks. To think the truth is to create that which is true, and when the true comes into being the false ceases to be.

There can be no darkness in the light; there can be no false conditions in the truth; therefore, when man is in the truth, the wholeness and the perfection of the truth will pervade his entire being through and through. Every part will be true to the truth, and every element will express the divinity of man.

When the mind thinks the truth, every mental conception of true being will formulate itself in a statement of truth; these statements will convey to man's intelligence the higher understanding of all that is. The mind will learn to see all things as they are in truth; the divine perfection of all things will be realized; all thought will contain the spirit of truth, and man, himself, will be the truth in every fiber of his being. Therefore, every mind should think statements of truth as frequently as possible, and with the deepest conviction possible.

The conditions of the personality are the direct effects of the states of the mind; therefore, the conditions of the personality will always be true, good and perfect so long as the states of the mind are true; and the states of the mind will always be true so long as the mind thinks the truth—thinks the truth about man as he is in the divine perfection of his real spiritual being.

To train the mind to think the real truth about man, statements of truth, of every possible description, should be employed extensively. In brief, the mind should be daily drilled, in the thinking of absolute truth; that is, the mental or verbal expression of statements of truth; and to enter into the spiritual understanding of the real significance of every statement should be the central purpose in view.

The mere mechanical repetition of such statements will not avail; the real truth of each statement is discerned only when the mind enters into the very soul of the statement; and it is the real truth that we wish to know, because it is the knowing of real truth that alone makes for freedom in life and that produces the fullness of life. To train the mind to think the real truth, the following statements of truth may be employed, though the wording may be changed to correspond with the state of each individual need, or the degree of conscious development in the spiritual life.

The perfection of my being is now realized in the spiritual understanding of truth

The understanding of truth reveals to the mind the divine perfection of all being, and the more spiritual this understanding is the more clearly can the divinity of man be discerned. Spirituality illumines, because to be spiritual is to live in the supreme light of the spirit. In the spirit there is no darkness, therefore, in the spirit all things can be seen as they are, and to see all things as they are is to see that all things are created in the likeness of God. The realization of the great truth that being is perfect, created in the image of God, will cause this perfection to be expressed. What we realize in the spirit will be expressed in the person. Therefore, when the real truth of this statement is understood, the personal life will be a manifestation of the spiritual life, and all will be well in body, mind and soul.

God is love, and in Him I live and move and have my being

To live the true spiritual life—the life of complete emancipation and high spiritual attainment—it is necessary to love all things with the pure, limitless love of the soul, but such a love cannot be realized so long as consciousness is personal only. It is when we **feel** that we live in the love of God that we gain consciousness of that love that loves all things at all times, and we shall invariably feel that we do live in the love of God when we know the real truth of the statement that God is boundless love, and that we have our being in Him. To realize that we live in God is to feel His presence, and when we do feel His presence we become absolutely filled with a love that is so tender, so beautiful, so high and so sublime, that we are placed completely at one with all the universe. We immediately transcend, and eliminate entirely, every adverse feeling; we are at peace with everything and that peace is animated with the spirit of that love that cannot be measured. To live in such a love is supreme joy, and it is the privilege of every soul now.

I am fixed on high in the spirit of truth

The I Am of every soul can truthfully make this statement, for real being is permanently established in the true life of the spirit, and as every individual is the I Am of his own being, every individual, to speak the truth, must make this statement about himself. To realize the truth of this statement is to enter more and more into the fixed state of true being, and to grow in the realization of this state is to gain that absolute safety and security where the soul finds complete divine protection. To be in the spirit of truth is to be in the very life of true existence, and to be fixed in this life is to occupy a permanent place in God's own beautiful world. In other words, to be fixed in the spirit of truth, is to be anchored in God, and we can readily realize how absolutely secure such a state of being must be. When we make this statement we should try to realize what existence in the truth must necessarily mean, how it must feel to be in the consciousness of the spirit of such an existence, and what a life must hold in store that is permanently established on the very heights of that existence. The more fully we enter into the soul of the truth that this statement conveys, the sooner we shall realize the truth itself; and when we do, we shall know that we are fixed on high, permanently established in the spirit of truth, forever anchored in God.

My spiritual being is the expression of eternal life

The life eternal is the whole of real, absolute, limitless life, and the real, spiritual man is this life individualized and expressed. The life eternal contains the whole complete existence; therefore, to live the life eternal is to live all that there is in absolute existence. It is the life eternal that the soul lives, and since man is the soul, he should affirm that he is living the life eternal now, and that his true being is the perfect expression of that life. The life eternal is the life of the divinity that is in man, and the true being of man constitutes that divinity; but we manifest in personal life only that which we become conscious of, therefore the mind must be unfolded to realize the true nature of the life eternal before we can enter into life now. To unfold the mind into this conscious realization, all thinking should be animated with the highest spiritual conception of the life eternal that we can possibly form, and the great truth that the true spiritual being of man is the perfect expression of that life, should be held before the mental vision constantly. In addition, every effort we make to live the life, that is, to live in the **soul** of real life, will cause this statement, not only to seem true in the ideal, but to prove itself to be true in the actual.

I am ever ascending into the greater and greater freedom of God

God is absolute freedom, and man is eternally becoming what God is. To realize this truth is to place life in that position where personal existence will, at every step in human advancement, be in full possession of that measure of freedom that present consciousness can possibly involve. This means that the life of every moment will be absolutely free, and that the measure of freedom will increase in perfect harmony with the increase of the mind's capacity for freedom. The real man is ever in possession of all the freedom that present development can comprehend and employ, and is ever ascending into the greater freedom of God; therefore, to enter into the realization of this truth is to keep the eye upon the supreme freedom, to steadily rise into more and more of that freedom, and this is the true path to complete emancipation. When we steadily grow into the freedom of God, we must necessarily grow out of everything that is limited, undesirable or adverse. The lesser passes away as we pass upward and onward into the ever expanding world of the greater.

God is health and wholeness, and I am his image and likeness

There can be no sickness in God; for the same reason there can be no sickness in the real being of man; and as each individual is what he is in his own real being, he must necessarily be well at all times. The real man cannot possibly be sick any more than light can be darkness, because he is as God is; therefore no man can truthfully say, at any time, that he is sick, weak or disabled. He cannot be any of these things, no matter what personal conditions may seem to be. The real man is always well, and I am the real man. I am not the body, nor the instrument, nor the garment. I am the I Am, the image of God, the exact likeness of the Most High. When adverse conditions appear in the personality, there are personal causes, either physical or mental, but these conditions can never enter the life of the real spiritual man. The real man continues to be well and strong at all times, and the life of the real man is perpetually a life of perfect health and wholeness. To live constantly in the conscious realization of the life of the real man is to always feel well, in body, mind and soul. There can be no sickness in the body so long as we live in the life of health, and we do live in the life of health so long as we continue in the realization of the great truth that God is health, and that we are as He is. Those adverse conditions that may exist in the body now will entirely disappear the moment we enter into the realization of real life, and begin to live in the spirit of the truth that we are as God is—perfect and whole, now and forever.

My Father and I are one

The mind that was in Christ Jesus, the same mind is in you, and this mind knows that My Father and I are One. When we enter into the spirit of the divine mind we realize that there is no separation whatever in the spirit. The spirit of the human soul is absolutely one with the spirit of the Infinite. There is no difference whatever in divine essence or soul life; only the Infinite is God while the human soul is an expression of God, the son of God, the only begotten of God.

When we enter into the very presence of God, we know that no separation can exist in the spirit, and we also learn that the Christ consciousness implies the highest consciousness of this divine oneness. The mind that was in Christ Jesus is conscious of the spiritual oneness that exists between God and man, and we enter into that mind whenever we feel that we are in the presence of God.

To realize that we are one with God, in spirit and in truth, is to realize that we are also one with the life, the divinity and the perfection of God; and therefore we are as God is; what is in God is in us; we live the same life that He lives, and since there can be no imperfection in His life, there can be no imperfection in our life.

The spiritual life of man is perfect, and when man enters fully into the consciousness of his spiritual life, his personal life will become the exact expression of His spiritual life. Then the Word will become flesh, and no ill can exist in the body any more. Nor can the untruth any longer exist in the mind.

To grow in the Christ consciousness is to grow in the consciousness of the spiritual life, and as the light of the spiritual life becomes stronger and stronger in mind, these elements of darkness, sickness, adverseness or imperfection that may remain in personal existence will entirely disappear. Then we shall realize the emancipated life, the freedom that comes from the knowing of the truth.

God is my strength. I am strong with His limitless life and power
To dwell perpetually in the conviction that the strength of the Infinite is our strength, is to steadily grow in the conscious realization of power, and the more power we become conscious of the more power we possess. To think of weakness in any sense of the term becomes impossible when we know that the limitless power of the Infinite is just as much ours as it is His. All that the Father hath is mine. And when we cease to think of weakness we shall never again be conscious of weakness.

To think of truth we can never admit that we are weak; we cannot even admit that it is possible for us to become weak. When we feel weak we are simply permitting ourselves to be untrue to ourselves; we ignore the reality of our own being and cause the mind to create conditions in our system that are false. Thus evil begins. But so long as we cause the mind to be fixed in that great truth that God is our strength, we shall not be conscious of anything that is not strength; nor will the mind create any condition that is not true to the truth.

When we realize that the strength of the Infinite is our strength, and that the strength of the Infinite is limitless, we must come to the conclusion that we are capable of doing anything that the living of a great life may demand. Whatever we are called upon to do, we are equal to it, because, have we not the power of the Supreme with which to work?

In the light of this truth we can never say that we are unable to do what the hour may require; nor can we say truthfully that we are ever tired, wearied or overcome. Such thoughts do not belong to the truth. While we are in the truth there is nothing that can make us tired; nor is there anything that is too much for us. God is our strength, and the power of Him that is within us is greater than anything in the world.

Though the flesh may seem to be weak, it seems so only because we have not fully accepted what is truly our own, the strength of the Infinite. But when we do accept this strength, the power of the spirit will manifest in the flesh; we shall then be strong, through and through, with power from on high. Every part of body, mind and soul will live with limitless life, because God lives with limitless life, and all that the Father hath is mine.

My being is sustained in the Word of Truth
The word of truth is the coming forth of truth into life; it is truth taking shape and form in the world of being, and to be sustained in the word of

truth is to so live that everything in life is shaped, formed and determined by the power of truth.

To think frequently of the great statement that we are sustained in the shaping and forming power of truth is to place the mind more and more perfectly in harmony with that power; in consequence, the mind will be shaped more and more in the exact likeness of truth.

When the mind assumes the form of truth, every action of the mind becomes an expression of truth; the mind itself becomes a true mind and all thinking will convey the elements of truth to every part of the being of man. When the mind is formed by the truth, only true conditions will be formed by the mind; and therefore, neither sickness, inharmony, weakness, adversity, pain nor want can possibly exist anywhere in the human system.

To feel that we are sustained in the word of truth is to produce that deep realization of the power of truth that is so conducive to the full understanding of truth; and as we grow in the understanding of truth we grow into the freedom that is produced by the truth.

The word of truth is the living truth; that is, the power of truth expressed in tangible action; and is therefore distinct from abstract truth, or the mere intellectual conception of truth. The intellectual aspect of truth does not sustain the true life because it has not become the word, or the power of true formation. But the realization of the world of truth takes life into what may be termed truth in action; and when we are in the truth in action we are acting in the truth.

To act, live or think in the truth is to give the sustaining power of truth to every action, and thus every action will not only be a true action, but it will contain the limitless power of truth. This is why no true action can fail, and also why no ill can possibly come to any human personality that lives in the word of truth, and that is consciously resolved into the pure spiritual essence of truth.

When the human system is sustained in the word of truth, every part of the system is fixed on high; that is, placed within that true state of being where everything is created in the image of God, and where everything is always well. In this state the good alone exists; everything has freedom because it is in the world of absolute freedom, and therefore everything will do what divine purpose planned that it should do. This is the true meaning of freedom, and it is such freedom alone that can give to every soul what the largest life and the greatest joy may need or desire.

"But let your speech be yea, yea; nay, nay." Every statement we make should either affirm that which is true or deny that which is not true. Statements that contain both the elements of truth and the elements of untruth are of the evil one; they confuse the mind, and lead to sin, sickness and death. Make no compromise with the untruth, and let no half-truth find expression in your life. Give positive expression, in thought, word, action and life, to that which you know to be real, and eliminate completely what you know to be unreal. Make your life a living affirmation of the great things that are before, and so live that everything you do will deny the lesser things that are passing away.

Spiritual consciousness is in the light of the truth, and can always see the truth clearly. To see the truth clearly is to know the truth, and to know the truth is to be free.

The spiritual understanding of truth is the direct consequence of the mind's insight into that realm where everything is what it is; where nothing can be added and nothing taken away.

When you inwardly feel what you say, you give spiritual power to your words; and what you say will surely come to pass.

CHAPTER XII

FINDING THE LOST WORD

Illumined minds in every age have declared their belief in what may be termed the sacred word; or that formulated statement of truth through which unbounded power could be expressed. According to this belief, anyone who knew this secret word or statement, could, by the use of that word, secure anything he might desire. Through this word the sick could be healed, adversity overcome, calamities prevented, enemies turned into friends, earnest desires realized, life prolonged, and everything gained that would tend to promote the comfort and joy of existence; and those who were high in the scale of spiritual attainments, could, with this word, perform miracles. This was the belief, and this is still the belief among nearly all who recognize divine power in man. But what this word really is, is a mystery in the minds of the many, and therefore it is usually called the lost word.

The great word is not a word, as many suppose, nor a definite statement of truth. The great word is the **soul** of every word, the **spirit** of every thought and the **inner power** of every expressed statement. In the minds of the great majority it is a lost word, because their speech does not have soul, their thought does not have spirit, and their statements of truth, or untruth, are devoid of inner power. But those who are learning to live, think and act, not as material personalities, but as Sons of God, are finding the great word; they are beginning to speak with authority, and there is hidden power in everything they say. What they say will come true, does come true; what they think they can do they gain the power to do, and their work invariably contains some exceptional quality that the ordinary mind cannot define. The spiritually minded, however, can understand; they know the secret; they realize that the great word is the supreme power of divine being coming forth into the speech, the thought and the actions of the fully awakened soul. And if these minds will continue to enter more and more deeply into the spirit of this supreme power they will find that the great word can do everything that the ages have declared that it could do. Thousands to-day do, at times, use this secret word; that is, they give **soul** to what they say, and they give **spirit** to what they think; in consequence, their words carry weight and their thoughts have extraordinary power. But they do not, as a rule, understand how the power of the soul is given to word and thought, and therefore do not secure results whenever they may so desire. The secret, however, is simple, so simple that it can be comprehended and applied by anyone.

To begin, train yourself to feel inner power whenever you give expression to a statement of truth; and whenever you think enter into the spirit of your thought. When you speak, do not simply say words; say more. Never indulge in empty speech; that is, place yourself, your whole self, your great self into every word you utter. Let the spoken word be the body of your speech, but see that every body has a great soul. The audible word itself has no power, but that word can carry all the power that you can inwardly feel at the time it is spoken. When you give soul to your speech every word will contain hidden power, and it is this hidden power of the spoken word that constitutes the secret word, the great word, the word that works wonders for those who understand. We realize, therefore, that there is nothing mystical or mysterious about the great word; it is simply a measure of supreme spiritual power taking expression in thought or speech. Jesus Christ was the greatest master in the use of the word that we know, though there have been hundreds in every age that have discerned its power and applied it to a great degree. In this age there are more than there ever were before who are consciously using the word, but as the general understanding of its nature is not clear, results are not as great as they might be. But it is predicted that we are to do the greater works, and it is our privilege to do so now because we have received the power.

There are thousands in the world to-day who are ready to do the greater works; they understand the law; they know the truth and their desire to live the truth is becoming stronger every hour; but there is one thing more needful. We must enter more deeply into the spirit. To believe in things spiritual is not sufficient; nor will the daily effort to conform with spiritual principles supply the necessary requirements. We must do all of these things and more. We must aim to enter into the very life of the innermost power of the spirit whatever we think, say or do. When we think the truth, we must mentally feel the **inner spirit** of that truth. When we desire the realization of some divine quality or perfect condition, we must mentally feel the deep invincible soul of that desire. And when we speak, we must not speak as personal men, but as spiritual Sons of the Most High, endued with limitless power from the Supreme. In brief, whatever we do in body, mind or soul, we must enter more deeply into the hidden powers of the spirit, and must try to realize that that power is the very soul of all power. When we think we can feel the soul of divine power, we must try to enter into the soul of that soul; and when we realize that a deeper soul state is being felt, we must try to enter into the soul of this deeper state, and so on, ever going deeper and deeper into the limitless vastness of the spirit. Thus we shall gain the great word, the word that gives **soul** to every word, **spirit** to every thought and **inner** power to every statement.

Give **soul** to every spoken word and you can heal yourself by saying, "I Am Well"; you can emancipate yourself from every adverse condition by saying, "I Am the Freedom of Divine Truth"; and you can cause every atom in your being to thrill with life and power by saying, "I Am the Strength of the Infinite." Give **spirit** to every thought you think and every condition you picture in the mind will be realized in the body. Every true desire you feel will be fulfilled, and every dream of greater things will positively come true. What you think you can do you will gain the power to do, because every thought that is filled with the spirit is also filled with the limitless power of the spirit. Give **inner** power to every statement, and whatever you affirm to be true you will cause to come true. The great word is creative, and if the hidden power of this word is **in** your statement, it will create whatever your statement may affirm. Therefore, select your statements with wisdom, and pray only for that which you know that you want. When you regain the lost word, all your prayers will be answered and all your desires come true. It is therefore advisable to pray for wisdom first, to desire spirituality first, and to seek first the kingdom of God.

The power of the spirit finds full expression only through the Word; but since mankind in general does not possess the Word, it is usually spoken of as the "lost word." To the mind that is only partly awakened this Word is something vague, almost incomprehensible, yet a jewel most earnestly desired. He feels that there is something within him that can know this Word, and speak the Word, but it seems to be lost to his mind in some mysterious manner. It is the speaking of the Word, however, that heals the sick and that makes man free; it is therefore most desirable to possess. When it is stated that the Word is lost, the idea is not that the human race possessed it once, and lost it later. The entire race never did possess the Word; never had the power to speak the Word. The Word has been lost to the race from the beginning of manifested existence in this sphere, but has been found in every age by the illumined minds of that age, and through those minds declared to the world. Instead of speaking of the Word as the "lost word," it would therefore be better to speak of it as the "hidden word," hidden from the mind of personal man, but revealed to the minds of illumined souls.

Those minds that are on the borderland of the great awakening realize that immediately beyond their present mental comprehension lies a world of wisdom and light, indescribable in its marvelousness and beauty. To some minds it is so near that at times the veil is parted, and they obtain a slight glimpse of the glory and splendor that was, is and is to be. Others have crossed the border at certain periods in their lives, and have actually entered, for a time, the Father's House of the Many Mansions. But the great purpose of every soul is to some day enter this celestial world and abide there always. Many have believed that we must leave the body before we can enter that sublime realm; the truth is, however, that we may enter today, if we are ready, and live in that higher world while still living upon earth in physical form. We shall then find that the earth is not outside of the kingdom, but that the real earth, spiritually discerned and understood in truth, is also one of His secret places.

To have the spiritual discernment to look into this beautiful world, these higher realms, and behold the sublime glory of the kingdom, the Father's House of the Many Mansions, is to regain the "lost word." "It is for you to know the mysteries of the kingdom"; and whoever has sufficient spiritual power to part the veil and see those things that are prepared for them that love Him, has found the "hidden word." Now he knows the mysteries; he has seen them as they are. He has crossed the border, he has trod the shining shore and his eyes have beheld eternity. He has seen the Word, because the One Divine Word is the revelation of all that Is Eternal. Whoever can see that which Eternally Is, that to which nothing can be added, nothing taken away, that which is the foundation of all, the life of all, the all in all, can see the Word. The Word is revealed to him; divine wisdom has inspired his soul, the light of the spirit has illumined his mind, and he speaks as one having authority. He speaks, not of that which others have told him, not as the scribes; he has seen the mysteries; he bears witness to the truth because he has witnessed and beheld the truth with his own illumined mind. The heavens have opened before him; he has not only had a vision; he has seen the truth that is beyond the vision and that truth is the Word.

To reach this sublime state the secret is faith; not the faith that believes, but the faith that knows—the faith that can see with the vision of the spirit. Every soul that has some discernment of higher things has a portion of faith. This faith increases as the soul ascends, and the soul ascends as the faith becomes larger, higher and more illumined. To feel the touch of the spirit is the beginning of real faith, and the nearer the soul lives to the spirit the larger the faith. In the first stages of faith, the way is opened for the power of the spirit to come forth and prepare the human temple for the greater things that are to follow. After this period, if the mind continues in spiritual growth, illumination begins, and will continue until the Christ state is attained.

During the first stages of spiritual illumination the mind feels the nearness of a higher world, and here is the soul's opportunity to take many steps toward the heights. Whenever these sublime moments appear, enter the stillness of the spirit, and place body, mind and thought in touch with the soul's eternal calm. Then when in the peace that passeth understanding, open the eyes of the spirit, and in faith, desire to meet Him face to face. He may not appear; but be not impatient; know that He will appear, and you can wait. You can wait an eternity for such a privilege, for a single moment in His Presence is a million heavens in one. But when you do draw near enough to behold His shining glory, give thanks with all the power of heart and soul. The Redeemer has entered your life; you have found the way; you have entered the great climax of human existence and now you may begin to live. Henceforth, give your highest thought and attention to every spiritual experience that may appear, no matter how insignificant it may seem to be. Know that every manifestation of Divine Presence indicates that you are growing in the spirit, that your spiritual eyes are being opened, that you are beginning to discern His omnipresence and to know that He is always here, closer than breathing, nearer than hands and feet.

To know God is the beginning of all wisdom. To know and feel that God is here, everywhere, that we live in His spirit, His life, His wisdom, His power, His light and His love now, is to awaken the mind to real wisdom. Then we shall find the "hidden word"; then we shall enter the inner sanctuary of the soul and behold the Word of God manifested in the true being of man, eternally creating the true being of man in the likeness of the image divine. And then we behold the Word of truth; in the being of truth we gain the power to speak the Word of truth. To know the Word is to have the power to speak the Word, and to speak the Word is to cause the Word to become flesh. Thus the life, the wholeness and the glory of the spirit is made real in the personal being of man.

To grow daily in the spirit is the way to the higher faith, the larger wisdom and the beautiful life. Aspire constantly to live the life of the spirit; turn all thought and attention to the more perfect understanding of the spirit; keep the eye single upon the divine perfection of the spirit, and there shall be many moments when His spirit will actually appear. When these moments come, grieve not the spirit away; receive its life and its power by entering into the stillness within; then open widely the door of the heart that the Guest from On High may come in. Soon He will come again. His coming will become more and more frequent, and when you are ready to actually live the life He lives, He will not go away any more.

Whenever the spirit comes and is received, the Word is being revealed to you, and you obtain a larger glimpse of that sublime state of being where you are about to enter, never to return. Never to return to the ways of the world; never to return to the bondage of sin; but to live in the light and the freedom of the spirit while still in personal form; to walk with God while still walking the earth; to be surrounded and protected by His invisible power while still living and working in the midst of visible things. In the world and yet above the world. Whenever you discern more clearly the glory of the kingdom it means that you are drawing nearer and nearer to the pearly gates. Press on; not with force and will, but with peace and faith, the eye ever single upon the Light that leads. It is the will of God that we should enter now "there is another and a better world." That world is not a future state of existence, but an eternal state of existence; it is therefore at hand here and now. To enter the "pearly gates" is to enter that better world—God's own true world where all is well. And those gates are ajar to all who can speak the Word.

Light within, guide thou my way,
I am seeking truth to-day;
Where thou leadest I will go,
And all wisdom I shall know.
Peace and joy and truth and love
Are the blessings from above
That will surely come to me
When I gently follow thee.

Light within, thou light divine,
Thou shalt never cease to shine;
Thou canst not depart from me;
We are one, for I am thee.
Darkness flies and sins depart,
Truth is reigning in my heart;
Endless day dispersed the night
When I found I was the Light.

CHAPTER XIII

THE ROYAL PATH TO WISDOM

Solomon prayed for wisdom and received it; any other soul may do the same. God is infinite wisdom; and "all that the Father hath is mine"; we need simply go and receive our own. We may receive from the supreme mind, at any time, as much wisdom, on any subject, as our own minds can possibly appropriate, and we may also receive, from the same source, the power to appropriate more.

The wisdom that comes from God does not simply pertain to the soul or to the life of some other world, because God is the original source of all wisdom, and therefore we may receive light directly from Him on any subject whatever. Nor does the wisdom that comes from God need special interpretation; it is sufficiently clear for anyone to understand who is in harmony with God.

When higher wisdom needs interpretation, it is not from God, but is simply the mystical ideas of minds that have not found the clear light of the Infinite mind. The mystical wisdom of man is complex and confusing; the wisdom of God is simple and illuminating; the former produces darkness and doubt; the latter produces that faith that knows.

When we learn that real wisdom comes directly from God, we shall no longer seek knowledge through the training of the senses to discriminate between illusions; nor shall we depend upon experience for instruction. Real wisdom does not come from experience; experience can only tell us how it feels to live in illusions and overcome illusions, but it tells us nothing about how it feels to live in the real and ascend into the greater and the greater life of the real.

The mind that lives in the light of the Most High, knows the result of any experience long before that experience arrives; therefore, to such a mind, experience can convey no information. If the experience is pleasant, it is welcomed and received for the joy it brings, but if it is not pleasant, it is avoided, and the mind that is taught of God, knows beforehand whether any particular experience will be desirable or not.

To live with God is to gain good from every source, be the source physical, mental or spiritual; but the wisdom that comes with this good does not come from these various sources; it may come through these sources because to live with God is to touch God everywhere, and thus receive wisdom from God through every channel in the world.

To be taught of God is to pray for wisdom, to depend upon God for wisdom, and to live so near to God that we shall be in the light of His wisdom. Whatever we wish to know, we should take it to God, and let His spirit lead us, guide us, and inspire our minds with the truth desired.

The mind that is led by the spirit will not go wrong; or if it should temporarily be on the verge of taking a misstep, something will interfere. This something may seem to be special providence, and in a certain sense it is, because the Infinite is ever ready to do for man whatever he may wish to have done.

When we place ourselves in the hands of the Infinite, He will find a way, and this way will be revealed to us before it is too late. Sometimes it may not appear until the eleventh hour, but it invariably comes in time. We may therefore rest assured in this faith and know, "That I will not forsake thee nor leave thee; I am thy Redeemer, I will care for thee."

The great secret of all the inspired minds of the ages may be found here; they seemed to have superhuman knowledge, they spoke with authority, and their words have been universally received as the truth; the reason being, they lived in the light of the Most High; they were taught of God.

To be taught of God it is necessary to live with God, walk with God, and open the mind completely to the great influx of supreme light from on high. It is necessary to be in such close spiritual touch with the Infinite mind that we can feel the thought of God, and think His thoughts after Him. And this any soul can do. To live with God is the simplest life of all, and also the most beautiful; and to walk with God requires no effort whatever. Any soul that can lift up the mind toward supreme spiritual realms can walk with God now.

When we place ourselves in that position where we can be taught of God, it is then that we begin to use the mind in the highest sense. It is then that the mind becomes so transparent that the light of Infinite wisdom can shine through and manifest itself in all its brilliancy and glory. It is then that the Word becomes flesh, and the truth of divine being is unfolded in the personal life of man.

The true function of the human mind is to think with the Infinite mind, because the human mind is an inseparable part of the Infinite mind. When the human mind tries to think alone, it becomes confused, and the ideas that it may form are mere illusions.

It is therefore evident that all the ideas in the world that have been formed while the human mind was trying to think apart from the Infinite mind, are illusions; and the wisdom of the world is full of such illusions. We can remove them completely, however, by turning to God, and opening our minds completely to the clear light from on high.

When we begin to receive the wisdom of God, we find that the wisdom of the world was the cause of our trouble; we were living in darkness and could not see the way, therefore took many missteps and made many mistakes; but when we open our minds to the wisdom of God we are in the light, the way is clear, and we shall not go wrong any more.

However, we are not required to ignore everything that man may say in order to receive the pure wisdom of God. God speaks through everything and most of all through man. When we desire, with the whole heart, to be taught of God, we shall constantly receive wisdom from God, and it may come through a million channels, including the mind of man, but we must remember that the mind of man does not simply mean the minds of other men; our own minds are included in the mind of man, and as we grow in the spirit we shall receive most of our divine wisdom with our own mentalities as the principal channel.

This is the great goal we have in view, but we cannot place our own minds in perfect touch with the Infinite mind unless we think of all minds and all things as being channels for the wisdom of God. When we can see God in all things, then we shall meet Him face to face. When we can receive His wisdom through all things, then we shall hear His voice, speaking directly to us, in the beautiful silence of our own soul.

When we enter this silence, as we may at any time, we know we are in communication with God, and we may learn the truth about anything that we have sought to understand. God is not a God of the future state alone. He is the God of all time, even the present, and He is at hand ready to lead us aright in everything that we may wish to do in the present. We may be taught now, by Him, in all things pertaining to physical and mental existence as well as the very highest spiritual existence. And the more we ask of God the more we please God.

"Lay not up for yourself treasures upon earth." Where the heart is there our treasures will be also, and when the heart is in the earth earthy, all that is beautiful in life will be lost. Our treasure is that which we love the best, but it is not wisdom to give our best love to things. Give your best love to the spirit of things and you will receive, not only the visible form, but also that sublime something that gives life and loveliness to the form. Seek the riches of the spirit and you gain wealth and happiness that shall never pass away. The richest man in the world is he who has found the diamond fields of the soul, while the poorest is he who is burdened with things that have not the spirit of things. It is our privilege to have abundance of all that is rich and beautiful in the visible world, but it is the wealth and the beauty of the soul that gives happiness; it is the treasures we lay up in the spiritual within that make all other treasures worth while.

When we know that God is life, power, health, harmony and joy, we will receive those blessings in boundless supply whenever we feel that His presence is here. When we attain the consciousness of the omnipresence of God, we will receive from God whatever we know to be in God.

CHAPTER XIV

THE GOLDEN PATH TO INCREASE

For whosoever hath, to him shall be given, and he shall have abundance, but whosoever hath not, from him shall be taken away even that which he hath.—Mat. 13:12.

The real element of possession exists in consciousness. What we possess in consciousness we inevitably will gain in the personal life; and no matter how well secured our external possessions may be, the moment we begin to feel in conscious that we may lose them, our hold on those things will weaken, and external loss will shortly begin unless this adverse state of mind is immediately changed.

To consciously feel that everything that you need or desire is for you—in brief, actually belongs to you in the real, is to be among those that hath, even though you may, at present, be empty handed in the external world. To you shall be given, and you shall have abundance both in spiritual possessions and in visible possessions. But to consciously feel that you do not have real or permanent possession of anything, is to be among those that hath not, even though you may have visible wealth in great measure. From you shall be taken away, and those external possessions that you seem to have shall pass to other hands.

This law is universal in its application and holds true in all matters, be they physical, mental or spiritual. The secret of gaining more on any plane is to consciously feel that you have more. Enter into the hath state of mind. Whether you desire life, health, power, wisdom, spirituality or greater abundance in external things, train your consciousness to feel that you have the real substance of the thing desired. Do not judge according to appearances, but continue to inwardly feel the possession of that which you claim as your possession.

When the mind enters the feeling of conscious possession, the first gain is the fuller possession of yourself and your powers; you immediately begin to feel stronger; this will strengthen and enlarge your consciousness of gain, which in turn, will increase the power of accumulation that has begun in your system. You thus not only become larger and stronger in your own nature, but you gain a more powerful hold upon everything with which you may come in contact. You awaken greater and superior qualities in your own mind and soul, and you inspire faith and confidence in the minds of others. You thus create those advantages and essentials, both in the within and in the without, that are conducive to gain.

When the mind enters the fear of loss and begins to feel that there is going to be loss, the first loss is the loss of self-possession. You lose your hold upon your own powers, and, in consequence, begin to weaken. Your faculties fail to do their best, your work becomes inferior, your personality does not attract as it did, and your power to inspire confidence in others, is on the wane. You suffer loss in all things, physical, mental and spiritual, and you are daily losing ground. Finally, everything that you seemed to possess is taken away. But the loss began in your own consciousness, and you could have stopped it there if you had known how.

The losing tendency can be stopped at any stage, but the only place where it can be immediately stopped is at its first appearance in consciousness. When you begin to feel that there is danger of loss, or when the general indications seem to predict loss, remove that feeling at once. Refuse to think of loss; refuse to admit the possibility of loss; refuse to recognize loss in any form whatever. Proceed to claim your own; give all the power of mind and thought to the great truth that you do possess now, in the real, everything that you can possibly need or desire. Give full recognition to the boundlessness of your own spiritual riches, and live in the conviction that whatever you claim possession of in the within you will gain possession of in the without.

The tide will turn before any real loss takes place; and instead of falling back into the world of the ones that hath not, you will advance farther into the richness of that world where dwell the ones that hath. In consequence, to you will be given, and you will have more than you ever had before. This method should be used with faith and perseverance whenever there is the least indication of loss; negative conditions should be replaced with positive conditions, fear should be annihilated by faith, and every downward tendency should be converted into a strong ascending tendency.

To live in the "hath" state of mind and grow steadily in the conscious feeling of possession, continuous growth in spirituality will be required. It is only through spirituality that we can grasp the reality of the inner substance of things, and we must gain consciousness of the inner substance of life before we can master those forces that make for perpetual increase in life.

To live in the "hath" state of mind it is also necessary to advance constantly into a deeper and larger conscious possession of those things that we already possess in abundance. There can be no inaction in consciousness; if we are not going forward into the larger and the more perfect we are going back and down into the lesser. Therefore, no matter how much power we actually possess, we should daily claim conscious possession of more; no matter how perfect our health may be, we should daily enter into the consciousness of higher perfections of health. When we cease to grow in health we prepare the system for sickness, but so long as we grow in health, sickness will be impossible.

The same law is applicable both to external possessions and spiritual possessions. To retain what we have we must daily develop the consciousness of more. The moment we decide to be satisfied with what we have we will begin to lose what we have. There is no limit to the riches of the kingdom of life, and it is the will of God that man shall enjoy more and more of these riches, every day, so long as eternity shall continue to be. And to do the will of God is to bring the highest happiness to man.

That the love of money is the root of all evil is true, providing we give the statement its true and full significance. When we speak of money we do not mean those things simply that pass for money, but we mean all external possessions. When we love external possessions the heart is in the without and not in the spirit as it always should be to be in the truth. When the heart is in external things, we begin to live for things; the mind comes to the surface and consequently becomes shallow and material. The mind that lives on the surface is not in touch with the deep things of life, is not conscious of the inner light of truth, and is therefore in darkness. To be in darkness is to go wrong, and to go wrong is to create evil. Every mind that is not led by the inner light of the spirit will go wrong; in fact, every wrong act comes because the mind follows external darkness instead of internal light; and it is only the love of other things that draws the mind out into the darkness of things. So long as we love the spirit the mind is in touch with the spirit and is illumined by the light of the spirit. When we are in this light we will not go wrong, we will not commit evil, because we can see the right, and we can see that the right is the very thing we have desired, longed for, prayed for.

The more deeply we love the inner life and the riches of the spirit, the more spiritual and illumined we become; accordingly, we can see more and more clearly how to do all things as they should be done; our mistakes will decrease, and wrongs and evil will disappear. To love the life is to enter into the spirit of truth, and in the truth there is freedom—freedom from sickness, evil, weakness and want. Evil can grow only in materiality; and materiality is produced simply by our own confused thinking. But when we are in touch with the spiritual life within, our thinking is not confused; we are then in the light of truth, and we think the truth. In consequence, we no longer produce the darkness and discord of materiality; instead we produce the peace and the harmony of spirituality, and all is well.

When your treasure, that is, that which you love the best, is in the without, in the earth, earthy, your whole life will be in the earth, earthy. You will thus live continually in wrong thought because you do not see how to create right thought. All mental light, even the light of reason, comes from within; therefore, when the mind is so absorbed in outer things that it ignores completely the within, all thinking will be more or less at variance with truth, and evils must necessarily follow. But when your treasure is in the spirit, and you love the riches of the soul better than anything else, you will live on the mountain top. You will dwell in realms sublime, in the very light of His infinite wisdom; all your thinking will be illumined with that light; you will thus think only the truth, and he produces no evil who always thinks the truth.

To lay up treasures in heaven is not to prepare for a heaven in the future, but to accumulate greater and greater spiritual riches now. That soul that is attaining real spiritual wisdom, that is growing daily in the love that loves everything, that is living in the peace that passeth understanding, that is being filled more and more with life and power from on high, that is gaining conscious realization of all the divine elements of pure, spiritual being— that soul is laying up treasures in heaven. Such a soul is actually coming into possession of those superior riches now, and is learning to use them today for the glory of God and the emancipation of man.

To become a strong soul, to attain the mastery of the spirit, to become a living inspiration to all the world, to unfold all that is lofty and beautiful and sublime in the spiritual life, to realize the joy everlasting and draw nearer and nearer to the Christ state—that is the purpose of him who is laying up treasures in heaven. And when we possess spirituality with all its qualities of high worth, we have the riches of all riches; we have that something that can produce all riches, not only in the spirit, but also in mind and body. That person who has found the riches of the within need never have any fear of external loss. Though all might disappear in the without, still, being in touch with the source of all supply, he could at once begin to regain everything. When we are in the spirit we are upon the solid rock of all good; we possess the key to unbounded riches on all planes, and so long as we live in the spirit we shall not lose that key. When one door closes we can open another, sometimes several, and all that the heart can wish for shall always be ours to possess and enjoy. When we are in the spirit, we not only possess the riches of the spirit—those riches that actually make every moment of existence a full realization of the highest joys of life—but we also possess the power to supply the without abundantly, being in perfect touch with the Giver of all that is good in the world.

There is no truth in the belief that we must necessarily relinquish external possessions the moment we begin to lay up treasures in heaven. That power that produces the riches of the spirit, can, and will, produce abundance in the external world as well. All outer things will invariably be added when the kingdom within is sought—actually sought, and sought first, not only at first but always. So long as we seek only the treasures of earth we get but little of those treasures, while we get an overabundance of the suffering and pain of material existence. But when we begin to lay up treasures in heaven, we obtain the peace, the joy, the contentment, the health, the strength, the wisdom, the power and the life we so greatly desire; in addition, we obtain higher spiritual possessions without number, and an abundance of everything that is necessary to make the outer life full and complete.

Live eternally in conscious unity with the Infinite; have faith in God, have faith in humanity, have faith in yourself; then live, think and act according to principles only, and there is nothing you may not accomplish.

Great deeds in life are invariably brought about by higher power. And if we would be constantly in touch with higher power, we must live in the perfect faith and consciousness of the great spiritual within, where higher power has its center and throne. This, however, is not possible so long as we think more of the person than of the soul. To be centered in the spirit we must live in the spirit, and give the spirit our first thought at all times. Then we shall be filled with the supreme power of the spirit, and our strength, both in mind and body, shall be daily renewed from on high.

"Resist not him that is evil." The true path to emancipation is to give so much thought, life and attention to the building of the good that we have not the time to even think of evil. Then evil will die for want of nourishment. The mind that is absolutely full of a strong, spiritual building power, has no room whatever for evil conditions of any kind.

CHAPTER XV

THE LIFE MORE ABUNDANT

I came that they may have life, and may have it abundantly.—John 10:10.

The greatest thing that man can do is to live. Everything that appears in any sphere of existence comes from life, and therefore everything increases with the increase of life. To live more is to become more and gain the power to accomplish more whatever the field of action may be; to live more is to enter more fully into the richness and joy of life itself, and there is no joy that is greater than that which comes from perpetual growth in real life.

The purpose of life is to live more life; the principal secret of perfection in any period of life is to live as large a life as that period can appreciate and employ, and to constantly add to the abundance of that large life is to make each period better than the one that went before. Growth in life means growth in health, growth in strength, growth in capacity, growth in mental brilliancy, growth in talent, growth in wisdom, growth in power, and, in brief, growth in everything that a normal state of existence can possibly need or desire. The mission of the Christ is therefore not purely transcendental, nor solely for some other world.

The teachings of the Christ are applicable to every part of personal existence, and may be applied with great profit in every circumstance or event that can arise in the great eternal now. What is more, no person can do full justice to anything he may undertake to do unless he enters into full harmony with the great mission of the Christ. The life more abundant can come only through the Christ, and we all need the life more abundant if we are to be true to our own marvelous nature.

The coming of the Christ, however, was not confined to a short period of time some two thousand years ago; the Christ comes now to every one who enters the spirit; and when He comes, He invariably brings the life more abundant. We may, at any time, enter the fullness of eternal life; and when we do, everything changes for the better. The life more abundant dispels the ills of existence in the same manner as light dispels darkness, and just as effectively, whatever those ills may be.

The ills of personal existence come principally from two causes: ignorance of divine law and false desire. The coming of the life more abundant gives the mind the necessary power to understand the laws of life; when we are in the life eternal we are in harmony with the laws of the life eternal, and will not misuse those laws any more. When we are filled with the richer life from within we no longer desire the lesser things in the without; we will not care for the wrong, having found everything that heart can wish for in the beautiful kingdom of the right.

To enter the life more abundant, first live the teachings of the Christ; not according to the letter but according to the spirit. The spirit is infinitely greater than the letter, and includes everything of worth that the letter may contain. Second, live now in the Christ consciousness. Know that the Christ is here, that His spirit is within you and all about you, and that you can be conscious of His presence at any time by simply opening your own mind to His kindness and tenderness and sublime love. Know that "I am with you, even to the end of the world," and think on these things.

The more attention we give to the great truth that the Christ is here with us now, the more we open the mind to the consciousness of His spiritual presence, and as we enter more and more into the consciousness of the Christ, we enter more and more into the limitless life of the Christ; thus we become filled, through and through, with the supreme power of that life that is eternal life.

The life eternal, however, is not distinct from any other form of life; it is the source of all life, and as we enter more and more into the life eternal we gain more life on every plane of being. We then begin to express the life more abundant through every part of body, mind and soul, and thus demonstrate conclusively that a strong soul does not mean a weak body.

The life of the soul is eternal life, and the more we unfold that life the more health, strength and vigor we give to the body; the mind becomes more brilliant, the personality more powerful, and the character more beautiful. And above all, we ascend to that sublime life on the heights that is fairer than ten thousand to the soul.

For whosoever would save his life shall lose it; and whosoever shall lose his life for my sake shall find it.—Mat. 16:25.

When you lose your life for the sake of Christ, you let go of the limited life that is living in you in order that the limitless life of the Christ may live in you. Likewise, when you deny yourself and follow the Christ you remove the personal self from the throne of your being and enthrone the superior spiritual self instead. There is therefore no sacrifice; you lose nothing but your limitations and your illusions, while you gain everything that the kingdom of God holds in store for man.

The belief that it is necessary to lose something of actual value in order to gain the life eternal is not the truth. Poverty in the personal life does not produce spiritual riches, nor does the sacrifice of temporal joys produce the bliss of heaven. The idea of self-sacrifice must be eliminated; so long as we think that we have to sacrifice all that is good in the visible world in order to gain the joys and the riches of the invisible, we are out of harmony with the beautiful order of the cosmos. In the true order of things all that is real is good, and all that is good, man has the privilege to enjoy now.

The only things that we are required to sacrifice are our ills, our defects, our weaknesses, our shortcomings, our limitations; in brief, we are required to remove the personal self and its imperfections from our world of existence. The true self-sacrifice is that which refuses to permit personal imperfections to rule in the personal life, and gives up to the light, the power and the life of the spirit.

When you deny yourself in the true manner, you deny your outer mind the privilege of rulership. You no longer follow the desires and the beliefs of the flesh; you no longer obey the dictates of the body; you declare that the body must serve the soul and the soul must serve the Christ. You thereby permit the supreme life of the Christ to live in you; the mind that was in Christ Jesus enters your mind, and His life and His power becomes your own. The lesser life is lost, the greater life has come in its place. The mere man in you is decreasing while the divine in you is increasing and will thus continue until you are perfect as your heavenly Father is perfect.

To try to save the personal life is to live exclusively for the limitations of external existence; in consequence, the mind becomes so absorbed in the lesser life without that it is wholly unconscious of the greater life within. But we cannot receive the greater life from within unless we are in conscious touch with that life, and since the within is the only source of life, we cease to receive life the moment we are consciously separated from the inner life.

To live entirely for the personal life is to be separated from the inner life, and therefore we are not receiving any more life. The personal life, however, that we are trying to save will be gradually used up, and thus we will lose what we are so anxious to save. But when we begin to live for the spirit, and begin to follow the Christ into the vast spiritual realms of limitless life, we will find more and more life; and the more life we find in the vast within the more life we will bring forth into the without. All the life that we become conscious of in the soul we will express in the mind and the body, and the personal self, instead of growing weaker, will grow stronger and stronger as it is filled more and more with life and power from on high. And thus, by losing ourselves in Christ we gain everything that exists in the supreme life of the Christ; we lose nothing, sacrifice nothing, while we find ourselves—all that we are in the image and likeness of God.

Live a beautiful life wherever you may be and you become a living benediction to all who may pass your way. You may see no immediate results; in fact, your beautiful life may have scattered its blessings so far and wide that you cannot find the exact places where the flowers grow that you planted; but that does not matter. You have given; in consequence, the world is better off and you are a stronger soul. You know that not a single good deed can be lost; somewhere it will bless somebody. You know that every good seed that you may sow in the garden of human life, will some day take root and grow. You may not remain long enough to see the flowers, but somebody will see those flowers, and the fact that your hand planted the seed is pleasure enough for you. To feel that you have given happiness to someone else, is the greatest happiness of all; and to know that millions will be inspired by the sublimity of your life ages after you are gone—could anything give a deeper joy to the soul? And yet, this is a privilege that is not given only to the few; there is not a soul that may not look forward to such a future and to such a life.

To be perfectly satisfied to let your light shine wherever you may go without ever looking back to see if there were results or no, is the mark of a great soul. So long as we do not wish to give unless we see visible results in exact places, our spirituality is not of the greatest; and so long as we require the personal testimony of those whom we have helped, to spur us on, our faith is nothing. He who has the true faith knows that spiritual living is a power wherever it is lived, and he never thinks of looking back to find if it was true. He scatters the seed and leaves results to Him that faileth not. He radiates the good and knows that that which is good can never cease to produce good.

When you realize that you are an entity through which God is expressed, and that your mind should be so transparent that the highest divine light may shine through and illumine the outer world, you have found your true place. To remain constantly in that beautiful place means that a higher power will be flowing through your being, radiating in every direction, giving the spirit of truth to everything you may think, say or do. You thus become a personal expression of the Word, and your life will be a message of truth to the race.

"Ye are the light of the world." Do not hide your spirituality in your feelings or your emotions. There is power in the spirit. Live this power, and give personal expression to everything that the spirit may contain. Then you will demonstrate to the world that the way of the spirit is the true way. When you are lifted up, hundreds and even thousands will come and go where you are going. Therefore, let the full glory of the spirit shine in your life; let power from on high manifest itself in everything that you may think or say or do, and great shall be your reward, both in this world and in the world to come. The spiritual life deprives you of nothing that has real worth, and gives you more and more of everything that has high worth.

"Agree with thine adversary quickly." There is a spiritual side to everything; enter into harmony with this spiritual side and the discord that seems to exist on the personal side will disappear. Forget those elements that are at variance and think only of those states that are perfectly at one with each other. You can easily find them; we find everything we seek, and whoever goes out to find harmony will discover that there is more harmony in the world than anything else, excepting life itself.

CHAPTER XVI

HUMAN NATURE
BECOMING DIVINE NATURE

There are thousands of people in the world today who have undertaken to live the spiritual life, and the majority of them understand, to a fair degree, the principles upon which such a life is based; nevertheless, there are too many who do not have as great results as they ought to have, and they are at a loss to find the reason why. With the spiritual wisdom which we now possess, we ought to do greater things than were ever known upon earth before; we ought to be able to overcome every wrong, not only in our own lives, but also in the lives of all who are receptive to our spiritual work; and we ought to realize an ever-increasing abundance of infinite good and infinite power from on high. We ought to do all these things and much more, and when we can see distinctly where the two ways part, we certainly shall.

When we know that we have such an exceptional opportunity for higher usefulness in this age, we can not be satisfied simply to use the power of divine truth for the attainment of physical health and personal prosperity. There are other and greater things to work for, but not many have the secret path to the world of these greater things. However, the reason why is simple; and likewise, the reason why the majority do not secure as great results as they should in the lesser things, is also simple. And the reason is we cannot serve two masters; we cannot take two paths at the same time; when we come to the parting of the ways we must take the one that leads into light and forget the other absolutely.

When we learn that man is created in the image and likeness of God, we enter a new realm of thought; we have made a new discovery, and we have found another way to think and live. The former belief taught us to think and live as a sinner, as a weak human body; the new truth has taught us to live as a spiritual being, as a child of God, as a strong, perfect, divine soul.

And here is the place where we must decide which way to go, as it is not possible to believe the old and the new at the same time and have result; nor is it possible to believe part of the old and part of the new at the same time and realize that power for good that the new may contain.

There are many minds who believe in divine truth, and who accept fully the great truth that man is the image of God, but still continue to think of themselves as weak, human creatures. When the difficult task comes, and they fail, they usually become discouraged, and this is their language: "Just as I expected; but then I am only human, only a weak, frail being, not able to cope with these things; some day I may be able to overcome, but as yet I am too weak; I must not expect too much of myself, as I am only human." This is the drift of the thought in many a mind, and it explains perfectly why they have not overcome the wrong and attained the good. They are trying to realize the perfection of the divine within while recognizing the imperfection of the human without. They expect to attain divine power while persisting in living in the world of human weakness. They are trying to serve both the truth and the untruth, but we cannot realize the power of truth until we eliminate the untruth completely.

The outer has seemed to be the only reality so long that the mind naturally thinks everything existing in the outer to be reality; and here is the difficulty; we think the outer to be substantial and the inner to be "mere mental mist," but it is when we reverse this belief that we find the real truth. The statement that the flesh is weak has been a race thought for ages, and it comes natural to think of the flesh as weak; but the truth is that the flesh is weak because we have made it so, and we have made is so by claiming human weakness as our heritage instead of spiritual strength. He who lives constantly in the conviction that unbounded, spiritual strength is his inheritance now, will never for one moment feel that the flesh is weak. The flesh is what we make it, and it is just as easy to make it strong as to make it weak. Think that you are a weak, frail, human creature and the flesh will become the dwelling place of weakness; but know that you are a strong, invincible, eternal soul, and the flesh will become the very embodiment of strength, and will be filled with life and power from on high.

We may philosophize learnedly about the beauty of spiritual thought, but that will serve no purpose unless the truth that is contained in our spiritual thought is stamped upon every word we express. We all realize the power of words; whenever we speak we send a life current through every part of the body; and if the words spoken are the expressions of material belief we give conditions of weakness to the body, and at times even disease. When we stamp every word, not with human thought, but with divine thought, every word will convey to the person the very spirit of life, power and wholeness. Through the power of speech a person can bring upon himself every wrong in the world; and through the same power he can bring upon himself every good in the world. Through the right use of words, uttered or unexpressed, a person can attain or obtain anything. Words are living forces; they create according to their nature, and they attract their kind. When we become as scrupulous about our words as we are about our clothes we shall become a superior race.

The parting of the ways is found where we can see the difference between human expression and divine expression. So long as our expressions are stamped with the belief that we are weak, frail or "only human," we shall continue in weakness and in that smallness of character that we call human nature. But human nature is simply an undeveloped condition; it is not a permanent factor in human existence; it seems to be permanent simply because practically no effort has been given to the unfoldment and expression of man's divine nature. To say that we are "human" and that we must ever remain so in this world is not only the untruth, but such expressions give weakness and adverse conditions to the personal life. We cause the flesh to become weak and remain weak by living in the belief that we are mere human creatures, and therefore when we meet adversity we "fall down," become sick, or otherwise manifest the imperfection of that life that is lived apart from the spirit.

When we take the other path, however, and begin to recognize our divine nature as our only nature, there will soon be a change in events. When this path is taken we recognize limitations no more, and the term "can not" is forgotten. You never again permit yourself to say that you are sick, tired, limited, easily tempted or merely human. Such expressions you simply will not employ under any circumstances whatever. You know your divine nature, and every thought you think and every word you speak must express what you know to be true. Your every expression of mind, tongue or being thrills with the life and the power of eternal spirit. Regardless of obstacles or adverse events, you stand by your convictions of truth whatever may happen or no. It matters not to you what happens in the exterior. You are not an exterior being; you are a spiritual being, created in the image of God. Nothing that happens can affect you, disturb you, or even touch you; you are in Him, in everlasting safety. You live in the spirit; you know what is true in the spirit, and you think and speak accordingly every moment of your endless existence. Ere long the word of truth becomes a living power in body, mind and soul, and your entire being becomes a perfect expression of that Divine Word that is of God.

There is a strong tendency to compromise with the undeveloped side of the person whenever we fail to demonstrate the absolute power of the spirit. But this must never be permitted. No matter how many times you fail in the person do not admit that you are weak. You are not the person; you are the soul—the perfect image of God, and the image of God is supreme strength regardless of what may happen in the person. Continue to think the absolute truth, even in the midst of sickness, failure, trouble and want, and those things will soon depart never to return any more.

Father I am one with thee,
One through all eternity;
One forever in the past,
One as long as time shall last.
Thou in me and I in thee,
Life of endless unity;
This my dearest song shall be,
Father, I am one with thee.

Father, I am one with thee,
Sweetest thought of truth to me.
I am filled with life divine,
Therefore boundless good is mine.
All my life is lived in thee,
Perfect life of harmony;
This my highest thought shall be,
Father, I am one with thee.

CHAPTER XVII

A SUBLIME STATE OF EXISTENCE

There never existed an awakened soul that did not believe in a spiritual state of being; and there never existed a soul in any condition of human understanding that did not have glimpses, at times, of what appeared to be another world. To those who had simply gained the simplest form of human consciousness, this other world seemed to be far away, a place we could not inherit until we had taken our departure from this visible state of existence; but to those who were on the verge of spiritual consciousness, this other world was not a far away place. Those awakened souls could discern that it was a spiritual realm in which all might dwell to-day—the kingdom of heaven that is ever at hand.

This other world is the soul of the universe, permeating the limitless vastness of the entire cosmos. It is the sublime essence of all reality, the real reality of all that is; it is the infinite spiritual sea in which we live and move and have our being, the divine counterpart of everything that was, is, or is to be. It is that world which we find on the supreme heights of all existence, and is therefore the cosmic world, orderly, harmonious, complete, perfect, transcendent, infinite, divine. To live in this cosmic world is to view the entire universe from the heights, and from that sublime view everything is beautiful and all is good. Therefore, the life of the cosmic is a life of perfected being, everlasting peace and eternal joy. It is the life victorious—the life of the spirit—that every exalted soul has revealed to man, but it is not a life that is apart from personal existence; it is the soul of personal existence.

The cosmic world permeates the physical world as spirit permeates substance; and what the physical world is to the body, the cosmic world is to the soul. According to the true purpose of life, the body should live in the physical world, enjoying everything that is good and beautiful in personal existence; while the soul should live in the cosmic world, enjoying everything that is good and beautiful in spiritual existence. This is complete existence, but the soul cannot consciously live in the cosmic until it is awakened, or until it has become conscious of its own exalted divinity.

The awakening of the soul into the world of its own spiritual nature, will not deprive the body of anything that is worthy in physical life. We are not required to leave the physical to enjoy the spiritual, nor is it necessary to sacrifice anything that can add to the welfare of the body in order to inherit the riches of the soul. The greatest good comes into the whole of life only when the body lives a complete physical life and the soul a complete spiritual life. The soul cannot fully express itself unless physical existence is all that it can be on the physical plane, and the body is not fully alive until the soul is awakened on the spiritual plane. We do not appreciate the beauty of the physical until we are illumined by the light of the spiritual, and we cannot comprehend the marvelousness of the visible world until we can see its splendor and vastness from the supreme heights of the cosmic world.

We must live in the cosmic world before we can live real life in any world. It is the soul of existence that unfolds the real beauty, the real worth and the real joy of every form of existence, but we do not become conscious of the soul of existence until we begin to live in the cosmic world. We cannot realize the fullness of life until we live in the source of life, and the source of life is spiritual. All life comes from above, therefore the nearer we live to that which is above, the more life we shall receive until we inherit real life itself—the life of the spirit—the life that is lived in the full consciousness of divine being. When we live almost wholly in the personal we live only in part, but when we live in the full consciousness of the spiritual as well as the personal, that which is in part passes away and the limitless life is realized instead. It is then that we inherit the life more abundant, and everything that life has the power to give.

To live in the cosmic world is to realize the purity and the absoluteness of the spiritual, the divinity of man's real nature and the absolute perfection of his true being. It is to know the truth about man—the truth that he is created in the image and likeness of God, and it is the knowing of this truth that makes man free, that produces complete emancipation. To enter into the cosmic world, therefore, is to enter into freedom, health, harmony and wholeness, and, in brief, everything that promotes the highest good for body, mind and soul. The cosmic life is the apex of all ascending life, the fulfillment of every true desire in life, the realization of everything that is ideal in life, the attainment of the one supreme goal in the living of divine life. To live in the cosmic is to live in the world of the great within, in the highest state of being, in the life of the soul, in tune with the Infinite, in the secret places of the Most High.

To enter the cosmic world is to ascend to the heights and live the spiritual life. The living of the spiritual life means the overcoming of spiritual death, and it is spiritual death that must be overcome before man can receive his inheritance, here or hereafter. The phenomena of physical death need not concern us; its coming produces no permanent effect upon real existence, nor is anything gained by prolonging personal existence so long as the soul is dead to spiritual existence. It is spiritual life that gives real worth to personal life, and it is the life of the living soul that prolongs indefinitely the life of the living body.

When the soul is not awakened, consciousness lives in a condition of spiritual death and mental darkness. The mind is deprived of the guidance of the spirit, and therefore follows blindly the changing desires of the flesh, those desires that are suggested by the world of things. In consequence, the person is almost buried in materiality, and goes wrong more frequently than otherwise, usually not knowing the reason why. The result is sickness, trouble and adversity, or the sum total of the ills of life. The real cause of all these ills is spiritual death, and the great, infallible remedy is the spiritual life. The ills of life are produced by the mind going wrong, but the mind will not go wrong when it is led by the spirit, and the mind invariably is led by the spirit when we live in the life of the spirit.

The higher we ascend in the true light of the spiritual life the more clearly we can see how to so live that we may be in perfect harmony with all the principles and laws of life. Our sins will cease, our mistakes will diminish, and consequently, ill effects will become more and more insignificant until we can truthfully say that we have gained complete emancipation. When we live in the spirit we live in the light, and when we live in the light we will not go wrong. We can then see where to find the greatest good, and no person will seek the lesser after having learned where to find the greater.

When consciousness acts almost entirely in conditions of spiritual death, nearly every action is at variance with the true order of things; in consequence, confusion, darkness and the downfall of the person follows. We always go down when darkness becomes our only guide, and as the spiritual light is the only guiding light, we will continue to go down so long as the spirit is not awakened. When spiritual death begins, downfall begins, not only in the lives of individuals, but also in the lives of nations, races and systems of thought. Therefore, the overcoming of spiritual death is the great hope of the world. It is this alone that can lead us out of the Egypt of sin, sickness, adversity and pain, into the promised land of peace, wholeness, happiness, freedom, power and truth. It is the awakening of the spirit that will take men and nations out of the powers of darkness, and place the whole of mankind upon those sublime heights where we shall live a life that is befitting the Sons of God.

The spiritualization of the world means the real salvation of the world; not salvation for the future alone but also salvation from sin, sickness and adversity now. When spiritualization begins, the mind is given a light, and that light invariably leads upward and onward into better things. To spiritualize the mind, the soul must be awakened, and to awaken the soul is to overcome and eliminate the conditions of spiritual death. Then real life begins—the life of an emancipated personal existence harmoniously blended with the life of an exalted spiritual existence. To awaken the soul, every act of consciousness must be animated with a strong, deeply felt desire to reach the heights; the eye must be kept single upon the supreme spiritual goal, and every thought must be formed by the highest spiritual understanding that can possibly be realized. To live must be the one ruling purpose, and that purpose must be inspired by the spiritual touch of that life that we know to be eternal life.

To awaken the soul and illumine the mind with the light of the spirit, one of the great essentials is to live by faith. To live by faith is to place your entire life, and everything that pertains to your life, in the hands of Supreme Power. This means that your life will be drawn toward the heights, because Supreme Power is ever ascending toward greater and greater heights. It also means that all things that pertain to your life will work together for the greatest good, because it is the purpose of Supreme Power to produce the greatest good. Whatever is placed in the hands of this power will be inspired and guided by this power, and consequently will do what this power is doing, that is, working in harmony with everything to produce the greatest good.

The secret of faith is therefore simple, and we can readily understand why all things become possible to him who has real faith. Supreme Power can do all things, and he who has faith places his life, his purpose, his plans, his desires—everything, in the hands of Supreme Power. That he should fail is impossible. When the Supreme is with us nothing can be against us, and the Supreme is with us when we place ourselves absolutely in the hands of His power.

When we live by faith, we are constantly on the verge of the great spiritual world, because the power into which we have given everything, is the power of the spiritual world. We are living, thinking and acting in constant recognition of the Supreme Power of the spirit, and are therefore constantly being touched by the spirit, and there is nothing that is more conducive to spiritual awakening than this tender touch of the spirit. To feel, through and through, that His presence is closer than breathing, nearer than hands and feet, is to arouse every spiritual element in our nature, and the soul will come forth into life clothed with the sublime glory of its own inherent divinity. Then we shall ascend into God's own beautiful world, and the life on the heights will begin.

When the soul discerns that My Father and I are One, the door to the kingdom of heaven within will be opened. To be with God is to be in heaven, and this is a privilege that any soul may enjoy now while yet in personal form.

To simply hope for health and freedom is to remain in our present condition however adverse that condition may be. But when we have faith in that power that can give us health and freedom we enter into the very life of that power, and we are healed at once. Faith moves on and on and enters directly into the very condition that is desired; it never ceases to press on until it is in the presence of that which is wanted, and therefore we can never fail. Hope stands on the outside; faith walks in; hope waits to be guided; faith trusts its own light and proceeds; hope waits for the right opportunity; faith creates its own opportunity; hope waits to see the solid rock appearing from out the seeming void; faith goes out upon the seeming void and finds the solid rock; hope stands upon the earth eagerly looking toward the heavens; faith mounts upon the wings of the spirit and ascends to the highest heavens.

CHAPTER XVIII

A FORETASTE OF HEAVEN

How to enter the silence is a problem that confronts every earnest seeker for that higher state of being, that more beautiful world of peace and joy, that inner realm where all is well, that secret place where dwells the soul with God. Prophets, illumined minds and great souls of every age have discovered that there exists a hidden somewhere in the cosmic life of man, the finding of which means the full realization of all the hopes of human life. In this inner realm there is healing for all ills, there is the peace that passeth understanding, the joy everlasting, and light, wisdom and power without end. To enter this sacred chamber of the soul is to find the answer to every prayer, the long sought fulfillment of every heart's desire; whatever the soul has longed for, the same will be found in this inner sanctuary of eternal life; and the path has been called the silence.

The will of the Father is to give us the kingdom; but we must go to Him if we would receive what is prepared for them that love Him. But how shall we go to God? We seem to be away from Him. There seems to be a gulf between our own life and the Infinite life. To bridge this gulf is the great need of the soul, and the silence seems to answer this need. Therefore, to know how to enter the silence becomes a great secret, both in the living of daily life and in the attainment of supreme spiritual life. To simply believe availeth nothing; we must actually go to God if we would receive what eternity holds in store. All things come from God, and he who enters into the presence of God will receive all that God can give. To go to God is to enter into the stillness of the spirit, into the silence of those secret places where the Infinite reigns in glory, where the Christ is enthroned On High.

Be still and know that I am God. This is the way, and no other path can be found. There are many who are trying to climb up some other way, but they will not find what they seek. The straight and narrow path alone leads to the Father's House. But there are few who find it, because the many try to reach the spirit without becoming spiritual. Man expects to gain the gifts of the spirit through methods, but never will he find the kingdom in this way. He alone receives the gifts of the spirit who becomes spiritual. He alone enters the kingdom who will live the life of the kingdom.

There are many who believe that psychical experiences constitute the "gates ajar" to the spiritual kingdom within, and multitudes have been lost in this sea of darkness and confusion. Such experiences never lead the soul to the kingdom, but they are, in many instances, the only obstacles in the way. So long as a person encourages those experiences and permits himself to be led by strange signs, he will remain in the without, and will suffer the usual ills of material man. The kingdom of heaven does not come by observation, neither tangible observations nor mysterious observations. The kingdom is found only in the spirit, and the spirit does not manifest itself in strange signs, but in the great and beautiful life. Jesus taught the existence of a spiritual realm within man, and emphasized again and again the necessity of living in this higher state if we would receive what real life can give. In this age, the entering of this secret place—the inner chamber of the soul, has been called the silence, or the true prayer of illumined faith—the prayer that not only asks of God but realizes eternal oneness with God. It is the prayer that is uttered in silence that is answered; it is the truth that is realized in the silence that gives freedom, peace and wholeness to man.

To enter the silence is to enter God's world, where everything is created in the image of God and manifests the likeness of God. To be in the silence is to know that you are spirit. To be in the silence is to know and feel that God is omnipresent and that you are one with God. To be in the silence is to actually be in the life eternal, and realize the divinity, the goodness and the perfection of all things. To enter the silence is to enter that sublime state where you know that God is in His Holy Temple and that all the world is silent before Him.

To enter the silence is not to have certain strange mental experiences for the space of a half an hour. You may have visions, you may realize the seeming reality of mystical realms, you may project thought, you may communicate with minds that are far away, you may have all kinds of super-physical sensations in mind and body; you may seemingly leave the form and be conscious of other worlds; you may imagine that your body is ether and that you can float upon the air; you may go into ecstacy and seem to receive wonderful revelations; you may have all of these experiences and many more, some of them real, some of them not, and never be in the silence for a single moment.

To enter the silence is to actually go to God; to enter into His presence and to know that He is ever with you. To enter the silence is to walk with God; to feel that His spirit protects you, leads you and keeps you, and that nothing but good can possibly come. To enter the silence is to awaken to the great truth that all that is real is good. To enter the silence is to become conscious of that cosmic state of existence where there is neither evil, sickness nor sin; where all is perfect and good; where life lacks nothing, and where the fullness of Infinite life reigns supremely through the all in all. To enter the silence is to see the soul-side of all things, to come face to face with the eternal, the changeless, the absolutely divine. In the silence you never look for experiences; you are above the world of experience; you are not in the presence of the passing; you are in the presence of the sublime stillness of that which ever and ever is as God is. When you are in a quiet state and have experiences you are not in the silence; but when passing thoughts are forgotten, and you find yourself face to face with the sublime stillness of eternal life, then you are in the silence. In that state all is silent and still; nothing is passing; all is; all is in Him; and all is illumined with the light and the glory of His radiant presence. Divine moments. Beautiful beyond human comprehension. A foretaste of heaven. A glimpse of the Many Mansions. Alone with God and the Great White Throne.

To enter the silence there are no special methods, but there are many things, which if done, will prepare the way. The first of these is to live the life of the spirit every day as far as you know; live in the spirit of the prayer without ceasing, and desire eternally the coming forth of the soul. And inspire this desire with the great truth that your soul is the throne of God. When the soul comes forth the Word becomes flesh, the perfection of divinity manifests in personal form, and the Mind that was in Christ Jesus the same Mind will be in you. Every day for a few moments be alone with the Most High. Let those moments be sacred, and think only of Him. Do not permit another thought to enter consciousness. Fill your being through and through with such strong spiritual aspirations that the thought of the Infinite reigns supremely in your mind. Try to realize His presence, His life and His love. Give yourself up wholly to God, and know that you are absolutely in His care. Enter so deeply into the spirit of this realization that you can actually feel divine nearness—that God is closer to you than your own life. To feel this is to enter into the greatest joy of sublime existence. To be touched by the Spirit of God, if but for a single moment, produces a million thrills of divine ecstacy, and so great is the joy that one short moment feels as if it were an eternity. In brief, when you are in that sublime state you are in real eternity; time passes no more; every moment appears to be an eternity because it is in eternity; and being in eternity it gives to you an eternity of bliss—unbounded bliss from the highest heaven.

There is nothing that will prepare the way to this sublime spiritual silence more than this—to give a few moments every day to God, to think of Him only, and to think of Him with your whole life, with your whole strength, with your whole mind, with your whole heart and with your whole soul. To give up to God is to enter into the kingdom of God, and to enter the kingdom of God is to receive everything that God has to give. To give up everything for God is to receive everything from God. To place everything in the hands of God is to be guided and led by the hands of God, and leads man into every good that the mind can imagine. God leads out of the lesser into the greater, out of limitations into the richness of the boundless, out of mere existence into the glories and splendors of empyrean heights. And it is the purpose of the silence to so deepen the consciousness of the spiritual life that we may live eternally in the very presence of God. Thus we shall ever walk with God and be guided by Him in all things.

To consecrate your entire being to the spiritual life and so live that everything you do draws you higher and higher into the very world of the spirit—this is another essential to the attainment of the true silence. When your life is consecrated to the spirit, all the powers of your being will constantly ascend toward the supreme heights of the spirit. Thus you become more and more spiritual, and to be truly spiritual is to be able to enter the secret places at any time. Another important essential is to live in the consciousness of the divine side of all things. Never for a moment permit the mind to forget that there is a divine side to everything in existence. No matter how imperfect things may seem to be on the surface, know that there is another and a better side, even to the least of these; and do not for a moment lose sight of the great truth that that better side is created in His image and likeness. This lofty mode of thought and life will not interfere in the least with the duties of every-day life, but will, instead, make all work and all life a great joy. To work when the mind is in the spirit is to work both wisely and well; and when you ascend to the supreme heights of the spirit your work becomes a great work. To live in the spirit is not to live apart from visible things, but to gain far greater mastery of things, and thus gain the power to do far greater things. To live in the silence is not to live in a dream; it is not to become oblivious to the realities of tangible existence, but to inspire tangible existence with all the power, with all the life, with all the truth, and with all of the beautiful that the soul can find when it soars to celestial realms on high. The purpose of the silence is to unite the world of things with the world of spirit, and thus give the fairest life in all the world to body, mind and soul.

Sun of my soul, eternal light,
Be thou my leader and my guide.
And I shall ever find the right
By walking truly by thy side.

Tho' clouds of doubt may hover near,
Darkness and wrong obstruct my way,
My faith in thee shall banish fear,
And give my soul the light of day.

Upward and onward I shall rise,
Treading the path of truth and right,
Passing through God's celestial skies,
Led by the Spirit of His Light.

CHAPTER XIX

THE VISION OF THE SOUL

Faith is the "gates ajar" to the Holy City, to the world celestial, to the many mansions, to the spiritual realms, to the beautiful life, to the inexhaustible source of all that is good. Faith is the path that leads to the soul's inheritance of all that the heart has prayed for, and to follow this path is to have faith in faith.

Thousands have undertaken to live by faith, but not having sufficient faith in faith have too soon adopted a different course. In the beginning of the spiritual life it is so easy to forget the vision of the soul, so easy to follow the dictates of the senses when this vision has seemingly faded away. And the cause is we have not sufficient faith in faith.

When we begin to live by faith we must have sufficient faith to go on and on, no matter how many obstacles or failures we may meet at first. Temptations are numerous and the soul that has resolved to employ spiritual methods in all things must be able to deal with the tempter as Jesus did. But this is not impossible, because the mind that is in Christ Jesus, the same mind is in you.

The greatest obstacle is the intended kindness of friends. They have our welfare at heart, and wish to do everything they can to promote that welfare; but they almost invariably employ the ways of the world; they do not know that faith is always sufficient. Here is a place where much strength is required. Here is the real parting of the ways, and the problem is, will you listen to those who love you with the love that knows not the way, or will you depend upon faith alone? Will you accept the kindness of the world or the unbounded love and the limitless power of the Infinite? Whoever loves brother or sister more than me is not worthy of me. Also, if thy right hand offend thee, cut it off. It is better to lose everything that is near and dear than to lose faith, but so long as we continue in faith, giving faith the first thought, and having abundant faith in faith, we shall not lose anything that we love.

The "right hand" is the sum-total of all those things in the world, that we feel we cannot get along without. They seem indispensable, and their loss seems irreparable; but they are insignificant compared with faith. We must be ready to dispense with them all if necessary to the realization of perfect faith, and we must depend absolutely upon faith regardless of the wishes of our dearest friends. But when we are ready to sacrifice everything that faith may have its way, we shall find that no sacrifice will be required of us.

When Abraham became absolutely willing to even sacrifice his own son in order to obey the spirit, he learned it was not required of him. And it is always thus; when we are willing to lose everything that spirit may reign, we find that we lose nothing, but gain much.

When we have faith in faith we find that faith can do anything; and we find that faith in the life, the power and the guidance of the spirit will take us safely through anything. If we are in trouble, faith will open the way out; if we have lost our friends, faith will give us more and better friends; if we have lost all of our possessions, faith will give us greater riches than we ever had before.

We have been told that the story of Job is an allegory; but even so, it illustrates what can be done, and what is being done in varying degrees in the lives of thousands where faith in faith is abundant and strong. He who has the faith that Job had will regain all he has lost and in addition, will receive much more. This is the law of faith and we can all prove the law by simply having faith in faith.

When we are in darkness and sin, faith will lead us into the full light; when we are in bondage to sickness and pain, faith will heal us and give us complete emancipation; and when we are in poverty or want, faith will lead us into the land of plenty.

The old thought has informed us that he who would live by faith must expect to live in poverty; many have believed this and have therefore been compelled to let go of almost everything of value and worth in the world. What we believe must come, will come. As your faith is, so shall it be unto you. If it is your faith that you must live in poverty in order to live by faith, in poverty you must live.

But it is the Father's will and desire to give us the riches of the kingdom; and to have faith is to live in harmony with Infinite will; therefore, when we begin to live by faith we shall leave the life of poverty and enter the world of abundance.

To live in poverty is not a mark of spirituality. If you are poor something is wrong either with you or with the society in which you live. But faith can take you out of that wrong and cause all things to become right. Faith can give you the best of everything that the whole of life can produce. Believe this and so it will be.

When things seem dark, and all that is near and dear seems to be slipping away from you, do not complain or weep. Have faith. Depend upon faith. Have faith in faith. Know that faith will change the course of events; turn darkness into light; turn hatred into love; turn chaos into order and harmony; and cause the best of all things to flow into your life in greater abundance than ever before. Faith can do anything. Have faith in faith and to you shall come the riches and blessings of the beautiful life.

The tendency of man is to turn to old methods when faith seems to fail; but why does faith ever fail? The reason is we have not sufficient faith in faith. When we have perfect faith in faith, it can never fail us. The power within faith is limitless, and it is our privilege to call into action as much of this power as we may need or desire.

We are called upon every day to decide upon something of importance; but how is this decision to be made? Are we to follow fear or faith? Fear declares that everything may go wrong; this is always the language of fear; but faith declares that everything will go right; and this is always the language of faith. Fear does not know; faith does know. Follow the verdict of fear and everything will go wrong, because the path of fear leads into wrong. But follow the superior insight of faith and everything will go right. The path of faith is the ever-ascending path to the greatest good that real life can give; therefore, no one can follow faith without finding the richer, the larger, the truer and the better.

Fear always expects the worst, because it can see only darkness; faith positively assures us of the best, because it can clearly see the light; and in the light the best is always found. But whether we decide to follow fear and live in darkness, or decide to follow faith and live in the light, will depend entirely upon how much faith we have in faith.

Millions are living lives that are not satisfactory; they long for a change, but they are in such complete bondage to fear that they are always afraid to even hope for something better. There is a power, however, that can break the bonds, and that power is faith. Are you living in Egypt? Are you in bondage to the king of evil, oppression and misery? Faith can lead you out. Depend upon faith, and begin this moment to follow wherever faith may go. Is there a Red Sea of mental materiality between yourself and the promised land of peace, happiness and plenty? Take the rod of faith in your hand and stretch it out over the sea; the waters will instantly divide, and you may walk safely to the other side. Faith can do anything. Have faith in faith.

There is not a single person in the world today that cannot enter the promised land, and do so now. Anyone may find peace, health, happiness, freedom, and the very best that life can give. These things are for you in your present state of existence. It is the will of God that life should be sweet to every soul; do not believe that you must suffer. There is freedom for you this very moment; there is a beautiful life that you may enter at once, and faith is the open door.

Have faith, and the veil of mystery is no more; you may see what has been hidden, and enter the secret chambers of life. Have faith, and the clouds of darkness will completely disappear; you will behold the light of the eternal sun, and the radiance of its glory will fill and illumine your entire sphere of existence. Have faith, and the barriers of limitations will fall to rise no more; and the invincible powers of the spirit will surge through and through your entire being, proclaiming in language divine, "Nothing shall be impossible unto thee, for I am thy strength and thy life forever."

Faith is the assurance of things hoped for, the evidence of things not seen; and the reason is that faith lives in the light. Faith knows that we may receive anything we ever hoped for, because faith discerns that power that makes all things possible. Faith is in the light, and therefore sees what has not been seen; it does not simply believe that the unseen is real, but proves the reality of everything by going out into the boundlessness of everything.

Faith is never sad, because it lives in the joy everlasting. Faith never grieves, because it knows that nothing is lost. Faith knows that what shall be united will be united; what shall be found will be found; and what belongs to us cannot long be kept away from us. Faith also knows that whatever we may need or desire now, exists for us now; and it is our privilege to enter through the door of faith and receive our own. The great secret is faith. Faith can do anything. Have faith in faith.

CHAPTER XX

THE INFINITE REVEALED

When we think of God as absolute and infinite, and try to picture His spirit as it fills the universe with His transcendental omnipresence, we seemingly lose, at first, that beautiful something that makes Him personal to us. God does not seem to be God unless we can think of Him as a friend, and go to Him as we would to some person that was very near and very dear. It seems difficult to speak to an Infinite Being, and there is no beauty or comfort in believing in God unless we can speak to Him at any time when we feel the need of His tender care. Nevertheless, our reason declares that God must be infinite or He would not be God; and our spiritual discernment concurs with reason upon this great, momentous theme; but since God is infinite, absolute and omnipresent, how can He be personal? And if He is not personal, how can we think of Him as being different from cold principle and law?

We cannot think of love as existing apart from personality, and God is love; therefore He must be personal; but how can God, who fills the universe, be personal? This is the problem that confronts nearly every mind that passes from the literal belief in truth to the spiritual understanding of truth. When we try to think that God is not personal, we feel as if we have lost a great friend, the very friend of all friends; there seems to be no use for prayer, because how can the limitless Soul of the universe be interested specially in one of us, a mere atom in the immensity of the cosmos? Besides, we find it practically impossible to pray to something that is nothing but changeless principle and immutable law. We therefore cease prayer and substitute affirmations; but something is lacking; the soul remains comfortless; the intellect may be satisfied, but the tender elements of love and sympathy are gradually disappearing, and finally we come to a place where nothing but cold intellect remains. Then we discover we are not on the path; we

The soul never acts alone; whenever the soul acts, God acts also, in the same place, at the same time, and for the same purpose. Whenever the soul undertakes anything, there is immediate and direct assistance from the Supreme. Therefore, the soul can never fail; nor can any personal undertaking fail that is prompted, directed and inspired by the soul. My Father worketh and I work; and I am the soul. So long as I know and feel that I am the soul, the soul will act in all my work, and where the soul acts there God will act also, because the two are One. What the soul begins, God will finish; what the soul aspires to be, God will cause it to be.

have gone astray, and everything the heart has wished for seems to be far in the distance.

With God all things are possible; therefore, it is not beyond His power to be personal as well as absolute; nor is it beyond the power of man to understand how this can be. God is the great Soul of the universe. He lives and acts everywhere, and there is no place where He is not; nevertheless, He is just as personal to any one of us as the very dearest friend; in truth, more so, because His personal nearness to us is closer than that of any friend, closer even than life itself. He is not limited and circumscribed as the form of a human personality; if He were, He could be personal only to those who lived in the same locality as He might happen to live; and therefore the vast throngs would receive no more comfort from His personal care than if they should try to worship principle and law. The very fact that God is infinite makes it possible for Him to be personal to all the souls in the universe; and the fact that He is present everywhere throughout the limitless vastness of space makes it possible for Him to give His personal care everywhere, thus ministering individually to every soul in existence.

God is individualized in every soul; that is, He actually lives in the very being of every soul. God is within us, closer than breathing, nearer than hands and feet; therefore it is not necessary to look to the great Soul of the universe whenever we think of God, to look within is sufficient. To contemplate the vastness of infinite life or the immensity of a universal soul is to lose sight of God. We can know Him only when we meet Him face to face within the sacred realms of our own divine spirit. Do not look toward the vastness of the without, but look toward the divinity of the within, and God will be there. He is always there, and His being there means that He is personal to us, ever ready to give personal attention to any need that we may have at the time. Being within us, and being in the very life of our own spirit, He is nearer than even our own personality, and can therefore give us His personal attention whenever we may so desire. Though He is not personal to any one or any special number alone, being omnipresent, He is personal to all souls at all times, and that is a truth that is beautiful indeed to think of. The vine is united with all its branches, and gives its very life to each individual branch at all times. The vine is personal to each branch, and yet is not confined to the personal form or personal limitations of any one branch. In like manner, the Infinite is personal to every soul, but is not localized as any one individual soul may be.

When we state that God is in His heaven, we do not mean that He occupies a certain local heaven, because God is everywhere, and where He is there heaven must be also. Nor do we mean that He has a local throne, because the Infinite is enthroned in every soul, and all souls are spiritually one; therefore the great throne of God is the spirit of all souls united in one perfect, universal divinity. But there is also a local heaven; there is a local heaven in every soul, and God lives there eternally; there is a local heaven wherever two or more are gathered in His name; there is a local heaven wherever there is a new heaven and a new earth; there is a local heaven on the spiritual heights of every word of divine existence, and there are heavens above heavens both in the great without and the great within, the higher we ascend upon the great eternal path of endless and limitless glory. God has provided everything that the life of man may desire. There are heavens for the senses and heavens for the soul; there are heavens that the eye can see and the person enjoy, and there are heavens that only the soul can discern while on the mountain tops of its own exalted divinity. And everywhere there is God giving His personal thought to every human desire or need.

God is not a personality, but He is personal to every personality in existence. He is personal to each one of us because He is in actual personal touch with each one of us. He lives in all, therefore he is personal to all, and can give personal attention to the needs of each and all. The soul knows this; the mind in its higher states of consciousness has discerned it, and thus the belief in a personal God has arisen. The mind has discerned only the personal presence of God in the soul at certain intervals, but the soul knows that God is personally present at all times in all souls. Thus the former belief in a personal God is not lost; it is only made infinitely larger. The feeling that we can speak to God as we speak to a personal friend continues, only that feeling has become infinitely more beautiful. To realize that God lives in us and we in Him, is to know that we are personally in touch, not with a part of God, but with all of God; and that all His power, all His wisdom and all His love is for each one of us now and eternally. All that the father hath is mine; and being infinite, He is personally interested in me even though He be personally interested in all the other souls in the universe at the same time. What He can be to one He can be to all, and He is. His eye is ever upon each one of us, and His hand is ever ready to guide whenever we may so desire.

God never ceases to think of you, nor should you cease to think of Him. He is personally interested in you and your welfare; then how can ill befall you? Why should any of us ever go wrong with the Infinite Hand so near? There are no reasons why unless it should be our endeavor to understand through reason that which the spirit alone can discern. Depend upon the spirit; follow the light of the spirit and every moment shall reveal the presence of God. Everything we do will be directed by His wisdom, and His power will see us through. Nothing need disturb us, neither need we ever be anxious. God wants us to reach our goal. He is personally interested in every undertaking we have in hand, and He is working with us, placing His limitless power at our command. Therefore, we need not be concerned when unexpected changes appear; every change will be a change for the better; every turn in events will lead us into greater events, and every door that may close on the left will open another door on the right through which we may pass to a greater world than we ever knew before. This is what will happen when God is with us; and He is always with us, only we must learn to receive everything that He has to give.

To know God is the beginning of wisdom, because God is the source of wisdom. The nearer we live to the source the more we receive of that which comes from the source. The mind that is not consciously living with God may have intellect and mental capacity, but the wisdom that knows can come only to that mind that is walking with God every moment of conscious existence. The mind that does not know God thinks in the darkness; the mind that does know God thinks in the light.

God is my light forever,
His spirit is shining within;
My home is the kingdom of heaven,
I'm free from all evil and sin.

God is my love and power,
My being is perfect and whole;
I'm living the life of the spirit,
The beautiful life of the soul.

God is my life eternal,
My truth and my wisdom divine,
I'm heir to His riches and glory,
His kingdom forever is mine.

CHAPTER XXI

RETURN YE UNTO GOD

Wherever we may be, whatever has happened or whatever may threaten to happen, it matters not; there is a power that can change everything. There are no reasons for sorrow, fear or regret; there are no occasions for anxiety, discouragement or despair; there is a path that leads to the world of the heart's desire, and anyone may find it. Great learning is not required, nor shall we find certain fixed beliefs necessary. The secret is simple, simple enough for any mind in the world, because it is the will of Infinite Love that every mind in the world shall know the way. None need stumble, none need go astray, none need ever be lost. All that is necessary is to follow the voice of the soul, and this voice is ever proclaiming in language divine, Return Ye Unto God.

The world has tried every imaginable method to gain freedom, but when all these methods fail, as they all will, Return Ye Unto God. The moment we return to Him, all that we have lost will return to us; and that which we do not wish for will vanish. When we return to Him we return to our own, because He is the source of everything that can possibly be our own. To be with Him is to be where we wish to be, and where we wish to be there we shall find the "gates ajar" to the heaven that is within. Before we can enter the heaven that is within us we must find perfect peace for mind and soul, and this peace we always find when we return to God. The more closely we live to His presence the deeper and more exalted the calm; and out from the silence of this calm comes the sacred symphonies of life, that music of the soul that we all recognize as the prelude to the kingdom of God. When we can hear it we know that His presence is near; we can discern through the spiritual vision those secret places that every returning soul has the privilege to enter. We learn what is in store, and life is not the same any more. We have had a vision, and all things have been glorified.

Return ye unto God. All other paths lead to sorrow and death, but in Him there is freedom and joy forever. In Him there is life, in Him there is peace, in Him there is wholeness and purity; in Him there is strength, in Him there is health, in Him there is power and truth; in Him there is all that life holds in store for man—all that the human heart can wish for. Seek no other source; follow no other path. There is only one place where the soul finds rest and contentment; only one place where every vision is realized, and every lofty dream made true. All may find it; the secret is simple. Return ye unto God.

But Jesus answered them, My Father worketh even until now, and I work.—John 5:17.

The significance of this statement is as large as the limitless sea of divinity in which we live and move and have our being. The Infinite is everywhere and works everywhere, and therefore He is with us working with us. To know this is to know one of the greatest truths in the world, and there is nothing that is more helpful in the living of everyday life than to live, think and act in harmony with this truth. Whatever our work may be, it ceases to be difficult the moment we realize that God is working with us. When we know that His power is with us, the burden disappears completely.

The undertaking we have in mind may be very large; it may seem to be more than we alone can carry through; but we need not be alone; the Infinite is at hand ready to work with us, and with Him there can be no failure. Depend upon the Supreme; ask God to work with you; live so near to the Spirit that you will be one with God, and when you choose to go with God, He will go with you. Then the work will almost do itself; you perform the most difficult task with perfect ease, and you can work as much as you desire, weariness will not even make an attempt to enter your world.

The average person works alone; his task is therefore difficult; he does nothing well, and his work is wearing and tearing to a degree that makes his life both bitter and disappointing. But he works alone, with almost every disadvantage in his way, simply because he has not ascended in the spiritual scale. He has not arisen to that lofty realm where he can be in harmony with Supreme power, and therefore must depend upon the limited power of mere man. This, however, is his own choice; he may rise in the spiritual scale whenever he may desire and as much as he may desire; and the higher he goes in this scale the more direct assistance he receives from the Infinite.

When we reach those same spiritual heights that Jesus had reached, we can also say as he did that my Father worketh and I work, and we will receive just as much power from God as he received. We shall thereby do the works that he did, and as we go on still farther with him, we shall do the greater works. Jesus declared that he could of himself do nothing. His great power came from God, and his spirituality was so high that he could both receive and apply this power. He had reached that state where he was in perfect harmony with Supreme power, and could manifest the fullness of that power in all his life and works.

And his command was: Follow me; what I have done, ye shall do. We are therefore not to remain content with simply believing that he was what he was and did what he did; we are to go and do likewise. Nor is the way difficult; to follow Christ is the simplest thing in the world, and there is nothing that produces such great results. Though we may not reach the heights that he reached at once, we can press on, and gain ground daily. Every step will bring added power, and this power we can use now in everything that we may be doing now. Spiritual power is not only for some other world; nor is its sole use in this world to keep us away from temptations. The power of the spirit is intended to be used in the living of a great life here and now, and in the doing of great things in this present world.

Those alone will enter the kingdom who do the will of the Father, and to do the will of the Father is to live the life that He lives now. Live the life of the Spirit now, and you are saved both for time and eternity. And one of the greatest essentials in the living of the spiritual life is to live so near to God that His power is in everything that we may do. Then God works with us; not simply in what the world calls great things, but in all things. Even in those things that seem to be insignificant, the power of the Supreme is with us, and everything we do brings joy.

The first step to be taken in anything we wish to do, is to seek divine assistance. To ask God to go with us and work with us, and to enter into such perfect spiritual harmony with God that we can feel His supreme power through and through—that is the first and most important, be it work pertaining to body, mind or soul. Whether we are beginners in the spiritual life or have reached the heights, God will work with us in whatever we have the understanding to do now; and as we rise in the scale, He will work with us in doing those greater things that spiritual giants have the privilege to perform. And with God working with us, we shall never fail; all work will be pleasure, and the days of weariness shall come no more.

The mind that understands the spirit of truth knows that it is the Father that does the work; that it is the power of the Infinite that produces all power; that this power comes into our life to be directed and used by us, and that we may receive as much of this power as we desire. Such a mind knows that it will profit nothing to force the limited power that we may seem to possess, but that more power from on high comes without fail when our thoughts are very high and very still. Therefore, the true mind creates all thought in the supreme stillness of higher spiritual realms, and leaves results to divine law. Those results will be far greater and better than the personal man, unaided, could have possibly produced, even with every external advantage at hand. When we have great things to do we are tempted to rush forward and force those things through; but this must never be permitted. Such methods are not only detrimental to the mind, but are wholly inadequate to fulfill the purpose we have in view. To be perfectly still at such times, and let Supreme Life do the great work is the secret.

To secure more power we must go up into those spiritual regions where power is limitless; and when we enter that high state our thoughts not only become enormously strong, but thinking becomes so smooth and easy that no effort whatever is required. We think God's thoughts after Him, and those thoughts are not only full of power, but also full of peace. To understand how an action can be perfectly still may be difficult to the mind that has never felt the perfect calm; but we must realize that stillness does not imply inactivity. Real stillness is the highest form of activity, where the strongest power acts in absolute harmony. To be in real stillness is to be in that power; therefore, the mind that is perfectly still thinks the highest thoughts, the greatest thought and the most powerful thought.

We may all demonstrate through personal experience that it is not strenuous metaphysical efforts that perform miracles, but the power of those high spiritual thoughts we create while in the secret places of the Most High. And when we learn to use that method only, and never permit ourselves to become mentally over-wrought, we shall develop healing powers that are extraordinary—powers that will do greater things than was ever seen upon earth before. "Greater things than these shall ye do." "I am with you always, even unto the end of the world."

When you live in the presence of the Infinite you are constantly in touch with higher power and superior guidance. You will therefore not only be able to accomplish far more in your chosen vocation, but you will be prevented from going astray. The very moment the person is tempted to take a misstep, the spirit from within interferes, and you are prompted to again proceed on the true path. When you are on the verge of doing something that is not best, higher power appears; something unexpected happens to upset all your proposed plans, and you are led to see, by the light from within, that there is something better in store. The nearer you live to the Infinite the more readily you are corrected and placed right whenever you are going to go wrong. Your seeming mistakes, therefore, are brought to naught in every instance, and you are awakened more and more to the realization of the great truth that God knows best. When in doubt or in darkness, leave it to God; the right way will open and the very best will come to pass.

The first principle in the unfoldment of the soul is to live in the spiritual attitude; that is, in the prayer without ceasing, or in that attitude where you feel that you are in the spirit. When you are in the spirit, or in the spirit of real prayer, and deeply desire certain things, you will certainly receive them. Everything that you can possibly pray for is in the spirit, and when you are in the spirit when you pray you will be in perfect spiritual touch with what you pray for. And what we spiritually touch, that we receive. Place human life in conscious contact with higher life and the latter will flow into the former. Soul unfoldment will place the being of man in higher and higher states of spiritual relationship with the Supreme Source of all things. Therefore, to unfold the soul is to open the way to every lofty goal that man may have in view.

"And if thy right hand cause thee to stumble, cut it off." The right hand symbolizes that which we think we cannot live without, and to think that anything in the visible world is indispensable, is to be in bondage to things. He who knows that he can live whether the universe lives or not, has found life itself—the eternal life of the spirit. He is therefore no longer in bondage to things because he is in that life that is infinitely greater than all things.

CHAPTER XXII

PRAYERS THAT ARE ANSWERED

The Infinite is changeless, therefore there is no special providence in the usual sense of that term, and yet in the higher sense, everything is special providence. Every act of the Supreme is a special act because it provides for a special need somewhere in the life of the human soul.

However, it is not necessary to ask God to go outside of His changeless laws to answer our particular prayer. Our particular prayer is already provided for; that is, God is already doing that which is required to supply what we desire. Therefore, God will not have to do something special to answer our special request. He is already and eternally doing everything; but we must do something special to secure what God has already provided for us.

What is called special providence is not the result of a special act of God, but the result of a special act of man; and this special act of man is the act of man **going to God** to present his request and receive his heart's desire.

The prayers that are answered are not the prayers that we express when we are away from God, but when we are with God. Our prayers are never answered when we think of God as far away; to receive an answer to our prayer we must go to God; we must enter into His very presence, and while we are in His presence there is no true request that we can possibly make that will not be granted.

The Infinite is limitless, both in power and in love; therefore, God is not only able to do everything that we ask Him to do, but He **wants** to do it. It is a great privilege for infinite love to do everything, and the love of God is infinite.

It is not the wish of God to withhold from us anything that we may desire; it is His supreme desire to give us everything, but we are created with a free will, therefore God gives only that which we, through our own free will, may select.

The average person thinks he is imposing upon God when he asks for much; but the fact is that the more we ask for the more we please God, provided we go to Him and receive it, and if we wish to please God in the highest measure we should pray without ceasing, pray for everything we can use in the building of a great and beautiful life.

The power of prayer, however, should not be used exclusively for the realization of what is usually termed spiritual things; all things become spiritual when animated with the spiritual life; and all things are good when used for a good purpose; therefore, we are free to pray for everything that can add to the whole of life, be it of the body, the mind or the soul.

The true spiritual life does not mean the riches of the soul combined with weakness of the body, poverty of the person and ignorance of the mind. The true spiritual life is an ideal life on all planes, and God is ready to provide us with everything that can make the whole of life ideal, if we only pray for it with the prayer that not only asks of God but also takes us to God.

The true prayer never doubts, but believes implicitly that the request will be granted; and this is natural, because we cannot possibly doubt when we know that the more we ask of God the more we please God. But it is not only natural for the true prayer to have perfect faith; it is necessary. Before our prayers can be answered we must go to God and receive what we have asked for; and it is only through perfect faith in God that we can enter into the presence of God.

The true prayer is always inspired with the thought "I know that thou wilt answer me"; and this thought is the spiritual product of faith—the faith that feels the love of God.

The true prayer is also animated with the highest form of spiritual gratitude, and is therefore always inspired with that beautiful thought, "My Father, I thank thee that thou hearest my prayer, and I thank thee, that thou hearest me always." The prayer of faith knows that God does hear every prayer, and that he will answer every prayer providing we come to Him in person with our request. In consequence, when we are in the spirit of true prayer, our gratitude must necessarily be boundless.

When we feel that God will give us anything we may ask for, that there is no doubt about it whatever, we cannot otherwise but give expression to the very soul of gratitude, and this gratitude is both limitless and endless; it is the soul's eternal thanksgiving.

To live in the spirit of that prayer that is ever asking God for everything, that believes that God is giving everything, and that is constantly giving thanks to God for everything, is, in itself, a life of the highest joy. In such a life everything is being taken to higher ground, because we are manifesting in body, mind and soul, more and more of the likeness of God. Personal existence is becoming ideal existence, while the soul is living in the full conscious realization of God's own beautiful world.

But thou, when thou prayest, enter into thine inner chamber, and having shut thy door, pray to thy Father which is in secret, and thy Father which seeth in secret shall recompense thee.—Mat. 6:6.

This is not a literal statement; the inner chamber is not some secluded place in some material structure, nor is the door referred to something that can be opened or closed with the power of physical hands. There is only one inner chamber; there is only one secret place; there is only one sacred realm where the human meets the divine, and that is in the soul of man. To enter the inner chamber is to enter the beautiful stillness within. God is enthroned in every human soul, and to enter into the secret places of the soul is to meet Him face to face.

The door that must be closed is the consciousness of the without, that something in the mind that takes cognizance of the world of things. When we enter into secret, the visible must be forgotten; we are upon holy ground and must remove the shoes of external existence. We cannot enter the silent within so long as we think of outer things, therefore the door must be closed. And we cannot pray to the Most High unless we enter His presence. To pray is not simply asking God, it is also going to God. The most beautiful prayer is not uttered in words but is felt in the sacred depths of the soul.

When we simply ask God our prayers are never answered; we do not pray unless we enter into secret; it will profit nothing to make a request of the Infinite unless we first enter our inner chamber and close the door. And no person ever prayed in secret that was not rewarded openly. No prayer that is uttered in the sublime stillness of the soul is ever disregarded. All such prayers are answered. What we ask of God when we meet Him face to face, that we invariably receive.

When we have learned to pray in secret we should never have occasion to doubt any more. We then know that every request will be granted. Even though the answer does not come until the eleventh hour and the last moment of that hour, we know that it will come. Our faith is as perfect as the word of truth, and as high as the heavens of the spirit, and in that faith we live. God will find a way; we have asked Him to do so and every request brings that beautiful response, "I will not forsake thee nor leave thee; I am thy Redeemer, I will care for thee."

To enter the inner chamber of the soul is to transcend everything, for the time being, that pertains to the visible world; but this requires spirituality. We cannot enter the spirit so long as we are subject to the body, and we are subject to the body so long as we live for the body. When we begin to live for the spirit we can enter the innermost chambers of the spirit whenever we so desire, and when we are in this spiritual state we may pray for anything that is needed in the body, the mind or the soul. What we pray for in secret we shall receive openly. Therefore, to live for the body is to neglect the body and to lose the soul. But to live for the spirit is to give the fullness of life to the entire being of man.

When we pray openly we do not pray, because we cannot be in the secret chambers of the soul so long as we are in the material world of external things; and no desire is a prayer unless it is uttered in that secret place within where we meet Him face to face. We must be with God to receive of God, and as He is enthroned within us, the perfect path to His presence is to enter the spiritual chamber within. There we shall find, not only the sublime stillness of the soul's communion with God, but also the secret power of faith—the faith that makes all things possible.

The secret power of faith is found in the soul's nearness to God; the nearer we are to God the more perfect our faith, the greater our power and the more beautiful our life; and when we enter into the sacred realms of the soul we are in the very presence of God. We are touched by the spirit, and to be touched by the spirit is to be filled with the spirit—to be filled with everything that the perfection of divine spirit may contain.

The prayer without ceasing is the living of that life that is so near to God that we can feel His power and His love at all times. In that life the mind is in constant touch with the soul and every true desire becomes a prayer uttered in secret. Therefore, when we so live that life itself becomes a beautiful prayer, there is nothing that we can desire or ask for that we shall not receive. When we live so near to God that we actually have our being in the spirit of His life, our every desire will be just and wholesome and true, and all such desires will be fulfilled; not in the distant future, but now. We shall begin to receive now that which is in store for them that

love Him and every day the measure will increase as long as eternity shall
continue to be.

**If ye abide in me, and my words abide in you, ask whatsoever ye will,
and it shall be done unto you.—John 15:7.**

There is no stronger statement to be found anywhere in the literature of
the world, and there is possibly no statement that has received less attention.
Nevertheless, those who understand the inner meaning of high spiritual
truth, know that this statement is not only based upon an exact scientific
principle, but that any spiritually minded person can demonstrate the whole
truth that is contained in that principle.

To abide in the Christ is not simply to live in the acceptance of some
belief about Jesus; but this is the current idea; and being purely literal it has
no power whatever; in consequence, those who claim to abide in the Christ
do not secure any greater results through their prayers than do those who
depend solely upon mere personal desire. To abide in the Christ is to actually **live** in the Christ consciousness, and every part of mind and soul is
permeated, through and through, with the life and the power of the Christ.
Your entire being is in the hands of higher power; you are in a world where
things are absolutely mastered by the spiritual will, and your mind is so
spiritualized that it responds perfectly to the power of divine will.

When the words of the Christ abide in you, your mind is in absolute
truth because those words are absolute truth. The mind that is in truth is in
the true state of being, and to be in the true state of being is to be so close to
God that anything desired can be received at any time. With God all things
are possible, and God will do anything for us if we live as He lives. This is
the secret, and we do live as God lives when we abide in the Christ with
His words abiding in us.

When the words of the Christ abide in us, every thought we think and
every word we utter will be animated with the spirit of the Christ; in like
manner, inner spiritual power will give **soul** to everything we do, and that
power that caused even the winds and the waves to obey will begin to work
through us. Supreme power will be with us at all times to answer our
prayers; our thoughts and our words will be living thoughts and words, and
will carry the power of the spirit wherever they may go. We are therefore
in that position where we not only can receive from God anything desired,
but where we have the power to make our own prayers come true.

To be in the Christ means more than to receive from his love what our hearts may desire; it means spiritual mastership. To be in the Christ is not a mere feeling of the emotions; it is a **life,** and in that life the power of the Christ is supreme. Nor is this power given to us temporarily; it becomes our own, and we become able to bring to ourselves anything we may ask for. It is the promise. "What I have done, ye shall do." This promise is not mere words; it means something; it means that any person may attain spiritual mastership and cause the world of things to respond to the power of the Christ within him.

We have believed this; the hour is at hand to prove it; and those who will try will find that God is with them. But we must remember that this supreme state does not come through personal effort. "I can of myself do nothing." We must enter the consciousness of the Christ, the inner life of the Christ, the very spirit of the Christ; and our thought must become identical with His word. When there is no difference whatever between our thoughts and the sublime words of the Christ, then we can truthfully say that His words are abiding in us.

When our thoughts become identical with the words of the Christ, the same power that was in His words will be in our thoughts; and also in our words; a principle of truth so extraordinary that when we first think of it we become awe-stricken with thoughts so great, so wonderful, so marvelous that no tongue can ever give them utterance. And as we penetrate further into the inner meaning of this great truth we meet thoughts more marvelous still; we are face to face with the statement that we, even we, shall in the near future hold in our own hands the same power that wrought such wonder works in the hands of the Christ. Every person that is living the spiritual life is steadily moving toward that supreme goal.

When we abide in the Christ and His words abide in us, we are living absolutely in the inner spiritual world; in that world there are no impossibilities, and everything that we can possibly ask for is even now at hand; that all our prayers should be answered is therefore most evident. God is more willing to give than we are to receive; the reason why we do not receive what we may desire or need is because we are not willing; that is, our will is not in harmony with the will of God and our desire is not in harmony with the desire of God. But this harmony with God is fully secured when we begin to live in the Christ and begin to think only those thoughts that are inspired by the words of the Christ. We are then absolutely in His power, in His life, in His love; we may ask what we will; His life contains everything; His power brings forth everything; His love gives everything.

Therefore I say unto you, all things whatsoever ye pray and ask for, believe that ye have received them, and ye shall have them.—Mark 11:24.

This great statement gives positive emphasis to the law that we can gain actual possession only of that which we have gained conscious possession. Or, in other words, we must become conscious of the existence of an object before we can gain personal possession of that object. We must enter consciously into the life of that which we desire to gain, but we cannot enter into the life of that which we doubt the existence of. Doubt invariably produces a gulf between ourselves and the object of doubt, while faith produces mental and spiritual unity.

Spiritual unity is always followed by actual or personal unity; that is, what we enter into conscious possession of in the spiritual life we will, ere long, gain actual possession of in the physical life. Believe that you have already received in the spirit what you desire to receive in the person, and you will receive it in the person in a very short time. This is a law that positively cannot fail. Claim your own in the ideal world and you will receive your own in the real world.

This law gives rise to the practice of affirmations, but affirmations as usually employed do not comply with all the elements of the law. To simply affirm that we **are** what we wish to be, or that we **have** what we wish to possess, is not sufficient. Our spiritual possessions do not express themselves unless there is a strong, positive, personal desire for expression. We must pray for that which we wish to realize, but our prayer should not be mere asking. The prayer that asks in the feeling of uncertainty as to whether the thing prayed for is for us or not, is not a prayer of faith; and it is only the prayer of faith that is answered.

To pray in the feeling that knows that what we pray for is, even now, ready to be given to us, is to combine the desire for expression with the realization of possession, and we thus comply fully with the law of supply. In this attitude we have faith, and it is only through faith that we can enter into the spirit of that which we desire to actually possess. We must awaken the spiritual cause before we can secure the physical effect, but it is only through faith that we enter into the world of spiritual cause. Faith produces spiritual unity, and when we are one with the spirit we become conscious of the life, the richness and the power of the spirit. In consequence, we cause that which is in the spirit to be brought forth in the body, because what we gain consciousness of in the within we invariably express in the without.

When we simply affirm that we have what we wish to possess, the mental action is quite liable to be merely intellectual or even mechanical; and we do not touch our interior, spiritual possessions in the least. But when the affirmation is animated with prayer and desire the mental action becomes so deep that the spiritual life is reached. Or, to express the same truth in another manner, when our prayer for that which we desire is strengthened by the positive faith that we have already received it, we remove all doubts and barriers and enter at once into actual and conscious possession.

To use affirmations alone is to ignore the great possibilities of Infinite assistance. Any person may, for a while, build himself up mentally and personally with affirmations alone, but the structure is artificial; it is built upon the sand and will surely fall when the storms of environments and changing circumstances become a trifle too strong. Without the conscious and continuous assistance of the Infinite no man can travel very far on the upward path nor go very high in the scale of true being. But any man who takes God with him can overcome any obstacle in the world, scale the highest heights in existence, and what he builds today he is building for eternity.

The proper course to pursue is to ask God for everything you desire; ask Him to be with you in everything you wish to accomplish; pray without ceasing, and while you pray and work and press on to the great goal you have in view, affirm with positive faith that God is with you, that He has given you everything you can possibly desire or need. Believe that you **have** what you pray for, believe that you **are** what you wish to become; then ask God to enlarge your realization, to give perpetual increase to your faith, and to be constantly with you in working out these great supreme convictions.

The true prayer is a high spiritual communion with God, but it is not an inactive state. True prayer is oneness with God and a strong living desire for the full realization of all that is in the life of God. Therefore, the true prayer is the perfect way to God. If we wish to be with God we must pray. If we wish God to be with us we must pray. Live in constant prayer to God and you secure the constant and conscious assistance of God in everything you do. But a prayer is not a prayer unless it incorporates the affirmation of the truth upon which the prayer or desire is based.

To simply affirm that God is with you will not give you the assistance of God. When you affirm a truth you are talking to yourself; when you pray you are talking to God, and God listens only to what we say to Him. If we want God to go with us we must ask Him, we must talk to Him consciously if we wish His personal assistance and power.

To affirm the truth is absolutely necessary because affirmations will train our own minds in right thinking, will remove doubt and will develop in us the power to know that all that we can pray for or desire is ours now. But in order to enter into the actual realization of our own we must enter the kingdom of God, because all things that are in store for man are now in the kingdom. And it is true prayer—the prayer that goes to God that constitutes the "gates ajar" to the riches and glory of that wonderful kingdom.

And Jesus lifted up his eyes, and said, Father, I thank thee that thou heardest me. And I know that thou hearest me always.—John 11:41.

This beautiful statement was given before the answer to the prayer was received, and is therefore an illustration of the very highest form of supreme faith. To thank God after you have received what you asked for is simple; any heart can, at such a time, be full of sublime gratitude; but to thank God before you have received what you intend to ask for, and **feel** the fullness of that gratitude thrill every fiber in your entire being—that is spirituality indeed. Likewise, to be able to say that you know that God hears you always; only the mind that is in the spirit can make such a statement, and pray in this manner; but that alone is real prayer.

To precede any prayer with doubt is to close the door between yourself and the spirit; there must be no uncertainty in our communion with God; we do not believe that God is God so long as we are uncertain as to whether our prayers will be heard or no, and we cannot enter into the presence of God until we believe that He verily is God. When we know that the power of God, the wisdom of God, the love of God—all is limitless, we can feel no doubt whatever, as to whether or no, our prayers will be answered. Divine power can do anything, but divine love cannot refuse anything.

When we know God as He is, we know that He hearest us always, and we feel it a privilege to thank Him every moment for this great truth. And when we thank Him in this manner before we begin our prayer, we not only enter into the very love of His spirit, but we also enter into that faith that makes all things possible. The faith that knows that God hearest us always is so close to God that it is animated with the very power of God; and therefore when we are in such a faith nothing can be impossible; we may then ask for what we will and it will be done unto us.

The more perfectly we realize that God hears us always the higher we ascend in the scale of true spirituality, because this supreme faith lifts the soul higher and higher until we are received at the very throne of the Most High. And to be in His presence is to receive whatever we may have asked or prayed for. God is everywhere, and we may enter into His presence anywhere. The Most High is enthroned in every soul, and pure spiritual faith is the "gates ajar" to His beautiful kingdom.

There is abundance of hope in the world, but what we need is more faith. Everybody is hoping for better things; the poor hope to get rich; the sick hope to get well; the sad hope to gain happiness; the troubled hope to find peace; everybody is hoping for something, but few have the faith that is necessary to secure that something. When we are in bondage, or keenly realize our bondage, we hope that the Great Deliverer will come; we pray that He may come; we hope that our prayers will be answered, and we are so absorbed in our hopes that we fail to hear Him knocking at the door even now. To have hope is to face the door, but hope stands still; it never moves toward the door. To live in hope is simply to face the great goal, but we may continue to face that goal for ages, and never move forward a step. "To live in hope is to die in despair," because hope remains stationary; it never gains what it hopes to gain. But when faith begins we remain stationary no more. We press on directly, and with power, toward the coveted goal; our hopes are soon realized; our desires are granted; what we wished for is withheld no more; through faith we have entered that world where every prayer is answered and every wish made true.

CHAPTER XXIII

THE FAITH THAT MOVES MOUNTAINS

To him who has faith nothing is impossible. It matters not what he may wish to realize or what he may wish to do; if he has faith, it can be done. But what do we mean by faith? Faith is not a passive belief; it is a positive action. It is the power of the spirit within man acting upon the life, the mind, the body and the nature of man; and by acting through man it acts upon everything with which man may come in contact. When we have faith we do not simply believe in the form, or that which may exist in the external; when we have faith we enter into the spirit of that in which we express our faith; the secret of real faith and the real power of such a faith is therefore found in the spirit.

When you proceed with something that you wish to accomplish, do not simply have confidence in yourself; and do not simply proceed in the mere conviction or assurance that your purpose will be realized; do more than that; have faith, and when you have faith, your mind will enter into the very spirit of that which you have undertaken to accomplish. This is the reason why nothing is impossible when you have faith, because when you enter the spirit you enter the power of the spirit, and to the power of the spirit there is no limit whatever. To have faith is to enter into the spirit; to enter into the spirit is to enter into the life and the power of the Most High; and with God all things are possible. The entire world of things is permeated with spirit, with infinite power; therefore, when we enter into the spirit of anything we enter in the one spirit that lives in all things, and gain possession of as much of the power of the one spirit as we can possibly receive. The greater our faith the greater our capacity to receive of the limitless power of the spirit, and, in consequence, the greater will be our realization of whatever we now may have in view.

To have more and more faith, the secret is to enter more and more deeply into the spirit of everything in which we express our faith. Do you have faith in yourself? Then try to enter mentally into the spirit of your entire being whenever you think of yourself. Do you have faith in your work? Then try to enter into the spirit of everything that is connected with your work. Do you have faith in every person you meet? Then try to enter into the spirit of his life, into mental contact with the greater man that lives within the personal man. Do you have faith in all things? Then enter into the spirit of things, into the real soul of things whenever you think of things or look upon things. Do you have faith in God? Then enter mentally and spiritually into the spirit of Infinite Spirit whenever you think of God; whenever you think of God, think of yourself as being in the spirit of God, and try to feel that God is closer than breathing, nearer than hands and feet. The more deeply, the more fully and the more completely you enter into the spirit of that of which you think, the greater your faith; and the greater your faith the greater your power.

There is not a person in the world who may not proceed in life with the full conviction that his ideals will be realized and that he will accomplish everything he has undertaken to do. If he lives and works in faith he simply cannot fail, because faith will give him all the power he may require, and anything may be accomplished when we have sufficient power. But the average person proceeds in the thought that he may possibly reach his goal; he is not certain; he concludes he will try, and will do his best; but as to the outcome he does not know. This, however, is not faith, and without faith nothing whatever can be accomplished. To fulfill any purpose, even the most insignificant, there must be some measure of faith, and the greater this measure, the greater will be the realization desired. He who proceeds in real, unbounded faith, will place his life in touch with invincible spirit, and he will continue unmoved, untouched and undisturbed, no matter what the circumstances may be. He will place his mental vision upon the highest light of supreme faith, and whatever may happen he will never waver from that light for a moment. He will continue with ceaseless perseverance and the most positive determination; he will continue in faith, and as he continues and grows in faith he will gain more and more power until he has sufficient power to do everything he is determined to do.

Faith does not always produce the expected miracle at once; it does not always convert a life of confusion, sickness and failure into a life of happiness, harmony and abundance without much waiting and watching and prayer; it does not always change a pathway of thorns into one of roses the very first day we begin to live by faith; and it does not always remove every obstacle in a minute. There are times when it requires months and even years of constant faith to realize what we pray for; but we may rest assured in the great truth that whoever fixes his attention upon a certain definite goal and continues to work toward that goal, in faith, will positively reach it. Work in faith, in continuous faith, in the spirit of unbounded faith, and you will reach your goal, you will accomplish your purpose just as surely as the coming of another day. Therefore, though you may not have results at once, nor even for some time, continue to work in the same unbounded faith; the results you desire will positively be gained; and the deeper and stronger your faith the sooner you will reach the object in view.

When faith seems to fail, the remedy is more faith. Do not become discouraged in the midst of seeming failure; do not give up the purpose you have undertaken to fulfill; do not doubt the possibilities of this purpose, nor come to the conclusion you are moving in the wrong direction. Continue to work in more and more faith, and if you should be on the wrong path, something will happen to set you right. Enter more and more into the light of faith, and all things will clear up. When you are on the wrong track doubt and uncertainty will but confuse you more, and cause you to go further into the wrong. But faith will increase your light; faith illumines the mind and clears the sky of your entire world; faith will lead you out of your mistakes and give you enough power to regain all that is lost and more. Continue, in faith, to press on toward your goal; discord will soon become harmony; uncertainty will soon become positive convictions; the crooked will be straightened out; obstacles will disappear; you will find your proper place; you will enter the work that is intended for you; all things in your life will work together for good, and you will press on and on, gaining ground steadily, drawing nearer and nearer toward the highest goal that your spiritual vision can possibly discern.

The majority of minds have many obstacles to meet, and almost invariably give emphasis to the belief that every seeming obstacle actually is an obstacle; but faith does not look upon obstacles as obstacles; faith does not call difficulties difficulties. When a person begins to live in faith, all things that come into his life are looked upon as opportunities, and they are. We all know very well that if we had no difficulties or obstacles to meet, or what would be more appropriately termed "great occasions," we should soon become nonentities. It is the difficult things that we meet that enable us to bring into action the greater power that is within us; difficulties, therefore, are the most valued of opportunities, and if taken advantage of as such, will always be met with joy. No obstacle should ever be called by that name or ever thought of as being an obstacle, for it is, in truth, something that will enable you to prove to yourself that the power that is within you is greater than anything in the world. When we no longer call obstacles obstacles or difficulties difficulties, we shall not be disturbed by obstacles or difficulties any more. Whatever we meet will be turned to good account and will call forth more and more of the greater power that is within us. Accordingly, all things will work together for greater good; every occasion will be welcome, no matter what it may be; every experience will be a pleasure, and everything that we pass through will add to our welfare and joy.

When a person thinks that every obstacle is an obstacle, he will frequently hesitate to proceed; and will, in many instances, on account of this hesitancy or doubt or fear, fail to reach his goal; but if he proceeds in the faith that there is something within him that is greater than all the obstacles in the world, there is no obstacle that can stand in his way. In fact, when he proceeds in such a faith, every obstacle that is met will simply call forth that greater something that is within him, and this "something" will give him all the power he may require to reach his goal.

Faith is that attitude of mind through which we come in conscious touch with the Infinite. When we are in the attitude of faith we are in the very spirit of life, and in the spirit of life God reigns supremely. The power of the Infinite is in the spirit, and when we are in the spirit we become one with that power; therefore, while we are in that oneness nothing can be impossible with us any more. But the power of the Infinite, expressed through us while we are in the spirit of faith, is not applicable to spiritual things alone; it is applicable to all things, and may be applied anywhere in life in the attainment of the higher, the greater and the better. If you wish to change your environment, or if you wish to better certain things in your life, determine precisely what you want; then have faith. Continue to say "I have the faith," and repeat that statement as frequently as possible. Believe that you will realize what you want and believe that your belief is absolute truth. Have faith, and also have faith in faith; and whenever you affirm the statement, "I have the faith," enter into the very spirit of that statement. When you say that you have the faith, and enter into the spirit of what you say, you awaken the power that can do what your faith has undertaken to do. That is how faith can never fail; the moment you begin to have faith in what you have undertaken to do you arouse all the power necessary to see that undertaking through. And the more frequently you affirm, in the spirit, "I have the faith," the sooner you will enter into the spirit of real faith, where the necessary power will be gained.

Our constant purpose should be to become conscious of the inner spirit of faith; and when we feel this inner spirit we should try to become conscious of the still deeper spirit that is within our first realization of the spirit. To go deeper and deeper into the realization of the spirit should be the ruling desire whenever we enter the attitude of faith; and as there is no end to the depth or the height of the spirit, there is no limit to that inner world of life, wisdom and power that may be realized through faith. However far we may enter into the spirit we can always go farther still; every step that we take in spiritual realization opens the door to a still higher spiritual realization, and whenever we proceed, through faith, to enter more deeply into the limitless spirit of faith, we open another door to the marvelous kingdom within. Faith goes into what seems to be unreality and finds that the deeper we enter the world of the spirit, the more real and the more substantial the spirit becomes. Faith goes out upon the seeming void and finds that there is no void; all is real, and the farther we go out into the vastness of limitless life the more real and the more beautiful life becomes. Therefore, to follow faith is always to pass from the lesser into the greater, into the better, the richer, the larger, the more wonderful and the more beautiful.

The mind that lives in doubt can see limitations everywhere; the mind that lives in faith can see no limitations, and, in fact, knows that there are no limitations anywhere. The mind that lives in doubt is in bondage to these seeming limitations and therefore realizes nothing more of life than what is confined within these seeming limitations; but the mind that lives in faith lives in the freedom of the all of life, and is daily realizing more and more of everything that is contained in the all of life. Faith can see that no matter how large or how beautiful life may be now, there is always a larger and a more beautiful life to live for, to work for and to realize in the days that are near at hand. In the life of faith there is no end to anything; there is always something more, always something richer, always something greater, always something better. The life of faith is therefore full of realization, full of promise, full of joy. What was promised by faith yesterday is realized today, because faith is not only the power to see the greater vision, but is also the power that can lead life into the very world of the greater vision; and thus the promise of yesterday is always fulfilled today.

Every person in the world, whatever his present position may be, can begin today, and through the power of faith, work himself up into any attainment or realization he may have in mind. Whatever his goal, he can reach it, if he works in faith. This may seem to be a strong statement, but Jesus Christ declared it was so; and it is certainly high time that we begin to believe and practice the great truths this Master Mind proclaimed. If the teachings of Jesus mean anything they mean that I can, through faith, overcome anything in my life, change anything in my life, better anything in my life, and realize any goal whatever to which I may aspire to reach in life. Though it may take months and years to reach certain things, those things that have exceptional worth, nevertheless I can do it, if I continue persistently to work in the spirit of unbounded faith. And, in the meantime, if I give this same faith to all my work, I shall be gaining ground daily, making my life larger, better, richer and more beautiful constantly. When I begin to work in the spirit of faith, I will always be in touch with the spirit; and to be in touch with the spirit is to be at one with God, because the kingdom of God is in the spirit; therefore, when I am in the spirit, I am with God; God is with me; God is on my side, and we two constitute a majority; we are greater than anything we shall ever meet, and we have the power to do anything we may desire, to work out anything, accomplish anything or realize anything that we may at any time have in view. Faith has made us one—the Infinite and myself, and together we hold, not simply the balance of power, but all power. Therefore, knowing this to be true, why should I ever doubt any more; why should I ever hesitate any more; why should I ever be fearful or afraid any more.

There are thousands of richly endowed minds in the world that accomplish nothing to speak of; and the reason is they live in the confusion of doubt, uncertainty and fear. Many of these minds would become giants in the world if all their powers were spurred to action by the invincible spirit of faith. In fact, there is not a single mind, whether naturally endowed or not, that would not come forth into a larger, richer life if inspired by the wonder-working power of faith. Faith awakens the all that is in human life, and makes that all a continuous power for good. Therefore, not a person in the world, whatever his work may be, can afford to live or work a single moment without faith, without the deepest, strongest faith that he can possibly arouse in his own soul. Faith is not for the spiritual world alone, but for every world. Not a muscle should move unless it moves in faith; not a thought should be formed unless it is filled with the spirit of faith; not a word should be uttered unless it comes directly from the limitless power of faith. This is what it means to live by faith, and such a life is a life indeed.

There is a belief among many that since every soul has the power to draw upon the limitless for any desired supply, it is not necessary to give special attention to physical or mental efforts. In other words, if they continue to live in faith they will receive what they want, their own will come, even though they be very inefficient as far as work is concerned. This is their spiritual theory, but it is a theory which, when applied, leads invariably into poverty both of body and mind. The fact that "all things are yours" on account of your divine heirship; and the fact that your spiritual nature is actually and permanently one with the limitless source of every good thing in existence, does not prove that you may receive all that you need by simply declaring, "My own cannot remain away from me." To fold your hands and wait in faith for your own to come, is not to wait in faith; hope stands and waits, but faith goes to work. Therefore, if you are waiting in faith you have no faith; and having no faith you will continue to wait; your own will not come. In the real, "all things are yours," but you can make no actual use of the riches of the kingdom within until they are brought forth into manifestation. The life, the power and the riches from within, however, will not manifest through a mind and body that is dormant; and the habit of waiting and hoping for supply to come, regardless of efficient personal effort, has a tendency to make the faculties and the elements of the human system more or less dormant.

To have faith is not simply to believe that everything will come to us, or that everything must come to us because everything already belongs to us. Faith is not simply belief; it is an attitude of mind and soul wherein you place your own life in perfect contact with infinite life; and, in consequence, when you live and work in faith every thought and every effort will be charged, so to speak, with the power of infinite life. To work in faith is to give more life and more power to your work; to think in faith is to animate and inspire your thought with a finer insight and a higher degree of understanding than you could ever receive in any other manner. The mission of faith, therefore, in practical life, is to give the individual that greater measure of wisdom and power through which he may make himself worthy of the very highest good that he may desire as his own. All things belong to us; that is, all things are ready for us whenever we can use them; but we can not use the greater things in life so long as we are living a small, partially dormant life. The riches of the kingdom are not for us "to have and to hold"; they are for us to use; and we can use them all only as we become alive with the life more abundant in every element of body, mind and soul.

The principle is this: Use the body, use the mind, use the soul, use every faculty, use every force, use every power that you can possibly find and arouse throughout your entire being; and use all these things in faith; that is, while you are using all these things, place your life, your mind and your consciousness in such perfect touch with the Supreme Source of life, power, wisdom and inspiration, that you become a perfect channel of expression for all that is great and worthy in the vastness of sublime existence. In this manner, you become so worthy, so competent and so efficient in your life that all that is great and worthy in the ideal can be naturally attracted and used by you in the real.

With regard to this subject, the human family divides itself into three classes. The first class is composed of the masses of men and women in the world, those who try to live and try to accomplish something in life by depending solely upon objective faculties. They proceed without paying any attention to the greater powers within them or to their relationship with infinite life; in consequence, they are constantly hemmed in by their own self-created limitations, and as a rule, merely exist. The second class is composed of those who go to the other extreme, depending almost entirely upon the power of the spirit to provide supply, while the true and full use of the powers of the personal man are either wholly or partially neglected. These people are buoyed up in the beginning with hopes and expectations, and for a time their spiritual theory of life seems to work; but ere long they find themselves drifting into adversity and want, and are forced to return to the ways of the world, as mere existence is better than annihilation. The third class is composed of those who combine the powers of the personal man with the powers of the spiritual man; they make a special effort to turn all their powers and faculties to practical use, and to all their work they invariably add the inspiring attitude of unbounded faith. The members of this class try to develop all their faculties to the very highest degree; they try to place body, mind and soul in the best working condition; they try constantly to increase their working capacity because they are not only believers, but doers; they are disciples of work—work that adds to the welfare of the world, and they always work in faith; they try to make the best use of everything in their possession, but while trying to push to the front, so to speak, the best that is in them, they try constantly to develop a higher and a finer conscious realization of the great truth that we live and move and have our being in the limitless power of the Supreme.

That all the great men and women that have appeared in the history of the world have come forth from this last mentioned class is most evident; and that no person can ever rise in the scale of life unless he applies the method of this class is equally evident. To depend solely upon the personal man is to merely exist; to depend solely upon the spiritual man is to be a dreamer, not a doer; but when the powers of the personal man are combined harmoniously and practically with the powers of the spiritual man, we cannot only dream; we can also make our dreams come true. What we discern in the ideal we can cause to come true in the real. We provide practical working capacity on the personal side and limitless power on the spiritual side; whatever we may wish to do, attain or accomplish in the great without, we may receive all the wisdom, all the understanding and all the power required from the great within. We shall thus demonstrate the great truth that "All that the Father hath is mine," not simply for spiritual contemplation, but for actual, personal possession and use in the tangible world today.

That the powers of the spiritual man can be readily combined with the powers of the personal man, in the producing of practical results, is a fact that is constantly being demonstrated in the lives of thousands. We all know of remarkable instances where people have, when in the midst of extreme want, sickness or despair, placed themselves in the hands of higher power, and secured emancipation under circumstances that have seemed miraculous. Many a person has found himself in a position where everything was lost, where all the elements were against him, and where not a single ray of light could be found anywhere; but by placing himself in touch with the power of the Supreme, and by going to work in full conscious oneness with that power, has caused everything to change in his favor. Many a person has demonstrated the great truth that by taking God with him in his work, he could overcome every obstacle, remove every barrier, vanquish every enemy, disperse everything that was against him, and come out victorious under circumstances that, in the beginning, seemed utterly hopeless. It has been demonstrated thousands of times that where the personal man alone was helpless, complete emancipation and victory were made possible where the powers of the spiritual man were combined with the efforts of the personal man. This is therefore a principle that no person can afford to ignore, no matter what his work may be.

Whatever we may wish to do or gain, there must be personal effort; but the more perfectly we are conscious of the limitless powers of the spirit within us, the greater will the results of those efforts be. And this is not true of certain special efforts alone; it is true of all efforts from the least significant on the physical plane to the most important on the sublime cosmic plane. It is true, not only in instances of man's extremity, but also in every state or degree of man's prosperity. If the power of the spirit, when combined with personal effort, can take man from death's door into perfect health, as has been done thousands of times, even when all hope was lost and every other method had failed; and if this same power, when combined with practical work, can take man out of the lowest depths of adversity, poverty and despair, and place him on the very heights of freedom, power and limitless supply, is there any reason why the power of the spirit can not be combined with personal effort in all the affairs of everyday life and thus give an ever-increasing measure of health, happiness and prosperity to man? Man calls upon God when everything else has failed; but he should call upon God before he tries anything else, and he would never fail.

Though we may be strong physically now, and be in possession of exceptional capabilities and advantages, we can not afford to ignore the fact for a moment that increase comes only from the within. "They that wait upon the Lord shall renew their strength"; none others. The present strength of the body will not hold out unless it is constantly replenished from on high. The present capabilities of the mind will shortly lose their brilliancy and power unless they are kept in the highest state of perfection through constant contact with the light and the life of the soul. It is not wisdom to use up the limited powers of the person and utterly ignore the great interior source of inexhaustible power. Yet man does this very thing; therefore, his person is weak, his days are short, and his life but a trifle better than mere existence. There is, however, a better way; let the powers of the spiritual man be constantly combined with the life, the powers and the efforts of the personal man, then shall the person of man never be weak; his days may be lengthened indefinitely, and his life will become richer, more beautiful and more inspiring, until a million joys are blended harmoniously in every moment of his endless existence.

We are all heirs to the kingdom, not only the spiritual kingdom but the entire kingdom of life; we can receive, however, only what we can use; we need only what we can use, therefore to receive more at any time would be superfluous, and there is no place for the superfluous in the realms of divine law. There are many that can use much, very much, but the majority do not receive as much as they can use because they do not live and work in the consciousness of the "all things are yours." Others receive but little at any time because they do not fully use what they already possess. We draw upon the universal for greater supply in proportion as we turn to good account our present supply; though we must remember, that no person can turn to good account the best that is in him now unless the efforts of the personal man are filled through and through with the powers of the spiritual man. The work that we do in faith is the only good work; and the faith that we apply in work is the only true faith.

The average person thinks that it is his privilege to continue to "hold" his possessions, regardless of use, and that he can accumulate as much as he

likes; but this is not true. The true life is not lived for the purpose of accumulating things. Many have realized this and have gone to the other
extreme, concluding that the only true life was the life that had no tangible
possessions whatever. There are only a few, however, who have taken the
path that lies directly between these two extremes, and that is one reason
why the power of the spirit to combine with the power of the person in
practical life has not been as extensively demonstrated as we should wish.
But it is our privilege to demonstrate the true law of complete existence,
and when we do, the reward will be great indeed.

Every individual is entitled to all the riches of the spiritual kingdom, and
in addition, to the possession of as many things, and as beautiful things, in
the visible kingdom, as we can possibly appreciate and use in the enrichment
of all the realms of his own entire existence. But before he can secure all
these things, he must cause his personal nature and his spiritual nature to
live together and work together as one. He must work for everything that
he may desire, and must work in the faith that every desire will be fulfilled.

To express the law of this principle more briefly, the first essential is to
make the best use possible of everything that we may possess now. The second essential is to live, think and work in faith. He who lives in faith lives
in the spirit, and he who lives in the spirit lives in God. No person can afford
to do anything without taking God with him; no person can afford to think
a single thought without realizing that that thought is created in the infinite
sea of divine thought; no person can afford to express a single desire without
realizing that that desire is the expression of some supreme, some great, some
beautiful state of interior existence.

It is extremely important to try, as much as possible and as frequently as
possible, to enter into the inner consciousness of the great truth that "All
things are yours." As we grow in this consciousness we actually enter into
real, limitless possession; and when we begin to "inwardly feel" that we
possess the rich and the beautiful in limitless supply, we will begin to attract
the rich and the beautiful from every source in the world.

Take the statement, "All that the Father hath is mine," and mentally
dwell upon the very innermost truth that can be found in this statement.
Try to realize what it means to possess everything that there is in the kingdom of the Infinite, and enter into the very soul of that meaning. Try to
feel the spirit of limitless, divine possession, and resolve to live perpetually
in the innermost life of that spirit. The consciousness of limitless supply will
soon become an actual factor in mind; and we can begin to draw upon the
limitless when we are actually conscious of the limitless.

When you actually realize that "All things are yours," you will never be anxious about the future any more. You know that there will be a ready way to supply every need at the proper time. You do not live in the possession of simply the barest necessities; you live in the life of abundance, and the rich and the beautiful in your life is constantly on the increase. But you are never disturbed about the greater needs that you know will come in the future. You live in the positive faith that when the greater needs are at hand, the greater supply will also be at hand. And your faith always comes true.

To live in this faith is to live in perfect peace; we are never disturbed about any threatening circumstance; we are never fearful or afraid any more; we know that the door will open when the time comes; we shall surely have what we need—enough to supply the greatest possible need. Having done our part we know that God will not fail in His; for as much greater is His faithfulness than ours as the entire cosmos is greater than a single drop in the sea. "I will not forsake thee nor leave thee"; upon this we may always depend.

When you look into the future, do not be anxious about methods or means to carry out what the future moment may demand. When you come to that place, God will be there; the limitless powers of infinite life will be there; the wisdom, the light and the luminous understanding of your highest spiritual nature will be there; all of you will be there, and the power of your faith to draw upon the limitless for any desire or need will also be there. Then why be fearful any more. Why be anxious about anything. All things are yours now, and the now that now is, is eternal.

Though your bark may be tempest-lossed, be not alarmed. The Christ is asleep in the ship. You may call Him at any time; and when you do the heavens will be cleared, and a beautiful stillness will come over the vastness of the deep. What does it matter to you what may threaten in days to be; the Christ will always be with you; wherever you may choose to sail upon the infinite sea of life, the Christ will always be in your ship. For lo, I am with you always. Whether He be asleep or awake, where you are, there He will be also. You may call upon Him as you will, and peace shall reign supremely in your life once more. For the winds and the waves shall obey my will. Then why be fearful or afraid any more. He can still any storm in the world, and bring the silence of the heavenly calm wherever His presence may be.

CHAPTER XXIV

THE WINDS AND THE WAVES
SHALL OBEY MY WILL

Then he arose and rebuked the winds and the sea; and there was a great calm. But the men marveled, saying, what manner of man is this that even the winds and the sea obey him.—Mat. 8:23–27.

We all come to places at times when the sea of life is tempest tossed, and the winds of adversity are mercilessly raging about us; we are all placed in circumstances at times when everything seems to go wrong, when everything seems to be against us, and when we fear lest we perish; but at such moments we should remember that the Christ is in the ship. No matter what the ship of life may be; no matter what manner of men may be sailing in that ship, or what their purpose may be, wherever man may be found sailing upon the sea of human existence there the Christ will be found also. Wherever we may be or wherever we may go, the Christ is in the ship. "For, lo, I am with you always." And it is our privilege, under every circumstance, to awaken the Christ. When we do, he comes forth invariably, and the winds and the waves will obey.

Whenever we enter into that higher and more sublime state of being where we meet him face to face, the consciousness of the Christ within us is awakened; we are in the Christ state; we are in the presence of Supreme Power; we are at one with God; and upon us comes a beautiful calm. The winds and the waves in our own minds are stilled, and upon the great sea of thought within us the billows are tossing no more; the storm has ceased; the black clouds have disappeared; all is beautiful and still; and the peaceful waters seem radiant with joy as they glitter in the sunbeams from the smile of God. We have opened our minds and souls to the strong and peaceful presence from on high; thus we have placed ourselves in the beautiful calm; and when we are stilled, all that is about us will be stilled also. As man is in the within, so will his life be in the without. When he can still the storms of his own mind he can also still the storms of adversity in his outer life. It matters not what is taking place in our own circumstances, all must change when we change; all must be stilled when we are stilled; and whenever we awaken the consciousness of the Christ within, upon us comes a beautiful calm.

When we know that the Christ is within at all times; when we know that whenever we call upon the Christ to come forth, the winds and the waves will obey; and when we know that the very hour the Christ is awakened, everything in life will be stilled, harmony will come out of everything, peace will come out of everything, good will come out of everything—when we positively know this, need we have any fear whatever concerning the future? Need we fear opposing circumstances or adversity? Need we fear any condition that might arise? Nothing can happen that need disturb us in the least. The Christ is **always** in the ship; we may call upon him at any time; he will never fail to come forth, and when he does, there will be a great calm; peace will reign once more, and all will be well again.

Those who do not know that the Christ is in the ship, are living constantly in fear; they reason that almost anything might happen to place obstacles in their way, or that certain conditions might arise to upset everything they had undertaken to do; and the things they fear usually come upon them; but when they know that there is a power within that can be awakened at any time—a power that is greater than anything in the world—fear may be banished for all time. When this great truth is realized we need never be concerned about the future any more, and anxious thought may be banished forever; whatever may happen in the future there is a power within that can change anything as we may desire, and turn anything to good account as we may desire. We may thus live in the conviction that all things will work together for good—for greater and greater good, and we may **know** that this conviction is based upon nothing less than eternal truth.

The Christ is always in the ship, always in every ship that may pass upon the sea of life; and he may seem to be asleep; we may not be aware of his presence within us, but our unconsciousness of his presence does not prove that he is asleep, or that he is never there. The Christ is never asleep. The only begotten son of God that is within all, within everything, that is the ruling power in every soul, the Supreme I Am in every soul, is never asleep. The statement that the Christ was asleep in the ship is metaphorical. It is not the Christ that is asleep, but our own consciousness of the Christ. When our own consciousness of the Christ is asleep we are not aware of his presence, and he seems to be asleep to us. When we are not aware of this great spiritual power within us, we are unconscious of that power; we are asleep, so to speak, as far as the existence of that power is concerned, and therefore will never think of awakening that power. But when we have attained sufficient spiritual discernment to know the power of the spirit in our own soul, we shall begin to call forth that power. From that moment higher power will be with us, and we shall no longer be victims of the tempest tossed sea; whenever the billows begin to toss or the storms begin to rage, we may call forth the Christ; he will always be with us, and will always respond to the call; he will answer our prayer with his own presence, and in his presence all is beautiful and still.

This same unconsciousness of the presence of the Christ within also explains the seeming loss of the soul. The soul is the Christ individualized, created in the image of God, and therefore can never be lost. The soul is co-existent with God, always is with God; and that which is eternally with God can never be lost. But the personal man is sometimes so engulfed in materiality that all view of the soul is lost. The soul is always there within us, ever abiding in the shining glory of the kingdom of God within us; the soul is safe, always was safe and always will be safe—safe in the life eternal; but if we are living in materiality, we do not see the soul, we do not feel the soul, we are utterly unconscious of the soul and therefore conclude that there is no soul. Or, if we are sufficiently awakened to feel the soul, but not sufficiently developed in spiritual discernment to know the divine nature of the soul, we may conclude that the soul is weak and imperfect as the flesh, and that it may go down into pain, bondage and misery at any time, now or in the future. And thus has arisen the seeming need of the doctrine of future salvation for the soul. Such a doctrine, however, is not based upon the spiritual conception of the soul, but was formed when we looked upon the soul through the confusion of materiality. The soul is never lost, never can be lost; and as you are the soul, you can never be lost. The soul is always safe with God, therefore you are always safe with God. Realize this truth, and you will find the soul; you will find that you are identical with the soul and that all is well with the soul now as all is well with God now.

To save the soul is not to save the soul, because the soul needs no salvation, but to restore the power of the soul as the supreme ruling power in your whole life. Enthrone the soul in every thought and action and you save the soul, not from sin, because it is free from sin, but you save the soul from your own personal neglect. The power of the soul is no longer neglected but is saved for actual use in the realization of health, freedom and mastery throughout your entire being; thus you gain emancipation for every element in your being, and that is the salvation we seek. We are saved in the true sense of the term when the divine power of the soul reigns so completely throughout the mind and the body that all the ills of life are completely banished from mind and body. We are saved in the true sense of the term when the body is filled with the power of health and wholeness, when the mind is illumined with the light of eternal truth, and when the soul is abiding forever in the splendors of the cosmic realms. And such a salvation is realized when we no longer ignore the soul, but place the soul upon the throne of being as complete master of everything that we may ever think or do or say. To enthrone the soul, the principle is to follow, not the desires or the tendencies of the person, but the supreme purpose of the spirit, and to depend absolutely upon the power of the soul in all things, knowing that the power of the soul can see you through no matter what your life, your work or your purpose may be.

The belief of the many is that whatever we may wish to accomplish we must depend wholly upon ourselves; and that we must depend upon ourselves as far as our ability and power may go, is very true, but it is not true that we should depend "wholly" upon ourselves. We can receive power and aid from sources that are above the personal self; and what is equally true, no one ever scaled the heights in life that did not depend constantly upon these higher sources. The best ideas, the noblest thoughts and the greatest truths that have ever appeared in the world, came to man when his mind was in the upper regions, in touch with the spirit sublime; and the power with which all great things have been wrought, has come from the same source. Men and women who depend wholly upon themselves—their personal selves, are weaklings; they come and go without doing anything aside from sustaining existence; but men and women who depend upon Supreme Power as well as their own ability to work out their purpose in harmony with that Power, invariably become giants in mind and soul. It is the deeds of such minds that become lights on the path to greater things; it is the lives of such souls that reveal to the race what true spiritual existence has in store; and it is the work of such men and women that has given us the light, the freedom and the happiness that we now enjoy.

You may live in absolute darkness today; you may not know where to turn; your sky may be black and a raging storm may be almost upon you; you can see nothing but destruction as you have no idea what to do; you are about to give up and perish, but as this thought passes through your mind you remember the "last resort"; you remember the great statement, Call upon me and I will answer thee. You then call upon that power that should be sought first, but that men usually seek last when in trouble. You turn to the Christ that is asleep in the ship. You open your mind to light and power from above, and almost at once there is a rift in the cloud. You are in absolute darkness no more, and the threatening storm is beginning to "break." You pass more completely into the spirit of the Christ, and you realize the beautiful calm. The clouds are gone; you are in the light! You can see everything clearly, and you know what to do. You are now in touch with that upper region from which you may receive better ideas, greater thoughts and more valuable truths than you ever received before; in consequence, you will find precisely what you may need in securing emancipation from external adversity, and in building for those greater things that alone can satisfy the aspirations of the soul.

The belief that the Christ within can still the winds and the waves of every condition that we may meet in life, and change every circumstance into one of calmness, harmony and well-being, is a truth that can be taken into every event of daily life. No matter what may come; no matter what the obstacle or the difficulty may be, there is something within us that is greater than anything in the world. The Christ is with us in the ship; we may call him at any time; he can still any storm, change any circumstance and remove every obstacle that we shall ever meet. His power is not applicable to conditions of mind and soul alone, but to physical conditions and circumstances as well. There is nothing that will not respond to the ruling will of the Christ within, and there is no place in practical life where the power of this will may not be applied to the greatest advantage. He who lives in constant touch with Supreme Power, is always in possession of the most power, and he may apply this added power in body, mind and soul. "They that wait upon the Lord shall renew their strength"; but this added strength does not simply appear in the spirit; it appears also in the mind and the body. Therefore, it is always profitable to be in touch with Supreme Power, and to depend upon Supreme Power, whether our work be physical, mental or spiritual. It is not wisdom to depend solely upon the lesser things of the person when we may constantly receive power and aid and inspiration from the greater things of the spirit. All things are for man; and the use of all things should ever be his purpose, no matter what his work may be.

We have found a perfect remedy for fear, because he who knows that the Christ is always in the ship will fear nothing. To him no ill can come whatever. Though the approaching storm may sweep everything before it, its fury will be dissipated into nothing when it comes to the ship where the Christ is awake. But the Christ is in every ship, and he will come forth in every ship and utterly put to naught the impending danger. Whatever our position in life may be, or whatever we may be called upon to do, when we know that the Christ is with us we may proceed calmly, peacefully and serenely in the full conviction that nothing but good will come. We need fear nothing because there will be nothing to fear. The turning of the tide may sometimes be delayed until the eleventh hour, and even until the fifty-ninth minute of that hour; but the turn will come without fail. We may continue positively in that faith. "I will not forsake thee or leave thee." This is the truth, and we can, under every circumstance, demonstrate this truth, providing we never fail to call the Christ. We must go to the Christ first; then he will come to us and answer our prayer whatever that prayer may be. We must place ourselves in touch with Supreme Power first; then that power will come with us; and when Supreme Power is with us we have nothing to fear. When the power of the Supreme is on our side all things will be on our side; and God will go with us the very moment we choose to go with God.

When the day is calm, it is well; but if it is not calm, it is also well; it will soon become calm if you call upon the Christ, for "the winds and the waves shall obey my will." If the future seems bright, you may rejoice; but if the future seems dark, as dark as the blackest night, you may also rejoice; there is a power within you that can put adversity to flight and turn misfortune and sorrow into the glory of a cloudless day. When all that is good is coming into your life you may be grateful; but when all that is good is passing out of your life you may also be grateful; the Christ that is within you can not only save your ship from every threatening storm and impending danger, but he can also guide your ship toward the shores of richer treasures and greater good than you ever knew before. Grieve not when in the midst of loss; rejoice with great joy, and be grateful from the deepest depth of your heart. Call upon the Christ and you will regain everything and more. There never was and never will be any real occasion for disappointment or tears; when the lesser disappears, turn to the greater; you will find the gates ajar, and you may enter at once into pastures green.

The power of that will that causes the winds and the waves to obey, comes invariably from the depths of spiritual existence. It is the power of the Christ enthroned in the soul, and whoever will recognize and call forth the reigning Christ within, will gain possession of such a will. But we can never gain such a will so long as we try to dominate the lives of others or try to forcefully control external circumstances or events. Nor can we gain such a will so long as we try to will with the outer mind. The real will comes from the great spiritual depths of being, and as it is coming forth it causes the being of man to become deeply calm and enormously strong. The difference between the man of real will power and the man of mere external force is readily discerned. When you meet the latter you find a great deal of domineering effort expressed through the most superficial of action; but you find the man, himself, weak and easily overcome by almost any adverse condition; when you meet the former, however, you will find yourself in the presence of a truly strong man, a man who is strong and alive all the way through to the very depths of his inexhaustible being, a man who is actually conscious of irresistible power; and you inwardly know that such a man cannot be moved by any power in the world; he has gained possession of that something that is greater than anything in the world, and wherever he may journey upon the sea of life, the winds and the waves must obey.

To depend exclusively upon the personality of Jesus and that power of the Christ that manifested through him twenty centuries ago, is to ignore the present power of the Christ within us. Thousands are doing this, and, in consequence, continue in sickness, trouble and sorrow. To depend upon any personality, no matter how sacred or how highly developed, is to depend upon the outer form and ignore the interior spirit. Such a practice leads into materiality away from spirituality, and materiality means bondage. To follow the Christ is not to worship the person of Jesus but to follow absolutely the light and the spirit of the Christ in your own soul today. The power that can calm the waves on every tempest-tossed sea does not come through any external personality; such a power can come only through the great spiritual depths of your own soul, or, to state it differently, from those sublime spiritual heights within where the Christ reigns eternally. When we follow the Christ that is here today, the Christ that reigns in the spiritual kingdom within today, we shall steadily grow in spirituality, emancipating mind and body from every form of bondage and from every condition of materiality, until that freedom that comes from the truth divine has been realized in its greatest measure. Then we may also say, My yoke is easy and my burden is light. Then we may also speak the great word, Peace, Be Still, and to us shall come the beautiful calm.

Rock of Ages, truth divine,
Strong foundation, ever mine;
Safe, secure, I here remain,
Free from evil, sin and pain;
Living ever in the right;
Fixed on high with souls of light.

On the rock of truth I stand,
Destiny at my command;
Filled with power from on high,
Boundless good forever nigh;
Far above the world of wrong,
Safe with truth, so firm and strong.

Every height in truth's domain,
I shall reach and thus obtain
Every wish within my heart
For no blessing can depart;
All of good is ever mine,
On the rock of truth divine.

CHAPTER XXV

FOR I HAVE OVERCOME
THE WORLD

These things have I spoken unto you, that in me ye may have peace. In the world ye have tribulation: but be of good cheer; I have overcome the world.—John 16:33.

There are two distinct worlds open to man in his present state of existence; in the one he finds tribulation; in the other he finds peace; the first is material; the other is spiritual, and it is man's privilege to choose which one he would have as his present place of abode. If he selects the material, he sacrifices everything that has real value in life; he secures a few fleeting pleasures and much pain; not a single moment gives real satisfaction, and nothing that he can do produces the results expected.

But when he selects the spiritual, he sacrifices nothing that is good; he secures all the joy that life can give; his pains are few, if any, and when they do come, they come to lift him higher; every moment is rich, every hour is thoroughly worth living, and there are many periods of time when his soul is lifted to the supreme ecstasies of the highest heavens; whatever he does he builds wiser than he knew, and he not only receives everything expected, but more.

Therefore, those who understand what the spiritual life holds in store, may be of good cheer; their sorrows and tribulations are over; better days are at hand; the words of the Christ have prepared the way, and that way leads to peace. No matter what external conditions may be; no matter what circumstances we may be in now; we may be of good cheer. "I have overcome the world"; and in Him we may live whenever we so desire. The power of the Christ can overcome anything and change anything, and that power is in us. Then why should we not rejoice, and rejoice in Him always?

There is something within us that is greater than things, and it is our privilege to claim the power of that something now. "I have overcome the world now, and every soul may live in Me now." That means emancipation now for all who will receive it. Freedom is not for some other world, but for the life we are living today. We are not required to live in tribulation at any time during present existence; the way to complete emancipation is before us at all times. **I am the way.** Whoever will transcend personal consciousness and enter into the consciousness of **I Am** will enter that life that is not of this world, and he will gain that power that can overcome anything that may exist in this world.

To enter the supreme life of the Christ is to gain the supreme power of the Christ; and to steadily grow in the consciousness of that life and power is to rise out of every tribulation until complete emancipation has been gained. That supreme life is in store for us; it already exists in the supreme **I Am** of our own being; this **I Am** is the Son of God, the only begotten of God, the Christ in us; and the Christ that is in each one of us is one with each one of us. That is how "I am in the Father, and ye in me."

This supreme oneness wherein the soul is one with the Son and the Son is one with the Father, is real; it is not merely in thought or in feeling; it is not solely an abstract state of being; it is as real and as tangible as life itself, and every element that pertains to that oneness is as real and as tangible as life itself. **I am the way,** and you are that **I Am**; you must be or you could not be one with the Father. If you are not that **I Am** you would be separated from God, and no soul can be separate from God and live. Claim your divine sonship; claim your divine inheritance; claim that supreme power that overcomes the world; it belongs to you; it is you; know this truth and this truth shall make you free.

To believe that you are a mere, weak, human being is not to be in the Christ; when you live in the Christ you are filled through and through, with supreme power, and you know neither weakness nor tribulation any more. This is evidence that you are in the Christ. When you live in Him you are stronger than any adversity that is in the world; you remain untouched, unmoved and undisturbed no matter what may threaten in the world; you are in Him and in Him you have found peace. You have entered the spiritual world, and **I Am** the door to that world; you have risen to that supreme state of being where you can say, in the spirit of eternal truth, **I Am,** and through the power of that truth you have overcome the world.

The attitude of overcoming is usually thought of as being inseparably connected with resistance, and as being directly antagonistic, in its action, toward that which is to be overcome. Nearly every person, when trying to overcome anything, begins to resist, begins to antagonize, begins to work against that which is not desired. Accordingly, he does not succeed because he must work in the opposite direction before his purpose can be fulfilled. The first principle in overcoming is to give no thought whatever to that which is not desired. The more completely we can forget that which we wish to overcome, the better. The second principle is to give our whole attention to that something which we know we shall realize when we have overcome. If a person is in adversity he knows that when this adversity is overcome certain most desirable conditions will be realized. Then let him begin at once to give his whole attention to those desirable conditions. By giving his whole time, thought and energy to the attainment of that which is desired, he will invariably overcome and rise out of that which is not desired. We overcome the wrong by turning completely away from the wrong, and giving all our life and power to the greater realization of the right. This is the secret of overcoming.

When we devote all the power of thought, all the power of soul, all the power of life to the constant attainment of greater and better things, we shall ascend perpetually in the scale of existence. This means perpetual growth, and, in consequence, the elimination of evil, because all evil is caused by retarded growth. The purpose of life is to move upward and onward forever; to live is to live more; but no person is actually living more unless he is living more every single moment. The moment he begins to live more he begins to ascend, and when he begins to grow into the greater he begins to grow out of the lesser. When he grows into the right he grows out of the wrong; he gains freedom from that which is not desired by entering more fully into the life and the spirit of that which is desired. But the moment he ceases to live more, he retards his growth; he violates the purpose of his life, and instead of supplying more life he supplies less life; his real nature, however, demands more and more life, and therefore, demand and supply will at once become unequal. There will, accordingly, be a lack of something in his life, and every evil that man has ever met came originally from a lack of something. Real life demands the living of more and more life; but when man fails to live more and more, the natural demand in life will not be fully supplied; the lack of one or more things in human existence will be the result, and conditions of evil invariably follow.

Real life is lived in the individuality, the soul, or the real man; and so long as we consciously live in the real man, or in the I Am of being we shall continue to live more and more. We shall thus realize the fullness of life constantly, and constantly grow into a larger measure of that fullness. Life will be full; there will be no lack of life, and no retarded growth in life; in consequence, there will be no evil in life; we shall have perfect freedom and there will be nothing to overcome. Accordingly, we shall fully comply with the great statement, **the true way to overcome is to so live that there is nothing to overcome.** However, when we do not consciously live in the individuality, or in the real man, but live consciously in the personality only, we are not in touch with the constantly ascending current of real life; we are not in touch with that greater measure of life that will enable us to live more and more life. A lack of life will at once be felt, and here we have the original cause of every ill, every wrong and every undesirable condition that man can know. This is the real fall; conscious living falling down from the living of unlimited life in the individuality to the living of limited life in the personality. But this fall did not take place only once ages ago; it is taking place every day in nearly every mind, and is taking place many times a day in most minds. To be saved from this fall, which is the only fall, proceed to live in the spirit, in the soul, in the real life of the I Am of being. Express the life more abundant in the personality, but live in the individuality. By living consciously and constantly in the individuality you will live in the life more abundant. You will live the limitless life, and what we live we express. We express in the personal man whatever we **live** in the real man; and therefore when we live the limitless life in the real man we express the limitless in the personal man; thus the personality is ever filled with the life more abundant; there will be no lack of life anywhere in the being of man; and there can be no evil where there is no lack of life.

To try to remove or overcome evil is nothing but wasted effort; evil is not a thing but a condition arising from a lack of life. When necessary life is supplied, there will be no further lack of life, and where there is no lack of life there can be no evil. To antagonize evil, to resist evil, to work against evil will not remove evil. Supply the life more abundant and evil will disappear of itself. Evil is simply emptiness, and no place can be empty when every place is full. To supply the life more abundant, live in the soul, in the real man. Do not establish yourself in the personality; establish yourself in the individuality and live in the source of life instead of in the partial manifestation of life. This is the simple secret. Go up into more life and you overcome everything that is not desirable in life. Do not try to overcome anything; simply begin to live more. Give no thought to evil; never try to remove evil; give all your thought to the attainment of the good, and direct all your effort toward the attainment of an ever-increasing measure of good. When you see evil, do not become indifferent; proceed at once to add to the good; when the good is on the increase evil is on the decrease; this is invariably the law; and the good will begin to increase the moment we begin to live more.

The same principle should be applied in every thought, action or relation in human life. We should never emphasize or ever recognize that which is not desired; but that which is desired should be recognized constantly and be emphasized most positively at every opportunity. When we meet others, their imperfections and shortcomings should be overlooked, while their good qualities should be given special attention. When we think of ourselves we should apply the same rule, and we should apply it universally in all physical, mental and spiritual training. The child that is trained in this manner from birth will naturally become extraordinary. When all the power that a person may possess is employed in the building of greater things, there must be great results, even though the power originally possessed be limited. The average person, however, employs but a fraction of his power in the upbuilding process; the remainder is employed in resisting evil and adversity. The reason why we are not higher in the scale of life, and not more perfectly developed in body, mind and soul, is because we have emphasized our imperfections, and have failed to give our good qualities special attention. You give your life to that which you emphasize; therefore give no thought to weakness or imperfection; give all your thought to those desirable qualities that you wish to build up; your worthy qualities will soon become so strong that weakness can no longer exist in your nature. Build up what you want; that is how you overcome and remove what you do not want. The more fully we can concentrate the whole of attention upon that which we desire, the sooner it will be realized; and when that which is desired is realized, that which is not desired can exist no more; therefore give all your thought, all your power, all your life, and the whole of your attention to that which is desired; do not try to remove the lesser but work uninterruptedly for the greater. The lesser is left further and further in the rear as you approach the greater goal that lies before you.

The process of overcoming is an ascending process, with the eye fixed upon the eternal mountain tops of spiritual supremacy. Give constant recognition to the very highest states of spiritual supremacy that you can possibly discern, and desire all the elements of your being to move perpetually toward those sublime states. You thus produce this ascending process; you will begin to grow out of, to rise out of everything that you have wished to overcome; and when this ascending process has been placed in full, continuous action, there will be nothing further to overcome. The wrongs that we wish to overcome have been produced by retarded growth, but when

we are ever rising into more and more life, growth will no longer be retarded; and, in consequence, there will be no further wrongs to overcome.
It is therefore evident that if you are still meeting things to overcome, you
have not learned to live more and more; you are still permitting yourself to
fall down from the world of real life into the world of temporary conditions;
you are still living in the body instead of manifesting in the body; and you
are still following the confused desires of the personal man, when the only
true desire can arise in the real man. To go up into more life, into the limitless life of eternal being, is the remedy.

Whenever you find yourself in any adverse condition, remember you will
not come out of it until you grow out of it. You may antagonize adversity
and cause it to disappear temporarily, but it will soon return in some other
form. Nothing, therefore, is ever gained by such a method. Train yourself
to grow out of that which is not good by constantly growing into the greater
good; and we invariably grow into that which we think of the most. Think
constantly of that which you desire, and you will grow into it. But your
thought must be of the heart; it must be deep and strong, and inspired by
the invincible power of soul. Do not give personal force to your thought
but try to feel that every thought you think has soul, and know that every
thought that has soul has the power to do whatever it was created to do.
And in all your efforts to grow into the better, the greater and the more
beautiful, consider the lilies of the field; grow like the flowers and you will
never fail. The flower resists nothing, antagonizes nothing, works against
nothing; it gently comes out of its gross and earthly environment, and grows
on peacefully, silently and serenely until it becomes an inspiration to all
the world. Human life can do the same, must do the same, if we wish to
realize the life beautiful and become conscious of the richness and glory of
the spiritual heights.

Spiritual consciousness never weeps; grief comes from the feeling of loss; spiritual consciousness knows that there is no loss; nothing ever can be lost; whatever was, is, and evermore shall be. To spiritual consciousness there are no tears; not because such consciousness is cold or indifferent, for he who has entered spiritual consciousness loves with a higher, a truer and a far more tender love than he ever knew before. He who has entered spiritual consciousness knows that all is well; and where all is well there can be no tears. Spiritual consciousness feels the existence, the presence and the unity of all things, visible and invisible. To be consciously in the spirit is to love all souls with the love of the spirit, and he who loves with the spirit is one with all souls, both in this realm and in realms beyond. He is conscious of the great white throng— those who are in the form and those who are in a higher form. His sublime love has given him a sublime vision, and through that vision he can see that nothing is lost, that all is well, and all that is well is eternal.

CHAPTER XXVI

THE SUPREME PURPOSE OF LIFE

The beliefs of the past have told us that we are now living in time, and that later on we shall enter eternity; but we are rapidly discarding this idea; first, because it is not true, and second, because we have discovered this idea to be one of the chief causes of age and premature death. By premature death we mean the passing away from this sphere before we have fulfilled the purpose for which we came, and since we are here for some special purpose, we must permit nothing that will take us away before our work is finished.

That we are living here for some great purpose we must all admit; that we have something very important to accomplish in this world we are all beginning to learn; and that we must necessarily remain here for a long time to rightly promote the divine plan is becoming more and more evident. When we think of this great theme from every viewpoint of consciousness we invariably come to the conclusion that man should remain here until he reaches such a high spiritual state that nothing in the world of things can serve him any more; and we shall find that when we begin to live for the attainment of this sublime state, every moment of existence will be perfect bliss. It is truly sweet to live when we live to promote the great divine plan.

We find, however, that but very few live a good life, and that only a limited number reach a high spiritual state before taking their departure. But what might the reason be? We all realize that old age is unnatural; and none of us require logic to demonstrate the great advantage of a life where eternal youth and eternal ascension in life are blended into one. Therefore we wish to find the fundamental cause of those conditions that produce age, that produce sickness, and that take us away from this sphere before our work is done. And this cause we find in the fact that man thinks he is living in time; when he should know that he is living in eternity.

When man fully realizes that he is living now in the great eternal now, and that he is already in eternity, he shall know age no more. Man grows old because he believes in the passing of time. He believes that he is living in a world where time is ever going, and that he is going with it—to the grave. He is conscious of the passing of years, and believes that the further he goes with the years the more years will be added to the burden of his life. He therefore thinks of himself as so many years old; but here he is mistaken. Time is not passing; time is; and the time that is, is eternity.

What we call time is only that period in eternity that we are conscious of now, and in truth we cannot call it a period of any definite length. To some it is long, to others it is short, to some it passes quickly, to others it drags, and it is variously interpreted by various minds; but the time itself continues to be the same—the eternity that we are conscious of now. It may be stated, however, that time must be passing because something certainly does appear to come and go. But this is only the changing attitude of consciousness as man ascends in the scale. We look at the sun; it appears to move, but we know that the sun is not moving from the earth's point of view; it is the earth that is moving. In like manner, we have looked upon time as passing, but now we know that time is standing still; we are moving upward and onward forever.

When man becomes conscious of the fact that time is standing still, that he is moving, and that the further on he moves the larger his life becomes, he will have attained the secret of that life that is ever young. It may be stated, however, that if man believes he is moving, that belief will cause him to think of advancing age; but the truth is that when man realizes that he is ever moving onward he will know that he is growing into life; and he will never pass into age so long as he is growing into life.

The many believe that time is passing—coming to man and going away from man, and that man himself is passing, not into life but out of life; in consequence, the life more abundant is not realized. What the race does realize in growth, advancement and higher attainment is produced partly by the natural power of life to ascend in the scale and partly by the efforts of great souls. The race belief, however, concerning time and man's relation to time, is a constant obstacle, both to emancipation from the imperfections of the lesser life, and the ascension into greater life. To secure emancipation now, to realize that youthful life now that is a necessary part of the spiritual life, and to rise daily into the greater spiritual life, the usual conception of time must be reversed. But we cannot accomplish this by trying to change our relations to those external devices that measure the movements of nature; nor will a denial of nature avail in the least. The change that is required must take place in our own consciousness.

Realize that time is, that the time that is is eternity, and that eternity is still, always here, forever giving forth her riches to man. Realize that there is no time except the eternal, therefore time does not pass because there is neither time to pass nor passing time. Realize this great truth in the depths of consciousness, and years will only add to your power, your youth, your life and your spiritual attainments. Then you shall remain upon earth until your work is finished—until you have reached the Christ state.

When this truth is realized, you will consciously feel the stillness and the calm of the eternity that forever is. You will no longer feel that you are passing on and on to some undesired end where adverse forces will rob you of the life you are here to live; you will no longer think of death or those periods of inability that have formerly preceded death; these mean nothing to you; they do not belong to your life; you are living in eternity; time is not adding years to your life; your life is eternal, and that which is eternal cannot be measured by years. The movements of nature in their circles and spirals may be measured; but that has nothing to do with life or time. Nature is forever moving around the great eternal now, and the eternal now is living in the deep silence of the life that forever is now. The life that you live—the real life, the eternal life, is the same life that is now; and in that life there is no time, no years, no age—only eternity.

Ascension in life means the appropriation of more and more of real life; it does not mean the changing of life from one state to another, nor the passing through periods of time. Growth does not come from the passing of time; growth comes from appropriation; besides, there is no passing of time. When we think of growth we usually think of so much gain in so much time, but that is a mistake. The soul that truly lives, appropriates all that it needs each moment; no more, no less; it does not deal with time; it deals only with that which has real, eternal existence; it never thinks of tomorrow because in eternity there is no tomorrow; it lives now, and it knows that the life that is now will never pass away.

When we become conscious of eternal life we no longer question the immortal existence of the soul. To feel eternal life is to know that life is eternal, and that every soul that lives lives the life eternal now. We cannot separate the life of the soul from the life that is eternal, and the moment that we discover that the two are one we know that we shall live forever. We need no external demonstration to prove to us that those that have gone before are still alive; we now know that no soul can possibly cease to exist, and we spiritually discern the immortal existence of all the souls in the world. We seek no visible sign because we are in the presence of that something from which every sign must proceed. We no longer ponder over the life after death; we know there is no death. That which is eternal life can never die, and to become conscious of the soul is to discover that the soul is eternal life. The soul is coexistent with God; what God is the soul is; the soul is the real man, the man that is forever in the image and likeness of God.

When we ask "If a man die, shall he live again?" we prove to those who understand that we are still living in the person, and that we still think of ourselves as being persons. The person passes away, and therefore so long as we think that we are persons we think that we shall also pass away; but we are not certain whether we shall pass into nothingness or into another life; we do not know because we are not awakened into that consciousness of eternal life that does know. We doubt no more, however, when we discover the real life of the soul, and find that we are not persons but spiritual entities, sons of the Most High. If you wish to convince yourself that you are to live after you have removed the physical body, do not seek after mysterious signs in the without; seek rather the real life in the within. The more deeply you enter into real life the more fully you realize that there is no end to your own life. The outer consciousness informs you that you have life; the inner consciousness informs you that there is no end to your life, and the one is as convincing to the mind as the other.

You know that you are living because you are conscious of life. Enter more deeply into the reality of your being and you become conscious of eternal life. Then you will not only know that you are living, but you will know that there can be no end to your living. To be conscious of life is to know that you are living now; to be conscious of eternal life is to know that you are living in eternity now, and that to live in eternity is to be eternal. To develop the consciousness of eternal life it is only necessary to grow daily in the spiritual life. Seek to understand the reality of your own divine being, and you will not only develop that spiritual discernment that knows the immortal existence of your own soul, but you will also develop that discernment that knows the present continued existence of all souls. You will know that you are destined to live eternally, and you will know that all souls, from ages past, are now living eternally. You know this, not through signs from without, or evidences that may appeal to physical senses or psychical senses, but through that spiritual understanding that is in conscious touch with every soul in God's unbounded cosmos. Neither the physical senses nor the psychical senses can know the soul; it is therefore impossible to demonstrate to any of those senses that the soul is immortal. Spiritual consciousness alone can know this great truth and to be spiritually conscious is to live in that sacred, interior realm where we know that man is perfect and divine, as God is perfect and divine. We know this when we are in the spirit, for nothing can be hidden in the light of the spirit. In that light we see all things as they are; therefore we know, and we speak with authority, not from ourselves but from God. In the spirit we are with God, and His thought becomes our thought, His word our word, His life our life.

When you see some one leaving the body you do not weep if you are spiritually awakened; you know that the leave-taking is but seeming; there is neither going nor coming in the spirit; there is no separation in spirit; in the spirit all are one in His love. Though the soul that seems to depart becomes invisible to physical sight, still that soul is ever visible to spiritual sight. To be consciously in the spirit is to see all those who live in the spirit whatever the form may be. In the consciousness of the spirit the manifestation of the form is secondary; whether the form be physical or ethereal is not of first importance; but to know the spirit, to be conscious of the spirit, and to know that all souls are eternally in the spirit—that is the first importance. That soul that seems to have gone, has not gone; you who are in the spirit, can feel her life, her presence and her love just the same; and you are wide awake to the fact that she still lives. Her existence is just as real to you as it was before, because in the spirit all is real. To you, who are in the spirit, all souls are real whether they manifest in this world or in some other world. They are all in God's sublime world, and when you are spiritually conscious your eyes are opened to the splendor and glory of that world.

CHAPTER XXVII

THE PSALM OF REJOICING

The Lord is my shepherd; I shall not want.

When we are led by the spirit of the Most High, the condition of want is removed completely; which means that **we shall want for nothing.** There is nothing that we may need or desire for the living of a complete life that we shall not receive when the Lord is our shepherd. We shall have abundance in every domain of existence, and no matter how great our demands may be the adequate supply will always be at hand; provided, however, that our demands are in accord with the ascending life—the life that leads to the heights.

We are not required to place limitations upon our demands or desires; the Supreme is not limited in His power to supply; it is our privilege to desire everything that we may need to make life as large, as perfect, and as beautiful as we possibly can; in brief, the more we desire the greater becomes the life we live, and the greatest life is the most acceptable life to God as well as to man. We do not please God by humbling ourselves into insignificance, the Infinite does not ask us to be small because He is great; He does not demand that we be satisfied with little because He has everything. This is not the nature of God because God is love, and love eternally declares, "Be as I am; come and enjoy everything that I have to enjoy; what is mine is thine; what is for me is for thee, and nothing shall be withheld whatever."

To want for nothing means that we shall be in possession of everything—everything that is necessary to a life that is all that real life is intended to be. This means that we shall have all the peace that the soul may require, even the peace that passeth understanding; we shall have all the wisdom and all the power that we may need to attain in life whatever our highest aspirations may have in view; we shall have sufficient joy to satisfy perfectly every element in the whole of being; we shall have happiness without measure, harmony as beautiful as the symphonies of heaven, and health in perfection forever. Not a moment shall your body know any ailment whatever, and not a moment shall your mind know sorrow or pain. This is the truth. It could not be otherwise when the Lord is your shepherd. God is love, and love leads away from ills and pains into the infinite delights of sublime existence.

God is equal to all your needs; He can give health and strength to the body; He can give peace and power to the mind; He can give wisdom and joy to the soul; He can surround your personal life with all that is rich and beautiful in physical existence; He can surround your spiritual life with all that is gorgeous and sublime in cosmic existence; and when you select Him as your shepherd He will. Take God at His word. Do not believe in His goodness and power and then act as if your belief was not true. Believe that He will actually supply your every need, then act accordingly. Have faith in abundance and expect your faith to come true. You shall not be kept waiting, nor shall you long remain empty-handed. Your prayers shall be answered, your needs shall be supplied, and all that your life may require shall now become your own.

Do not depend upon yourself alone. The belief that man must depend wholly upon himself to rise to the heights of being is not true. Man alone can do nothing of real worth; it is only when we work with God and God works with us that we can do what the ideal within us desires to do. The greatest things in the world are done by those who constantly depend upon God, who walk with God and live with God, and then make the fullest, the largest and the best use of those powers they are eternally receiving from God. Wherever you may go, or whatever you may wish to do, take the Lord for your shepherd and you shall positively gain what you have in view. Failure becomes impossible because God is equal to any condition that may arise, and so long as you are with God, God is with you. Though you may meet adversity, you need not be disturbed; something will happen; God will cause something to happen so that things will take a turn; you shall be led into pastures green where all your desires shall be granted. Then you shall want for nothing. Remember, **you shall want for nothing**. This is the great truth to understand fully and demonstrate fully in the actual living of life.

The secret is absolute trust and faith in the goodness and the power of the Supreme. Believe that God is your shepherd; believe that you can want for nothing so long as He is with you; then act accordingly. Live as if you actually believed that your belief was true, and you shall find it to be true. It is only when we live the truth that the truth proves itself to be the truth. Do not wait for external evidence before you proceed to act upon your faith. Real faith has any amount of internal evidence, and any principle that proves itself to be true in the within can be demonstrated to be true in the without. What the vision of the soul may declare, the powers of the personal man can supply; and daily life can be made as true, as beautiful and as sublime as the life that is lived on the heights.

He maketh me to lie down in green pastures; he leadeth me beside the still waters.

To be led by the spirit of the Most High is to pass through perpetual change—to pass from the good to the better, from the better to the best, and then higher and higher into those richer realms that infinite love has in store. In such a life there is always something new to live for, always something higher, something better to enjoy. Such a life can never be wearisome nor monotonous, for it is nothing less than a continuous feast—the richest imaginable feast, and all the elements of that feast are changed as often as we desire. It is in this feast that we partake of "the meat that ye know not of," and it is in this feast that the soul is nourished unto eternal life. Then comes the great spiritual strength that gives us the power to transcend the seeming and enter into the realms of existing sublime. And how beautiful to enter the pastures green of those lofty worlds, there to lie down and rest in the peace that passeth understanding, in the deep eternal calm that touches the soul with the symphonies of heaven. And how beautiful to be led beside the still waters, the living waters of celestial kingdoms on high, peacefully flowing onward and onward into that fairer kingdom, wherein we shall enter some golden morn, there to behold what eternity has in store for man.

When we follow the spirit, countless worlds are constantly opening before us, and in those worlds there are pastures green everywhere. In these we shall find nourishment for the soul; in these we shall find rest for the spirit. Then shall the soul come forth with new strength; then shall the spirit arise with power, and the spiritual life within us shall begin its great eternal reign. And when the spirit begins its reign, the outer world takes upon itself the peace, the wholeness, the harmony and the perfection of the beautiful life within. Adversity disappears; wrongs give place to the purity of the life divine; imperfections are lost in the dimness of the past, and the richness that we find in the pastures green of realms sublime, is reproduced in personal existence. Then we shall realize in the without what the soul has discerned in the within; then the joys of the spirit shall be made known to the person, and life in this world shall become the image and likeness of that other life that our most lofty moments have so beautifully revealed.

When the Infinite leads you and guides you, you will constantly be led into the larger, the greater and the better. Pastures green will always be ready for you the very moment you are ready for a larger, richer life. You will never have to remain in the lesser for a single moment after you are ready for the greater; the Most High will open the way for you, and the increase you desire in your life shall speedily become your own. All the world rests upon the Great law of perpetual increase; and the pathway of all life is upward and onward forever; therefore to follow the law of life is to ever ascend into a greater and a greater measure of the highest good that life can give. The great law of life is the law of infinite life because God is the source of all law and all life; and since God lives as His own laws direct, we understand that when we follow the laws of life we shall live as He lives. And we always follow His laws when we are led by Him. We therefore conclude that all life that is led by the spirit of infinite life will ever live in perpetual increase. In such a life the greatest good in life will be enjoyed now, and that good will become higher and greater without any end.

The great truth to remember is that God always leads into the greater, never to the lesser. When the Lord is your shepherd you will eternally be led into pastures green, and every new pasture will be richer than the one you knew before. Walk with God; live in the presence and the power of His spirit and follow the light of the Supreme in all things; then you shall be led eternally into greater and greater things. The boundless will ever be at your door and your faith will open that door. This is a great truth; it is a truth that we must always remember and always apply because we can receive from infinite supply only what we believe that we will receive. Believe with heart and soul that you will receive everything that is necessary to the fullness and completeness of ideal living, and you will receive all these things if you have taken the Lord for your shepherd. He will lead you into pastures green, and your faith will open your life to all the richness that those newer worlds may contain.

The Infinite never leads into trouble, sickness, adversity or pain. When we enter such conditions we are not led by the spirit of the Most High; we are simply going away from His spirit, and thus create the very ills from which we soon must suffer. When we go away from God we create evil; this is the only way that evil can be created, and the evil we thus create is the only evil that can ever come to us. Therefore the one great remedy that can heal all the ills of human life is found in that wonderful statement, "Return Ye Unto God."

When people who claim to be spiritual, are led into sickness and trouble, they are either mistaking emotionalism for spirituality, or their spirituality is as yet but a negative quality. When we begin to walk with God we begin to gain real spirituality, but such a spirituality is not simply a beautiful vision of the perfect and the divine; nor is it simply an esthetic feeling or a tender sentiment; it is the great spiritual life within coming forth with living power. Spirituality is sweet and tender and beautiful, but it is also immensely strong. Therefore when we are in possession of real spirituality the ills of life must vanish just as darkness disappears with the coming of the light. No ill can exist in the living power of the spirit, and we are always filled through and through with that power when we are **in** the spirit, when we are living in that life that God lives. And when the Lord is our shepherd He invariably leads us into His life, His world, His kingdom, and into His light, wherein we shall know the truth—the truth that gives freedom to all that is in the being of man.

When you are led "beside the still waters" everything in your life will move smoothly, and all your efforts, experiences and modes of existence will work together harmoniously for greater and greater good. At first, or for some time, there may be conditions in your life that are not as they should be, but these will soon pass away, and while they do remain you will be so strong, if you live in God, that no adversity can disturb you in the least. When you are led by the spirit of the Most High, adversity will become less and less, while you will gain in strength, more and more, so that whatever adversity you may for awhile meet will be as nothing in your life. You thus become able to master whatever may appear in the present, and you are, at the same time, rising out of every condition that is in any manner undesirable or adverse. You are led beside the still waters into the peace, the contentment and the joy of complete emancipation.

The life that is led by the spirit is the most peaceful, the most comfortable and the most sweetly serene of all life; it is ever beside the still waters, and is ever in touch with the great eternal calm. But it is also the most interesting as well as the most beautiful, for it is ever moving onward and onward.

And here we find a great secret. The great life is not the life that imitates the storm-tossed sea, but the life that is deep and strong and yet always peaceful and still. Such a life is great in power, limitless in capacity and wonderful in efficiency, but in all things and at all times, is forever sweetly serene. Such a life sounds the very depth of real being and calmly brings to the surface the rich treasures of those inexhaustible realms within. And thus the entire domain of human existence is made larger, richer and more beautiful without any end. We shall ever find pastures green both in the within and in the without, and beside the still waters we shall be led into that peaceful life that we have sometimes felt when the soul was attuned to God.

He restoreth my soul; he leadeth me in the paths of righteousness for his name's sake.

When we enter into the life of the Infinite, all that is high, all that is perfect and all that is beautiful in the soul will be restored to consciousness. The glory, the divinity and the sublime majesty of the soul will be revealed; the veil of mystery will be removed and we may behold the gorgeous splendor of the spiritual life as it truly is. The soul is no longer lost from view; we are no longer ignorant of the wonderful life within us; the heavens are opened, so to speak, and we may see most clearly and most perfectly that eternal something within us that is created in the image and likeness of God. Our divine nature is restored to us; we learn what we are; we discover our great inheritance; we find that we are not mere human creatures, but sons of the Most High, destined to reign with Him on the heights of glory, and to live in His sublime kingdom during countless ages yet to be.

When the soul is restored, our inner spiritual nature becomes the ruling power in life; mind and body becomes servants to the soul, and we no longer live for circumstances, conditions and things; we begin to live for life itself, and we thus gain, in an ever increasing measure, all the richness, all the beauty and all the power that life can give. When we live for life we can gain everything of worth that is in life, and we invariably live for life when the soul is the ruling power in life. In the life of the soul all is perfect and all is well because the soul lives the same life that God lives. Therefore when the soul becomes the ruling power in personal life, we will live as God lives in our entire domain of life, and throughout that domain all will always be well. When the soul is the master in human life, all will be well in human life, and the soul is always restored to its high place in life when we elect to be led by the spirit of God.

The soul is perfect, being created in the image of God; therefore, the elimination of the imperfect in life must begin when the soul becomes the ruling power. When the soul rules in mind and body it will live in every part of mind and body; and where the soul lives there can be neither sickness nor pain, neither weakness nor want. When the soul is restored to its high place of majesty and power in life, all the ills of life must inevitably disappear. When the light returns, the darkness is no more. When the wholeness of the spirit becomes a living power in mind and body, the life of the person must necessarily become as clean, as strong and as wholesome as the life of the soul. And such a state of being is invariably secured when the soul is selected to reign in the wonderful kingdom of man. The ills of life come only when we follow those desires of the person that are not inspired from within; but when the soul is restored, every desire of the person will be true to the life of the spirit. We shall then no longer follow darkness into wrong and distress, but we shall follow divine light into peace, wholeness, freedom and joy. We naturally follow our desires in everything that we may think or do; therefore when all our desires are born from above, we shall naturally keep the eye single upon the light from above, and in consequence, will ever be led by the wisdom of God.

When the soul is restored to complete mastership in the human domain, everything changes for the better; a new life begins and all the elements of this new life contain possibilities for greater things than we ever knew before. We actually enter a new world, and the former things are passing away. What was against us either disappears or changes so completely that all its power is given to the promotion of what we have in view; and those things that always were for us become stronger and stronger until we feel that limitless power is on our side. When the soul rules the destiny of human life all the forces of life will build for a greater and a greater destiny; all things will move toward the heights; want will give place to perpetual increase; sickness will give place to wholeness and strength, and adversity will give place to harmony and joy. Restore the soul to mastery in your life and your entire being will be restored to its birthright divine; all that is worthy and beautiful in sublime existence will begin to accumulate in your world, and life to you will be rich indeed.

Follow the spirit and you will always go right. He will lead you in the paths of righteousness, and whatever you think or do will always be for the best. In brief, nothing but the best can happen to you because the Lord is your shepherd and He will surely care for His own. The spirit never leads into anything but that which is right, that which is good, that which is best. When you do not follow the spirit, you are either going wrong or you are drifting into channels that will finally take you into the wrong. You may not be consciously following the spirit now, and yet you may be seemingly going right now, but this does not mean that you are on the true path. Those who are not following the spirit now are going wrong, and to them adversity will come sooner or later. Present conditions, however favorable, do not prove that you are on the path that leads to freedom and the greater life. You are on that path only when you know that you are led by His spirit in all things and at all times. We cannot judge according to appearances; the truth comes only from the supreme light within; and when we know the truth and live accordingly, we know that all will be right—in the within and in the without—all will be right.

We all follow the inner light to some degree; the soul is awakened in us all and is prompting us all; but in many instances we are led by those personal desires that are not in harmony with real life, and we are influenced by external conditions and things; thus we go wrong, and here is the cause of our troubles and pains. Whenever we go right, we go right because we have followed the higher promptings from within; and whenever we go wrong, we go wrong because we have followed those external conditions that are not in harmony with the real life within. But do we know when we are prompted by the soul? Do we know when we are led by the spirit? Do we know when we are guided by the Infinite and by Infinite Wisdom alone? At first we may not know; we may follow the spirit at times without knowing that it is the spirit, and at times we may think we are led by the spirit and yet be mistaken. But every person who fully and absolutely decides to follow the spirit in all things, henceforth and forever, will not long remain unconscious to the radiant presence of the Most High. If you will take this great step your spirit will soon be attuned to the tender music of the still small voice, and your mind will be illumined more and more with the glory of His sight. Then you will know, and never be mistaken, whenever He speaks to you; then you will see His light at all times and you will always know that it is the light divine. You will readily discern the meaning of His will in all things, and you will find that to follow His will is to go where glory is waiting. Not to some other world, but to His world, here and now. "There is another and a better world" here and now wherein we all may dwell in the never-ending today; and the light of His spirit leads directly into the freedom and joy of that beautiful world.

Yea, though I walk through the valley of the shadow of death, I will fear no evil: For thou art with me; thy rod and thy staff they comfort me.

When God is with us nothing but that which is good can happen. It matters not what we may meet or what we may be required to pass through, good will be the final outcome. We need fear no condition that can possibly arise; Supreme Power is with us, and we may overcome and surmount anything. We shall come out of every experience uninjured and unharmed; nothing can hurt us because there can be no hurt in the presence of infinite goodness, infinite power, infinite love. Wherever we are called we may safely go; whatever we are expected to do we may proceed. So long as we feel and know that God is with us, all will be well. We shall be led, guided, directed and protected; we may, without doubt or fear, proceed to do our part, and leave results to higher power; the very best will come to pass. Even though things happen for a short time that seem adverse, the outcome of everything will be good—very good. The light of divine wisdom is guiding our life, our thought, our actions, our destiny, and therefore all things will work together for the very highest good that we can possibly realize in every state of continued existence.

What is here spoken of as the valley of the shadow of death is the most extreme condition of danger that a person can possibly pass through; there can be no worse state of threatening calamity than the "dark valley," yet even there "I will fear no evil, for thou art with me." It matters not to what extreme we may be taken by circumstances or fate, God is equal to all our needs. He can protect us and guide us anywhere, and He will. He can take us out in safety, and He will surely do so if we have selected Him as our shepherd. And not simply because His power is supreme, but also because where God is there can be no evil. There is no evil to fear where God is because there can be no evil where God is. Be with God and God will be with you; and when God is with you, you are ever in the presence of the good and the beautiful. You are in a world where freedom is complete, where truth is omnipresent, and where all the elements of life are in touch with higher and better things.

When we are in the presence of danger we almost invariably shrink into dread or fear of some kind; and when called upon to do what seems beyond us, or what we personally dislike, we usually hesitate, or refuse absolutely; but this is all a mistake. God is with us; we need fear nothing, for He will protect us in everything. God is our strength, and with His strength we can surely do anything that life may require of us. When we feel weak we should remember that His rod and His staff are at our service. If we must have something to lean upon, His staff is ever at hand, and with such a staff we shall not fall down; no matter how heavy the burden, or how difficult the task, we shall **not** fall down. His staff will support us whenever we may need support; His rod will hold us up whatever the circumstances may be, and the power of His presence will give us all the strength we may require to reach any goal we may have in view. We should rather look upon difficulties as opportunities through which we may demonstrate to others the great truth that nothing is impossible when God is with us. And when called upon to do what seems beyond our capacity, we shall proceed nevertheless, pressing on in the full faith that we can. God is with us, and when He is with us we can do anything that our present sphere of existence may require.

If we have a great purpose to carry through we need never hesitate. Though the opposition may be great and the obstacles seemingly insurmountable, we may safely proceed. We need fear neither danger nor defeat, **for Thou art with me.** God will see us through. The Lord is our shepherd; we shall want for nothing; indeed, we shall receive everything we may need to accomplish what we have undertaken. When the task seems hard and the flesh seems weak, then we should remember, **Thy rod and Thy staff they comfort me.** And in that comfort our strength shall return, even more than enough to carry through the task that lies before us. We are equal to any occasion when God is with us, and God will always be with us if that is our deepest prayer of the heart. Therefore, we should never complain, and never give up to weariness or defeat. When it seems as if we could do nothing more, God will do the rest; and if we take heart again and proceed in unison with Him, we shall become stronger than we ever were before. When it seems as if everything would be lost, we should refuse to judge according to the seeming. "The Lord is my shepherd." The seeming loss will not take place. The tide will turn. God can turn anything in our favor, and if we accept Him as our shepherd He always will.

When God is our strength how great indeed is that strength. With Him at our side we have our own life in our own hands, and may do with it whatsoever we will. The present is ours to enjoy, the future is ours to create.

Adverse indications mean nothing; threatening ills or failures mean nothing; we need fear none of these things. God is greater than all outward indications, and His greatness is with us, on our side, working for our happiness and welfare. We should never recognize that which seems to be against us, for when God is with us His strength is our strength, His life is our life, and the wisdom that illumines His mind the same wisdom shall illumine our minds also. We therefore can never have any occasion to fear, to hesitate or to entertain doubts in any form or manner. The Lord is our shepherd. He will surely care for His own, and whatever is necessary to give fullness, perfection and completeness to the great eternal now, that we shall all receive.

God is with us when we choose to be with God. This is the simple secret. When we select Him as our shepherd, then we become His own; then He will care for us, guide us and protect us; then He will place the gates ajar so we may enter into pastures green; then He will lead us beside the still waters into the peace and the joy of the beautiful life. It will all be as we desire. The Infinite is ever ready, and it is our privilege to accept His goodness today. But to accept Him as our shepherd does not mean that we must completely relinquish our own will and our own way. When we decide to go God's way we shall find that He is helping us to gain our way; and when we decide to follow His will we shall find that He is giving us all the power required to carry out our will. Thus we shall find that the goodness of God is far greater than we thought, and that His love is as boundless as the infinite sea.

Thou preparest a table before me in the presence of mine enemies: Thou anointest my head with oil; my cup runneth over.

When God is with us we shall continue to enjoy the best that life can give regardless of what surrounding conditions may be. Though things may seemingly be against us, and though we may be in the presence of enmity and adversity, nevertheless, those things shall neither touch us nor disturb us. In the midst of such circumstances, or any kind of circumstances, God will prepare a table of everything that is rich and desirable in life. Whatever may happen in the world in which we live, God will protect us from loss. His table will always be richly laden, and it will be our privilege to partake according to our largest and most heart-felt need. When the Lord is our shepherd we need fear neither persons nor things that may seem to be against us. When God is with us, nothing can be against us. We have a place at His table, and those who are guests at His table shall want for nothing. He will provide for His guests and provide richly; therefore if we accept Him as our everlasting host we need never be disturbed about any condition, circumstance or event. The best will happen, and all will always be well.

When things go wrong with those who are living only for the world, things will go right with us. Misfortune can not overtake us. In His presence the power of evil is powerless, and we are ever in His presence so long as we elect that we so shall be. When we take God with us, and leave all our plans and desires with God before we decide, there will not even be indications of misfortune or adversity in our world. He will continue to prepare His table before us, and we shall continue to enjoy, both the good things of this world, and "the meat that ye know not of." We shall continue in prosperity even though all who live in the material world go down into adversity. The Lord is our shepherd, and we shall not want. However, if we should meet what would seem to be the indications of a threatening misfortune, we need not be disturbed. There may be temporary losses, and adverse conditions may come so near as to almost enter into our very lives, nevertheless we need not be disturbed. Whatever may threaten to happen, we need fear no evil, for Thou art with me. The entire experience will simply prove to be an open door to better things and greater things than we ever knew before. Such experiences sometimes come to those who are in His care; not often, but sometimes; and they come to test our faith, our spiritual strength and our dependence upon Him; they come to prepare us for a greater life, for pastures green, for new fields of endeavor and for a higher mission in the world. Count it all joy; so long as we are with God, God will be with us; and He will cause all things to work together for greater good than we ever dreamed.

Whatever may come to the world, the best alone can come to us. And we shall thus, not only realize the richness and the beauty of that life that is lived in God, but we shall become living examples to the world, proving to the world that God's way is best. We shall then demonstrate to all who have eyes to see, that to follow the light of the spirit is to follow that light that leads into everything that is worthy and beautiful in endless existence. The world believes that the spiritual life leads away from happiness and abundance; we must prove to everybody that the spiritual life leads into greater happiness and a richer life than we have ever known before. And we can prove this when we take the Lord for our shepherd. When we accept a place at His table, we shall demonstrate in the most tangible and the most convincing manner that to go with God is to go where every person may supply his every need; and not only be supplied, but supplied in the richest, the most worthy and the most ideal manner conceivable. To go with God is to find everything that heart can wish for in this world, and in addition, the infinite glory, the gorgeous splendor and the supreme joy of His kingdom on the heights.

To be anointed with oil is to have everything that is worthy and superior come down upon us. The oil of all things is the richest essence of all things, and when we are anointed with this richest essence, our minds become enriched with all that has quality and worth, all that is high in the scale of being. And it is but natural that that mind that lives and thinks with God, should be constantly enriched. Everything that comes from God has quality; everything that we receive from God has high worth, and everything that pertains to the spiritual life contains all the elements of real superiority; therefore, to follow God is to rise eternally in the scale of superior being. When we elect to go with God we leave behind us all that is common, ordinary or inferior; and we put on the royal garments of true quality and high worth. We become superior in body, mind and soul, and every element in our being becomes a living expression of that quality that reveals the royal presence of God.

When we are actually living in the spirit, and can fully appreciate all that is good and beautiful in real life, we become so filled with gratitude and joy that neither thoughts nor words can express what we feel. It is then that we wish as never before "that the mind could fathom and the tongue could utter the thoughts that arise in me." Our cup is running over; we have everything that can fill the fullness of life with the richness of life, and our joy is great indeed. Words fail us, but that something within that is far more eloquent than words gives utterance to what we wish to say. And as we listen, this language divine becomes heavenly music, repeating again and again that tender refrain, "God's beautiful gift to me."

To always live in the realization of that sublime state of being where our cup is running over, is to become conscious more and more of the great truth that real life has everything that man can wish for, and infinitely more. And as we grow in the conscious realization of this truth, the power of this truth will manifest itself in our external world. Then we shall find increase everywhere; wherever we may go in the physical world, in the mental world or in the spiritual world, God will prepare His table before us, and we shall enjoy the richest feast that His infinite goodness can possibly provide. In every domain of existence His bountiful hand will be our supply, and our cup will always be running over. What we feel and realize in the world of the spirit that we shall gain in the world of things. Thus our joy becomes complete; all that we need is always at hand, all that we desire for a greater existence shall be speedily supplied, and wherever our place in life may be, God will appear and prepare His table before us. He will be our supply always and everywhere; and existence will be rich indeed.

Surely goodness and mercy shall follow me all the days of my life; and I will dwell in the house of the Lord for ever.

When the soul enters the faith that leads eternally into the kingdom, the entire being of man is placed in the keeping of the spirit of goodness. That power that works for the good and the good only, will henceforth be with man under every circumstance and condition; and all his actions will be attended by the angel of mercy. His life will be lived in the consciousness of the Infinite presence, and this consciousness is the open door to the house of the Lord. The moment we feel that God is closer than breathing, nearer than hands and feet, we are upon the threshold of the sublime spiritual world—the Father's House of the Many Mansions, and from that moment we may dwell in His house forever. From that moment all will be changed; life will never seen ordinary, commonplace or mere existence any more; we have seen the House Beautiful, we have felt the touch of the life that God lives, we have been on the heights, and we have had a glimpse of the glory that eternity holds in store. Henceforth, there is so much to live for, that simply to think of the ever ascending destiny that lies before us, is in itself a source of unspeakable joy. Then who can measure the peace, the joy, in brief, the unbounded ecstasy that must follow the living of the life? Those who have been led beside the still waters know the meaning of such a life. Those who have entered the house of the Lord know what is prepared for them that love Him. But tongue can never tell, and only the mind of the soul can understand.

To follow the spirit is to enter the glorified vastness of the great spiritual mind within; and here is wisdom. Spiritual things must be spiritually discerned; we must enter spiritual light in order to know the reality of our own divine being, and the mind of the soul is eternally illumined with this light. There are no mysteries in spiritual consciousness; all is clear; the meaning of life is perfectly understood; the purpose of it all is distinctly revealed, and the soul knows what it is about every step of the way. Every soul that goes with God in all things and at all times, will ever live in this consciousness, and will ever rise higher and higher into the greater brilliancy and the more sublime beauty of the spiritual light. To live such a life is to dwell in the house of the Lord, and whosoever will may dwell in that house forever.

The world in which we live may not, at present, contain everything that the heart can wish for; but "there is another and a better world" that does contain everything. Our human dwelling place may not be perfect, it may not be complete, it may not satisfy the soul's longing for the ideal and the beautiful; but the house of the Lord can satisfy. We therefore need not be unhappy; personal life need not be incomplete because there are seeming limitations among external conditions. The fact that we manifest in visible form does not mean that we should live wholly among visible things. The law of true being is to manifest in the personal but to always live in the spiritual. The house of the Lord is our true dwelling place now and forever. And as there are many mansions in the Father's House—innumerable mansions, we shall not be confined to one place, or one state of existence; we shall live in each of these mansions; we shall enjoy them all, we shall pass through them all as eternity goes on. No matter how lofty the present abode of the soul, there is always something higher; no matter how unspeakable our spiritual joys today, or any time in eternity, there are always greater joys coming in days that are yet to be. We thus realize what it means to dwell in the house of the Lord forever.

When we have entered to dwell permanently in the house of the Lord, existence, both personal and spiritual, becomes perpetual joy. Whatever external conditions may be, or whatever may come and go in personal life, we are always in the joy everlasting, in the peace that passeth understanding, in the world on high where all is forever well. We no longer depend upon things, and we are no longer moved by things; we have transcended the world of things; we have gained the power to perfectly use things, and we are attaining the mastery of all things. We are living in God's world—the world of limitless richness, happiness and power; therefore, the world of things constitutes but a small part of our vast and wonderful domain. We have found so many sources of joy, so many states of being that can add to the value of life, that though other things should sometimes fail, we are never affected in the least. Confusion and failure in the outer world mean no more to us than the loss of a penny would mean to a man who owns a mountain of gold. Things may come and go in the outer world, but we are living in the house of the Lord. In that house there is never confusion, trouble nor pain; in that house there can be neither failure nor want. The Most High provides for that house; therefore so long as we dwell in His house we shall want for nothing. Whatever may come or go, we shall always have abundance, both in the within and in the without. We need fear nothing; we may rejoice always, for in His house all is well, and for evermore shall be.

―――――――――――――

Dream on fair soul, dream on. Thy visions are not in vain. Other and greater worlds are waiting for thee. Dream on fair soul, dream on. Let thy spirit ascend to the supreme heights of those greater worlds where thou shalt behold the glory and splendor of that sublime existence that is in store for thee. And let nothing that may come or go in thy waking hours cause thee to forget what thou hast seen. For the time is near when the dreams of the night shall rise with the morning but shall not depart with the setting sun. What thou hast seen in thy visions shall come to remain; and what thy lofty moments have revealed to thee shall become thine own forever.

―――――――――――――

CHAPTER XXVIII

GOD'S BEAUTIFUL GIFT TO ME

The great goal is cosmic consciousness, and every soul that endeavors to live according to the highest light that is known in the world, is daily drawing nearer and nearer to that sublime state. To such a soul the heavens may be opened at any time, and the splendors of the cosmic world revealed. Then everything will change. Life will not be the same any more. The meaning of it all will be discerned, and no fault can be found anywhere. When we look at life from the heights of the cosmic realm we can see only the divine side of existence; we therefore can see no evil; in brief, when we are in the cosmic we have absolutely forgotten everything about evil; we do not know that there is such a thing as evil because we are in that exalted world where we can be conscious only of the good. And here is the real evidence of cosmic consciousness. When you have entered the peace that passeth understanding and the joy that can only be described as a million heavens in one, you are in the cosmic state, providing you have forgotten every ill and every wrong you ever knew. In the cosmic world everything is as God made it; nothing has been changed in any way; absolute perfection and absolute divinity reign supremely, and the glory of it all no power in man can ever attempt to picture. It is beyond all the powers of the personal man; it is for the soul only to understand and enjoy.

When we enter the cosmic state we transcend that part of man that takes cognizance of the imperfect and incomplete; we enter a realm that never knew anything less than absolute, divine perfection, and therefore when we are in that realm we can know no evil. In the cosmic state our eyes are too pure to see evil, and the mind too high in divine consciousness to even think of evil. We are thinking the thoughts of the Infinite and everything we are conscious of is manifesting the shining glory of the Most High. In the cosmic state we think the truth, the absolute truth, because in that state everything is the expression of absolute truth. Therefore, the more frequently we enter into the realization of cosmic consciousness the more fully will the mind discern the truth, and the more readily can we think the truth whatever the field of our thought may be.

There are many minds that think that they have frequent experiences in cosmic consciousness, but not all of these have judged those experiences correctly. The great within is filled with wonderful realms of every description, and some have mistaken one or more of these realms for the home of the soul when the body has been removed. Many have thought they have seen heaven after beholding the gorgeous splendor of these inner realms, while others, after meeting the beautiful thoughts that take human shape in the great within, believe they have conversed with angels. But this is not the cosmic world. Though we may find peace and joy and ecstasy without measure in many of these beautiful interior realms, still we also find imperfection in one or more of its many forms. We do not forget evil while we are in the ecstasy of the great within; nor do we become unconscious of everything but that which is pure shining divinity. This, however, is precisely what happens when we are in the cosmic state; we meet only that which is wholly in the likeness of God, and our joy at times becomes so great that our feelings cannot contain themselves. Our cup overflows and the person bursts forth in tears. We have found that for which we have waited and prayed so long; we are inwardly moved as never before, and it is but natural that the person should weep for joy. We have found eternal life, we have felt His presence, we have touched the hem of His garment, we have met Him face to face.

The greater number of those who are spiritually inclined are almost constantly on the verge of the cosmic state, and at intervals they receive glimpses of that wondrous world. Could they but see themselves at such moments, they would discover that their faces are also shining as the sun, for their minds are illumined with radiant glory from on high. But such moments do not usually come when the senses expect them, nor can they be produced at will. We gain glimpses of the cosmic only when the soul occupies the supreme state in consciousness, and we begin to live within the pearly gates of the cosmic when the soul has gained full supremacy in every domain in consciousness. Therefore, to attain cosmic consciousness, we must give the spiritual life the first place in everything; we must do everything to the glory of God, and follow the light of the spirit in everything we may think or do. The eye must be single, and to see and to know only that which is wholly divine must be the one supreme desire.

The ruling spirit in the cosmic world is divine perfection; therefore the more we think of divine perfection, and the more we try to see divine perfection in all things, the more we develop the consciousness of divine perfection; and the development of this form of consciousness will finally culminate in divine consciousness which is synonymous with cosmic consciousness. To keep the eye single upon the great truth that every creation of God is good is to draw nearer and nearer to that state where we became conscious only of the absolutely good; then follows the limitless joy of the cosmic world. But when we permit the eye to become double, and begin to see the evil as well as the good, the unreal as well as the real, we fall from our lofty state; and this is the only fall of man. When we partake of the fruit from the tree of the knowledge of good and evil, we fall from the cosmic world, and we have to leave paradise. We cannot live in the garden of bliss, in the joys of cosmic consciousness, so long as we know evil as well as good; but when we become unconscious of evil, with the eye single upon His supreme goodness alone, then the gates of paradise shall open for us once more. Then we shall forget everything but that which is good and beautiful and true; we shall enter the new heaven and the new earth, the new heaven in the within, and the new earth in the without, and while still in personal form we shall live in the cosmic world.

To rise daily into a higher and better understanding of the reality of the cosmic state of existence is to become conscious, more and more, of the real sweetness of existence. Life becomes so rich and so beautiful that to live is in itself absolutely sufficient. In the cosmic state every moment seems to be an eternity of bliss, and every movement of consciousness produces a million pleasures. In comparison, the joys of sense have no significance whatever. Therefore, when the mere living of life gives all the joy that heart and soul may desire, it is evidence conclusive that the cosmic state has been reached; and the joys that are to follow, the soul on the heights alone can know.

The cosmic world is that highly refined, spiritualized world all about us, permeating everything, encompassing everything; the great divine sea in which we live and move and have our being; a world of pure light, gorgeous splendor and celestial brilliancy. The cosmic world is the world sublime; it is everywhere, and we live in it now and eternally, but only those who are spiritually awakened can discern its reality and behold the shining glories of its fair transcendent realms. When the true spiritual awakening begins we discover the cosmic world, and we enter cosmic consciousness. The heavens are opened and the vision before us reveals splendors and glories that tongue can never describe, joys that cannot be measured, and life that is a million heavens in one.

When we are in the cosmic state the entire world is clothed with the sun; the waters of the deep reflect the radiant glory of celestial kingdoms, and the mountains proclaim the majesty and the power of the life that is lived on the heights. Nature sings the everlasting praises of Him who is closer than breathing, nearer than hands and feet, and every human countenance beams with the beautiful smile of God. The flowers declare the thoughts of the Infinite; the forest chants the silent prelude to worship, while the birds inspire the soul to ascend to the vast empyrean blue. We are speechless with ecstasy, but as we behold the beauty and glory of it all the spirit within speaks from out the fullness of the heart and sweetly proclaims in language divine—"God's beautiful gift to me."

There is an upper realm in the spiritual life of man where the reality and perfection of divine existence is revealed. In this realm all is truth, all is purity, all is love. To enter this realm is to become conscious of eternal truth and understand the truth as it manifests everywhere. In the cosmic state the spiritual understanding of truth is complete, therefore every step in the spiritual understanding of truth is a step toward cosmic consciousness. All understanding is spiritual that discerns the spirit of truth as well as the reality of truth; and the mind develops in the discernment of truth when every effort to understand truth enters into the very innermost life of truth. When you think of truth, think of the spirit of truth; that is, that spiritual life or soul that is within truth; and desire with all the power of life, thought and feeling to enter into the soul of truth. To enter into the soul of truth is to enter into the cosmic state, and you not only gain an illumined understanding of the truth itself, but you become conscious of the entire cosmic world. The heavens are opened, for I Am the door, the way, the truth—the spirit of truth.

To enter the cosmic state is to become conscious of that divinity within us that is too pure to behold anything but that which is absolute purity. "To the pure all things are pure," and in the cosmic state we become pure; we enter into the world of shining purity; we do not recognize evil, and to us, iniquity has no significance whatever. While we are in the cosmic state we are in a pure state and can know only the boundless world of sublime purity that is all about us and all within us everywhere. Therefore, to enter the cosmic state the mind must be pure; that is, the mind must face the divinity that is in all things, and must, at all times, keep the eye single upon the shining purity of that divinity.

The cosmic realm is filled through and through with love, and to enter this realm is to love every living creature with all the power of heart and soul. When you are in the cosmic state you are in the universal; all life is divine to you; all life is beautiful, all life is precious, all life is sacred; your sympathy is as large as the universe and as touching as the innermost tenderness of the soul. To love everybody, no matter what they are or what they have done, is a part of your own life. You are above personal conditions; you are above personal deeds; you can see through the imperfect and behold the shining glory that reigns supremely in all that is. You see the divine reality in all things and you love it with all the tenderness of heart and soul. This divine loveliness in all things is the all in all in all things; to you it is beautiful, "fairer than ten thousand to the soul."

To love in the spirit of the universal is not to disregard the person. You love the person infinitely more because when you are in the cosmic every atom in the person is glorified with the presence of Him who is closer to life than breathing, nearer than hands and feet. You love the person because all that is true in that person is the coming forth of the divine. That which may not be true you do not see; your eyes are too pure to behold iniquity; besides, the imperfect in any person is insignificant and does not belong to the real person himself. Even in the most sinful of persons the evil is but a fragment compared with the good that is inherent in every fiber of his being. Take the worst person in the world and you will find the good and the right in him a thousand times greater than the wrong. When you are awakened to the truth you know this; therefore it becomes so easy to love; and since your heart is simply overflowing with love, you must love—love everything and everybody. And what a supreme joy is found in such a love.

To enter the cosmic state and develop cosmic consciousness, the soul must be given perfect freedom to love in the universal. It is a part of the life of the soul to love everything in existence, therefore the physical senses must not interfere with this love by impressing the mind to think that some things are evil and not worthy of love. Everything is worthy of love because in everything the good is infinitely greater than that which appears not to be good. The senses must be trained to recognize this great truth and the mind must be trained to harmonize all thinking with the sublime desires of the soul. When you meet a person see the all in all in that person; you will then see the shining purity of divine loveliness animating every fiber of his being; his countenance will be glorified before you, and you will love him with that beautiful love that reigned in the tenderness of the Christ. Meet all things in this sublime spiritual attitude, and the material veil will be removed more and more until all the splendors of the cosmic world are revealed to your vision.

To develop cosmic consciousness, place yourself in the hands of higher power. Depend upon higher power in all things; do nothing without first calling upon higher power; and so live that every thought, word and action is inspired by the spirit of higher power. Feel that higher power is always with you; deeply desire higher power to direct you, and open consciousness so completely to the limitless life of higher power that you actually realize that you live, move and have your being in the infinite power of the Most High. To enter the cosmic state you must transcend all belief in limitations; you must enter the universal where you clearly discern that all things are possible, for God is everywhere; and when your life is filled through and through with the presence of higher power you are lifted to the mountain tops of this lofty state. You rise above personal conditions and enter the limitless—where life is limitless, where power is limitless, where truth is limitless, where light is limitless, where the good is limitless, where love is limitless—where everything is limitless; and that is the cosmic world.

To live by faith is another supreme essential in the attainment of this sublime state. It is the very nature of faith to go out upon the limitless, and wherever faith may go, better things, higher things and greater things are found than were ever known before. Faith invariably leads upward and onward; faith always inspires the soul to ascend; while the spirit of faith illumines the way. To enter into the true spirit of faith, have faith in the innermost life of faith. There is a hidden power in faith; this power is the power of the Infinite; it is the soul of faith, the spirit of faith, and is eternally one with the spirit of the Most High. To enter into the spirit of faith is to enter into the spirit of the Most High, and thus be filled through and through with the power of the Most High. And this is the reason why all things are possible to him who has faith.

When you use the power of faith, have faith with the spirit of faith. You thus enter into the real power of faith and the illumined world of faith. In consequence, you not only gain the power to make all things possible, but you also enter into the spiritual light, and in the spiritual light the shining glory of the cosmic is revealed. To have faith with the spirit of faith, think of that supreme spiritual life and power that is in faith. Mentally dwell upon this inner life of faith, and whenever you use your faith, which should be every moment of existence, enter into the spirit of faith with all the power of feeling, thought and soul. You thus place yourself in perfect spiritual touch with the world of celestial light, with the world of divine wisdom, with the world of eternal life, with the world of limitless power, with the world of shining purity, with the world of that love that loves everything and everybody with the most touching tenderness of the Most High. You are in the Mind that was in Christ Jesus; you are in the same Spirit that He was when His face did shine as the sun and His garment became white as the light.

YOUR
FORCES *and*
HOW *to*
USE THEM

CONTENTS

FOREWORD

"There are a million energies in man. What may we not become when we learn to use them all." This is the declaration of the poet; and though poetry is usually inspired by transcendental visions, and therefore more or less impressed with apparent exaggerations, nevertheless there is in this poetic expression far more actual, practical truth than we may at first believe.

How many energies there are in man, no one knows; but there are so many that even the keenest observers of human activity have found it impossible to count them all. And as most of these energies are remarkable, to say the least, and some of them so remarkable as to appear both limitless in power and numberless in possibilities, we may well wonder what man will become when he learns to use them all.

When we look upon human nature in general we may fail to see much improvement in power and worth as compared with what we believe the race has been in the past; and therefore we conclude that humanity will continue to remain about the same upon this planet until the end of time. But when we investigate the lives of such individuals as have recently tried to apply more intelligently the greater powers within them, we come to a different conclusion. We then discover that there is evidence in thousands of human lives of a new and superior race of people—a race that will apply a much larger measure of the wonders and possibilities that exist within them.

It is only a few years, not more than a quarter of a century, since modern psychology began to proclaim the new science of human thought and action, so that we have had but a short time to demonstrate what a more intelligent application of our energies and forces can accomplish. But already the evidence is coming in from all sources, revealing results that frequently border upon the extraordinary. Man can do far more with himself and his

life than he has been doing in the past; he can call into action, and successfully apply, far more ability, energy and worth than his forefathers ever
dreamed of. So much has been proven during this brief introductory period
of the new age. Then what greater things may we not reasonably expect
when we have had fifty or a hundred years more in which to develop and
apply those larger possibilities which we now know to be inherent in us all.

It is the purpose of the following pages, not only to discuss these greater
powers and possibilities in man, but also to present practical methods
through which they may be applied. We have been aware of the fact for
centuries that there is more in man than what appears on the surface, but it
is only in recent years that a systematic effort has been made to understand
the nature and practical use of this "more," as well as to work out better
methods for the thorough and effective application of those things on the
surface which we have always employed. In dealing with a subject that is so
large and so new, however, it is necessary to make many statements that
may, at first sight, appear to be unfounded, or at least exaggerations. But if
the reader will thoroughly investigate the basis of such statements as he goes
along, he will not only find that there are no unfounded statements or exaggerations in the book, but will wish that every strong statement made had
been made many times as strong.

When we go beneath the surface of human life and learn what greater
things are hidden beneath the ordinary layers of mental substance and vital
energy, we find man to be so wonderfully made that language is wholly
inadequate to describe even a fraction of his larger and richer life. We may
try to give expression to our thoughts, at such times, by employing the
strongest statements and the most forceful adjectives that we can think of;
but even these prove little better than nothing; so therefore we may conclude that no statement that attempts to describe the "more" in man can
possibly be too strong. Even the strongest fails to say one thousandth of what
we would say should we speak the whole truth. We shall all admit this, and
accordingly shall find it advisable not to pass judgment upon strong statements but to learn to understand and apply those greater powers within
ourselves that are infinitely stronger than the strongest statement that could
possibly be made.

Those minds who may believe that the human race is to continue weak
and imperfect as usual, should consider what remarkable steps in advance
have recently been taken in nearly all fields of human activity. And then
they should remember that the greater powers in man, as well as a scientific
study of the use of his lesser powers, have been almost wholly neglected.

The question then that will naturally arise is, what man might make of himself if he would apply the same painstaking science to his own development and advancement as he now applies in other fields. If he did, would we not, in another generation or two, witness unmistakable evidence of the coming of a new and superior race, and would not strong men and women become far more numerous than ever before in the history of the world?

Each individual will want to answer these questions according to his own point of view, but whatever his answer may be, we all must agree that man can be, become and achieve far more than even the most sanguine indications of the present may predict. And it is the purpose of the following pages to encourage as many as possible to study and apply these greater powers within them so that they may not only become greater and richer and more worthy as individuals, but may also become the forerunners of that higher and more wonderful race of which we all have so fondly dreamed.

Promise Yourself

To be so strong that nothing can disturb your peace of mind.

To talk health, happiness and prosperity to every person you meet.

To make all your friends feel that there is something in them.

To look at the sunny side of everything and make your optimism come true.

To think only of the best, to work only for the best, and to expect only the best.

To be just as enthusiastic about the success of others as you are about your own.

To forget the mistakes of the past and press on to the greater achievements of the future.

To wear a cheerful countenance at all times and give every living creature you meet a smile.

To give so much time to the improvement of yourself that you have no time to criticize others.

To be too large for worry, too noble for anger, too strong for fear; and too happy to permit the presence of trouble.

To think well of yourself and to proclaim this fact to the world, not in loud words but in great deeds.

To live in the faith that the whole world is on your side so long as you are true to the best that is in you.

CHAPTER I

THE RULING PRINCIPLE IN MAN

The purpose of the following pages will be to work out the subject chosen in the most thorough and practical manner; in brief, to analyze the whole nature of man, find all the forces in his possession, whether they be apparent or hidden, active or dormant, and to present methods through which all those forces can be applied in making the life of each individual richer, greater and better. To make every phase of this work as useful as possible to the greatest number possible, not a single statement will be made that all cannot understand, and not a single idea will be presented that any one cannot apply to every-day life.

We all want to know what we actually possess both in the physical, the mental and the spiritual, and we want to know how the elements and forces within us can be applied in the most successful manner. It is results in practical life that we want, and we are not true to ourselves or the race until we learn to use the powers within us so effectively, that the greatest results possible within the possibilities of human nature are secured.

When we proceed with a scientific study of the subject, we find that the problem before us is to know what is in us and how to use what is in us. After much study of the powers in man, both conscious and subconscious, we have come to the conclusion that if we only knew how to use these powers, we could accomplish practically anything that we may have in view, and not only realize our wants to the fullest degree, but also reach even our highest goal. Though this may seem to be a strong statement, nevertheless when we examine the whole nature of man, we are compelled to admit that it is true even in its fullest sense, and that therefore, not a single individual can fail to realize his wants and reach his goal, after he has learned how to use the powers that are in him. This is not mere speculation, nor is it simply a beautiful dream. The more we study the lives of people who have achieved, and the more we study our own experience every day, the more convinced we become that there is no reason whatever why any individual should not realize all his ambitions and much more.

The basis of this study will naturally be found in the understanding of the whole nature of man, as we must know what we are, before we can know and use what we inherently possess. In analyzing human nature a number of methods have been employed, but there are only three in particular that are of actual value for our present purpose. The first of these declares that man is composed of ego, consciousness and form, and though this analysis is the most complete, yet it is also the most abstract, and is therefore not easily understood. The second analysis, which is simpler, and which is employed almost exclusively by the majority, declares that man is body, mind and soul; but as much as this idea is thought of and spoken of, there are very few who actually understand it. In fact, the usual conception of man as body, mind and soul will have to be completely reversed in order to become absolutely true. The third analysis, which is the simplest and the most serviceable, declares that man is composed of individuality and personality, and it is this conception of human nature that will constitute the phases of our study in this work.

Before we pass to the more practical side of the subject, we shall find it profitable to examine briefly these various ideas concerning the nature of man; in fact, every part of our human analysis that refers to the ego, simply must be understood if we are to learn how to use the forces we possess, and the reason for this is found in the fact that the ego is the "I Am," the ruling principle in man, the center and source of individuality, the originator of everything that takes place in man, and that primary something to which all other things in human nature are secondary.

When the average person employs the term "ego," he thinks that he is dealing with something that is hidden so deeply in the abstract that it can make but little difference whether we understand it or not. This, however, does not happen to be true, because it is the ego that must act before any action can take place anywhere in the human system, and it is the ego that must originate the new before any step in advance can be taken. And in addition, it is extremely important to realize that the power of will to control the forces we possess, depends directly upon how fully conscious we are of the ego as the ruling principle within us. We understand therefore, that it is absolutely necessary to associate all thought, all feeling and all actions of mind or personality with the ego, or what we shall hereafter speak of as the "I Am."

The first step to be taken in this connection, is to recognize the "I Am" in everything you do, and to think always of the "I Am," as being you—the **supreme you.** Whenever you think, realize that it is the "I Am" that originated the thought. Whenever you act, realize that it is the "I Am" that gives initiative to that action, and whenever you think of yourself or try to be conscious of yourself, realize that the "I Am" occupies the throne of your entire field of consciousness.

Another important essential is to affirm silently in your own mind that you are the "I Am," and as you affirm this statement, or as you simply declare positively, "I Am," think of the "I Am" as being the ruling principle in your whole world, as being distinct and above and superior to all else in your being, and as being you, yourself, in the highest, largest, and most comprehensive sense. You thus lift yourself up, so to speak, to the mountain top of masterful individuality; you enthrone yourself; you become true to yourself; you place yourself where you belong.

Through this practice you not only discover yourself to be the master of your whole life, but you elevate all your conscious actions to that lofty state in your consciousness that we may describe as the throne of your being, or as that center of action within which the ruling "I Am" lives and moves and has its being. If you wish to control and direct the forces you possess, you must act from the throne of your being, so to speak; or in other words, from that conscious point in your mental world wherein all power of control, direction and initiative proceeds; and this point of action is the center of the "I Am." You must act, not as a body, not as a personality, not as a mind, but as the "I Am," and the more fully you recognize the lofty position of the "I Am," the greater becomes your power to control and direct all other things that you may possess. In brief, whenever you think or act, you should feel that you stand with the "I Am," at the apex of mentality on the very heights of your existence, and you should at the same time, realize that this "I Am" is **you**—the **supreme you.** The more you practice these methods, the more you lift yourself up above the limitations of mind and body, into the realization of your own true position as a masterful individuality; in fact, you place yourself where you belong, over and above everything in your organized existence.

When we examine the mind of the average person, we find that he usually identifies himself with mind or body. He either thinks that he is body or that he is mind, and therefore he can control neither mind nor body. The "I Am" in his nature is submerged in a bundle of ideas, some of which are true and some of which are not, and his thought is usually controlled by those ideas without receiving any direction whatever from that principle within him that alone was intended to give direction. Such a man lives in the lower story of human existence but as we can control life only when we give directions from the upper story, we discover just why the average person neither understands his forces nor has the power to use them. He must first elevate himself to the upper story of the human structure, and the first and most important step to be taken in this direction is to recognize the "I Am" as the ruling principle, and that the "I Am" is **you.**

Another method that will be found highly important in this connection is to take a few moments every day and try to feel that you—the "I Am"—are not only above mind and body, but in a certain sense, distinct from mind and body; in fact, try to isolate the "I Am" for a few moments every day from the rest of your organized being. This practice will give you what may be termed a perfect consciousness of your own individual "I Am," and as you gain that consciousness you will always think of the supreme "I Am" whenever you think of yourself. Accordingly, all your mental actions will, from that time on, come directly from the "I Am"; and if you will continue to stand above all such actions at all times, you will be able to control them and direct them completely.

To examine consciousness and form in this connection is hardly necessary, except to define briefly their general nature, so that we may have a clear idea of what we are dealing with in the conscious field as well as in the field of expression. The "I Am" is fundamentally conscious; that is, the "I Am" knows what exists in the human field or in the human sphere and what is taking place in the human sphere; and that constitutes consciousness. In brief, you are conscious when you know that you exist and have some definite idea as to what is taking place in your sphere of existence. What we speak of as form, is everything in the organized personality that has shape and that serves in any manner to give expression to the forces within us.

In the exercise of consciousness, we find that the "I Am" employs three fundamental actions. When the "I Am" looks out upon life we have simple consciousness. When the "I Am" looks upon its own position in life we have self consciousness, and when the "I Am" looks up into the vastness of real life we have cosmic consciousness.

In simple consciousness, you are only aware of those things that exist externally to yourself, but when you begin to become conscious of yourself as a distinct entity, you begin to develop self consciousness. When you begin to turn your attention to the great within and begin to look up into the real source of all things, you become conscious of that world that seemingly exists within all worlds, and when you enter upon this experience, you are on the borderland of cosmic consciousness, the most fascinating subject that has ever been known.

When we come to define body, mind and soul, we must, as previously stated, reverse the usual definition. In the past, we have constantly used the expression, "I have a soul," which naturally implies the belief that "I am a body"; and so deeply has this idea become fixed in the average mind that nearly everybody thinks of the body whenever the term "me" or "myself" is employed. But in this attitude of mind the individual is not above the physical states of thought and feeling; in fact, he is more or less submerged in what may be called a bundle of physical facts and ideas, of which he has very little control. You cannot control anything in your life, however, until you are above it. You cannot control what is in your body until you realize that you are above your body. You cannot control what is in your mind until you realize that you are above your mind, and therefore no one can use the forces within him to any extent so long as he thinks of himself as being the body, or as being localized exclusively in the body.

When we examine the whole nature of man, we find that the soul is the man himself, and that the ego is the central principle of the soul; or to use another expression, the soul, including the "I Am," constitutes the individuality, and that visible something through which individuality finds expression, constitutes the personality.

If you wish to understand your forces, and gain that masterful attitude necessary to the control of your forces, train yourself to think that you are a soul, but do not think of the soul as something vague or mysterious. Think of the soul as being the individual you and all that that expression can possibly imply. Train yourself to think that you are master of mind and body, because you are above mind and body, and possess the power to use everything that is in mind and body.

Man is ever in search of strength. It is the strong man that wins. It is the man with power that scales the heights. To be strong is to be great; and it is the privilege of greatness to satisfy every desire, every aspiration, every need. But strength is not for the few alone; it is for all, and the way to strength is simple. Proceed this very moment to the mountain tops of the strength you now possess, and whatever may happen do not come down. Do not weaken under adversity. Resolve to remain as strong, as determined and as highly enthused during the darkest night of adversity as you are during the sunniest day of prosperity. Do not feel disappointed when things seem disappointing. Keep the eye single upon the same brilliant future regardless of circumstances, conditions or events. Do not lose heart when things go wrong. Continue undisturbed in your original resolve to make all things go right. To be overcome by adversity and threatening failure is to lose strength; to always remain in the same lofty, determined mood is to constantly grow in strength. The man who never weakens when things are against him will grow stronger and stronger until all things will delight to be for him. He will finally have all the strength he may desire or need. Be always strong and you will always be stronger.

CHAPTER II

HOW WE GOVERN THE
FORCES WE POSSESS

Whenever you think or whenever you feel, whenever you speak, whenever you act, or whatever may be taking place in your life, your supreme idea should be that you are above it all, superior to it all, and have control of it all. You simply must take this higher ground in all action, thought and consciousness before you can control yourself and direct, for practical purposes, the forces you possess. Therefore, what has been said in connection with the "I Am," the soul and the individuality as being one, and as standing at the apex of human existence, is just as important as anything that may be said hereafter in connection with the application of the forces in man to practical action. And though this phase of the subject may appear to be somewhat abstract, we shall find no difficulty in understanding it more fully as we apply the ideas evolved. In fact, when we learn to realize that we, by nature, occupy a position that is above mind and body, this part of the subject will be found more interesting than anything else, and its application more profitable.

We can define individuality more fully by stating that it is the invisible man and that everything in man that is invisible belongs to his individuality. It is the individuality that initiates, that controls or directs. Therefore to control and use a force in your own system, you must understand and develop individuality. Your individuality must be made distinct, determined and positive. You must constantly know what you are and what you want, and you must constantly be determined to secure what you want. It is individuality that makes you different from all other organized entities, and it is a highly developed individuality that gives you the power to stand out distinct above the mass, and it is the degree of individuality that you possess that determines largely what position you are to occupy in the world.

Whenever you see a man who is different, who seems to stand out distinct, and who has something vital about him that no one else seems to possess, you have a man whose individuality is highly developed, and you also have a man who is going to make his mark in the world. Take two men of equal power, ability and efficiency, but with this difference. In the one individuality is highly developed, while in the other it is not. You know at once which one of these two is going to reach the highest places in the world of achievement; and the reason is that the one who possesses individuality, lives above mind and body, thereby being able to control and direct the forces and powers of mind and body. The man, however, whose individuality is weak, lives more or less down in mind and body, and instead of controlling mind and body, is constantly being influenced by everything from the outside that may enter his consciousness.

Whenever you find a man or a woman who is doing something worth while, who is creating an impression upon the race, who is moving forward toward greater and better things, you find the individuality strong, positive and highly developed. It is therefore absolutely necessary that you give your best attention to the development of a strong, positive individuality if you wish to succeed in the world and make the best use of the forces in your possession. A negative or weak individuality drifts with the stream of environment, and usually receives only what others choose to give, but a firm, strong, positive, well-developed individuality, actually controls the ship of his life and destiny, and sooner or later will gain possession of what he originally set out to secure. A positive individuality has the power to take hold of things and turn them to good account. This is one reason why such an individuality always succeeds. Another reason is that the more fully your individuality is developed, the more you are admired by everybody with whom you may come in contact. The human race loves power, and counts it a privilege to give lofty positions to those who have power, and every man or woman, whose individuality is highly developed, does possess power— usually exceptional power.

To develop individuality, the first essential is to give the "I Am" its true and lofty position in your mind. The "I Am" is the very center of individuality, and the more fully conscious you become of the "I Am" the more of the power that is in the "I Am" you arouse, and it is the arousing of this power that makes individuality positive and strong. Another essential is to practice the idea of feeling or conceiving yourself as occupying the masterful attitude. Whenever you think of yourself, think of yourself as being and living and acting in the masterful attitude. Then in addition, make every desire positive, make every feeling positive, make every thought positive, and make every action of mind positive. To make your wants distinct and positive, that is, to actually and fully know what you want and then proceed to want what you want with all the power that is in you, will also tend to give strength and positiveness to your individuality; and the reason is that such actions of mind will tend to place in positive, constructive action every force that is in your system.

A most valuable method is to picture in your mind your own best idea of what a strong, well-developed individuality would necessarily be, and then think of yourself as becoming more and more like that picture. In this connection it is well to remember that we gradually grow into the likeness of that which we think of the most. Therefore, if you have a very clear idea of a highly developed individuality, and think a great deal of that individuality with a strong, positive desire to develop such an individuality, you will gradually and surely move toward that lofty ideal.

Another valuable method is to give conscious recognition to what may be called the bigger man on the inside. Few people think of this greater man that is within them, but we cannot afford to neglect this interior entity for a moment. This greater or larger man is not something that is separate and distinct from ourselves. It is simply the sum-total of the greater powers and possibilities that are within us. We should recognize these, think of them a great deal, and desire with all the power of heart and mind and soul to arouse and express more and more of these inner powers. Thus we shall find that the interior man, our real individuality, will become stronger and more active, and our power to apply our greater possibilities will increase accordingly. The value of individuality is so great that it cannot possibly be over-estimated. Every known method that will develop individuality, therefore, should be applied faithfully, thoroughly and constantly. In fact, no one other thing we can do will bring greater returns.

The personality is the visible man. Everything that is visible in the human entity belongs to the personality, but it is more than the body. To say that some one has a fine personality may and may not mean that that personality is beautiful, in the ordinary sense of the term. There might be no physical beauty and yet the personality might be highly developed. There might be nothing striking about such a personality, and yet there would be something extremely attractive, something to greatly admire. On the other hand, when the personality is not well developed, there is nothing in the visible man that you can see, besides ordinary human clay. Everything existing in such a personality is crude and even gross; but there is no excuse for any personality being crude, unrefined or undeveloped. There is not a single personality that cannot be so refined and perfected as to become strikingly attractive, and there are scores of reasons why such development should be sought. The most important reason is that all the forces of man act through the personality, and the finer the personality, the more easily can we direct and express the forces we possess. When the personality is crude, we find it difficult to apply in practical life the finer elements that are within us, and here we find one reason why talent or ability so frequently fails to be its best. In such cases the personality has been neglected, and is not a fit instrument through which finer things and greater things can find expression. The personality is related to the individual as the piano is to the musician. If the piano is out of tune, the musician will fail, no matter how much of a musician he may be; and likewise, if the piano or instrument is crude in construction, the finest music cannot be expressed through it as a channel. To develop the personality, the principal essential is to learn how to transmute all the creative energies that are generated in the human system, a subject that will be given thorough attention in another chapter.

When we proceed to apply the forces within us, we find three fields of action. The first is the conscious field, the field in which the mind acts when we are awake. The second field is the subconscious, that field in which the mind acts when it goes beneath consciousness. It is also the field in which we act when asleep. The term, "falling asleep," is therefore literally true, as when we go to sleep, the ego goes down, so to speak, into another world—a world so vast, that only portions of it have thus far been explored. The third field is the superconscious, the field in which the mind acts when it touches the upper realm, and it is when acting in this field that we gain real power and real inspiration; in fact, when we touch the superconscious, we frequently feel as if we have become more than mere man. To know how to act in the superconscious field, is therefore highly important, even though the idea may at first sight seem to be vague and somewhat mystical.

We are constantly in touch, however, with the superconscious, whether we know it or not. We frequently enter the superconscious when we listen to inspiring music, when we read some book that touches the finer intellect, when we listen to someone who speaks from what may be termed the inner throne of authority, when we witness some soul-stirring scene in nature. We also touch the superconscious when we are carried away with some tremendous ambition, and herein we find practical value in a great measure. When men of tremendous ambition are carried away, so to speak, with the power of that ambition, they almost invariably reach the higher and finer state of mind—a state where they not only feel more power and determination than they ever felt before, but a state in which the mind becomes so extremely active that it almost invariably gains the necessary brilliancy to work out those plans or ideas that are required in order that the ambition may be realized.

It can readily be demonstrated that we get our best ideas from this lofty realm, and it is a well-known fact that no one ever accomplishes great or wonderful things in the world, without touching frequently this sublime inspiring state. When we train the mind to touch the superconscious at frequent intervals, we always find the ideas we want. We always succeed in providing the ways and means required. No matter what the difficulties may be, we invariably discover something by which we may overcome and conquer completely.

Whenever you find yourself in what may be termed a difficult position, proceed at once to work your mind up into higher and higher attitudes, until you touch the superconscious, and when you touch that lofty state you will soon receive the ideas or the methods that you need. But this is not the only value connected with the superconscious. The highest forces in man are the most powerful, but we cannot use those higher forces without acting through the superconscious field. Therefore, if you want to understand and apply all the forces you possess, you must train the mind to act through the superconscious as well as the conscious and the subconscious.

However, we must not permit ourselves to live exclusively in this lofty state; though it is the source of the higher forces in man, those forces that are indispensable to the doing of great and important things; nevertheless, those forces cannot be applied unless they are brought down to earth, so to speak, and united with practical action. He who lives exclusively in the superconscious, will dream wonderful dreams, but if he does not unite the forces of the superconscious with practical action, he will do nothing else but dream dreams, and those dreams will not come true. It is when we combine mental action in the conscious, subconscious and superconscious, that we get the results we desire. In brief, it is the full use of all the forces in mind through all the channels of expression that leads to the highest attainment and the greatest achievements.

When we proceed with the practical application of any particular force,

we shall not find it necessary to cause that force to act through what may
be termed the psychological field, and the reason is that the psychological field in man is the real field of action. It is the field through which
the undercurrents flow, and we all understand that it is these undercurrents
that determine, not only the direction of action, but the results that follow
action. This idea is well illustrated in the following lines:

> "Straws upon the surface flow;
>   He who would seek for pearls must dive below"

The term "below" as applied to the life and consciousness of man, is
synonymous with the psychological field, or the field of the undercurrents.
Ordinary minds skim over the surface. Great minds invariably sound these
deeper depths, and act in and through the psychological field. Their minds
dive below into the rich vastness of what may be termed the gold mines of
the mind, and the diamond fields of the soul.

When we enter the psychological field of any force, which simply means
the inner and finer field of action of that force, we act through the undercurrents, and thereby proceed to control those currents. It is in the field of
the undercurrents that we find both the origin and the action of cause,
whether physical or mental. It is these currents, when acted upon intelligently, that remove what we do not want and produce those changes that
we do want. They invariably produce effects, both physical and mental,
according to the action that we give to them, and all those things that pertain to the personality will respond only to the actions of those currents;
that is, you cannot produce any effect in any part of the mind or body unless you first direct the undercurrents of the system to produce those effects.
To act through the undercurrents therefore is absolutely necessary, no matter what we may wish to do, or what forces we may wish to control, direct
or apply; and we act upon those undercurrents only when we enter the
psychological field.

In like manner, we can turn to good account all things in practical everyday life only when we understand the psychology of those things. The
reason is, that when we understand the psychology of anything, we understand the power that is back of that particular thing, and that controls it and
gives it definite action. In consequence, when we understand the psychology
of anything in our own field of action or in our own environment, we will
know how to deal with it so as to secure whatever results that particular
thing has the power to produce. But this law is especially important in deal-

ing with forces within ourselves, whether those forces act through the mind or through any one of the faculties, through the personality or through the conscious, subconscious or superconscious fields. In brief, whatever we do in trying to control and direct the powers we possess, we must enter the deeper life of those powers, so that we can get full control of the undercurrents. It is the way those undercurrents flow that determines results, and as we can direct those currents in any way that we desire, we naturally conclude that we can secure whatever results we desire.

Man lives to move forward. To move forward is to live more. To live more is to be more and do more; and it is being and doing that constitutes the path to happiness. The more you are the more you do, the richer your life, the greater your joy. But being and doing must always live together as one. To try to be much and not try to do much, is to find life a barren waste. To try to do much and not try to be much, is to find life a burden too heavy and wearisome to bear. The being of much gives the necessary inspiration and the necessary power to the doing of much. The doing of much gives the necessary expression to the being of much. And it is the bringing forth of being through the act of doing that produces happiness that is happiness. Being much gives capacity for doing much. Doing much gives expression to the richest and the best that is within us. And the more we increase the richness of that which is within us, the more we increase our happiness, provided we increase, in the same proportion, the expression of that greater richness. The first essential is provided for by the being of much; the second, by the doing of much; and the secret of both may be found by him who lives to move forward.

CHAPTER III

THE USE OF MIND
IN PRACTICAL ACTION

In the present age, it is the power of mind that rules the world, and therefore it is evident that he who has acquired the best use of the power of
mind, will realize the greatest success, and reach the highest places that
attainment and achievement hold in store. The man who wins is the man
who can apply in practical life every part of his mental ability, and who can
make every action of his mind tell.

We sometimes wonder why there are so many capable men and admirable women who do not reach those places in life that they seem to deserve,
but the answer is simple. They do not apply the power of mind as they should.
Their abilities and qualities are either misdirected or applied only in part.
These people, however, should not permit themselves to become dissatisfied
with fate, but should remember that every individuality who learns to make
full use of the power of his mind will reach his goal; he will realize his
desire and will positively win.

There are several reasons why, though the principal reason is found in
the fact that when the power of the mind is used correctly in working out
what we wish to accomplish, the other forces we possess are readily applied
for the same purpose, and this fact becomes evident when we realize that
the power of mind is not only the ruling power in the world, but is also the
ruling power in man himself. All other faculties in man are ruled by the
power of his mind. It is the action of his mind that determines the action
of all the other forces in his possession. Therefore, to secure the results desired, he must give his first thought to the scientific and constructive
application of mental action.

In a preceding chapter, it was stated that the "I Am" is the ruling principle in man, and from that statement the conclusion may be drawn that the
"I Am" is the ruling power as well, but this is not strictly correct. There is

a difference between principle and power, though for practical purposes it is not necessary to consider the abstract phase of this difference. All that is necessary is to realize that the "I Am" directs the mind, and that the power of the mind directs and controls everything else in the human system.

It is the mind that occupies the throne but the "I Am" is the power behind the throne.

This being true, it becomes highly important to understand how the power of the mind should be used, but before we can understand the use of this power, we must learn what this power actually is. Generally speaking, we may say that the power of mind is the sum-total of all the forces of the mental world, including those forces that are employed in the process of thinking. The power of mind includes the power of the will, the power of desire, the power of feeling, and the power of thought. It includes conscious action in all its phases and subconscious action in all its phases; in fact, it includes anything and everything that is placed in action through the mind, by the mind or in the mind.

To use the power of the mind, the first essential is to direct every mental action toward the goal in view, and this direction must not be occasional, but constant. Most minds, however, do not apply this law. They think about a certain thing one moment, and about something else the next moment. At a certain hour their mental actions work along a certain line, and at the next hour those actions work along a different line. Sometimes the goal in view is one thing, and sometimes another, so the actions of the mind do not move constantly toward a certain definite goal, but are mostly scattered. We know, however, that every individual who is actually working himself steadily and surely toward the goal he has in view, invariably directs all the power of his thought upon that goal. In his mind not a single mental action is thrown away, not a single mental force wasted. All the power that is in him is being directed to work for what he wishes to accomplish, and the reason that every power responds in this way is because he is not thinking of one thing now and something else the next moment. He is thinking all the time of what he wishes to attain and achieve. The full power of mind is turned upon that object, and as mind is the ruling power, the full power of all his other forces will tend to work for the same object.

In using the power of mind as well as all the other forces we possess, the first question to answer is what we really want, or what we really want to accomplish; and when this question is answered, the one thing that is wanted should be fixed so clearly in thought that it can be seen by the mind's eye every minute. But the majority do not know what they really want. They may have some vague desire, but they have not determined clearly, definitely and positively what they really want, and this is one of the principal causes of failure. So long as we do not know definitely what we want, our forces will be scattered, and so long as our forces are scattered, we will accomplish but little, or fail entirely. When we know what we want, however, and proceed to work for it with all the power and ability that is in us, we may rest assured that we will get it. When we direct the power of thinking, the power of will, the power of mental action, the power of desire, the power of ambition, in fact, all the power we possess on the one thing we want, on the one goal we desire to reach, it is not difficult to understand why success in a greater and greater measure must be realized.

To illustrate this subject further, we will suppose that you have a certain ambition and continue to concentrate your thought and the power of your mind upon that ambition every minute for an indefinite period, with no cessation whatever. The result will be that you will gradually and surely train all the forces within you to work for the realization of that ambition, and in the course of time, the full capacity of your entire mental system will be applied in working for that particular thing.

On the other hand, suppose you do as most people do under average circumstances. Suppose, after you have given your ambition a certain amount of thought, you come to the conclusion that possibly you might succeed better along another line. Then you begin to direct the power of your mind along that other line. Later on, you come to the conclusion that there is still another channel through which you might succeed, and you proceed accordingly to direct your mind upon this third ambition. Then what will happen? Simply this: You will make three good beginnings, but in every case you will stop before you have accomplished anything. There are thousands of capable men and women, however, who make this mistake every year of their lives. The full force of their mental system is directed upon a certain ambition only for a short time; then it is directed elsewhere. They never continue long enough along any particular line to secure results from their efforts, and therefore results are never secured.

Then there are other minds who give most of their attention to a certain ambition and succeed fairly well, but give the rest of their attention to a number of minor ambitions that have no particular importance. Thus they are using only a fraction of their power in a way that will tell. The rest of it is thrown away along a number of lines through which nothing is gained. But in this age high efficiency is demanded everywhere in the world's work, and any one who wants to occupy a place that will satisfy his ambition and desire, cannot afford to waste even a small part of the power he may possess. He needs it all along the line of his leading ambition, and therefore should not permit counter attractions to occupy his mind for a moment.

If you have a certain ambition or a certain desire, think about that ambition at all times. Keep that ambition before your mind constantly, and do not hesitate to make your ambition as high as possible. The higher you aim, the greater will be your achievements, though that does not necessarily mean that you will realize your highest aims as fully as you have pictured them in your mind; but the fact is that those who have low aims, usually realize what is even below their aims, while those who have high aims usually realize very nearly, if not fully, what their original ambition calls for. The principle is to direct the power of mind upon the very highest, the very largest and the very greatest mental conception of that which we intend to achieve. The first essential therefore, is to direct the full power of mind and thought upon the goal in view, and to continue to direct the mind in that manner every minute, regardless of circumstances or conditions.

The second essential is to make every mental action positive. When we desire certain things or when we think of certain things we wish to attain or achieve, the question should be if our mental attitudes at the time are positive or negative. To answer this we only have to remember that every positive action always goes toward that which receives its attention, while a negative action always retreats. A positive action is an action that you feel when you realize that every force in your entire system is pushed forward, so to speak, and that it is passing through what may be termed an expanding and enlarging state of feeling or consciousness. The positive attitude of mind is also indicated by the feeling of a firm, determined fullness throughout the nervous system. When every nerve feels full, strong and determined, you are in the positive attitude, and whatever you may do at the time will produce results along the line of your desire or your ambition. When you are in a positive state of mind you are never nervous or disturbed, you are never agitated or strenuous; in fact, the more positive you are the deeper your calmness and the better your control over your entire system.

The positive man is not one who rushes helter-skelter here and there regardless of judgment or constructive action, but one who is absolutely calm and controlled under every circumstance, and yet so thoroughly full of energy that every atom in his being is ready, under every circumstance, to accomplish and achieve. This energy is not permitted to act, however, until the proper time arrives, and then its action goes directly to the goal in view.

The positive mind is always in harmony with itself, while the negative mind is always out of harmony, and thereby loses the greater part of its power. Positiveness always means strength stored up, power held in the system under perfect control, until the time of action; and during the time of action directed constructively under the same perfect control. In the positive mind, all the actions of the mental system are working in harmony and are being fully directed toward the object in view, while in the negative mind, those same actions are scattered, restless, nervous, disturbed, moving here and there, sometimes under direction, but most of the time not. That the one should invariably succeed is therefore just as evident as that the other should invariably fail. Scattered energy cannot do otherwise but fail, while positively directed energy simply must succeed. A positive mind is like a powerful stream of water that is gathering volume and force from hundreds of tributaries all along its course. The further on it goes the greater its power, until when it reaches its goal, that power is simply immense. A negative mind, however, would be something like a stream, that the further it flows the more divisions it makes, until, when it reaches its goal, instead of being one powerful stream, it has become a hundred small, weak, shallow streams.

To develop positiveness it is necessary to cultivate those qualities that constitute positiveness. Make it a point to give your whole attention to what you want to accomplish, and give that attention firmness, calmness and determination. Try to give depth to every desire until you feel as if all the powers of your system were acting, not on the surface, but from the greater world within. As this attitude is cultivated, positiveness will become more and more distinct, until you can actually feel yourself gaining power and prestige. And the effect will not only be noticed in your own ability to better direct and apply your talents, but others will discover the change. Accordingly, those who are looking for men of power, men who can do things, will look to you as the one to occupy the position that has to be filled.

Positiveness therefore, not only gives you the ability to make a far better use of the forces you possess, but it also gives you personality, that much admired something that will most surely cause you to be selected where men of power are needed. The world does not care for negative personalities. Such personalities look weak and empty, and are usually ignored, but everybody is attracted to a positive personality; and it is the positive personality that is always given the preference. Nor is this otherwise but right, because the positive personality has better use of his power, and therefore is able to act with greater efficiency wherever he is called upon to act.

The third essential in the right use of the mind is to make every mental action constructive, and a constructive mental action is one that is based upon a deep seated desire to develop, to increase, to achieve, to attain— in brief, to become larger and greater, and to do something of far greater worth than has been done before. If you will cause every mental action you entertain to have that feeling, constructiveness will soon become second nature to your entire mental system; that is, all the forces of your mind will begin to become building forces, and will continue to build you up along any line through which you may desire to act.

Inspire your mind constantly with a building desire, and make this de- sire so strong that every part of your system will constantly feel that it wants to become greater, more capable and more efficient. An excellent practice in this connection is to try to enlarge upon all your ideas of things whenever you have spare moments for real thought. This practice will tend to produce a growing tendency in every process of your thinking. Another good prac- tice is to inspire every mental action with more ambition. We cannot have too much ambition. We may have too much aimless ambition, but we can- not have too much real constructive ambition. If your ambition is very strong, and is directed toward something definite, every action of your mind, every action of your personality, and every action of your faculties will become constructive; that is, all those actions will be inspired by the tre- mendous force of your ambition to work for the realization of that ambition.

Never permit restless ambition. Whenever you feel the force of ambition direct your mind at once in a calm, determined manner upon that which you really want to accomplish in life. Make this a daily practice, and you will steadily train all your faculties and powers not only to work for the realization of that ambition, but become more and more efficient in that direction. Ere long your forces and faculties will be sufficiently competent to accomplish what you want.

In the proper use of the mind therefore these three essentials should be applied constantly and thoroughly. First, direct all the powers of mind, all the powers of thought, and all your thinking upon the goal you have in view. Second, train every mental action to be deeply and calmly positive. Third, train every mental action to be constructive, to be filled with a building spirit, to be inspired with a ceaseless desire to develop the greater, to achieve the greater, to attain the greater. When you have acquired these three, you will begin to use your forces in such a way that results must fol- low. You will begin to move forward steadily and surely, and you will be constantly gaining ground. Your mind will have become like the stream mentioned above. It will gather volume and force as it moves on and on, until finally that volume will be great enough to remove any obstacle in its way, and that force powerful enough to do anything you may have in view.

In order to apply these three essentials in the most effective manner, there are several misuses of the mind that must be avoided. Avoid the forceful, the aggressive, and the domineering attitudes, and do not permit your mind to become intense, unless it is under perfect control. Never attempt to control or influence others in any way whatever. You will seldom succeed in that manner, and when you do, the success will be temporary; besides, such a practice always weakens your mind. Do not turn the power of your mind upon others, but turn it upon yourself in such a way that it will make you stronger, more positive, more capable, and more efficient, and as you develop in this manner, success must come of itself. There is only one way by which you can influence others legitimately, and that is through the giving of instruction, but in that case, there is no desire to influence. You desire simply to impart knowledge and information, and you exercise a most desirable influence without desiring to do so.

A great many men and women, after discovering the immense power of mind, have come to the conclusion that they might change circumstances by exercising mental power upon those circumstances in some mysterious manner, but such a practice means nothing but a waste of energy. The way to control circumstances is to control the forces within yourself to make a greater man of yourself, and as you become greater and more competent, you will naturally gravitate into better circumstances. In this connection, we should remember that like attracts like. If you want that which is better, make yourself better. If you want to realize the ideal, make yourself more ideal. If you want better friends, make yourself a better friend. If you want to associate with people of worth, make yourself more worthy. If you want to meet that which is agreeable, make yourself more agreeable. If you want to enter conditions and circumstances that are more pleasing, make yourself more pleasing. In brief, whatever you want, produce that something in yourself, and you will positively gravitate toward the corresponding conditions in the external world. But to improve yourself along those lines, it is necessary to apply for that purpose, all the power you possess. You cannot afford to waste any of it, and every misuse of the mind will waste power.

Avoid all destructive attitudes of the mind, such an anger, hatred, malice, envy, jealousy, revenge, depression, discouragement, disappointment, worry, fear, and so on. Never antagonize, never resist what is wrong, and never try to get even. Make the best use of your own talent and the best that is in store for you will positively come your way. When others seem to take advantage of you, do not retaliate by trying to take advantage of them. Use your power in improving yourself, so that you can do better and better work. That is how you are going to win in the race. Later on, those who tried to take advantage of you will be left in the rear. Remember, those who are dealing unjustly with you or with anybody are misusing their mind. They are therefore losing their power, and will, in the course of time, begin to lose ground; but if you, in the mean time, are turning the full power of your mind to good account, you will not only gain more power, but you will soon begin to gain ground. You will gain and continue to gain in the long run, while others who have been misusing their minds will lose mostly everything in the long run. That is how you are going to win, and win splendidly regardless of ill treatment or opposition.

A great many people imagine that they can promote their own success by trying to prevent the success of others, but it is one of the greatest delusions in the world. If you want to promote your own success as thoroughly as your capacity will permit, take an active interest in the success of everybody, because this will not only keep your mind in the success attitude and cause you to think success all along the line, but it will enlarge your mind so as to give you a greater and better grasp upon the fields of success. If you are trying to prevent the success of others, you are acting in the destructive attitude, which sooner or later will react on others, but if you are taking an active interest in the success of everybody, you are entertaining only constructive attitudes, and these will sooner or later accumulate in your own mind to add volume and power to the forces of success that you are building up in yourself.

In this connection, we may well ask why those succeed who do succeed, why so many succeed only in part, and why so many fail utterly. These are questions that occupy the minds of most people, and hundreds of answers have been given, but there is only one answer that goes to rock bottom. Those people who fail, and who continue to fail all along the line, fail because the power of their minds is either in a habitual negative state, or is always misdirected. If the power of mind is not working positively and constructively for a certain goal, you are not going to succeed. If your mind is not positive, it is negative, and negative minds float with the stream. We must remember that we are in the midst of all kinds of circumstances, some of which are for us and some of which are against us, and we will either have to make our own way or drift, and if we drift we go wherever the stream goes. But most of the streams of human life are found to float in the world of the ordinary and the inferior. Therefore, if you drift, you will drift with the inferior, and your goal will be failure.

When we analyze the minds of people who have failed, we invariably find that they are either negative, non-constructive or aimless. Their forces are scattered, and what is in them is seldom applied constructively. There is an emptiness about their personality that indicates negativeness. There is an uncertainty in their facial expression that indicates the absence of definite ambition. There is nothing of a positive, determined nature going on in their mental world. They have not taken definite action along any line. They are dependent upon fate and circumstances. They are drifting with some stream, and that they should accomplish little if anything is inevitable. This does not mean, however, that their mental world is necessarily unproductive; in fact, those very minds are in many instances immensely rich with possibilities. The trouble is, those possibilities continue to be dormant, and what is in them is not being brought forth and trained for definite action or actual results.

What those people should do, is to proceed at once to comply with the three essentials mentioned above, and before many months there will be a turn in the lane. They will soon cease to drift, and will then begin to make their own life, their own circumstances, and their own future.

In this connection, it is well to remember that negative people and non-constructive minds never attract that which is helpful in their circumstances. The more you drift, the more people you meet who also drift, while on the other hand, when you begin to make your own life and become positive, you begin to meet more positive people and more constructive circumstances. This explains why "God helps them that help themselves." When you begin to help yourself, which means to make the best of what is in yourself, you begin to attract to yourself more and more of those helpful things that may exist all about you. In other words, constructive forces attract constructive forces; positive forces attract positive forces. A growing mind attracts elements and forces that help to promote growth, and people who are determined to make more and more of themselves, are drawn more and more into circumstances through which they will find the opportunity to make more of themselves. And this law works not only in connection with the external world, but also the internal world. When you begin to make a positive determined use of those powers in yourself that are already in positive action, you draw forth into action powers within you that have been dormant, and as this process continues, you will find that you will accumulate volume, capacity and power in your mental world, until you finally become a mental giant.

As you begin to grow and become more capable, you will find that you will meet better and better opportunities, not only opportunities for promoting external success, but opportunities for further building yourself up along the lines of ability, capacity and talent. You thus demonstrate the law that "Nothing succeeds like success," and "To him that hath shall be given." And here it is well to remember that it is not necessary to possess external things in the beginning to be counted among them "that hath." It is only necessary in the beginning to possess the interior riches; that is, to take control of what is in you, and proceed to use it positively with a definite goal in view. He who has control of his own mind has already great riches. He has sufficient wealth to be placed among those who have. He is already successful, and if he continues as he has begun, his success will soon appear in the external world. Thus the wealth that existed at first in the internal only will take shape and form in the external. This is a law that is unfailing, and there is not a man or woman on the face of the earth that cannot apply it with the most satisfying results.

The reason why so many fail is thus found in the fact that they do not fully and constructively apply the forces and powers they possess, and the reason why so many succeed only to a slight degree is found in the fact that only a small fraction of their power is applied properly. But any one can learn the full and proper use of all that is in him by applying faithfully the three essentials mentioned above. The reason why those succeed who do succeed is found in the fact that a large measure of their forces and powers is applied according to those three essentials, and as those essentials can be applied by any one, even to the most perfect degree, there is no reason why all should not succeed.

Sometimes we meet people who have only ordinary ability, but who are very successful. Then we meet others who have great ability but who are not successful, or who succeed only to a slight degree. At first we see no explanation, but when we understand the cause of success as well as the cause of failure, the desired explanation is easily found. The man with ordinary ability, if he complies with the three essentials necessary to the right use of mind, will naturally succeed, though if he had greater ability, his success would of course become greater in proportion. But the man who has great ability, yet does not apply the three essentials necessary to the right use of mind, cannot succeed.

The positive and constructive use of the power of mind, with a definite goal in view will invariably result in advancement, attainment and achievement, but if we wish to use that power in its full capacity, the action of the mind must be deep. In addition to the right use of the mind, we must also learn the full use of mind, and as the full use implies the use of the whole mind, the deeper mental fields and forces, as well as the usual mental fields and forces, it is necessary to understand the subconscious as well as the conscious.

When you think of yourself do not think of that part of yourself that appears on the surface. That part is the smaller part and the lesser should not be pictured in mind. Think of your larger self, the immense subconscious self that is limitless both in power and in possibility.

Believe in yourself but not simply in a part of yourself. Give constant recognition to all that is in you and in that all have full faith and confidence.

Give the bigger man on the inside full right of way. Believe thoroughly in your greater interior self. Know that you have something within you that is greater than any obstacle, circumstance or difficulty that you can possibly meet. Then in the full faith in this greater something proceed with your work.

CHAPTER IV

THE FORCES OF THE SUBCONSCIOUS

In using the power of the mind, the deeper the action of thought, will and desire, the greater the result. Accordingly, all mental action to be strong and effective, must be subconscious; that is, it must act in the field of the mental undercurrent as it is in this field that things are actually done. Those forces that play upon the surface of mind may be changed and turned from their course by almost any outside influence, and their purpose thus averted. But this is never true of the undercurrents. Anything that gets into the mental undercurrents will be seen through to a finish, regardless of external circumstances or conditions; and it is with difficulty that the course of these currents is changed when once they have been placed in full positive action. It is highly important therefore that we permit nothing to take action in these undercurrents that we do not wish to encourage and promote; and for the same reason, it is equally important that we cause everything to take action in these currents that we do wish to encourage and promote.

These undercurrents, however, act only through the subconscious, and are controlled by the subconscious. In consequence, it is the subconscious which we must understand and act upon if we want the power of mind to work with full capacity and produce the greatest measure possible of the results desired.

In defining the subconscious mind, it is first necessary to state that it is not a separate mind. There are not two minds. There is only one mind in man, but it has two phases—the conscious and the subconscious. We may define the conscious as the upper side of the mentality, and the subconscious as the under side. The subconscious may also be defined as a vast mental field permeating the entire objective personality, thereby filling every atom of the personality through and through. We shall come nearer the truth, however, if we think of the subconscious as a finer mental force, having distinct powers, functions and possibilities, or as a great mental sea of life energy and power, the force and capacity or which has never been measured.

The conscious mind is on the surface, and therefore we act through the conscious mind whenever mental action moves through the surface of thought, will or desire, but whenever we enter into deeper mental action and sound the vast depths of this underlying mental life we touch the subconscious, though we must remember that we do not become oblivious to the conscious every time we touch the subconscious, as the two are inseparably united.

That the two phases of the mind are related can be well illustrated by comparing the conscious mind with a sponge, and the subconscious with the water permeating the sponge. We know that every fiber of the sponge is in touch with the water, and in the same manner, every part of the conscious mind, as well as every atom in the personality is in touch with the subconscious, and completely filled, through and through, with the life and the force of the subconscious.

It has frequently been stated that the subconscious mind occupies the Fourth Dimension of space, and though this is a matter that cannot be exactly demonstrated, nevertheless, the more we study the nature of the subconscious, as well as the Fourth Dimension, the more convinced we become that the former occupies the field of the latter. This, however, is simply a matter that holds interest in philosophical investigation. Whether the subconscious occupies the Fourth Dimension or some other dimension of space will make no difference as to its practical value.

In order to understand the subconscious, it is well at the outset to familiarize ourselves with its natural functions, as this will convince ourselves of the fact that we are not dealing with something that is beyond normal, mental action. The subconscious mind controls all the natural functions of the body, such as the circulation, respiration, digestion, assimilation, physical repair, etc. It also controls all the involuntary actions of the body, and all those actions of mind and body that continue their natural movements without direction from the will. The subconscious perpetuates characteristics, traits, and qualities that are peculiar to individuals, species or races. What is called heredity therefore is altogether a subconscious process. The same is true of what is called second nature. Whenever anything has been repeated a sufficient number of times to have become habitual, it becomes second nature, or rather a subconscious action. It frequently happens, however, that a conscious action may become a subconscious action without repetition, and thus becomes second nature almost at once.

When we examine the nature of the subconscious, we find that it responds to almost anything the conscious mind may desire or direct, though it is usually necessary for the conscious mind to express its desire upon the subconscious for some time before the desired response is secured. The subconscious is a most willing servant, and is so competent that thus far we have failed to find a single thing along mental lines that it will not or cannot do. It submits readily to almost any kind of training, and will do practically anything that it is directed to do, whether the thing is to our advantage or not.

In this connection, it is interesting to learn that there are a number of things in the human system usually looked upon as natural, and inevitable, that are simply the results of misdirected subconscious training in the past. We frequently speak of human weaknesses as natural, but weakness is never natural. Although it may appear, it is invariably the result of imperfect subconscious training. It is never natural to go wrong, but it is natural to go right, and the reason why is simple. Every right action is in harmony with natural law, while every wrong action is a violation of natural law.

It has also been stated that the aging process is natural, but modern science has demonstrated that it is not natural for a person to age at sixty, seventy, or eighty years. The fact that the average person does manifest nearly all the conditions of old age at those periods of time, or earlier, simply proves that the subconscious mind has been trained through many generations to produce old age at sixty, seventy, eighty or ninety, as the case may be; and the subconscious always does what it has been trained to do. It can just as readily be trained, however, to produce greater physical strength and greater mental capacity at ninety than we possess at thirty or forty. It can also be trained to possess the same virile youth at one hundred as the healthiest man or woman of twenty may possess. In fact, practically every condition that appears in the mind, the character and the personality of the human race, is the result of what the subconscious mind has been directed to do during past generations. It is therefore evident that as the subconscious is directed to produce different conditions in mind, character, and personality— conditions that are in perfect harmony with the natural law of human development, such conditions will invariably appear in the race. Thus we understand how a new race or a superior race may appear upon this planet.

There are a great many people who are disturbed over the fact that they have inherited certain characteristics or ailments from their parents, but what they have inherited is simply subconscious tendencies in that direction, and those tendencies can be changed absolutely. What we inherit from our parents can be eliminated so completely that no one would ever know it had been there. In like manner, we can improve so decidedly upon the good qualities that we have inherited from our parents that any similarity between parent and child in those respects would disappear completely. The subconscious mind is always ready, willing and competent to make any change for the better in our physical or mental make-up that we may desire, though it does not work in some miraculous manner, nor does it usually produce results instantaneously. In most instances its actions are gradual, but they invariably produce the results intended if the proper training continues.

The subconscious mind will respond to the directions of the conscious mind so long as those directions do not interfere with the absolute laws of nature. The subconscious never moves against natural law, but it has the power to so use natural law that improvement along any line can be secured. It will reproduce in mind and body any condition that is thoroughly impressed and deeply felt by the conscious mind. It will bring forth undesirable conditions when directed to produce such conditions, and it will bring forth health, strength, youth and added power when so directed. If you continue to desire a strong physical body, and fully expect the subconscious to build for you a stronger body, you will find that this will gradually or finally be done. You will steadily grow in physical strength. If you continue to desire greater ability along a certain line and expect the subconscious to produce greater mental power along that line, your ability will increase as expected, but it is necessary in this connection to be persistent and persevering. To become enthusiastic about these things for a few days is not sufficient. It is when we apply these laws persistently for weeks, months and years that we find the results to be, not only what we expected, but frequently far greater.

Everything has a tendency to grow in the subconscious. Whenever an impression or desire is placed in the subconscious, it has a tendency to become larger and therefore the bad becomes worse when it enters the subconscious, while the good becomes better. We have the power, however, to exclude the bad from the subconscious and cause only the good to enter that immense field. Whenever you say that you are tired and permit that feeling to sink into the subconscious, you will almost at once feel more tired. Whenever you feel sick and permit that feeling to enter the subconscious, you always feel worse. The same is true when you are weak, sad, disappointed or depressed. If you let those feelings sink into your subconscious, they will become worse. On the other hand, when we feel happy, strong, persistent and determined, and permit those feelings to enter the subconscious, we always feel better. It is therefore highly important that we positively refuse to give in to any undesirable feeling. Whenever we give in to any feeling, it becomes subconscious, and if that feeling is bad, it becomes worse; but so long as we keep undesirable feelings on the outside, so to speak, we will hold them at bay, until nature can readjust itself or gather reserve force and thus put them out of the way altogether.

We should never give in to sickness, though that does not mean that we should continue to work as hard as usual when not feeling well, or cause mind and body to continue in their usual activities. When we find it necessary, we should give ourselves a complete rest, but we should never give in to the feeling of sickness. The rest that may be taken will help the body to recuperate and when it does the threatening ailment will disappear. When you feel tired or depressed, do not admit it, but turn your attention at once upon something that is extremely interesting—something that will completely turn your mind toward the pleasing, the more desirable or the ideal. Persist in feeling the way you want to feel, and permit only wholesome feelings to enter the subconscious. Thus wholesome feelings will live and grow, and after awhile your power to feel good at all times will have become so strong that you can put out of the way any adverse feeling that may threaten at any time.

In this connection, we may mention something that holds more than usual interest. It has been stated by those who are in a position to know, that no one dies until he gives up; that is, gives in to those adverse conditions that are at work in his system, tending to produce physical death. So long as he refuses to give in to those conditions, he continues to live. How long a person could refuse to give in even under the most adverse circumstances is a question, but one thing is certain, that thousands and thousands of deaths could be prevented every year if the patient in each case refused to give in. In many instances, the forces of life and death are almost equally balanced. Which one is going to win depends upon the mental attitude of the patient. If he gives over his mind and his will to the side of the forces of life, those forces are most likely to win, but if he permits the mind to act with death, the forces of death are most certain to win. So long as he continues to persist in living, refusing absolutely to give in to death, he is throwing the full power of mind, thought and will on the side of life. He thereby increases the power of life, and he may increase that power sufficiently to overcome death. Again we say that it is a question how many times a person could overcome death by this method, but the fact remains that this method alone can save life repeatedly in the majority of cases; and all will admit after further thought on this subject that the majority will be very large. This is a method, therefore, that deserves the best of attention in every sickroom. No person should be permitted to die until all available methods for prolonging life have been exhausted, and this last mentioned method is one that will accomplish far more than most of us may expect; and its secret is found in the fact that whenever we give in to any condition or action, it becomes stronger, due to the tendency of the subconscious to enlarge, increase and magnify whatever it receives. Give in to the forces of death, and the subconscious mind will increase the powers of that force. Give in to the forces of life, and the subconscious mind will increase the power of your life and you will continue to live.

Concerning the general possibilities of the subconscious, we should remember that every faculty has a subconscious side, and that it becomes larger and more competent as this subconscious side is developed. This being true, it is evident that ability and genius might be developed in any mind even to a remarkable degree, as no limit has been found to the subconscious in any of its forces. In like manner, every cell in your body has a subconscious side, and therefore, if the subconscious side of the personality were developed, we can realize what improvement would become possible in that field. There is a subconscious side to all the faculties in human nature, and if these were developed, we understand how man could become ideal, even far beyond our present dreams of a new race.

It is not well however to give the major portion of our attention to future possibilities. It is what is possible now that we should aim to develop and apply, and present possibilities indicate that improvement along any line, whether it be in working capacity, ability, health, happiness and character, can be secured without fail if the subconscious is properly directed.

To direct the subconscious along any line, it is only necessary to desire what you want and to make those desires so deep and so persistent that they become positive forces in the subconscious field. When you feel that you want a certain thing give in to that feeling and also make that feeling positive. Give in to your ambitions in the same manner, and also to every desire that you wish to realize. Let your thought of all those things that you wish to increase in any line get into your system, because whatever gets into your system, the subconscious will proceed to develop, work out and express.

In using the subconscious, we should remember that we are not using something that is separated from normal life. The difference between the man who makes scientific use of the subconscious and the one who does not, is simply this; the latter employs only a small part of his mind, while the former employs the whole of his mind. And this explains why those who employ the subconscious intelligently have greater working capacity, greater ability and greater endurance. In consequence they sometimes do the work of two or three men, and do excellent work in addition. To train the subconscious for practical action is therefore a matter of common sense. It is a matter of refusing to cultivate only a small corner of your mental field when you can cultivate the entire field.

When you have made up your mind what you want to do, say to yourself a thousand times a day that you will do it. The best way will soon open. You will have the opportunity you desire.

If you would be greater in the future than you are now, be all that you can be now. He who is his best develops the power to be better. He who lives his ideals is creating a life that actually is ideal.

There is nothing in your life that you cannot modify, change or improve when you learn to regulate your thought.

Our destiny is not mapped out for us by some exterior power; we map it out for ourselves. What we think and do in the present determines what shall happen to us in the future.

CHAPTER V

TRAINING THE SUBCONSCIOUS FOR SPECIAL RESULTS

When we proceed to train the subconscious along any line, or for special results, we must always comply with the following law: The subconscious responds to the impressions, the suggestions, the desires, the expectations and the directions of the conscious mind, provided that the conscious touches the subconscious at the time. The secret therefore is found in the two phases of the mind touching each other as directions are being made; and to cause the conscious to touch the subconscious, it is necessary to feel conscious action penetrating your entire interior system; that is, you should feel at the time that you are living not simply on the surface, but through and through. At such times, the mind should be calm and in perfect poise, and should be conscious of that finer, greater something within you that has greater depth than mere surface existence.

When you wish to direct the subconscious to produce physical health, first picture in your mind a clear idea of perfect health. Try to see this idea with the mind's eye, and then try to feel the meaning of this idea with consciousness, and while you are in the attitude of that feeling, permit your thought and your attention to pass into that deep-quiet, serene state of being wherein you can feel the mental idea of wholeness and health entering into the very life of every atom in your system. In brief, try to feel perfectly healthy in your mind and then let that feeling sink into your entire physical system. Whenever you feel illness coming on, you can nip it in the bud by this simple method, because if the subconscious is directed to produce more health, added forces of health will soon begin to come forth from within, and put out of the way, so to speak, any disorder or ailment that may be on the verge of getting a foothold in the body. Always remember that whatever is impressed on the subconscious will after a while be expressed from the subconscious into the personality; and when the physical conditions that you wish to remove are only slight, enough subconscious power can be aroused to restore immediate order, harmony and wholeness. When the condition you wish to remove has continued for some time, however, repeated efforts may be required to cause the subconscious to act in the matter. But one thing is certain, that if you continue to direct the subconscious to remove that condition, it positively will be removed.

The subconscious does not simply possess the power to remove undesirable conditions from the physical or mental state. It can also produce those better conditions that we may want, and develop further those desirable conditions that we already possess. To apply the law for this purpose, deeply desire those conditions that you do want, and have a very clear idea in your mind as to what you want those conditions to be. In giving the subconscious directions for anything desired in our physical or mental makeup, we should always have improvement in mind, as the subconscious always does the best work when we are thoroughly filled with the desire to do better. If we want health, we should direct the subconscious to produce more and more health. If we want power, we should direct the subconscious not simply to give us a great deal or a certain amount of power, but to give us more and more power. In this manner, we shall secure results from the very beginning. If we try to train the subconscious to produce a certain amount, it might be some time before that amount can be developed. In the meantime, we should meet disappointment and delay, but if our desire is for steady increase along all lines from where we stand now, we shall be able to secure, first, a slight improvement and then added improvement to be followed with still greater improvement, until we finally reach the highest goal we have in view.

No effort should be made to destroy those habits or qualities that we may not desire. Whatever we think about deeply or intensely, the subconscious will take up and develop further. Therefore, if we think about our failings, shortcomings or bad habits, the subconscious will take them up and give them more life and activity than they ever had before. If there is anything in our nature therefore that we wish to change, we should simply proceed to build up what we want and forget completely what we wish to eliminate. When the good develops the bad disappears. When the greater is built up, the lesser will either be removed or completely transformed and combined with the greater.

That the subconscious can increase your ability and your capacity is a fact that is readily demonstrated. Whenever the subconscious mind is aroused, mental power and working capacity are invariably increased, some times to such an extent that the individual seems to be possessed with a superhuman power. We all know of instances where great things were accomplished simply through the fact that the individual was carried on and on by an immense power within him that seemed to be distinct from himself and greater than himself; but it was simply the greater powers of the subconscious that were aroused and placed in positive, determined action. These instances, however, need not be exceptions. Any man, under any circumstances, can so increase the power of his mind, his thought and his will as to be actually carried away with the same tremendous force; that is, the power within him becomes so strong that he is actually pushed through to the goal he has in view regardless of circumstances, conditions or obstacles.

This being true, we should arouse the subconscious no matter what it is we have to do. No day is complete unless we begin that day by making alive everything that we possess in our whole mind, conscious and subconscious. Whenever you have work to do at some future time, direct the subconscious to increase your ability and capacity at the time specified, and fully expect the desired increase to be secured. If you want new ideas on certain studies or new plans in your work, direct the subconscious to produce them and you will get them without fail. The moment the direction is given, the subconscious will go to work along that line; and in this connection, we should remember that though we may fail to get the idea desired through the conscious mind alone, it is quite natural that we should get it when we also enlist the subconscious, because the whole mind is much greater, far more capable and far more resourceful than just a small part of the mind.

When demands are urgent, the subconscious responds more readily, especially when feelings at the time are also very deep. When you need certain results, say that you must have them, and put your whole energy into the "must." Whatever you make up your mind that you must do, you will in some manner get the power to do.

There are a number of instances on record where people were carried through certain events by what seemed to be a miraculous power, but the cause of it all was simply this—that they had to do it, and whatever you have to do, the subconscious mind will invariably give you the power to do. The reason for this is found in the fact that when you feel that you must do a thing and that you have to do it, your desires are so strong and so deep that they go into the very depths of the subconscious and thus call to action the full power of that vast interior realm.

If you have some great ambition that you wish to realize, direct the subconscious several times each day and each night before you go to sleep, to work out the necessary ways and means; and if you are determined, those ways and means will be forthcoming. But here it is necessary to remember that we must concentrate on the one thing wanted. If your mind scatters, sometimes giving attention to one ambition and sometimes to another, you will confuse the subconscious and the ways and means desired will not be secured. Make your ambition a vital part of your life, and try to feel the force of that ambition every single moment of your existence. If you do this your ambition will certainly be realized. It may take a year, it may take five years, it may take ten years or more, but your ambition will be realized. This being true, no one need feel disturbed about the future, because if he actually knows what he wants to accomplish and trains the subconscious to produce the idea, the methods, the necessary ability and the required capacity, all these things will be secured.

If there is any condition from which you desire to secure emancipation, direct the subconscious to give you that information through which you may find a way out. The subconscious can. We all remember the saying, "Where there is a will there is a way," and it is true, because when you actually will to do a certain thing, the power of the mind becomes so deep and so strong along that line, that the entire subconscious mind is put to work on the case, so to speak; and under such circumstances, the way will always be found. When you put your whole mind, conscious and subconscious, to work on any problem, you will find the solution. If there is any talent that you wish to develop further, direct the subconscious every day, and as frequently as possible, to enlarge the inner life of that talent and to increase its brilliancy and power.

When you are about to undertake anything new, do not proceed until you have submitted the proposition to the subconscious, and here we find the real value of "sleeping over" new plans before we finally decide. When we go to sleep, we go more completely into the subconscious, and those ideas that we take with us when we go to sleep, especially those that engage our serious attention at the time, are completely turned over, so to speak, during the period of sleep, and examined from all points of view. Sometimes it is necessary to take those ideas into the subconscious a number of times when we go to sleep, as well as to submit the matter to the subconscious many times in the day during the waking state, but if we persevere, the right answer will finally be secured. The whole mind, conscious and subconscious, does possess the power to solve any problem that may come up, or provide the necessary ways and means through which we can carry out or finish anything we have undertaken.

Here, as elsewhere, practice makes perfect. The more you train the subconscious to work with you, the easier it becomes to get the subconscious to respond to your directions, and therefore the subconscious mind should be called into action, no matter what comes up, in other words make it a practice to use your whole mind, conscious and subconscious, at all times, not only in large matters, but in all matters. Begin by recognizing the subconscious in all thought and in all action. Think that it can do what you have been told it can do, and eliminate doubt absolutely. Take several moments every day and suggest to the subconscious what you want to have done. Be thoroughly sincere in this matter; be determined; have unbounded faith, and you can expect results; but do not permit the mind to become wrought up when giving directions. Always be calm and deeply poised when thinking out or suggesting to the subconscious, and it is especially important that you be deeply calm before you go to sleep. Do not permit any idea, suggestion or expectation to enter the subconscious unless it is something that you actually want developed or worked out, and here we should remember that every idea, desire or state of mind that is deeply felt will enter the subconscious. When there are no results, do not lose faith. You know that the cause of the failure was the failure of the conscious to properly touch the subconscious at the time the directions were given, so therefore try again, giving your thought a deeper life and a more persistent desire.

Always be prepared to give these methods sufficient time. Some have remarkable results at once, while others secure no results for months; but whether you secure results as soon as you wish or not, continue to give your directions every day, fully expecting results. Be determined in every effort you may make in this direction, but do not be over-anxious. Make it a point to give special directions to the subconscious every day for the steady improvement of mind, character and personality along all lines. You cannot give the subconscious too much to do because its power is immense, and as far as we know, its capacity limitless. Every effort you may make to direct or train the subconscious, will bring its natural results in due time, provided you are always calm, well balanced, persistent, deeply poised and harmonious in all your thoughts and actions.

The Path to Greater Things

Dream constantly of the ideal; work ceaselessly to perfect the real.

Believe in yourself; believe in everybody; believe in all that has existence.

Give the body added strength; give the mind added brilliancy; give the soul added inspiration.

Do your best under every circumstance, and believe that every circumstance will give its best to you.

Live for the realization of more life and for the more efficient use of everything that proceeds from life.

Desire eternally what you want; expect eternally what you desire; and act always as if every expectation were coming true.

CHAPTER VI

THE POWER OF
SUBJECTIVE THOUGHT

The first important factor to consider in connection with the study of thought is that every thought does not possess power. In modern times, when thinking has been studied so closely a great many have come to the conclusion that every thought is itself a force and that it invariably produces certain definite results; but this is not true, and it is well, for if every thought had power we could not last very long as the larger part of ordinary human thinking is chaotic and destructive.

When we proceed to determine what kinds of thought have power and what kinds have not, we find two distinct forms. The one we call objective, the other subjective. Objective thought is the result of general thinking, such as reasoning, intellectual research, analysis, study, the process of recollection, mind-picturing where there is no feeling, and the usual activities of the intellect. In brief, any mental process that calls forth only the activities of the intellect is objective, and such thinking does not affect the conditions of mind and body to any extent; that is, it does not produce direct results corresponding to its own nature upon the system. It does not immediately affect your health, your happiness, your physical condition nor your mental condition. It may, however, affect these things in the long run, and for that reason must not be ignored.

Subjective thinking is any form of thinking or mind-picturing that has depth of feeling that goes beneath the surface in its action that moves through the undercurrents, that acts in and through the psychological field. Subjective thought is synonymous with the thought of the heart, and it is subjective thought that is referred to in the statement. "As a man thinketh in his heart so is he." Subjective thought proceeds from the very heart of mental existence; that is, it is always in contact with everything that is vital in life. It is always alive with feeling, and originates, so to speak, in the heart of the mind. The term "heart" in this connection has nothing to do with the physical organ by that name. The term "heart" is here used in its metalphysical sense. We speak of the heart of a great city, meaning thereby, the principal part of the city, or that part of the city where its most vital activities are taking place; likewise, the heart of the mind is the most vital realm of the mind, or the center of the mind, or the deeper activities of the mind as distinguished from the surface of the mind.

Subjective thinking being in the heart of the mind is therefore necessarily the product of the deepest mental life, and for this reason every subjective thought is a force. It will either work for you or against you, and has the power to produce direct effects upon mind or body, corresponding exactly with its own nature. But all thinking is liable to become subjective at times. All thoughts may sink into the deeper or vital realms of mind and thus become direct forces for good or ill. Therefore, all thinking should be scientific; that is, designed or produced with a definite object in view. All thought should be produced according to the laws of right thinking or constructive thinking. Though objective thinking usually produces no results whatever, nevertheless there are many objective thoughts that become subjective and it is the objective mind that invariably determines the nature of subjective thinking. Every thought therefore should have the right tendency, so that it may produce desirable results in case it becomes subjective, or may act in harmony with the objective mind whenever it is being employed in giving directions to the subjective.

In this connection, it is well to remember that subjective thinking invariably takes place in the subconscious mind, as the terms subjective and subconscious mean practically the same; though in speaking of thought, the term subjective is more appropriate in defining that form of thought that is deep, vital and alive, or that acts through the mental undercurrents.

To define scientific thinking, it may be stated that your thinking is scientific when your thought has a direct tendency to produce what you want, or when all the forces of your mind are working together for the purpose you desire to fulfil. Your thinking is unscientific when your thought has a tendency to produce what is detrimental, or when your mental forces are working against you.

To think scientifically, the first essential is to think only such thoughts and permit only such mental attitudes as you know to be in your favor; and the second essential is to make only such thoughts subjective. In other words, every thought should be right and every thought should be a force. When every thought is scientific, it will be right, and when every thought is subjective it will be a force. Positively refuse to think of what you do not wish to retain or experience. Think only of what you desire, and expect only what you desire, even when the very contrary seems to be coming into your life. Make it a point to have definite results in mind at all times. Permit no thinking to be aimless. Every aimless thought is time and energy wasted, while every thought that is inspired with a definite aim will help to realize that aim, and if all your thoughts are inspired with a definite aim, the whole power of your mind will be for you and will work with you in realizing what you have in view. That you should succeed is therefore assured, because there is enough power in your mind to realize your ambitions, provided all of that power is used in working for your ambitions. And in scientific thinking all the power of mind and thought is being caused to work directly and constantly for what you wish to attain and achieve.

To explain further the nature of scientific thinking, as well as unscientific thinking, it is well to take several well-known illustrations from real life. When things go wrong, people usually say, "That's always the way"; and though this may seem to be a harmless expression, nevertheless, the more you use that expression the more deeply you convince your mind that things naturally go wrong most of the time. When you train your mind to think that it is usual for things to go wrong, the forces of your mind will follow that trend of thinking, and will also go wrong; and for that reason it is perfectly natural that things in your life should go wrong more and more, because as the forces of your mind are going wrong, you will go wrong, and when you go wrong, those things that pertain to your life cannot possibly go right.

A great many people are constantly looking for the worst. They usually expect the worst to happen; though they may be cheerful on the surface, deep down in their heart they are constantly looking for trouble. The result is that their deeper mental currents will tend to produce trouble. If you are always looking for the worst, the forces of your mind will be turned in that direction, and therefore will become destructive. Those forces will tend to produce the very thing that you expect. At first they will simply confuse your mind and produce troubled conditions in your mental world; but this will in turn confuse your faculties, your reason and your judgment, so that you will make many mistakes; and he who is constantly making mistakes will certainly find the worst on many or all occasions.

When things go wrong, do not expect the wrong to appear again. Look upon it as an exception. Call it past and forget it. To be scientific under these circumstances, always look for the best. By constantly expecting the best, you will turn the different forces of your mind and thought to work for the best. Every power that is in you will have a higher and finer ideal upon which to turn its attention, and accordingly, results will be better, which is perfectly natural when your whole system is moving toward the better. A number of people have a habit of saying, "Something is always wrong"; but why should we not say instead, "Something is always right"? We would thereby express more of the truth and give our minds a more wholesome tendency. It is not true that something is always wrong. When we compare the wrong with the right, the wrong is always in the minority. However, it is the effect of such thinking upon the mind that we wish to avoid, whether the wrong be in our midst or not. When you think that there is always something wrong, your mind is more or less concentrated on the wrong, and will therefore create the wrong in your own mentality; but when you train yourself to think there is always something right, your mind will concentrate upon the right, and accordingly will create the right. And when the mind is trained to create the right it will not only produce right conditions within itself, but all thinking will tend to become right; and right thinking invariably leads to health, happiness, power and plenty.

The average person is in the habit of saying, "The older I get"; and he thereby calls the attention of his mind to the idea that he is getting older. In brief, he compels his mind to believe that he is getting older and older, and thereby directs the mind to produce more and more age. The true expression in this connection is, "The longer I live." This expression calls the mind's attention to the length of life, which will, in turn, tend to increase the power of that process in you that can prolong life. When people reach the age of sixty or seventy, they usually speak of "the rest of my days," thus implying the idea that there are only a few more days remaining. The mind is thereby directed to finish life in a short period of time, and accordingly, all the forces of the mind will proceed to work for the speedy termination of personal existence. The correct expression is "from now on," as that leads thought into the future indefinitely without impressing the mind with any end whatever.

We frequently hear the expression, "I can never do anything right," and it is quite simple to understand that such a mode of thought would train the mind to act below its true ability and capacity. If you are fully convinced that you can never do anything right, it will become practically impossible for you to do anything right at any time, but on the other hand, if you continue to think, "I am going to do everything better and better," it is quite natural that your entire mental system should be inspired and trained to do things better and better. Hundreds of similar expressions could be mentioned, but we are all familiar with them, and from the comments made above, any one will realize that such expressions are obstacles in our way, no matter what we may do.

In right thinking the purpose should be never to use any expression that conveys to your mind what you do not want, or what is detrimental or unwholesome in any manner whatever. Think only what you wish to produce or realize. If trouble is brewing, think about the greater success that you have in mind. If anything adverse is about to take place, do not think of what that adversity may bring, but think of the greater good that you are determined to realize in your life. When trouble is brewing, the average person usually thinks of nothing else. His mind is filled with fear, and not a single faculty in his possession can do justice to itself. And as trouble is usually brewing in most places, more or less, people have what may be called a chronic expectation for trouble; and as they usually get more or less of what they expect, they imagine they are fully justified in entertaining such expectations. But here it is absolutely necessary to change the mind completely. Whatever our present circumstances may be, we should refuse absolutely to expect anything but the best that we can think of. The whole mind, with all its powers and faculties, should be thrown, so to speak, into line with the optimistic tendency, and whatever comes or not, we should think only of the greater things that we expect to realize. In brief, we should concentrate the mind absolutely upon whatever goal we may have in view, and should look neither to the left nor to the right.

When we concentrate absolutely upon the greater things we expect to attain or achieve, we gradually train all the forces of the mind and all the powers of thought to work for those greater things. We shall thereby begin in earnest to build for ourselves a greater destiny; and sooner or later we shall find ourselves gaining ground in many directions. Later on, if we proceed, we shall begin to move more rapidly, and if we pay no attention to the various troubles that may be brewing in our environment, those troubles will never affect us nor disturb us in the least.

The mental law involved in the process of scientific thinking may be stated as follows: The more you think of what is right, the more you tend to make every action in your mind right. The more you think of the goal you have in view, the more life and power you will call into action in working for that goal. The more you think of your ambition, the more power you will give to those faculties that can make your ambitions come true. The more you think of harmony, of health, of success, of happiness, of things that are desirable, of things that are beautiful, of things that have true worth, the more the mind will tend to build all those things in yourself, provided, of course, that all such thinking is subjective.

To think scientifically, therefore, is to train your every thought and your every mental action to focus the whole of attention upon that which you wish to realize, to gain, to achieve or attain in your life.

In training the mind along the lines of scientific thinking begin by trying to hold the mind upon the right, regardless of the presence of the wrong, and here we should remember that the term "right" does not simply refer to moral actions, but to all actions. When the wrong is coming your way, persist in thinking of the right; persist in expecting only the right. And there is a scientific reason for this attitude, besides what has been mentioned above. We know that the most important of all is to keep the mind right or moving along right lines, and if we persistently expect the right, regardless of circumstances, the mind will be kept in the lines of right action. But there is another result that frequently comes from this same practice. It sometimes happens that the wrong which is brewing in your environment, has such a weak foundation that only a slight increase in the force of the right would be necessary to overthrow that wrong completely; in fact, we shall find that most wrongs that threaten can be overcome in a very short time, if we continue to work for the right in a positive, constructive, determined manner. It is when the individual goes all to pieces, so to speak, that adversity gets the best of him; but no individual will go to pieces unless his thinking is chaotic, destructive, scattered, confused and detrimental. Continue to possess your whole mind and you will master the situation, no matter what it may be, and it is scientific thinking that will enable you to perform this great feat.

To make thinking scientific, there are three leading essentials to be observed. The first is to cultivate constructive mental attitudes, and all mental attitudes are constructive when mind, thought, feeling, desire and will constantly face the greater and the better. A positive and determined optimism has the same effect, and the same is true of the practice of keeping the mental eye single on the highest goal in view. To make every mental attitude constructive the mind must never look down, and mental depression must be avoided completely. Every thought and every feeling must have an upward look, and every desire must desire to inspire the same rising tendency in every action of mind.

The second essential is constructive mental imagery. Use the imagination to picture only what is good, what is beautiful, what is beneficial, what is ideal, and what you wish to realize. Mentally see yourself receiving what you deeply desire to receive. What you imagine, you will think, and what you think, you will become. Therefore, if you imagine only those things that are in harmony with what you wish to obtain or achieve, all your thinking will soon tend to produce what you want to attain or achieve.

The third essential is constructive mental action. Every action of the mind should have something desirable in view and should have a definite, positive aim. Train yourself to face the sunshine of life regardless of circumstances. When you face the sunshine, everything looks right, and when everything looks right, you will think right. It matters not whether there is any sunshine in life just now or not. We must think of sunshine just the same. If we do not see any silver lining, we must create one in our own mental vision. However dark the dark side may seem to be, we cannot afford to see anything but the bright side, and no matter how small or insignificant the bright side may be, we must continue to focus attention on that side alone. Be optimistic, not in the usual sense of that term, but in the real sense of that term. The true optimist not only expects the best to happen, but goes to work to make the best happen. The true optimist not only looks upon the bright side, but trains every force that is in him to produce more and more brightness in his life, and therefore complies with the three essentials just mentioned. His mental attitudes are constructive because they are always facing greater things. His imagination is constructive because it is always picturing the better and the ideal, and his mental actions are constructive because he is training the whole of his life to produce those greater and better things that his optimism has inspired him to desire and expect.

In this connection, we must remember that there is a group of mental forces at work in every mental attitude, and therefore if that attitude is downcast, those forces will become detrimental; that is, they will work for the lesser and the inferior. On the other hand, if every mental attitude is lifted up or directed toward the heights of the great and the true and the ideal, those forces will become constructive, and will work for the greater things in view.

In the perusal of this study, we shall find it profitable to examine our mental attitudes closely, so as to determine what our minds are actually facing the greater part of the time. If we find that we are mentally facing things and conditions that are beneath our expectations, or find that our imaginations are concerned too much about possible failure, possible mistakes, possible trouble, possible adversity, etc., our thinking is unscientific, and no time should be lost in making amends.

When you are looking into the future, do not worry about troubles that might come to pass. Do not mentally see yourself as having a hard time of it. Do not imagine yourself in this hostile condition or that adverse circumstance. Do not wonder what you would do if you should lose everything, or if this or that calamity should befall. Such thinking is decidedly unscientific and most detrimental. If you entertain such thoughts you are causing the ship of your life to move directly toward the worst precipice that may exist in your vicinity. Besides, you are so weakening this ship through wrong treatment, that it will some day spring a leak and go down.

Think of the future whenever it is unnecessary for you to give your attention to the present, but let your thought of the future be wholesome, constructive, optimistic and ideal. Mentally see yourself gaining the best that life has to give, and you will meet more and more of the best. Think of yourself as gaining ground along all lines, as finding better and better circumstances, as increasing in power and ability, and as becoming more healthful in body, more vigorous and brilliant in mind, more perfect in character, and more powerful in soul. In brief, associate your future with the best that you can think of along all lines. Fear nothing for the days that are to be, but expect everything that is good, desirable, enjoyable and ideal. This practice will not only make your present happier, but it will tend to strengthen your mind and your life along wholesome constructive lines to such a degree that you will actually gain the power to realize, in a large measure, those beautiful and greater things that you have constantly expected in your optimistic dreams.

In living and building for a larger future, we should remember that our mind and thoughts invariably follow the leadership of the most prominent mental picture. The man who clearly and distinctly pictures for himself a brilliant future will inspire the powers of his entire mental world to work for such a future; in fact, all the forces of thought, mind, life, personality, character and soul will move in that direction. He may not realize as brilliant a future as he has pictured, but his future is certainly going to be brilliant, and it is quite possible, as is frequently the case, that it may become even more brilliant than he dreamed of in the beginning.

When the average mind thinks of the future, he usually pictures a variety of conflicting events and conditions. He has nothing definite in mind. There is no actual leadership therefore in his mind, and nothing of great worth can be accomplished.

When we look into the lives of men and women who have reached high places, we always find that they were inspired with some great idea. That idea was pictured again and again in their mental vision, and they refused to let it go. They clung tenaciously to that idea, and thereby actually compelled every force and element within them to enlist in the working out of that idea. It is therefore simple enough that they should realize every aim and reach the highest places that achievement has in store. Such men and women possibly did not understand the science or the process, but they were nevertheless thinking scientifically to a most perfect degree. Their ambition pictured only that lofty goal which they wanted to reach. All their mental attitudes were constantly facing that lofty goal, and thereby became constructive; and all the actions of mind were directed toward the same goal. Accordingly, everything within them was trained to work for the realization of their dream, and that is what we mean by scientific thinking; that is what we mean by thinking for results. And any one who will train himself to think for results in this manner, will positively secure results; though in this connection it is well to remember that persistence and determination are indispensable every step of the way.

When we do not secure results at once, we sometimes become discouraged, and conclude that it is no use to try. At such times, friends will usually tell us that we are simply dreaming, and they will advise us to go to work at something practical, something that we really can accomplish; but if we ignore the advice of our friends, and continue to be true to the great idea that we have resolved to work out, we shall finally reach our goal, and when we do, those very same friends will tell us that we took the proper course. So long as the man with ambition is a failure, the world will tell him to let go of his ideal; but when his ambition is realized, the world will praise him for the persistence and the determination that he manifested during his dark hours, and everybody will point to his life as an example for coming generations. This is invariably the rule. Therefore pay no attention to what the world says when you are down. Be determined to get up, to reach the highest goal you have in view, and you will.

There are a great many ambitious men and women, who imagine that they will succeed provided their determination is strong and their persistence continuous, regardless of the fact that their thinking may be unscientific; but the sooner we dispel this illusion, the better. Unscientific thinking, even in minor matters, weakens the will. It turns valuable thought power astray, and we need the full power of thought, positively directed along the line of our work if we are going to achieve, and achieve greatly.

The majority of the mental forces in the average person are working against him, because he is constantly entertaining depressed mental states or detrimental habits of thought; and even though he may be ambitious, that ambition has not sufficient power to work itself out, because most of the forces of his mind are thrown away. We therefore see the necessity of becoming scientific in all thinking, and in making every mental habit wholesome and beneficial in the largest sense of those terms. But scientific thinking not only tends to turn the power of thought in the right direction; it also tends to increase mental power, to promote efficiency and to build up every faculty that we may employ.

To illustrate the effect of right thinking upon the faculties, we will suppose that you have musical talent, and are trying to perfect that talent. Then, we will suppose that you are constantly expressing dissatisfaction with the power of that talent. What will be the result? Your mental action upon that faculty will tend to lower its efficiency, because you are depressing its action instead of inspiring those actions. On the other hand, if you encourage this talent, you will tend to expand its life, and thereby increase its capacity for results.

In this respect, talents are similar to people. Take two people of equal ability and place them in circumstances that are direct opposites. We will suppose that the one is mistreated every day by those with whom he is associated. He is constantly being criticized and constantly being told that he will never amount to anything; he is blamed for everything that is wrong, and is in every manner discouraged and kept down. What would happen to the ability and efficiency of that man if he continued under such treatment year after year? He simply could not advance unless he should happen to be a mental giant, and even then, his advancement would be very slow; but if he was not a mental giant, just an average man, he would steadily lose ambition, self-confidence, initiative, judgment, reasoning power, and in fact, everything that goes to make up ability and capacity.

We will suppose the other man is encouraged continually. He is praised for everything, he is given every possible opportunity to show and apply what ability he may possess; he is surrounded by an optimistic atmosphere, and is expected by everybody to advance and improve continually. What will happen to this man? The best will be brought out in his power and ability. He will be pushed to the fore constantly and he will climb steadily and surely until he reaches the top.

Treat your talents in the same way, and you have the same results in every case. To state it briefly, make it a point to encourage your talents, your faculties and your powers. Give every element and force within you encouragement and inspiration. Expect them all to do their best, and train yourself to think and feel that they positively will. Train yourself to think of your whole system as all right. Deal with your mental faculties in this manner, under all circumstances, and deal with your physical organs in the same way.

Most people among those who do not have perfect health, have a habit of speaking of their stomachs as bad, their livers as always out of order, their eyes as weak, their nerves as all upset, and the different parts of their systems as generally wrong. But what are they doing to their physical organs through this practice? The very same as was done to the unfortunate man just mentioned, and we shall find, in this connection, one reason why so many people continue to be sick. They are keeping their physical organs down, so to speak, by depressing the entire system with unwholesome thinking; but if they would change their tactics and begin to encourage their physical organs, praise them and expect them to do better, and to treat them right from the mental as well as a physical standpoint, they would soon be restored to perfect health.

In training the mind in scientific thinking, the larger part of attention should be given to that of controlling our feelings. It is not difficult to think scientifically along intellectual lines, but to make our feelings move along wholesome, constructive, optimistic lines requires persistent training. Intellectual thought can be changed almost at any time with little effort, but feeling usually becomes stronger and stronger the longer it moves along a certain line, and thus becomes more difficult to change. When we feel discouraged, it is so easy to feel more discouraged; when we feel dissatisfied, it is only a step to that condition that is practically intolerable. It is therefore necessary to stop all detrimental feeling in the beginning. Do not permit a single adverse feeling to continue for a second. Change the mind at once by turning your attention upon something that will make you feel better. Resolve to feel the way you want to feel under all circumstances, and you will gradually develop the power to do so. Depressed mental feelings are burdens, and we waste a great deal of energy by carrying them around on our mental shoulders. Besides, such feelings tend to direct the power of thought toward the lower and the inferior. Whenever you permit yourself to feel bad, you will cause the power of mind and thought to go wrong. Therefore, persist in feeling right and good. Persist in feeling joyous. Persist in feeling cheerful, hopeful, optimistic and strong. Place yourself on the bright side and the strong side of everything that transpires in your life, and you will constantly gain power—power that will invariably be in your favor.

Life is growth and the object of right thinking is to promote that growth.

Give less time trying to change the opinions of others, and more time trying to improve your own life.

Life becomes the way it is lived; and man may live the way he wants to live when he learns to think what he wants to think.

Create your own thought and you become what you want to become because your thought creates you.

We all know that man is as he thinks. Then we must think only such thoughts as tend to make us what we wish to be.

The secret of right thinking is found in always keeping the mind's eye stayed upon the greater and the better in all things.

CHAPTER VII

HOW MAN BECOMES
WHAT HE THINKS

Scientific research in the metaphysical field has demonstrated the fact that man is as he thinks, that he becomes what he thinks, and that what he thinks in the present, determines what he is to become in the future; and also that since he can change his thought for the better along any line, he can therefore completely change himself along any line. But the majority who try to apply this law do not succeed to a great degree, the reason being that instead of working entirely upon the principle that man is as he thinks, they proceed in the belief that man is what he thinks he is.

At first sight there may seem to be no difference between the principle that man is as he thinks and the belief that man is as he thinks he is, but close study will reveal the fact that the latter is absolutely untrue. Man is not what he thinks he is, because personality, mentality and character are not determined by personal opinions. It is the thought of the heart, that is, the mental expression from the subconscious that makes the personal man what he is; but the subconscious is effected only by what man actually thinks in the real field of creative thought, and not by what he may think of himself in the field of mere personal opinion.

It is subjective thought that makes you what you are; but to think that you are thus or so, will not necessarily make you thus or so. To create subjective thought you must act directly upon the subconscious, but it is not possible to impress the subconscious while you are forming opinions about your personal self. A mere statement about yourself will not affect or change the subconscious, and so long as the subconscious remains unchanged, you will remain unchanged. While you are thinking simply about your external or personal self you are acting upon the objective, but to change yourself you must act upon the subjective.

Man may think that he is great, but so long as he continues to think small thoughts, he will continue to be small. No matter how high an opinion he may have of himself, while he is living in the superficial, his thoughts will be empty, and empty thoughts are not conducive to high attainments and great achievements. Man becomes great when he thinks great thoughts, and to think great thoughts he must transcend the limitations and circumscribed conditions of the person, and mentally enter into the world of the great and the superior. He must seek to gain a larger and a larger consciousness of the world of real quality, real worth and real superiority, and must dwell upon the loftiest mountain peaks of mind that he can possibly reach. He must live in the life of greatness, breathe the spirit of greatness, and feel the very soul of greatness. Then, and only then, will he think great thoughts; and the mind that continues to think great thoughts will continue to grow in greatness.

It is not what you state in your thought but what you give to your thought that determines results. The thought that is merely stated may be empty, but it is the thought with something in it that alone can exercise real power in personal life. And what is to be in your thought will depend upon what you think into your thought. What you give to your thought, your thought will give to you, and you will be and become accordingly, no matter what you may think that you are. The cause that you originate in the within will produce its effect in the without, regardless of what your opinions may be. Your personal life will consequently be the result of what you think, but it will not necessarily be what you think it is.

Having discovered the fact that the physical body is completely renewed every eight or ten months, you will naturally think that you are young, but to simply think you are young will not cause the body to look as young as it really is. To retain your youth you must remove those subconscious tendencies and conditions that produce old age, and you must eliminate worry. So long as you worry you will cause your personality to grow older and older in appearance, no matter how persistently you may think that you are young. To simply think that you are young will not avail. You must think thoughts that produce, retain and perpetuate youth. If you wish to look young, your mind must feel young, but you will not feel young until the whole of your mind produces the feeling of youth.

To develop the feeling of youth in the whole mind, you must become fully conscious of the fact that youth is naturally produced in your entire system every minute, and you must train the mind to take cognizance only of the eternal now. So long as we feel that we are passing with time, we will imagine that we feel the weight of more and more years, and this feeling will invariably cause the body to show the mark of years, growing older and older in appearance as more years are added to the imaginary burden of age. You will look young when you feel young, but to simply feel that you are young will not always cause you to feel young. The real feeling of youth comes when we actually think in the consciousness of youth and give the realization of the now to every thought.

You may think that you are well, but you will not secure health until you think thoughts that produce health. You may persistently affirm that you are well, but so long as you live in discord, confusion, worry, fear and other wrong states of mind, you will be sick; that is, you will be as you think and not what you think you are. You may state health in your thought, but if you give worry, fear and discord to that thought, your thinking will produce discord. It is not what we state in our thoughts, but what we give to our thoughts that determine results. To produce health, thought itself must be healthful and wholesome. It must contain the quality of health, and the very life of health. This, however, is not possible unless the mind is conscious of health at the time when such thought is being produced. Therefore, to think thoughts that can produce health, the mind must enter into the realization of the being of health, and not simply dwell in the objective belief about health. Again, to produce health, all the laws of life must be observed; that is, the mind must be in that understanding of law, and in that harmony with law where the guiding thought will naturally observe law. To simply think that you are well will not teach the mind to understand the laws of life and health, nor will that thinking place you in harmony with those laws. That thinking that does understand the laws of life will not come from the mere belief that you are well, but from the effort to enter into the understanding of all law, the spirit of all law, the very life of health, and into the very soul of all truth.

You may think that your mind is brilliant and may undertake most difficult tasks in the belief that you are equal to the occasion, but the question is if your conception of brilliancy is great or small. If your conception of brilliancy is small, you may be right to that degree in thinking you are brilliant; that is, you may be brilliant as far as your understanding of brilliancy goes. Whether that is sufficient or not to carry out the task that is before you is another question. Your opinion of your mental capacity may be great, but if your idea of intelligence is crude, your intelligence-producing thought will also be crude, and can produce only crude intelligence. It is therefore evident that to simply think that you are brilliant will not produce brilliancy, unless your understanding of brilliancy is made larger, higher and finer. What you understand and mentally feel concerning intelligence, mental capacity and brilliancy, is what you actually think on those subjects, and it is this understanding or feeling or realization that will determine how much intelligence you will give to your thought. Your thought will be as brilliant as the brilliancy you think into your thought, and how much brilliancy you will think into your thought will depend upon how high your realization of brilliancy happens to be at the time. When your thinking is brilliant, you will be brilliant, but if your thinking is not brilliant you will not be brilliant, no matter how brilliant you may think you are.

To make your thinking more brilliant, try to enter into the consciousness of finer intelligence, larger mental capacity, and the highest order of mental brilliancy that you can possibly realize. Do not call yourself brilliant at any time, or do not think of yourself as lacking in brilliancy. Simply fix the mental eye upon absolute brilliancy, and desire with all the power of mind and soul to go on and on into higher steps of that brilliancy.

When all the elements and forces of your system are working in such a way that beauty will naturally be produced, you will be beautiful, whether you think you are beautiful or not, and it is the actions of the subconscious that determine how the elements and forces of the system are to work. Therefore, the beautiful person is beautiful because her real interior thinking is conducive to the creation of the beautiful. That person, however, who is not beautiful, does not necessarily think ugly thoughts, but her interior mental actions have not been brought together in such a way as to produce the expression of beauty; that is the subconscious actions have not been arranged according to the most perfect pattern. But these actions can be arranged in that manner, not by thinking that one is beautiful, but by thinking thoughts that are beautiful.

When you think that you are beautiful, you are liable to think that you are more beautiful than others, and such a thought is not a beautiful thought. To recognize or criticize ugliness and inferiority in others is to create the inferior and the ugly in yourself, and what you create in yourself will sooner or later be expressed through your mind and personality. So long as you worry, hate or fear, your thought will make you disagreeable in mind and character, and later on in the person as well; and no amount of affirming or thinking that you are beautiful will overcome those ugly states of mind that you have created. You will thus be as you think—worried, hateful and ugly, and not beautiful as you may try to think you are.

The personal man is the result, not of beliefs or opinions, but of the quality of all the mental actions that are at work throughout the whole mind. Man is as he thinks in every thought, and not what he thinks he is in one or more isolated parts of his personal self. You may think that you are good, but your idea of goodness may be wrong. Your thought therefore will not be conducive to goodness. On the contrary, the more you praise yourself for being good, the less goodness you will express in your nature. In addition, to think of yourself as good will have a tendency to produce a feeling of self-righteousness. This feeling will cause the mind to look down upon the less fortunate, and a mind that looks down will soon begin to go down, and you will be no better than those whom you criticized before. You are only as good as the sum total of all your good thoughts, and these can be increased in number indefinitely by training the mind to perpetually grow in the consciousness of absolute goodness.

To grow in the consciousness of goodness, keep the mental eye upon the highest conception of absolute goodness. Try to enlarge, elevate and define this conception or understanding of goodness perpetually. Pattern your whole life, all your thoughts and all your actions after the likeness of this highest understanding. Then never look back nor try to measure the goodness that you may think you now possess. Press on eternally to the higher and larger realization of absolute goodness, and leave results to the law. More and more real goodness will naturally appear in all your thoughts and actions. You will therefore become good, not by thinking that you are good, but by thinking thoughts that are created in the image and likeness of that which is good.

From the foregoing it is evident that man is as he thinks, and not necessarily what he thinks he is. But there is still more evidence. That your personal self is the result of your thought has been demonstrated, but what thought? To make yourself thus or so, the necessary thought must first be created, but to think that you are thus or so, will not create the thought that can make you thus or so. The reason is because it is subconscious thought alone that can produce effects in your nature, physical or mental, and you cannot enter the subconscious while you are thinking exclusively of your personal self. What you think about yourself is always objective thought, and mere objective thought is powerless to effect or change anything in your nature. To think thoughts that can give you more life, you must enter into the consciousness of absolute life, but you cannot enter the absolute while you are defining or measuring the personal. If you wish to possess more quality, you must give your thoughts more quality and worth, you must forget the lesser worth of the personal and enter into the consciousness of the greater worth of absolute worth itself.

So long as you think that you are thus or so in the personal sense, your thought will be on the surface. You will mentally live among effects. You will not create new causes, therefore will not produce any changes in yourself. You will continue to be as you are thinking deep down in the subconscious where hereditary tendencies, habits, race thoughts and other mental forces continue their usual work, regardless of your personal opinion or empty thoughts on the surface.

To change yourself you must go to that depth of mind where the causes of your personal condition exist. But your mind will not enter the depth of the within so long as your thought is on the surface and your thought will be on the surface so long as you are thinking exclusively about your personal self. The secret therefore is not to form opinions about yourself or to think about yourself as being thus or so, but to form larger conceptions of principles and qualities. Enter the richness of real life and you will think richer thoughts. Forget the limitations, the weaknesses and the shortcomings of your personal self as well as your superficial opinions of your personal self, and enter mentally into the greatness, the grandeur, the sublimity and the splendour of all things. Seek to gain a larger and a larger understanding of the majesty and marvelousness of all life, and aspire to think the thoughts of the Infinite.

This is the secret of thinking great thoughts, and he will positively become great whose thoughts are always great. In like manner, he who thinks wholesome thoughts, and wholesome thoughts only, will become healthful and wholesome. Such thoughts will have the power to produce health, and thoughts never fail to do what they have the power to do. Place in action the necessary subconscious thought and the expected results will invariably follow.

Man therefore is not what he thinks he is because such thinking is personal, and consequently superficial and powerless. The thought that determines his personality, his character, his mentality and his destiny is his subjective thought, the thought that is produced in the subconscious during those moments when he forgets his personal opinions about himself and permits his mind to act with deep feeling and subjective conviction. But those thoughts that enter the subconscious are not always good thoughts. Man's subjective thinking is not always conducive to the true, the wholesome and the best, as his thinking is not always right. For this reason, man himself is not always good, nor his life as beautiful as he might wish to be. His thinking is in his own hands, however. He can learn to think what he wants to think, and as he is and becomes as he thinks, we naturally conclude that he may, in the course of time, become what he wants to become.

The greatest remedy in the world is change; and change implies the passing from the old to the new. It is also the only path that leads from the lesser to the greater, from the dream to the reality, from the wish to the heart's desire fulfilled. It is change that brings us everything we want. It is the opposite of change that holds us back from that which we want. But change is not always external. Real change, or rather the cause of all change, is always internal. It is the change in the within that first produces the change in the without. To go from place to place is not a change unless it produces a change of mind—a renewal of mind. It is the change of mind that is the change desired. It is the renewal of mind that produces better health, more happiness, greater power, the increase of life, and the consequent increase of all that is good in life. And the constant renewal of mind— the daily change of mind—is possible regardless of times, circumstances or places. He who can change his mind every day and think the new about everything every day, will always be well; he will always have happiness; he will always be free; his life will always be interesting; he will constantly move forward into the larger, the richer and the better; and whatever is needed for his welfare to-day, of that he shall surely have abundance.

CHAPTER VIII

THE ART OF
CHANGING FOR THE BETTER

Personal man gradually but surely grows into the likeness of that which he thinks of the most, and man thinks the most of what he loves the best. This is the law through which man has become what he is, and it is through the intelligent use of this law that man may change for the better and improve in any way desired. The thought you think not only effects your character, your mind and your body, but also produces the original cause of every characteristic, every habit, every tendency, every desire, every mental quality and every physical condition that appears in your system. Thought is the one original cause of the conditions, characteristics and peculiarities of the human personality, and everything that appears in the personality is the direct or indirect effect of the various actions of thought. It is therefore evident that man naturally grows into the likeness of the thought he thinks, and it is also evident that the nature of his thought would be determined by that which he thinks of the most.

The understanding of this fact will reveal to all minds the basic law of change, and though it is basic, its intelligent use may become simplicity itself. Through the indiscriminate use of this law, man has constantly been changing, sometimes for the better, sometimes not, but by the conscious, intelligent, use of this law he may change only for the better and as rapidly as the sum total of his present ability will permit.

The fact that mental conditions and dispositions may be changed through the power of thought, will readily be accepted by every mind, but that mental qualities, abilities, personal appearances and physical conditions may be changed in the same way all minds may not be ready to accept. Nevertheless, that thought can change anything in the human system, even to a remarkable degree, is now a demonstrated fact. We have all seen faces change for the worse under the influence of grief, worry and misfortune, and we have observed that all people grow old who expect to do so, regardless of the fact that the body of the octogenarian is not a day older than the body of a little child. We have unlimited evidence to prove that ability will improve or deteriorate according to the use that is made of the mind. A man's face reveals his thought, and we can invariably detect the predominating states of the mind that lives in a groove. When a person changes his mental states at frequent intervals, no one state has the opportunity to produce an individual, clear-cut expression, and therefore cannot be so readily detected, but where one predominating state is continued in action for weeks or months or years, any one can say what that state is, by looking at the face of him who has it. Thus we can detect different kinds of disposition, different grades of mind, different degrees of character and different modes of living, and convince ourselves at the same time, that man in general, looks, acts and lives the way he thinks.

The fact that every mental state will express its nature in body, mind and character, proves that we can, through the intelligent use of mental action, cause the body to become more beautiful, the mind more brilliant, character more powerful and the soul life more ideal. To accomplish these things, however, it is necessary to apply the law continuously in that direction where we desire to secure results. When a person thinks of the ordinary for a few weeks, he invariably begins to look ordinary. Then when something impels him to think for a while of the ideal, the true and the beautiful, he begins to look like a new creature; but if reverses threaten, he will feel worried, dejected and afraid, and everybody observes that he looks bad. Then if the tide turns in his favor, he will begin to look content, and if something should suggest to his mind the thought of the wholesome, the sound and the harmonious, he will begin to look remarkably well. In this manner he is daily using the law of change, but never intelligently. He does not take the law into his own hands, but uses the law only as suggestions from his environment may direct. He advances one day and falls back the next. One week his physical mansion is painted with colors of health and beauty; the next week only the conditions of age and disease are in evidence. He plants a flower seed to-day, and to-morrow hoes it up to plant a weed in its place. Thus the average person continues to live, and every change comes from the unconscious, indiscriminate use of the power of his thought. This power, however, can be employed more wisely, and when the many begin to do so, the progress of the race will be remarkable indeed.

The basic law of change must be taken into our own hands, and must be employed directly for producing the change we have in view; and to accomplish this the love nature must be so trained that we shall love only what we want to love, only what is greater and better than that which we have realized up to the present time. In this respect strong, highly developed souls will have no difficulty, because they have the power to see the great, the beautiful and the ideal in all things, but those who have not as yet acquired that power, must train their feelings with care, lest love frequently turns thought upon the low, the common or the ordinary.

What you admire in others will develop in yourself. Therefore, to love the ordinary in any one is to become ordinary, while to love the noble and the lofty in all minds is to grow into the likeness of that which is noble and lofty. When we love the person of someone who is in the earth earthy, we tend to keep ourselves down in the same place. We may give our kindness and our sympathies to all, but we must not love anything in any one that is not ideal. It is a misdirection of love to love exclusively the visible person. It is the ideal, the true and the beautiful in every person that should be loved, and as all persons have these qualities, we can love everybody with a whole heart in this more sublime manner.

In this connection a great problem presents itself to many men and women who aspire to a life of great quality. These people feel that they cannot give their personal love to husbands, wives, relatives or friends that persist in living in the mere animal world; but the problem is easily solved. We must not love what is ordinary in any one; in fact, the ordinary must not be recognized, but we can love the real life in every one, and if we will employ our finer perceptions we will find that this real life is ideal in every living creature in the world. We need not love the perversions of a person, but we can love the greater possibilities and the superior qualities that are inherent in the individual. It is not the imperfections or appearances that should be loved, but the greatness that is within; and what we love in others we not only awaken in others, but we develop those very things more or less in ourselves.

To promote the best welfare of individuals under all sorts of circumstances, personal loves should be exchanged only by persons who live in the same world. When the woman has found the superior world, the man must not expect her personal love unless he also goes up to live in the same world. It is simply fair that he should do so. The woman who lives in a small world must not expect the love of a man who lives in a great world. He would lose much of his greatness if he should give his personal love to such a woman.

The tendency of all life is onward and upward. Therefore, to ask anything to come down is to violate the very purpose of existence. If we wish to be with the higher, the greater and the superior, we must change ourselves and become higher, greater and superior; and this we all can do.

In the application of the basic law of change, no factor is more important than that of pleasure. We are controlled to a great extent by the pleasures we enjoy, ofttimes so much so that they may even determine our destiny. The reason why is found in the fact that we deeply love what we thoroughly enjoy, and since we think the most of what we love the best, we naturally become like the pleasures we thoroughly enjoy, because man gradually grows into the likeness of his predominating thought. It is therefore unwise to permit ourselves to enjoy anything that is beneath our most perfect conception of the ideal, and it is likewise unwise to associate personally with people who care only for the ordinary and the common. What we enjoy becomes a part of ourselves, and for the good of everybody, we cannot afford to go down; but when we love only those pleasures that are as high as our own ideal of joy, then we are truly on the great ascending path.

To overlook the wrongs, the defects and the perversions of life, and to look only for that beautiful something in every soul that we simply want to love, even without trying, is one of the greatest things that we can do; but we must not permit our conception of the beautiful within to become a mere, cold abstraction. It is most important that we be as emotional as we possibly can without permitting ourselves to be controlled by our emotions. The heart should be most tender and warm, and every feeling constantly on fire; but if all such feelings are turned into the secret realms of soul life, we shall find that the forces of love are drawn insistently toward the highest, the truest, and most noble and the most beautiful that our inspired moments have revealed. When this is done we can readily love with the whole heart any noble quality, or high art, or great work upon which we may direct our attention, and what we can love at will, that we can think of as deeply and as long as we may desire.

When we have formulated in our minds what changes we wish to make, the course to pursue is to love the ideal that corresponds to those changes. This love must be deep and strong, and must be continued until the desired change has actually taken place. Know what better qualities you want; then love those qualities with all your mind and heart and soul.

To love the higher and the greater qualities of life is to cause the creative qualities of mind to produce those same qualities in our own nature; and in consequence, we steadily grow into the likeness of that which we constantly love. This is the great law—the law that governs all change for the better. But to use this law intelligently the power of love must cease to respond to every whim or notion that the suggestibility of environment may present to the mind.

The power of love is the greatest power in the world, but it can cause persons or nations to fall to the lowest state, as well as rise to the highest state. Every fall in the history of the race has been caused largely by the misdirection of love, while every step in advance has been prompted largely by the power of love turned upon better things. To misdirect love is to love that which is beneath our present stage in advancement; it is turning the forces of life backward, and retrogression must inevitably follow.

In the average person, love is directed almost exclusively upon the personal side of life. In consequence, the love nature becomes so personal, so limited and so superficial, that materialism follows. In many other minds, it is mere appearances that attract the power of admiration, and the finer things in mind, soul and character, are wholly ignored. The result is that the finer qualities of such people gradually disappear, and grossness, both in thought and in appearance, naturally follows. But we must not conclude in this connection that it is wrong to admire the beautiful wherever it may be seen in the external world. We should love the beautiful everywhere, no matter where it may be found; we should admire the richness of life, both in the external and in the internal; and by living a complete life, we shall enjoy more and more of the richness and the beautiful in life, in the within as well as in the without. But the power of love must direct the greater part of its attention upon that which is rich and beautiful in mind and soul. It is that which is finer than the finest of external things that must be loved if man is to grow into the likeness of the great, the superior and the ideal, because man is as he thinks, and he thinks the most of what he loves the best.

When any individual begins to love the finer qualities in life, and gives all the power of mind and soul to that love, he has taken the first step in the changing of his destiny. He is laying the foundation for a great and a better future, and if he continues as he has begun, he will positively reach the loftiest goal that he may have in view. There are many laws to apply in the beginning of a great life, but the law that lies at the foundation of them all is the law of love. It is love that determines what we are to think, what we are to work for, where we are to go, and what we are to accomplish. Therefore, among all great essentials, the principal one is to know how to love.

To apply this essential for all practical purposes, the secret is to love the great, the beautiful, and the ideal in everybody and in everything; and to love with such a strong, passionate love that its ascending power becomes irresistible. The whole of life will thus change and go up with the power of love into the great, the superior and the ideal; everything, both in the being of man and in his environment will advance and change accordingly, and the dreams of the soul will come true. The ideal will become real, the desires of the heart will be granted, and what man has hoped to make his own will be absent no more.

When failure comes be more determined than ever to succeed.

The more feeling there is in your thought the greater its power.

You steadily and surely become in the real what you constantly and clearly think that you are in the ideal.

The more you believe in yourself the more of your latent powers and possibilities you place in action. And the more you believe in your purpose the more of your power you apply in promoting that purpose.

To him who thinks he can everything is an opportunity.

Depend only upon yourself but work in harmony with all things. Thus you call forth the best that is in yourself and secure the best that external sources have to give.

CHAPTER IX

HE CAN WHO THINKS HE CAN

The discovery of the fact that man is as he thinks, has originated a number of strange ideas concerning the power of thought. One of the principal of these is the belief that thought is a domineering force to be used in controlling things and in compelling fate to come our way. But that this belief is unscientific in every sense of the term has been demonstrated any number of times.

Those who have accepted this belief, and who have tried to use thought as a compelling force, have seemingly succeeded in the beginning, but later on have utterly failed, and the reason is that the very moment we proceed to apply thought in this manner, we place ourselves out of harmony with everything, both within ourselves and in our environment. The seeming success that such people have had in the beginning, or for a season, is due to the fact that a strong compelling force can cause the various elements of life to respond for a while, but the force that compels, weakens itself through the very act of compelling, and finally loses its power completely; and then, whatever has been gathered begins to slip away.

This explains why thousands of ardent students of metaphysics have failed to secure the results desired, or have succeeded only in spurts. They have taken the wrong view of the power of thought, and therefore have caused their power to work against them during the greater part of the time. The power of thought is not a compelling force. It is a building force, and it is only when used in the latter sense that desirable results can be produced. The building capacity of thought, however, is practically unlimited. Therefore there is actually no end to what might be accomplished, so long as this power is employed intelligently.

To apply the full building power of thought, we should proceed upon the principle that he can who thinks he can, and we should act in the full conviction that whatever man thinks he can do, he can do, because there is no limit to the power that such thinking can bring forth. The majority among intelligent minds admit that there is some truth in the statement that he can who thinks he can, but they do not, as a rule, believe it to be a very large truth. They admit that we gain more confidence in ourselves when we think that we can do what we have undertaken to do, and also that we become more determined, but aside from that, they see no further value in that particular attitude of mind. They do not realize that he who thinks he can, develops the power that can; but this is the truth, and it is one of the most important of all truths in the vast metaphysical domain.

The law that governs this idea, and its process while in action, is absolutely unlimited in its possibilities, and therefore is in a position to promise almost anything to him who is faithful. When a man begins to think that he can do certain things that he desires to do, his mind will naturally proceed to act on those faculties that are required in the working out of his purpose; and so long as the mind acts upon a certain faculty, more and more life, nourishment and energy will accumulate in that faculty. In consequence, that faculty will steadily develop. It will become larger, stronger and more efficient, until it finally is competent to do what we originally wanted done. Thus we understand how he who thinks he can develops the power that can.

When a man begins to think that he can apply the power of invention, his mind will begin to act upon the faculty of invention. The latent powers of this faculty will be aroused. These powers will accordingly be exercised more and more, and development will be promoted. This, however, is not all. Whenever the mind concentrates its attention upon a certain faculty, additional energy will be drawn into that faculty; thus power will be added to power, much will gather more, and as this may continue indefinitely there need be no end to the capacity and the ability that can be developed in that faculty. In the course of time, be it in a few months or in a few years, that man will actually have developed the power of invention to such a degree that he can invent successfully; and through the application of the same law, he can further develop this same faculty, year after year until he may finally become an inventive genius. When a man has some inventive power in the beginning, he will secure, through the application of this law, more remarkable results and in less time than if there were originally no indications of that faculty; but even if there were no original indications of individual power, that power can be developed to a high degree through the faithful application of the great law—he can who thinks he can, or to state it differently—he who thinks he can develops the power that can.

There is no faculty that we all do not possess, either in the active or in the latent state. Every faculty that naturally belongs to the human mind is latent in every mind, and it can be awakened and developed, provided the proper laws are faithfully applied. It should be our object, however, to accomplish as much as possible in the present. It is therefore advisable to proceed in the beginning to work through, and develop, those faculties that already indicate considerable power. The mind that has some talent for invention should proceed to think that he can invent. Thus he will accumulate more and more inventive ability or genius. The mind that has some talent for music, should proceed to think that he can master the art of music. He will thereby cause the creative energies of his mentality to accumulate more and more in the faculty of music, until that faculty will be developed to a greater and greater degree. The mind that has some talent for art should apply the same law upon that talent. The mind that has literary ability should proceed to think that he can write what he wants to write, and he will finally secure that literary ability or genius with which he can write what he wants to write. The mind that has ability in any line of business should proceed to think that he can conduct that business in the most successful manner. Should he enter that business and continue to think that he can, combining such thought with good work, enterprise and the full use of his personal ability, his success will continue to grow indefinitely.

Whatever a man may think that he can do, let him proceed to carry out that undertaking, constantly thinking that he can. He will succeed from the beginning, and his advancement will be continuous. However, no mind need be confined to a single purpose. If we have talent for something better than we are doing now, or if we wish to awaken some talent that we long to possess, we may proceed now to think that we can do what we long to do. We shall thus give more and more power to that faculty until it becomes sufficiently strong to be applied in actual practice. In the mean time, we should continue to think that we can do better and better what we are doing now. We shall thereby advance steadily in our present work, and at the same time, prepare ourselves for a greater work in the coming days.

When we think that we can, we must enter into the very soul of that thought and be thoroughly in earnest. It is in this manner that we awaken the finer creative energies of mind, those forces that build talent, ability and genius—those forces that make man great. We must be determined to do what we think we can do. This determination must be invincible, and must be animated with that depth of feeling that arouses all the powers of being into positive and united action. The power that can do what we think we can do will thus be placed at our command, and accordingly we may proceed successfully to do what we thought we could do.

The fact that you have failed to get the lesser proves conclusively that you deserve the greater. So therefore, dry those tears and go in search of the worthier prize.

Count nothing lost; even the day that sees "no worthy action done" may be a day of preparation and accumulation that will add greatly to the achievements of to-morrow. Many a day was made famous because nothing was done the day before.

Know what you want and continue to want it. You will get it if you combine desire with faith. The power of desire when combined with faith becomes invincible.

Some of the principal reasons why so many fail to get what they want is because they do not definitely know what they want, or because they change their wants almost every day.

CHAPTER X

HOW WE SECURE WHAT
WE PERSISTENTLY DESIRE

The purpose of desire is to inform man what he needs at every particular moment to supply the demands of change and growth in his life; and in promoting that purpose, desire gives expression to its two leading functions. The first of these is to give the forces of the human system something definite to do, and the second is to arouse those forces or faculties that have the natural power to do what is to be done.

In exercising its first function, desire not only promotes concentration of action among the forces in man, but also causes those forces to work for the thing that is wanted. Therefore, it is readily understood why the wish, if strong, positive, determined and continuous, will tend to produce the thing wished for. If you can cause all the elements and powers in your being to work for the one thing that you want you are almost certain to get it. In fact, you will get it unless it is so large that it is beyond you, or beyond the power of your present capacity to produce; though in that case you have exercised poor judgment; you have permitted yourself to desire what lies outside of your sphere; and what you could neither appreciate nor use were you to get it.

What you can appreciate, enjoy and use in your present sphere of existence, you have the power, in your present state of development, to produce; that is, you can produce it if all your power is applied in your effort to produce it; and when you desire any particular thing with the full force and capacity of your desire you cause all your power to be applied in producing that particular thing.

In exercising its second function, desire proceeds directly into that faculty or group of forces that can, if fully applied, produce the very thing that is desired. In its first function it tends to bring all the forces of the system together, and inspires them with the desire to work for what is wanted. It

acts upon the system in general and gives everything in the system something definite to do, that something definite in each case being the one
thing desired. In its second function it acts upon certain parts of the system
in particular; always upon those parts that can do what is wanted done; and
it tends to arouse all the life and power that those particular parts may contain. How desire proceeds, and how it secures results in this respect is easily
illustrated.

We will take, for example, a man who is not earning as much as he feels
that he needs. Naturally, he will begin to desire more money; and we will
suppose that this desire becomes stronger and stronger until it actually stirs
every atom of his being. Now what happens? He is not only arousing a great
deal of latent and unused energy, but all of his active energy is becoming
more and more alive. But what becomes of all this energy? It goes directly
into his money-making faculties, and tends to increase decidedly the life,
the power, the capacity and the efficiency of those faculties.

There is in every mind a certain group of faculties that is made by nature
for financial purposes. In some minds these faculties are small and sluggish,
while in other minds they are large and active. And that the latter kind
should be able to make more money and accumulate things in a greater
measure is quite natural. But is it possible to take those faculties that are
small and sluggish and make them large and active? If so, those who now
have limited means may in the course of time have abundance.

To answer this question, we will ask what it is that can arouse any faculty
to become larger and more active, and we find that it is more energy, and
energy that is more alive. No matter how sluggish a faculty may be, if it is
thoroughly charged, so to speak, with highly active energy, it simply must
become more active. And no matter how small it may be, if it continues to
receive a steady stream of added life, energy and power, day after day, month
after month, year after year, it simply must increase in size and capacity. And
whenever any faculty becomes greater in capacity and more alive in action
it will do better work; that is, it will gradually gain in ability and power
until it has sufficient ability and power to produce what you wished for.

Returning to the man in our illustration, we will see how the principle
works. His money-making faculties are too small and too sluggish to produce as much money as he needs. He begins to desire for more. This desire
becomes strong enough to arouse every element and force in his money-
making faculties; for here be it remembered that the force of any desire goes
directly into that faculty that can, by nature, produce the thing desired. This
is one of the laws of mind. In addition, the action of his desire tends to

arouse all the other forces of his system, and tends to concentrate those forces upon the idea of making more money.

In the beginning, no important change in his financial ability may be noticed, except that he feels more and more confidence in his power to secure the greater amount desired. In a short time, however, possibly within a few months, he begins to get new ideas about the advancement of his work. His mind is beginning to work more actively upon the idea of increased gain. Accordingly, suggestions as to how he might increase the earning capacity of his business are constantly coming up in his mind, and ways and means and plans are taking shape and form more and more completely.

The actions of his money-making faculties are also beginning to change; that is, they are becoming finer, more penetrating, and more keen so that his insight into financial matters is steadily improving. He is therefore securing the necessary essentials to greater financial gain, and as he applies them all things will naturally begin to take a turn. To state it briefly, his strong, persistent desire for more money has aroused his money-making faculties. They have become stronger, more active, more wide-awake and more efficient. And as a strong, wide-awake faculty can do many times as good work as one that is only partly alive, we understand how his desire for more money has given him the ability to make more money. As he continues this desire, making it stronger and more persistent, his financial ability will increase accordingly, and his financial gains continue to increase in proportion.

Many may doubt the efficiency of the plan just presented, because as is well known, most people desire more money but do not always get it. But do they always wish hard enough? It is not occasional desire, or half-hearted desire that gets the thing desired. It is persistent desire; and persistent desire, not only desires continually, but with all the power of life and mind and soul. The force of a half alive desire, when acting upon a certain faculty, cannot cause that faculty to become fully alive. Nor can such a desire marshal all the unused forces of the system and concentrate them all upon the attainment of the one thing wanted. And it is true that the desires of most people are neither continuous nor very deep. They are shallow, occasional wishes without enough power to stir to action a single atom.

Then we must also remember that results do not necessarily follow the use of a single force. Sometimes the force of persistent desire alone may do wonders, but usually it is necessary to apply in combined action all the forces of the human system. The force of desire, however, is one of the greatest of these, and when fully expressed in connection with the best talents we may possess, the thing desired will certainly be secured.

We may take several other illustrations. Suppose you have a strong desire for more and better friends. The action of that desire, if deep, whole-hearted and persistent will tend to impress the qualities of friendship upon every element of your character. In consequence, you will in time become the very incarnation of friendship; that is, you will become a better and a better friend, and he who becomes a better friend will constantly receive more and better friends. In other words, you become like the thing you desire, and when the similarity has become complete, you will get what you want through the law of like attracting like.

You may desire to succeed in a certain line of work; we will say, in the literary field. If your desire for success in that field is full and persistent, the power of that desire will constantly increase the life, the activity and the capacity of your literary faculties, and you will naturally do better work in that field. The same is true with regard to any other line of work, because your desire for greater success in your work will arouse to fuller action those faculties that you employ in that work. But, in every case, the desire must be deep, whole-souled, persistent and strong.

It is therefore evident that results in all lines of endeavor depend very largely upon the power of desire, and that no one can afford to let his desires lag for a moment. The law should be: Know what you want, and then want it with all the life and power that is in you. Get your mind and your life fully aroused. Persistent desire will do this. And that it is most important to do this is proven by the fact that in thousands of instances, a partly alive mind is the only reason why the goal in view has not been reached.

It is necessary, however, that your desires continue uninterruptedly along the lines you have chosen. You may desire a score or more of different things, but continue each desire without change, unless you should find that certain changes are necessary to secure the greater results you have in mind. To desire one thing to-day and another to-morrow means failure. To work for one thing this year and another thing next year is the way to empty handedness at the end of every year.

Before you begin to apply the power of desire, know with a certainty what you want because when you get what you have desired, you may have to take it. If you do not know definitely what you really do want, desire a better judgment, a clearer understanding and a more balanced life. Desire to know what is best for you, and the force of that desire will tend to produce normal action in every part of your system. Then you will feel distinctly what the highest welfare of your nature actually demands.

In deciding upon what you want, however, do not be timid, and do not measure the possible with the yard-stick of general appearances. Let your aspirations be high, only be sure that you are acting within the sphere of your own inherent capacity; though in this connection it is well to remember that your inherent capacity is many times as great as it has been supposed to be; and also that it can be continuously enlarged.

In choosing what you are to desire, act within reason, but go after the best. If the full power of desire is applied upon all the elements of your mind and character, what is latent within you will be aroused, developed and expressed; you will become much more than you are and thereby will not only desire the best, but be able to be of service to the best. And this latter fact is important. When we desire the great and the wonderful we must ask what we have to give the great and the wonderful in return. It is not only necessary to get the best—to realize our ideal, but it is also necessary to be so good and so great that we can give to the best as much as we are receiving from the best. Before we begin to wish for an ideal, we must ask what that ideal is going to get when it comes.

Coupled with our desire for the ideal, therefore, we must have an equally strong desire for the remaking of ourselves so that we may become equal to that ideal in every respect. If we want an ideal companion, we must not only wish for such a companion, but we must also desire the development of those qualities in ourselves that we know would make us agreeable to that companion. If we want a different environment we should wish for such an environment with all the life and soul we possess, and should at the same time wish for the increase of those powers in our own talents that can earn such an environment. If we want a better position we should desire such a position every minute and also desire that we may become more competent to fill it when it comes.

The power of desire not only tends to arouse added life and power in these faculties upon which it may act, but it also tends to make the mind as a whole more alert and wide-awake along those lines. This is well illustrated by the fact that when we have a strong, continuous desire for information on a certain subject, we always find someone or something that can give us that information. And the reason is that all the faculties of the mind are prompted by the force of this desire to be constantly on the look-out for that information.

That the same law will apply in the desire or search for wisdom, new ideas, better plans, better opportunities, more agreeable environments and more ideal companions, is clearly understood. And when we couple this fact with the fact that the power of desire tends to increase the life, the ability, the working capacity and the efficiency of these faculties or forces that can produce what we desire, we must certainly admit that those who have found the secret of using desire have made a great find indeed. But, as stated before, and it cannot be repeated too often, the desire must be persistent and strong, as strong as all the life and soul we possess.

In other words, we must wish hard enough, and we wish hard enough when our desires are sufficiently full and deep and strong to thoroughly arouse those faculties that have the natural ability to fulfil those desires. Many desires are only strong enough to arouse their corresponding faculties to a slight degree—not enough to increase the activity or working capacity of these faculties, while most desires are too weak to arouse any force or faculty in the least.

The act of wishing hard enough, however, does not imply hard mental work. If you make hard work of your wishing, you will use up your energy instead of turning it into those channels where it can be applied to good account. It is depth of desire and fullness of desire combined in an action that is directed continuously upon the one thing desired that constitutes true desire. To wish hard enough is simply to wish for all that you want with all that is in you. But we cannot wish with all that is in us unless our wish is subconscious as well as conscious because the subconscious is a part of us— the larger part of us.

To make every desire subconscious, the subconscious mind should always be included in the process of desire; that is, whenever we express a desire we should think of the subconscious, and combine the thought of that desire with our thought of the subconscious mind. Every desire should be deeply felt as all deeply felt mental actions become subconscious actions.

It is an excellent practice to let every desire sink into the deeper mental life, so to speak; and also to act in and through that deeper mental life, whenever we give expression to desire; or, in other words, when we turn on the full force and power of that desire. To become proficient in these methods requires some practice, though all that is necessary to become proficient is to continue to try. No special rule is required.

Begin by feeling your desires through and through. Make them as strong and as deep as you can, and always combine the living action of your desire with your thought of those faculties through which you know that desire is to work. To illustrate: If you desire greater success in your work, think of those faculties that you are using in your work whenever you give full expression to your desire. If you are a business man, think of your business faculties whenever you desire greater business success. If you are a musician, think of your musical faculties whenever you desire greater proficiency in your music. Though in case your desires should be such that you do not know through what kinds of faculties it will naturally be expressed, never mind. Continue to desire what you want; the power of that desire, if persistent and strong, will find a way to make your wish come true.

When we understand how desire works, and know that it works only when it is persistent, we realize that we have found, not only a great secret, but also a simple explanation for many of the failures in life as well as many of its greatest achievements. And from the facts in the case we conclude that no matter what a man's condition or position may be to-day, if he will decide upon that something better that he wants, he may get it, provided his wish for it is as strong as his own life and as large as his own soul.

The optimist lives under a clear sky; the pessimist lives in a fog. The pessimist hesitates, and loses both time and opportunity; the optimist makes the best use of everything now, and builds himself up, steadily and surely, until all adversity is overcome and the object in view realized. The pessimist curbs his energies and concentrates his whole attention upon failure; the optimist gives all his thought and power to the attainment of success, and arouses his faculties and forces to the highest point of efficiency. The pessimist waits for better times, and expects to keep on waiting; the optimist goes to work with the best that is at hand now, and proceeds to create better times. The pessimist pours cold water on the fires of his own ability; the optimist adds fuel to those fires. The pessimist links his mind to everything that is losing ground; the optimist lives, thinks and works with everything that is determined to press on. The pessimist places a damper on everything; the optimist gives life, fire and go to everything. The optimist is a building force; the pessimist is always an obstacle in the way of progress. The pessimist lives in a dark, soggy unproductive world, the optimist lives in that mental sunshine that makes all things grow.

CHAPTER XI

CONCENTRATION AND
THE POWER BACK OF SUGGESTION

The purpose of concentration is to apply all the active forces of mind and personality upon that one thing which is being done now, and it may therefore be called the master key to all attainments and achievement. In its last analysis, the cause of all failure can be traced to the scattering of forces, and the cause of all achievement to the concentration of forces. This does not imply, however, that concentration is the only essential, but it does imply that concentration must be perfect, or failure is inevitable no matter how many good methods one may employ. The ruling thought of concentration is, "This one thing I do," and it can be stated as an absolute truth that whenever the mind works completely in the attitude of that thought, concentration is perfect.

The value of concentration is very easily illustrated by taking, for example, a wheel of twenty spokes with every spoke a pipe, and all those pipes connected with another conveying steam. The steam will thereby pass out through twenty channels. Then connect an engine with one of the pipes. That engine will accordingly receive only one-twentieth of the steam conveyed through the wheel, while nineteen-twentieths will pass out in waste. But suppose the other nineteen pipes were plugged so that all the steam would pass out through the one pipe connected with the engine. The engine would then have twenty times as much power as before.

The average mind is quite similar to such a wheel. An enormous amount of energy is generated at the hub, so to speak, or at the vital center of mental life; but as a rule, that power passes out through a score of channels, so that the channel of action receives only a fraction of the power generated in the human system. But here we must remember that you can apply your power effectively only in one direction at a time; therefore, if all your power is to be applied in that one direction, all other channels must be closed up for the time being; or in other words, all the power of mind and thought must be concentrated where you are acting at the time.

In learning how to concentrate, it is necessary in the beginning to remember that the usual methods are of no value. You cannot develop concentration by fixing thought or attention upon some external object. Real concentration is subjective, and subjective thought is deep; that is, it acts through the deeper or interior realms of mind. When you fix your attention, however, upon some external object, like a spot on the wall, as has been suggested by some would-be instructors in this field, your thought goes out toward the surface, so that you are actually getting away from the true field of concentration. Any method, or any line of thinking that tends to draw the mind out toward the surface, will produce a superficial attitude, and when the mind is in such an attitude, deep mental action is not possible; but deep mental action is absolutely necessary in all concentration. There is no use trying to concentrate unless the action of the mind is deep. That is the first essential. In other words, the mind must go into the psychological field; the mind must act, not on the surface of things, but through the deeper life of its thought process.

To develop concentration, all that is necessary is to apply consciously those two factors that are invariably found in natural concentration. In the conscious application of these two factors, the following two methods will be found sufficient; in fact, nothing further will be required in the attainment of concentration to any degree desired.

The first method is to train the mind to act in the subjective or psychological field; in other words, cause all thinking, all feeling and all actions of thought, will and desire to become deeper and finer; in fact, deepen as far as possible all mental action. Whenever you concentrate or turn your attention upon any subject or object, try to feel deeply, try to think deeply and try to turn thought into deeper realms of feeling. The moment your mental action begins to deepen, you will find your attention directed upon the object in mind with perfect ease and with full force. Whenever you are thinking about anything, try to feel your thought getting into the vital life of that something, and wherever you turn your attention, try to feel that the force of that attention acts through your whole mind instead of simply on the surface of your mind. To state it briefly, whenever you concentrate, deepen your thought, and the deeper your thought becomes, the more perfectly will the full force of your mind and thought focus upon the point of concentration. Whatever you have to do, deepen your thought while giving that work your attention. You will find that you will thereby give all your energy to that work and this is your purpose.

The second method is to become interested in that upon which you desire to concentrate. If you are not interested in that subject or object, begin at once to look for the most interesting point of view. You will be surprised to find that no matter how uninteresting a subject may seem, the very moment you begin to look for the most interesting viewpoints of that subject, you will almost immediately become interested in that subject itself. And it is a well-known fact that whenever we are thoroughly interested in a subject we concentrate thoroughly and naturally upon that subject.

To make concentration perfect, so that you can turn all the power of mind and thought upon any subject or object desired, these two methods should be combined. Always look for the most interesting points of view, and while you are looking for those viewpoints, deepen the action of your mind by trying to feel the real vital life of those actions. You thereby become interested in the subject on the one hand, and you make every action of the mind subjective on the other hand; and when perfect interest is combined with subjective mental action, you have perfect concentration.

The constant practice of these two methods will develop the power of concentration to such an extent that you can concentrate completely at any time and for any length of time, by simply deciding to do so; and that such an attainment is of enormous value is evident when we understand how much power there is in man, and how concentration can turn all of that power upon the one thing that is being done now.

All modern psychologists agree that there is enough power in any man to accomplish what he has in view, provided it is all constructively applied in that one direct. And when man can concentrate perfectly, he can use all of his power wherever he may choose to act. Then, if he combines scientific thinking and constructive mental action with concentration, nothing can prevent him from realizing his very highest ambition.

Another important essential in the use of the forces of mind and thought, is that of understanding suggestion and the power back of suggestion; and this becomes especially true when we realize that there is no factor or condition that we may come in contact with anywhere or under any circumstances, that does not suggest something.

To define suggestion, it may be stated that anything is a suggestion that brings into mind some thought, idea or feeling that tends to undermine some similar idea, thought or feeling that happens to be in the mind at the time. When you have certain ideas or feelings, and you meet circumstances that tend to remove those ideas or feelings, the power of suggestion is working in your mind. If your mind is in a wholesome state and an unwholesome picture removes that wholesome state by replacing something that is degrading, your mind is in the power of suggestion. If you feel joyous and some idea given to you makes your mind depressed, you are in the hands of suggestion; in fact, when anything enters your mind in such a manner as to remove certain similar or opposite states already in your mind, it exercises the power of suggestion.

It is therefore necessary to understand how this power works, so that we can take advantage of good suggestions and avoid those that are not good. The great majority are receiving all sorts of suggestions every hour, and they respond to a very large number of them; in fact, we can truthfully say that most people are controlled, most of the time, by suggestions that come to them from their environment. Those minds, however, who understand the power of thought, and who know the difference between detrimental and beneficial suggestions, can close their minds to the former and open them fully to the latter. And the method to apply is this, that whenever you are in the presence of an adverse suggestion, concentrate your attention upon some idea or mental state which you know will act as a counter suggestion; in other words, when adverse suggestion is trying to produce in your mind what you do not want, persist in suggesting to yourself what you do want. This practice, if employed frequently, will soon make you so strong in this direction that you will unconsciously, so to speak, be on your guard; in fact, the very moment that an adverse suggestion is given, your mind will spring up of its own accord with a wholesome suggestion to meet the requirements. To avoid becoming a victim to adverse suggestions—and we have such suggestions about us almost constantly—fill your mind so full of good, wholesome thoughts and suggestions that there is no room for anything else. Feel right at all times, and nothing from without can tempt you to think wrong. Make every good thought subconscious, and no adverse thought from without can possibly get into your subconscious mind at any time.

A great many suggestions do not produce results, a fact which should be perfectly understood, because every thought that we think does contain some suggestion. When we are trying to impress good thoughts upon our minds, we want the good suggestions conveyed by those thoughts to take effect, but frequently they do not, and the reason is that a suggestion takes effect only when we exercise the power that is back of suggestion. The outward suggestion itself is simply the vehicle through which another power is acting, and that other power is nothing more nor less than the real life of that idea which the suggestion intends to convey.

To simplify this matter, we will suppose that you are suggesting to yourself that you are well. The suggestion itself is simply a vehicle conveying the idea of health, but if your mind is not in touch with the interior or living force of that idea of health at the time you are giving the suggestion, you have not exercised the power back of suggestion, and the idea of health will not be conveyed to your subconscious mind. On the other hand, if you can actually feel the power of this interior idea of health when you are giving the suggestion, you are in mental touch with the power back of that suggestion, and whenever you touch the power back of suggestion you use that power. Results, therefore, will be forthcoming. To explain further, we might say that you use the power back of suggestion whenever you mentally feel that vital idea which the suggestion aims to convey. When you feel that idea, you respond to the suggestion, but when you do not feel it, you do not respond.

This explains why the power of suggestion so frequently fails, not only in every day life, but also in mental healing. When you think health, you will produce health in your system if you feel the real or interior life of health at the time. When you think harmony you will produce harmony in your system, if your mind actually goes into the soul of harmony at the time. When you place yourself in the mental world of happiness, whenever you are thinking happiness, you will actually produce happiness in your mind, because you are applying the power that is back of the thought that suggests happiness.

Two men may present the same proposition under the same circumstances, and you will accept the proposition from the one, while ignoring the arguments of the other completely. The reason will be that while the one is talking about his proposition, the other is talking through his proposition. The mind of the one goes on the outside of his arguments and his suggestions, while the mind of the other goes through the real inner life of those arguments and suggestions. Therefore, the one is only using suggestion, while the other is also using the power back of suggestion; and it is the power back of suggestion that produces results, whenever results are secured. The same idea is illustrated when a person is speaking on a certain subject. If his description deals simply with the shell of that subject, he does not attract attention, but the moment he touches the vital or inner factors of that subject, everybody is interested. The reason is, he has touched the power back of his theme. But we all have ideas or suggestions to present at frequent intervals. Therefore, if we can use the power back of our suggestion at such times we may receive a hearing, but if we cannot, we attract little or no attention.

Thus we understand the value of knowing how to use the power back of suggestion, and we can learn to use this power by training ourselves to get into the real life of every idea and every thought that we may try to think or convey. When we try to live our ideas and thoughts, we will begin to express that interior power, and we shall succeed in living our ideas when we try to feel consciously and constantly the real life and the real truth that is contained in those ideas.

To secure the best results from the power of thought in its various modes of application, we must understand that there is something back of everything that takes form or action in life, and that it is through this something that the actions of mind should move whenever we use thought or suggestion in any manner whatever. When we are conscious only of the body of our ideas, those ideas convey no power. It is when we become conscious of the soul of those ideas that we have aroused that something within that alone produces results in the mental world. Any thought or suggestion that conveys simply the external form, invariably falls flat. There is nothing to it. It is entirely empty, and produces no impression whatever. But our ideas and suggestions become alive with the fullness of life and power when we also convey the real life or the real soul that is contained within the body of those thoughts. We have, at such times, entered the depths of mental life. We are beginning to act through undercurrents, and we are beginning to draw upon the immensity of that power that exists in the vast interior realms of our own mental world.

Say to yourself a hundred times every day and mean it with all your heart: I will become more than I am. I will achieve more and more every day because I know that I can. I will recognize only that which is good in myself; only that which is good in others; only that in all things and places that I know should live and grow. When adversity threatens I will be more determined than ever in my life to prove that I can turn all things to good account. And when those whom I have trusted seem to fail me, I will have a thousand times more faith in the honor and nobleness of man. I will think only of that which has virtue and worth. I will wish only for that which can give freedom and truth. I will expect only that which can add to the welfare of the race. I will live to live more. I will speak to give encouragement, inspiration and joy. I will work to be of service to an ever-increasing number. And in every thought, word and action my ruling desire shall be, to enrich, ennoble and beautify existence for all who come my way.

CHAPTER XII

THE DEVELOPMENT OF THE WILL

No force in the human system can be properly used unless it is properly directed, and as the will is the only factor in man that has the power to direct or control, a thorough development of the will, as well as a clear understanding of its application under every circumstance, becomes absolutely necessary if we are to use all the forces within us to the very best advantage.

To define the will with absolute exactness is hardly possible, though a clear knowledge as to its general nature and special functions must be secured. In a previous chapter, it was stated that the "I Am" is the ruling principle in man, and it may be added here that when the "I Am" exercises this function of rulership anywhere in the human system, will power is the result; or, it may be stated that the will is that attribute of the "I Am" which is employed whenever there is a definite intention followed by actual action, with a view of initiating, controlling or directing. To state it briefly therefore, will power is the result of the "I Am" either taking initiative action or controlling and directing any action after it has been taken.

Among the many functions of the will, the principal ones are as follows: The will to initiate; the will to direct; the will to control; the will to think; the will to imagine; the will to desire; the will to act; the will to originate ideas; the will to give expression to those ideas; the will to will into action any purpose; the will to carry through that purpose; the will to employ the highest and most perfect action of any force or faculty in mind; and the will to push up, so to speak, any talent in the mind to its highest point of efficiency. This last mentioned function has been ignored, but it is by far the most important in the practical life of attainment and achievement.

To illustrate this idea, we will suppose that you have a group of faculties, all of which are well developed, and contain a great deal of ability and power.

But how can those faculties be caused to act? The fact is they will not act in the least until the will wills them into action. The will therefore must first be applied, but the act of initiating action among those faculties is not its only function. To illustrate again, we will suppose that your will is very weak. It therefore stands to reason that the original impulse given those faculties will also be weak. Then when we understand that it is necessary for the will to continue to prompt or impel the continued action of any faculty we realize how weak, half-hearted and limited such an action will necessarily be when the will is weak. On the other hand, if your will is very strong, the original impulse given to the faculty will be strong and the continued action of that faculty will be much stronger, larger and more efficient. In brief, when a faculty is backed up, so to speak, with a powerful will, it easily doubles its capacity and efficiency; in other words, it is pushed up to a higher state of action. We understand therefore the great importance of having a strong will, though such a will is not only an advantage in promoting a fuller and larger expression of any faculty we may possess, but also in promoting a larger and more perfect expression of any force that may be applied, either in the personality, in character or in mind.

A powerful will, however, is never domineering or forceful. In fact, a domineering will is weak. It may be seemingly strong on the spur of the moment, but it cannot be applied steadily for any length of time. A strong will, however, is deep, continuous, and persistent. It calls into action your entire individuality, and as you exercise such a will you feel as if a tremendous power from within yourself had been calmly, though persistently aroused.

When we analyze the human mind, in the majority we find the will to be weak, and in fact, almost absent in a great many. Such people do not have the power to take a single original step. They have no initiative, and accordingly drift with the stream. Among others, who are a little higher in the mental scale, we find a will somewhat stronger, but not sufficiently strong to exercise with any degree of efficiency a single one of its functions. Among what can be called "the better class," we invariably find the will to be fairly well developed, and among the great leaders in all the different phases of human life and action, we find the will to be very strong; in fact, there is not a single mental or spiritual giant in history, who did not have a tremendous will, and this was one of his great secrets.

To illustrate further with regard to the last mentioned of the special functions, we will suppose that you have some talent for music. If you should will to exercise that talent to a slight degree only, it is evident that your efficiency along that line would not be marked. On the other hand, if your will was so strong that you could push up, so to speak, your musical faculty to its very highest point of efficiency, you would soon find yourself on the verge of musical genius; in fact, musical genius is absolutely impossible unless you have a strong will, no matter how much musical talent you may possess. Though it must be remembered in this connection that it is not sufficient simply to have a strong will.

The majority do not possess a strong will, and most of those who do have a strong will, have not learned how to apply it so as to secure greater efficiency in anything they may do; and here it is important to state that any one who will increase the power of his will, and properly train it for the purpose just indicated, may expect to increase his efficiency anywhere from twenty-five to two hundred percent. The majority have many times as much ability and working capacity as they are using at the present time; in fact, they apply only a small fraction of what is in them, and the principal reason why they do not apply all that is in them, is that they do not have sufficient power of will to act on this larger scale.

In this connection, we find another condition which is very important, and especially with regard to overcoming circumstances. A great many people have good intentions, and they have sufficient will power to originate those intentions, but they have not sufficient will power to carry them out; in other words, they have the will to think, but not the will to act. And here we can use our own imagination in picturing that state of human affairs that would inevitably come into being if all good intentions became actions.

Thousands of people start out right, but they have not the power of will to continue, so that where ten thousand make a good beginning, less than a score finish the race. We find this condition in all walks of life and in all undertakings, and it illustrates most eloquently the necessity of a strong will in every mind.

Realizing the importance of a strong will, and knowing that the will is weak in the minds of the great majority, we may well ask what might be the cause of this weakness; and the answer is that there are several marked causes, all of which we shall proceed to consider.

The first among these causes is alcohol. The use of alcohol weakens the will, not only in the individual who partakes of it, but in his children and grandchildren, and many generations following. It has been estimated by those who have studied this subject carefully, that the use of alcohol from generation to generation through the centuries is one of the principal causes for this weakness in the human will that we find to be almost universal. And when we study the psychology of the subject we soon discover the reason why.

Nearly every nation, as far back in history as we can go, has been using alcohol in some form or other, and as its weakening effect upon the will is transmissible from one generation to another, we realize that practically every member of the race has been burdened, more or less, with this adverse inheritance. But in this connection, we must remember that it is not necessary to be disturbed by this dark picture, because no matter what we have inherited, we can overcome it absolutely. However, we do not wish to do anything that will be in our own way, or in the way of generations that are to follow. It is therefore necessary that we consider this subject thoroughly, and act upon it accordingly.

The fact that the human race has transmitted a weak will from generation to generation explains why the human family does not have enough power to produce more than an occasional mental giant. Here and there we find in history, men and women who tower above the rest. Their minds are strong, their wills powerful, and their souls invincible; but how different is the condition among the majority. Most of them constitute mere driftwood, and follow blindly the leadership of these mental giants the race has produced. This, however, is not the intention of nature. Nature intends all men and women to be mental and spiritual giants, and does not intend that any one should follow the will of another. But the human race has, in this respect, ignored the intentions of nature.

The reason why the use of alcohol weakens the will, is very easily explained. When you take anything into the system that tends to take control over your desires, feelings or intentions, you permit yourself to be controlled by an outside agency, and accordingly the will for the time being is laid aside; and the law is, that whenever the will is laid aside by anything whatever it is weakened; that is, you undermine, so to speak, that element of the will which gives it the power to direct and control. When this practice is continued and repeated a number of times, we can readily understand how the power of the will is gradually decreased more and more, until its very foundation has been practically removed.

When you permit an outside agency to control your feelings and emotions at frequent intervals for a prolonged period, your system will soon get into the habit of submitting to the control of this outside agency, and will not respond any longer to any effort that the will may make to regain its original power of control. This being true, we find an explanation for a number of perplexing questions. We learn why great men and women are not more numerous. We learn why the majority are so easily influenced by temptations. We learn why powerful characters are found only here and there, and we also learn why every great nation of past history has fallen.

When we study history, we find that every great nation, after coming to a certain point of supremacy, began to decline, and there are several reasons for this strange termination of national power. But there is only one reason that stands out as the most vital of them all, and as possibly the cause of them all. We refer to the fact that a decrease of great men and women invariably precedes the decline of a nation. To keep any great nation up to a high standard of civilization there must be enough superior characters to hold the balance of power, but the very moment the balance of power gets into the hands of second grade men and women, a decline of that nation is inevitable. Therefore, if any great nation in the present age is to continue to grow in real greatness and real power, we must make a special effort to increase the number of great men and women in every generation. The greater a nation becomes, the more great men and women are required to govern and direct the forces of progress and growth that are at work in that nation. We therefore understand what is required of us in this generation if we want present civilization to advance and rise in the scale.

Another cause of this weakness in the will is found in what may be called psychical excess. And it is unfortunate that so many people have permitted themselves to be placed under psychical influences during the last fifty or seventy-five years; though it is a fact that a great many people have permitted their minds to be controlled or influenced by the psychical or the occult in every age. Another tendency therefore toward weakness in the will has been transmitted from generation to generation down through the ages, and we all have the effect of this misuse of mind also to overcome at the present time; but again let us remember that we have the power to overcome anything that we might have inherited.

Whenever you give up your individuality, or any part of your mind or thought, to some unknown force or influence that you know little or nothing about you are permitting an outside agency to usurp the function of the will. You lay the will aside, you undermine its power to some extent, and thereby weaken those elements in its nature that constitute self-mastery and self-control. That psychical excess has this tendency to a most pronounced degree is well illustrated by the fact that every individual, who is fascinated with psychical experience, invariably lacks in self-control. Such people are usually so sensitive that they are swayed in every direction by every suggestion or influence or environment with which they may come in contact.

But here we may well ask what we are living for—if we are living to give up to the influence of environment, visible or invisible, or if we are living to attain such full control over the powers and talents that are within us, that we can not only control, modify, and perfect environment, but also so perfectly control ourselves that we can become all that nature intends that we should become. If we are to rise in the scale, we must attain greater degrees of self-mastery, but we cannot learn to master ourselves so long as we are constantly permitting ourselves to be mastered by something else; and those who indulge in psychical experiences to any degree whatever, are permitting themselves to be mastered by something else. They are therefore losing ground every day. Their characters are becoming weaker, their standards of morality and rightness becoming more and more lax, as we all have discovered, and their power to apply those faculties and forces in their natures through which they may accomplish more and achieve more, are constantly decreasing, both in working capacity and in efficiency.

If man wants to live his own life as it should be lived; if he wants to master circumstances and determine his own destiny, he must have the power to say under all sorts of conditions what he is going to think and what he is going to do; but he cannot exercise this power unless his own will is permitted to have absolute control over every thought, effort and desire in his life.

Emotional excess is another cause that weakens the will, and by emotional excess we mean the act of giving way to uncontrolled feelings of any kind. To give way to anger, hatred, passion, excitability, intensity, sensitiveness, grief, discouragement, despair, or any other uncontrolled feeling, is to weaken the will. The reason is that you cannot control yourself through your will when you permit yourself to be controlled by your feelings; and any act that rules out the will, weakens the will.

Whenever you permit yourself to become angry, you weaken the will. Whenever you permit yourself to become offended or hurt you weaken your will. Whenever you permit yourself to become despondent or discouraged, you weaken your will. Whenever you give way to grief, mental intensity or excitability, you weaken your will. You permit some artificial mental state to take possession of your mind, and your will at the time is put aside. We therefore should avoid absolutely all emotional excess. We must not permit any feeling whatever to take possession of us, or permit ourselves to be influenced in any form or manner by anything that may enter the mind uncontrolled through the emotions; but this does not mean that we should ignore emotion. Emotion is one of the most valuable factors in human life, and should be used and enjoyed under every normal circumstance, but should never become a ruling factor in mind, thought or feeling.

You may look at a beautiful picture, and lose yourself, so to speak, in its charms. You may listen to exceptional music, and be carried away, or be thrilled through and through by the joy of its harmony; or you may witness some scene in nature that causes your soul to take wings and soar to empyrean heights. You may permit yourself to enjoy any or all of these ecstasies at any time, provided you have conscious control over every movement of your emotions at the time.

Whenever you feel the touch of some sublime emotion, try to direct the force of that emotion into a finer and a higher state of expression; thus you will not be controlled by it, but will exercise control over it, and accordingly will enjoy the pleasure of that emotion many times as much. It is a well-known fact that whenever we control any feeling, whether it be physical or mental or spiritual, and try to turn it into a larger sphere of expression, we enjoy far more the pleasure that naturally comes through the exercise of that feeling. To control our emotions therefore is to lose nothing and gain much.

Another cause of weakness in the will is what might be called mental dependence. To depend upon anybody or anything outside of yourself, is to weaken the will, for the simple reason that you let the will of some one else rule your actions, while your own will remains dormant. Nothing, however, that remains dormant can grow or develop. On the other hand, it will continue to become weaker and weaker, like an unused muscle, until it has no strength whatever. We therefore understand why those multitudes of people, who have followed blindly the will and leadership of others, not only in religion but in all other things, have practically no will power at all. And here we wish to state that it is positively wrong for any individual or any group of individuals to follow any one man or any one woman or any group of men or women under any circumstances whatever. We are here in this life to become something. We are here to make the best use of what we possess in mind, character and personality; but we cannot cause any element, faculty or power within us to express itself to any extent so long as we are mere dependent weaklings.

In everything, depend upon yourself, but work in harmony with all things. Do not depend even upon the Infinite, but learn to work and live in harmony with the Infinite. The highest teachings of the Christ reveal most clearly the principle that no soul was created to be a mere helpless instrument in the hands of supreme power, but that every soul should act and live in perfect oneness with that power. And the promise is that we all are not only to do the things that Christ did, but even greater things. Man is no credit to supreme creative power if he remains in the puppet stage, but he is a credit to that power if he becomes a giant in character, mind and soul. In our religious worship we have given unbounded praise to God for his wonderful power in creating man, and the very next moment we have announced the hymn, "Oh To Be Nothing." The absurdity of it all is too evident to need comment, but when we understand that character and man-hood, as well as practical efficiency in life, are the products of strength and not of weakness, we must come to the conclusion that every system of thought in the present age, be it religious, moral, ethical, or philosophical, needs complete reconstruction.

We are here to become great men and women, and with that purpose in view, we must eliminate everything in our religion and philosophy that tends to make the human mind a dependent weakling. If you would serve God and be truly religious, do not kneel before God, but learn to walk with God, and do something tangible every day to increase the happiness of mankind. This is religion that is worth while, and it is such religion alone that can please the Infinite.

Another cause which is too large and diversified to outline in detail, is that of intemperance; that is immoderation in anything in life. To indulge excessively any desire or appetite, be it physical or mental, is to weaken the will. Partake only of that which is necessary and good, and observe moderation. Control yourself under all circumstances, and resolve never to go too far in anything, because too much of the good may be more of an evil than not enough of it.

The effects of weakness in the will are numerous, but there are two in particular that should receive marked attention. The first is that when the will is weak, the human system becomes incapable of resisting temptations, and therefore moral weakness or a complete moral downfall is inevitable. Character in the largest sense of the term is impossible without a strong will, and it is impossible to accomplish anything that is of permanent value without character.

The second is that weakness in the will inevitably implies weak mental actions; that is, no matter how much ability you may possess, if your will is weak, you will apply only a fraction of that ability; and there are thousands of able men and women who are failures in life simply because they have not the will to apply all their ability. If they would simply increase the power of their will, and properly train that will, they would immediately pass from failure to success, and in many instances, remarkable success. It is the power of the strong will alone that can give full expression to every talent or faculty you may possess, and it is only such a power that can push up the actions of every faculty to a point of high efficiency.

In learning to develop the will and to use the will, realize what the will is for. Understand clearly what its functions actually are, and then use it in all of those functions. Avoid anything and everything that tends to weaken the will, and practice every method known that can strengthen the will. Do not give in to any feeling or desire until you succeed in directing that feeling or desire as you like. Feel only the way you want to feel, and then feel with all the feeling that is in you. Whatever comes up in your system, take hold of it with your will and direct it so as to produce even greater results than were at first indicated. Use the will consciously as frequently as possible in pushing up your faculties to the highest point of efficiency; that is, when you are applying those faculties that you employ in your work, try to will them into stronger and larger actions. This is a most valuable practice, and if applied every day will, in the course of a reasonable time, not only increase the capacity and ability of those faculties, but will also increase decidedly the power of the will.

Whenever you will to do anything, will it with all there is in you. If no other practice than this were taken, the power of the will would be doubled in a month. Depend upon the power that is in you for everything, and determine to secure the results you desire through the larger expression of that power. Never give in to anything that you do not want. When a certain desire comes up that you do not care to entertain, turn your attention at once upon some favorable desire, and give all the power of your will to that new desire. This is very important, as the average person wastes more than half of his energy entertaining desires that are of no value, and that he does not intend to carry out. Whenever any feeling comes up in the system ask yourself if you want it. If you do not, turn your attention in another direction; but if you do want it, take hold of it with your will and direct it toward the highest states of mind that you can form at the time. In brief, every action that enters the system, whether it comes through thought, feeling, desire or imagination, should be redirected, by the power of the will and turned into higher and greater actions.

Whenever you think, make it a practice to think with your whole mind.

Make your thinking whole-hearted instead of half-hearted. Whenever you act, act with all there is in you. Make every action firm, strong, positive and determined; in other words, put your whole soul into everything that you feel, think or do. In this way, you turn on, so to speak, the full current of the will, and whenever the will is used to its full capacity, it will grow and develop.

Try to deepen every action of mind and thought; that is, do not think simply on the surface, but also think subconsciously. Think and act with your deeper mental life. You thereby give the power of the will a deeper field of action, and it is established in the larger life of your individuality instead of in the surface thought of your objective mind. The difference between a superficial will and a deeply established will is readily found in everyday experience. When you will to do anything and your intentions are easily thwarted by the suggestion of some one else, your will is on the surface. But when your intentions are so deeply rooted in the subconsciousness of your mind that nothing can thwart those intentions, your will has gained that great depth which you desire.

The more easily you are disturbed, the weaker your will, while the stronger the will, the more difficult it is for anything to disturb your mind. When the will is strong, you live and exercise self-control in a deeper or interior mental world, and you look out upon the confusions of the outer world without being affected in the least by what takes place in the external.

Whenever you exercise the will, try to place the action of that will as deeply in the world of your interior mental feeling as you possibly can; that is, do not originate will-action on the surface, but in the depth of your own supreme individuality. Try to feel that it is the **"I Am"** that is exercising the power of the will, and then remember that the **"I Am"** lives constantly upon the supreme heights of absolute self-mastery. With this inspiring thought constantly in mind, you will carry the throne of the will, so to speak, farther and farther back into the interior realms of your greater mental world, higher and higher up into the ruling power of the supreme principle in mind. The result will be that you will steadily increase the power of your will, and appropriate more and more the conscious control of that principle in your greater nature through which all the forces in your possession may be governed and directed.

He who would become great must live a great life.

Happiness adds life, power, and worth to all your talents and powers. It is most important, therefore, that every moment should be full of joy.

However much you may do, always remember you have the ability to do more. No one has as yet applied all the ability in his possession. But all of us should learn to apply a greater measure every year.

While you are waiting for an opportunity to improve your time, improve yourself.

The man who never weakens when things are against him, will grow stronger and stronger until he will have the power to cause all things to be for him.

CHAPTER XIII

THE BUILDING OF A GREAT MIND

A great mind does not come from ancestors, but from the life, the thought and the actions of the individual himself; and such a mind can be constructed by any one who understands the art of mind building, and who faithfully applies his art.

You may have a small mind to-day, and your ancestors for many generations back may have been insignificant in mental power; nevertheless, you may become even exceptional in mental capacity and brilliancy if you proceed to build your mind according to the principles of exact science; and those principles any one can apply.

There are two obstacles, however, that must be removed before this building process can begin, and the first one of these is the current belief in heredity. That we inherit things is true, but the belief that we cannot become any larger or any better than our inheritance is not true. As long as a man believes that greatness is not possible to him because there were no great minds among his ancestors, he is holding himself down, and cannot become any more than he subconsciously thinks he can; while on the other hand, the man who expects to become much because he had remarkable grandfathers is liable to be disappointed because he depends too much upon his illustrious forefathers and not enough upon himself. Blood will tell when combined with ambition, energy and enterprise, but the very best of blood will prove worthless in the life of him who expects ancestral greatness to carry him through. When we have received good things we must turn them to good account or nothing is gained. Our success will not come from the acts of our forefathers, but can come alone from what we are doing now.

Those who have inherited rich blood can use that richness in building greatness in themselves, but those who have not the privilege of such inheritance need not be discouraged. They can create their own rich blood and make it as rich as they like. Whether your forefathers were great or small matters not. Do not think of that subject, but live in the conviction that you may become what you wish to become by using well the good you have received, and by creating those essentials that you did not receive. If you have inherited undesirable traits, remember that evil is but valuable power misdirected. Learn to properly direct all your forces and your undesirable traits will be transformed into elements of growth, progress and advancement.

We all have met men and women with remarkable talents, who persisted in thinking that they would never amount to anything because there was no genius among their ancestors. But if there had been a genius in the family some time during past generations, the question would be where that genius actually received his genius. If we all have to get greatness from ancestors, where did the first great ancestor get his greatness? There must be a beginning somewhere to every individual attainment, and that beginning might just as well be made by us now. What others could originate in their time, we can originate in our time.

The belief that we must inherit greatness from some one in order to attain greatness is without any scientific foundation whatever, and yet there are thousands of most promising minds that remain small simply because they entertain this belief.

To believe that heredity is against you and that you therefore will not accomplish anything worth while, is to make your work a wearing process instead of a building process. In consequence, you will not advance, and you will constantly remain in the rear; but the moment you realize that it is in your power to become as much as you may desire, your work and study will begin to promote your own growth and advancement. When you live, think and act in the belief that you can become much, whatever you do will cause you to become more. Thus all your actions will develop power and ability, and living itself will become a building process.

That man may become great regardless of the fact that there were no great minds among his ancestors many thinkers will admit, provided there are indications of exceptional ability in the man himself, but they entertain no hope if they see nothing in the man himself. And here we have the second obstacle to the building of a great mind. This obstacle, however, must be removed in every mind that aims to rise above the ordinary, because the belief that the average person has nothing in him is the cause of fully three-fourths of the mental inferiority we find in the world. But the new psychology has conclusively demonstrated the fact that the man who has nothing in him does not exist. All minds have the same possibilities, though most of those possibilities may be dormant in the minds of the majority.

The difference between a great mind and a small mind is simply this, that in the former the greater possibilities have come forth into objective action, while in the latter those possibilities are still in subjective inaction. When we say that a man has nothing in him we are contradicting the very principle of existence, because to be a man, a man must have just as much in him as any other man. What is in him may not be in action, and his mentality may appear to be small, but the possibilities of greatness are there. There is a genius somewhere in his mind, because there is a genius in every mind, though in most minds that genius may as yet be asleep.

When every child is taught the great truth that it has unlimited possibilities within its own subconscious mind, and that it can, through the scientific development of those possibilities, become practically what it may desire to become, we shall have laid the foundation for the greatest race of people that the ages have known. But we need not wait for future generations to demonstrate the possibilities of this truth. Every mind that begins to apply the principle of this truth now may begin to enlarge his mind now, and he may continue this process of enlargement indefinitely.

When we have removed the two obstacles mentioned, and have established ourselves firmly in the conviction that we have unlimited possibilities within us, more than sufficient to become whatever we may desire, we are ready to proceed with the building of a great mind.

To promote the building of a great mind, the two prime essentials, scope and brilliancy, must be constantly kept in the foreground of consciousness. The mind that is not brilliant is of little value even though its scope may be very large. Likewise, the mind that is narrow or circumscribed is extremely limited, however brilliant it may be. A great mind is great both in capacity and ability. It can see practically everything and see through practically everything. To see everything is to have remarkable scope. To see through everything is to have exceptional brilliancy.

To give scope to the mind, every action of mind must be trained to move toward that which is greater than all persons or things. Those feelings or desires that cause the mind to become absorbed in some one thing or group of things, will limit the mental scope. Therefore in love, sympathy, and purpose the sphere of action must be universal. When we live only with that love that centers attention upon a limited number of persons, one of the greatest actions of mind will work in a limited world. When our sympathies go only to a chosen few, the same thing occurs, and when our purpose in life has a personified goal, we keep the mind within the limitations of that personification.

To give universality to our feelings and actions, may require considerable training of the mental tendencies, but it is absolutely necessary if we will develop a great mind. It is only those mental forces that move toward the verge of the limitless in every direction that can cause the mind to transcend limitations; therefore, all the forces of the mind should be given this transcending tendency.

To develop mental scope, consciousness must move in every direction, and it must move along right lines, so that no obstacle may be met during that continuous expansive process. Such obstacles, however, are always produced by limitations of thought. Therefore, they may be avoided when all the actions of mind are placed upon a universal scale. In the mental actions of love, we find many forces, all of which are true in their own places, but all of these forces must be exercised universally; that is, they must act upon a scale that is without bounds in the field of your own consciousness. The mind must go in every direction as far as it possibly can go in that direction, and must act in the conviction that wherever it may go it can go farther still. The understanding must know that there is no obstacle where the mind may seem to cease in its onward action, and that the mind is forever growing, thereby going as far each day as that day's development requires.

When this idea is applied to a personal love between man and woman, the feeling of love must be based upon the principle that those two souls have the power to love each other more and more indefinitely; that the larger the love becomes the more lovable will the objects of that love become, and that the consciousness of perfect unity in pure affection increases constantly as the two souls become more and more individualized in their own sublime nature. It is possible to make conjugal love universal and continuous between one man and one woman when the love of each is directed toward the sublime nature of the other. Through this law, each individual develops through the consciousness of the largeness of the real nature of the other, and the more the two love each other in this universal sense, the more they will see in each other to love. In addition, the minds of both will constantly enlarge in scope, because when love acts upon this larger scale, the whole mind will act upon this larger scale, as there is no stronger power in mind than love.

The love between parent and child can, in like manner, be made universal. In this attitude, the parent will love all of the child, not only the visible person, but the undreamed-of wonders that are waiting in that child-mind for expression. The child already loves the parent in this larger sense, and this is one reason why the child-mind lives so much nearer to the limitless, the universal, the ideal and the beautiful. And when the parent will do likewise, there will arise between the two a love that sees more and more to love the more love loves in this larger, sublime sense.

The idea is not only to love the tangible, but also that other something that transcends the tangible—that something that appears to the soul in visions, and predicts wonders yet to be. That such a love will expand and enlarge the mind anyone can understand, because practically all the elements of the mind will tend to follow the actions of the love nature, when that nature is exceptionally strong. But we must not imagine that we shall, through this method, love the person less. The fact is, we shall love the person infinitely more, because we shall discern more and more clearly that the person is the visible side of that something in human life that we can only describe as the soul beautiful—that something that alone can satisfy the secret longings of the heart.

The love of everything can, through the same law, become universal. Even friendship, which is always supposed to be confined to a small world, may become universal and limitless in the same way; and when it does, you will see more to admire in your friend every day. You will both have entered the boundless in your admiration for each other, and having entered the boundless, you will daily manifest new things from the boundless, and thus become delightfully surprised at each other constantly. The same may be employed in making sympathy universal; that is, never sympathize with the lesser, but always sympathize with the greater. The lesser is combined in the greater, and by sympathizing with the greater, the mind becomes greater.

In the fields of motives, objects, aims and purposes, we find that nearly every mental action is occupying a limited scope, and is acting in such a manner that its own limitations are being perpetuated. This tendency, however, must be removed if a greater mind is to be constructed, because every action of the mind must aim to change itself into a larger action. To cause every aim or purpose to become universal in its action, the mind must transcend shape, form, space and distance in its consciousness of everything that it may undertake to do. When we confine our thought to so far or so much, we place the mind in a state of limitations, but when we promote every object with a desire to go as far as the largest conception of the present may require, and proceed to attain as much as present capacity can possibly appropriate, we are turning all purposes and aims out upon the boundless sea of attainment. And we shall not only accomplish all that is possible in our present state of development, but we will at the same time constantly enlarge the scope of the mind.

It is absolutely necessary to have a fixed goal whatever our purpose in life may be, but we must never give special shape or size to that goal. We must think of our goal as being too large to be measured, even in the imagination. When we have a goal in mind that is only so and so large, all the creative energies of the mind will limit themselves accordingly. They will create only so and so much, regardless of the fact that they may be able to create many times as much. But when we think of our goal as being too large to be measured, the creative energies will expand to full capacity, and will proceed to work for the largest attainment possible. They will act constantly on the verge of the limitless, and will cause the mind to outdo itself every day.

In the field of desire, the same law should be applied, and applied constantly, as there are no actions in the mind that exercise a greater influence over the destiny of man than that of desire. When desire is low or perverted, everything goes down or goes wrong, but when desire changes for the better, practically everything else in the human system changes to correspond. To train desire to become universal in action, every individual desire should be changed so as to act only for the promotion of growth. Those desires which when fulfilled, do not make for the enlargement of life, are detrimental. The power of all such desires therefore must be changed in their course. Your object is to become more and achieve more, and to constantly promote that object, development and growth must be perpetual throughout your system. For this reason, every action must have growth for its purpose, and as every action is the result of some desire, no desire must be permitted that is not conducive to growth. It is not necessary, however, to remove a single desire from the human system to bring about this change, because every desire can be trained to promote the building of a greater life.

When every desire is caused to move toward the larger and the greater through the mind's irresistible desire for the larger and the greater, all the creative forces of the mind will move toward the same goal, and will constantly build a greater mind. The principle is this, that when all the actions of mind are trained to move toward the larger, they will perpetually enlarge. The first essential to the building of a great mind will thereby be promoted.

To promote the second essential, mental brilliancy, the actions of mind must be made as high and as fine as possible; that is, the vibrations of the

mental life must be in the highest scale attainable. To see through everything the mind will require the very finest rays of mental light, and as this
mental light is produced by the vibrations of the actions of mind, these actions should be as high in the scale as we can possibly reach at every stage
of our mental ability. The light of intelligence is created by the mind itself,
and the more brilliant this light becomes, the greater will become the powers of intelligence, discernment, insight, understanding, ability, talent and
genius. And the power of mind to create a more brilliant mind increases as
the mind places itself more and more in the consciousness of the absolute
light of universal intelligence.

To cause the mind to become more brilliant, all the tendencies of mind
should fix their attention upon the highest mental conception of mental
brilliancy. Every expression of the mind should be animated with a refining
tendency. Every force of the mind should rise toward the absoluteness of
mental light. Those states of mind that tend to magnify the inferior must
be eliminated, and this is accomplished by thinking only of the superior that
is possible in all things. All mental actions that are critical, depressing or
depreciative must be replaced by their constructive opposites, as every action of the mind must concentrate its attention upon the largest and the best
in all fields of consciousness. The mind must be kept high in every respect,
because the higher in the mental scale the mind functions, the more brilliant
will become the mental light.

To increase the rapidity of the vibrations in these higher mental states,
creative energy must be supplied in abundance, and to comply with this
requirement, all that is necessary is to retain in the human system all the
energy that is already created. The human system creates and generates
an enormous amount of creative energy every day. Therefore, when all this
energy is retained and transmuted into finer mental elements, the mind will
be abundantly supplied with those finer energies that can increase both
the power and the brilliancy of thought and mind. The mind that is animated with a strong desire to constantly refine itself, and that is thoroughly
charged with creative energy, will always be brilliant, and will become
more and more brilliant as the laws given above are faithfully and thoroughly applied.

Remove the sting; remove the whine; remove the sigh. They are your enemies. They are never conducive to happiness; and we all live to gain happiness, to give happiness. From every word remove the sting. Speak kindly. To speak kindly and gently to everybody is the mark of a great soul. And it is your privilege to be a great soul. From the tone of your voice remove the whine. Speak with joy. Never complain. The more you complain, the smaller you become, and the fewer will be your friends and opportunities. Speak tenderly, speak sweetly, speak with love. From all the outpourings of your heart, remove the sigh. Be happy and contented always. Let your spirit sing, let your heart dance, let your soul declare the glory of existence, for truly life is beautiful. Every sigh is a burden, a self-inflicted burden. Every whine is a maker of trouble, a forerunner of failure. Every sting is a destroyer of happiness, a dispenser of bitterness. To live in the world of sighs is to be blind to everything that is rich and beautiful. The more we sigh, the less we live, for every sigh leads to weakness, defeat, and death. Remove the sting, remove the whine, remove the sigh. They are not your friends. There is better company waiting for you.

CHAPTER XIV

HOW CHARACTER DETERMINES
CONSTRUCTIVE ACTION

All the elements of life are good in themselves; and should produce good results when in action; that is, when the action is properly directed; but when any action is misdirected, evil follows, and this is the only cause of the ills of human existence.

Everything that is wrong in the world has been produced by the perversion and the misuse of the good. Therefore, to eliminate wrong, man must learn to make the proper use of those things that exist in his sphere of action. The misuse of things comes either from ignorance or lack of character, or both. That person who does not understand the elements and the forces of the world in which he lives will make many mistakes, and he will make the wrong use of nearly everything unless he is guided by instructions of those who understand. The leadership of greater minds is therefore necessary to the welfare of the race, but this leadership is not sufficient. Guidance from great minds will help to a limited degree so long as the actions of the individual are simple, but when greater development is sought, with its more complex actions, the individual himself must learn to master the laws of life. He can no longer depend upon others.

Therefore, though the leadership of greater minds be necessary to the welfare of the race, it is also necessary for that leadership to be used, not for keeping the multitude in a state of simple-mindedness and dependence, but for promoting the intelligence of each individual until external guidance is needed no more. The true purpose of the strong is to promote greater strength in the weak, and not to keep the weak in that state where they are at the mercy of the strong. Our united purpose should be to develop more great men and women, and to do everything possible to lead the many from dependence to independence.

Every state of individual attainment is preceded by a childhood period, but this period should not be unnecessarily prolonged, nor will it be, when every strong mind seeks to develop strength in the weak instead of using the weakness of the weak for his own gain. Those who understand the laws of life may inform the ignorant what to do and what not to do, and may thereby prevent most of the mistakes that the ignorant would otherwise make. But this guidance will not prevent all the mistakes, as experiences demonstrate, because it requires a certain amount of understanding to even properly apply the advice of another. Those who do not have the understanding will therefore misuse the elements of life at every turn, no matter how well they are guided by wiser persons, while those who do have this understanding will invariably begin to do things without consulting their so-called superiors. It is therefore evident that more understanding for everybody is the remedy, as far as this side of the subject is concerned, but there is also another side.

A great many people go wrong because they do not know any better. To them, a better understanding of life is the path to emancipation. They will be made free when they know the truth, but the majority of those who go wrong do know better. Then why do they go wrong? The cause is lack of character. When you fail to do what you want to do, your character is weak. The same is true when you preach one thing and practice another. When you fail to be as perfect, as good or as ideal as you wish to be, or fail to accomplish what you think that you can accomplish, your character is at fault. It is the character that directs the action of the mind. It is the lack of character, or a weak character that produces misdirections; and when you fail to accomplish what you feel you can accomplish, something is being misdirected.

What you feel that you can do that you have the power to do. Therefore, when you fail to do it, some of the powers of your being are being misdirected. To be influenced to do what you would not do if you were normal, means that your character is weak, and to be affected by surroundings, events, circumstances and conditions against your will, indicates the same deficiency. A strong character is never influenced against his will. He is never disturbed by anything, never becomes upset, offended or depressed. No one can insult him because he is above small states of mind, and is stronger than those things that may tend to produce small states of mind. All mental tendencies that are antagonistic, critical or resisting indicate a deficiency in character. The desire to criticize becomes less and less as the character is developed. It is the mark of a fine character never to be critical and to mention but rarely the faults of others. A strong character does not resist evil, but uses his strength in building the good. He knows that when the light is made strong, the darkness will disappear of itself. A strong character has no fear, never worries and never becomes discouraged. If you are in the hands of worry, your character needs development. The same is true if you have a tendency to submit to fate, give in to adversity, give up in the midst of difficulties, or surrender to failure or wrong. It may be stated, without any exceptions or modifications whatever, that the more temper, the less character. Anger is always a misdirection of energy, but it is the function of character to properly direct all energies. Therefore, there can be no anger when the character is thoroughly developed.

The mind that changes easily, that is readily carried away by every new attraction that may appear, and that does not retain a well-balanced attitude on any subject lacks character. A strong character changes gradually, orderly, and only as each step is thoroughly analyzed and found to be a real step forward. The more individuality, the more character, and the more one is oneself, the stronger the character. Practice being yourself, your very best self, and your very largest self, and your character will be developed. The more one is conscious of flaws and defects, the weaker the character, and the reason is because nearly everything is being misdirected when the character is weak. The strong character is conscious only of the right because such a character is right, and is causing everything in its sphere of action to do right.

To the average person, character is not important as far as this life is concerned; and as most theological systems have declared that it was repentance and not character that would insure human welfare in the world to come, the development of character has naturally been neglected. But when we realize that it is character that determines whether our actions in daily life are to go right or wrong and that every mistake is due to a lack of character, we shall feel that the subject requires attention.

It is the power of character that directs everything that is done in the human system or by the human system. Character is the channel through which all expressions must pass. It is character that gives human life its tone, its color and its quality, and it is character that determines whether our talents and faculties are to be their best or not.

The man who has a well developed character is not simply good. He is good for something, because he has the power to turn all his energies to good account. A strong character not only turns all the elements and energies of life to good account, but has the power to hold the mind in the right attitude during the most trying moments of life, so that he will not make mistakes nor fall a victim to insidious temptation. A strong character will keep all the faculties and forces of life moving in the right direction, no matter what obstacles we may meet in the way. We shall turn neither to the right nor to the left, but will continue to move directly toward the goal we have in view, and will reach that goal without fail.

Thousands of people resolve every year to press on to higher attainments and greater achievements. They begin very well, but ere long they are turned off the track. They are misled or switched off by counter attractions. They have not the character to keep right on until they have accomplished what they originally set out to do. True, it is sometimes wisdom to change one's plans, but it is only lack of character to change one's plans without reason, simply because there is a change of circumstance. To change with every circumstance is to drift with the stream of circumstance, and he who drifts can only live the life of a log. He will be a victim of every external change that he may meet. He will control little or nothing, and he will accomplish little or nothing.

We all can develop the power to control circumstances or rather to cause all circumstances to work with us and for us in the promotion of the purpose we have in view; and this power is character. Never permit circumstances to change your plans, but give so much character to your plans that they will change circumstances. Give so much character to the current of your work that all things will be drawn into that current, and that which at first was but a tiny rivulet, will thus be swelled into a mighty, majestic stream.

When the various forces of the system are properly directed and properly employed, the development of the entire mentality will be promoted; and this means greatness. The power that directs the forces of the system is character, and it is character that causes the mind to use those forces in the best and most constructive manner. There must be character before there can be true greatness, because any deficiency in character causes energy to be wasted and misdirected. It is therefore evident that the almost universal neglect in the development of character is one of the chief reasons why great men and women are not as numerous as we should wish them to be. Many may argue, however, that great minds do not always have good characters, and also that some of our best characters fail to manifest exceptional ability. But we must remember that there is a vast difference between that phase of character that simply tries to follow the moral law, and real character— the character that actually is justice, virtue and truth. Then we must also remember that character does not mean simply obedience to a certain group of laws, but the power to use properly all the laws of life. That person who uses mental laws properly, but fails to comply with moral laws does not possess a complete character. Nevertheless, the character of this person is just as good as that of the person who follows moral laws while constantly violating mental laws.

In the study of character, it is very important to know that the violation of mental laws is just as detrimental as the violation of moral laws, though we have been in the habit of condemning the latter and excusing the former. That person who uses properly the mental laws, will to a degree promote the development of the mind even though he may neglect the moral laws; and this accounts for the fact that a number of minds have attained a fair degree of greatness in spite of their moral weakness. But it is a fact of extreme importance, that those minds who attain greatness in spite of their moral weakness could become two or three times as great if they had also developed moral strength. That person who complies with the mental laws but who violates the moral laws, wastes fully one-half of the energies of his mind, and sometimes more. His attainment and achievement will, therefore, be less than one-half of what they might be if he had moral character as well as mental character.

The same is true, however, of that person who complies with the moral laws, but who violates the mental laws; fully one-half of his energy is wasted and misdirected. This explains why the so-called good characters are not any more brilliant than the rest, for though they may be morally good, they are not always mentally good; that is, they do not use their minds according to the laws of mind, and therefore cannot rise above the level of the ordinary.

The true character tries to turn all the energies of the system into the best and most constructive channels, and it is the mark of a real character when all the various parts of the being of man are working together harmoniously for the building of greatness in mind and soul. When the character is weak, there is more or less conflict among the mental actions. Certain actions have a tendency to work for one thing, while other actions are tending to produce the very opposite. The same is true of the desires. A character that lacks development will desire one thing today, and something else to-morrow. Plans will change constantly, and little or nothing will be accomplished. In the strong character, however, all actions work in harmony and all actions are constructive. And this is natural because it is the one supreme function of character to make all actions in the human system constructive—to make every force in the human life a building force.

Be good and kind to everybody and the world will be kind to you. There may be occasional exceptions to this rule, but when they come pass them by and they will not come again.

Ideals need the best of care. Weeds can grow without attention, but not so with the roses.

Not all minds are pure that think they are. Many of them are simply dwarfed.

It does not pay to lose faith in anybody. It is better to have faith in everybody and be deceived occasionally than to mistrust everybody and be deceived almost constantly.

When you meet a person who does not look well, call his attention to the sunny side of things, and aim to say something that will give him new interest and new life. You will thereby nip in the bud many a threatening evil, and carry healing with you wherever you go.

CHAPTER XV

THE ART OF BUILDING CHARACTER

Character is developed by training all the forces and elements of life to act constructively in those spheres for which they were created, and to express themselves in those actions only that promote the original purpose of the being of man.

Every part of the human system has a purpose of its own—a purpose that it was created to fulfil. When those elements that belong to each part express themselves in such a way that the purpose of that part is constantly promoted, all actions are right; and it is character that causes those actions to be right. Character is therefore indispensable, no matter what one's object in life may be. Character is the proper direction of all things, and the proper use of all things in the human system. And the proper use of anything is that use that promotes the purpose for which that particular thing was created.

To develop character it is therefore necessary to know what life is for, to know what actions promote the purpose of that life, and to know what actions retard that purpose. When the secret of right action is discovered, and every part of man is steadily trained in the expression of right action, character may be developed. But whatever is done, character must be applied in its fullest capacity. It is only through this full use, right use and constant use that anything may be perpetuated or developed.

Character develops through a constant effort to cause every action in the human system to be a right action; that is, a constructive action, or an action that promotes the purpose of that part of the system in which the action takes place. This is natural because since character is the power of right action, every effort to extend the scope of right action will increase the power of character. To have character is to have the power to promote what you know to be the purpose of life, and to be able to do the right when you know the right. To have character is to know the right, and to be so well established in the doing of the right that nothing in the world can turn you into the wrong.

The first essential is therefore to know the right; to be able to select the right; to have that understanding that can instinctively choose the proper course of action, and that knows how each force and element of life is to be directed so that the original purpose of human life will be fulfilled. The understanding of the laws of life will give this first essential in an intellectual sense, and this is necessary in the beginning; but when character develops, one inwardly knows what is right without stopping to reason about it. The development of character enables one to feel what is right and what course to pursue regardless of exterior conditions or intellectual evidence. The intellect discerns that the right is that which promotes growth and development; character inwardly feels that the right leads to greater things and to better things, and that the wrong leads invariably to the inferior and the lesser.

The presence of character produces a consciousness of growth throughout the system; and the stronger the character, the more keenly one can feel that everything is being reconstructed, refined, perfected and developed into something superior. This is but natural because when the character is strong, everything in the system is expressed in right action, and the right action of anything causes the steady development of that particular thing.

To distinguish between the right and the wrong becomes simplicity itself when one knows that the right promotes growth, while the wrong retards growth. Continuous advancement is the purpose of life; therefore, to live the right life is to live that life that promotes progress and growth, development and advancement in everything that pertains to life. For this reason, that action that promotes growth is in harmony with life itself, and must consequently be right. But that action that retards growth is at variance with life; therefore it is wrong; and wrong for that reason alone. Everything that promotes human advancement is right. Everything that interferes with human advancement is wrong. Here we have the basis of a system of ethics that is thoroughly complete, and so simple to live that no one need err in the least.

An intellectual understanding of the laws of life will enable any one to know what action promotes growth and what action retards growth, but as character develops, one can feel the difference between right and wrong action in his own system, because the consciousness of right becomes so keen that anything that is not right is discerned at once. It is therefore evident that the power to distinguish the right from the wrong in every instance will come only through the development of character. No matter how brilliant one may be intellectually, he cannot truly know the right until he has a strong character. The external understanding of the right can be misled, but the consciousness of the right is never mistaken; and this consciousness develops only as character develops.

The second essential is to create a subconscious desire for the right—a desire so deep and so strong that nothing can tempt the mind to enter into the wrong. When this desire is developed, one feels a natural preference for the right; to prefer the right, under all circumstances becomes second nature, while every desire for the wrong will disappear completely. When every atom in one's being begins to desire the right, the entire system will establish itself in the right attitude, and right action will become the normal action in every force, function and faculty. In addition, this same desire will produce mental tendencies that contain the power of right action, which always means constructive action.

It is a well known fact that all the forces and energies of the system, and all the movements of mind follow mental tendencies; therefore, when the mental tendencies are right actions, everything that takes place in the system will produce right action; and everything will be properly directed.

The desire for the right may be developed by constantly thinking about the right with deep feeling. Every thought that has depth, therefore, will impress itself upon the subconscious, and when that thought is inspired with a strong desire for the right, the conscious impression will convey the right to the subconscious. Every impression that enters the subconscious will cause the subconscious to bring forth a harvest of that which the impression conveyed; therefore, when the right is constantly held in mind with deep feeling, the right thought will soon become the strongest in the mind; and our desires are the results of our strongest thoughts.

You always desire that which is indicated in your strongest thought. You can therefore change those desires completely by thinking with deep feeling about that which you want to desire. No desire should be destroyed. All desires should be transmuted into the desire for the right, and when you subconsciously desire the right, every action in your being will be a right action.

The two fundamental essentials, therefore, to the development of character are to know the right and to desire the right, but the term "right" as employed here must not be confounded with that conception of right which includes only a few of the moral laws. To be right, according to the viewpoint of completeness, is to be in harmony with all the principles of life, and all the laws of the present sphere of human existence. To know the right, it is necessary not simply to memorize rules that other minds have formulated, but to inwardly discern what life is for, and what mode of thought and action is conducive to the realization of that which is in life. To desire the right, according to this view of the right, the mind must actually feel the very soul of right action, and must be in such perfect touch with the universal movement of right action, that all lesser and imperfect desires are completely swallowed up in the one desire—the desire that desires all that is in life, and all that is in perfect harmony with that which is in life.

It is the truth, that when we come into perfect touch with the greater, we cease to desire the lesser, and the closer we get to the one real desire, the less we care for our mistaken desires. Therefore, to remove an undesirable desire, the course is not to resist that desire, but to cultivate a greater and a better desire along the same line. In this connection, we must remember that the adoption of a greater desire does not compel us to sacrifice those things that we gain from the lesser desires. He who adopts the greater loses nothing, but is on the way to the gaining of everything.

To know the right and to desire the right, according to the complete significance of the right we must interiorly discern the very right itself. We cannot depend upon another's definition of the right, but must know fully the spirit of the right with our own faculties. That faculty that knows and feels the right, and that naturally knows and desires the right is character. Therefore, it is through the development of character that each individual will know for himself how to live, think and act in perfect harmony with the laws of all life.

When the consciousness of right action has been attained, a clear mental picture should be deeply impressed upon mind and every desire should be focused upon that picture. This concentration should be made as strong as possible, so that all the energies of the system are not only aroused, but caused to move toward the ideal of right action. And by right action, we mean that action that is thoroughly constructive, that builds for greater things and greater things only. Everything is right that builds for greater things. If it were not right, it could not produce the greater.

To clearly picture upon the mind the image of right action, and to concentrate with strong desire the whole attention upon that mental image, will cause all the tendencies of mind to move in the same direction. There will therefore be perfect harmony of mental action, and that action will be right action, because everything that moves toward the right must be right. This mental picture of right action should always be complete; that is, one's mental conception of the right should not be confined to certain parts of the system only, but should include every action conceivable in the being of man.

That person who pictures himself as virtuous, but forgets to picture himself above anger, fear and worry, is not forming a complete picture or ideal of the right. He is not giving the creative energies of the system a perfect pattern; the character that those energies are to build will therefore be one-sided and weak.

First ask yourself what you would have all the energies, powers, functions and faculties in your system do. Answer that question in the best manner possible, and upon that answer, base your picture of right action. Whenever a new line of action is undertaken, the mind should continue in that original line of action until the object in view has been reached. To do this in all things, even in trivial matters, will not only cause every action to produce the intended results, but real character will steadily be made stronger thereby.

The habit of giving up when the present task is half finished and try something else is one of the chief causes of failure. The development of a strong character, however, will remove this habit completely. To constantly think of the highest and the greatest results that could possibly follow the promotion of any undertaking or line of action will aid remarkably in causing the mind to keep on. To expect much from what we are doing now is to create a strong desire to press on toward the goal in view. To press on toward the goal in view is to reach the goal, and to reach the goal is to get what we expected.

An essential of great importance in the building of character is the proper conception of the ideal. No mind can rise higher than its ideals, but every mind can realize its ideals no matter how high they may be. Our ideals therefore cannot be too high. The ideal should not only be a little better than the present real, but should be perfection itself. Have nothing but absolute perfection in all things as the standard and the goal, and never think of your goal as anything less. Do not simply aim to improve yourself in just one more degree. Aim to reach absolute perfection in all your attainments and all your achievements, and make that desire so strong that every atom in your being thrills with its power.

To form all one's ideals in accordance with one's mental conception of absolute perfection, will cause the mind to live above the world of the ordinary, and this is extremely important in the building of character. A great character cannot be developed so long as the mind continues to dwell on the ordinary, the trivial or the superficial. Neither can true quality and true worth find expression so long as thought continues on the common plane; and the life that does not continue to grow into higher quality and greater worth has not begun to live. When character is highly developed, both the personality and the mentality will feel the stamp of quality and worth. High mental color will be given to every characteristic, and the nature of man will cease to be simply human. It will actually be more.

In building character, special attention must be given to hereditary tendencies or those traits of character that are born in us. But as all such traits are subconscious, they can be changed or removed by directing the subconscious to produce the opposite characteristics or tendencies. It matters not in the least what we may have inherited from our ancestors. If we want to change those things, we can do so. The subconscious will not only respond to any direction that we may make, but is fully capable of doing anything in the world of mind or character that we may desire to have done. Examine the tendencies of your mind and character, and fix clearly in consciousness which ones you wish to remove and which ones you wish to retain. Those that you wish to retain should be made strong by daily directing the subconscious to give those tendencies more life, more power and more stability. To remove those tendencies that you do not wish to retain, forget them. Do not resist them nor try to force them out of the mind. Simply forget them and direct the subconscious to create and establish new tendencies that are directly opposite to the nature of the ones that you wish to remove. Build up those qualities that constitute real character, and every bad trait that you have inherited from your ancestors will disappear.

To build up those qualities, picture in your mind the highest conceptions of those qualities that you can possibly form; then impress those conceptions and ideas upon the subconscious. Such impressions should be formed daily, and especially before going to sleep, as the building process in the subconscious is more perfect during sleep.

By impressing the idea of spotless virtue upon the subconscious every day for a few months, your moral tendencies will become so strong that nothing can tempt you to do what you know to be wrong. Not that physical desire will disappear; we do not want any natural desire to disappear, but your control of those desires will be so complete that you can follow them or refuse to follow them just as you choose. And your desire to remain absolutely free from all wrong will become so strong that nothing can induce you to do what your finer nature does not wish to have done.

There are millions of people who are morally weak in spite of the fact that they do not wish to be, but if these people would employ this simple method, their weakness would soon disappear, because by impressing the idea of spotless virtue upon the subconscious, the subconscious will produce and express in the personality the power of virtue; and if this process is continued for some time, the power of virtue in the person will become so strong that it can overcome and annihilate instantly every temptation that may appear.

Impress upon the subconscious the idea of absolute justice, and your consciousness of justice will steadily develop until you can discriminate perfectly between the right and the wrong in every imaginable transaction. Whatever quality you wish to develop in your character, you can increase its worth and its power steadily by applying this subconscious law; that is, what is impressed upon the subconscious will be expressed through the personality, and since the seed can bring forth ten, thirty, sixty and a hundred fold, one tiny impression, therefore, may have the power to bring forth a great and powerful expression. Everything multiplies in the subconscious, whether it be good or otherwise. Therefore, by taking advantage of this law and giving to the subconscious only those ideas and desires that have quality and worth, we place ourselves in the path of perpetual increase of everything good that the heart may desire.

The two predominating factors in character are justice and virtue. The former gives each element in life its proper place. The latter turns each element to proper use. The consciousness of justice is developed through the realization of the fact that nothing can use what is not its own. To try to use what is not one's own will result in misuse.

When the consciousness of justice is thoroughly developed, everything in the human system will be properly placed. That very power of the mind that feels justice—the true placing of things—will cause all things within man to be properly placed. And when justice rules among all things in the interior life of man, that man will naturally be just to all things in the exterior life.

It is not possible for any person to deal justly with men and matters in the external world until he has attained the consciousness of justice within himself. He may think he is just, or he may try to be just, but his dealings will not be absolutely just until he can feel justice in his own life. To feel justice within oneself is to keep the entire system in a state of equilibrium. The mentality will be balanced and no force or element will be misplaced. It is therefore something for which we may work with great profit.

To be virtuous in the complete sense of the term, is to use all things properly, and the proper use of things is that use that works for greater things. Virtue is therefore applicable to every force, function and faculty in the being of man, but in its application there must be no desire or effort to suppress or destroy. Virtue means use—right use—never suppression.

When things cannot be used in their usual channels, the energies in action within those things should be turned in their courses and used elsewhere. When creative energy cannot be properly applied physically, it should be employed metaphysically; and all energy can be drawn into mind for the purpose of building up states, faculties, talents or powers. (Practical methods through which this may be accomplished will be given in the next chapter.)

When a certain desire cannot be expressed with good results in its present purpose, the power of that desire should be changed and caused to desire something else—something of value that can be carried out now. The power of that desire therefore is not lost, neither is enjoyment sacrificed, because all constructive forces, give joy to the mind. "And the greatest of joys shall be the joy of going on."

The desire for complete virtue is developed through the realization of the fact that the greatest good comes only when each part fulfils, physically and metaphysically, what nature intended. In the application of virtue, the purpose of nature may be fulfilled metaphysically when the physical channel does not permit of true expression at the time; though when physical expression may be secured, the metaphysical action should always be in evidence, because the greatest results always follow when physical and metaphysical actions are perfectly combined.

In the building of character, the two principal objects in view should be the strong and the beautiful. The character that is strong but not beautiful may have force, but cannot use that force in the building of the superior. The character that is beautiful but not strong will not have sufficient power to carry out its lofty ideals. It is the strong and the beautiful combined that builds mind and character, and that brings into being the superior man.

When the creative energies are daily transmuted, and turned into muscle, brain and mind, a virtuous life can be lived without inconvenience. Besides, the body will be healthier, the personality stronger and the mind more brilliant.

Hold yourself constantly in a positive, masterful attitude, and fill that attitude with kindness. The result will be that remarkable something that people call personal magnetism.

Creative energy when retained in the system will give vigor to the body, sparkle to the eye, and genius to the brain.

There is enough power in any man to enable him to realize all his desires and reach the highest good he has in view. It is only necessary that all of this power be constructively applied.

CHAPTER XVI

THE CREATIVE FORCES IN MAN

The human system may well be termed a living dynamo, as the amount of energy, especially creative energy, generated in the mind and personality of man is simply enormous. If we should try to measure the amount produced in the average healthy person, we should become overwhelmed with surprise; though we should naturally become even more surprised after learning how much power nature gives to man, and then finding that he applies only a fraction of it. We shall soon see the reason for this, however, and learn exactly why all of this vast amount of energy is not turned to practical use.

What is called creative energy in its broadest, largest sense, is that power in man that creates, forms or reproduces anywhere in the human system, and it divides itself into a number of groups, each one having its special function. One group creates thought, another brain cells, another nerve tissues, another muscular tissues, another manufactures the various juices of the system, another produces ideas, another creates talent and ability, another reproduces the species, and a number of other groups produce the various chemical formations in the system. We therefore have all kinds of creative processes going on in the human system, and corresponding energies with which these processes are continued.

One of the most interesting facts in connection with this study is that Nature generates more energy for each group than is required for normal functioning through its particular channel. In consequence, we find a great deal of surplus energy throughout the system. Each function supplies a certain percentage, and as it is not used by the function itself, the larger part of it naturally goes to waste. And here is where our subject becomes decidedly important. All kinds of creative energy are so closely related that they can be transformed and transmuted into each other. What is wasted in one function can therefore be turned to actual use in another function. An extra supply can thereby be secured for the creation of thoughts and ideas if such should be necessary, or an extra supply can be secured for the manufacture of the different juices of the system, or for the increase of muscular activity or functional activity in any one of the vital organs. Each group will readily change and combine with any other group, thus producing additional power in any part of the system at any time.

More than half of the energy generated in the human system is surplus energy, and is not needed for normal functioning, either in mind or body, though there are many personalities that generate so much energy that fully three-fourths of the amount generated is surplus. The question is therefore what shall be done with this surplus energy, and how any amount of it can be applied through any special function or faculty desired? If a person can accomplish a great deal, sometimes remarkable things by only using a fraction of his energy, it is evident that he could accomplish a great deal more if some means could be found through which he might apply all of his energy. In fact, if such means were found, his working capacity, as well as his ability, might be doubled or trebled, and his achievements increased in proportion. If a certain amount of energy produces a certain degree of working capacity, twice as much energy would naturally double that working capacity, and this has been demonstrated a number of times. A great many people, who have tried to transmute their creative energies, and direct those energies into some special faculty, have found that the working capacity of that faculty has been increased for the time being to a remarkable degree, but this is not the only result secured. The same process will also increase the brilliancy of the mind, and here let us remember that genius, in most instances, is accounted for by the fact that practically all of the surplus energy of the personality flows naturally into that faculty where genius is in evidence.

To illustrate the idea further, take two men of equal personal power. Let one of them permit his surplus energy to flow into the different functions as usual, giving over a part to normal requirements, and the other to mere waste. We shall not find this man doing anything extraordinary. But let the other man give over to normal functions only what is actually required, and then turn the remainder into his mind, or those parts of his mind that are being applied in his work. We shall find in this second case that ability will rapidly increase, and that in the course of time actual genius be developed. That genius could be developed by this process in every case, has not been demonstrated, though it is quite probable that it could be demonstrated without a single exception. However, no individual can turn surplus energy into any faculty without becoming more able, more efficient and more competent in that faculty. To learn how this process can be carried out successfully under any circumstances is therefore thoroughly worth while.

To proceed, we must first learn how these different groups of creative energy naturally act; and we find that each group goes, either naturally or through some habit, into its own part of mind or body; in other words, we find in the human system, a number of streams of energy flowing in different directions, performing certain functions on their way, using up a fraction of their power in that manner, the rest flowing off into waste. Knowing this, the problem before us is to learn how to redirect those streams of energy so as to turn them to practical use where they can be used now, and thus not only prevent waste, but increase the result of our efforts in proportion. In brief, we want to know how we can take up all surplus energy, that is, all energy that remains after normal functioning has been provided for, and use that surplus in promoting more successfully the work in which we are engaged. And to learn how to do this, we must study the art of transmutation.

What we call transmutation is not some mysterious something that only a few have the power to understand and apply, but one of the simplest things in Nature, as well as one of the most constant of her processes. Nature is continually transmuting her energies, and it is in this manner that extraordinary results are found anywhere in the realms of Nature, or anywhere in human nature where unconscious actions along greater lines have been the cause. Whenever any individual has accomplished more than usual, it is the law of transmutation through which the unusual has been secured. The use of the law may have been unconscious, though everything that is applied in part and unconsciously, can be applied fully and thoroughly through conscious action.

When anyone is using his mind continually along a certain line, and is so thoroughly absorbed in that line of action that it takes up his whole attention, we invariably find that the mind while in that condition, draws an extra amount of energy from the body. Sometimes it draws too much, so that every desire of the body is, for the time being, suspended and the vitality of the different physical organs decreased below normal. A man while in this condition frequently loses desire for food, and we all know of inventors who have been so absorbed in their experiments that they have neither taken nor desired food for days. We have also found the same condition in many others, especially among authors, composers and artists, where the mind was given over completely to the subject at hand. And what is the cause but transmutation? When the mind takes up for its own use a great deal of the energy naturally employed in the body, the power of normal functioning will have so decreased that the desire for normal functioning will have practically disappeared for the time being.

Another illustration with which we are all familiar, is where every natural desire of the body disappears completely, for a time, when the mind is completely absorbed in some entirely different desire; and here we find the law that underlies the cure of all habits. If you would turn your mind upon some desire that was directly opposite to the desire that feeds your habit, and if you would give over your whole attention to that opposite desire, you would soon draw all the energy away from that desire which perpetuates the habit. The habit in question therefore would soon die of starvation. In the same way, people who are inclined to be materialistic could overcome that tendency entirely by concentrating attention constantly and thoroughly upon the idealistic side of life. In this case, those forces of the system that are perpetuating materialistic conditions would be transmuted into finer energies, and would thereby proceed to build up idealistic or more refined conditions of body, mind and personality. Both Nature and human experience are full of illustrations of transmutation, so that we are not dealing in this study with something that lies outside of usual human activity. We are dealing with something that is taking place in our systems every minute, and we want to learn how to take better control of this something, so that we can apply the underlying law to the best advantage.

In learning to apply the law of transmutation, our first purpose should be to employ all surplus energy either in promoting our work or in developing faculties and talents. This process alone would practically double the working capacity of any mind, and would steadily increase ability and talent; and also to turn energy to good account that cannot be used in its own channel now.

To illustrate, suppose you have a desire for a certain physical or mental action, and you know that it would not be possible to carry out that desire at the time. Instead of permitting the energy that is active in that desire to go to waste, you would turn that energy into some other channel where it could be used to advantage now. Our second purpose should be to direct all surplus energy into the brain and the mind in case we had more energy in our body than we could use, or that was required for physical functioning, and thereby become stronger and more efficient in all mental activities.

Our third purpose should be to transmute all reproductive energy into talent and genius when there was no need of that energy in its own particular sphere. And in this connection, it is well to mention the fact that a man who is morally clean, other things being equal, has in every instance, greater agility, greater capacity, and greater endurance by far than the man who is not. While the latter is wasting his creative energies in useless pleasures, as well as in disease producing habits, the former is turning all of his creative energy into ability and genius, and the result is evident. In carrying out these three purposes we can prevent all waste of mental and personal power. We can control our desires completely; we can eliminate impurity, and we can turn life and power into channels that will invariably result in greater mental power and brilliancy, if not marked ability and rare genius.

To experiment, turn your whole attention upon your mind for a few minutes, and desire gently to draw all your surplus energy into the field of mental action. Then permit yourself to think along those lines where the mind is inclined to be most active. In a few moments you will discover the coming of new ideas; and in many instances, you will for several hours receive ideas that are brighter and more valuable than what you have received for some time. Repeat the process later, and again and again for many days in succession, and it will be strange indeed, if you do not finally secure a group of ideas that will be worth a great deal in your special line of thought or work. Whenever you feel a great deal of energy in your system, and try to direct it into the mind, you will have the same result. Ideas will come quickly and rapidly, and among them all you will surely find a few that have exceptional merit.

In learning the art of transmutation, the first essential is to train your mind to think that all surplus energy is being turned into the channel you have decided upon; that is, if you are a business man, you naturally will want all your surplus energy to accumulate in your business faculties. To secure this result, think constantly of your surplus energy as flowing into those faculties. This mode of thinking will soon give your energies the habit of doing what you desire to have done. It is a well-known law, that if we continue to think deeply and persistently along a certain line, Nature will gradually take up that thought and carry it out. Another law of importance in this connection is that if we concentrate attention upon a certain faculty or upon a certain part of the system, we create a tendency among our energies to flow toward that faculty or part. We understand therefore the value of constantly bearing in mind the idea that we wish to realize. What we constantly impress upon the mind through our thoughts and desires, finally becomes a subconscious habit, and when any line of action becomes a subconscious habit, it acts automatically; that is, it works of itself.

Before taking up this practice, however, it is necessary to determine positively what you actually desire your surplus energy to do. You must know what you want. Then continue to want what you want with all the power of desire that you can arouse. Most minds fail in this respect. They do not know with a certainty what they wish to accomplish or perfect. Their energies therefore are drawn into one channel to-day and another to-morrow, and nothing is finished. If you are an inventor, train your mind to think that all your surplus energy is constantly flowing into your faculties of invention. If you are a writer, train your mind to think that all your surplus energy is flowing into your literary talents; or whatever it is that you may be doing or want to do, direct your energy accordingly. You will soon find that you will increase in power, ability, and capacity along the lines of your choice, and if you continue this process all through life, your ability will continue to increase, no matter how long you may live.

The second essential is to desire deeply and persistently that all your surplus energy shall flow into those functions or faculties that you have selected for greater work. Wherever your desire is directed, there the force of your system will also tend to go, and herein we find another reason why persistent desire has such extreme value. The use of desire in this connection, however, must always be deep and calm, and never excited or overwrought.

The third essential is to place your mind in what may be termed the psychological field, and while acting in that field, to concentrate upon that part or faculty where you want your surplus energy to accumulate. This essential or process constitutes the real art of transmutation, though it is by no means the easiest to acquire. To master this method a great deal of practice will be required, but whenever you can place your mind in the psychological field and concentrate subjectively upon any part of your system where you want surplus energy to accumulate, all your surplus energy positively will accumulate in that part within a few moments' time. Through the same process, you can annihilate any desire instantaneously, and change all the energy of that desire into some other force. You can also, in the same way, reach your latent or dormant energies, and draw all of those energies into any channel where high order of activity is desired; in fact, through this method, you can practically take full possession of all the power, active or latent, in your system, and use it in any way that you may wish. That you should, after you learn to apply this method successfully, become highly efficient in your work, is therefore evident, though this is not all. Extraordinary capacity, mental brilliancy and genius can positively be developed through the constant use of this method, provided, however, that nothing is done, either in thought, life or conduct, to interfere with the underlying law of the process.

To place your mind in the psychological field, try to turn your conscious actions into what may be termed the finer depths of the personality; that is, try to become conscious of your deeper life; try to feel the undercurrents of mind and thought and consciousness, and try to act in perfect mental contact with those deep, underlying forces of personality and mentality that lie at the foundation of your conscious activity. An illustration in this connection will be found valuable. When you listen to music that seems to touch your soul, so that you can feel the vibrations of its harmony thrill every atom of your being, you are in the psychological field. You are alive in another and a finer mental world, a mental world that permeates your entire personal existence. You are also in the psychological field when you are stirred by some emotion to the very depth of your innermost life. A deepening of thought, feeling, life and desire will take the mind, more or less, into the psychological field; and whenever the mind begins to act in that field, you should concentrate your attention upon that faculty or part of your system where you wish extra energy to accumulate. Make your concentration alive, so to speak, with interest, and make every action of that concentration as deep as possible, and all your surplus energy will positively flow toward the point of concentration.

The power of this process can be demonstrated in a very simple manner. Place your mind in the psychological field, and then concentrate subjectively upon your hand, arousing at the time a deep desire for the increase of circulation in your hand. In a few moments, the veins on the back of your hand will be filled to capacity, and your hand, even though it might have been cold in the beginning, will become comfortably warm. Another experiment that is not only interesting in this connection, but may prove very valuable, is to concentrate in this same manner upon your digestive organs, in case the digestive process is retarded. You will soon feel more energy accumulating throughout the abdominal region, and any unpleasant sensation that you might have felt on account of indigestion will disappear entirely; in fact, even chronic indigestion can be cured in this way if the method is applied for a few minutes immediately before and after each meal. The idea is simply this, that when you give extra energy to an organ, it will be able to perform its function properly, and whenever any function is performed properly, any ailment that might have existed in the organ of that function, will disappear. A number of similar experiments may be tried, all of which will prove equally interesting, and besides, will train the mind to apply this great law of transmutation.

The following effects may be secured through transmutation: Working capacity in any part of the personality or mentality may be constantly increased; all the energy generated in the system may be employed practically and successfully; the mind may be made more brilliant, as it is an extraordinary amount of creative energy going into the mind that invariably causes mental brilliancy. Any faculty selected can be given so much of this surplus energy of the system, that it will almost from the beginning, manifest an increase in ability, and will, in the course of time, manifest rare talent and even genius. Moral purity may become second nature, as all that energy that was previously squandered in impure thought, impure desire or impure action can be transmuted readily, and applied in the building of a more vigorous personality and a more brilliant mind. A better control of all the forces of the personality may be obtained, and that mysterious something called personal magnetism may be acquired to a remarkable degree.

The attainment or accumulation of personal magnetism is something that we all desire, and the reason why is evident. What is called personal magnetism is the result of an extra amount of creative energy stored up in the personality and caused to circulate harmoniously throughout the personality. And the effect of this power is very marked. People who possess it are invariably more attractive, regardless of shape and form, and they are invariably more successful, no matter what their work may be. Hundreds of illustrations could be mentioned proving conclusively the extreme value of personal magnetism, though we are all so familiar with the fact that we do not require proof in the matter. What we want to know is what this power really is, how it may be produced, and why those who possess it have such a great advantage over those who do not possess it.

To illustrate, we may take two women who look alike in every respect; who have the same character and the same mentality, and who are equals in every respect but one, and that is that the one has personal magnetism while the other has not. But we need not be told of the fact. The woman who does not possess this power cannot be compared in any way with the woman who does possess it. The woman who does possess this power is far more attractive, far more brilliant, and seems to possess qualities of far greater worth; and the reason is that personal magnetism tends to heighten the effect of everything that you are, or that you may do. If we should compare two business men of equal ability and power, the one having personal magnetism and the other one not, we should find similar results. The one having this power would be far more successful, regardless of the fact that his ability and power in other respects were the same as his associate. Even men of ordinary ability succeed remarkably when they have personal magnetism; and we all know of women who are as plain as nature could make them, and yet being in possession of personal magnetism, are counted among the most attractive to be found anywhere. The most ordinary human form becomes a thing of beauty if made alive with this mysterious power, and a personality that had no attraction whatever, will fascinate everybody to a marked degree if charged with this power. We all know this to be true; we are therefore deeply interested to know how this power might be secured.

In the first place, we must remember that personal magnetism does not exercise its power by controlling or influencing other minds as many have supposed. The fact is if you try to influence others, you will lose this power, and lose it completely, no matter how strong it may be at the present time. The secret of personal magnetism simply lies in the fact that it tends to bring out into expression the best that is in you, and tends to heighten the effect of every expression; or, in other words, it causes every expression to act to the best advantage; though we find this power exercising its peculiar effect, not only in the personality and in the mentality of the individual, but also in his work.

When a musician has this power, his music charms to a far greater degree than if he does not possess it. There is something not only in the singing voice, but also in the speaking voice that indicates the absence or presence of this power. What it is no one can exactly describe, but we know it is there, and it adds immeasurably to the quality of what is expressed through the voice. In the field of literature we find the action of this power to be very marked. A writer who does not possess this mysterious force may write well, but there is something lacking in what he has written. On the other hand, if he has this power, he gives not only added charm to what he has written, but his ideas invariably appear to be more brilliant. In fact, there seems to be a power in everything he writes that is not ordinarily found on the printed page. On the stage this power is one of the principal factors, and we frequently find that the only difference between the good actor and a poor one, is the possession of a high degree of personal magnetism. No matter how well an actor may act, if he lacks in this power, he cannot succeed on the stage. When we go into the social world, we find the same fact.

Those who possess this power are invariably the favorites, even though they may be lacking in many other qualities. In the business world we find in every case that a man who is lacking in personal magnetism is at a disadvantage, while the one who has an abundance of this power will have no difficulty, other things being equal, in working himself to the fore.

In a deeper study of this force, we find that it affects every movement of the body, every action of the mind, and every feeling or expression that mind and personality may produce; that is, it seems to give something additional to every action or movement, and makes everything about the individual more attractive. We might say that this force sets off everything about the person to a greater advantage. This power therefore does not act directly upon others, but acts directly upon the one who has it, and thereby makes the individual more striking, as well as more attractive, both in appearance and in conduct. What is good in you is made better if charged with this force, and every desirable effort that you may make produces a better effect in proportion. Added charm, added attractiveness, and added efficiency—these invariably follow where the individual is in possession of a marked degree of this power. That which is beautiful is many times as beautiful where personal magnetism is in action, and that which is brilliant, becomes far more brilliant when combined with this mysterious force. Many people are born with it and apply it unconsciously, though the majority who have it, have acquired it through various forms of training. Any system of exercise that tends to harmonize the movements of the body, will tend to increase to some extent the power of this force; though when such exercises are combined with the transmutation of creative energy, the results will be far greater. The reason for this is found in the fact that what is called personal magnetism is the result of a great deal of creative energy held in the system, or transmuted into harmonious muscular or mental activity.

The development of this power depends upon the proper training of the body in rhythmic movements, and the training of the surplus energy in the system to act harmoniously along the lines of constructive action in mind and body. A very important essential is to cultivate poise, which means peace and power combined. Try to feel deeply calm throughout your entire system, and at the same time, try to give full and positive action to every power in your system. Try to hold in your system all the energy generated, and the mere desire to do this will tend to bring about what may be called accumulation of energy. To experiment, try for several minutes to hold all your energy in your personality, and at the same time, try to give all of that energy harmonious action within your personality. In a few moments, you will actually feel alive with power, and if you have succeeded very well with your experiment, you will really feel like a storage battery for the time being. You will have so much energy that you will feel as if you could do almost anything. Experiment in this way at frequent intervals until you get your system into the habit of carrying out this process unconsciously. You will thereby cause your surplus energy to accumulate more and more in your system, and you will produce what may be called a highly charged condition of your personality, a condition that invariably means the attainment of personal magnetism. To secure this result, however, it is necessary to keep the mind in an undisturbed attitude, to avoid all bad habits, physical or mental, to be in harmony with everything and everybody, and to exercise full self-control under every circumstance.

In cultivating this power, realize that it is the result of surplus energy held in the system, and caused to circulate harmoniously through every part of the system; remember that it is a power that does not act intentionally upon persons or circumstances; that its aim is not to control or influence anybody, but simply to act within the individual self, and heighten the effect of everything that he may be or do.

Never think or speak of that which you do not wish to happen.

The whine, the sting, and the sigh—these three must never appear in a single thought or a single word.

You can win ten times as many friends by talking happiness as you can by talking trouble. And the more real friends you have the less trouble you will have.

Speak well of everything good you find and mean it. When you find what you do not like keep quiet. The less you think or speak of what you do not like the more you have of what you do like.

Magnify the good; emphasize that which has worth; and talk only of those things that should live and grow.

When you have something good to say, say it. When you have something ill to say, say something else.

CHAPTER XVII

THE BUILDING POWER OF
CONSTRUCTIVE SPEECH

There is a science of speech, and whoever wishes to promote his welfare and advancement must understand this science thoroughly and regulate his speech accordingly. Every word that is spoken exercises a power in personal life, and that power will work either for or against the person, depending upon the nature of the word. You can talk yourself into trouble, poverty or disease, and you can talk yourself into harmony, health and prosperity. In brief, you can talk yourself into almost any condition, desirable or undesirable.

Every word is an expression and every expression produces a tendency in some part of the system. This tendency may appear in the mind, in the body, in the chemical life of the body, in the world of desire, in character, among the various faculties, or anywhere in the personality, and will work itself out wherever it appears. Our expressions determine largely where we are to go, what we are to accomplish, and how we are to meet those conditions through which we may pass.

When our expressions produce tendencies toward sickness and failure, we will begin to move toward those conditions, and if the tendency is very strong, all the creative energies in the system will move in the same direction, focusing their efforts upon sickness and failure, or taking those conditions as their models, and thereby producing such conditions in the system. On the other hand, when our expressions produce tendencies toward health, happiness, power and success, we will begin to move toward those things, and in like manner create them in a measure.

Every word has an inner life force, sometimes called the hidden power of words, and it is the nature of this power that determines whether the expression is to be favorable or not. This power may be constructive or destructive. It may move toward the superior or the inferior. It may promote your purpose in life or it may retard that purpose, and it is the strongest when it is deeply felt. Therefore the words which we inwardly feel are the words that act as turning points in life. When you feel that trouble is coming, and express that feeling in your speech, you are actually turning in your path and are beginning to move toward that trouble. In addition you are creating troubled conditions in your system. We all know that the more trouble we feel in the midst of trouble, the more troublesome that trouble will become. And we also know that that person who retains poise and self-control in the midst of trouble, will pass through it all without being seriously affected; and when it is over, is much wiser and stronger for the experience.

When you feel that better days are coming, and express that feeling in your speech, you turn all the power of your being toward the ideal of better days, and those powers will begin to create the better in your life. Whenever you talk about success, advancement, or any desirable condition, try to express the feeling of those things in your words. This inner feeling determines the tendencies of your creative powers; therefore, when you feel success in your speech, you cause the creative powers to create qualities in yourself that can produce success, while if you express the feeling of doubt, failure or loss in your words, those creative powers will produce inferiority, disturbance, discord, and a tendency to mistakes. It is in this way that the thing we fear comes upon us. Fear is a feeling that feels the coming of ills or other things we do not want; and as we always express through our words the feelings that we fear, we form tendencies toward those things, and the creative powers within us will produce them.

Whether the inner life force of a word will be constructive or destructive depends upon several factors, the most important of which are the tone, the motive and the idea. The tone of every word should be harmonious, wholesome, pleasing, and should convey a deep and serene expression. Words that express whines, discontent, sarcasm, aggressiveness and the like are destructive; so much so, that no one can afford to employ them under any circumstance whatever. Nothing is ever gained by complaints that are complaining, nor by criticisms that criticize. When things are not right, state so in a tone of voice that is firm and strong, but kind. A wronged customer who employs sweetness of tone as well as firmness of expression is one who will receive the first attention and the best attention, and nothing will be left unturned until the matter is set right. The words that wound others do far more injury to the person who gives them expression. No one therefore can afford to give expression to a single word that may tend to wound. Words of constructive power are always deeply felt. They are never loud or confusing, but always quiet and serene, filled with the very spirit of conviction.

Never give expression to what you do not wish to encourage. The more you talk about a thing the more you help it along. The "walls have ears" and the world is full of minds that will act upon your suggestion. Never mention the dark side of anything. It will interfere with your welfare. To tell your troubles may give you temporary relief, but it is scattering seed broadcast that will produce another crop of more trouble. If you have troubles, turn your back upon them and proceed to talk about harmony, freedom, attainment and success, and feel deeply the spirit of these new and better conditions. Thus you will begin to create for yourself a new life, new opportunities, new environment and a new world. Never speak unless you have something to say that gives cheer, encouragement, information or wholesome entertainment. To talk for the mere sake of talking is to throw precious energy away, and no human chatterbox will ever acquire greatness.

The motive back of every word should be constructive, and the life expressed in every word should convey the larger, the better, and the superior. Such words have building power, and are additions to life of extreme value. Every word should express, as far as possible, the absolute truth, and should never convey ideas that are simply indicated by appearances.

What is meant by speaking the absolute truth, however, is a matter that the majority do not understand, and as it is a very large subject, it would require pages to give even a brief scientific definition. But for practical purposes, the subject can be made sufficiently clear through the use of a few illustrations taken from the world's daily speech. People who think they have to say something and have nothing in particular to say, always take refuge in a brief description of the weather. In their descriptions they usually employ such expressions as "It is terribly hot," "It is an awful day," "This is terrible weather," "This is a miserably cold day," and so on. But such expressions do not change the weather, and there is no use of talking if your words are not to be of value in some way. You may say all sorts of disagreeable things about the weather without changing the weather in the least, but will such expressions leave you unchanged? Positively not! Whenever you declare that something is horrible, you cause horrible thoughts to send their actions all through your nervous system. These actions may be weak, but many drops, no matter how small, will finally wear away a rock.

When people talk about themselves, they seldom fail to give expression to a score of detrimental statements. Here are a few: "I can't stand this," "I feel so tired," "I cannot bear to think of it," "I am thoroughly disgusted,"

"I am so susceptible to climatic changes," "I am so sensitive and so easily disturbed," "I am getting weak and nervous," "My memory is failing," "I am getting old," "I cannot work the way I used to," "My strength is gradually leaving me," "There is no chance for me any more," "Everything in life is uphill work," "I have passed a miserable night," "This has been a hard day," "I have nothing but trouble and bad luck," "You know I am human and so very weak," "There is always something wrong no matter how hard you try," "You know I have to be so very careful about what I eat as nearly everything disagrees with me."

A thousand other statements, all of them destructive, might be mentioned, but any one who understands the power of thought will realize at once that such statements can never be otherwise but injurious and should therefore be avoided absolutely. But these statements are not only injurious—they are also untrue—absolutely untrue in every sense of the term.

The fact is you can stand almost anything if you forget your human weakness and array yourself in spiritual strength. You do not have to get tired. Work does not make any one tired so long as he gets eight hours of sleep every night. It is wrong thinking that makes people tired. These are scientific facts. That person who permits himself to become disgusted at anything whatever is talking himself down to the plane of inferiority. When you feel disgusted you think disgusting thoughts, and such thoughts clog the mind. You cannot afford to think disgusting thoughts simply because something else is disgusting, because we daily become like the thoughts we think. We cannot improve disagreeable things by making ourselves disagreeable. Two wrongs never made a right. The proper course is to forgive the wrong-doer, forget the wrong and then do something substantial to right the whole matter. When we think kindly of the weather, place ourselves in harmony with Nature, think properly and dress properly, we shall not be susceptible to changes in the atmosphere; but so long as we say that we are affected by changing atmospheres, we not only make ourselves negative and susceptible, but we also produce detrimental effects in our systems through our own unwholesome beliefs. The man who constantly thinks he is easily disturbed disturbs himself. When we are in harmony with everything including ourselves and refuse to be otherwise, nothing will ever disturb us. That person who is nervous can make the matter worse by saying that he is nervous, because such a statement is a nervous statement and is full of discord. When we begin to feel nervous, we can remedy the matter absolutely by resolving to remain calm, and by employing only quiet, wholesome and constructive speech. Your words will cause you to move in the direction indicated by the nature of those words, and it is just as easy to use words that bring calmness and poise, as those that bring inharmony and confusion.

Modern science has demonstrated conclusively that there is nothing about a person that gets old. Therefore, to say that you are getting old is to persist in speaking the untruth, and it is but natural that you should reap as you sow. We must remember that a false appearance comes from the practice of judging from appearances. To state that your strength is failing is likewise to speak the untruth. There is but one strength in the universe—the strength of the Supreme—and that strength can never fail. You may have as much of that strength as you desire. All that is necessary for you to do is to live in perfect touch with the Supreme, and never think, do or say anything that will interfere with that sublime oneness. The strength of the Supreme is just as able to fill your system with life and power now as it was at any time in the past. Therefore, there is no real reason whatever why your power should diminish. Be true to the truth and your power will perpetually increase.

The belief that there are no opportunities for you is caused by the fact that you have hidden yourself in a cave of inferiority. Go out into the life of worth, ability and competence, and you will find more opportunities than you can use. The world is ever in search of competent minds, and modern knowledge has made it possible for man to develop his ability. No one therefore has any legitimate reason for speaking of hard luck or hard times unless he prefers to live in want. The more you complain about hard times, the harder times will become for you, while if you resolve to forget that there is such a thing as failure and proceed to make your own life as you wish it to be, the turn in the lane will surely come.

The idea that the pathway of life is all uphill work is also a false one, and if we give that idea expression we are simply placing obstacles in our way. Nothing is uphill work when we approach it properly, and there is nothing that helps more to place us in true relationship with things than true expression.

If the night has been unpleasant, never mention the fact for a moment. To talk about it will only produce more unpleasantness in your system. There is nothing wrong about the night. The unpleasantness was most likely produced by your own perverse appetite, or by some reckless inexcusable act. Forgive yourself and declare that you will never abuse nature any more. Such powerful words if repeated often, will turn the tendency of your habits, and your life will become natural and wholesome.

No day would be hard if we met all things with the conviction that we are equal to every occasion. Live properly, think properly, work properly and talk properly, and trouble and ill-luck will not trouble you seriously any more. That person who declares that there is always something wrong is always doing something to make things wrong. When we have wrong on the brain we will make many mistakes, so there will always be something wrong brewing for us. When wrong things come, set them right and look upon the experience as an opportunity for you to develop greater mastership.

When you agree with yourself, all wholesome and properly prepared food will agree with you. But you cannot expect food to agree with you so long as you are disagreeable; and to declare that this or that always disagrees with you, is to fill your system with disagreeable thoughts, disturbed actions and conditions of discord. That nature can digest food under such circumstances no one can justly expect. There is nothing that injures digestion more than the habit of finding fault with the food. If you do not think that you can eat this or that, leave it alone, but leave it alone mentally as well as physically. It is not enough to drop a disagreeable thing from your hands; you must also drop it from your mind.

Remember, you are mentally living with everything that you talk about, and there is nothing that affects us more than that which we take into our mental life. It is therefore not only necessary to speak the truth about all things, but also to avoid speaking about those things that are unwholesome. To speak about that which is wrong or inferior is never wholesome, no matter how closely we think we stand by the facts. Seeming facts, or what is called relative truth, should never receive expression unless they deal with that which is conducive to higher worth; and when circumstances compel us to make exceptions to this rule, we should avoid giving any feeling to what we say.

The greatest essential, however, is to make all speech constructive. Search for the real truth that is at the foundation of all life, and then give expression to such words as convey the full significance to that truth. The results, to say the least, will be extraordinary.

In daily conversation, the law of constructive speech should be most conscientiously applied. What we say to others will determine to a considerable degree what they are to think, and what tendencies their mental actions are to follow; and since man is the product of his thought, conversation becomes a most important factor in man.

We steadily grow into the likeness of that which we think of the most, and what we are to think about depends largely upon the mode, the nature and the subject matter of our conversation. When conversation originates or intensifies the tendency to think about the wrong, the ordinary or the inferior, it becomes destructive, and likewise it tends to keep before mind the faults and defects that may exist in human nature. To be constructive, conversation should tend to turn attention upon the better side, the stronger side, the superior side of all things, and should give the ideal the most prominent place in thought, speech or expression. All conversation should be so formed that it may tend to move the mind toward the higher domains of thought, and should make everybody more keenly conscious of the greater possibilities that exist within them. No word should ever be spoken that will, in any way, bring the person's faults or short-comings before his mind, nor should any form of speech be permitted that may cause sadness, offense, depression or pain. Every word should convey hope, encouragement and sunshine.

To constantly remind a person of his faults is to cause him to become more keenly conscious of those faults. He will think more and more about his faults, and will thereby cause his faults to become more prominent and more troublesome than they ever were before. The more we think about our weakness, the weaker we become; and the more we talk about weakness, the more we think about weakness. Conversation therefore should never touch upon those things that we do not wish to retain or develop. The only way to remove weakness is to develop strength, and to develop strength we must keep attention constantly upon the quality of strength. We develop what we think about provided all thinking has depth, quality and continuity.

Conversation has exceptional value in the training of young minds, and in many instances may completely change the destinies of these minds. To properly train a child, his attention should be directed as much as possible upon those qualities that have worth and that are desired in his development; and the way he is spoken to will largely determine where he is to give the greater part of his attention. To scold a child is to remind him of his faults. Every time he is reminded of his faults he gives more attention, more thought, and more strength to those faults. His good qualities are thereby made weaker while his bad qualities are made worse. It is not possible to improve the mind and the character of the child by constantly telling him not to do "this" or "that." As a rule, it will increase his desire to do this other thing, and he will cease only through fear, or after having wasted a great deal of time in experiences that have become both disgusting and bitter.

It is the tendency of every mind to desire to do what it is told not to do, the reason being that negative commands are nearly always associated with fear; and when the mind is in the attitude of fear, or dread or curiosity, it is very easily impressed by whatever it may be thinking about.

When we are warned we either enter a state of fear or one of curiosity, and while in those states, our minds are so deeply and so easily impressed by that from which we are warned, that we give it our whole attention. The result is we think so much about it that we become almost completely absorbed in it; and we are carried away, so to speak, not away from the danger, but into it.

When any one is going wrong, it is a mistake to warn him not to go further. It is also a mistake to leave him alone. The proper course is to call his attention to something better, and frame our conversation in such a way that he becomes wholly absorbed in the better. He will then forget his old mistakes, his old faults and his old desires, and will give all his life and power to the building of that better which has engaged his new interest.

The same law may be employed to prevent sickness and failure. When the mind becomes so completely absorbed in perfect health that all sickness is forgotten, all the powers of mind will proceed to create health, and every trace of sickness will soon disappear. When the mind becomes so completely absorbed in higher attainments and in greater achievements that all thought of failure is forgotten, all the forces of mind will begin to work for the promotion of those attainments and achievements. The person will be gaining ground every day, and greater success will positively follow.

To cause the mind to forget the wrong, the lesser and the inferior, constructive conversation may be employed with unfailing results; in fact, such conversation must be employed if the mind is to advance and develop. Our conversation must be in perfect accord with our ambitions, our desires, and our ideals, and all our expressions must aim to promote the real purpose we have in view.

It is the tendency of nearly every mind to try to make his friends perfect according to his own idea of perfection, and he usually proceeds by constantly talking to his friends about their faults, and what they should not do in order to become as perfect as his ideal. Parents, as a rule, do the same with their children, not knowing that through this method many are made worse; and it is only those who are very strong in mind and character that are not adversely affected by this method.

To help our friends or our children to become ideal, we should never mention their faults. Our conversation should deal with the strong points of character and the greater possibilities of mind. We should so frame our conversation that we tend to make everybody feel there is something in them. Our conversation should have an optimistic tendency and an ascending tone. It should deal with those things in life that are worth while, and it should always give the ideal the greatest prominence. Weaknesses of human nature should be recognized as little as possible, and should seldom, if ever, be mentioned. When people engage in destructive conversation in our midst we should try to change the subject, by calling their attention to the better side. There always is another and a better side; and when examined closely will be found to be far greater and infinitely more important than the ordinary side. Admirable qualities exist everywhere, and it will prove profitable to give these our undivided attention.

The first mark of a master mind is that he is able to promote his own perpetual improvement. The second is that he is able to be strong, joyous and serene under every circumstance.

The imagining faculty is the creative faculty of the mind, the faculty that creates plans, methods and ideas. Our imagination therefore must always be clear, lofty, wholesome, and constructive if we would create superior ideas and build for greater things.

Before you can have greater success you must become a greater man. Before you can become a greater man you must reach out toward the new and the greater along all lines; and this is possible only through the constructive use of imagination.

You get your best ideas when your mind acts in the upper story. And in all fields of action it is the best ideas that win.

CHAPTER XVIII

IMAGINATION AND THE MASTER MIND

The forces of the human system must have something definite to work for; that is, they must have an ideal upon which to concentrate their attention, or some model or pattern to follow as they proceed with their constructive actions.

To form this model, it is the power of imagination that must be employed, and that power must, in each case, be applied constructively. What we imagine becomes a pattern for the creative energies of mind and personality, and as the creations of these energies determine what we are to become and attain, we realize that the imaging faculty is one of the most important of all our faculties. We therefore cannot afford to lose a moment in learning how to apply it according to the laws of mental construction and growth.

To proceed, imagine yourself becoming and attaining what you wish to become and attain. This will give your energies a model, both of your greater future self and your greater future achievements. When you think of your future, always imagine success and greater things, and have no fear as to results. If you fear, you give your creative energies a model of failure, and they will accordingly proceed to create failure. Then we must also remember if we wish to succeed, our faculties must work successfully, but no faculty can work successfully when filled with fear. It is only when constantly inspired by the idea of success that any faculty or power in the human system can do its best.

To inspire our faculties with this idea, we should always imagine ourselves obtaining success. The picture of success should be placed upon all the walls of the mind, so that the powers within us will see success, and success only as their goal. Hang up pictures in your mind that will inspire you to do your best; hang up pictures in your mind that will cause you to think constantly of that which you desire to accomplish, and this you may do by imagining yourself being that greater something that you want to be and doing that greater something that you want to do.

An excellent practice is to use your spare moments in creating such pictures in your imagination and placing them in the most conspicuous position of your mind, so that all your faculties and powers can see them at all times. We are always imagining something. It is practically impossible to be awake without imagining something. Then why not imagine something at all times that will inspire the powers within us to do greater and greater things?

To aid the imagination in picturing the greater, the higher and better, we should "hitch our wagon to a star." The star may be something quite out of reach as far as present circumstances indicate, but if we hitch our wagon to something in such a lofty position, our mind will begin to take wings. It will no longer be like a worm crawling in the dust. We shall begin to rise and continue to rise.

The only thing that can cause the mind to rise is imagination. The only thing that can make the mind larger than it is, is imagination. The only thing that can make the mind act along new lines is imagination. This being true, it is unwise to use the imagination for any other purpose than for the best that we can think or do.

In this connection, there are a few suggestions that will be found of special value. First, make up your mind as to what you really want in every respect. Determine what surroundings or environment you want. Decide upon the kind of friends you want and what kind of work you would prefer. Make all those ideals so good and so perfect that you will have no occasion to change them. Then fix those ideals so clearly in mind that you can see them at all times, and proceed to desire their realization with all the power of mind and soul. Make that your first step.

Your second step should be to imagine yourself living in those surroundings that you have selected as your ideal; then make it a point to live in that imagination every moment of every day. Instead of imagining a number of useless things during spare moments, as people usually do, imagine yourself living in those surroundings and those ideals. Imagine yourself in the presence of friends that are exactly what you wish your ideal friends to be, and permit your fancy to run as far as it may wish along all of those idealistic lines. If you have not found your work, proceed to imagine yourself doing what you wish to do. If you have already found your work, imagine yourself doing that work as well as you would wish, and imagine the coming of results as large as your greatest desires could expect. Devote every moment of your spare time to the placing of those ideals before your attention, and you will give your power and forces something strong and definite to work for. Every mental force is an artist, and it paints according to the model. What you imagine is the model, and there is not a single mental action that is not inspired or called forth into action by some picture or model which the imagination has produced.

The imagination can call forth the ordinary or the extraordinary. It can give the powers of your being an inferior model or an extraordinary model, and if the imagination is not directed to produce the extraordinary and the superior, it is quite likely to produce the ordinary and the inferior. Your second step, therefore, should be to imagine yourself actually living in those surroundings that you have selected as your ideal, and in actually becoming and doing what you are determined to become and do.

This practice would, in the first place, give you a great deal of pleasure, because if you have definite ideals and imagine yourself attaining those ideals, you will certainly enjoy yourself to a marked degree for the time being. But in addition to that enjoyment, you will gradually and steadily be training your mind to work for those greater things. The mind will work for that which is uppermost in thought and imagination. Therefore, we should invariably place our highest ideals uppermost, so that the whole of our attention may be concentrated upon those ideals, and all the powers of our mind and personality directed to work for those ideals.

Your third step should be to proceed to apply the power of desire, the power of will, the power of scientific thought, and in brief, all your powers, in trying to realize those beautiful ideals that you continue to imagine as your own. Do as the ancient Hebrews did. First make your prediction. Then go to work and make it come true. What you imagine concerning your greater future is your prediction, and you can cause that prediction to come true if you apply all the power in your possession in working for its realization every day.

The constructive use of imagination therefore will enable you to place a definite model or pattern before the forces of your system, so that those forces may have something better and greater to work for. In brief, instead of permitting most of your energies to go to waste and the remainder to follow any pattern or idea that may be suggested by your environment, or your own helter-skelter thinking, you will cause all your energy to work for the greatest and the best that you may desire.

This is the first use of imagination, and it easily places this remarkable faculty among the greatest in the human mind. Another use of the imagination is found in its power to give the mind something definite to think about at all times, so that the mind may be trained to always think of that which you really want to think; that is, through this use of the imagination, you can select your own thought and think your own thought at all times; and he who can do this is gradually becoming a master mind.

The master mind is the mind that thinks what it wants to think, regardless of what circumstances, environment or associations may suggest. The mind that masters itself creates its own ideas, thoughts and desires through the original use of imagination, or its own imaging faculty. The mind that does not master itself forms its thoughts and desires after the likeness of the impressions received through the senses, and is therefore controlled by those conditions from which, such impressions come; because as we think, so we act and live. The average mind usually desires what the world desires without any definite thought as to his own highest welfare or greatest need, the reason being that a strong tendency to do likewise is always produced in the mind when the desires are formed in the likeness of such impressions as are suggested by external conditions. It is therefore evident that the person who permits himself to be affected by suggestions will invariably form artificial desires; and to follow such desires is to be misled.

The master mind desires only that which is conducive to real life and in the selection of its desires is never influenced in the least by the desires of the world. Desire is one of the greatest powers in human life. It is therefore highly important that every desire be normal and created for the welfare of the individual himself. But no desire can be wholly normal that is formed through the influence of suggestion. Such desires are always abnormal to some degree, and easily cause the individual to be misplaced.

A great many people are misplaced. They do not occupy those places wherein they may be their best and accomplish the most. They are working at a disadvantage, and are living a life that is far inferior to what they are intended to live. The cause is frequently found in abnormal or artificial desires. They have imitated the desires of others without consulting their present needs. They have formed the desire to do what others are doing by permitting their minds to be influenced by suggestions and impressions from the world, forgetting what their present state of development makes them capable of doing now. By imitating the lives, habits, actions and desires of others, they are led into a life not their own; that is, they are misplaced.

The master mind is never misplaced because he does not live to do what others are doing, but what he himself wants to do now. He wants to do only that which is conducive to real life, a life worth while, a life that steadily works up to the very highest goal in view.

The average mind requires a change of environment before he can change his thought. He has to go somewhere or bring into his presence something that will suggest a new line of thinking and feeling. The master mind, however, can change his thought whenever he so desires. A change of scene is not necessary, because such a mind is not controlled from without. A change of scene will not produce a change of thought in the master mind unless he so elects. The master mind changes his thoughts, ideals or desires by imaging upon the mind the exact likeness of the new ideas, the new thoughts, and the new desires that have been selected.

The secret of the master mind is found wholly in the intelligent use of imagination. Man is as he thinks, and his thoughts are patterned after the predominating mental images, whether those images are impressions suggested from without, or impressions formed by the ego acting from within. When man permits his thoughts and desires to be formed in the likeness of impressions received from without, he will be more or less controlled by environment and he will be in the hands of fate, but when he transforms every impression received from without into an original idea and incorporates that idea into a new mental image, he uses environment as a servant, thereby placing fate in his own hands.

Every object that is seen will produce an impression upon the mind according to the degree of susceptibility. This impression will contain the nature of the object of which it is a representation. The nature of this object will be reproduced in the mind, and what has entered the mind will be expressed more or less throughout the entire system. Therefore, the mind that is susceptible to suggestions will reproduce in his own mind and system conditions that are similar in nature to almost everything that he may see, hear or feel. He will consequently be a reflection of the world in which he lives. He will think, speak and act as that world may suggest; he will float with the stream of that world wherever that stream may flow; he will not be an original character, but an automaton.

Every person that permits himself to be affected by suggestion is more or less an automaton, and is more or less in the hands of fate. To place fate in his own hands, he must use suggestions intelligently instead of blindly following those desires and thoughts that his surroundings may suggest. We are surrounded constantly by suggestions of all kinds, because everything has the power to suggest something to that mind that is susceptible, and we are all more or less susceptible in this respect. But there is a vast difference between permitting oneself to be susceptible to suggestion and training oneself to intelligently use those impressions that suggestions may convey.

The average writer on suggestion not only ignores this difference, but encourages susceptibility to suggestion by impressing the reader with the remark that suggestion does control the world. If it is true that suggestion controls the world, more or less, we want to learn how to so use suggestion that its control of the human mind will decrease steadily; and this we can accomplish, not by teaching people how to use suggestion for the influencing of other minds, but in using those impressions conveyed by suggestion in the reconstruction of their own minds. Suggestion is a part of life, because everything has the power to suggest, and all minds are open to impressions. Nothing therefore can be said against suggestion by itself. Suggestion is a factor in our midst; it is a necessary factor. The problem is to train ourselves to make intelligent use of the impressions received, instead of blindly following the desires produced by those impressions as the majority do.

To proceed in the solution of this problem, never permit objects discerned by the senses to reproduce themselves in your mind against your will. Form your own ideas about what you see, hear or feel, and try to make those ideas superior to what was suggested by the objects discerned. When you see evil do not form ideas that are in the likeness of that evil; do not think of the evil as bad, but try to understand the forces that are back of that evil—forces that are good in themselves, though misdirected in their present state. By trying to understand the nature of the power that is back of evil or adversity, you will not form bad ideas, and therefore will feel no bad effects from experiences that may seem undesirable. At the same time, you will think your own thought about the experiences, thereby developing the power of the master mind.

Surround yourself as far as possible with those things that suggest the superior, but do not permit such suggestions to determine your thought about the superior. Those superior impressions that are suggested by superior environment should be used in forming still more superior thoughts. If you wish to be a master mind, your thought must always be higher than the thought your environment may suggest, no matter how ideal that environment may be. Every impression that enters the mind through the senses should be worked out and should be made to serve the mind in its fullest capacity. In this way the original impression will not reproduce itself in the mind, but will become instrumental in giving the mind a number of new and superior ideas.

To work out an impression, try to see through its whole nature. Look at it from every conceivable point of view, and try to discern its actions, tendencies, possibilities and probable defects. Use your imagination in determining what you want to think or do, what you are to desire and what your tendencies are to be. Know what you want, and then image those things upon the mind constantly. This will develop the power to think what you want to think, and he who can think what he wants to think is on the way to becoming what he wants to become.

The principal reason why the average person does not realize his ideals is because he has not learned to think what he wants to think. He is too much affected by the suggestions that are about him. He imitates the world too much, following desires that are not his own. He is therefore misled and misplaced. Whenever you permit yourself to think what persons, things, conditions or circumstances may suggest, you are not following what you yourself want to think. You are not following your own desires but borrowed desires. You will therefore drift into strange thinking, and thinking that is entirely different from what you originally planned. To obey the call of every suggestion and permit your mind to be carried away by this, that or the other, will develop the tendency to drift until your mind will wander. Concentration will be almost absent and you will become wholly incapable of actually thinking what you want to think. One line of constructive thinking will scarcely be begun when another line will be suggested, and you will leave the unfinished task to begin something else, which in turn will be left incomplete. Nothing, therefore, will be accomplished.

To become a master mind, think what you want to think, no matter what your surroundings may suggest; and continue to think what you want to think until that particular line of thought or action has been completed. Desire what you want to desire and impress that desire so deeply upon consciousness that it cannot possibly be disturbed by those foreign desires that environment may suggest; and continue to express that desire with all the life and power that is in you until you get what you want. When you know that you are in the right desire, do not permit anything to influence your mind to change. Take such suggestions and convert them into the desire you have already decided upon, thereby giving that desire additional life and power. Never close your mind to impressions from without. Keep the mind open to the actions of all those worlds that may exist in your sphere and try to gain valuable impressions from every source, but do not blindly follow those impressions. Use them constructively in building up your own system of original thought. Think what you want to think, and so use every impression you receive that you gain greater power to think what you want to think. Thus you will gradually become a master mind.

Follow the vision of the soul. Be true to your ideals no matter what may happen now. Then things will take a turn and the very things you wanted to happen will happen.

The ideal has a positive drawing power toward the higher, the greater, and the superior. Whoever gives his attention constantly to the ideal, therefore, will steadily rise in the scale.

Take things as they are to-day and proceed at once to make them better.

Expect every change to lead you to something better and it will. As your faith is so shall it be.

To be human is not to be weak. To be human is to be all that there is in man, and the greatness that is contained in the whole of man is marvelous indeed.

CHAPTER XIX

THE HIGHER FORCES IN MAN

It is the most powerful among the forces of the human system that we least understand, and though this may seem unfortunate, it is not unnatural. All advancement is in the ascending scale. We learn the simplest things first and the least valuable in the beginning. Later on, we learn that which is more important. We find therefore the greatest forces among those that are almost entirely hidden, and for that reason they are sometimes called the hidden forces, the finer forces, or the higher forces.

As it is in man, so it is also in nature. We find the most powerful among natural forces to be practically beyond comprehension. Electricity is an illustration. There is no greater force known in nature, and yet no one has thus far been able to determine what this force actually is. The same is true with regard to other natural forces; the greater they are and the more powerful they are, the more difficult it is to understand them. In the human system, there are a number of forces of exceptional value that we know nothing about; that is, we do not understand their real nature, but we can learn enough about the action, the purpose and the possibilities of those forces to apply them to practical life; and it is practical application with which we are most concerned.

The field of the finer forces in mind may be termed the unconscious mental field, and the vastness of this field, as well as the possibilities of its functions, is realized when we learn that the greater part of our mental world is unconscious. Only a fraction of the mental world of man is on the surface or up in consciousness; the larger part is submerged in the depths of what might be called a mental sea of subconsciousness. All modern psychologists have come to this conclusion, and it is a fact that any one can demonstrate in his own experience if he will take the time.

In the conscious field of the human mind, we find those actions of which we are aware during what may be called our wide-awake state; and they are seemingly insignificant in comparison with the actions of the vast unconscious world, though our conscious actions are found to be highly important when we learn that it is the conscious actions that originate unconscious actions. And here let us remember that it is our unconscious actions that determine our own natures, our own capabilities, as well as our own destiny. In our awakened state we continue to think and act in a small mental field, but all of those actions are constantly having their effect upon this vast unconscious field that is found beneath the mental surface.

To realize the existence of this unconscious mental world, and to realize our power to determine the actions of that world, is to awaken within us a feeling that we are many times as great and as capable as we thought we were, and the more we think of this important fact, the larger becomes our conscious view of life and its possibilities.

To illustrate the importance of the unconscious field and your finer forces, we will take the force of love. No one understands the nature of this force, nor has any one been able to discover its real origin or its actual possibilities; nevertheless, it is a force that is tremendously important in human life. Its actions are practically hidden, and we do not know what constitutes the inner nature of those actions, but we do know how to control those actions in a measure for our own good; and we have discovered that when we do control and properly direct the actions of love, its value to everybody concerned is multiplied many times. It is the same with a number of other forces with which we are familiar. They act along higher or finer lines of human consciousness, and they are so far beyond ordinary comprehension that we cannot positively know what they are. But we do know enough about them to control them and direct them for our best and greatest good. In like manner, the unconscious mental field, though beyond scientific analysis, is sufficiently understood as to its modes of action, so that we can control and direct those actions as we may choose. When we analyze what comes forth from the unconscious field at any time, we find that it is invariably the result of something that we caused to be placed in that field during some past time. This leads up to the discovery of unconscious mental processes, and it is not difficult to prove the existence of such processes.

Many a time ideas, desires, feelings or aspirations come to the surface of thought that we are not aware of having created at any time. We come to the conclusion, therefore, that they were produced by some unconscious process, but when we examine those ideas or desires carefully, we find that they are simply effects corresponding exactly with certain causes that we previously placed in action in our conscious world. When we experiment along this line we find that we can produce a conscious process at any time, and through deep feeling cause it to enter the unconscious mental world. In that deeper world, it goes to work and produces according to its nature, the results coming back to the surface of our conscious mentality days, weeks or months later. The correspondence between conscious and unconscious mental processes may be illustrated by a simple movement in physical action. If a physical movement began at a certain point, and was caused to act with a circular tendency, it would finally come back to its starting point. It is the same with every conscious action that is deeply felt. It goes out into the vastness of the unconscious mental field, and having a circular tendency, as all mental actions have, it finally comes back to the point where it began; and in coming back, brings with it the result of every unconscious experience through which it passed on its circular journey.

To go into this subject deeply, and analyze every phase of it would be extremely interesting; in fact, it would be more interesting than fiction. It would require, however, a large book to do it justice. For this reason, we can simply touch upon the practical side of it, but will aim to make this brief outline sufficiently clear to enable any one to direct his unconscious process in such a way as to secure the best results.

Every mental process, or every mental action, that takes place in our wide-awake consciousness will, if it has depth of feeling or intensity, enter the unconscious field, and after it has developed itself according to the line of its original nature, will return to the conscious side of the mind. Here we find the secret of character building, and also the secret of building faculties and talents. Everything that is done in the conscious field to improve the mind, character, conduct or thought will, if it has sincerity and depth of feeling, enter the unconscious field; and later will come back with fully developed qualities, which when in expression, constitutes character. Many a man, however, after trying for some time to improve himself and seeing no results, becomes discouraged. He forgets that some time always intervenes between the period of sowing and the period of reaping. What he does in the conscious field to improve himself, constitutes the sowing, when those actions enter the conscious field to be developed; and when they come back, it may be weeks or months later, the reaping time has arrived. Many a time, after an individual has given up self-improvement, he discovers, after a considerable period, that good qualities are beginning to come to the surface in his nature, thereby proving conclusively that what he did months ago along that line was not in vain. The results of past efforts are beginning to appear. We have all had similar experiences, and if we would carefully analyze such experiences, we would find that not a single conscious process that is sufficiently deep or intense to become an unconscious process will fail to come back finally with its natural results. Many a time ideas come into our minds that we wanted weeks ago, and could not get them at that time; but we did place in action certain deep, strong desires for those ideas, at that particular time, and though our minds were not prepared to develop those ideas at once, they finally were developed and came to the surface.

The fact that this process never fails indicates the value of giving the mind something to work out for future need. If we have something that we want to do months ahead, we should give the mind definite instruction now and make those instructions so deep, that they will become unconscious processes. Those unconscious processes will, according to directions, work out the ideas and plans that we want for that future work, and in the course of time, will bring results to the surface. To go into detail along the line of this part of our study would also be more interesting than fiction, but again, a large book would be required to do it justice. However, if we make it a practice to place in action our best thoughts, our best ideas and our best desires now and every moment of the eternal now, we will be giving the unconscious mental field something good to work for at all times; and as soon as each product is finished, or ready to be delivered from the unconscious world, it will come to the surface, and will enter the conscious mind ready for use.

Some of the best books that have been written have been worked out during months of unconscious mental processes; the same is true with regard to inventions, dramas, musical compositions, business plans, and in fact, anything and everything of importance that could be mentioned. Every idea, every thought, every feeling, every desire, every mental action, may, under certain circumstances, produce an unconscious process corresponding with itself, and this process will in every instance bring back to consciousness the result of its work. When we realize this, and realize the vast possibilities of the unconscious field, we will see the advantage of placing in action as many good unconscious processes as possible. Give your unconscious mental world something important to do every hour. Place a new seed in that field every minute. It may take weeks or months before that seed brings forth its fruit, but it will bring forth, after its kind, in due time without fail.

We understand therefore, how we can build character by sowing seeds of character in this field, and how we can, in the same way, build desirable conduct, a different disposition, different mental tendencies, stronger and greater mental faculties, and more perfect talents along any line. To direct these unconscious processes, it is necessary to apply the finer forces of the system, as it is those forces that invariably determine how those processes are to act. Those forces, however, are very easily applied, as all that is necessary in the beginning is to give attention to the way we feel. The way we feel determines largely what our finer forces are to be and how they are to act, and there is not an hour when we do not feel certain energies at work in our system. All the finer forces are controlled by feeling. Try to feel what you want done either in the conscious or the unconscious mental fields, and you will place in action forces that correspond to what you want done. Those forces will enter the unconscious mental world and produce processes through which the desired results will be created.

Whenever you want to redirect any force that is highly refined, you must feel the way you want that force to act. To illustrate, we will suppose you have certain emotions in your mental world that are not agreeable. To give the energies of those emotions a new and more desirable force of action, change your emotions by giving your whole attention in trying to feel such emotions as you may desire. And here let us remember that every emotion that comes up in the system is teeming with energy; but as most emotions continue to act without any definite control, we realize how much energy is wasted through uncurbed emotions. We know from experience, that whenever we give way to our feelings, we become weak. The reason is that every uncontrolled feeling wastes energy. A great many people who are very intense in their feelings, actually become sick whenever they give way to strong or deep emotions. On the other hand, emotions that are controlled and properly directed, not only prevent waste, but will actually increase the strength of mind and body. Here is a good practice. Whenever you feel the way you do not wish to feel begin to think deeply and in the most interesting manner possible, of those things that you wish to accomplish. If you can throw your whole soul, so to speak, into those new directions, you will soon find your undesired feelings disappearing completely. Every individual should train himself to feel the way he wants to feel, and this is possible if he will always direct his attention to something desirable whenever undesired feelings come up. Through this practice he will soon get such full control over his feelings that he can always feel the way he wants to feel, no matter what the circumstances may be. He will thus gain the power not only of controlling his emotions and using constructively all those energies that invariably appear in his emotions, but he will also have found the secret of continued happiness. Whenever mental energy moves in a certain direction, it tends to build up power for good along that line. We realize therefore the value of directing all our attention upon those things in mind, character and life that we wish to build and develop.

In building character we find the results to be accumulative; that is, we make an effort to improve our life or conduct, and thereby produce an unconscious process, which will later on, give us more strength of character to be and live the way we wish to be and live. This in turn will enable us to produce more and stronger unconscious processes along the line of character building, which will finally return with a greater number of good qualities. The result of this action will be to give us more power to build for a still greater character, and so this process may be continued indefinitely.

The same is true with regard to building the mind. The more you build the mind, the greater becomes your mental power to build a still greater mind; but in each case, it is the unconscious process that must be produced in order that the greater character or greater mind may be developed from within. In this connection, it is well to remember that the principal reason why so many people fail to improve along any line is because their desires or efforts for improvement are not sufficiently deep and strong to become unconscious processes. To illustrate, it is like placing seed on stony ground. If the seed is not placed in good, deep soil it will not grow. You may desire self-improvement for days, but if those desires are weak or superficial, they will not enter the unconscious field; and no action, however good it may be, if it fails to enter the unconscious field, will also fail to produce results along the line of self-improvement.

With regard to the building of character, we must also remember that character determines in a large measure the line of action of all the other forces in the human system. If your character is strong and well developed, every force that you place in action will be constructive; while if your character is weak, practically all your forces will go astray. This is not true in the moral field alone, but also in the field of mental achievement. If the character is weak, your ability will be mostly misdirected no matter how hard you may work, or how sincere you may be in your effort to do your best. This explains why a great many people do not realize their ideals. They have paid no attention to character building, and therefore, nearly every effort that they may have made in trying to work up toward their ideals, has been misdirected and sent astray. Whatever our ideals may be therefore, or how great our desires may be to realize those ideals, we must first have character; and even though we may be able to place in action the most powerful forces in the human system, we will not get results until we have character. It is character alone that can give the powers of man constructive direction, and it is a well-known fact that those people who have a strong, firm, well-developed character easily move from the good to the better, no matter what the circumstances.

What may be called the higher forces in man act invariably through our most sublime states of consciousness, and as it is these higher forces that enable man to become or accomplish more than the average, it is highly important that we attain the power to enter sublime consciousness at frequent intervals. No man or woman of any worth was ever known, who did not have experience in these sublime states; in fact, it is impossible to rise above the ordinary in life or achievement without drawing, more or less, upon the higher realms of consciousness. People are sometimes criticized for not being on the earth all the time, but it is necessary to get above the earth occasionally in order to find something worth while to live for and work for while upon earth. The most powerful forces in human life can be drawn down to earth for practical use, but to get them we must go to the heights frequently. No one can write music unless his consciousness touches the sublime. No one can write real poetry unless he has the same experience. No one can evolve ideas worth while unless his mind transcends the so-called practical sphere of action, and no individual can rise in the world of attainment and achievement unless his mind dwells almost constantly on the verge of the sublime. Examine the minds of people of real worth, people who have something in them, people who are beyond the average, people who are rising in the scale, people whom we truly admire, people that we look up to, people who occupy high positions—positions that they have actually won through merit—and we find in every instance, that their minds touch frequently the sublime state of consciousness. When we touch that state, our minds are drawn up above the ordinary, and mental actions are developed and worked out that are superior to ordinary or average mental actions. It is therefore simply understood that experience in sublime consciousness if properly employed, will invariably make man greater and better.

When we look upon a man that we can truthfully say is a real man, we find that something unusual has been or is being expressed in his personality; and that something unusual is hidden in every personality. It is a hidden power, a hidden force, which, when placed in action, gives man superior worth, both as to character, ability and life. Real men and real women, people who are real in the true sense of the term, are always born from the sublime state of consciousness; that is, they have, through coming in contact with higher regions of thought, evolved greater worth in their own minds and personalities; and as this possibility is within reach of every man or woman, we see the importance of dealing thoroughly with these higher powers in human nature.

Whenever we touch those finer states in the upper regions of the mind, we invariably feel that we have gained something superior, something that we did not possess before; and the gaining of that something invariably makes life stronger as well as finer. The ordinary has been, in a measure, overcome, and that which is beyond the ordinary is being gradually evolved. If we would rise in the scale in the fullest and best sense of the term, we must pay close attention to those higher forces and make it a practice to enter frequently into close touch with higher states of consciousness; in fact, we simply must do it, because if we do not we will continue to move along a very ordinary level. Then we must also bear in mind that it is our purpose to use all the forces we possess, not simply those that we can discern on the outside or that we are aware of in external consciousness, but also those finer and more powerful forces which we can control and direct only when we ascend to the heights.

In dealing with these greater powers in man, it will be worth our while to reconsider briefly the psychological field. As long as the mind acts on the surface of consciousness, we have very little control of those finer elements in human life, but when the mind goes into the depths of feeling, into the depths of realization, or into what is called the psychological field, then it is that it touches everything that has real worth or that has the power to evolve, produce or develop still greater worth. It is the active forces of the psychological field that determine everything that is to take place in the life of man, both within himself and in his external destiny. We must therefore learn to act through the psychological field if we would master ourselves and create our own future.

The psychological field can be defined as that field of subconscious action that permeates the entire personality, or that fills, so to speak, every atom of the physical man on a finer plane. The psychological field is a finer field, permeating the ordinary tangible physical elements of life, and we enter this field whenever our feelings are deep and sincere. The fact that the psychological field determines real worth, as well as the attainment of greater worth, is easily demonstrated in every day experience. When a man has anything in him, his nature is always deep. The same is true of people of refinement or culture; there is depth to their natures, and the man of character invariably lives in that greater world of life and power that is back of, or beneath, the surface of consciousness. If there is something in you, you both live and act through the deeper realms of your life, and those realms constitute the psychological field.

Among the many important forces coming directly through emotion or feeling, one of the most valuable is that of enthusiasm. In the average mind, enthusiasm runs wild, but we have found that when this force is properly directed it becomes a great constructive power. When you are enthusiastic about something, it is always about something new or something better— something that holds possibilities that you did not realize before. Your enthusiasm, if properly directed, will naturally cause your mind to move toward those possibilities, and enthusiasm is readily directed when you concentrate attention exclusively upon that something new that inspires enthusiasm. By turning your attention upon the thing that produces enthusiasm, the mind will move forward toward those greater possibilities that are discerned. This forward movement of the mind will tend to renew and enlarge the mind so that it will gain a still greater conception of those possibilities. This will increase your enthusiasm, which will in turn impel your mind to move forward still further in the same direction. Thus a still larger conception of those possibilities will be secured, which in turn will increase your enthusiasm and the power of your mind to take a third step in advance. We thus realize that if enthusiasm is directed upon the possibilities that originally inspired that enthusiasm, we will not only continue to be enthused, but we will in that very manner, cause the mind to move forward steadily and develop steadily, so that in time it will gain sufficient power to actually work out those possibilities upon which attention has been directed. In this connection, we must also remember that we can grow and advance only as we pass into the new. It is new life, new thought, new states of consciousness that are demanded if we are to take any steps at all in advance, and as enthusiasm tends directly to inspire the mind to move toward the new, we see how important it is to continue, not only to live in the spirit of enthusiasm, but to direct that spirit upon the goal in view. It is invariably the enthusiastic mind that moves forward, that does things, and that secures results.

Two other forces of great value, belonging to this group, are appreciation and gratitude. Whenever you appreciate a certain thing you become conscious of its real quality, and whenever you become conscious of the quality of anything, you begin to develop that quality in yourself. When we appreciate the worth of a person, we tend to impress the idea of that worth in our own minds, and thereby cause the same effect to be produced, in a measure, in ourselves. The same is true if we appreciate our own worth, in a sensible and constructive manner. If we appreciate what we already are, and are ambitious to become still more, we focus our minds upon the greater, and employ what we already possess as stepping stones toward the greater attainment; but when we do not appreciate ourselves, there are no stepping stones that we can use in attaining greater things. We thus realize why people that do not appreciate themselves never accomplish much, and why they finally go down grade in nearly every instance.

When we appreciate the beautiful in anything, we awaken our minds to a higher and better understanding of the beautiful. Our minds thus become, in a measure, more beautiful. The same is true with regard to any quality. Whatever we appreciate, we tend to develop in ourselves, and here we find a remarkable aid to the power of concentration, because we always concentrate attention perfectly, naturally and thoroughly upon those things that we fully appreciate. Thus we understand why it is that we tend to develop in ourselves the things that we admire in others.

Whenever you feel grateful for anything, you always feel nearer to the real quality of that particular thing. A person who is ungrateful, however, always feels that there is a wall between himself and the good things in life. Usually there is such a wall, though he has produced it himself through his ingratitude. But the man who is grateful for everything, places himself in that attitude where he may come in closer contact with the best things everywhere; and we know very well that the most grateful people always receive the best attention everywhere. We all may meet disappointment at some time and not get exactly what we wanted, but we shall find that the more grateful we are, the less numerous will those disappointments become. It has been well said that no one feels inclined to give his best attention to the man who is always "knocking," and it is literally true. On the other hand, if you are really grateful and mean it, it is very seldom that you do not receive the best attention from everybody wherever you may go.

The most important side of this law, however, is found in the fact that the more grateful you are for everything good that comes into your life, the more closely you place your mind in contact with that power in life that can produce greater good.

Another among the finer forces is that of aspiration. No person should fail to aspire constantly and aspire to the very highest that he can possibly awaken in his life. Aspiration always tends to elevate the mind and tends to lift the mind into larger and greater fields of action. And when the mind finds itself in this larger field of action, it will naturally gain power to do greater things. We all realize that so long as we live down in the lower story, we can not accomplish very much; it is when we lift our minds to the higher stories of the human structure that we begin to gain possession of ideas and powers through which greater things may be achieved.

The same is true of ambition. Ambition not only tends to draw the mind up into higher and larger fields, but also tends to build up those faculties through which we are to work. If you are tremendously ambitious to do a certain thing, the force of that ambition will tend to increase the power and ability of that faculty through which your ambition may be realized. To illustrate, if you are ambitious to succeed in the business world, the force of that ambition is very strong, will constantly make your business faculties stronger and more able, so that finally your business ability will have become sufficiently great to carry your ambition through. You cannot be too ambitious, provided you are ambitious for something definite and continue to give your whole life and soul to that which you expect or desire to accomplish through that ambition.

When we know the power of ambition, and know that anybody can be ambitious, we realize that any one can move forward. No matter what his position may be, or where he may be, he can, through the power of ambition begin to gain ground, and continue to gain ground indefinitely. The average mind, however, has very little ambition, and makes no effort to arouse this tremendous force; but we may depend upon the fact that when this force is fully aroused in any mind, a change for the better must positively come before long.

The force of an ideal is another among the finer forces that should receive constant and thorough attention. When you have an ideal and live for it every second of your existence, you place yourself in the hands of a drawing power that is immense, and that power will tend to draw out into action every force, power and faculty that you may possess, especially those forces and qualities that will have to be developed in order that you may realize that ideal.

Have an ideal, and the highest that you can picture. Then worship it every hour with your whole soul. Never come down, and do not neglect it for a moment. We all know very well that it is the people who actually worship their high ideals with mind and heart and soul that finally realize those ideals. It is such people who reach the high places and the reason why is easily explained. Give your attention, or rather, your whole life to some lofty ideal, and you will tend to draw into action all the finer and higher forces of your system—those forces that can create greater ability, greater talent, greater genius—those forces that can increase your capacity, bring into action all your finer elements and give you superior power and superior worth in every sense of the term—those forces which, when aroused, cannot positively fail to do the work you wish to have done.

A fact well known in this connection is that when the mind is turned persistently upon a certain ideal, every power that is in you begins to flow in that direction, and this is the very thing you want. When we can get all that is in us to work for our ideals and to work toward our ideals, then we shall positively reach whatever goal we have in view.

Closely connected with our ideals, we find our visions and dreams. The man without a vision will never be anything but an ordinary man, and the people who never dream of greater things, will never get beyond ordinary things. It is our visions and dreams that lift our minds to lofty realms, that make us feel that there is something greater and better to work for; and when we become inspired with a desire to work for greater and better things, we will not only proceed to carry out those desires, but will finally secure sufficient power to fulfil those desires. "The nation that has no vision shall perish." This is a great truth that we have heard a thousand times, and we know the reason why; but the same truth is applicable to man. If he has no vision, he will go down; but if he has visions, the highest and most perfect visions he can possibly imagine, and lives constantly for their realization, he will positively ascend in the scale. He will become a greater and a greater man, and those things that were at one time simply dreams, will, in the course of time, become actual realities.

The power of love is another force in this higher group that is extremely valuable, and the reason is that it is the tendency of love to turn attention upon the ideal, the beautiful and the more perfect. When you love somebody, you do not look for their faults; in fact, you do not see their faults. Your whole attention is turned upon their good qualities, and here, let us remember that whatever we continue to see in others, we develop in ourselves. The power of real love always tends to draw out into expression the finer elements of mind, character and life. For that reason, we should always love, love much, and love the most ideal and the most perfect that we can discover in everybody and in everything that we may meet in life. We have all discovered that when a man really loves an ideal woman, or the woman that constitutes his ideal, he invariably becomes stronger in character, more powerful in personality, and more able in mind. When a woman loves an ideal man, or her ideal, she invariably becomes more attractive. The beautiful in her nature comes forth into full expression and many times the change is so great that we can hardly believe that she is the same woman. The power of love, if genuine, constant and strong, tends to improve everything in human life; and as this power is one of the higher forces in human nature, we readily understand the reason why. We can therefore without further comment, draw our own conclusions as to how we will use this power in the future.

The last of these finer forces that we shall mention, and possibly the strongest, is that of faith; but we must remember if we wish to use this force, that faith does not constitute a belief or any system of beliefs; it is a mental action—an action that goes into the very spirit of those things which we may think of or apply at the time we exercise faith. When you have faith in yourself you place in action a force that goes into the very depth of your being and tends to arouse all the greater powers and finer elements that you may possess. The same is true when you have faith in a certain faculty or in a certain line of action. The power of faith goes into the spirit of things and makes alive, so to speak, the all that is in you. The power of faith also produces perfect concentration. Whenever you have faith along a certain line, you concentrate perfectly along that line, and you cause all the power that is in your mind or system to work for the one thing you are trying to do. It has been discovered that the amount of energy latent in the human system is nothing less than enormous, and as faith tends to arouse all this energy, we realize how important and how powerful is faith.

The effect of faith upon yourself therefore is beneficial in the highest and largest sense, but this is not its only effect. The more faith you have in yourself, the more faith people will have in you. If you have no confidence in yourself you will never inspire confidence in anybody; but if you thoroughly believe in yourself, people will believe in you and in your work. And when people believe in you, you can accomplish ten times as much as when they have no confidence in you whatever.

When a man has tremendous faith in himself, he becomes a live wire, so to speak. It is such a man that becomes a real and vital power wherever he may live or go. It is such a man who leads the race on and on. It is such a man who really does things, and it is people of such a type that we love the best. They invariably inspire others to love the nobler life and to attempt greater things in life, and for this reason their presence is of exceptional value to the progress of the race. To go into details, however, is not necessary. We all know and appreciate the value of faith. We all know that it is one of the highest and one of the greatest forces that man can exercise; we therefore realize how important it becomes to train ourselves to have unbounded faith in everything and in everybody at all times, and under all circumstances.

With All Thy Faults I Love Thee Still

   Thus sings the poet, and we call him sentimental; that is, at first thought we do. But upon second thought we change our minds. We then find that faults and defects are always in the minority, and that the larger part of human nature is so wonderful and so beautiful that it needs must inspire admiration and love in everybody. With all their defects there is nothing more interesting than human beings; and the reason is that for every shortcoming in man there are a thousand admirable qualities. The poet, being inspired by the sublime vision of truth, can see this; therefore, what can he do but love? Whenever his eyes are lifted and whenever his thoughts take wings, his soul declares with greater eloquence than ever before, "What a piece of work is man!" Thus every moment renews his admiration, and every thought rekindles the fire of his love.

CHAPTER XX

THE GREATEST POWER IN MAN

It is the conclusion of modern psychology that the powers and the possibilities inherent in man are practically unbounded. And this conclusion is based upon two great facts. First, that no limit has been found to anything in human nature; and second, that everything in human nature contains a latent capacity for perpetual development.

The discovery of these two facts—and no discovery of greater importance has appeared in any age—gives man a new conception of himself, a conception, which, when applied, will naturally revolutionize the entire field of human activity.

To be able to discern the real significance of this new conception becomes, therefore, the greatest power in man, and should, in consequence, be given the first thought in all efforts that have advancement, attainment or achievement in view. The purpose of each individual should be, not simply to cultivate and apply those possibilities that are now in evidence, but also to develop the power to discern and fathom what really exists within him. This power is the greatest power, because it prepares the way for the attainment and expression of all other powers. It is the power that unlocks the door to all power, and must be understood and applied before anything of greater value can be accomplished through human thought or action.

The principal reason why the average person remains weak and incompetent is found in the fact that he makes no effort to fathom and understand the depths of his real being. He may try to use what is in action on the surface, but he is almost entirely unconscious of the fact that enormous powers are in existence in the greater depths of his life. These powers are dormant simply because they have not been called into action, and they will continue to lie dormant until man develops his greatest power—the power to discern what really exists within him.

The fundamental cause of failure is found in the belief that what exists on the surface is all there is of man, and the reason why greatness is a rare exception instead of a universal rule can be traced to the same cause. When the mind discovers that its powers are inexhaustible and that its faculties and talents can be developed to any degree imaginable, the fear of failure will entirely disappear. In its stead will come the conviction that man may attain anything or achieve anything. Whatever circumstances may be to-day, such a mind will know that all can be changed, that the limitations of the person can be made to pass away, and that the greater desires of the heart can be realized.

That mind that can discern what exists in the depths of the real life of man does not simply change its views as to what man may attain and achieve, but actually begins to draw, in a measure, upon those inexhaustible powers within; and begins accordingly to develop and apply those greater possibilities that this deeper discernment has revealed. When man can see through and understand what exists beneath the surface of his life, the expression of his deeper life will begin, because whatever we become conscious of, that we tend to bring forth into tangible expressions, and since the deeper life contains innumerable possibilities as well as enormous power, it is evident that when this deeper life is clearly discerned and completely taken possession of in the consciousness, practically anything may be attained or achieved. The idea that there is more of man than what appears on the surface should be so constantly and so deeply impressed upon the mind that it becomes a positive conviction, and no thought should be placed in action unless it is based upon this conviction. To live, think and act in the realization that "there is more of me" should be the constant aim of every individual, and this more will constantly develop, coming forth in greater and greater measure, giving added power and capacity in life to everything that is in action in the human system.

When the average individual fails, he either blames circumstances or comes to the conclusion that he was not equal to the occasion. He therefore easily gives up and tries to be content with the lesser. But if he knew that there was more in him than what he had applied in his undertaking he would not give up. He would know by developing and applying this more, he positively would succeed where he had previously failed. It is therefore evident that when man gives attention to his greater power—the power to discern the more that is in him—he will never give up until he does succeed, and in consequence he invariably will succeed.

That individual who knows his power does not judge according to appearances. He never permits himself to believe that this or that cannot be done. He knows that those things can be done, because he has discovered what really exists within him. He works in the conviction that he must, can and will succeed, because he has the power; and it is the truth—he does have the power—we all have the power. To live, think and work in the conviction that there is more of you within the real depths of your being, and to know that this more is so immense that no limit to its power can be found, will cause the mind to come into closer and closer touch with this greater power within, and you will consequently get possession of more and more of this power.

The mind that lives in this attitude opens the door of consciousness, so to speak, to everything in human life that has real quality and worth. It places itself in that position where it can respond to the best that exists within itself, and modern psychology has discovered that this best is extraordinary in quality, limitless in power, and contains possibilities that cannot be numbered.

It is the truth that man is a marvelous being—nothing less than marvelous; and the greatest power in man is the power to discern the marvelousness that really does exist within him.

It is the law that we steadily develop and bring forth whatever we think of the most. It is therefore profitable to think constantly of our deeper nature and to try to fathom the limitlessness and the inexhaustibleness of these great and marvelous depths.

In practical life this mode of thinking will have the same effect upon the personal mind as that which is secured in a wire that is not charged when it touches a wire that is charged. The great within is a live wire; when the mind touches the great within, it becomes charged more and more with those same immense powers; and the mind will constantly be in touch with the great within when it lives, thinks and works in the firm conviction that "there is more of me"—so much more that it cannot be measured.

We can receive from this deeper life only that which we constantly recognize and constantly realize, because consciousness is the door between the outer life and the great within, and we open the door to those things only of which we become conscious.

The principal reason therefore why the average person does not possess greater powers and talents, is because he is not conscious of more; and he is not conscious of more because he has not vitally recognized the great depths of his real life, and has not tried to consciously fathom the possibilities that are latent within him. The average person lives on the surface. He thinks that the surface is all there is of him, and consequently does not place himself in touch with the live wire of his interior and inexhaustible nature. He does not exercise his greatest power—the power to discern what his whole nature actually contains; therefore, he does not unlock the door to any of his other powers.

This being true, we can readily understand why mortals are weak—they are weak simply because they have chosen weakness; but when they begin to choose power and greatness, they will positively become what they have chosen to become.

We all must admit that there is more in man than what is usually expressed in the average person. We may differ as to how much more, but we must agree that the more should be developed, expressed and applied in everybody. It is wrong, both to the individual and to the race, for any one to remain in the lesser when it is possible to attain the greater. It is right that we all should ascend to the higher, the greater and the better now. And we all can.

MASTERY
of SELF

MASTERY OF SELF

MAN is made for attainment and achievement; to ever become greater and greater than he is now—that is the purpose of his life; and to promote that purpose he must ever advance in the mastery of self. To move forward in the path of attainment, everything in the being of man must be employed constructively; every process in mind or body must become a building process, and all the elements and forces in the human system must work together toward the great goal in view; but to direct the whole of self to work for a greater self demands the mastery of self.

No power in man can do what it is created to do, and what it has the capacity to do, until it is directed by man himself; powers, elements, forces, and things are at the disposal of man; they can do only what he directs them to do; they respond only to his control, but before man can gain the power to master forces and things, he must gain the power to master himself.

When man has gained the power to control himself he can control everything in his world without trying to control anything. It is therefore evident that he who is trying to control everything has not learned how to control anything. The true master never tries to master anything, not even himself. He does not have to try to be a master—he is a master.

Nor is it necessary to try to be a master in order to reach that state where one is a master; in fact, no person can learn to control himself so long as he tries to control himself.

To eliminate every desire to master oneself is the first step toward the attainment of the mastery of self. He who does not wish to control anything is alone prepared to gain the power to control everything.

He who tries to control himself, or who tries to control anything that exists outside of himself gives everything in his being the tendency to work toward the surface; the power that produces the mastery of self, however, can only be gained by training the mind to move in the opposite direction.

To master self is to have the power to produce any effect desired in any part of mind or body, and to produce any effect desired it is necessary to produce the corresponding cause; but to produce any cause the mind must act in the world of cause—a world which exists, not on the surface of thought or being, but in the great within.

The harder one tries to control himself the nearer to the surface will the mind act, and the further will mental action be separated from that interior mental state from which one may gain the power to control himself.

He who tries to attain the mastery of self will act entirely upon the outer mental world of effect, and will therefore be unable to create the cause that can produce the mastery of self. The mind must act back of, beneath and above the effect in order to change or produce the cause.

The state of self-mastery is an effect; it is the result of certain attainments; therefore, to produce the state of self-mastery, one must not act upon the state of self-mastery, but must proceed to promote those attainments that naturally result in self-mastery.

It is not possible, however, to promote these attainments while the mind is trying to exercise control over things; to try to control things is to think about things and act directly upon things, and no mind that is acting upon things can act upon the power that controls things.

Each power in the being of man will, when expressed, do the very thing that it is naturally adapted for; that is, it will produce its own natural effect; therefore, to secure any desired effect, the secret is to awaken that power that will, of itself, produce that effect.

However, to awaken any power in the being of man, the mind must act directly upon that state where the power originates; and every power in man originates in the great within.

There is an inner source of everything that appears in the human personality, and to master self is to have the power to cause this inner source to bring forth into the personal self whatever we desire to have expressed through the self.

What the self is to be, and to do, is determined by what is expressed through the self; therefore, when we can cause the inner source to bring forth into the self whatever we may desire, the self will be and do whatever we may desire. And when we can cause the self to be what we wish it to be, and do what we wish it to do, at any time and under any circumstance, then it is that we have gained the mastery of self.

THE mastery of self is an attainment that has no end. Though everything in mind and body may be mastered to-day, to-morrow will bring forth from the great within new forces, new talents, new powers, and new fields of consciousness, all of which demand control and direction if they are to serve their purpose and be of the greatest possible use to man.

Everything that exists in the being of man is created for some purpose, and the whole of life is not lived as it is intended to be lived unless every such purpose is fulfilled; but nothing in man can fulfil its purpose unless it is mastered by the ruling power in man.

The attainment of self-mastery is therefore indispensable to the living of life, and the promotion of the greatest welfare of the whole of life.

Those elements, forces, faculties, talents, and functions that are only partially under control do not serve the life of man as extensively as they might; in fact, many of these, even those that we have been conscious of for ages, serve us but little; and the cause is deficiency in the art of self-mastery.

There are only a few minds that accomplish as much with their talents as it is possible to accomplish at present; the majority, even among the most gifted, seldom use their ability in its full capacity because they have only a limited control over that ability.

That person who has perfect control of himself can accomplish from two to five times as much with a given talent as those who have no more self-control than is found among the average.

To those who seek to attain much and achieve much, self-mastery is therefore invaluable, though it is equally important in the minor affairs of every-day life; a fact that will readily be admitted when we realize how much distress comes hourly to millions because they cannot control their feelings, emotions, thoughts, and actions.

A large share of the mistakes that are made every moment, can be traced directly to a lack of self-control; and the same can be said of sickness, trouble and failure. To have health, happiness and harmony, peace, power and plenty, self-mastery, to a high degree, is necessary; in brief, the only life that is worth while is the life that is lived in the mastery of self.

To attain the mastery of self, it is first necessary to establish firmly in mind the fundamental purpose of mastery. This is extremely important, because to proceed with the wrong purpose in view is to make every effort useless. This, however, is what has been done by nearly everyone who has undertaken the attainment of self-mastery; and nearly all the books that have been written on the subject have been based upon the wrong purpose; they have therefore retarded the very thing which they aimed to promote.

This being true, it is simple to understand why it is practically impossible to find a single person who has attained complete mastery over self.

Nearly every system purporting to teach the art of self-mastery has been based upon the purpose of controlling something, or exercising arbitrary rulership over mind, body, circumstances, and things. But so long as the mind is trying to control something, the power that can control that something will not be gained.

We must remember, at the very beginning, that before the power of self-mastery can be developed and the state of complete mastery attained, all desire to exercise control over anything or anybody must be eliminated absolutely.

The purpose of self-mastery is to give the mind the power to make the fullest and the most perfect use of all the gifts that one may possess now; to be one's best in every sense of the term, at all times, and under all circumstances; to fulfil the purpose of life thoroughly during every passing moment; to live a larger life, a better life, and a more beautiful life every day; to be all that one can be now, and to do all that one can do now; to bring forth continually the very best that may exist in the great within, and to use that best in such a way that the very best will always come to pass.

The true purpose of self-mastery is to make yourself more perfect, more competent, and more useful. In other words, to become much and accomplish much, in order that you may not only be your complete self, but also be an inspiration to all those who believe in the new race, the superior race, the race of mental mastery and soul supremacy.

THE problem of causing everything in life to become right will easily be solved when man becomes great enough to produce only that which is right; and this greatness will inevitably come when the mastery of self is attained.

That man may become infinitely more than he is now, and that he can do far greater things than has ever been done before, we know with a certainty; we also know that it is the purpose of human life to go on to greatness and greater greatness, but every step must be preceded by another degree in the mastery of self.

When we understand life we invariably gain a strong desire to develop superiority; first, because it is right to attain superiority, and second, because we may thereby inspire thousands to press on to those same magnificent heights.

We desire to demonstrate superiority, however, not for the sake of applause, but to prove by example what man can do. We seek greatness, not that we may rule over anything or anybody, but that we may fulfil the law of life which declares that man is created to become greater and greater so long as eternity shall continue to be.

Our object is not to control those things that exist about us, but to develop those things that exist within us. We seek the fulness of life, and the power to be of the greatest possible use in life; and we seek self-mastery because through mastery alone can these things be promoted to the very highest degree.

When the true purpose of self-mastery is firmly established in mind, we may proceed to develop the power that does produce self-mastery; but the true purpose must never be ignored, because growth in mastery will awaken new forces, new states of consciousness, and new possibilities, and these must all be properly directed.

The higher the power the stronger its force; therefore, the higher we go in the scale of attainment the more important it becomes to properly direct everything.

The misdirection of the higher forces will not only produce all manner of ills, troubles, and failures, but will produce mental phenomena that is misleading. The understanding of truth or any phase of truth will thereby become extremely difficult; in fact, it will be practically impossible to know the real truth about anything so long as such misdirections prevail.

To avoid absolutely the misdirection of any power, fix attention upon development; seek the mastery of self and everything that exists in yourself because you desire to promote greatness in yourself, and you will continue to remain on the right path.

When every thought is animated with a strong desire for a more perfect body, a larger mind, and a more beautiful soul, every effort toward the attainment of self-mastery will become constructive, and only good results can possibly follow.

The less you think about the outer self, and the more you think about the inner self, the better, because it is through the perfect expression of the inner self that you will gain the power to master the outer self.

To clearly, firmly, and permanently establish in mind what one desires to master is extremely important; also, what self-control will mean when it is attained, and what will happen to mind and body when the power of mastery is exercised.

There is a current belief among many that to master oneself is to have the power to interfere with natural functions at will; to suspend the action of this or that organ without producing serious results, and to violate natural laws without having to undergo any of the natural consequences. Others believe that mastery consists in the forceful control of anything and everything that may exist in one's system or in one's circumstances; but such conclusions are the very opposites to the truth.

The majority, however, entertain those very ideas concerning self-mastery; and this is one of the principal reasons why their efforts to attain self-mastery cannot possibly succeed.

He who has attained the mastery of self never tries to suspend the action of any organ; he never thinks of interfering with natural functions in any way whatever, nor does he ignore or violate a single natural law. He never tries to control anything or anybody, not even himself. In fact, the desire to control has been eliminated completely from his mind. His object is not to control himself, but to make the best possible use of himself; and to try to exercise control over something is to interfere with the best use of that something.

The greatest use of self comes directly from the greatest mastery of self, but it is not possible to attain the greatest mastery of self unless the greatest use of self is made the one sole purpose in view.

He who has no desire to control anything, but is inspired with a strong, irresistible desire to make the greatest use of everything, has entered the path to the mastery of self. Without trying to control anything, everything will naturally and willingly come under his control, and will do whatsoever he may wish to have done.

TO master oneself means to direct all the elements, forces, functions, and faculties in the system for the purpose of promoting their natural activities to the highest degree of perfection.

To master one's desires does not mean to suspend those desires, but to give those desires more life and power than ever before, and then direct them into channels of action where the greatest and best results can be obtained under present circumstances.

When you have a desire to do a certain thing and the force of that desire is at hand in the system ready to act, but present circumstances will not permit the expression of that desire, instead of suspending that desire, thereby wasting the energy that was ready for action, you simply turn the force of that desire into some other channel. In this way, valuable results may be secured from the force of every desire that appears in the system, whether the original impulse of that desire can be carried out or not.

Whenever a desire is crushed or suspended all the energy that was alive in that desire will be wasted; and the same waste takes place when a desire is carried in the system for hours, days or weeks, to wear itself out, so to speak, without having its active power turned into any channel of constructive action.

To feel a desire is simply to feel the presence of energy; a desire conveys to the mind the fact that there is energy in the system ready to do something; and if this energy is not given the opportunity to do something it will be wasted.

Through the attainment of self-mastery all the energy that comes into action in the system can be turned into any channel of constructive expression that may be convenient at the time; in fact, to master a desire does not mean to suspend that desire so that it is not felt any more, but to change the course of the force that is active in that desire, so that something of value may be accomplished now while that force is in working condition.

The master-mind never destroys a single desire; he not even thinks of putting down a single feeling that may arise in the system; when he cannot carry out the original desire, or when he finds that the original desire is not normal, which is frequently the case, he redirects the forces that are felt in the system causing them to do something else, something that is normal, and that is possible now.

To master the natural functions is not to interfere with the purpose of those functions, but to promote that purpose to the very highest degree of perfection.

You can master a natural function when you can cause that function to perform its work perfectly under all sorts of conditions, and thereafter, to continue to further perfect the perfection of its perfect work.

To master the organs and functions of digestion does not mean that you can cause those organs to digest anything that you might take into the system; self-mastery does not violate law, neither does it willfully admit an enemy in order that it may demonstrate its power to overcome that enemy. Self-mastery does not resist what is not wanted, but gives man the power to create and secure that which is wanted.

To master the organs of digestion would mean to keep those organs continually in such a perfect state of action that whatever the system needs could be digested perfectly, and without the slightest unpleasant sensation at any time or under any circumstance.

To master the heart does not mean that you can increase or decrease the heart-beats at will, but that you can keep the heart constantly in its true, normal action, no matter how much confusion or excitement there may be in your immediate environment.

The attainment of mastery, therefore, does not mean to interfere with natural action, but to promote natural action to the highest possible degree of perfection.

The idea of mastery is perfect action of all things at all times, regardless of circumstances or events. When you attain self-mastery, all things in your system will be doing their work perfectly, at all times, no matter what your work or your environment may be. And, in addition, this perfect action will constantly develop higher degrees of perfect action.

To master the elements and the forces of the system is not only to promote normal action in the chemical world, but to increase the quality and the power of that action by producing new and superior compounds.

Every mind forms different compounds, unconsciously, as the various grades of vibration are entered by the predominating mental states; but what is formed unconsciously is not always desirable, and when it is desirable it is always inferior to what might have been produced through a similar, intelligently directed conscious action.

Mental states of anger usually produce poisonous elements in the system, while states of fear and depression convert healthy tissues into useless, foreign matter. Such matter always clogs the system, thus interfering with natural functions, and producing, directly or indirectly, a number of ills.

Mental states that are lofty, true, and constructive produce chemical compounds in the system that are nourishing and vitalizing, and that have a strong, refining tendency.

Through the power of self-mastery, undesirable compounds may be prevented entirely because the mind that masters self will not create other than wholesome mental states. Through the same power we may so direct and blend the elements of the system that the formation of the most beneficial and the most highly refined compounds may be constantly taking place.

The possibilities of this law are marvelous to say the least; it is through this law that false chemical conditions in the system may be transformed instantaneously into normal and wholesome actions, and it is through this law that all the elements of the physical body may be constantly refined, until absolute regeneration and spiritualization has taken place.

Through this law the physical body can be developed to the very highest degree of purity, wholeness, refinement, and perfection, and made as beautiful as the Ideal Form itself. The application of this law, however, is possible only to those who have attained the mastery of self.

TO master the forces of the system, the principal object in view is to gain power to accumulate those forces in any part of mind or body where important work is to be done now; because, by giving all the power at hand now to the work we are doing now, that work will invariably result in a superior product.

To employ this method at all times would not only cause all things to be done well, but all things would constantly be done better, and failure would be a thing of the past.

If we would give the greater part of our active energy to the organs of digestion during meals, and for a short time after meals, we should never have anything but the most perfect digestion.

If we would give all the forces of intelligence and genius to the faculty that is in action now, that faculty would invariably do the work of genius, and would never fail to improve upon its own previous record.

The possibilities of self-mastery as applied to the forces of the system are therefore extraordinary; but we cannot master the forces of the system by trying to control those forces; to master any force, the will must act, not upon the force itself, but upon the interior cause of that force.

In the mastery of faculties, the purpose must be expansion and enlargement of conscious action; the average mind needs expansion of consciousness because most of its faculties are too small to give expression to all the energy of the system when concentration and accumulation take place. When this expansion has begun, however, quality, efficiency, and volume may always be secured through the action of any faculty or talent.

Consequently, in the mental world one of the principal objects of self-mastery will be to lead consciousness into the realization of new and greater realms of perception and illumination, and to awaken a greater and greater measure of the great within.

The first real step in the mastery of self is to eliminate all desire to control what is exterior to yourself. Train your mind to desire only the mastery of your own being, and refuse absolutely to even think of controlling anything else. We cannot possibly master ourselves so long as there is the slightest desire to control others.

This may seem to be a contradiction of terms, because when one is master, he ought to be master of everything, whether it be in the without or in the within. But though mastery implies the mastery of everything, the fact must not be forgotten that the mastery of the without is simply an effect of the mastery of the within.

The mastery of environments, circumstances, and external things, naturally follows when one has mastered himself; but so long as we try to control external things we cannot control ourselves, because we cannot produce causes while trying to interfere with effects.

The mastery of self can only be attained through the control of the inner side of mind, consciousness, thought, and action; and to control the inner side constantly, the whole of attention must constantly be given to the inner side.

You control the exterior by causing the interior to become exactly what you wish the exterior to be.

The principle is, produce the cause you want and you will have the effect you want. The cause can be produced only by acting upon the subjective, because it is only the subjective side that has the power to originate cause; and to act upon the subjective, the forces of the mind must be trained to move toward the within.

However, whenever we try to control that which is exterior to ourselves, the forces of the mind will begin to move toward the without; and it is not possible for the forces of mind to go in while they are going out, neither can the tendency to act upon the within be established in mind so long as the outward movement of mind is permitted in the least.

The mind of the average person has already a strong tendency to move toward the surface; therefore, to remove that tendency completely, the opposite tendency must be given the whole of attention; all the forces of mind must move toward the within at all times, and attention must be concentrated upon the subjective side absolutely without any cessation whatever.

It is not possible to form a tendency toward the inner life while the mind is acting more or less upon external things; a tendency is a continuous movement in a certain direction; therefore, while the mind is acting more or less upon the surface, the continuous movement toward the within will be interrupted and there will be no tendency toward the within.

We cannot train mental tendencies to move in opposite directions; no two forces, directly opposed to each other, can exist in the mind at the same time.

If the entire mind is to be harmonious and constructive, all the forces of the mind must move toward the within; that is, they must move into the mind and not out of the mind. The person, however, who is trying to control external things while he is trying to develop the mastery of self, will cause his mind to be divided against itself. He will consequently control nothing.

When we realize the difference between the control of self and the control of others, and how they are direct opposites in purpose and action, we shall understand why the two cannot exist in the mind together. And since the methods employed in the control of persons and things are antagonistic to those employed in the control of self, it will not be possible to develop self-mastery so long as there is the least attempt to influence others.

It may seem impossible, however, to deal with other minds, especially with younger minds, without exercising some form of influence; but we must remember that there is a great difference between trying to control a mind and trying to instruct a mind.

To control a mind is to compel that mind to neglect its own power; to instruct a mind is to inspire in that mind the desire to use its own power.

To train another mind in the line of right thought and action, do not try to compel that mind to think right or act right; place before that mind ideas that will naturally produce right thought and right action. And this can be done without having the slightest desire to influence or control.

It is upon this principle that the new education is based—the education that will not simply train small minds to remember what great minds have thought, but will train all small minds to become great minds.

GREAT is the mind that can leave everybody alone, that can be friendly to those who think what he cannot accept, and that can desire with his whole heart to have everybody be free to be themselves; but it is necessary to have such a mind if we would attain mastery of self.

If we are not to influence anyone it may be a problem to know how far we may go in persuading others to examine the desirability of the good things we have found in life. There is a natural tendency among us all to wish that everybody had all the good that we have, but we frequently go too far in trying to make people accept what they cannot appreciate. From this we observe that the human race is not depraved at all, but is somewhat lacking in judgment.

The best way and the simplest way to persuade others to take advantage of the good that you may have found, is to prove in your own life that what you have found is better.

Never try to compel others to change; leave them free to change naturally and orderly because they want to; and they will want to change when they find that your change was worth while.

To inspire in others a desire to change for the better is truly noble; but this you can do only by leaving them alone, and becoming more noble yourself.

Make the most of yourself in your way, and leave everybody free to make the most of themselves in their way; they will when they find that it is better to enter the greater than to remain in the lesser; and that that is better you can prove by the way you live.

All minds want the best, and they will soon know the best when it is constantly before them as a living reality. People may not accept your theories, but if your life is better than theirs, they will soon do their utmost to live as you do.

After all, what would one have? Is it not life, the best life, the most beautiful life that we all seek?

To completely eliminate all desire to control persons and things, impress upon mind the great fact that it is not what others do, but what you, yourself do, that determines whether good or ill shall come to you.

When this fact is realized, your one desire will be to perfect your own life, thought, and action; you will find that the mastery of yourself will require all of your time and the whole of your attention, and you will interfere with others no more.

The true understanding of freedom will also help a great deal in removing the desire to interfere with others. When one finds that he cannot receive what he is not willing to give, and that so long as we deny freedom to others, others cannot give freedom to us, the relations between man and man become so clear that anyone can understand how to relate himself to the human race.

The best way, however, is to have so much faith in others that you know they will do the best they can without your telling them to do so. Such a faith may not always bring forth the best from everybody, but it will produce a strong tendency in that direction; and besides, it will make of you a superior being. You will advance constantly through such a faith, and thousands will follow your example.

To eliminate all desire to control others, however, is not the only essential; you must also eliminate all desire to control your own person. Nor is this a contradiction; to control the person you must act upon that inner power that can control the person; but it is not possible to act upon the power that is back of the person while attention is centered upon the person itself.

You cannot control the within while trying to control the without; the within is the world of cause, while the person is but the effect of what is being expressed from the inner cause.

As the subjective is, so is the objective; the subjective is the inner life, and originates everything that appears in the objective or outer life.

We must not try to control the person, whether that person belongs to us or to some other soul.

True, we are to master the person, but we cannot master the person by concentrating attention upon the person; we master the person by expressing through the person those conditions and actions that we desire to see in the person, and those can be brought forth only from the within.

You can produce any change desired in the person by creating the cause of that change in the subconscious; and you can make the person express any desired action by creating the subconscious cause of that action. Nothing can be done, however, in the person, or through the person, unless the necessary cause is first produced in the subconscious, or what is frequently termed the subjective side of mind.

It is therefore evident that all effort to control the person or act upon the person, is wasted effort; results can be secured in the person only through that action that deals with the power back of the person, because what this power does, that the person will do also.

THE mastery of self implies the power to make the greatest and the best use of self, and to exercise this power is the real purpose of mastery; therefore, those mental states through which this power can act with the greatest efficiency must be cultivated.

The first essential mental state is harmony; complete and universal harmony, harmony with oneself, with everybody, and with everything.

To be in harmony is to be properly related to that with which we may come in contact; and to be properly related to anything is to meet that something in its own world without disregarding the purpose of our world.

To be in harmony with everything is to adapt yourself to everything, and though this is an art requiring much thought and effort, it is absolutely necessary, because when one is not in harmony he is in discord, and discord misdirects energy.

To cultivate harmony, concentrate attention frequently upon the interior principle of harmony, the soul of harmony as it exists in the ideal within.

There is a state in the within that not only is in harmony, but that is harmony; and to mentally grow in the consciousness of that state is to unfold the life of harmony throughout one's entire personality.

The second essential mental state is poise, and its chief value in self-mastery is the part it plays in holding together the energies of the system.

The mastery of self implies the possession of self, the conscious possession of one's entire self; that is, the holding together of the various activities, forces, and elements in the system so that they may all work in unison in promoting the purpose the mind may now have in view. And this is poise.

Through the law of harmony you may change your mental attitudes at will, because when the consciousness of harmony is attained, you have not only the power to change your attitude so as to harmonize yourself with everything, but you also discern instantaneously when to change, and in what way.

Through the law of poise, however, you gain the power to prevent mental change, which at times, and in a certain sense is absolutely necessary.

To be ever the same and yet never the same is to be on the perfect path to the greater life.

All the energies of the system must be held together in poise even when you are changing your mental attitudes to harmonize with something that is different.

Every change demands a law through which to produce its change; but this law does not change. The law is ever the same, and yet he who applies this law will be never the same.

The attitude of poise is the changeless attitude through which all energies must pass if constructive results and change for the better are to be secured. It is therefore indispensable to the attainment of self-mastery, because to master the forces of the system is to have conscious possession of those forces, and that is poise.

To cultivate the attitude of poise, combine in consciousness the feeling of power and the feeling of peace. To feel immensely strong, and perfectly serene at the same time, is to be in poise.

The feeling of poise produces the feeling of self-possession, and to concentrate attention frequently upon our most perfect mental conception of the state of self-possession will develop the attitude of poise.

The third essential mental state is non-resistance; and the value of this state in the mastery of self is beyond measure.

To practice resistance is to direct attention upon the objective; it is trying to force things, and this causes the mind to act directly upon things; consciousness is brought to the surface, and the mental forces will begin to move toward the without instead of toward the within.

What we try to resist we try to control; and so long as we try to control anything we cannot attain the mastery of self.

The mental actions of resistance employ the external will altogether, something that must be eliminated completely before mastery can take place.

The external will, that is, ordinary will-power, is one of the principal obstacles to the attainment of self-mastery, and so long as we practice resistance this will-power will live and grow.

The stronger the power of the ordinary will, the larger will be the time required to attain the mastery of self, unless that form of will-power is eliminated completely at the beginning.

Resistance, however, is the chief promoter of this form of will-power; therefore, non-resistance must be made the one great rule in everything, whether in life, thought, or action.

To practice resistance is to try to overcome by going against; to practice non-resistance is to overcome by going above. Resistance wastes its energy by fighting what it does not want; non-resistance leaves behind what it does not want, and proceeds serenely to employ its energy in creating what it does want.

It is therefore evident that resistance never can succeed while non-resistance always does succeed.

To enter the attitude of non-resistance is not to bring your life to a stand-still, nor to fold your arms, permitting persons, circumstances, and things to do to you what they like. Non-resistance is a forward movement, while resistance is never anything but retrogression.

The non-resisting mind does not antagonize the wrongs that are behind, and all wrongs are behind, but proceeds in peace to realize the greater good that is before.

The attitude of non-resistance makes man a stronger individuality, and he who becomes stronger will not remain in the hands of the weaker.

To resist what is against us is to continue to be small, and he who is small cannot overcome those obstacles that may seem to be great.

Resistance scatters and wastes energy; non-resistance accumulates and constructively employs energy. Therefore, to practice the former is to re-main weak, while to practice the latter is to develop strength and power in greater and greater measure.

To use your power in resisting wrongs is to continue in bondage to those wrongs, because we give our power to that which we resist. To use your power for self-development and self-mastery is to rise superior to every circumstance and condition, which means inevitable victory and complete emancipation.

THE fourth essential mental state is receptivity, or the attitude of responsiveness—that attitude that places the mind in perfect touch with everything that it may desire to receive.

The objective or personal life is controlled by causing the objective to respond to the subjective, and there is positively no other law through which the person may be controlled.

It is not necessary to act upon the person to control the person, nor would such action produce any results whatever; the person will respond only to that which is taking place in the within; therefore, to create the desired subjective action, and train the person to respond to that action, is to secure the desired objective action.

The mastery of the personal self depends entirely upon the degree of responsiveness that exists in the person; but how can responsiveness be cultivated in the person if we are not to act upon the person? And if this quality is developed from within, how can the person, in the beginning, respond even to responsiveness?

The fact is that receptivity has its existence primarily in consciousness, and as consciousness fills the personal self, everything that is developed in consciousness will be active in the person.

When you become conscious of the state of receptivity, the person will respond to everything with which you may come in contact, whether the contact be with the without or with the within.

The receptive mind is easily influenced and affected by everything, both good and otherwise; for this reason, no mind should place itself in sympathetic contact with environments that are contrary to its own ideals.

What enters mind from adverse environments or inferior associations will manifest in the person according to the degree of receptivity that may be present at the time; but since it is possible to control the attitude of receptivity so that we come in mental contact only with that which is desirable, every person may determine what he is to receive, and what he is not to receive, from the physical or mental worlds in which he may be living now.

The power that environment may exercise in the life of any person depends entirely upon himself, how receptive he may happen to be; but since anyone can train himself to respond only to those things that are superior to himself, he may eliminate completely every form of influence that may come from those circumstances, persons, or things that are inferior.

It is absolutely necessary that the person should respond to the mind if it is to be mastered by the mind, but since the person, when highly receptive, will respond to everything that enters the mind, nothing that is inferior or undesirable must be permitted to enter the mind.

To prevent this, however, another, and a corresponding state of mind, viz., positiveness, must be cultivated.

The person that is not receptive is barely alive, and can accomplish nothing of real value; receptivity is, therefore, indispensable, and the fact that the receptive person responds to that which is not good, as well as to that which is good, should not cause any hesitancy in the cultivation of receptivity.

The person does not respond directly to anything that exists in the without, but only to that which has first entered the mind, and the mind has the power to select from every source what it wants to accept, and reject what it does not wish to use.

To cultivate the state of receptivity, encourage the actions of the finer forces and the finer vibrations in the system. Whenever these forces are felt, the mind should become quiet and should enter more deeply into the feeling of those forces.

It is the finer forces to which the person responds; therefore, to promote the development of receptivity the action of these forces should be increased perpetually through the entire personality.

Another essential to the cultivation of receptivity is to enter into the closest possible mental touch with the finer elements that permeate all things; mentally live with the soul of things; and this is the true receptivity.

When we realize the great value of receptivity, and find that the person can respond to the low as well as to the high, it becomes necessary to find a method through which this delicate faculty may be so guarded and directed that it will respond only to the superior.

In other words, how shall the mind protect itself from being impressed with the many inferior things with which we come in daily contact?

What we see, hear, or feel, or meet in any way, produces some impression upon the mind; in fact, everything that enters through the senses will impress the mind, and every impression, if sufficiently strong, will affect the mind, and then the person.

We cannot close our eyes to what we see; we must, therefore, find a method through which we may prevent what we do see from impressing the mind when we so elect.

We want all our senses to be thoroughly alive, and we want consciousness to be wide-awake to everything that is taking place in our present state of existence, but we also want the power to close the mental door to every impression from without that is not worthy of being entertained.

This power is found in the state of positiveness, the fifth essential mental state.

So long as the mind is in a positive state, nothing can impress the mind unless that impression is deeply desired, and the reason why is simple.

It is the creative energies of mind that produce the mental impressions, but these energies will do only what they are directed to do by the vibrations that enter the mind. These vibrations may come from without, through

the senses, or they may come from within, through the mind's own thinking, and the creative energies will obey those vibrations that have the greatest power.

When the vibrations from without are the strongest, as is the case in the
average mind, the creative energies will proceed to form impressions, states,
conditions, and thoughts that are exactly similar to the ideas that are being
conveyed by the vibrations from without; and the mental world will be created in the likeness of the exterior environment.

However, when the mind is in a positive state, the vibrations from within
are the strongest, and no vibration from without can produce an impression
upon the mind unless the mental door is consciously opened to that particular idea.

When you are in a positive state, nothing that you may see, hear, or feel
will impress your mind unless you so desire. It is therefore evident that so
long as you remain in a positive state, you will never be controlled by environments, circumstances, persons, or things.

Positiveness is that state wherein the mind generates its own vibrations
and its own mental life; forms its own mental attitudes, thinks consciously
its own thoughts, and is so strong in its own individualized being that no
power can act in the mental domain unless it is wanted.

To be positive, however, does not mean to domineer over anything, but
to feel the fullness of invincible life and power, and to fill the mind with
the fullness of that life and power.

You do not have to exercise control over the forces of the mind; you do
not have to compel the creative energies to ignore the vibrations, the influences, and the ideas that come from without; it is simply necessary to fill
your own mind with your own mental vibrations, and to make those vibrations stronger than those that may try to enter from without.

So long as you fill your mind with your own mental vibrations, and you
always do when in a positive state, the creative energies will produce only
those thoughts and impressions that you desire to have produced; the desires
of your own true self will be obeyed by the powers within you, and those
desires alone.

The value of positiveness lies, first, in its power to protect the mind from
being impressed by inferior, external conditions; and secondly, in its power
to keep the creative energies under the complete control of the mind.

The positive mind has the power to think whatever it may want to think,
and this is the real secret of the mastery of self.

He alone can master himself who can master his mind; and he alone can master his mind who can think what he wants to think, at any time and under any circumstance.

To develop positiveness, simply be positive at all times; that is the whole secret, and it is something that any one can do with perfect ease.

Feel the fullness of invincible life and power, and fill your mind with this life and power. Resist nothing, domineer over nothing, and try to control nothing. Feel positively that you are a master, because that is what you are.

The sixth essential mental state to the attainment of the mastery of self, is the consciousness of superiority.

It is not possible to attain self-mastery so long as one thinks that he is an inferior creature, because through that thought mind goes down and functions below its true level.

We can control only that which we have risen above; therefore, no mastery is possible until we live in the mental world of superiority.

The idea, however, is not that we are to think of ourselves as being superior to others; we know that the same superiority that exists in us exists in every person, and it is this superiority into which we desire to enter.

The idea is to dwell constantly upon the mountain top of your being; to live consciously and perpetually at the very apex of all your aspirations, and to constantly function in the most perfect spheres of those present possibilities that you can now realize.

The purpose of self-mastery is to make all of life just as high as our highest vision of the ideal; and we have attained mastery when we can make everything in life become exactly what we wish it to be.

The act of mastering oneself implies the power to bring oneself up to the state of superiority; to make everything superior to what it was, and then press on to still greater heights.

The purpose of mastery is not to control faculties, talents, forces, or elements, but to direct them all toward greater attainments and greater achievements—toward superiority.

It is not possible, however, to cause everything in one's being to move toward superiority unless the mind is established in the consciousness of superiority; to produce mental tendencies toward the superior, consciousness must feel the life, the spirit, and the soul of the superior, and this feeling may be cultivated by frequently concentrating attention upon the most perfect conception of superiority that the mind can possibly form.

Whatever we frequently think of, with depth and feeling, that we shall gain the consciousness of; this is a law through which any hidden secret may be brought into the light of a clear, positive understanding.

The seventh essential mental state is the realization of supremacy; the knowing of the truth that you, yourself, are the supreme ruler over everything in your being and in your world.

We must remove the idea of exercising control over the person through the use of objective will-power, and in the place of that idea establish the realization of supremacy.

When one knows that he is the supreme master of his being, he rules supremely without trying to do so; and herein we learn why he who has attained the mastery of self never tries to master or control anything, not even himself.

It is not necessary to try to be that which you are; and as you are created with the power to master yourself, you do not have to try, at any time, to master yourself. You are the supreme master of your being, and to think the truth, you must think of yourself as such.

He *is* what he is who knows that he *is*; and he who knows *what* he is, does what he *can* do by the virtue of being what he *is*.

He who knows that he is supreme in his own being exercises supremacy by the virtue of being supreme.

He who is supreme cannot do otherwise but exercise supremacy; and since man is supreme in his own being he must necessarily exercise supremacy in his own being; that is, when he knows that he is what he *is*.

Man in the real is a master; therefore, when in the consciousness of the real, he does master; and does not have to try. He who tries to be a master does not know that he really is a master; when he knows that he is, he will do that which he has the power to do, not by trying, but by doing what he is in being.

The sun does not try to shine; it is light; therefore, it does shine. The sun does not have to control the sunbeams: the sun creates the sunbeams by being the cause of sunbeams; the sunbeams are created to give light because they proceed from that which is light; and that which is created to give light will give light because it is light; it will not have to be controlled to do so.

A piece of ice *is* cold, therefore, it makes everything cold with which it comes in contact; it does not have to try to produce cold. It is not necessary for any force or element in nature to try to produce in itself that which already exists in itself; neither is it necessary for man to try to do this.

So long as we try to master ourselves we shall not succeed in mastering anything; but when we discover that we in truth *are* masters, we shall succeed in mastering everything without trying in the least to do so.

The realization of supremacy is therefore of the highest value, because this realization will reveal man to himself. He will *know* that he is supreme in his own being; he will know that he is created with that power, and when man knows what he is he will act accordingly.

To cultivate the mental state of supremacy, impress the mind as frequently as possible with the truth that you are supreme in your own being. If you were not, you could not exist; your being would be chaos; the fact that you exist as an individualized entity proves that you are supreme in the being of that entity, and to be just to yourself you must exercise the whole of that power.

Therefore, to impress the mind with the idea that you are supreme in your being, is simply to train your mind to understand a great truth; and when that truth is realized, the realization of supremacy will have been attained; you will know what you are and you will act with supremacy in everything that is done within yourself.

When the mind acts with supremacy in the within, all the creations of mind will be patterned after the highest ideals that may now exist in consciousness; and the progress of the individual will be remarkable.

The reason why so many fail to reach their ideals is because they do not act with supremacy in the inner world of creation; they, therefore, do not recreate themselves in the likeness of their ideals, and no person can realize his ideals until he grows into the exact likeness of those ideals.

When the mind has not attained the consciousness of supremacy it cannot act with supremacy; the creative energies will, consequently, follow lower ideals, and will not do what is wanted done.

To enter fully into the consciousness of supremacy, all knowledge that reveals the unlimited possibilities of man will prove of great value, because the more deeply we can penetrate the greatness already existing within us, the more firmly we can establish the consciousness of supremacy.

To constantly feel that one is supreme in his own domain is absolutely necessary, and as this feeling would simply be the conscious expression of what is the truth, no one should hesitate for a moment to enter that attitude, and to dwell therein forever.

The person may feel weak, but that does not prove that you are weak; the weakness of the person is felt because you have failed to bring forth your own real strength.

Know that you are strong, and all weakness will disappear; know that you are supreme in your own domain, and you will rule supremely in your own domain. You will rule with supreme power because you are the individualization of supreme power.

HAVING established the mind in the seven states that are necessary to the attainment of self-mastery, the next essential is to train the will to perform its true function.

To begin, we must discard the current belief that the will was made to rule; the very opposite is its function; the true will never attempts to rule anything, but holds itself constantly in that attitude through which it can be ruled by the mind's highest conception of law, principle, and truth.

Man attains self-mastery not by trying to rule, but by permitting himself to be ruled by that which is greater than his present conception of himself.

That personality is always the most powerful that lets go of its own personal power and gives itself up completely to superior power.

He who is willing to lose the smaller life for the sake of the larger, will gain the larger; and he who is willing to lose his limited personal power for the sake of unlimited impersonal power, will gain the unlimited.

In like manner, he who disposes of the will that tries to rule, for the sake of the will that is *the* ruler, will receive the latter, which is the real will. And this is necessary, because the mastery of self cannot be attained so long as will-power is exercised in the usual way.

The true will never tries to rule; it already is the ruling power; and it never tries to gain supremacy; it already is supreme.

Since the true will already is supreme, it would be a misuse of will to try to become supreme. Through such actions an inferior imitation of the real will would be employed, and that imitation would not contain any will-power whatever, but would simply be some aimless use of superficial mental force.

What is usually termed the personal will, that is, that something that we employ when we try to rule or domineer, is not will-power in any form; the personal will is nothing but the misuse of mental forces.

In the average person the real will is never employed; what passes for will in those minds is a more or less uncertain expression of those states of consciousness that have gained some imperfect conception of the real will.

Through every mental conception of the will a temporary state of consciousness is established having a tendency to direct, and to take initial steps. This is natural, because since the will itself is the ruling power every mental conception of the will would have a tendency to rule.

Each mental conception of the will bears a slight resemblance to the will, and receives a tendency to act accordingly. Consequently, a mental conception of the will, by virtue of this slight resemblance, imitates the will with imperfect attempts to rule.

When we take initial steps, we are said to use the will, but we do not; we simply express our latest mental conception of the will; and since all such conceptions have tendencies to rule, direct, or take initial steps, initial steps, however imperfect, will accordingly be taken.

It is the truth, well-known to everybody, that the average initial step is a mistake; and it could not very well be otherwise, because it is not taken by the real will, but by an inferior imitation. It is also well known that most of our attempts at exercising the power to rule are complete failures, and lead both object and subject into confusion.

It is also the truth, easily demonstrated, that practically all the mistakes of the world come originally from the tendency of the mind to follow imitations of the will instead of the real will itself.

The ills of life are wholly due to the mistakes we make when trying to control and direct our actions by the personal will; while the great and the good things that are done are done only when the mind gives way to a superior power, and acts under the direction and inspiration of the supreme will.

The pronounced individualist may object to the idea that we are to give up to a superior power, but such objections will disappear when we realize that this superior power is our own power, and that we are simply discarding the false and the limited in order that we may take possession of the limitless and the true.

In like manner, all objections to the idea that the will must place itself in that attitude where it can be ruled by the superior, will disappear when we realize that through that attitude of the will, the will is permitted to be itself.

In order that the will may be itself, it should make no effort to rule, but should remain what it is—*the power that does rule*.

The will is properly performing its true function when it is eternally giving way to the superior; that is, the superior that is in itself, that is in man, and that is in the expression of the infinite in man.

The true function of the will is to hold the mind in such a state that the higher may find a full and free expression at all times. In other words, to keep the mind open to the perpetual influx of life and power from on high—that is what the true will is created to do; and that is sufficient; the mind that is constantly being filled with the superior, will receive everything that it may desire to receive because the superior contains everything.

Such a mind will also become what it may wish to become, because to be filled with the superior is to become superior. It will also achieve anything that may be undertaken, because there is no limit to the power from which the superior eternally proceeds.

The difference, therefore, between the real will and its man-made imitations is immense, and any one can understand that man has nothing to lose and everything to gain by eliminating the latter and giving up completely to the power of the former.

THE purpose of the personal will is to try to compel things to do thus or so; but this is not necessary, neither can anything but undesirable results proceed from such efforts.

Things will do that which they are created to do when left to themselves; and since everything has the inherent right to be itself and itself only, we cannot try to make them do or be different without violating the law of freedom.

When we desire different things we should cause different things to be created, and not try to make things already created different from what they are. This, however, is constantly being done; the result is, we not only misplace things, but we interfere, more or less, with the natural inclinations and best motives of nearly every person with whom we come in contact.

This practice leads to the violation of the law of freedom on every hand, and since we cannot expect to receive from others what we do not wish to give to others, there can be no freedom for ourselves until we interfere with persons and things no more.

The leading purpose of the personal will is to change things in the with-out; to try to make over what has already been created. In brief, the ordinary will-power is simply a meddler, and is engaged principally in the work of interference, trying to prevent persons and things from being themselves.

This purpose, however, is contrary to all the laws of life, because the very first principle in life is to give everything the freedom to be what it is.

When we wish to change things we must not misplace them, but proceed to transmute them; and transmutation is brought about, not by interfering with the present external condition of things, but through the expression of superior power into the interior life of things.

When things are not as they should be, we can change them, not by trying to remake the present external condition of things, but by creating a new internal condition for things.

We remove evil, not by resistance nor by interference, but by permitting evil to be itself, which is nothing. Evil, being mere nothingness or emptiness, would never disturb us if we did not make "something" out of it.

The more we interfere with evil the more we make of evil and the more we disturb the development of the good, thus retarding the growth of the very thing that *can* remove evil.

We cannot remove evil; this the good alone can do; but we can create the good in sufficient abundance to cause all evil to disappear.

We have no time to create the good while constantly interfering with evil; and since it is the creation of the good and the good alone that can remove evil, we understand perfectly why we should not disturb the tares.

We have given ages of time to the pulling up of tares, but there are just as many tares in the world now as there ever were. Nothing has been gained; we have not removed the ills of life by constantly interfering with those ills; the method is a complete failure, and should be abandoned absolutely.

It can be demonstrated conclusively that evil invariably disappears when left to itself, to be itself, which is nothing; but to leave evil alone, the mind must give the whole of its attention to the creation of the good.

The personal will, however, cannot leave evil alone; its nature is to interfere; therefore, it must be eliminated, and the entire mind placed absolutely in the hands of Supreme Will.

When we compare, briefly, the two methods for dealing with adverse conditions, we find that the old method, the method of the personal will, through a constant interference with evil, never succeeds in eliminating evil, while the new method, through a constant creation of the good, soon eliminates all the evil there is.

Employ the new method, and evil will continue but a short time, and it is no more; but so long as the old method is employed, evil will live and grow, with no promise of cessation whatever.

When we examine evil we find that it is a condition of emptiness or incompleteness, and can live only until the fullness and the completeness of the opposite good appears.

The harvest of tares, which we have been told not to prevent, is therefore not some future fixed time, but any time when the true life-forces of growth are made sufficiently strong to bring evil conditions to an end.

This end can be brought about by any person, in his own life, at any time, by the giving of all his power and the whole of his attention to the creation of those good things that are necessary to fill the conditions of nothingness that may exist in the world.

The harvest of tares, that is, the end of evil conditions in any personal life, can be produced at once, and complete emancipation secured now; but the personal will must first give way to the ruling power of the real will.

To use the will for the purpose of interfering with things, as they are, not only perpetuates evil, but also prevents everything in life from being its best.

Nothing can be its best unless it is given freedom to be itself, its true and complete self; and in order that we may enter that attitude wherein we naturally give all things the freedom to be themselves, we must permit both the perfect and the imperfect to be what they are.

Our tendency to interfere with the imperfect will disappear of itself when we realize that the imperfect will not pass away until we create something better to take its place.

However, to create that something better it is necessary to attain a higher understanding of the superior, and also to bring into action the finer creative forces. The present states of mind must give place to states that have all the essentials required for the creation of the better; but this becomes possible only when the will is employed in its true function.

***

THE purpose of self-mastery is the attainment of superiority; to employ all the elements of being in such a way that perpetual growth becomes the principal factor in existence.

You have attained mastery of all the forces and elements of your being when you have caused all of these to work together constantly for the higher development of your entire self.

To simply make certain forces in your system obey your desires does not indicate any degree of self-mastery; in fact, every attempt to control your forces according to personal desires will pervert the will, and thus prevent the attainment of mastery. But when any force has been made constructive and constructive only, then you are the master of that force.

It is the true purpose of all forces to be constructive; they are, therefore, not in their true sphere of action until they have become permanently constructive; and he who has accomplished this has mastered the powers of his being.

To master yourself is to cause all things in yourself to enter their true sphere of action, and the very moment that the will proceeds to direct all things in being into their true spheres of action, the first step in mastership has been attained.

The will cannot direct things, however, until it has given up completely to that superior power that is the ruling power; and its direction of things into their true spheres of action consists in the placing of things in the hands of this same power.

When analyzing the true will and its true function, we find that its one and only purpose is to act upon consciousness; not to control consciousness, but to act upon consciousness.

The will was not made to act upon the body, nor upon any of the forces and elements in the body; neither was it made to act upon the mind, nor upon any of the states, the tendencies, or the desires of the mind.

The will should act upon consciousness only, and the reason why is found in the fact that everything that appears in body or mind is but the effect of conscious states.

Whatever you become conscious of, that you will express in the personality, and mind and body will become what those expressions are. The conditions of those expressions will be externalized in the personality, and the person will feel, act, and behave exactly as those expressions feel, act, and behave.

Every change that actually takes place in consciousness will produce a corresponding change in the personality, and every step in advance that is realized in consciousness will cause the personality to advance and develop in a similar manner.

Every cause that is formed in consciousness will produce its own effect in the personality, and as any cause desired may be produced in consciousness, any effect desired may be secured in mind or body.

There is nothing, however, except the true will that can produce causes in consciousness, therefore the will must be trained for this work.

In training the will for practical purposes, the mind should be centered as much as possible upon the true function of the will; the personal will should be ignored completely, and no thought whatever should be given to the exercise of control over anything, nor should the slightest desire to rule be permitted.

To feel a desire to rule, control, antagonize, or resist, means that the true will is not recognized, and that the mind is permitting itself to be misled by inferior imitations.

The true will always moves toward the superior; it acts upon consciousness for the purpose of causing consciousness to gain a higher and a larger conception of the superior, and as these superior conceptions are realized in mind, they become patterns for the creative energies. Superior thoughts, desires, tendencies, actions, and conditions will thereby be created throughout the entire system.

The will is created to take the initial step in everything that transpires in human existence; and since all the elements of life follow the will, it is of the highest importance that every step be a step in advance, because if it is not, the elements of life will produce the inferior; retrogression will then take place, and the very things that are not wanted will appear in life.

However, when the will is true every step that is taken will be a step in advance, a step toward the consciousness of greater superiority; the true will is superior, therefore can will act only in the life of superiority.

The will is superior now; it is above all other functions and attributes; nothing takes place until the will acts; it is the master over all, and therefore occupies the highest place in mind. Consequently, when we recognize the will in its true state, we recognize something that is superior, and all our thoughts will ascend toward the superior.

When all the actions of mind are moving toward the superior, greatness is being developed and the purpose of mastery is being fulfilled.

We master any particular part of the system when that part is made to perform its true function under all sorts of conditions; and we further master the same part when we have trained it to perform its function much better than it ever did before.

To cause this perfect action, and the more perfect action, to take place in any particular part of the system, this action must first be caused in consciousness, because each part of the system simply carries out what consciousness holds for it to do. The various forces, elements, organs, and states are mere channels of expression for conscious action.

Change a certain phase of consciousness, and the corresponding mental or physical expression changes likewise; but no change can possibly take place in any part of the personality until the necessary change is produced in consciousness; and nothing can produce this change in consciousness but the true action of the true will.

The prevailing state of consciousness is the only one cause in the personal being of man; all other things are effects of this one cause; it is therefore useless for the will to act upon anything else but consciousness, because it is only through consciousness that the purpose of the will can be promoted.

To train the will to will in harmony with the real will, form in mind a clear conception of the real will; then will only the larger, the higher, and the better.

As the consciousness of the real will is developed, the will-power becomes immensely strong; and there are two reasons why; first, because the true will does not destroy its strength through the desire to rule; and second, because it gives itself up to the influx of real power—the power that proceeds from the source of limitless power.

As this power fills the system more and more, a deep stillness is gained, a state of being that is not only perfectly serene, but immensely strong; peace and power united; and when this state of being is felt, one may know that the path to self-mastery has been found.

To enter this state is to begin the mastery of self, and to continue in this state is to continue to develop the mastery of self to the very highest possible degree.

To step outside of this state is to cease, for the time being, to master oneself, and herein one may know whether he is on the path to mastery or not.

To hold the mind and every part of the mind in this serene, strong state, and to hold it there at all times, is a very high art, and is made possible only through the training of the will to act upon the principle of the real will.

When the will wills to be what it *is*—the ruling power, and wills to feel the action of this power, the mind will enter the strong, serene state, because the action of the real will is perfectly serene, and its power is immensely strong.

TO master oneself is to cause oneself to be what one wishes to be. To eternally become what one desires to become means a perpetual transformation of self because all becoming is change—eternal change for the better; and to perpetually transform the self, a higher order of life and thought must be constantly expressed in the self.

This, however, is made possible only through awakening of higher and larger states of consciousness, and as consciousness responds only to the actions of the will, the true use of the will becomes indispensable in the attainment of the mastery of self.

To train the will to act upon consciousness, will-power should be concentrated upon every individualization of consciousness in the personality as well as upon consciousness in general.

If we wish to produce a certain effect in any part of the personality, the will should act upon the consciousness that permeates that part, and the cause that can produce the desired effect should be impressed upon that state of consciousness.

Consciousness permeates every atom in your entire being, and every atom responds to the action of that part of consciousness that is centered within the atom; it is therefore possible to produce any desired physical or chemical effect in any part of the personality by producing in the consciousness within that part the desired cause.

There is a special center of consciousness in every organ of the body, and in every faculty of the mind; therefore, to produce any desired effect upon any special organ or faculty, the will must act, not upon the organ or faculty itself, but upon the center of consciousness that is within that organ or faculty.

The reason why the average person fails to control his body or mind is because he uses will-power upon the body and the mind instead of upon the consciousness that permeates both.

Control the consciousness that permeates the body and you control the body as well; and consciousness is readily controlled when the will acts directly upon consciousness while strongly desiring to secure certain results.

To cause the will to act directly upon consciousness, concentrate attention upon the finest substance or life that you can picture as permeating that part of mind or body where you desire the effect to be produced.

To illustrate, when concentrating upon the brain do not think of the brain itself, nor use will-power upon the brain, but turn will and attention upon the finer life-forces that permeate the brain. Likewise when concentrating upon any organ in the body, do not direct the will upon the physical organ, but upon the finer forces that permeate that organ. In this way you will act directly upon the center of consciousness within that organ, and whatever you impress that center of consciousness to do, the organ itself will do.

Through the same process the center of consciousness in any organ or faculty may be so strongly individualized that it will respond instantaneously to any action that may be made by the will. The stronger the center of consciousness in any part of the personality the stronger the subconscious action of the will in that center; and as it is the subconscious action of the will that controls, the value of developing strong centers of consciousness in every part of the personality becomes evident.

When attention is being concentrated upon the various centers of consciousness, the will must never try to control those centers, or domineer, in any way, over consciousness itself. The object of the will is to impress upon consciousness those actions or qualities that are desired in personal expression.

To promote this object, the force of will and the force of desire should be combined into one action, and this action should be directed where results are to be secured.

The true will and the true desire are the two halves of the same whole; they are therefore indispensable to each other, and the more thoroughly they are trained to work as one, the sooner will the mastery of self be attained.

Desire receives, and the will directs action upon the object that the mind wishes to receive. Before the mind can receive, consciousness must come in contact with the object desired, and to direct consciousness into that contact, the will is required, because the will is the only power that can direct.

When desire acts without the will, it fails to bring consciousness into contact with the object desired; nothing is therefore received; and this explains why most desires are never fulfilled.

When the will acts without desire, the mental attitude that receives and appropriates is absent; there is no receptivity, therefore, nothing is received; and this explains why mere will-power is powerless to gain the object in view.

When the will acts upon a certain state of consciousness, there should be a very strong desire to awaken into positive action what may be latent in that state; and, conversely, whenever the mind feels a strong desire for something, the will should act directly upon the inner or subjective state of that center of consciousness that contains that something.

Through these methods, what we desire to receive will be received, and what we will to accomplish will be accomplished.

The desire that is aimless, and the will that domineers but never directs—these two actions in mind are responsible for nearly all the failures in life; it is therefore evident that failure could be reduced to a minimum in every sphere of life when the force of desire and the force of will were combined into one perfect action.

Such an action would be irresistible, and would invariably gain what it willed and desired to gain. It would be the action of complete mastery wherever it willed and desired to act.

We may desire power for ages, but so long as consciousness is not placed in touch with the inner source of power, we shall desire in vain. We can receive nothing from any source, until we place mind in contact with that source, and to produce that contact, the will must direct consciousness to become conscious of that source.

It is the truth that we may gain possession of anything in the external world that we may require, if we unfold the necessary capacity and ability from the internal world; but again, it is only the true use of the will, combined with a strong desire, that can place mind in touch with the limitless power of this internal ability.

To use will-power without desire is to stupify the mind; and here we have one reason why so many minds lack brilliancy.

To use desire without will is to place the mind in a negative state, where it may be controlled by anything that may appear in its environment.

To combine the force of will and the force of desire into one action no particular method is required, except to will to desire whatever you desire to desire, and to desire to accomplish whatever you will to accomplish.

Whenever you desire to unfold and express a certain condition, state, or quality in your being, cause the will to act upon the inner consciousness of that condition, state, or quality; and when you employ the will in any way whatever, desire something definite at the time, with the very strongest desire that you can possibly arouse.

When causing the will to act upon consciousness, think of the soul of things; consciousness is always reached when attention is concentrated upon the *soul* of things, because consciousness is that finer something that permeates the soul of things. It has neither shape nor form, yet it is *in* all shapes and forms.

WHAT is termed the soul of things is the inner world of limitless possibility; therefore, by causing will and desire to act upon the inner world of consciousness, the greater things that are latent within are unfolded, developed, and expressed.

We thereby train ourselves to promote the purpose of self-mastery to a greater and a greater degree, because we attain the mastery of self only by eternally bringing forth a superior self.

It is therefore evident that every attempt toward self-mastery must have the superior self always in view; and this is accomplished perfectly when the forces of will and desire act invariably upon the inner consciousness of everything in the human system.

When the self is perfect, as far as its present requirements are concerned, it needs no control; it will be right and do right because it is right. When a certain organ in the body performs its function perfectly, it needs no attention; it needs no control in order that it may do its work; it is already subconsciously controlled by its own state of harmony with the real will.

It is the same with everything in the system; no mastery is needed over anything while it is doing its work perfectly, because it is already in the hands of mastery; but if it is not doing its work perfectly, it needs transformation, not control.

You cannot control the wrong to be right; but you can transmute and transform the wrong into the right; you can gradually transform the inferior into the superior, and it has been demonstrated that when the entire system is being steadily transformed, every part of the system will not only perform its function properly, but will perpetually improve the work of that function.

The best way to keep the entire system in order, is to constantly improve the entire system; and this is the purpose of self-mastery.

To master self is not to try to control self, but to perpetually transform self; it means continuous advancement for every part of the being of man; it is the elimination of evil through a constant growth in the realization of the good; it is overcoming the imperfect by creating the perfect; it is the passing out of the lesser through the passing into the greater; it is the prevention of retrogression through the perpetual promotion of progression.

The law of continuous advancement, however, is based upon the principle that every change or improvement that is to be produced in life must come from the unfoldment of the greater possibilities that are latent in life. We advance in the without by unfolding and expressing the greater from the within; and we master the self by causing the self to eternally become what is latent in the superior life within the self.

The mastery of self may therefore be promoted only through the practical application of this principle; that is, every action of mind, desire, or will must act upon the greater within. Before a desired effect can be secured in the without, the corresponding cause must be created in the within; and to create this cause, action must be concentrated upon the consciousness of the within.

To control the forces of the system, the mind, through the united action of will and desire, must act upon the finer forces that permeate the finer elements throughout the system. Produce any desired impression upon the finer forces while mentally entering into the inner world of the finer forces, and the outer forces of the personality will act exactly as the impression desired.

Discord, confusion, irritability, restlessness, or pain among the forces of the system can be removed instantaneously by impressing upon the finer forces the desire for peace, serenity, harmony, and poise.

When the mind enters the finer forces while in the attitude of harmony, perfect harmony will immediately be established throughout the personality.

This is how adverse conditions in the system may be mastered; not by trying to control those conditions, but by entering into the finer consciousness and creating there more perfect conditions.

Whenever you wish to change physical action, direct attention upon the subjective side, that is, the finer consciousness that permeates that part of the physical form through which the new action is to appear, and desire that subjective side to act the way you wish the physical part to act; and as soon as the desired subjective action is produced the corresponding physical action will immediately follow.

In this way, the body can be controlled completely, and caused to act in any way that we may desire.

To remove physical pain or disease, concentrate attention upon the finer consciousness of that part of the body where the pain is felt. Do not think of the body itself, nor the ailment, but cause the mind to enter into the finer elements and the finer forces that permeate that part of the body where the adverse condition appears.

While in the attitude of concentration, use the will in drawing all the forces of that part of the body into the finer vibrations, and desire, with deep feeling, to realize the health and the wholeness of this finer life into which the mind has entered.

The reaction will soon follow, and the adverse condition will be caused to disappear by the coming forth of a strong, wholesome life from within.

Every unpleasant sensation in the physical system can be removed by refining the vibrations in those parts where the sensations are felt; and the vibrations of any part of the system will be refined when attention is concentrated upon the finer forces that permeate those parts.

To master your mental attitudes, turn attention upon the silent within. There is a state in the inner field of consciousness where absolute peace prevails at all times; to become conscious of this state is to become calm and serene, and by directing attention upon this state the realization of peace will immediately follow.

When in the midst of confusion, do not permit your mental forces to run toward the surface; to do this is to become confused, and thus be controlled by the confusion that exists about you.

Draw all your mental forces toward the within, while in such surroundings, and think toward the peaceful within; you will thereby realize peace, and be in peace. You will master yourself in the midst of the storm; you will remain untouched, unmoved, and undisturbed.

To control your thoughts, do not try to control those thoughts that you are thinking now, but use the will in producing a new line of thinking. If the will is well trained this can be done at once, and as the mind becomes active in new fields of consciousness, those thoughts that we did not wish to entertain will disappear of themselves.

To think of something different becomes simplicity itself when the mind enters into the finer consciousness of new thought. It is only when the mind continues to act upon the surface that it is difficult to change the mind.

To control your feelings, enter into the finer feeling of the opposite states of feeling. Having decided upon the way you want to feel, turn attention upon the finer consciousness of the state of feeling desired. The desired state will soon be felt in every part of the system.

To control desires, transmute the forces that are trying to express themselves through those desires; then turn the transmuted energy into those parts of mind or body where expression may legitimately take place now.

To transmute the energies that are alive in any desire, concentrate attention upon that part of mind or body where the desire is centralized, and with the action of desire and will draw all the finer forces of that part toward the subjective side.

When the finer forces are felt, attention may be turned upon any part of the body or into any faculty where added power can be used with profit. Wherever attention is directed, there the finer forces will accumulate, that is, when the consciousness of those forces has been attained.

Through this same process all the finer elements and forces in the personality or the mentality may be called into action, and superior results secured in everything one may undertake to do.

All the forces of the system are creative, and the creative process may be promoted anywhere in the system by any of the forces of the system; therefore, if the creative function cannot now take place in the personality, the same force may be employed now in any part of the mentality. This being true, it is wasted effort to try to subdue one's physical passions; when physical desires are felt, and it is not possible to express them physically at the time, the force of those desires should be transmuted, and concentrated upon some mental creative process.

To apply the principle of self-mastery to the moral nature, the true method is, not to say no to the wrong, but to say yes to the right.

To control yourself in the midst of temptation, divert your attention from those things that you do not want, and cause the will to act upon the inner consciousness of those qualities and virtues that you do want.

To resist temptation is to fix attention upon the very thing that you do not wish to do; the mind will think more and more of the wrong until it becomes oblivious to the right, and will consequently do what it was tempted to do.

To concentrate the whole of attention upon the wrong is to cause all the tendencies of mind to move toward the wrong; the mind will think the wrong and be placed in bondage to the wrong; it will follow the wrong and act accordingly.

The secret of overcoming temptation is to refuse to give the wrong step a single moment of attention; do not resist it; do not even think about it, but give the whole of attention to the right step.

This will not be difficult if the mind, when concentrating upon the right step, will look within and view the superior side of the right step; because when its superiority is discerned, the interest in the right step will become so great that nothing could persuade the mind to think of anything else.

The various mental states of depression, gloom, despondency, worry, etc., are produced by the mind coming down to inferior planes of action. To control those states, that is, to remove them completely, turn all the forces of mind upon the highest state of consciousness that the imagination can picture. Then direct the will to act upon the finer consciousness of this state, and into the finer state the entire mind will go.

No attempt should be made to control the temper; this will simply place the mind more completely in bondage to the forces of temper. It will also give life and power to the present personal will.

When a person becomes angry he throws his thoughts out toward the object of his ill-will, thereby bringing consciousness to the surface, away from the real will and into the personal will. His energies are wasted, poise is lost, and practically all the actions of mind are misdirected; to try to control anything while in such a state would, therefore, be useless.

To avoid becoming angry under every circumstance, do not permit the actions of the mind to move outwardly against anything when antagonized, but direct all the forces of mind inwardly at once. This will prevent the antagonistic attitude, and so long as there is no antagonistic attitude there will be no feeling of anger.

To prevent thoughts from going out when provocations appear, impress daily upon mind the most perfect conception of a wholesome nature that can be formed, and train all the tendencies of mind to focus upon this ideal.

This will not only cause the creative energies of mind to build a sweet and wholesome nature, but the tendency of all feelings and emotions to move toward this inner ideal will become so strong that nothing can cause the force of feeling to go out against anything.

When this state has been established, all temper has been mastered, because all those forces that were previously wasted in temper have been turned in their courses, and are now engaged in the development of kindness, sympathy, tenderness, and love.

To master anything is to turn it to better use; and all things are turned to better use that are trained to work in harmony with the law of continuous advancement.

To control circumstances, the principle is to establish in yourself what you wish your circumstances to be. The mind that has created the ideal mental world will gravitate, through absolute law, into an ideal physical world.

However, before man can create an ideal internal world he must attain that state of self-possession where he will not be influenced by the adverse in the external world. He must control himself in the midst of circumstances before circumstances will respond to his control.

In the midst of adverse circumstances, it is your thought and feeling that must be controlled, and to control thought under such circumstances all thought must be given to the ideal circumstance that you have in view.

To meet and overcome adversity it must be approached, not as an enemy, but as a force that can be turned to a better use. Adversity is but misdirected energy; but if you remain calm and strong, it will follow you, and do what you may desire to have done.

When you become stronger in your own conscious being than the forces that are about you, those forces will obey your will. For this reason, he who has mastered himself has mastered the universe.

The forces about you will not obey your will when you try to control them; they will follow you and obey you only when you have become stronger than they.

Circumstances do not have to be controlled; when the forces that are active in our circumstances are used intelligently, which means constructively, those circumstances will be in our hands without our trying to place them there.

It is necessary, however, to be calm and self-possessed in order to use those forces intelligently; therefore, the principal essential in the midst of circumstances is to control the mode of thinking. He who can do this can turn everything to good account that may enter his path.

There is only one mode of thinking that is conducive to self-mastery, and that is scientific thinking; therefore, to control thinking is to think scientifically.

To think scientifically is to cause all the forces of mind to work together for the object that one has in view; and when all the forces of mind work for this object, the forces of circumstance will work for the same object; that is, if the force of mind is stronger than the force of circumstance.

Every person that thinks scientifically, and that unites all his forces upon the one object in view, will be stronger than his circumstances, and will thereby control those circumstances absolutely.

In the last analysis, therefore, the control of everything depends upon the control of self, and must necessarily follow the control of self; but he who would control himself must not try to control himself; he must not try to control anything; in brief, he must eliminate completely every desire that desires to exercise the power to rule. Instead, he must place himself absolutely in the consciousness of that power within that does rule—the power that is supreme.

He who gives himself to supreme power, will give expression to his own supreme power; and the expression of supreme power through every part of the self constitutes the mastery of self.

The IDEAL MADE REAL

CONTENTS

FOREWORD

The purpose of this work is to present practical methods through which anyone, the beginner in particular, may realize his ideals, cause his cherished dreams to come true, and cause the visions of the soul to become tangible realities in every-day life.

The best minds now believe that the ideal can be made real; that every lofty idea can be applied in practical living, and that all that is beautiful on the heights of existence can be made permanent expressions in personal existence. And so popular is this belief becoming that it is rapidly permeating the entire thought of the world. Accordingly, the demand for instructive knowledge on this subject, that is simple as well as scientific, is becoming almost universal.

This book has been written to supply that demand. However, it does not claim to be complete; nor could any work on "The Ideal Made Real" possibly be complete, because the ideal world is limitless and the process of making real the ideal is endless. To know how to begin is the principal secret, and he who has learned this secret may go on further and further, forever and forever, until he reaches the most sublime heights that endless existence has in store.

No attempt has been made to formulate the ideas, methods and principles presented, into a definite system. In fact, the tendency to form a new system of thinking or a new philosophy of life, has been purposely avoided. Closely defined systems invariably become obstacles to advancement, and we are not concerned with new philosophies of life. Our purpose is the living of a greater and a greater life, and in such a life all philosophies must constantly change.

In preparing the following pages, the object has been to take the beginner out of the limitations of the old into the boundlessness of the new; to emphasize the fact that the possibilities that are latent in the human mind are nothing less than marvelous, and that the way to turn those possibilities to practical use is sufficiently simple for anyone to understand. But no method has been presented that will not tend to suggest new and better methods as required for further advancement. The best ideas are those that inspire new ideas, better ideas, greater ideas. The most perfect science of life is that science that gives each individual the power to create and recreate his own science as he ascends in the scale of life.

Great souls are developed only where minds are left free to employ the best known methods according to their own understanding and insight. And it is only as the soul grows greater and greater that the ideal can be made real. It is individuality and originality that give each person the power to make his own life as he may wish it to be; but those two important factors do not flourish in definite systems. There is no progress where the soul is placed in the hands of methods; true and continuous progress can be promoted only where all ideas, all methods and all principles are placed in the hands of the soul.

We have selected the best ideas and the best methods known for making the ideal real, and through this work, will place them in your hands. We do not ask you to follow these methods; we simply ask you to use them. You will then find them all to be practical; you will find that every one will work and produce the results you desire. You will then, not only make real the ideal in your present sphere of life, but you will also develop within yourself that Greater Life, the power of which has no limit, the joy of which has no end.

CHAPTER I

THE IDEAL MADE REAL

To have ideals is not only simple but natural. It is just as natural for the mind to enter the ideal as it is to live. In fact, the ideal is an inseparable part of life; but to make the ideal real in every part of life is a problem, the solution of which appears to be anything but simple. To dream of the fair, the high, the beautiful, the perfect, the sublime, that everyone can do; but everyone has not learned how to make his dreams come true, nor realize in the practical world what he has discerned in the transcendental world. The greatest philosophers and thinkers in history, with but few exceptions, have failed to apply their lofty ideas in practical living, not because they did not wish to but because they had not discovered the scientific relationship existing between the ideal world and the real world. The greatest thinker of the past century confessed that he did not know how to use in every day life the remarkable laws and principles that he had discovered in the ideal. He knew, however, that those laws and principles could be applied; that the ideal could be made real, and he stated that he positively knew that others would discover the law of realization, and that methods would be found in the near future through which any ideal could be made real in practical life; and his prophecy has come true.

To understand the scientific relationship that exists between the real and the ideal, the mind must have both the power of interior insight and the power of scientific analysis, as well as the power of practical application; but we do not find, as a rule, the prophet and the scientist in the same mind. The man who has visions and the man who can do things do not usually dwell in the same personality; nevertheless, this is necessary. And every person can develop both the prophet and the scientist in himself. He can develop the power to see the ideal and also the power to make the ideal real. The large mind, the broad mind, the deep mind, the lofty mind, the properly developed mind can see both the outer and the inner side of things. Such a mind can see the ideal on high, and at the same time understand how to make real, tangible and practical what he has seen. The seeming gulf between the ideal and the real, between the soul's vision and the power of practical action is being bridged in thousands of minds to-day, and it is these minds who are gaining the power to make themselves and their own world as beautiful as the visions of the prophet; but the ideal life and the world beautiful are not for the few only. Everybody should learn how to find that path that leads from the imperfections of present conditions to the world of ideal conditions—the world of which we have all so frequently dreamed.

The problem is what beginners are to do with the beautiful thoughts and the tempting promises that are being scattered so widely at the present time. The average mind feels that the idealism of modern metaphysics has a substantial basis. He feels intuitively that it is true, and he discerns through the perceptions of his own soul that all these things that are claimed for applied metaphysics are possible. He inwardly knows that whatever the idealist declares can be done will be done, but the problem is how. The demand for simple methods is one of the greatest demands at the present time—methods that everyone can learn and that will enable any aspiring soul to begin at once to realize his ideals. Such methods, however, are easily formulated, and will be found in abundance on the following pages. These methods are based upon eternal laws; they are as simple as the multiplication table and will produce results with the same unerring precision. Any person with a reasonable amount of intelligence can apply them, and those who have an abundance of perseverance can, through these methods, make real practically all the ideals that they may have at the present time. Those who are more highly developed will find in these methods the secret through which their attainments and achievements will constantly verge on the borderland of the marvelous. In fact, when the simple law that unites the ideal and the real is understood and applied, it matters not how lofty our minds and our visions may be—we can make them all come true.

To proceed, the principal obstacle must first be removed, and this obstacle is the tendency to lose faith whenever we fail to make real the ideal the very moment we expect to do so. This tendency is present to some degree in nearly every mind that is working for greater things, and it postpones the day of realization whenever it is permitted to exercise its power of retrogression. Many a person has fallen into chronic despondency after having had a glimpse of the ideal, because it was so very beautiful, so very desirable, in fact, the only one thing that could satisfy, and yet seemingly so far away and so impossible to reach. But here is a place where we must exercise extraordinary faith. We must never recognize the gulf that seems to exist between our present state and the state we desire to reach. On the other hand, we must continue in the conviction that the gulf is only seeming and that we positively shall reach the ideal that appears in the splendors of what seems to be a distant future, although what actually is very near at hand.

Those who have more faith and more determination do not, as a rule, fall down when they meet this seeming gulf; they inwardly know that every ideal will some time be realized. It could not be otherwise, because what we see in the distance is invariably something that lies in the pathway of our own eternal progress, and if we continue to move forward we must inevitably reach it. But even to these the ideal does at times appear to be very far away, and the time of waiting seems very long. They are frequently on the verge of giving up and fears arise at intervals that many unpleasant experiences may, after all, be met before the great day of realization is gained; however, we cannot afford to entertain such fears for a moment nor to think that anything unpleasant can transpire during the period of transition; that is, the passing from the imperfections of present conditions to the joys and delights of an ideal life. We must remember that fear and despondency invariably retard our progress, no matter what our object in view may be, and that discouragement is very liable to cause a break in the engine that is to take our train to the fair city we so long have desired to reach.

The time of waiting may seem long during such moments as come when the mind is down, but so long as the mind is on the heights the waiting time disappears, and the pleasure of pursuit comes to take its place. In this connection we should remember that the more frequently we permit the mind to fall down into fears and doubts the longer we shall have to wait for the realization of the ideal; and the more we live in the upper story of life the sooner we shall reach the goal in view. There are many who give up temporarily all efforts toward reaching their ideals, thinking it is impossible and that nothing is gained by trying, but such minds should realize that they are simply making their future progress more difficult by retarding their present progress. Such minds should realize the great fact that every ideal can be made real, because nothing is impossible.

To reach any desired goal the doing of certain things is necessary, but if those things are not done now they will have to be done later; besides, when we give up in the present we always make the obstacles in our way much greater than they were before. Those things that are necessary to promote our progress become more difficult to do the longer we remain in what may be termed the "giving up" attitude, and the reason why is found in the fact that the mind that gives up becomes smaller and smaller; it loses ability, capacity and power and becomes less and less competent to cope with the problems at hand. Whenever we give up we invariably fall down into a smaller mental state. When we cease to move forward we begin to move backward. We retard progression only when we cease to promote progression. On the other hand, so long as we continue to pursue the ideal we ascend into larger and larger mental states, and thus increase our power to make real the ideals that are before us. The belief that it is impossible to make real the ideal has no foundation whatever in truth. It is simply an illusion produced by fear and has no place in the exact science of life. When you discern an ideal you discover something that lies in your own onward path. Move forward and you simply cannot fail to reach it; but when you are to reach the coveted goal depends upon how rapidly you are moving now. Knowing this, and knowing that fear, doubt, discouragement and indifference invariably retard this forward movement, we shall find it most profitable to remove those mental states absolutely.

The true attitude is the attitude of positive conviction; that is, to live in the strong conviction that whatever we see before us in the ideal will positively be realized, sooner or later, if we only move forward, and we can make it sooner if we will move forward steadily, surely and rapidly during every moment of the great eternal now. To move forward steadily during the great eternal now is to realize now as much of the ideal as we care to appropriate now; no waiting therefore is necessary. To begin to move forward is to begin to make real the ideal, and we will realize in the now as much of the ideal as is necessary to make the now full and complete. To move forward steadily during the great eternal now is to eternally become more than you are; and to become more than you are is to make yourself more and more like your ideal; and here is the great secret, because the principle is that you will realize your ideal when you become exactly like your ideal, and that you will realize as much of your ideal now as you develop in yourself now. The majority, however, feel that they can never become as perfect as their ideal; others, however, think that they can, and that they will sometime, but that it will require ages, and they dwell constantly upon the unpleasant belief that they may in the meantime have to pass through years and years of ordinary and undesirable experience; but they are mistaken, and besides, are retarding their own progress every moment by entertaining such thoughts.

If all the time and all the energy that is wasted in longing and longing, yearning and yearning were employed in scientific, practical self-development, the average person would in a short time become as perfect as his ideal. He would thus realize his ideal, because we attract from the without what corresponds exactly to what is active in our own within. When we attain the ideal and the beautiful in our own natures, we shall meet the ideal and the beautiful wherever we may go in the world, and we will find the same things in the real that we dreamed of in the ideal. When we see an ideal we usually begin to long for it and hope that something remarkable may happen so as to bring it into our possession, and we thus continue to long and yearn and wait with periods of despondency intervening. We simply use up time and energy to no avail. When we see an ideal the proper course to pursue is to begin at once to develop that ideal in our own nature. We should never stop to wait and see whether it is coming true or not, and we should never stop to figure how much time it may require to reach our goal. The secret is, begin now to be like your ideals, and at the proper time that ideal will be made real.

The very moment you begin to rebuild yourself in the exact likeness of your ideal you will begin to realize your ideal, because we invariably gain possession of that of which we become conscious; and to begin to develop the ideal in ourselves is to begin to become conscious of the ideal. To give thought to time is to stop and measure time in consciousness, and every stop in consciousness means retarded progress. Real progress is eternal; it is a forward movement that is continuous now, and in the realization of such a progress no thought is ever given to time. To live in the life of eternal progress is to gain ground every moment. It means the perpetual increase of everything that has value, greatness and worth, and the mind that lives in such a life cannot possibly be discouraged or dissatisfied. Such a mind will not only live in the perpetual increase of everything that heart can wish for, but will also realize perpetually the greatest joy of all joys, the joy of going on. The discouraged mind is the mind that lives in the emptiness of life, but there can be no emptiness in that life that lives in the perpetual increase of all that is good and beautiful and ideal.

The only time that seems long is the time that is not well employed in continuous attainment, and the only waiting time, that seems the hardest time of all, is the time that is not fully consecrated to the highest purpose you have in view. When we understand that we all may have different ideals we will find that we have an undeveloped correspondent in ourselves to every ideal that we may discern, and if we proceed to develop these corresponding parts there will be some ideals realized every day. To-day we may succeed in making real an ideal that we first discovered a year ago. To-morrow we may reach a goal toward which we have been moving for years, and in a few days we may realize ideals that we have had in view during periods of time varying from a few weeks to several years; and if we are applying the principles that underlie the process of making real the ideal, we may at any time realize ideals of which we have dreamed for a life time. Consequently, when we approach this subject properly we shall daily come into the possession of something that is our own. All the beautiful things of which we have dreamed will be coming into our world and there will be new arrivals every day.

This is the life of the real idealist, and we cannot picture a life that is more complete and more satisfying; but it is not only complete in the present. It is constantly growing larger and more desirable, thus giving us daily a higher degree of satisfaction and joy. When we discern an ideal that ideal has come within the circle of our own capacity for development, and the power to develop that ideal in ourselves is therefore at hand. The mind never discerns those ideals that are beyond the possibility of present development. Thus we realize that when an ideal is discerned it is proof positive that we have the power to make it real now.

Those who have not found their ideals in any shape or form whatever have simply neglected to make their own ideal nature strong, positive and pronounced. To live in negative idealism is to continue to dream on without seeing a single dream come true; but when the ideals we discern in our own natures become strong, positive working-forces our dreams will soon come true; our ideals will be realized one after the other until life becomes what it is intended to be, a perpetual ascension into all that is rich, beautiful and sublime.

Whether we speak of environments, attainments, achievements, possessions, circumstances, opportunities, friends, companions or the scores of things that belong in our world, the law is the same. We receive an ideal only when we become just like that ideal. If we seek better friends, we shall surely find them and retain them, if we develop higher and higher degrees of friendship. If we wish to associate with refined people, we must become more refined in action, thought and speech. If we wish to reach our ideals in the world of achievement, we must develop greater ability, capacity and power. If we desire better environments, we must not only learn to appreciate the beautiful, but must also develop the power to produce those things that have true quality, high worth and real superiority. The great secret is to become more useful in the world; that is, useful in the largest and highest sense of that term. He who gives his best to the world will receive the best in return.

The world needs able men and women; people who can do things that are thoroughly worth while; people who can think great thoughts and transform such thoughts into great deeds; and to secure such men and women the world will give anything that it may hold in its possession. To make real the ideal, proceed to develop greatness, superiority and high worth in yourself. Train the mind to dwell constantly upon the borderland of the highest ideals that you can possibly picture; but do not simply yearn for what you can see, and do not covet what has not yet become your own. Proceed to remake yourself into the likeness of that ideal and it will become your own. To proceed with this great development, the whole of life must be changed to conform with the exact science of life; that is, that science that is based upon the physical and the metaphysical united as the one expression of all that is great and sublime in the soul. The new way of thinking about things, viewing things and doing things must be adopted in full, and this new way is based upon the principle that the ideal actually is real, and therefore should be approached not as a future possibility, but as a present actuality. Think of the ideal as if it were real and you will find it to be real. Meet all things as if they contained the ideal, and you will find that all things will present their ideals to you, not simply as mere pictures, but as realities. View the whole of life from the heights of existence; then you will see things as they are and deal with things accordingly; you will see that side of the whole of existence that may be termed the better side, and in consequence, you will grow into the likeness of that better side. When you grow into the likeness of the better side of all things, you will attract the better side of all things, and the ideal in everything in the world will be made real in your world.

CHAPTER II

HOW TO BEGIN:
THE PRIME ESSENTIALS

To formulate rules in detail that will apply to each individual case is neither possible nor necessary. All have not the same present needs nor the same previous training; but there are certain general principles that apply to all, and these, if followed according to the individual view-point, will produce the results desired. If the proper beginning is made, the subsequent results will not only be greater and be realized in less time, but much useless experience and delay will be avoided. These principles, or prime essentials, are as follows:

1. **Learn to be still.** When you undertake to live an ideal life and seek to promote your advancement in every direction, you will find that much cannot be gained until your entire being is placed in a proper condition for growth; the reason being that the ideal is ever advancing toward higher ideals, and you must improve yourself before you can better your life. It has been found that all laws of growth require order, harmony and stillness for proper action; therefore, to live peacefully, think peacefully, act peacefully and speak peacefully are important essentials. This will not only put the entire being into proper condition for growth, but will also conserve energy, and when you begin to live the larger life you will want to use properly all your forces; neither misusing or wasting anything. To acquire stillness never "try hard," but simply exercise general self-control in everything you do. Never be anxious about results, and they will come with less effort, and in less time. Whenever you have a moment to spare relax the whole person, mind and body; just let everything fall into the easiest position possible. Make no effort to relax, simply let go. So long as you try to relax you will not succeed. While in this relaxed condition be quiet; do not move a muscle; breathe deeply but gently, and think only of peace and stillness. Before you go to sleep at night relax your entire system, and fall asleep with

peace in your mind; bathe your mind and body, so to speak, in the crystal sea of the beautiful calm. These methods alone will work wonders in a few weeks. While you are at work hold yourself from anxious hurry or disturbed action; work in the attitude of poise and you will accomplish much more in the same given time and you will be a far better workman. Train yourself to come into the realization of perfect peace by gently holding a deep strong desire for peace and by ordering all your actions to harmonize with the peaceful goal in view. The result will be "the peace that passeth understanding," and for this alone your gratitude will be both boundless and endless.

2. **Rejoice and be glad.** Cheerfulness is not only a good medicine, but it is food for mind and body. The cheerful life will fill every atom with new life, and it is to the faculties of the mind what sunshine is to the flowers and trees. To be happy always is one of the greatest things that man can do, and there are few things that are more profitable in every sense of that term. No matter what comes, be glad; and live in the conviction that all things are working together for good to you. As your conviction is so is your faith; and as your faith is so it shall be unto you. When you live in the conviction that all things are working together for good you will *cause* all things to work together for good, and you will understand the reason why when you begin to apply the real science of ideal living. No matter how dark the cloud, look for the silver lining; it is there, and when you always look at the bright side of things you develop brightness in yourself. This brightness will strengthen all your faculties so that you can easily overcome what obstacles may be in your way, and thus gain the victory desired. Direct your attention constantly to the bright side of things; refuse absolutely to consider any other side. At first this may not be possible in the absolute sense, but perseverance never fails to win. However, do not try hard; gently direct your attention to the bright side and know that you can. Ere long it will be second nature for you to live on the sunny side. The value of this attainment is very great; first, because joyousness will increase life, power, energy and force; this we all know from personal experience, and we wish to have all the life and power that we can possibly secure; second, because the happiest soul never worries, which is great gain. Worry has crippled thousands of fine minds and brought millions to an early grave. We simply cannot afford to worry and must never do so under any condition whatever. If we have that habit we can remove it at once by the proper antidote, which is joyousness. After you have trained yourself to look only for the bright and the best, the bright and the best will come to you, because you will be using your powers to bring those very things to pass; therefore, rejoice and be glad

every moment. Let your heart and your soul sing at all times. When you do not feel the joyous music within, produce it with your own imagination, and ere long it will come of itself with greater and greater abundance; your soul will *want* to sing because it *feels* music, and there are few joys that equal the joy that comes when music is felt in the soul. There are so many things that are sweet and beautiful in life that when we once find the key to harmony we shall always rejoice. In the meantime, be happy for the good you have found, and through that very attitude you will develop the power to attract better things than you ever had before. This personal existence is brimful of good things and happy souls will find them all.

3.   **Love everybody and be kind.** If you wish your path to be strewn with roses, just be kind. Give your best to the world, and the best will come to you without fail; if it does not come to-day, never mind; just go on being kind and refuse to consider disappointments. Never hold in mind those things that you do not wish to retain; you thus cause those things to pass away. This "shall also pass away" is true of everything that is not pleasant; but unpleasant things will not pass away so long as we hold them in thought. That which you let go from your mind will pass away from you entirely. Train yourself to be kindness in a permanent state of mind, because you cannot afford to criticize, condemn or be angry at any time. We know that anger not only disturbs the mind, but also destroys the cells of the body, and no one can be angry without losing a great deal of life and energy. To find fault never pays; it simply brings enmity, discord and criticisms; besides, the faults we constantly see in others will develop in ourselves. The critical mind is destructive and the critical attitude is weakening to the entire system; therefore, no one can be his best who permits himself to think or talk about the flaws of life. Be good and kind to everybody; it is one of the royal paths to happiness and peace. When anyone does wrong, do not condemn; help him out; help him find the better way. "Cast your bread upon the waters;" it will surely return; sometimes more quickly than you expect it. Therefore, give abundantly of all that is best in your life, and nothing is better than kindness and love. When you begin to live an ideal life you will desire more and more to live the largest life possible, and to accomplish this you must learn to be much to everybody. Your purpose must be to be useful in the largest and truest sense of that term; and nothing can promote this purpose so thoroughly and so extensively as universal kindness. This does not imply, however, that you are to permit yourself to be imposed upon or unjustly used by the unscrupulous. It is our duty, as well as our privilege to demand the right at all times, and to demand justice for everybody and from

everybody, but this should be done in kindness, with the antagonistic attitude eliminated. The love that loves everybody is not the love that seeks to gain personal possession of some object of affection. We refer to that larger kindness that excludes no one from our whole souled good wishes. This form of love is the greatest power in the world, and the one who loves the most in this larger, truer sense will accomplish the most. The reason why is found in the fact that a great love invariably brings out all that is large, great and extraordinary in human nature. To state that the one who takes the greatest interest in the welfare of the world does the most to promote his own interests may seem to be a contradiction of terms; but it is true, and it proves conclusively that the one who gives his best to the world will invariably receive the best in return. Never permit yourself to say that you cannot love every creature that lives; say that you do love everything that lives, and mean it. What you say you are doing that you will find yourself doing. This greater love illumines the mind, gives new life to every fiber in your being, removes almost every burden and eases the whole path of existence. Love removes entirely all anger, hatred, revenge, ill-will, and similar states, a matter of great importance, for no one can live an ideal life while such states of mind remain. To have a sweet temper and loving disposition and a kind heart is worth more than tons of gold. We are all finding this to be true, and we realize fully that the person who loves everybody with that larger loving kindness has taken a long step upward into that life that is real life. This is not mere sentiment, but the expression of an exact scientific fact. A strong, continuous love will bring all good to any one who lives and acts as he inwardly feels.

4.   **Have faith in abundance.** Have faith in God; have faith in man; have faith in yourself; have faith in faith. Believe in everything, and you relate yourself to the best that is in everything. We all know the value of self-confidence, but faith is infinitely deeper, larger and higher. Self-confidence helps us to believe in ourselves, as we are at present, and thus helps us to make a better use of the talents we now possess; but faith elevates the mind into the consciousness of our larger and superior possibilities, and thus increases perpetually the power, the capacity and the efficiency of the talents we now possess. Faith brings out the best that is within us and puts that best to work now. He who follows faith may frequently go out upon the seeming void, but he always finds the solid rock. The reason is that faith has superior vision and goes instinctively to the very thing we desire to find. Faith does not expect things to come of themselves. Faith never stands and waits; it does things; but while at work *believes* that the goal will be

reached and the undertaking accomplished. The person who works in the attitude of faith can never fail; because through faith he draws upon the inexhaustible. The person who works in the attitude of doubt can never be at his best. Through the feeling of doubt he lowers his own ability; he holds back his best power and employs but a portion of his capacity; but the one who works in faith will press on to the very limit of his present capacity and then go on further still, because the more faith he has the more fully he realizes that there is no limit to his capacity, that the seeming void that lies before is positively solid rock all the way and he may safely proceed. Whatever you do *believe* that you can succeed in; do not for a moment permit yourself to doubt; know that the Infinite is your source, that you live in the universal and have the boundless upon which to draw for supply. If people or things do not come up to your ideal never mind; give them time; continue to have faith in their better selves; they will also scale the heights. Expect them all to do their best, and most of them will do so now; the others will soon follow, if you live in the faith that they will. The unbounded faith of one soul can elevate the lives of thousands. This is a statement that is just as true as it is great, and we should constantly give it the highest place in mind. The man who has faith in the whole race is an inspiration to everybody. Many a person has risen rapidly in the scale because some one had faith in him. Faith is the greatest elevating power that we know in the world. Faith can convert any failure into success and can promote the advancement of everybody, no matter what the circumstances may be. Have faith in yourself and you will advance as you never advanced before. Have faith in others and they will inevitably follow. Have faith in the Infinite and the Supreme Power will always be with you. This power will see you through, whatever your goal may be. Therefore, if you would enter the new life, the better life, the ideal life, and inspire others to do the same, have faith in abundance.

5. **Pray without ceasing.** The true prayer is the whole-souled desire for the larger, the higher and the better while the mind is stayed upon the Most High; and to pray without ceasing is to constantly live in that lofty desire. The forces of mind and body always follow our desires; therefore, if we would use our powers in building up a larger life we must have high desires and true desires. Turn your desires upward and keep them there; desire the greater things only; never desire anything less. Those powers within you will cause you to become as true, as great and as perfect as your heart has prayed that you might become. To cause our desires, thoughts and states of consciousness to rise to the very highest states of being, we should

employ the silence daily; that is, we should enter into the absolute stillness of the secret life of the soul. Through the silence we shall find the secret of secrets, the path to that inner world from which everything proceeds. To begin, be alone and comfortably seated. Or, you may enter the silence in association with someone that is in perfect harmony with yourself. Relax mind and body; close your eyes and be perfectly quiet; turn your attention upon the inner life of the soul and gently hold your mind upon the thoughts of stillness and peace. Affirm with deep, quiet feeling, "Peace is mine." "I am resting in the stillness of the spirit." "I have entered the beautiful calm." "I am one with the Infinite." "I am in the kingdom of the great within." "I am in the secret places of the Most High," and similar states. While you make these statements *feel* that you are peaceful and still and that you are now in that inner world where all is quiet and serene. When you feel this deep, sublime stillness you can use other affirmations according to your present needs. You may affirm that you are well and strong and happy and harmonious, and that you have full possession of all those qualities that you know have existence in real life. To feel the perfect peace of the soul, however, is the first essential. After that is attained your consciousness will deepen and you will enter the great within to a greater and greater degree. While the mind is in this interior state of being every thought you think will be a power, and every desire you express will modify or change every-thing in your life according to the nature of that desire and in proportion to its depth and unity with the Supreme. For this reason you should train yourself to think only right thoughts and create only the truest desires while you are in the silent state. That which you think or do while in the silence will have a greater effect upon your life than that which you may attempt while on the surface of outer consciousness. Therefore, everything that is important should be taken into the silence and through the silence to the Infinite. This corresponds perfectly with the statement "Take it to the Lord in prayer." The real purpose of the silence is to enable the mind to enter the inner life and not only re-create all thought according to the higher truth, but to enter into a more perfect touch with the divine source of things. The silence should be entered every day for ten, twenty or thirty minutes. This is a daily practice of extreme value. Though you may not have any real results at first, simply continue; you will reach your goal. When you begin to become conscious of your interior life and begin to live more or less in touch with the world beautiful that is within you, you will find that you can live in this high, peaceful state the greater part of the time and thus be in the silence almost constantly. This is not only a most desirable attainment, but it is *the one great* attainment toward which every soul should work. When a person can live in these higher realms always and constantly, and desire the realization of the highest and the best that he knows, the prayer without ceasing, the true spiritual prayer is being fulfilled. Such a prayer will be answered eternally. Every day will bring us something that we truly wished for, and every moment will be supplied with all that is necessary to make the present full and complete.

6.   **Think the truth.** When we learn to think the truth we have actually come to the "parting of the ways." Here we find where the old leaves off and the new begins. In this state the wrong disappears and the right is discerned and realized in an ever increasing manner. The foundation of all truth is expressed in the basic statement—MAN IS A SPIRITUAL BEING CREATED IN THE IMAGE AND LIKENESS OF GOD. Being created in the image of God man is now divine and in possession of all the divine attributes. Each individual is now in possession of infinite wisdom, infinite power, infinite love, eternal life, perfect peace, everlasting joy, universal truth, universal freedom, universal good, divine wholeness, spotless virtue, boundless supply. True, these attributes exist principally in the potential state, that is, they are possibilities waiting in the within for unfoldment, development and expression; nevertheless, they do exist in every soul and to a degree that is limitless. Therefore, every soul does actually possess those attributes, and to speak the truth we must recognize their existence and even now claim their possession. To think the truth you must think that you are divine in your true being, and that you possess these attributes, because this is the truth. You *are* divine in your true being, because you are created in the image of God, and you *do* possess the divine attributes just mentioned because that which is divine must necessarily possess the attributes of the divine. To think contrary to this would be wrong thought, and from wrong thought comes all the wrong in the world. The average person does think contrary to this thought; therefore, he is almost constantly in bondage to sin, sickness or trouble of some kind. Divine wholeness, that is, perfect health of body and mind is yours now, always was and always will be; therefore it would be wrong for you to say, "I am sick." Your real being is never sick, never will be, because it is divine and you are the real being; you are not the body; you possess a body, and that body may be indisposed, if you create wrong thought, but that body is not you. You are a spiritual being created in the image of God, therefore you are always well. When sickness appears on the surface, that is, in the body, know that it is on the surface only; that sickness is not in you; you are real being, and in real being perfect

health reigns absolutely and eternally. The sickness that sometimes appears in the body is the result of a recognition of untruth, either expressed in wrong thinking or wrong living. Right thought, that is, that thought that invariably follows the recognition of absolute truth, would not produce sickness; and no person could become sick that is always filled and protected with the power of right thought. When the light reigns supremely, darkness cannot enter. Wrong thought comes from a false conception of yourself, and false conceptions will continue to form in mind so long as you are ignorant of the truth. When you know the truth, that you are the image of God, perfect in your own true being, you will think this truth and all your thought will be right; consequently, only right conditions can exist in your life, and all will henceforth be well with you. When you see yourself as you are in your true being, that you are even now strong and well, in full possession of peace, love, power, wisdom, freedom and all the good that is in God you will think of yourself accordingly, and such thought is right thought. The result will be right conditions in mind and body. From center to circumference your entire being will be well and perfect, as it always was and ever will be in the truth. To think the absolute truth at first seems a contradiction of known facts, because we are so used to judging from appearances, but when we find that appearances are simply the result of thought, that right thought produces good appearances, and wrong thought produces adverse appearances, and learn that true being is the image of God, we shall no longer see contradiction in thinking absolute truth. When we think the truth about ourselves we shall always think the truth about others; we shall, therefore, not think of them as they appear on the surface but as they are in the perfection of real spiritual being. We shall overlook, forgive and forget the wrong appearance, knowing that it is but a temporary effect of wrong thought, and we shall proceed to inspire everyone to change that appearance by thinking right thought, the thought of truth.

7.   **Live in the spirit.** To express this statement in its simplest terms, we would say that to live in the spirit is to live in the upper story of mind and thought, or to live on the good side, the bright side and the true side of everything. To the beginner this is sufficient, because this simple change in living must come before the higher spiritual consciousness can be realized; but the change though simple at first will completely revolutionize life. Ere long, however, the consciousness of the true side and the better side will become so clear that to live in the spirit will mean infinitely more than to simply dwell in the upper story of mind, and when this larger experience comes we shall know from our own illumined understanding what it means

to live in the spirit. When we begin to think the truth all kinds of illusions and false beliefs will gradually vanish, and we shall not only understand that we are spiritual beings, but we shall feel that we are all that divine life can be. We shall positively know that we are eternal souls living in a spiritual world now, expressing ourselves in a physical world, and we shall realize that we are actually created in the image and likeness of the Infinite, united with the Infinite and living in the life of Infinite being. Through the fuller realization of truth we will learn that the spiritual is not some vague, far away something that saints alone can know, but that spirit is the essence of all things, the very life of all things visible and invisible, and that spirit is in itself absolutely good and perfect. We will realize that there is but one substance from which all things proceed and that substance is the expression of spirit; we will see that there is but one life, the spiritual life, and that there is but one law, the eternal coming forth in a greater and greater measure of life. We will find that spirit is the basis of all things, the *soul* of all things, and that therefore all things are in reality very good and very beautiful. We will find through the spirit that evil is but a temporary condition produced by man's misunderstanding of the goodness and the completeness of real being and that to so live that we realize the absolute goodness and the perfect harmony of the whole universe is to live in the spirit. When we realize this we are on the true side of all things and we feel that we are. When we are in harmony with all things we are in harmony with the Infinite and can feel His presence always; and we also find that to "dwell in the secret places of the Most High" is to realize that we are in that great sea of life, the great spiritual sea, the universal state of being, the world of divine existence. While we are in this upper state, that is, in the spirit, we are away from the false, and actually in the true. We are in the spirit, and from the light of the spirit we can see clearly the truth concerning everything. From this place we may ascend to other and greater heights and enter into the ever increasing realms of life where existence becomes fairer and higher, too beautiful for tongue to ever describe. What is held in store for the soul that lives in the spirit, eternity alone can reveal, but that the life that is lived in the spirit is the only true life thousands have learned, both in this age and in ages gone by. To the beginner, however, the first essential is to get away from material life, that is, the common, the gross, the superficial, the ordinary, the perverted and the wrong; then to go up higher, to enter the world of light and live in the more beautiful realms of sublime existence. To live in the spirit, live in the highest and most perfect state now, and do not for a moment come down. At first this state will simply be a life that is finer, larger and more harmonious, where things move more smoothly and where the value of life seems to constantly increase; but ere long living in the spirit will mean far more than merely a pleasing state of existence, and the further we advance the more this wonderful life will be, until we begin to under-stand the great soul who declared: "Eye hath not seen nor ear heard, neither hath it entered into the heart of man what God has prepared for them that love Him." In this connection we must bear in mind that it is not necessary to reach the supreme heights in spiritual life before we can live in the spirit. We can live in the spirit no matter where me may be in the scale of life, because the spiritual life has just as many degrees as there are human souls. Live in the realization that this universe has *soul*, that this soul is divine, and that you live and move and have your being in that great soul. Realize this as fully as your present state of development will permit, and you have begun to live in the spirit. The realization of the divinity of the soul-side of all things will reveal to your mind the great truth that all things are perfect in their real state of being, and that the real of everything lives in a universe of spirit, a universe that is everywhere within us all and about us all. However, before we begin we must be convinced of the great truth that the spiritual life is not mere sentiment nor a mere feeling of mind and soul. The spiritual life is the real life, the foundation of all life, the essence of all life, the soul of all life, and every true statement concerning the spiritual life is an exact scientific fact readily demonstrated by anyone who will apply the principle. And happy is the soul that does apply this principle, for such a soul will find life in the spirit, not only to be real, but to be infinitely more perfect, more wonderful and more beautiful than anyone has ever dreamed.

CHAPTER III

THE FIRST STEPS IN IDEAL LIVING

Give your best to the world no matter how insignificant that best may be, and the world will invariably give its best to you. There was nothing great or remarkable about the widow's mite, but it did produce remarkable results, and the reason was she gave her very best. When we give our best we not only receive the best in return from the outer world, but we also receive the best from the inner world. When you give your best you bring forth your best, and it is the bringing forth of your best that causes you to become better and better. When you become better you will meet better people and enter into better environments, and everything in your life will change for the better, because like does attract like. To give much is to become much, provided we give our best and give with the heart. The giving that comes simply from the hand does not count, no matter how large it may be. It brings nothing back to us nor does it bring permanent good to anybody else. When you give your best you do not give from your over-supply or from that which you cannot use. If you have something that you cannot use, it does not belong to you, and you cannot give, in the true sense of the term, what is not your own. To give does not mean simply to give money, unless that is the best you have; but rather to give your own service, your own talents, your ability, your own true worth and your own real self. The man who lives a real life at all times and under all circumstances is giving his best and the very best possible that can be given. A real life truly lived in the world is a power, and the person who lives such a life is a power for good wherever he may be. The presence of such a person is an inspiration and a light, as we all know. The man who loves the whole world with heart and soul, and loves without ceasing is doing far more for the race than he who endows universities, and will receive a far greater reward. We must remember, however, that such a love is not mere sentiment. Real love is a power and will cause the person who has it to do his very best for everybody under every possible circumstance. That person whose heart is with the race will never be satisfied with inferior work. He will never shirk nor leave the problems of life to somebody else; he will go in and push wherever something good is being done, and he will constantly endeavor to render better and better service where-ever his field of action may be. Such a person will give his best to the world, whether he gives through the channels of art or mechanics, music or literature, physical labor or intellectual labor, ideas or real living. What he does will be the best, and what he receives in return will be the best that the world is able to give. Give the best that you are through every thought, word and deed; that is the principle; and your life will be constantly enriched both from without and from within. Through the daily application of this principle you will develop superiority in mind, soul, character and life, and the world will be better off because you are here.

Expect the best from everybody and everybody will do their best for you. There may be occasional exceptions to this rule, but through close examination we shall find that these exceptions are due solely to our own negligence in applying the law to every occasion. The man who expects the best from everybody and has faith in everybody will certainly receive more love, more kindness, better friendship, better service and more agreeable associates by far than the one who has little or no faith in anyone. But our faith in people must be alive, and our expectations must have *soul*. To live constantly in the fear that people will do this or that, and that such and such mistakes may be made, is to live in a confused mental world, and where there is much confusion there will be many mistakes. Mental states are contagious; how that can be is not a matter for present discussion, but the fact that they are is extremely important, and we all know that they are; therefore, if we live in fear and confusion we will be a disturbing element among all those with whom we associate, and if our associates are not mentally strong and positive, they will be more or less confused by our presence, and they are very liable to produce the very mistakes we feared. On the other hand, when we have faith in people we help them to have faith in themselves, and the more faith a person has in himself the fewer his mistakes and the better his work. When we have faith in everybody and are constantly expecting the best from everybody we create wholesome conditions in our own minds, conditions that will tend to develop the best in ourselves; that person, however, who has no faith in others will soon lose faith in himself, and when he does there will be a turn for the worse in his life. True, he may continue to possess a mechanical self-confidence or an exaggerated state of egotism, but such a state will soon produce a reaction, and failure will follow. The self-confidence that brings out the best that is within us is always founded upon a living faith in the inherent greatness of man; therefore, no one can have real faith in himself unless he also has faith in the greater possibilities of the race, and no one can expect the best from himself and give soul to that expectation unless he also expects the best from others. This is a scientific fact that anyone can prove in his own daily experience. To expect the best from everybody will cause everybody to do their best for you.

Look for the best everywhere and you will find the best wherever you go. Why this is so is a matter upon which many delight to speculate, but the why does not concern us just now. It is the fact that this law works that concerns us, and concerns us very much. Not everybody can fully understand why the best is always found by him who never looks for anything but the best, but everybody *can* look for the best everywhere and thereby find the best; and it is the finding of the best that attracts our attention. It is real results that we are looking for, and the simpler the method the better. The man who will constantly apply this law will not remain in undesirable environments very long, nor will he occupy an inferior position very long; better things will positively come his way and he will not have to wait an age for the change. The man who looks for the best is constantly thinking about the best and constantly impressing his mind with the best thought about everything; and since man is as he thinks we can readily understand why such a man will become better and better; therefore, by looking for the best everywhere he will not only find the best in the external world, but he will create the best in his mental world; this will give him a greater mind, which in turn will produce higher attainments and greater achievements. That man, however, who is always looking for the worst will constantly think about the worst and will fill his mind with inferior thoughts; that he, himself, will become inferior by such a process is a foregone conclusion. We shall positively find, sooner or later, what we constantly look for; it is, therefore, profitable to look for the best everywhere and at all times; we become like those things that we constantly and deeply think about; it is, therefore, profitable to think only of the best whatever may come or not. The average person may not find the best the very first day this principle is applied. Most of us have strayed so far away from this mode of thinking and living that it may take some time to get back to the path that leads to the best; but one thing is certain, whoever will look for the best everywhere, and continue to do so for a reasonable length of time,

THE IDEAL MADE REAL 447

will find that path; besides, he will have more delightful experiences while he is training himself to apply this principle than he has had for any similar period before. This, however, will be only the beginning; the future has far greater things in store, if he will continue to look for the best and never look for anything else.

When things are not to your liking, like them as they are. In other words, while you are working for greater things make friends with the lesser things, and they will help you to reach your goal. The person who is dissatisfied with things as they are and discontented because things are not to his liking is standing in his own way. We cannot get away from present conditions so long as we antagonize those conditions, because we are held in bondage to that which we resist. If you want present conditions to become stepping-stones to better things, you must get on the better side of present conditions, and you do that by liking things as they are while they remain with you. We must be in harmony with the present if we wish to advance, because in order to advance we must use the present, but we cannot use that with which we are not in harmony. This is a fact that deserves the most thorough attention and will, when understood, explain fully why the average person seems powerless to rise above his surroundings. We must be on friendly terms with everything that exists in our present world if we wish to gain possession of all the building material that our present world can give, and we cannot secure too much material if we desire to build a larger life and a greater future. That which we dislike becomes detrimental to us, no matter how good it may be; nevertheless, it will always be with us because it is impossible to eliminate permanently that which we antagonize; when we run away from it in one place we shall meet it elsewhere in some other form; but that which we love will constantly serve us and help us on to greater things; when it can serve us no longer it will disappear. To like those things, however, that are not to our liking may seem difficult, but the question is why they are not to our liking; when we know that everything in our present world is a stepping-stone to something still better it will be natural for us to like everything. Those things may not come up to our ideals, but that is not their real purpose; it is not the mission of present things to serve as ideals, their mission is to help us to reach our ideals, and they positively can do this if we will take them into friendly co-operation. When you take a drive to an ideal country place you do not dislike the horse because he is not that country place; if you are humane, you will love that horse because he is willing and able to take you where you wish to go. If you should dislike and mistreat that horse or should fail to hitch him to the vehicle, you would not reach your destination. This, however, is the very thing that the average person does with the things of his present world; these things are the horses and the vehicles that can take us to the ideal places we desire to reach; but we must hitch them up; we must treat them right and use them. To cause all things that are about us now to work together with us, we must be in perfect harmony with them; we must like them as they are, and that becomes comparatively easy when we know that it is necessary for them to be what they are in order that they may serve as our stepping-stones; if they were different there would be no stepping-stones, and we would have to remain where we are. When we realize that everything that exists in our present world has the power to promote our advancement, if we properly use that power, and when we realize that it is necessary to be in harmony with all things to use the power that is within those things, we shall no longer dislike anything; we shall even make friends with adversity, because the power that is in adversity can be tamed by kindness and love; and when that power is tamed it becomes our own. These are great facts and easily demonstrated by anyone, and whoever will apply these principles will find that by liking everything that he finds he will secure the co-operation of everything, and anyone can move forward rapidly when all things are working with him; consequently, by liking what he finds he will find what he likes.

When you do not get what you want take what you can get and call it good. It is better to have something than nothing; besides, we must use what we can get before we can become so strong and so able that we can get whatever we may want. When a person fails to realize his ideals, there is a reason; usually the cause is this: He simply longs for the ideal but does not work himself up to the ideal. And to work himself up to the ideal he needs everything that he can get and use now; by taking what he can get he secures something to work with in promoting his present progress, and by looking upon this something as good he will turn it to good account. It is a well-known fact that we get the best out of everything when we meet everything in the conviction that it is *good for something*, because this attitude invariably brings the mind into conscious touch with the real value of that which is met. What we constantly look for we are sure to find, therefore, by calling everything good that we get and by constantly looking for the real worth of that which we get, the good in everything that we get will be found; the result is that everything we receive or come in contact with will be good for something to us and will have something of value to give us. Gradually, the good will so accumulate that we shall have all that we want; life will be filled with that which has quality and worth, which means that the development toward greater worth will constantly take place, and development toward greater worth means the constant ascension into the realization of our ideals. By accepting and using the good that we can now secure we add so much to the worth of our own life that we become worthy of the greater good we may desire; in consequence, we shall positively receive it. This process may not satisfy those who expect to reach the top at once or expect to receive the better without making themselves better, but it will satisfy those who would rather move forward gradually and surely than stand empty handed waiting and waiting for ages hoping that some miraculous secret may be found through which everything can be accomplished at once. The idea, however, is not that we should meekly submit to things as they are and be satisfied with what little fate may seem willing to give us; that is the other extreme and is just as detrimental to human welfare. Take everything that legitimately comes your way; do not refuse it because it seems too small; take it and call it good, because it is good for something; then make the best possible use of it with a view of getting greater good through that use; expect everything to multiply in your hands; have that faith; accept little things, as well as large things in that conviction, and every good that you do accept will be instrumental in bringing greater good to you. To live in the attitude of turning everything to good account has a most wholesome effect upon mind and character, because that mental attitude will tend to turn everything within yourself to good account; the result will be the constant development of a finer character and a more capable mind. By combining all the results from this mode of living and by noting the greater results that will invariably come from these combined results we must conclude that the total gain will be great, and that he who turns to good account everything that comes into his life, will positively receive everything that he may require to live an ideal life.

Live in the cheerful world, even if you have to create such a world in your own imagination. Resolve to be happy regardless of what comes; you cannot afford to be otherwise. Count everything joy; meet everything in the spirit of joy, and expect everything to give you joy. By creating a cheerful world in your own imagination you develop the tendency to a sunny disposition, and by meeting everything in the attitude of joy you will soon meet only those things that naturally produce joy. Like does attract like. Much sunshine will gather more sunshine, and the happiest mind meets the most delightful experiences. When exceptions occur pass them by as of no consequence, because they are of no consequence to you; you are interested only in happy events; it is only such events that you desire to meet; therefore, there is no reason whatever why you should pay any attention to the other kind. It is a fact that the less attention we pay to unpleasant conditions the less unpleasantness we meet in life. That person who looks for the disagreeable everywhere and expects to find it everywhere will certainly find what he is looking for in most places, if not in all places. On the other hand, the person who expects only the pleasant will seldom find anything else. We attract what we think of the most. There is no better medicine than cheerfulness, especially for the circulation and the digestive functions. Keep your mind full of living joy and your circulation will be strong in every part of your being, and a strong full circulation is one of the secrets to perfect health. Another great secret to health is a good digestion, and it is well to remember that so long as you are thoroughly bright and happy you can digest almost anything. The greatest value of cheerfulness, however, is found in its effect upon the mind; that is, in its power to make faculties and talents grow, just as sunshine makes flowers grow. It is a well-known fact that the most cheerful mind is the most brilliant mind, other things being equal, and that the brightest ideas always come when you are in the brightest frame of mind. This makes cheerfulness indispensable to those who wish to improve themselves and develop superior mental power. The depressed mind is always dull and never sees anything clearly; while the cheerful mind learns more readily, remembers more easily and understands more perfectly; but we must not conclude that cheerfulness is all that is necessary to the development of a fine intelligence; there must be mental power and mental quality as well; but the power and the quality of the mind, however great, cannot be fully expressed without an abundance of mental sunshine. Though the warmest sunshine may fail to make a gravel-knoll productive, still the most fertile soil will remain barren so long as the sunshine is absent. There are thousands of fertile minds in the world that are almost wholly unproductive, because they lack mental sunshine. If these would cultivate real genuine mental brightness every part of the world would sparkle with brilliant ideas. What the acorn is to the oak bright ideas are to a great and successful life, and we all can produce bright ideas through the development of mental ability and the cultivation of mental sunshine. Cheerfulness keeps the body in the best condition and brings out the best that there is in the mind. To attain the cheerful state we must remember that it is a product of the inner life and does not come from circumstances or conditions; therefore, the first essential is to create a cheerful world in the imagination; picture in mind the brightest states of existence that you can think of and impress joy upon mind at all times; feel joy, think joy, and make every action of mind and body thrill with joy; ere long you will have created within yourself the subconscious cause of joy, and when this is done cheerfulness and brightness will become permanent elements in yourself.

Live in the present only, and seek to make the great eternal now as full and complete as possible. It is what we do for the present that counts; the past is gone, and the future is not ready to be acted upon. Give your time, your talent and your power to that which is now at hand and you will do things worth while; you will not waste thought upon what you expect to do, but you will turn all your energies upon that which you now can do; results will positively follow. The man who does things worth while in the present will not have to worry about the future; for such a man the future has rich rewards in abundance. The greater the present cause the greater the future effect. Nine-tenths of the worries in the average life are simply about the future; all of these will be eliminated when we learn to live in the present only. Instead of giving anxious thought to the bridge we may have to cross we should give scientific thought to the increase of present ability and power; thus we make ourselves fully competent to master every occasion that may be met. To judge the present by the past is not sound doctrine, because if we are advancing, the present is not only larger than the past, but quite different in many if not all respects. To follow the past is to limit one's self to the lesser accomplishments of the past and thus prevent the very best from being attained in the present. The present moment should be dealt with according to the needs of the present moment regardless of what was done under similar conditions in the past. There is sufficient wisdom at hand now to solve all the problems of the present moment, if we will make full, practical application of that wisdom. He who lives for the present only will live a larger life, a happier life, a far more useful life; this is perfectly natural, because he will not scatter his forces over past ages and future ages, but will concentrate his whole life, all his power, all his ability upon that which he is trying to do now; he will be his best to-day, because he will give all of his best to the life of to-day, and he who is his best to-day will be still better to-morrow.

Never complain, criticize or condemn, but meet all things in a constructive attitude of mind. The critical mind is destructive to itself, and will in time become wholly incompetent to even produce logical criticism. To complain about everything is to constantly think about the inferior side of everything, thus impressing inferiority upon the mind; this will cause the entire process of thinking to become inferior; in consequence, the retrogression of the man himself will inevitably follow. Refuse to complain about anything; complaints never righted a wrong and never will. When you seek to gain justice through complaint you temporarily gain something in one place and permanently lose something in another; besides, you have harmed your own mind. The fact is that the more you complain the worse things will become; and the more you criticize what you meet to-day the more adverse and inferior will be the things you are to meet to-morrow. The reason why is simple; the complaining mind attracts the cheap and the common, and the critical spirit goes directly down into weakness and inferiority. However, we must remember in this connection that there is a marked difference between the critical attitude and the discriminating attitude. When things are not right we should say so, but while saying so we should not enter into a "rip and tear" frame of mind; the facts should be stated firmly but gently and without the slightest trace of ill feeling or condemnation; simply discriminate between the white and the black and state the facts, but let no hurt whatever appear in your voice. What we say is important, but the way things are said is far more important; even truth itself, can be expressed in such a way that it hurts, harms and destroys; this, however, is not true expression. It is truth misdirected, and always produces undesirable effects. To state your wants in a friendly manner is not complaint, but when there are hurts and whines in your voice you are making complaints and you are harming yourself; besides, you are producing unfavorable impressions upon those with whom you come in contact. It is far better to have faith in people than to criticize and complain, even though everything seems to go wrong, because when we have faith in people we shall finally attract those who are after our own hearts, and who are competent to do things the way we wish to have them done. Instead of complaining, or stating that there is always something wrong, we should live constantly in the strong faith that everything is eternally coming right; we thus place ourselves in harmony with those laws that can and will make things right. This is no idle dream, nor shall we have to wait a long time to secure results. The very day we establish faith in the place of complaints, criticisms and distrust, the tide will turn; things will change for the better in our world, and continue to improve perpetually.

Make the best use of every occasion, and nothing but opportunities will come your way. He who makes the best of everything will attract the best of everything, and it is always an opportunity to meet the best. There are occasions that seem worthless, and the average person thinks he is wasting time while he is passing through such states, but no matter how worthless the occasion may seem to be the one who makes the best use of it while he is in it will get something of real value out of it; in addition, the experience will have exceptional worth, because whenever we try to turn an occasion to good account we turn everything in ourselves to good account. The person who makes the best use of every occasion is developing his mind and strengthening his own character every day; to such a person every occasion will become an opportunity and will consequently place him in touch with the greater world of opportunities. Much gathers more and many small opportunities will soon attract a number of larger ones; then comes promotion, advancement and perpetual increase. "To him that hath shall be given." Every event has the power to add to your life, and will add to your life, if you make the best use of what it has to give; this will constantly increase the power of your life, which will bring you into greater occasions and better opportunities than you ever knew before. Make the best use of everything that comes your way; greater things will positively follow; that is the law, and he who daily applies this law has a brilliant future before him.

Never antagonize anything, neither in thought, word nor deed, but live in that attitude that is non-resisting to evil while positively and continuously inclined toward the good. You give your energy to that which you resist; you thereby give life to the very thing you seek to destroy. To resist evil is to increase the power of evil, and at the same time take life and power away from that good which you wish to develop or promote. The antagonistic mind develops bitterness in itself and thereby becomes just as disagreeable as the thing disliked; frequently more so, and we cannot expect to be drawn into the more delightful elements of the ideal while we ourselves are becoming less and less ideal. To live in the antagonistic attitude is to perpetuate a destructive process throughout mind and body, and at the same time suffer a constant loss of energy. We therefore cannot afford to be antagonistic at any time, nor even righteously indignant, no matter how perfectly in the right we may be; though in this connection it is well to remember that indignation never can be righteous. There are a number of minds that have the habit of feeling an inner bitterness toward those beliefs or systems of thought which they cannot accept. Frequently there can be no logical grounds for such a feeling. In many instances it is simply hereditary, or the result of foundationless prejudice; nevertheless, it is there and is actually sapping life and power out of the mind that has it. This habit is therefore responsible for much mental weakness, inability and consequent failure; and as everything that tends to decrease the life and the power of the individual tends to shorten his life, as well as decrease the value and usefulness of his life, it is evident that we cannot afford to feel bitter toward any religion, any belief, any doctrine, any party or any person whatever; we harm ourselves by so doing and do not add to the welfare or happiness of anybody. Be on friendly terms with the entire universe and feel kindly toward every creature in existence; leave the ills of perverted life to die; let the "dead bury their dead." It is our privilege to press on and promote the greatest good that we know; and when we give our whole time and attention to the highest attainment of the greatest good, evil will die of itself. This is what it means to overcome evil with good, and it is the one perfect path to complete emancipation, both for the individual and for the race. If you wish to serve the race do not antagonize systems, doctrines, methods or beliefs; be an inspiration to the race by actually *living* the very best you know now.

CHAPTER IV

THE FIRST THOUGHT IN
IDEAL THINKING

But seek ye first his kingdom, and his righteousness; and all these things shall be added unto you.—Mat. 6:33.

The kingdom of God is a spiritual kingdom within man and manifests through man as the spiritual life. His righteousness is the right use of all that is contained in the elements of the spiritual life. The spiritual life being the complete life, the full expression of life in body, mind and soul, it is evident that the right use of the spiritual life will produce and bring everything that man may need or desire. The source of everything has the power to produce everything, provided the power within that source is used according to exact spiritual law. The spiritual life being the source of all that is necessary to a full and perfect life, and the kingdom within being the source of the spiritual life, we can readily understand why the kingdom should be sought first; and also why everything that we may require will be added when the first thought is given to spiritual living, ideal thinking and righteous action. Righteous action, however, does not simply imply moral action, but the right use of the elements of life in all action.

The kingdom of God is the spiritual side of all things. This spiritual side is within the manifested or visible side; that is, everything is filled with an inner, finer something that is perfect and complete. Every part of the outer world is filled and permeated with an inner world, and everything that appears in the outer world is a partial manifestation or expression of what exists in a perfect and complete state in the inner world. This inner world is the kingdom referred to, and as it is inexhaustible in every sense of that term, there is nothing we cannot receive when we learn to draw upon the riches of this vast inner realm. In the life of man we have the outer and the inner worlds; the personal life in the without and the great spiritual life in the within. What appears in the outer world of man, that is, in his personal existence, is the result of what he has sought and brought forth from his inner world. According to one of the greatest of metaphysical laws we express whatever we become conscious of. We, therefore, understand clearly why the personal man, or his outer world, is the direct result of what he has become conscious of in his interior world. Man is what he is in the without, because he has sought the corresponding elements in the within, and he may change the without in any manner desired by seeking first in the within those qualities and attributes that he may desire.

To seek and find the within is to become conscious of the within, and what is thus sought and found will express itself in personal life; but its real value will depend upon whether it is properly used or not. To seek the richer kingdom within is the first essential, but to promote the righteous use of these greater riches is the second essential, and is just as important as the first. To give the first thought at all times to the great spiritual kingdom within, it is not necessary to withdraw attention from the outer world nor to deny one's self the good things that may exist in the outer world. To seek the kingdom first is to give one's strongest thought to the spiritual life, and to make spiritual thought the predominating thought in everything that one may do in life; in other words, live so closely to the spiritual kingdom within that you are fully conscious of that kingdom every moment, and depend absolutely upon supreme power to carry you through whatever you may undertake to do. To seek the kingdom first the heart must be in the spirit; that is, to live in the full realization of the inner spiritual life at all times must be the one predominating desire. However, the mental conception of the spiritual life must not be narrow, but must contain the perfection of everything that can possibly appear in life.

To think of the spiritual life as being distinct from mind and body, is to prevent the elements of the great interior life from being expressed in mind and body, and what is not expressed cannot be lived. The spiritual life in this larger sense must be thoroughly lived in mind and body. The power of the spiritual must be made the soul of all power, and the law of spiritual action must be made the rule and the guide in all action. When the spiritual is lived in all life the richness and the quality and the worth of the spiritual will be expressed in all life, and spiritual worth means the sum-total of all worth. There are any number of minds in the world who now realize this greater worth and who have found the spiritual riches within to an extraordinary degree, but they have not in every instance sought righteousness; therefore, these spiritual riches have been of no use; frequently they have become obstacles in the living of a life of personal welfare and growth.

Real righteousness means right living and exact scientific thinking; that is, the correct expression of everything of which we are now conscious. To be righteous does not simply mean to be moral and truthful and just, but to live in harmony with all laws, physical, mental, moral and spiritual. To be in harmony with physical law, is to adapt one's self orderly to everything in the external world; to resist no exterior force, but to constructively use every exterior force in such a manner that perpetual physical development may take place. To be in harmony with mental laws is to promote scientific thinking; that is, to think the truth about everything and to see everything from the universal view-point. Scientific thinking is that mode of thinking that causes all the forces of mind and thought to constantly work for greater things. To be in harmony with moral laws is to live a life of complete purity; and purity in the true sense of the term is the doing of all things at the right time, in the right place and with the right motive; in other words, every action is a pure action that leads to higher and better things. All other actions are not pure, therefore not moral. To be in harmony with spiritual laws is to live in constant conscious touch with the inner or higher side of everything. To apply the spiritual law is to seek the spiritual first, no matter what the goal in view may be; to seek first the spiritual counterpart that is within everything, to make the spiritual thought the predominating thought and to dwell constantly in the spiritual attitude. We enter the spiritual attitude when we enter the upper story of the mind and mentally face that supreme side of life that is created in the likeness of the Supreme. Briefly stated, to be righteous is to be in harmony with the outer side of life, to think the truth, to live in real purity, to dwell on the spiritual heights and to give full and complete expression to the highest and the best of which we are now conscious. When this is done we shall rightly manifest whatever we may find in the kingdom within. Righteousness, however, is not a definite goal but a perpetual process of attainment that involves the entire being of man. The righteous man is right and perfect as far as he has ascended in the scale of life at present, though not simply in a moral sense, but in every sense, including body, mind and soul.

The righteous man is never weak, never sick, and is never in a state of discord or disorder. This is a great truth that we should not fail to remember. Sickness, weakness, discord and all other adverse conditions come from the violation of law somewhere in human life, but the righteous man violates no law. He is true to life as far as he has ascended in the scale of life. To be righteous in the absolute sense of the term is to use everything in our present world as God uses everything in His world, which means in harmony with its own nature, in harmony with its sphere of action, and in harmony with that law that leads upward and onward forever. Righteous action is that action that is always harmonious and that always works for better things, greater things, higher things. The great majority of those minds that are awakened to the reality of the spiritual side of things have already found an abundance of good things in the vast interior life that is ready for manifestation in personal life, but as most of these have neglected the law of real righteousness this abundance remains inactive in the potential state and all other things as promised are not added. That all other things will be added when His kingdom and His righteousness are sought first may not seem clear to everybody, because the kingdom of God has been looked upon as a far away place that we are to enter when we leave the body, and righteousness has been looked upon as simply a moral, just and honest mode of living. But when we realize that the kingdom is the great spiritual world within us, and that from this world comes all wisdom, all power, all talent, all life; in brief, everything that we now possess in body, mind and soul, and that everything we are to receive in the future must come from the same source, we understand clearly why the kingdom must be sought first.

We cannot secure anything unless we go to the source, and the spiritual kingdom within us is the one only source of everything that is manifested in human life. When we desire more wisdom and a greater understanding it is evident that we can obtain these things only by entering real mental light, and that light is within us in the spirit. By entering into the consciousness of the illumined world within we naturally receive more light. We, ourselves, become illumined to a degree, frequently to a great degree, and we thus gain the power to understand perfectly what we could neither desire nor comprehend before. When we seek more life and power we can find the greater life only in the eternal life, and the eternal life is the life of the spirit in the kingdom within.

"They that wait upon the Lord shall renew their strength." To wait upon the Lord is to enter into the spiritual presence of the Infinite, and whenever we enter into the presence of the Infinite we enter into the life of the Infinite and we are thus filled through and through with the supreme power of that life. When we enter into the spiritual kingdom within we enter into the Christ consciousness and in that consciousness we receive the life more abundant, because to be in the Christ consciousness is to be in the very spirit of the limitless life of the Christ. When we seek health we can find it in the kingdom, because in the spirit all is always well. There is a realm within man where perfect health reigns supremely and eternally. In that realm everything is always perfectly whole and to enter into that realm is to enter into absolute health and wholeness. No one who lives constantly in the spirit can possibly be sick, because sickness can no more enter the spiritual state than darkness can enter where there is absolute light. To enter the kingdom within is to enter health, happiness and harmony in the highest, largest degree; therefore, by seeking the kingdom, health will be added, happiness will be added, harmony will be added. It is impossible, however, to gain health, happiness and harmony, in the true sense, from any other source. But to seek these qualities in the kingdom is not sufficient. We must also seek righteousness or the right expressions of those things. If we misuse any organ, faculty, function or power anywhere in body, mind or soul, we cannot remain in health, no matter how spiritual we may try to be.

To enter the kingdom within is to enter the perpetual increase of power, because there is no limit to the power of the spirit, and the more power we enter into or become conscious of the more power we shall give to mind and body; in consequence, the more spiritual we become the stronger we become, the more able we become, the more competent we become and the more we can accomplish whatever our work may be; and he who can do good work in the world invariably receives the good things of the world. To his life will be added all those things that can make personal existence rich and beautiful. To enter the kingdom within is to enter the life of freedom. There is no bondage in the spirit, and as we grow in the spirit we grow out of every form of bondage. One adverse condition after another disappears until absolute freedom is gained. Therefore, when we seek first His kingdom and His righteousness we shall find the life of complete emancipation. Perfect freedom in all things and at all times will positively be added.

There are thousands of aspiring souls in this age that are trying to develop their powers and talents so that they might be of greater use in the world, but if these would seek the kingdom first, they would find within themselves the real source of every talent; and as the only way to permanently increase anything is to increase the expressions of its source we understand perfectly why greatness can come only when we begin to live in the great within. We must always bear in mind that what we become conscious of we bring forth into personal expression, but we cannot become conscious of the larger source of any quality or talent unless we enter into the spirit of that quality and talent, and as the spirit of all things has its source of real existence in the kingdom within, we must enter this interior world if we wish to become conscious of a larger and a larger measure of those things that we wish to express.

That any person can improve his environment or overcome poverty by seeking the kingdom first may not seem possible, but the truth is that adverse conditions will positively disappear after one begins to actually live the full spiritual life. Poverty has two causes; lack of ability and the misplacing of ability. To improve ability to any degree the within must be awakened. We must learn to draw upon the inexhaustible sources of the inner life and become conscious of the greater capacity that lies latent within us. This is accomplished by seeking the kingdom first. By giving your first thought, your predominating thought to the great and mighty world within, your mind will gradually enter more deeply into the life of this inner world. You thus become conscious of the larger powers within, because consciousness always follows the predominating thought. What you think of the most develops in yourself. When you think the most of the spiritual, consciousness will follow your spiritual thought and thus enter more deeply into the spirit. The result is you become conscious of a larger spiritual domain every day, you become conscious of a greater capacity within yourself every day, and since you always express what you become conscious of you will cause greater ability and capacity to be developed and expressed in yourself every day; you thereby remove the first cause of poverty and place yourself in a position where you will be in greater demand, and the greater the demand for your service the greater will be your recompense.

There are a number of people who have misplaced their talents that may have considerable ability, but they are not in the work for which they are adapted, and therefore do not succeed. They may have been forced into their present positions by necessity, or they may have chosen their present places through inferior judgment, but both of these causes may be changed by seeking the kingdom first. When we enter the spiritual everything clears up. We not only see our mistakes, but also how to correct them; therefore, if you are in the wrong place, enter the spiritual light of the kingdom within, and you will see clearly where you belong. If you do not know whether you are in the proper sphere or not, enter the spirit. Constantly live in the spirit and you will soon know; you will also know when and how to change. By entering this state where the outlook is infinitely greater you will see opportunities, open doors, possibilities, and pastures green that you never saw before, and you will also see clearly which one you have the power and the capacity to take advantage of now. If you have been forced into the wrong place by necessity, the larger mental life that will come when you seek the kingdom will give you the power to command something better, and the superior wisdom that comes through the light of the spirit will guide you in your choice. Instead of adversity and constant need you will have peace, harmony and abundance. You will pass from the world of poverty and limitations to a world that can offer a future as brilliant as the sun.

The man who fights adversity and complains of his lot will continue in poverty and need. He will remain in mental darkness; he will be daily misled, and will always be doing the wrong thing at the wrong time. Such a life breeds ill luck and misfortune and perpetuates the poverty that already exists. However, let this person enter into harmony with his present fate, count everything joy, and realize that he can make his present misfortune a stepping-stone to better things; then let him give his first thought to the kingdom, to the greater life and power and capacity within, to the superior creative powers of his own mind, those powers that are able even now to create for him a better fate, if he will but place before them a better pattern; the results will be peace of mind first, then hope of the better, then the vision of great changes near at hand, then the faith that the new life, the new time and the better days are now being created for his world. And when a person begins to inwardly feel that things are taking a turn, that better days are coming and that the good is beginning to accumulate in his life, the victory is nearly won. A little more faith and perseverance and the crowning day is at hand. From that moment all things will begin to work together for good things and for still greater things, providing the mind is held in constant conscious touch with the spiritual kingdom within, and all the laws of life are employed according to the highest ideal of righteousness.

Many a person, however, has failed while on the very verge of his victory, because he neglected the kingdom when he began to see the change coming. By giving his first thought to the material benefits that he expected to secure, his consciousness is taken away from the spirit and becomes confused in those things that had not as yet been placed in the true order of perpetual increase. The result is a scattering of forces and his loss upon the hold of the good things that were beginning to gravitate toward his world. While ascending this upward path we must at every step keep the eye single upon the kingdom, upon the spiritual, upon the larger and the higher life within. When the other things are being added we must not forget the kingdom and give our first thoughts to the other things. We shall enjoy these other things so much the more, if we continue to give the first thought to the spirit. This is evident, because while giving the first thought to the spirit everything that comes into our world will be spiritualized, refined and perfected, and will thus be given added power and worth. When we continue to give the first thought to the spiritual kingdom those other things that are added will enter our world at their best and we shall thus receive the best that those things may have to give.

We are always at our best when we are on the heights, and we gain the power to create, produce and attract those things from every part of life that correspond to the life on the heights. Therefore, by living on the heights in the spiritual kingdom we gain everything that we may require; we gain the best of everything that we may require, and we are in that condition where we can make the best use of what comes, and enjoy what comes to the highest and most perfect degree. We can thus readily understand that when we seek the kingdom of God constantly, giving our first thought to the spiritual and seeking to live righteously according to this larger view of righteousness, all problems of life will be solved. All the crooked paths of life will be made straight; obstacles will disappear; our circumstances will change to correspond with our ideas, and we will daily enter into a better life and a greater state of existence than we ever knew before. The problems of the world can be solved in the same way. Therefore, the greatest thing that we can do for the human race is to make clear this law, that is, the law through which His kingdom and His righteousness may be sought first by any individual, no matter what the degree of that individual's understanding may be. To promote a real spiritual movement on the largest possible scale is to cause the ills of humanity to gradually, but surely, pass away. This planet will then become, not a vale of tears, but what it is intended to be, the kingdom of heaven realized upon earth.

The human race, however, is the product of human thought; therefore, the prime essential is to inspire the human mind with the power to give His kingdom and His righteousness the first thought. To make the ideal real upon earth, all thinking must be ideal; and to cause all things to become ideal the foundation of all things must be based upon pure spiritual thought; that is, every thought that is created in the mind must be animated with this great first thought, the thought of the kingdom within and the full righteous expression of that kingdom.

When we seek first the kingdom and his righteousness all other things are added, not in some mysterious manner, nor do they come of themselves regardless of conscious effort to work in harmony with the law of life. We receive from the kingdom only what we are prepared to use in the living of a great life and in the doing of great and worthy things in the world. We receive only in proportion to what we give, and it is only as we work well that we produce great results; but by entering the spiritual life we receive everything that we may require in order to give as much as we may desire, to do as much as we may desire. We gain the power and the talent to do everything that is necessary to give worth and superiority to our entire state of existence. When we enter the spiritual life we gain every quality that is necessary in making life full and complete now, and we gain the power to produce and create in the external world whatever we may need or desire. In other words, we receive everything we want from within and we gain the power to produce everything we want in the without. We, therefore, need never take anxious thought about these other things. By seeking first His kingdom and His righteousness we shall positively receive these other things. The way will be open to all that is rich, beautiful and superior in life, and we shall be abundantly supplied with the best that life can give.

CHAPTER V

THE IDEAL AND THE
REAL MADE ONE

When the elements of the ideal are blended harmoniously with the elements of the real the two become one; the ideal becomes real and the real gives expression to the qualities of the ideal. To be in harmony with everything at all times and under all circumstances is therefore one of the great essentials in the living of that life that is constantly making real a larger and larger measure of the ideal; and so extremely important is continuous harmony that nothing should be permitted to produce confusion or discord for the slightest moment. Discord wastes energy, while harmony accumulates energy. If we wish to be strong in mind and body and do the best possible work, harmony is absolutely necessary and we must be in the best possible condition to make real the ideal. The person who lives in perpetual harmony with everything will accomplish from ten to one hundred percent more than the average during any given period of time; a fact that gives the elements of harmony a most important place in life. When harmony is absent there is always a great deal of mental confusion, and a confused mind can never think clearly, therefore makes mistakes constantly. To establish complete and continuous mental harmony will reduce mistakes to a minimum in any mind; another fact that makes the attainment of harmony one of the great attainments.

The mind that is living in continuous harmony is realizing a great measure of heaven upon earth regardless of his personal attainments or external possessions. He has made real that ideal something that makes existence thoroughly worth while, and he is rich indeed. To live in harmony is to gain the joy everlasting, the contentment that is based upon the real value of life, and that satisfaction that grows larger and better for every day that passes by. On the other hand, to live in discord is to live in perpetual torment, even though our personal attainments may be great and our personal possessions as large as any mind could wish.

To live the good life, the ideal life, the beautiful life, we must be at peace with all things, including ourselves, and every thought, word and deed must be harmonious. Whatever we wish to do or be it is wisdom to make any sacrifice necessary for the sake of harmony, although that which we sacrifice for the sake of harmony is not a sacrifice. When we enter into harmony we will regain everything that we were willing to lose in order that we might possess harmony. When we establish ourselves in perfect harmony we shall be reunited with everything that we hold near and dear and the new unity will be far sweeter, far more beautiful than the one we had before. "My own shall come to me" is a favorite expression among all those who believe that every ideal can be made real, and many of these are waiting and watching for their own to come, wondering in the meantime what can be done to hasten that coming. There are many things to be done, however, but one of the most important is the attainment of harmony. No person who lives in perpetual harmony will be deprived very long of his own whatever that own may be. Whatever you deserve, whatever you are entitled to, whatever belongs to you will soon appear in your world, if you are living in perfect harmony.

To enter harmony is to enter a new world where everything is better, where opportunities are greater and more numerous, and where persons, conditions and things are more agreeable. You will not only enter a better world, however, but the attitude of harmony will relate your life so perfectly to the good things in all worlds that may exist about you, that the best from every source will naturally gravitate toward your sphere of existence. But harmony will not only cause the good things of life to gravitate toward you; it will also cause you to radiate the good qualities in your own being and thus become a perpetual benediction to everybody. To be in the presence of a person who dwells serenely in the beautiful calm is, indeed, a privilege, especially to those who can appreciate the finer elements of a truly harmonious life. Whenever we are in touch with real harmony, whether it comes from the music of human life, the music of nature or the music of the spheres, we are one step nearer the Beautiful. We can therefore realize the great value of being able to actually live in perfect harmony at all times. The life of harmony is the foundation of happiness and health and is one of the greatest essentials to achievement and real success. When we look into the past we can always find that our failures originated in confusion;

likewise our troubles and ills. On the other hand, all the good things that have happened to us in the past, or that are happening in the present, had their origin and their growth in the elements of continuous harmony; the ideal and the real were made one, and we consequently reached the goals we had in view.

The mind that works in perpetual harmony does more work and far better work than is possible in any other condition; besides, harmonious work is invariably conducive to higher development and growth. To work in harmony is to promote increase and development in all the qualities and powers of the personality; while to work in confusion is to weaken the entire system and thus originate causes that will terminate in failure. The majority state that they have no time for self-development, but to live in harmony and work in harmony is to promote self-development every moment, and this development will not be confined simply to those muscles or faculties that we use directly, but will express itself throughout the entire system; and the mind especially will, under such conditions, steadily gain both in power and in worth. In the presence of these facts we can realize readily that no person can afford to permit discord, disturbance or confusion at any time. The many declare, however, that they cannot help it, but we must help it and we can. There is no reason why our minds should be excited or our nerves upset at any time. We can prevent this just as easily as we can refuse to eat what we do not want.

To proceed, we must apply exact reason to this great subject. We should learn to understand that no wrong will be righted because we permit ourselves to "fly to pieces"; also that the act of becoming nervous over a trouble will never drive that trouble away. To live in a constant strain will not promote our purpose nor arrange matters the way we want them. This is a fact that we should impress deeply upon our minds, and then impress our minds to take another and a better course. The average person feels that it is a religious duty to be as excited as possible, and to string up all his nerves as high as possible, whenever he is passing through some exceptional event; in consequence, he spoils all or practically all of that which might have been gained; besides, he places his system in a condition where all sorts of ills may gain a foothold. There are many reasons why such a large number of undertakings fail, but one of the principal reasons is found in the fact that few people have learned to retain perfect harmony under all kinds of circumstances. Discord and confusion are usually present to a great degree, and in consequence, something almost invariably goes wrong. But when a person is in perfect harmony and does his very best, he will succeed at least in a

measure every time, and he will thus prepare himself for the greater opportunities that are sure to follow. To believe that intelligent, well educated
people almost daily break down over mere trifles is not mere simplicity, but
the fact that it is the truth leads us to question why. Intelligence and education should give those who possess it the power to know better. Modern education, however, does not teach us how to use ourselves. We have
learned how to mix material substances so as to satisfy every imaginable
taste, and we have learned how to use the tangible forces of nature so as to
construct almost anything we like in the physical world, but we have not
learned how to combine the elements of mind so as to produce health, happiness, strength, brilliancy and harmony whenever we may so desire. A few,
however, have made the attempt, but the elements of the mind will not
combine for greater efficiency and higher states of expression unless the
mind is in perfect harmony.

We have all learned to remember, but few have learned to think. To
repeat verbatim what others have thought and said is counted knowledge
and with such borrowed knowledge the majority imagine they are satisfied,
the reason being they have not discovered the art of thinking thoughts of
their own. This is an art that every person must learn; the sooner the better,
if the ideal is to be made real. Original thinking is the secret of all greatness,
all high attainments, all extraordinary achievements and all superior states
of being; but no mind can create original thought until a high state of mental harmony is attained. To produce mental harmony we must first bear in
mind the great fact that it is not what happens that disturbs us, but the way
we think about that which happens; and our thought about anything depends upon our point of view. The way we look at things will determine
whether the experience will produce discord or harmony, and it is in our
power to look at things in any way that we may desire. When we are face
to face with those things that usually upset the mind we should immediately
turn our attention upon the life and the power that is back of the disturbing
element, having the desire to find the better side of that life and power
constantly in view. Everything has its better side, its ideal side, its calm and
undisturbed side, and a mere desire to gain a glimpse of that better side will
turn the mind away from confusion and cause attention to be centered upon
that calm state that is being sought. This will decrease discord at once, and
if applied the very moment we are aware of confusion we will entirely prevent any mental disturbance whatever. To meet all circumstances and events
in this way is to develop in ourselves a harmonious attitude toward all
things, and when we are established in this harmonious attitude nothing

whatever disturbs us; no matter what may happen we will continue to remain in harmony, and will consequently be able to deal properly with
whatever may happen.

The mind that is upset by confused circumstances will lose ground and
fail, but the mind that continues calmly in harmony with everything, no
matter what the circumstances may be, will master every occasion and
steadily rise in the scale. He will continue to make real the ideal, because
he is living in that harmonious state of being where the ideal and the real
are harmoniously blended into one. To promote the highest and most perfect state of continuous harmony we must learn to meet those persons,
things and events, with which we come in daily contact, in the right mental attitude. The result of such an attitude is determined directly by the
nature of our own attitude of mind, and as we can express ourselves through
any attitude we desire, it is in our power either to spoil the most promising
prospects, or convert the most unpromising conditions into the greatest
success. We should train ourselves to meet everything in that attitude of
mind that expects all things to work out right. When we deeply and continually expect all things to work out right we relate ourselves more perfectly with that with which we come in contact; we take things, so to
speak, the way they ought to be taken, and we thereby promote harmony
and co-operation among all things concerned.

Though this be extremely important, it is insignificant, however, in
comparison with another great fact in this connection; that is, the way
things respond to the leading desires of the ruling mind; whether it is the
exercise of the mysteries of mental force or the application of a mental law
not generally understood, does not concern us just now; but it is a fact that
things will do, as a rule what we persistently expect them to do. To understand why this is so may require some study of the great laws of mind and
body, and everybody should seek to understand these laws perfectly; but in
the meantime anyone can demonstrate the fact that things will work out
right if we constantly expect them to do so. No matter what may happen
we should continue in the faith that all things will come right, and as our
faith is so it shall be. To place ourselves in perfect harmony with all things,
the domineering attitude of mind must be eliminated completely. The mind
that tries to domineer over things will not only lose control of things, but
will lose control of its own faculties and forces. At first it may seem that the
domineering mind gains ground, but the gain is only temporary. When the
reaction comes, as it will, the loss will be far greater than the temporary
gain. When you try to domineer over persons and things you gain posses-

sion and control of those things only that are too weak to control themselves. That is, you gain a temporary control over negatives, and negatives have no permanent value in your life; in fact, they soon prove themselves to be wholly detrimental. Occasionally a domineering mind may attract the attention of better things, but as soon as his domineering qualities are discovered those better things will part company with him at once. The law of attraction is at the foundation of all natural constructive processes; therefore, to promote construction, growth, advancement and real success we must work in harmony with that law. If we wish to attain the superior, we must become superior, because it is only like that attracts like. If we wish to gain the ideal, we must become ideal. If we wish to make real the ideal, we must live the ideal in the real.

When you want good things, make yourself better, and better things will naturally be attracted to you; but good things do not submit to force. Therefore, to try to secure better things through forceful methods, or through the domineering attitude can only result in failure; such methods gain only the inferior, those things that can add neither to the welfare nor the happiness of any one. This fact holds good, not only among individuals, but also among nations and institutions. The more domineering an institution is the more inferior are its members, and the more autocratic the nation the weaker its subjects. On the other hand, we find the best minds where the individual is left free to govern himself and where he is expected to act wisely, to be true to the best that is within him. In order that the individual may advance he must steadily grow in the mastery of himself, and must so relate himself to the best things in life that he will naturally attract the best things; but these two essentials are wholly interfered with by the domineering attitude. Such an attitude repels everything and everybody that has any worth. It spoils the forces of mind, thus weakening all the mental faculties, and it steadily undermines whatever self-control a person might possess. Never try to control anything or domineer over anything, but aim to live in perpetual harmony with the highest, the truest and the best that is in everything.

Whatever happens we should approach that event in that attitude that believes it is all right. We should never permit the attitude that condemns, not even when the things concerned have proved themselves to be wrong. The attitude that condemns is detrimental to our own minds, because it invariably produces discord. When you meet all things in the expectation of finding them right, you always find something about them that is right. This something you may appropriate and thus gain good from everything that happens. That person, however, who expects to find most things wrong will fail to see the good that may exist among the things that come his way; therefore, he gains far less from life than his wiser neighbor. But what is equally important, the man who expects to find everything right wherever he may go, will gradually gravitate toward those people and circumstances that are right. The man who expects to find everything wrong usually finds what he expects. The effect of these two attitudes upon mind and character is even more important, because the man is as his mind and character, and as the man is so is his destiny. The man who expects to find most things wrong and meets the world in that attitude is constantly impressing the wrong upon his mind, and as we gradually grow into the likeness of that which we think of the most, he is building upon sinking sand. The mind that is constantly looking for the wrong cannot be wholesome. Such a mind is not in harmony with the law of growth, power, and ability; therefore, can never do its best. Unwholesome thoughts will steadily undermine the finest character and mind, and the world is full of illustrations. There is always something wrong in the life of that person who constantly expects to find things wrong, and the reason why is simple. His own expectations are reacting upon himself; by thinking about the wrong he is creating the wrong and thus bringing forth the wrong in every part of his life.

The man, however, who expects to find everything right and meets the world in that attitude is daily nourishing his mind with right thoughts, wholesome thoughts and constructive thoughts; he thinks the most of that which is right, and is therefore steadily growing more and more into the likeness of that which is right, perfect, worthy and good; he is daily changing for the better, and through this constant change he steadily rises in the scale and thereby meets the better and the better at every turn. By expecting to find everything right he finds more and more of that which is right, and as he is becoming stronger in mind, character and soul he is affected less and less by those few things that may not be as they should be. When you meet a disappointment meet it in the conviction that it is all right, because through this attitude you enter into harmony with the power that is back of the event at hand, and you thus convert the disappointment into a channel through which greater good may be secured. Those who doubt this should try it; they will find that it is based upon exact scientific fact. Transcend disappointment, and all the powers of adversity will begin to rise with you and will begin to work with you and help you reach the goal you have in view. You will thus find that it is all for the best, because through the right mental attitude you made everything work out in such a way that the best transpired as a final result.

To live in what may be termed the "all right" attitude, that is, in that attitude that expects to find everything all right and that constantly affirms that everything is all right, is to press on to the realization and the possession of those things that are as you wish them to be. Disappointments and failures, when met in this attitude, simply become open doors to new worlds where you find better opportunities and greater possibilities than you ever knew before. When the average person meets disappointment he usually declares, "Just my luck"; in other words, he enters that mental attitude that faces ill luck; he thus fails to see anything else but misfortune in that which has happened; and so long as that person consciously or unconsciously expects misfortune, into more and more misfortune he will go. He who believes that he is fated to have bad luck will have bad luck in abundance. The reason is he lives in that mental attitude that places his mind in constant contact with those confused elements in the world that never create anything else but bad luck. That person, however, who thoroughly believes that everything that happens is simply a step to greater good, higher attainments and greater achievements, will steadily rise into those greater things that he expects to realize; the reason being that he is living in that mental attitude that places his mind in contact with the building power of life. Those powers will always build for greater things to those with whom they are in harmony, and we all can place ourselves in harmony with those powers; therefore, we can all move upward and onward forever, eternally, making real more and more of that which is ideal.

What we expect comes if our expectation is filled with all the power of life and soul, and what we believe our fate to be, that is the kind of a fate we will create for ourselves. To meet ill luck in the belief that it is your luck, your particular kind of luck, and that it is natural for you to have that kind of luck is to stamp your own mind as an unlucky mind. This will produce chaotic thinking, which will cause you to do everything at the wrong time, and all your energies will be more or less misdirected; in consequence, bad luck and misfortune must necessarily follow. Bad luck comes from doing the wrong thing, or from being your worst; while good luck comes from being your best and from doing the right thing at the right time. It is therefore mere simplicity to create good luck at any time and in the measure that we may desire. The person that fears misfortune or expects misfortune and faces life in that attitude is concentrating attention upon misfortune; he thereby creates a world of misfortune in his own mind; and he who lives in mental misfortune will produce misfortune in his external life. Like causes produce like effects; and this explains why the things we fear always come upon us. We create mental causes for those things, and corresponding tangible effects always follow. Train the mind to expect the right and the best, regardless of present circumstances, conditions or events. Call everything good that is met. Declare that everything that happens, happens for the best. Meet everything in that frame of mind, and no matter how wrong or adverse conditions seem to be, you cause them all to work out right.

When the mind expects the best, has the faith that the right will prevail, and constantly faces the superior, the true mental attitude has been gained. Through that attitude all the forces of mind and all the powers of will become constructive, and will build for man the very thing that he expects or desires while his mind is fixed upon the ideal. He relates himself harmoniously to the best that is in all things and thus unites the ideal with the real in all things; and when the ideal becomes one with the real, the ideal desired becomes an actual fact in the real; and this is the goal every true idealist has in view. He takes those elements that have been revealed to him through the vision of the soul and blends them harmoniously with the actions of daily life. He thus brings the ideal down to earth and causes the real of every day life to express the ideal in everything that he may undertake to do. His life, his thought, his action, his attainments, his achievements, all contain that happy state where the ideal and the real are made one. His dreams have become true. The visions of the soul are actually realized, and the tangible is animated with that ideal something that makes personal existence all that any one could wish it to be.

CHAPTER VI

THE FIRST STEP TOWARD COMPLETE EMANCIPATION

To forgive everybody for everything at all times, regardless of circumstances, is the first step toward complete emancipation. Heretofore, we have looked upon forgiveness as a virtue; now we know it to be a necessity. To those who possessed the spirit of forgiveness we have given our highest praise, and have thought of such people as being self-sacrificing in the truest sense of that term. We did not know that the act of forgiving is the simplest way to lighten one's own burdens. According to our former conception of this subject, the man who forgives denies himself a privilege, the privilege of indignation and revenge; for this reason we have looked upon him as a hero or as a saint, thinking that it could not be otherwise than heroic and saintly to give up the supposed pleasure of meting out revenge to those who seemed to deserve it. According to the new view, however, the man who forgives is no more saintly than the one who insists upon keeping clean, because in reality the act of forgiving simply constitutes a complete mental bath. When you forgive everybody for everything you cleanse your mind completely of every wrong thought or adverse mental attitude that may exist in your consciousness. This explains why forgiveness is a necessity and why the man who forgives everything emancipates himself from all kinds of burdens. It is therefore profitable, most highly profitable, to forgive everybody, no matter what they have done, and this includes also ourselves. It is just as necessary to forgive ourselves as to forgive others, and the principal reason why forgiveness has seemed to be so difficult is because we have neglected to forgive ourselves.

We cannot let go of that which is not desired until we have acquired the mental art of letting go, and to acquire this art we must practice upon our own minds. That is, we must learn to let go from our own minds all those things that we do not wish to retain. When you forgive yourself completely you wash your mentality perfectly clean. You let go of everything in your mental system that is not good. You emancipate yourself completely. Whatever you held against yourself or others you now drop entirely out of your mind; in consequence, you are freed from your mental burdens, and when mental burdens disappear all other burdens will disappear also. The ills that we hold in mind are the only things that can actually burden our lives. Therefore, when we forgive everybody for every ill we ever knew we no longer hold a single ill in our own minds; we thus throw off every burden and are perfectly free. This also includes disease, because disease is nothing but a temporary effect of a wrong that we mentally hold in the system. Forgive everybody, including yourself, for everything, and all disease will vanish from your system. This may at first sight appear to be a startling statement, but it is the truth, and anyone can prove it to be the truth. "As a man thinketh in his heart so is he." Therefore, when every wrong is eliminated from the heart of man there can be no wrong in the man himself, and every wrong is eliminated from that heart that forgives everything in everyone. Many persons, however, will state that they hold no ill against anyone yet suffer just the same. So they may think, nevertheless they are mistaken and will see their mistakes when they learn the truth about mental laws. You may not hold direct ill against any person just now, but your mind has not always been absolutely pure and absolutely free from every wrong thought. You have had many wrong desires in your heart, and have had many mistaken ideas. To hold a mistaken idea is to hold a wrong in your heart. To have wrong desires is to hold ills against yourself, as well as others. To blame yourself, criticize yourself, feel provoked at yourself or condemn yourself for your shortcomings is to hold ills against yourself, and there are very few who are not doing this every day to some degree.

When we forgive all and still suffer we may not believe that forgiveness produces emancipation; but the fact is that suffering is impossible when forgiveness is absolute. When we forgive completely we shall also eliminate completely every trouble or ill that may exist in our world. When you have trouble forgive those who have caused the trouble; forgive yourself for permitting yourself to be troubled, and your troubles will pass away. When you have made a mistake do not condemn yourself or feel upset; simply forgive yourself, and resolve that you will never make the mistake again. As you make that resolution, desire more wisdom, and have the faith that you will secure the wisdom you require. "According to your faith so shall it be." There are many who will think that the practice of forgiving everybody for everything will produce mental indifference and thus weaken character, but it is the very opposite that will take place. To forgive is to eliminate the useless, everything that is not good; and to free the mind from obstacles and adverse conditions is to enable that mind to be its best, to express itself fully and completely. This will not only strengthen the character and enlarge the mind, but will cause the greatness of the soul to come forth. There is many a character that appears to be strong on account of its open hostility to wrongs, but such a character is not always strong. Too often it is composed of a few borrowed ideas about morality backed up by mere animal force. The true character does not express hostility and does not resist or antagonize, but overcomes evil by giving all its power to the building of the good. A strong character meets evil with a silent indifference; that is, indifference in appearance only. The true character does not pass evil by because he does not care, but because he does care. He cares so much that he will not waste one single moment in prolonging the life of the wrong; therefore gives his whole time and attention to the making of good so strong that evil becomes absolutely powerless in the presence of that good. No intelligent person would antagonize darkness. By giving his time to the production of light he causes the darkness to disappear of itself.

When we apply the same principle to the elimination of evil a marvelous change for the better will come over the world. No person can forgive everybody for everything until he desires the best from every person and from every source. In other words, we cannot forgive the wrong until we desire the right. Therefore, the letting go of the inferior and the appropriation of the superior constitutes one and the same single mental process. We cannot eliminate darkness until we proceed to produce light, and it requires only the one act for removing the one and bringing forth the other. From these facts it is evident that when we let go of the wrong we gain more of that power that is right, and we thus increase the strength of character. To eliminate diseased conditions from the body will increase the strength of the body and will place the body in a position for further development, if we desire to promote such development. Likewise, to eliminate all ill feelings, all hatred, all wrong thoughts and all false beliefs from the mind will increase the power of the mind and place every mental faculty in proper condition for higher development. The same effect will be produced in the character, and all awakened minds know that the greatness of the soul can begin to come forth only when we have completely forgiven everybody for everything.

The man who finds it easier to forgive than to condemn is on the verge of superior wisdom and higher spiritual power. He has entered the path to real greatness and may rapidly rise in the scale by applying the laws of true human development. Instead of producing weakness and indifference the act of absolute forgiveness will produce a more powerful character, a more brilliant mind and a greater soul. Try this method for a year. Forgive everybody for everything, no matter what happens, and do not forget to forgive yourself. You will then conclude that forgiveness, absolute forgiveness, is not only the path to complete emancipation, but is also the "gates ajar" to a better life, a larger life, a richer life, a more beautiful life than you ever knew before. You will find that you can instantaneously remove disease from the body, perversion and wrong from the mind by complete and unrestricted forgiveness; and you can in the same way steadily recreate yourself into a new and better being. Forgive the imperfect, and with heart and soul desire constantly the realization of the perfect; the imperfect will thus pass away and the more perfect will be realized in a greater and greater abundance.

Whatever our place in life may be, we must eliminate every burden of mind or body, if we wish to rise in the scale, and the first step in this direction is to forgive everybody for everything. When you begin to practice forgiveness on this extensive scale you will find obstacles disappearing one after the other. Those things that held you down will vanish and that which was constantly in your way will trouble you no more; your pathway will be cleared. You will have nothing more to contend with, and everything in your life will move smoothly and harmoniously toward greater and greater things. This is perfectly natural, because by forgiving everybody and everything you have let every form of evil go. You have invited all the good, and have therefore populated your own world with persons and things after your own heart. Through perpetual and complete forgiveness your mind will be kept perfectly clean. Not a single weed will ever appear in the beautiful garden of your mind, and so long as the mind is clean neither sickness nor adversity can exist in human life. This may be a strong statement, but those who will try the principle and continue to live it will find it to be the truth.

Since forgiveness is a necessity to all who wish to eliminate the lesser and retain the greater, or in other words make real the ideal, it will be highly important to present the simplest methods through which anyone may learn to practice this great art. It has been said that to know all is to forgive all; but it is not possible for anyone to know all. Therefore, if we wish to forgive absolutely, we must proceed along a different line. When we ask ourselves why people live, think and act as they do we meet the great law of cause and effect. In our study of this law we find that every cause is an effect of a previous cause, and that that previous cause is also an effect of a cause still more remote. We may continue to trace these causes and effects far back along the chain of events until we are lost in the dimness of the past; but what do we learn by such a process of analysis? Nothing whatever. We fail to find anything definite about anybody, and consequently cannot fix the blame for anything; but it is not possible to justly blame anybody when we cannot fix the blame for anything. Therefore, we have only one alternative, and that is to forgive. We can never find the real cause of a single thing. We may first blame the individual, but when we discover the influence of environment, heredity and early training we cannot wholly blame the individual. If we blame the parents, we must find the reason why those parents were not different, also why previous generations were not different. If we accept the theory that the individual has lived before and that he came into his present environments because he was what he was in a previous state of existence, we must explain why he did not live a different life in that other existence; why did he act in such a manner in the past that he should merit adversity and weakness in the present. If he knew no better in the past, what is the reason that he did not know any better? If we accept the belief that we have all inherited our perverted tendencies from Adam and Eve, we must explain why those two souls were not strong enough to rise above temptation. If they were tempted, we must explain why; we must explain why the original man who was created in the image and likeness of God did not express his divine nature in the midst of temptation. But there is no way in which we can explain these things; therefore, to fix the blame for anything is absolutely impossible.

The more we try to find the original cause of anything the more convinced we become that to look for sin or the cause of sin is nothing but a waste of time. Every individual is himself a cause, and his life comes constantly in touch with a number of other causes; therefore, it is never possible to say which one of these causes or combination of these causes produced the original action. Back of every action we find other actions that lead us to the one that we may now consider, but we do not know how those other actions were produced. To trace them back to their original source simply leads us into what appears to be a beginningless beginning. For this reason it is the height of wisdom to let the "dead bury its dead," to let the past go, to forgive every sinner and forget every sin, and to use our time, talent and power for the building of more lofty mansions in the great eternal now. To look for the blame is to find that we are all more or less to blame, and also to find that there is no real fixed blame anywhere. We may then ask what we are to do with this great subject; are we to talk, theorize, speculate, condemn and punish? We know too well that all of that is but a waste of time. The sensible course to pursue is to forgive everybody for everything, to drop ills, mistakes, wrongs, disagreeable memories and proceed to use those laws of life that we understand now in making life better for everybody now.

The man who is habitually doing wrong is mentally or morally sick. Punishment is a waste of time; besides, it is absolutely wrong, and one wrong cannot remove another. Such a person should be taken where he can be healed and kept there until he is well. We should not hate him or condemn him any more than those who are physically sick. Sickness is sickness whether it appears in the body, the mind or the character, and he who is sick does not need a prison; he needs a physician. To absolutely remove this hatred for the wrong-doers in the world we must cultivate a higher order of love, that love that loves every living creature with the true love of the soul, and such a love is readily attained when we train ourselves to look for the ideal soul of life that exists in everything everywhere in the world. This idea may cause many to come to the conclusion that the act of forgiving the wrong-doer will have an undesirable effect upon society, because we may be liable to let people in general do as they please; but in this they are wholly mistaken. Reason declares that you cannot justly blame anyone, and love does not wish to blame anyone; forgiveness must therefore inevitably follow when reason and love are truly combined; but reason and love will never permit man in general to do as he pleases. When we love people we are not indifferent about their future. We do not wish them to go down grade. We want them to improve, to do the right and the best and we will do everything in our power to emancipate and elevate the entire race. Reason understands how the laws of life can be applied in producing those results we may have in view; therefore, the desires of love can be carried out through the understanding of reason, and thus every high purpose may be promoted by the right spirit and the proper methods. Others may declare that these methods are in advance of our time and cannot be carried out at present; therefore, it is useless to even talk about it. However, be that as it may, the fact remains that forgiveness is a necessity to the true life, the emancipated life, the superior life, the ideal life. For that reason every person who desires to make real the ideal in his world must begin to practice absolute forgiveness at once. If we can forgive everybody for everything now, we should do so, whether the world in general can do so or not. The man who wishes to move forward must not wait for the race. It is his privilege to go in advance of the race; thus he prepares the way for millions.

When he has demonstrated by example that there are better ways of living, the race will follow. What the few can do to-day the many will do to-morrow, but if the few should wait until tomorrow, the many would have to wait until the day following, or possibly longer still. Be what you can be now. Do what you can do now, no matter how far in advance of this age such actions may be. If you are capable of greater things to-day, you owe it to the race to demonstrate those greater things now. You sprung from the race. You are composed of the finer elements that exist in the race, and should consider it a privilege to cause those elements to shine as brilliantly as possible; and one of the greatest of all demonstrations in this age is that of absolute forgiveness, to demonstrate the power of forgiving everybody for everything at all times and under every possible circumstance. We therefore conclude that complete emancipation from everything that is not desired in life can be realized only when we forgive absolutely in this great universal sense; and when we have forgiven everybody for everything, then we can say with the great Master Mind, "My yoke is easy and my burden is light."

CHAPTER VII

PATHS TO PERPETUAL INCREASE

The universe is overflowing with all manner of good things and there is enough to supply every wish of every heart with abundance still remaining. How every heart is to proceed, however, that its every wish may be supplied, has been the problem, but the solution is simple. In consequence, everybody may rejoice. This world is not a "vale of tears," but is in truth a most delightful place, and is endowed with everything that is needful to make the life of man an endless song. We now know that we do not live to be miserable, but to rejoice. The bitterness that sometimes appears in life is not a real part of life. The greatness of existence alone is intended for man. To know the bitter from the sweet and to appropriate the latter and always reject the former is a matter, however, that is not clearly understood. There may be thousands who know the bitter when they see it, but they do not always know how to reject it. To throw off the ills of life is an art that few have mastered. But those who can eliminate the wrong are not always able to distinguish the right from the wrong, the reason being that we have not looked at things from the view-point of that power that produces things. The philosophers, the theologians and the scientists, as a rule, make life very complex and difficult to live. Their profound expressions confuse the multitudes, while ills and troubles continue as before; but to live is simple. Even a child can be happy; it therefore should not be difficult for anyone else.

When we realize happiness in its highest, broadest sense, we find that it comes in its fulness only when we have everything that the heart desires; and since the desires of the heart increase in size and number with the enlargement of life, the joy of living will increase in proportion providing all the desires of the heart are supplied. This fact, however, may at first sight seem to make happiness very difficult to secure. If we cannot enjoy the allness of joy until we have everything that heart can wish for, then happiness is far away; so it may seem, but things are not always what they seem. All things are possible, and the most difficult things become comparatively easy when we know how; therefore, the way of wisdom is not to look for those difficulties that ignorance has connected with things, but look for that simplicity that is the soul of all knowledge. When we learn to do things as they should be done, all difficulties disappear, and even the largest life becomes simple.

The doing of things is the universal theme in this age. Those who simply tell us what to do are no longer acceptable. We want practical instructions that tell us how. The greatest man of this age and of the future will not be the one who can move as he wishes the emotions of multitudes by the magic art of eloquence and bring whole nations to his feet by the artistic juggling of eloquent phrases. The great man will henceforth be the man who can tell us how, and who can express himself so clearly that anyone can understand. This, however, we are now beginning to do, and ere long the many will come back to the truth itself and understand the real truth in all its original simplicity. The path of truth and life is perfectly straight and is illumined all the way. It is therefore simplicity itself to follow this path when we find it, but the many have strayed into the jungles of illusions and misconceptions. These must all come back to the simple path, and when they do the difficulty of living will wholly disappear.

To teach the race how to find the simple things, the true things and the real things is now the purpose of every original thinker, and whoever can add to the world's wisdom in this respect becomes a light to the race, indeed. One of the first principles in this new understanding of things is that which deals with man's power to place himself in perfect touch with the source of limitless supply; in other words to enter the path of perpetual increase. As previously stated, the world is overflowing with good things, because life is in touch with the limitless source of all good things, and there is so much of everything that the wish of every heart can be gratified. We do not have to take from another to have abundance, because there is more than sufficient for all. The fact that some one has abundance does not prove that he has taken some or all of his wealth from others, although this is what a great many believe to be the truth. Whenever we see some one in luxury we wonder where and how he got it, and we usually add that many are in poverty because this one is in wealth. Such doctrine, however, is not true. It is thoroughly false from beginning to end. The world is not so poverty stricken that the few cannot have plenty without stealing from the many. The universe is not so bare and so limited that multitudes are reduced to want whenever a few persons undertake to surround themselves with those things that have beauty and worth. True, there is injustice in the world. There are people who have secured their wealth, not upon merit, but through the art of reducing others to want; but the remedy is not to be found in the doctrine that thousands must necessarily become poor when one becomes very rich. This doctrine is an illusion, and illusions cannot serve as foundations for a better order. There is enough in life to give every living person all the wealth and all the luxury that he can possibly appropriate.

God is rich; the universe is overflowing with abundance. If we have not everything that we want, there is a reason; there is some definite cause somewhere, either in ourselves or in our relations to the world, but this cause can be found and corrected; then we may proceed to take possession of our own. Among the many causes of poverty and the lack of a full supply there is one that has been entirely overlooked. To overcome this cause is to find one of the most important paths to perpetual increase, and the remedy lies within easy reach of everyone who has awakened to a degree the finer elements in his life.

There may be exceptions to the rule, but there are thousands who are living on the husks of existence because they were not grateful when the kernels were received. Multitudes continue in poverty from no other cause than a lack of gratitude, and other thousands who have almost everything that the heart may wish for do not reach the coveted goal of full supply because their gratitude is not complete.

We are now beginning to realize more and more that the greatest thing in the world is to live so closely to the Infinite that we constantly feel the power and the peace of His presence. In fact, this mode of living is the very secret of secrets revealing everything that the mind may wish to know or understand in order to make life what it is intended to be. We also realize that the more closely we live to the Infinite the more we shall receive of all good things, because all good things have their source in the Supreme; but how to enter into this life of supreme oneness with the Most High is a problem. There are many things to be done in order to solve this problem, but there is no one thing that is more important in producing the required solution than deep, whole-souled gratitude. The soul that is always grateful lives nearer the true, the good, the beautiful and the perfect than anyone else in existence, and the more closely we live to the good and the beautiful the more we shall receive of all those things. The mind that dwells constantly in the presence of true worth is daily adding to his own worth. He is gradually and steadily appropriating that worth with which he is in constant contact; but we cannot enter into the real presence of true worth unless we fully appreciate the real worth of true worth; and all appreciation is based upon gratitude.

The more grateful we are for the good things that come to us now the more good things we shall receive in the future. This is a great metaphysical law, and we shall find it most profitable to comply exactly with this law, no matter what the circumstances may be. Be grateful for everything and you will constantly receive more of everything; thus the simple act of being grateful becomes a path to perpetual increase. The reason why is found in the fact that whenever you enter into the mental attitude of real gratitude your mind is drawn into much closer contact with that power that produces the good things received. In other words, to be grateful for what we have received is to draw more closely to the source of that which we receive. The good things that come to us come because we have properly employed certain laws, and when we are grateful for the results gained we enter into more perfect harmony with those laws and thus become able to employ those laws to still greater advantage in the immediate future. This anyone can understand, and those who do not know that gratitude produces this effect should try it and watch results.

The attitude of gratitude brings the whole mind into more perfect and more harmonious relations with all the laws and powers of life. The grateful mind gains a firmer hold, so to speak, upon those things in life that can produce increase. This is simply illustrated in personal experience where we find that we always feel nearer to that person to whom we express real gratitude. When you thank a person and truly mean it with heart and soul you feel nearer to that person than you ever did before. Likewise, when we express whole-souled thanksgiving to everything and everybody for everything that comes into life we draw closer and closer to all the elements and powers of life. In other words, we draw closer to the real source from which all good things in life proceed.

When we consider this principle from another point of view we find that the act of being grateful is an absolute necessity, if we wish to accomplish as much as we have the power to accomplish. To be grateful in this large, universal sense is to enter into harmony and contact with the greatest, the highest and the best in life. We thus gain possession of the superior elements of mind and soul and, in consequence, gain the power to become more and achieve more, no matter what our object or work may be. Everything that

will place us in a more perfect relation with life, and thus enable us to appropriate the greater richness of life, should be employed with the greatest
of earnestness, and deep whole-souled gratitude does possess a marvelous
power in this respect. Its great value, however, is not confined to the laws
just mentioned. Its power is exceptional in another and equally important field.

To be grateful is to think of the best, therefore the grateful mind keeps
the eye constantly upon the best; and, according to another metaphysical
law, we grow into the likeness of that which we think of the most. The
mind that is always dissatisfied fixes attention upon the common, the ordinary and the inferior, and thus grows into the likeness of those things. The
creative forces within us are constantly making us just like those things
upon which we habitually concentrate attention. Therefore, to mentally
dwell upon the inferior is to become inferior, while to keep the eye single
upon the best is to daily become better. The grateful mind is constantly
looking for the best, thus holding attention upon the best and daily growing
into the likeness of the best. The grateful mind expects only good things,
and will always secure good things out of everything that comes. What we
constantly expect we receive, and when we constantly expect to get good
out of everything we cause everything to produce good. Therefore, to the
grateful mind all things will at all times work together for good, and this
means perpetual increase in everything that can add to the happiness and
the welfare of man. This being true, and anyone can prove it to be true, the
proper course to pursue is to cultivate the habit of being grateful for everything that comes. Give thanks eternally to the Most High for everything
and feel deeply grateful every moment to every living creature. All things
are so situated that they can be of some service to us, and all things have
somewhere at sometime been instrumental in adding to our welfare. We
must therefore, to be just and true, express perpetual gratitude to everything that has existence. Be thankful to yourself. Be thankful to every soul
in the world, and most of all be thankful to the Creator of all that is. Live
in perpetual thanksgiving to all the world, and express the deepest, sincer-
est, most whole-souled gratitude you can feel within whenever something
of value comes into your life.

When other things come, pass them by; never mind them in the least.
You know that the good in greater and greater abundance is eternally coming into your life, and for this give thanks with rejoicing; you know that
every wish of the heart is being supplied; be thankful that this is true, and
you will draw nearer and nearer to that place in life where that can be real-

ized that you know is on the way to realization. Live according to this principle for a brief period of time, and the result will be that your life will change for the better to such a degree that you will feel infinitely more grateful than you ever felt before. You will then find that thanksgiving is a necessary part of real living, and you will also find that the more grateful you are for every ideal that has been made real, the more power you gain to press on to those greater heights where you will find every ideal to be real. And when this realization begins you are on the path to perpetual increase, because the more you receive the more grateful you feel, and the more grateful you feel for that which has been received the more closely you will live to that Source that can give you more.

CHAPTER VIII

CONSIDER THE LILIES

Consider the lilies of the field, how they grow; they toil not, neither do they spin; yet I say unto you, that even Solomon in all his glory was not arrayed like one of these.—Mat. 6: 28, 29.

The greatest service that anyone can render to the race is to properly fill the place he occupies now, to be himself to-day; but it is not only others that will benefit by such individual actions. The individual himself will receive greater good from life through this method than through all other methods combined. The great secret of secrets is to live your own life in your own world as well as you possibly can now. In this age thousands are seeking the path of spiritual growth and high intellectual attainments, while millions are dreaming of the life beautiful; accordingly, systems almost without number are springing up everywhere, claiming to reveal the hidden path to these greater goals; but it is the truth that when everything has been said, the one statement that rises above them all is this: *Be all that you are to-day and you shall be even more to-morrow.* If you are in search of higher spiritual and intellectual attainments enter into every form of wisdom that surrounds you to-day and fill your life with as much spirit as you can possibly realize. If you wish to live an ideal life, then aim to make real the most beautiful life that you can think of to-day. If you are longing for greater accomplishments and a larger sphere of usefulness, then be your very best in the place that you occupy now.

The mighty oak grows great because it grows in the present; it does not think of the past or the future; it is what it is now; it does not wish to become mighty; it simply grows on silently and continually. The lily of the field is beautiful because it is perfectly satisfied to be a lily, but it is not satisfied to be less than all a lily can be. It does not strive or work hard to become beautiful; it simply goes on being what it is, and the result is it has been made immortal by the greatest mind that ever lived. When we follow the example of the lily we find the real secret of life, so simply and clearly stated that any one can understand. Be what you are to-day. *Do not be satisfied to be less than you can to-day and do not strive to be more.* Progress, growth, advancement, attainment—these do not come through overreaching. The mind that overreaches will have a reaction; he will fall to the bottom and will have to begin all over again. Real attainment comes by being your best where you are just for to-day, by filling the pesent moment with all the life you are conscious of; no more. If you try to express more life than you can comfortably feel in consciousness, you are overreaching and you will have a fall. The great mistake of the age is to strive, to go about our work as if it were extremely difficult. The man who works the hardest usually accomplishes the least; while the truly great man is the man who has trained his life and his power to work through him.

The lilies of the field are not engaged in hard labor, and yet their usefulness cannot be measured; they are fulfilling their true purpose; they are making real the ideal in their own world and they are living inspirations to every soul in existence. They live to be beautiful and they become beautiful, not by being ambitious for beauty, but by permitting all the beauty they possess to come forth. What is within us is constantly pressing for expression. We do not have to call it forth nor labor so much to bring it into action. All we are required to do is to permit ourselves to be what we are, to permit what is within to express itself fully and completely. We do not have to work so hard to become great. We are all naturally great, and our potential greatness is ever ready to manifest, if we would only cease our striving and let life live. The lily is beautiful because it does not hinder its own inherent beauty from coming forth to be seen; but if the lily should take up the strenuous life it would in one generation become a despised weed. The human race to-day resembles in too many instances the useless weed. Millions in every generation come and go without accomplishing anything whatever. They do not even live a life that gives contentment. The reason is they strive too much, and in their striving destroy the very powers that can produce greatness. We have worked hard for results, not knowing that the only cause of results was within us, ready to produce the very results we desired, just for the asking. We have in many instances destroyed our brains trying to invent methods for producing health, happiness, power and success, not knowing that these things already existed within us in abundant supply, and that by wholesome thinking they would appear in full external expression.

The secret of secrets is to let the best within us have full right of way; this, however, most of us have failed to do. In consequence, the majority are undeveloped weaklings of little use to themselves or to the world. The lily permits that which *is* to have right of way. It does not interfere, but man does interfere. He usually refuses to accept the gifts which nature wishes to bestow upon him, and he hardly ever accepts assistance from a higher power. He sets out for himself and works himself into old age and death trying to gain what was actually given to him in the beginning. He leaves the real riches of life and enters the world of personal ambition expecting to find something better and create something superior through his own efforts, but he fails because man alone can do nothing. The average person does not realize that to create something from nothing is impossible, nor has he learned that the necessary something can come only from the life that is within. He may try to accomplish much and become much through personal ambition and hard work, but no one can build without material, and the material that is needed in building greatness can be secured only by giving right of way to the life and the power of the inner world. The man who expects to build greatness upon personal limitations will pass away in the effort, leaving his unfinished work to be taken up by some one else who will possibly build upon the same useless foundation. Thus one generation after another comes and goes, each expecting to succeed where predecessors failed; in the meantime very little is accomplished by man, and he fails to receive what infinite life is ever waiting to give.

This is the truth about man in general. The multitudes have come and gone during countless ages and have accomplished but little. There have been a few great exceptions in every age, but these were exceptions because they refused to follow the ways of the world. They learned the lesson that the lilies have taught, and they chose to let life live, to let the greatness from within come forth, to let power work, and to let that which *is* in the real of man have full right of way. When a person discovers what he is and permits that which he is to have full expression, his days of weariness, trouble and failure are gone. Henceforth he will live as the flower. His life will be full. He will fulfill his purpose and eternally become more and more of that which already is in the great within. When a flower, which has so little of soul within itself, can become so much by permitting itself to be itself, how much more might man become if he would permit himself to be himself. Man is created in the image of God, therefore marvels are hidden within his wonderful soul. When these marvels are given full expression then man begins to become that which the Infinite intended that he should be. In the soul of the lily is hidden the spirit of beauty; nothing more. But the lily does not hinder this spirit from appearing in visible form; therefore, it becomes an inspiration of joy to all the world. In the soul of man even the Infinite is hidden; we can therefore imagine what man will become when he permits the spirit of divinity to express itself in his personal form. This is a great truth, indeed, and deserves constant attention from every mind that has learned to think.

We may believe that every step forward that we have taken has been produced through personal efforts and hard work, but in this we are mistaken. In the first place, those achievements that have followed hard work are always insignificant and never of any permanent value, but those steps forward that have permanent value and that are truly great we find were taken during those moments when we permitted real life to live. We therefore find that striving accomplishes nothing, while we may through *living*, accomplish anything. There are times when many of us cease our strenuous labor for a few moments and unconsciously open our souls to that higher something that we feel so much the need of when wearied with misdirected labors, and the influx of real life that comes at such times is the cause of those real steps upward and onward that we have taken. At such times we chose to be like the lily; we permitted the good that was to come forth; we gave up, so to speak, to higher power and did not interfere with its highest, fullest expression. What we gain at such moments is always with us and never fails to give us strength, power and inspiration even when we decide for the time being to adopt the ways of the world once more. But since every step in advance comes when we refuse to go the way of the world, we should now understand that the way of the world is a mistake. We should therefore free ourselves from that mode of life, thought and action absolutely.

The world seeks to gain greater things through personal ambition and hard work. The true way to attain greater things is to permit the greatness that is within to have full expression; likewise when we seek health, happiness and harmony or a beautiful life, the true course is to permit those things to come forth and act through us; they are ready to appear. We do not have to work for them or strive so hard to secure them. They are now at hand and will express themselves through us the very moment we grant them permission. We have all discovered that whenever we become perfectly still and permit supreme life to live in us we can feel power accumulating in our system until we feel as if we could move mountains. We have also felt that while turning attention to the everlasting joy within and opening the mind fully to this joy that there came into being a state of happiness, comfort and contentment that seemed infinitely more perfect than the imagination has ever pictured the joys of heaven to be. Likewise when we failed to find health in the without or through external means we invariably found the precious gift coming from within, the moment we gave up, so to speak, to its wholesome life and power.

In this age personal ambition is one of the ruling factors, and nearly everybody is trying to outdo some one else. The result is we build up and tear down in the outer world, but as a race we improve but little. The great within is ignored, held back or prevented from free expression, while there are few things in the great without that are really worth while. There never was a time when we should consider the lilies of the field more than now. The human race is breaking itself down striving to gain hold upon phantoms, while the great prize that has already been given is lost sight of in the dust and confusion. But to inspire the present generation with a desire to return to nature and her beautiful ways cannot be done to any extent, however, except through living examples. It is the living of life that will change the life of the world. The world at large does not listen to reason, nor can those who are in the mad rush stop to think; besides, such minds are not sufficiently clear to understand the principles upon which the living of life is based. Seeing is believing, as far as the world is concerned, and therefore they require living examples of those who have proven the superiority of the better way; accordingly, those who know how to live as the lilies live should consider it a privilege to place their light wherever it can be seen. When you can prove through your own life and experience that personal ambition and hard work are not necessary to greater things, but are actual hindrances, and that greater things come of themselves to those who will permit themselves to *be* themselves, you have caused a great light to spring up, and few there are who will not see it.

Those who take everything literally may wonder how anything can be accomplished without work, but they must bear in mind that there is work, and work. The work that is done by those who are down in the world's way is hard, wearing and tearing. It is destructive to human life and builds up one thing by tearing down another, and in the end it brings no lasting good, neither to the individual nor to the race; but the work that is done by those who have found the better way is neither hard nor wearisome. It is not done through strenuous living nor external striving, but is done by the power of the great within coming forth into expression in personal life. In this mode of work you first give your inner power right of way, then you direct it consciously and intelligently. You do not depend upon personal power and difficult personal efforts. You place yourself in the hands of higher power, and as you receive higher power you cause it to do that which you wish to have done. You have all felt power working through you, and at such times work was pleasure. You gave the commands, of course, and you knew it was your own power, your own higher power, but no hard personal effort was required. You simply opened the way somehow, then decided firmly but gently what you wished to have done; and you could feel a mighty power coming forth, seemingly from an inexhaustible source, taking full possession of thought and muscle, and doing the very thing you desired to have done. After the work was finished you discovered it was superior work, and although you had engaged in the task for many hours you actually felt stronger than when you began.

The reason why is simple. You did not depend upon personal limitations and strenuous efforts; and you did not try to make those limitations do a great deal more than they had the capacity to do. You opened your life to all the power of your life and you thus received enough power to do what you wished to have done, and more; and so long as you have power to spare you can be neither weak nor tired. When the system is thoroughly full of energy, work is a pleasure; and so long as that fullness continues weariness is impossible; and there is enough power in real life to cause your system to be full of energy, and more, at all times no matter how much you may do or how great your task may be.

When we consider the lilies of the field, how they grow, we find that they naturally permit the life that is within them to unfold; they do not try to grow; they have, as everything has, the power of growth within them and they grow because they do not hinder that interior power and growth from having their way. Likewise, when we know that divinity reigns within us we do not have to work hard nor many years to reach that state. We will grow and develop, both mentally and spiritually, when we permit the divinity within to unfold. Everything seeks self-expression. Nothing in nature, visible or invisible, will have to be forced into expression, because at the very heart of all things there is the deep, strong desire to come forth and be. Therefore, if we wish to ascend in the scale of life, we must cease those confused and destructive states of mind that hinder expression, and become as the lilies of the field. Give the life within permission to really live in us. The life within will live our life and give us a beautiful life. The power within will do our work and do that work extremely well. The divinity within will make us God-like in all things, and never cease to give us the things of the spirit so long as we permit those things to come forth and abide in personal existence.

What we are required to do that such things may come to pass is to live, think and act in the likeness of the Infinite. God *is*, and He permits Himself to be what He *is*. Man must do likewise, and all shall be well with him. Those who do not understand may think that the individuality of man might diminish, if he were to give himself up to the life and the power within, but such a conclusion will disappear when we realize that the power from within is our own. We are simply causing ourselves to become more and more of what we already are in reality. By giving free expression to our own higher, interior powers we naturally become more powerful, and by giving free expression to our own inherent divinity we naturally become more God-like and more spiritual on every plane of being. The lilies of the field do not become inferior lilies by permitting the spirit of the beautiful to unfold from within their gentle lives. It is by this method that they become what they are, and they become so much that the glory of artificial man can never compare with theirs. It is the same with the human soul. The soul becomes great and beautiful by permitting its own greatness and loveliness to come forth unhindered and undisturbed.

Thousands of people are at present trying to develop higher powers. Many of these actually try to work hard in their efforts to gain the various gifts of mind and soul, and because they do not succeed to any great extent they frequently become discouraged and give up, wondering whether or no the real truth has been found. Others being ambitious to become great in the world try to employ spiritual laws in the furthering of their personal aims, but they find the reactions so disagreeable that the prize is not worth the labor. To fly to the top at once is the ruling passion among many and when they fail with whatever methods they may employ they conclude that what passes for truth is nothing but man-made doctrines. The fact is, however, that the truth always appears to be the untruth when misdirected. To apply the principles of real truth in the furthering of any lofty aim we may have in mind, the first essential is to establish life in perfect touch with eternal life; the second essential is to positively determine what we expect to attain and become in actual personal living; and the third essential is to proceed in the attainment of health, happiness and harmony. Without health nothing of permanent value can be accomplished. Without happiness our talents will be as the flowers without sunshine, and without harmony most of the power we might receive would be thrown away.

To obtain health, happiness and harmony we need simply let life live. Real life already has these things, and when we let life live in us those things will be expressed through us. The next essential is to resolve that we will be fully contented simply to live. To shine in the world, to acquire fame or to do something wonderful that mankind may long remember us, that we will not think of. Many a person has worked hard for fame and died early, in obscurity. Fame in itself, however, is of no value. When you are neither happy nor well, fame cannot make your life worth while. If you are miserable, it will profit nothing if everybody may know your name. It is not the praise of man that we should seek, but the life of the Infinite. The praise of the world can give us nothing, but life from within can give us everything that the heart can wish for.

True fame comes to him who deserves it without his trying to get it, but those only can deserve the honor of the race who have always been their best, who have not neglected a single opportunity to be of service, and who have lived constantly for the one purpose of being an inspiration to every soul. We may look at this phase of the subject as we may, we can come to only one conclusion. He alone is great and deserving of honor who so lives that he always is all that God made him to be; and it is such a life that is lived by the lilies of the field. When man will be as true to his large world as the lilies are to their small world, mankind will become a race of gods indeed, and the Utopian dreams of the prophets will come true. This, however, the ordinary thinker may declare to be impossible, but nothing is impossible. If a flower can be true to itself in its world, man can be true to himself in his world.

Those who are accustomed to the worldly methods of thinking and working may feel that it is hardly possible to apply these new ideas while associated with worldly minds, but we must remember that it is not where we work or at what we work, but how we work that determines what results are to be. To so work that you permit the boundless power within to work through you is the secret, and this will not only cause your work to be pleasant, but will also cause you to do better and better work every day. It is therefore the royal path to pleasantness to-day and greater things to-morrow. In the old way you are compelled to almost wear yourself out to-day in order that you might provide for to-morrow; but not so in the new. While you are providing for tomorrow you are not only enjoying life to-day, but you are, through the expression of greater and greater power from within, making yourself larger, stronger and greater to-day. In the development of talents you employ the same principle. You do not strive for greatness; you know that you are potentially great already, and by permitting this greatness to become alive in you, you will accomplish great things.

When you apply this principle in everything that you do, you will find your advancement to be steady and even rapid; you will move forward in all things, making the ideal real as you ascend in the scale. The very moment you find a new ideal you find that power within you that can make that ideal real; thus your advancement becomes continuous, your progress eternal. To live the life beautiful we simply let life live. We know that life, itself, is beautiful and when we permit that life that is beautiful to live in us, we will live consciously and personally the most beautiful life that we can picture in the ideal without making any personal effort to do so. When we begin to live, think and act according to these principles we feel that we are carried on and on by some mysterious presence that seems to be doing everything for us while giving us the pleasure and the glory. We soon learn, however, that this presence is ourself, our own larger, superior self created in the image of God; therefore, able to do everything that we may wish to have done; and it is a joy, indeed, to feel everything moving so smoothly and gently, so harmoniously and pleasantly, and at the same time producing such great results.

To engage in some extraordinary work becomes one of our greatest pleasures, because nothing is hard or difficult any more; obstacles disappear the very moment we enter their presence, and we realize inwardly that whatever we undertake to do will be accomplished. We no longer tremble when in the midst of events that require exceptional wisdom and power; we know that wisdom is ready to speak whatever may be necessary now, and that power is at hand to do whatever may be necessary to be done now. We are in touch with the greatness of the great within and may draw upon that great, inexhaustible source whatever we may need at any time. Fear takes flight, while faith becomes stronger, higher and more perfect; sorrow and despair are no more, because all things are working for the best. Even in the presence of death and loss we see more life and greater gain. We know that what passes away merely ascends that it may live more and be itself in a larger, higher measure than it ever was before. We know that whatever comes will bring the new and the more beautiful. It could not be otherwise, because having chosen to be all that we are, the all can never cease to come, and the more the all continues to come the more the all will continue to bring. We have laid aside the illusions of the world and adopted the ways of truth. We have beheld the beauties of nature and have opened our minds to the visions of the soul. These have given us the secret, and like the lilies of the field, we have learned to be still and live.

CHAPTER IX

COUNT IT ALL JOY

We meet something at almost every turn that we think ought to be different. If we have high ideals, we may not feel satisfied to permit those conditions to remain as they are; we may even complain or antagonize. On the other hand, if our ideals be low, we may feel wholly indifferent, but then we find that those things go from bad to worse. What we seek, however, is our present comfort on the one hand and the betterment of everything about us on the other hand, and we wish to know how this may be brought about in the midst of the confusion, the ignorance and the ills that we find in the world. When we are indifferent to the wrong it becomes worse; therefore, even for our own good we must do something with those adverse conditions that exist in the home, in society, or in the state. We must meet all those things and meet them properly, but the problem is, how?

To antagonize, criticize or condemn never helps matters in the least; besides, such states of mind are a detriment to one's own peace and health. The critical mind wears itself out while thinking about the wrong, but the wrong in the meantime goes on becoming worse. To feel disappointed because the universe does not move according to our fancy will not change the universe, but it will produce weakness in our own mind and body. That person who lives constantly in the world of despondency will soon lose all hold upon life; he consequently does nothing in the world but bring about the end of his own personal life. The usual way of dealing with the problems of life solves nothing. The ordinary way of meeting temptation gives the tempter greater power, while the person who tries to resist is usually entrapped in adversity and trouble. But St. James has told us what to do under all such circumstances. *Count it all joy.* That is the secret. Count it all joy no matter what may come, agreeing with all adversity at once, antagonizing nothing, condemning no one, leaving criticism alone. Never be disappointed or discouraged, and have nothing whatever to do with worry. Whatever comes, count it all joy. He who meets adversity in the attitude of peace, harmony and joy will turn enemies into friends and failures into greater good.

When things do not come your way, never mind. Continue to count everything joy, and everything will change in such a manner as to give you joy. If you are seeking the best, all things will work together in such a way as to give you the best, and your heart's desire shall be realized; possibly not to-day, but life is long; you can wait. That which is good is always good; it is always welcome whenever it comes. In the meantime you are living in harmony and joy, and that in itself is surely a great good. That person who lives constantly in gloom drives even the sunshine out of his own mind; the clouds of gloom are so heavy that he fails to see the brightness that is all about him. That person, however, who counts everything joy will change everything to brightness and thus receive joy from everything. When you fail to receive what you sought, never for a moment be disappointed. Count it all joy. In fact, be supremely happy; you have a reason so to be. When you fail to get what you seek it simply means that there is something still better in store for you; then why should you not count such an event great joy. This is always the case when your whole desire is to receive the best; and when you train yourself to count everything joy, your mind develops that desire that always desires the best.

When you seek only the best, the best only will come, and you must not feel disappointed when you are taken away from a hovel in order that you may enter a palace. When you meet enemies or adversaries do not resist them or enter into warfare; look for terms of agreement. Possibly they may seem to get the best of the bargain now, but you can afford to give them the terms they ask. The Infinite is your supply. When one door closes another opens, and if you depend upon the Supreme to open that other door, it will be a door opening into far greater and far better things than what you seemingly lost; besides, by being kind to your adversary you lifted yourself up. You are now a higher and a greater being. That means that you will now draw to yourself higher and better things; consequently, it was not the enemy that got the best terms; it was you.

Whatever you are called upon to do, do it and be happy. Count it all joy that you are given the opportunity to bring sunshine into dark places and develop your own latent power by doing what seemed difficult. You are equal to the occasion, if you think so; therefore you should consider it a privilege to prove it. The world is waiting for great souls—souls that are ready to do what others failed to accomplish. You can become one of these great souls by proving to yourself that you are equal to every occasion; and you will be equal to every occasion, if you count everything joy. When you are in the midst of temptations, rejoice with your whole heart. You have found a great opportunity to turn wrong into right, and to turn wrong into right is always a mark of greatness. Millions of people have died unhonored and unsung who might have arisen to greatness and become leaders and saviors in the world, if they would have demonstrated their superiority in the midst of temptation, tribulation and wrong. Look upon all temptations and troubles as opportunities to make wrong right, and be glad that such opportunities have been presented to you. Count it all joy; besides, the result will not only produce joy to yourself, but possibly to millions. He who changes wrong into right rises in the scale, and you can think of no greater good coming to you than this. He who remains below must be counted with the small and the ordinary. He who goes up higher shall gain everything that his heart may wish for. Therefore, whatever comes, or whatever you meet, or whatever you are called upon to do, proceed with peace and joy. Be glad that you have the opportunity to prove your own power, and thus elevate yourself thereby. Be supremely happy to know that you may change many things for the better through this attitude, and thus bless the lives of multitudes.

Train yourself to look at things according to this principle, and you will find that everything can produce joy. Everything can give cause for rejoicing; that is, providing everything is met in that attitude that counts everything joy. The same principle may be employed to great advantage in overcoming difficulties. When you are asked to do what seems to be very difficult, or when you are called upon to perform duties you do not like, never refuse. Count it all joy. To excuse yourself when such occasions appear is to lose most valuable opportunities. Every person desires to make the most of himself, but to accomplish this all latent power must be awakened, and there is nothing that will bring forth our latent powers more thoroughly than the doing of what seems difficult. When you find yourself shrinking from certain tasks you have discovered a weak faculty within yourself. Refuse to let that faculty remain in such a condition. Go and do what you feared to do and let nothing hold you back. In this way the weak faculty will be made strong and your entire nature will pass through most valuable discipline and training. Nothing is really disagreeable unless we think so. That is, we may approach the disagreeable in such a way that it ceases to be disagreeable; and the secret is, count everything joy. You may enter darkness and gloom, but if you are living in a world of brightness and cheer, that darkness will not be darkness to you, nor will gloom enter your mind for a moment. You can remain in your own happy world, no matter what may happen, no matter what may take place in your immediate environment.

When you resolve to do certain things and proceed with a conviction that you will enjoy the work thoroughly, you will find real pleasure in that work; besides, you will do the work very well. Pleasure comes from within, and when the fountain of joy within is overflowing, it will give joy to everything that exists about us. To cause this fountain within to overflow at all times, count everything joy at all times. We should never look for weakness, but when we find it we should proceed at once to change it into strength. Whenever we meet difficulties, or whenever we are called upon to do what we dislike we have found a weakness. We may remove that weakness by doing with a will what the moment demands, and resolve to enjoy it. Never permit such occasions to pass by without being changed. The opportunity is too valuable. Whatever your present sphere of action may require of you, that you are able to do; and the present demand upon your life and your talents must be supplied by you if you would bring out the best that is in you, and make the great eternal now full and complete.

Tasks that seem difficult and demands that seem unreasonable are after all neither difficult nor unreasonable. They are simply golden opportunities for you to become what you never were before. They are but paths to greater achievements, sweeter joys and a larger life. Therefore, when you meet such occasions, count it all joy. When you fail to gain or realize in the present what you expected, do not feel disappointed. Make up your mind to be just as happy in those conditions that are, as you expect to be in those conditions that you are looking for. The feeling of disappointment is not produced by events. It is produced by your own attitude toward events. You can meet all events in such a frame of mind that you never feel disappointed in the least, and that frame of mind is the result of counting everything joy. When you know that eternity is long and that countless joys are in store for you, you will not feel sad now because one insignificant event has been postponed. And when you have full control of your mind you will have the power to produce just as much happiness in the absence of that event as in its presence, because events themselves cannot produce happiness.

The same is true of things. We do not gain joy from things, but from the way we think about things, and we can think as we choose at any time no matter what the circumstance may be. When the present demands happiness from something different than what you were looking for in the present, grasp the opportunity to prove that you are equal to this occasion. You thus develop latent ability. When you count everything joy you know that you can always produce joy. You know that whatever happens is best, because you have the power to cause it to become the best. The best always happens to those who seek only the best; therefore, whatever comes should be received as the best, and we must give it the opportunity to prove that it is better than anything that could have happened. You are not dependent upon events for happiness. Happiness does not come from what we do or where we go. Happiness comes from what we are now or what we create out of what is present now. Whether we be alone in a garret or in a gorgeous ball room the amount of happiness we are to receive in either place will depend entirely upon our own frame of mind. The frame of mind that you desire for the present moment you may have; if it does not come of itself, you can create it; you are the master.

When things do not come the way we like, we can like them the way they are coming. This is how we agree quickly with our adversaries; we thus *receive* the enemy instead of fighting the enemy; and that which we receive in the true attitude of mind becomes our own. Count everything joy and every adversity will give up its power to you. That which is evil becomes good when we meet it in such a way that we draw out of it the best that it may contain, and we always attract the best from everything when we meet everything in the conviction that all things work together for good. When nothing comes to give us happiness in the external we can open the fount of everlasting joy in the great within. The heaven of the soul is ever ready to open its pearly gates, but we must look toward the soul if we would pass through those gates. We shall fail to see the fountain of joy within, however, so long as our whole attention is fixed upon those worldly pleasures that failed to come into our world; but if we count everything joy we no longer feel disappointed about what did not happen; on the other hand we enter into that joyous state of mind that will place us in direct contact with the source of limitless joy within the mind. When people speak unkindly of you, you will become offended if you thought they spoke unkindly, but if your eyes are too pure to behold iniquity you will go on your way as if nothing had been said; you count everything joy and thus you will receive joy from your own lofty position in the matter.

When you are asked to do certain things do not proceed with a feeling that you are compelled to. Go and do it because you want to; say that you want to, and count it all joy. We should never say, "I have a duty to perform," but rather, "Here is an opportunity which I have the privilege to embrace."

Train yourself to want to do whatever your present sphere of life may demand. He who loves and thoroughly enjoys what he is doing to-day will be asked to do greater things to-morrow. The large soul never asks if things are unpleasant or difficult; such thoughts never enter his mind. Whatever he finds to do he proceeds to do, with his mind full of will and his heart full of joy. If you dislike anybody, you have found a weakness in yourself. You have found a difficulty that must be overcome at once. Do not permit such obstacles to remain in your way. The soul that knows no weakness loves everything that God has created. The strong soul never considers those imperfections in life that man has created. Intelligence was not intended to be used in the study of nothingness, illusions or mistakes. When we hate anything we recognize the existence and the power of those things that have neither real existence nor real power; we therefore enter into a confused state of mind. What God has created we cannot help but love, but if we see something else and dislike that something else we are seeing something that God has not created. In other words, we are giving attention to illusions and mistakes, and the mind is not intended for that purpose. Remove the illusion by transforming that hate into love; this will change the point of view. You will thus see things from the upper side, the divine side, and when we look at things from the divine side we find that everything is altogether lovely.

Therefore, when you dislike anybody overcome that weakness by giving that person all the love of your heart. Love that person and *mean* it, no matter what he has said or done. There is nothing in the world that lifts the soul so high above darkness and illusion as strong, pure, spiritual love; and it is not difficult to love a person when you know that he is God's creation, while his mistakes are simply man's creation. Mistakes must be forgiven. Our desire is to do the will of God, and to do the will of God is to love every creature in existence, and to love everything as God loves everything.

CHAPTER X

THE TRUE USE OF
KINDNESS AND SYMPATHY

The ordinary use of sympathy is responsible for a very large portion of the ills and the troubles we find in the world; the reason being that nearly all suffering is mental before it is physical, and that mental suffering is almost invariably produced when we enter into sympathetic touch with the ills that we meet among relations, friends or associates. The average person would suffer but little if he suffered only from the troubles that arise in his own system. It is the pain that is felt through sympathy for others that gives him most of the burdens he finds it necessary to bear. It is considered a sign of kindness, goodness and high regard, however, to sympathize with others in this manner, or rather to suffer with others, but this is not the true use of kindness.

We do not help others by entering into the same weakness that is keeping them in a world of distress. We do not help the weak by becoming weak. We do not relieve sickness by becoming sick. We do not right the wrong by entering into the wrong, or doing wrong. We do not free man from failures by permitting ourselves to become failures. We do not emancipate those who are in bondage to sin by going and committing the same sin. This is very simple; but ordinary sympathy is based upon the idea that we sympathize with a person only when we suffer with that person. We expect to relieve pain by proceeding to produce the same pain in our own systems; but we cannot remove darkness by entering into the dark. We can remove wrong only by removing the cause of that wrong, and to remove the cause of wrong we must produce the cause of right. Darkness disappears when we produce light; likewise, sickness and trouble will vanish when we produce health and harmony, but we cannot produce health and harmony by entering into disease and trouble. This, however, is what ordinary sympathy does; it has, therefore, failed to relieve the world. The ordinary use of sympathy multiplies suffering by making suffering contagious. It causes the suffering of the one to give pain to the many, and then in turn causes the pain of the many to give additional pain to each individual person whose sympathy is aroused in the same connection. We must remove everything that tends to make ills contagious, whether it is physical or mental, and it is very evident that ordinary sympathy does spread pains and ills to a very great degree. Therefore, one of the first essentials in producing emancipation or in making real the ideal is to find the true use of sympathy.

Sympathy itself must not be removed, because it is one of the highest virtues of the soul. The average person, however, misapplies this virtue continuously, and in consequence brings pains and ills both to himself and others, that could easily have been prevented. There is a better use for sympathy, and through this better use we cause all the good things in life to become contagious. Instead of entering into sympathetic touch with the weakness that may temporarily exist in the personality of man we enter into sympathetic touch with the strength that permanently exists in the soul of man. Instead of morbidly dwelling upon the ills and the wrongs which we find we proceed to gain the highest possible realization of the good, the right, the superior and the beautiful that we know has existence back of and above the superficial life of human nature. According to a metaphysical law, when we enter into mental contact with the good in man we awaken the power of that which is good in man, and the most perfect mental contact is produced by sympathy.

To sympathize with the soul is to increase the active power of the soul, because we always arouse into greater action that with which we sympathize, and when the active power of the soul is increased the weakness of the personality will become strength. To sympathize with the power of health and harmony in man will increase the power of health and harmony throughout his entire system and the elimination of sickness and trouble must inevitably follow. To sympathize with the pain a person may feel is to do nothing to relieve that person. You take the pain to yourself, but you do not take the pain away from the person with whom you sympathize. You thus double the suffering instead of removing it entirely, as you should. On the other hand, when we refuse to recognize the suffering itself and proceed to awaken in that person that something that can remove the suffering we protect ourselves from pain, while we actually do something to relieve that person from pain. We do not suffer with the person that suffers, but we do something to remove suffering absolutely from everybody concerned; instead of entering into the pain we take that person out of pain. That is sympathy that *is* sympathy. That is kindness that really results in a kind act. It does not weep, but does better. It removes both the cause and the effect of the weeping. It awakens that superior power in man that positively does produce emancipation. It does not cause suffering to be transmitted to a score of other persons who have done nothing to merit that suffering, but it stops the pain where it is and puts it out of existence absolutely.

Every form of suffering comes from the violation of some law in life. It is therefore wrong, but it cannot be righted by making a special effort to spread the results of that wrong among as many others as possible. This, however, ordinary sympathy does; it makes a special effort to make every-body feel bad because some one is not feeling as he should; but the pains of the many cannot give ease and comfort to the one, nor can many minds in bondage set one mind free. When any one is feeling bad it will not help him to have a group of morbid minds suffer with him. When any one is sorry it will not remove the cause of his grief to have others decide to be sorry also. Do something so that person will not feel bad any more. Take him out of his trouble. That is real sympathy; and while you are helping him out make him feel that your heart is as tender as tenderness itself. Do something so that the grief may be removed through the realization of that greater truth that knows that all is well. That is kindness worthy of the name.

Those, however, who are in the habit of sympathizing in the ordinary way may think the new way cold, and devoid of feeling or love, but the fact is that it is the ordinary form of sympathy that is devoid of love. When you love a person who is in pain you will not stand around and weep pretending that you are also feeling bad. You will put on the countenance of light and cheerfulness and actually do something tangible to remove his pain. That's love; and if you have real sympathy, you will minister to him with so much depth of feeling and tender kindness that you will touch the very innermost life of his soul. All love, all tenderness, all kindness and all real feeling come from the soul. Therefore, he whose sympathy is of the soul will receive his love and his kindness directly from the true source; in consequence, he will have more love and more kindness by far than the one whose sympathy is a form of morbid feeling.

The real purpose of true sympathy is two-fold; first, to arouse in a greater measure that finer something in life that is not only tender and sweet and beautiful, but is also immensely strong—strong with the strength of the Infinite; and second, to awaken everything in man that has quality, superiority and worth; that is, to make man feel the supreme power of his own inherent divinity. There is something in man that is greater than all weakness, all ills, all wrongs, and when this something is awakened, developed and expressed, all weakness, all ills and all wrongs must disappear. To sympathize with this greater something in everybody with whom one may come in contact will arouse this greater something, not only in others, but also in him who lives in this form of sympathy. In other words, to sympathize with the superior in man is to banish the wrong and the inferior by causing the expression of that divine something within that has the power to make all things well. Such a sympathy will tend to build a stronger life, a better life, a superior life, a more beautiful life; and to give such a sympathy to everybody is kindness indeed.

There may seem to be kindness in weeping with those who weep, but it is a far greater kindness to give those people the power to banish their sorrows completely, and he who does this is not cold; he is the very essence of the highest and most beautiful love. There is no joy in having sorrow. There is no pleasure in having pain. Therefore, what greater good can man do for man than to help him gain complete emancipation from all those things, and this is the purpose of this higher use of sympathy. True sympathy is neither cold nor purely intellectual. It is real soul-feeling, while ordinary sympathy is simply a morbid mental feeling. True sympathy is the very fire of real spiritual love, because it springs from the very soul of love and is in constant touch with the unbounded power of that love. That such a sympathy should have extraordinary emancipating power is therefore most evident. The ordinary use of sympathy may appear to be kind. It may mean well, but it is usually misdirected kindness, and is nearly always weak. The higher use of sympathy, that is, the expression of divine sympathy, is not only kindness itself, but it has the spiritual understanding and the spiritual power to do what kindness wants to do. Ordinary kindness is usually crippled. It lacks both the power to do and the understanding to know what to do. The true sympathy, however, not only has the power to feel kindly, but has the power to act kindly. It not only gives love and makes everybody feel that they are in the presence of real love, but it also gives that something that can cause the purpose of love to come true. Real love invariably aims to produce comfort, peace and emancipation. That is its purpose, and real sympathy can fulfill that purpose. Therefore, this higher sympathy is the sympathy that *is* sympathy.

The same principle should be employed in the use of every form of emotion, because every emotion is a movement of the mind conveying mental elements and powers with certain definite objects in view. Therefore, the way the emotion acts will determine to a very great extent whether these mental powers will build for better things, or produce undesirable conditions. Those movements of the mind or emotions that express themselves in love, heart-felt joy and spiritual feeling have a beneficial effect; while that mental feeling that is usually termed emotionalism is never wholesome. True spiritual feeling is calm, but extremely beautiful and awakens orderly and harmoniously all the finer elements of human life. It is true spiritual feeling, or what may be termed emotions sublime, that gives action and expression to personal quality, mental worth and individual superiority. In other words, it is these actions of mind and soul that elevate thought, action, feeling, consciousness and desire above the planes of the ordinary. Such emotions should therefore be cultivated to the very highest and finest degree.

What is spoken of as heartfelt joy is that wholesome joy that comes directly from the heart and that has depth, reality and joyous feeling; but that joy that runs into uncontrolled ecstasy is never wholesome. Every feeling of joy that causes the mind to be carried away into excited or overwrought ecstasy is not joy, but mental intoxication. Such joy does not produce genuine happiness, and the reaction always disturbs the equilibrium of the mind. Depth of thought, clear thinking, intellectual brilliancy, good judgment, mental poise, all of these will diminish in the mind that indulges in uncontrolled ecstasy, emotionalism or pleasure that produces excitability and overwrought emotional feeling. The feeling of love, when it is love, is always wholesome and elevating, but passionate desire is weakening unless it is permeated through and through with genuine love. A deep, strong feeling of love will turn all desires, whether mental or physical, into constructive channels, but we must be certain that it is real love and not an artificial feeling temporarily produced by the misuse of the imagination. Here every mental movement that is intense, forced, overwrought or worked up to an abnormal pitch of excited enthusiasm leads to emotionalism, and emotionalism burns up energy. Nearly all kinds of nervous diseases can be traced directly or indirectly to emotionalism in one or more of its many forms; and as physical and mental weakness always follows the burning up of energy, a number of physical and mental ills can be traced to this source.

When emotionalism, fear, anger and worry are eliminated, all kinds of insanity and all kinds of nervous diseases will be things of the past; while the power, the capacity and the brilliancy of the average mind will increase to an extraordinary degree. Strong emotional feelings and intense enthusiasm will sometimes arouse a great deal of dormant, mental power. In consequence, people sometimes do exceptional things while under the emotional spell, but the entire process, as well as the final results, is very similar to that produced by alcoholic stimulants and other drugs. The system seems to be charged with a great deal of extra power for a while, but when the reaction comes the entire system becomes much weaker than it ever was before. The mind that permits itself to be aroused by intense, emotional feeling will gradually lose its power of clear thought. The understanding will become so weakened that the principles of real truth cannot be fully comprehended, while the judgment will follow more and more the illusions of an overwrought imagination. The fact that religious feeling among millions is so closely associated with this overwrought state of emotionalism proves the importance of a better understanding of the use of these finer mental elements. Emotionalism compels the mind to follow mere feeling, and mere feeling, when not properly blended with clear understanding, will be misdirected at every turn. Emotionalism also stupefies the finer perceptions by intoxicating the mind, and by burning up the finer mental energies; and since these finer perceptions are required to discern real truth we understand readily why highly emotional people cannot comprehend the principles of pure, spiritual metaphysics. Having been trained toward materialistic literalism instead of away from it, they are not to blame, however, for their present state and deserve no criticism. Nevertheless, those who wish to find real religion and real spirituality must learn to understand the psychology of emotion and must learn the true use of all the finer feelings of the mind.

There is something in man that is called religious feeling. It is present to a greater or lesser degree in everybody and cannot be removed, because it is a part of life itself. When in action, and it is never inactive very long, it expresses itself in some power of emotion. When this emotion or delicate mental movement is permitted to act without any definite purpose it becomes emotionalism; that is, mental energy running rampant, and becoming more and more intense until it destroys itself, as well as all the energy it originally contained. On the other hand, when this feeling is directed toward the highest and the most perfect conception of truth, life and being that the mind can possibly picture, all that is lofty, ideal and beautiful will be developed in the mind and soul of that individual. This is natural, because there is nothing that has greater developing power than deep, spiritual feeling; a fact that those who desire to develop remarkable ability, extraordinary talent and rare genius will do well to remember.

There is no mental faculty that is more readily affected by the emotions than the imagination, and since the imagination is such a very important faculty, no mental or physical action that in any way interferes with the constructive work of the imagination should be permitted. Emotionalism, however, invariably excites the imagination, and an excited imagination will imagine all sorts of things that are not true. The mind will thus be filled with illusions, and in consequence, false beliefs, wrong thoughts, perverted states and misdirected mental energy will follow. The result will be sickness, trouble, mistakes and failures in one or more of their many forms. It is now a well demonstrated truth that every thought has a definite power of its own, and that that power will produce its natural effect in some part of the human system. If the thought is not good the effect will naturally be undesirable, and conditions will be produced in mind or body that we do not want. But whatever we imagine, that we think; therefore, when we excite the imagination we imagine all manner of things that are untrue, unreal or abnormal; we produce false or perverted thought action in the mind; we think the wrong, and wrong thoughts invariably produce wrong conditions in mind or body, or both.

What we imagine we reproduce in ourselves to some degree, frequently to a marked degree; but an excited imagination simply cannot imagine what is good and wholesome. In every form of development, whether in the body, the mind or the soul, the imagining faculty is employed extensively. All growth is promoted by combining and recombining the elements of life in higher and higher forms, and since it is one of the functions of the imagination to produce these higher, more complex and more perfect combinations, development cannot take place unless the imagination works orderly, constructively and progressively. An excited imagination will produce false mental combinations or may waste energy by attempting to combine mental elements that will not combine. An orderly imagination may be likened to a skilled workman who builds a beautiful mansion out of his bricks, while an excited imagination might be likened to some one who can do nothing more than pile those bricks into a heap. The fact that emotionalism always excites the imagination proves therefore how impossible it is for minds with uncontrolled emotions to develop the greatness that is latent within them.

Another fact of great importance in this connection is that emotionalism will intensify every mental tendency that may be active in mind at the time. If there is a tendency toward abnormal desires, emotionalism will intensify those desires so that it will be very difficult to resist temptation should it appear. On the other hand, pure spiritual feeling would transmute those desires, and produce instead, an ascending tendency, thus leading all the forces of mind toward higher ground. To overcome emotionalism, intense mental feeling, anger, excitability and all overwrought or abnormal mental states, turn attention upon the spiritual heights of the soul whenever such mental feelings are felt. By training all mental feelings and emotions to move toward the deeper and the higher spiritual state of being these same feelings will become stronger, deeper, finer and more beautiful than they ever were before. We thus establish the foundation upon which we can build an ideal character, and through such a character all the qualities of mind and soul can be used beneficially in the midst of every experience, whatever the nature of that experience may be.

To cause all the emotions to follow ascending tendencies will increase remarkably the power, the fineness, the life and the rapture of every phase of feeling, not only in the soul, but in the mind and the body as well. Every trace of coldness, indifference or lack of feeling will entirely disappear, and we shall develop instead that higher form of kindness, sympathy and spiritual emotion that is created in the likeness of divine emotion. Whoever employs this method will not permit his feelings to run wild at any time, but will cause the life and the power of every feeling to accumulate in his system. He will hold them all in poise and use their energies intelligently in the building up of his whole life and in adding to the joy, the rapture and the delight of the living of a full, strong, ever-ascending state of existence. That person who controls his feelings and turns all the energies of those feelings upon the spiritual heights of the soul will actually become a living flame of love, sympathy and sublime emotion. Such a person will enjoy everything intensely, but his joy will be in such a high state of harmony that he will waste nothing in his life; instead, all the elements and powers of his life will continue to accumulate, thus giving added strength, worth and superiority to everything that he may physically, mentally or spiritually possess.

CHAPTER XI

TALK HEALTH, HAPPINESS,
AND PROSPERITY

Talk happiness. When things look dark, talk happiness. When things look bright, talk more happiness. When others are sad, insist on being glad. Talk happiness, and they will soon feel better. Talk happiness; it pays in every shape and form and manner. Give sunshine to others, and others will be more than pleased to give sunshine to you. Talk happiness, and your health will be better, your mind will be brighter and your personality far more attractive; but the qualities that happiness will give to you will also be given to those who have the pleasure to listen to you when you talk happiness.

Talk happiness, and you will always remain in a happy frame of mind. You will encourage thousands of others to do the same. You will become a fountain of joy in the midst of the garden of human life, and who can tell how many flowers of kindness and joy unfolded their rare and tender beauty because you were there. When others have lost courage, talk happiness. The future is bright for everybody. Talk happiness, and you turn on the light in their pathway, and they will see the better things that are before them. When the mind is depressed it is blinded; it sees only the darkness; but when the light of joy is admitted everything is changed. Therefore, talk happiness to all persons and on all occasions.

We cannot have too much light in the world, and the more we talk happiness the more light we produce wherever we may be. What greater pleasure could anyone desire than to realize that he has eased the way of life for thousands and sent the sunbeams and joy into the mental world of tens of thousands? You can do this by talking happiness. Thus by constantly talking happiness you produce perpetual increase in your own happiness. What we give in abundance always returns in abundance; that is, when we give in the right spirit; and he who talks happiness is always in the right spirit. When in the midst of discord, trouble or confusion, talk happiness. Harmony will soon be restored. The majority can easily change their minds for the better when some one takes the lead. You can take the lead by talking happiness.

Talk prosperity. When times are not good, man himself must make them better, and he can make them better by doing his best and having faith in that power that produces prosperity. When men have faith in prosperity they will think prosperity, live prosperity and thus do that which produces prosperity; and you can give men faith in prosperity by constantly talking prosperity. They may not listen at first, but perseverance always wins. Prosperity is extremely attractive, and the more you impress it upon the minds of others the more attractive it becomes until no one can resist it; and when we admit the idea of prosperity into our own minds we will from that moment begin to produce prosperity. Think prosperity, talk prosperity, and live prosperity; and you will rise in the scale no matter what the circumstances may be. Hold to the power that produces abundance by having unbounded faith in that power and you will overcome all adversity and reach the highest goal you have in view. The fear of failure produces more failure than all other causes combined. You can remove that fear by talking prosperity.

Talk health. It is the best medicine. When people stop talking sickness they will stop getting sick. Talk health and stay well. Talk health to the person who is sick and you will cause him to think health. He who thinks health will live health, and he who lives health will produce health. When your associates take delight in relating minutely everything they know about the ills of the community, purify the muddy waters of their conversation by talking health. Insist on talking health. Prove that there is more health than sickness, and that therefore health is the more important subject. The majority rules. Health is in the majority. Increase that majority by talking more health. Take the lead in this manner of conversation, and be positively determined to continue in the lead. Others will soon follow, and when they do, sickness will diminish more and more until it becomes practically unknown among those who have the privilege to live in your circle.

When the sins of the world are in evidence, talk virtue. When the power of virtue is in evidence, talk more virtue. Eternally emphasize the good; give it more and more power, and it will soon become sufficiently strong to produce that ideal of power that you wish to make real. Talk virtue, and people will think of virtue; they will dwell more and more upon the beauty of virtue. 'Ere long they will desire virtue, and that desire will become

stronger and stronger until it thrills every atom in human life. To desire
virtue is to become virtuous. To live for the attainment of purity is to place
in action all the purifying elements in your being, and you will soon realize
that perfectly clean condition that every awakened mind has learned to
worship. You can purify the minds of thousands by constantly talking virtue, and these thousands will in turn convey the power of virtue to as many
thousand times thousands more.

Talk virtue eternally and there is no end to the good that you may do.
When the world seems bad, talk virtue. The power of good is not gone; it
is just as great as it ever was, and it is here and there and everywhere. You
can open the mind of man to the mighty influx of this power by eternally
talking virtue. You can, through the proper use of your own words, change
the tide of human thought. You can cause all mankind to desire virtue by
forever talking virtue. On the surface many things may seem to be what
they ought not to be, but the surface is not all there is. It is an insignificant part of the whole. There is a hidden richness in life that the many do
not see, because their attention has never been turned in that direction. You
can lead mankind into the gold mines of the mind and into the diamond
fields of the soul, and the secret lies in the words you speak. You can guide
the mind of man by the way you talk. Talking therefore should not be
empty, but should ever have a sublime goal in view. Your words point the
way and they who hear what you have to say will, to some degree, be influenced to go whatever way your words may point. Your power, therefore,
in directing other minds toward greater and better things is hidden in every
word you speak, and how important that that power be wisely employed.

We are responsible for every word we express. It will affect somebody
either for good or otherwise. Talk sin, sickness and trouble, and you will
cause many to go directly into more sin, sickness and trouble. Talk health,
happiness and prosperity, and you will cause many to find health, happiness
and prosperity in greater and greater abundance. When the world complains, do not forget to emphasize the great fact that universal good is even
now at hand. The complaining mind wears colored glasses. He cannot see
things as they are. You can help him to remove those glasses by calling his
attention to the fact that things are not what they seem to him. Everything
lies in the point of view. Look at things from the right point of view and
you will be happy, cheerful and optimistic under all sorts of circumstances.
But look at things from the wrong point of view, and you will see nothing
clearly; everything will appear to be what it is not. You will thus live in
confusion and your mistakes will be many. Remove this confusion by plac-

ing yourself in harmony with eternal good, and you can do this by talking about the good, thinking about the good and emphasizing most positively every expression of good with which you may come in contact. That which we think of and talk of constantly will multiply and grow in our own world.

Talk peace. You will thus not only prevent confusion, but you will remove those confused conditions that may already exist. You can still the storms of life everywhere by talking peace. When man thinks the most of peace he will be in peace, and he cannot fail to think of peace so long as he is faithfully talking peace. Talk success, and you will inspire everybody with the spirit of success. You will help to turn the energies of life upon the goal of success, and thus you will help all minds to move toward success. Never say that anything is impossible. Talk success, and you help to make everything possible. Everybody should succeed. It is not only the privilege of everybody to succeed, but every person, to be just to himself, must succeed. The fear of failure, however, is the greatest obstacle. You can remove that fear by talking success. Hold the idea of success before every mind with which you come in contact; you will thus become one of the greatest philanthropists in the world.

New and greater opportunities may be found everywhere. Talk of these things and forget the missteps of the past. We can leave the lesser that is behind only by pressing on toward the greater that is before. Talk success to everybody, and everybody will press on toward the greater goal of success. Be an inspiration among all minds; and you can be by holding up the light of success, prosperity and attainment at all times. Use your words in promoting advancement, in awakening new interest in the better side, the brighter side, the sunny side, and turn the mind of man upon those things that *can* be done. He can who thinks he can, and you help every person to think that he can by talking prosperity and success. Impress the greater upon every mind, and every mind will think the greater; and he who thinks the greater is constantly building for greater things. Emphasize the sunny side in all your speech and you provide a never failing antidote for complaints; and since the complaining mind soon becomes the retrogressing mind, this antidote has extreme value. It may change for the better the destiny of anyone when brought squarely before his attention, and this your words can do.

When one door closes another opens; sometimes several. This is the law of life. It is the expression of the law of eternal progress. The whole of nature desires to move forward eternally. The spirit of progress animates everything. Whenever a person loses an opportunity to move forward this great law proceeds to give him another. This proves that the universe is kind, that everything is for man and nothing against him. This being the truth, the man who talks health, happiness, prosperity, power and progress is working in harmony with the universe, and is helping to promote the great purpose of the universe; and who would not occupy a position of such value and importance? Whenever you talk trouble, failure, sickness or sin you arraign your own mind against the law of life and the purpose of the universe. You will thereby be against everything, and everything will, in consequence, be against you. You must, therefore, necessarily fail in everything you undertake to do. But how different everything will be when you turn and move in the other direction. Go with the universe, and all the power of the universe will go with you, and will help you to reach whatever object you may have in view.

Harmonize yourself with the laws of life and you will steadily rise in the scale of life. Nothing can hold you down. Everything you undertake to do you will accomplish, because everything will be with you. You will reach every ideal, and at the best time and under the best circumstances cause that ideal to become real. When you cease to talk failure and begin to talk success you invariably meet the turn in the lane. You find that a new world and a better future is in store. Things will take a turn when you take a turn, and you will take a turn when you begin to talk about those things that you desire to realize. Never talk about anything else. The way you talk you go. The way you talk others will go. Therefore, talk health, happiness and prosperity, and help everybody, yourself included, to move toward health, happiness and prosperity. The power of words is immense, both in the person that speaks and in the person that is spoken to. The simplest way to use this power is to train yourself to talk the things you want; talk the things that you expect or desire to realize; talk the things you wish to attain and accomplish. You thus cause the power of words to work for you and with you in gaining the goal you have in mind. Whatever comes, talk health, happiness and prosperity. Say that you are well; say that you are happy; say that you are prosperous. Emphasize everything that is good in life, and the power of the Supreme will cause your words to come true.

CHAPTER XII

WHAT DETERMINES
THE DESTINY OF MAN

The destiny of every individual is being hourly created by himself, and what he is to create at any particular time is determined by those ideals that he entertains at that time. The future of a person is not preordained by some external power, nor is fate controlled by some strange, mysterious force that master-minds alone can comprehend and employ. It is ideals that control fate, and all minds have their ideals wherever in the scale of life they may be. To have ideals is not simply to have dreams or visions of that which lies beyond the attainments of the present; nor is idealism a system of ideas that the practical mind may not have the privilege to entertain. To have ideals is to have definite objects in view, be those objects very high or very low, or anywhere between those extremes.

The ideals of any mind are the real wants, the real desires or the real aims of that mind, and as every normal mind invariably lives, thinks and works for that which is wanted by his present state of existence, it is evident that every mind must necessarily, either consciously or unconsciously, follow his ideals. When those ideals are low, ordinary or inferior the individual will work for the ordinary and the inferior, and the products of his mind will correspond in quality with that for which he is working. Inferior causes will originate in his life and similar effects will follow; but when those ideals are high and superior, he will work for the superior; he will develop superiority in himself, and he will give superiority to everything that he may produce. Every action that he originates in his life will become a superior cause and will be followed by a similar effect.

The destiny of every individual is determined by what he is and by what he does; and what any individual is to be or do is determined by what he is living for, thinking for or working for. Man is not being made by some outside force. Man is making himself with the power of those forces and elements that he employs in his thought and his work; and in all his efforts, physical or mental, he invariably follows his ideals. He who lives, thinks and works for the superior becomes superior; he who works for less, becomes less. It is therefore evident that any individual may become more, achieve more, secure more and create for himself a greater and a greater destiny by simply beginning to live, think and work for a superior group of ideals. To have low ideals is to give the creative forces of the system something ordinary to work for. To have high ideals is to give those forces something extraordinary to work for, and the fate of man is the result of what his creative forces hourly produce. Every force in the human system is producing something, and that something will become a part of the individual. It is therefore evident that any individual can constantly improve the power, the quality and the worth of his being by directing the forces of his system to produce that which has quality and worth. These forces, however, are not directed or controlled by the will. It is the nature of the creative forces in man to produce what the mind desires, wants, needs or aspires to attain, and the desires and the aspirations of any mind are determined by the ideals that are entertained in that mind.

The forces of the system will begin to work for the superior when the mind begins to attain superior ideals, and since it is the product of these forces that determines both the nature and the destiny of man, a superior nature and a greater destiny may be secured by any individual who will adopt the highest and the most perfect system of idealism that he can possibly comprehend. To entertain superior ideals is to picture in mind and to hold constantly before mind the highest conception that can be formed of everything of which we may be conscious. To mentally dwell in those higher conceptions at all times is to cause the predominating ideas to become superior ideas, and it is the predominating ideas for which we live, think and work. When the ruling ideas of any mind are superior the creative force of that mind will produce the superior in every element, faculty, talent or power in that mind; greatness will thus be developed in that mind, and the great mind invariably creates a great destiny.

To entertain superior ideals is not to dream of the impossible, but to enter into mental contact with those greater possibilities that we are now able to discern; and to have the power to discern an ideal indicates that we have the power to realize that ideal. We do not become conscious of greater possibilities until we have developed sufficient capacity to work out those possibilities into practical, tangible results. Therefore, when we discern the greater we are ready to attain and achieve the greater; but before we can proceed to do what we are ready to do we must adopt superior ideals, and superior ideals only. When our ideals are superior we shall constantly think of the superior, because as our ideals are so is our thinking, and to constantly think of the superior is to steadily grow into the likeness of the superior.

When the ideals are very high all the forces of the system will move toward superior attainments; all things in the life of the individual will work together with greater and greater greatness in view, and continued advancement on a larger and larger scale must inevitably follow. To entertain superior ideals is not simply to desire some larger personal attainment or to mentally dwell in some belief that is different from the usual beliefs of the world. To entertain superior ideals is to think the very best thoughts and the very greatest thoughts about everything with which we come in contact. Superior idealism is not mere dreaming of the great and the beautiful, but is actual living in mental harmony with the very best we can find in all things, in all persons, in all circumstances and in all expressions of life. To live in mental harmony with the best we can find everywhere is to create the best in our own mentality and personality; and as we steadily grow into the likeness of that which we think of the most, we will, through ideal thinking, perpetually increase our power, capacity and worth. In consequence, we will naturally create a greater and a more worthy destiny.

The man who becomes much will achieve much, and great achievements invariably build a great destiny. To think of anything that is less than the best, or to mentally dwell with the inferior is to neutralize the effect of those superior ideals that we have begun to entertain. To secure the greatest results it is therefore absolutely necessary to entertain superior ideals only and to cease all recognition of inferiority or imperfection. The reason why the majority fail to secure any tangible results from higher ideals is because they entertain too many of the lower ideals at the same time. They may aim high; they may adore the beautiful; they may desire the perfect; they may live for the better and work for the greater, but they do not think their best thoughts about everything, and this is the reason why they do not reach the goal they have in view. Some of their forces are building for greater things, while other forces are building for lesser things, and a house divided against itself cannot stand.

Superior idealism contains no thought that is less than the very greatest and the very best that the most lofty states of mind can possibly produce, and it entertains no desire that has not the very greatest worth, the greatest power, and the highest attainment in view. Superior idealism does not recognize the power of evil in anything or in anybody,; it knows that adverse conditions exist, but it gives the matter no conscious thought whatever. It is not possible to think the greatest thought about everything while mind is giving conscious attention to adversity or imperfection. The true idealist, therefore, gives conscious recognition to the power of good only, and he lives in the conviction that all things in his life are constantly working together for good. This conviction is not mere sentiment with the idealist. He knows that all things positively will work together for good when we recognize only the good, think only the good, desire only the good and expect only the good; likewise, he knows that all things positively will work together for greater things when all the powers of life, thought and action are concentrated upon the attainment and the achievement of greater things.

To apply the principles of superior idealism in all things means advancement in all things. To follow the superior ideal is to move toward the higher, the greater and the superior, and no one can continue very long in that movement without creating for himself a new world, a better environment and a greater destiny. To create a better future begin now to select a better group of ideals. Select the best and the greatest ideals that you can possibly find, and live those ideals absolutely. You will thus cause everything in your being to work for the higher, the better and the greater, and the things that you work for now will determine what the future is to be. Work for the greatest and the best that you know in the present, and you will create the very greatest and the very best for the future.

CHAPTER XIII

TO HIM THAT HATH SHALL BE GIVEN

The statement that much gathers more is true on every plane of life and in every sphere of existence; and the converse that every loss leads to a greater loss is equally true; though we must remember that man can stop either process at any time or place. The further down you go the more rapidly you will move toward the depths, and the higher up you go the easier it becomes to go higher still. When you begin to gain you will gain more, because "To him that hath shall be given." When you begin to lose you will lose more, because from "Him that hath not, even that which he hath shall be taken away." This is a great metaphysical law, and being metaphysical, man has the power to use it in any way that he may desire. As man is in the within, so everything will be in his external world. Therefore, whether man is to lose or gain in the without depends upon whether he is losing or gaining in the within.

The basis of all possession is found in the consciousness of man, and not in exterior circumstances, laws or conditions. If a man's consciousness is accumulative, he will positively accumulate, no matter where he may live; but whether his riches are to be physical, intellectual or spiritual will depend upon the construction of his mind. When the mind has the greatest development on the physical plane an accumulative consciousness will gather tangible possessions. When the mind has the greatest development on the intellectual or metaphysical plane, an accumulative consciousness will gather abundance of knowledge and wisdom. When the mind has the greatest development on the spiritual plane an accumulative consciousness will gather spiritual riches. However competent you may be on the physical plane, if your consciousness is not accumulative, you will not gain possession of a great deal of this world's goods. Likewise, no matter how diligently you may search for wisdom in the higher spiritual possessions, if your consciousness is not accumulative you will gain but little. In fact, you will constantly lose the knowledge of truth on the one hand while trying to gain it on the other. Therefore, to gain abundance in the world of things or tangible possessions, the secret is to become competent in our chosen vocations, and then acquire an accumulative consciousness.

To gain the riches of the mind and the soul, the secret is to develop the same accumulative consciousness and to consecrate all the powers of mind and thought to spiritual things. There are thousands in this age who have consecrated their whole lives to the higher state of being, but there are very few who have gained the real riches of the spiritual kingdom, and the reason is they have neglected the development of the accumulative consciousnesss. In other words, they have overlooked the great law, "To him that hath shall be given." Those who have nothing will receive nothing, no matter how devotedly they may pray or how beautifully they may live. But to have is not simply to possess in the external sense. Those who are conscious of nothing have nothing. Those who are conscious of much have much, regardless of external possession. Before we can gain anything we must have something, and to have something is to be conscious of something.

We must be conscious of possession in the within before we can increase possession in any sphere of existence. All possession is based upon consciousness and is held by consciousness or lost by consciousness. All gain is the result of an accumulative consciousness. All loss is due to what may be termed the scattering consciousness; that is, that state of consciousness that lets go of everything that may come within its sphere. When you are conscious of something you are among those that hath and to you shall be given more. As soon as you gain conscious hold of things you will begin to gain possession of more and more things. As soon as you gain conscious hold upon wisdom and spiritual power, wisdom and spiritual power will be given to you in greater and greater abundance. On the other hand, when you begin to lose conscious hold of things, thoughts or powers you will begin to lose more and more of those possessions, until all are gone.

When you inwardly feel that things are slipping away from you, you are losing your conscious hold of things, and all will finally be lost if you do not change your consciousness. When you inwardly feel that you are gaining more and more, or that things are beginning to gravitate toward your sphere of existence, more and more will be given to you until you have everything that you may desire. How we feel in the within is the secret, and it is this interior feeling that determines whether we are to be among those that have or among those that have not. When you feel in the within that you are gaining more you are among those that have, and to you shall be given more. When you feel in the within that you are losing what you have, you are among those that have not, and from you shall be taken away even that which you have.

When we learn that mind is cause and that everything we gain may come from the action of mind as cause, we discover that all possession is dependent upon the attitude of mind, and since we have the power to hold the mind in any attitude desired, all the laws of gain and possession are in our own hands. When this discovery is made we begin to gain conscious possession of ourselves, and to him that hath himself all other things shall be given. To feel that you, yourself, are the power behind other powers, and that you may determine what is to come and what is to go, is to become conscious of the fact that you are something. You thus become conscious of something in yourself that is real, that is substantial and that is actually supreme in your world. To become conscious of something in yourself is to have something, and to have something is to gain more; consequently, by gaining consciousness of that something that is real in yourself you become one of those that hath, and to you shall be given.

To gain consciousness of the real in yourself is to gain consciousness of the real in life, and the more you feel the reality of life the more real life becomes. The result is that your consciousness of the reality of life becomes larger and larger; it comprehends more and takes in more. In other words, it is becoming accumulative. When this realization is attained you gain conscious hold upon life and are gradually gaining conscious hold upon everything that exists in life. This means a greater and greater mastery of life, and mastery is always followed by an increase in possession. Whatever you become conscious of in yourself, that you gain possession of in yourself. Whatever you gain possession of in yourself, that you can constructively employ in your sphere of existence, and whatever is constructively employed is productive; it produces something. Therefore, by becoming conscious of something you gain the power to produce something, and products on any plane constitute riches on that plane.

The more you become conscious of in yourself and in your life the greater your power to create and produce in your sphere of action, and the more wealth you produce the greater your possession, providing you have learned how to retain the products of your own talent. When we analyze these laws from another point of view we find the consciousness of the real in ourselves produces an ascending tendency in the mind, and whenever the mind begins to go up, the law of action and reaction will continue to press the mind up further and further indefinitely. Every upward action of mind, produces a reaction that pushes the mind upward still farther. As the mind is pushed upward a second upward action is expressed that is stronger than the first; this in turn produces a second reaction stronger than the first reaction, and the mind is pushed upward the second time much farther than it was the first time. The fact is, when the mind enters the ascending scale the law of action and reaction will perpetuate the ascension so long as the mind takes a conscious interest in the progress made; but the moment the mind loses interest in the movement the law will reverse itself and the mind enters the descending scale. Therefore, become conscious of the law in yourself and take a conscious interest in every step in advance that you make, and you will go up in the scale of life continually and indefinitely.

When the mind is in the ascending scale it is steadily becoming larger, more powerful and more competent, and will consequently be in demand where recompense is large and the opportunities more numerous. Such a mind will naturally gain step by step in rapid succession. To such a mind will be given more and more continually, because it has placed itself in the world of those who have. The great secret of gaining more, regardless of circumstances, is to continue perpetually to go up in mind. No matter how things are going about you, continue to go up in mind. Every upward step that is taken in mind adds power to mind, and this added power will produce added results in the tangible world. When these added results are observed mind gains more faith in itself, and more faith always brings more power. On the other hand, when we permit ourselves to go down in mind, because things seem to go down, we lose power. This loss of power will prevent us from doing our work properly or from using those things and conditions about us to the best advantage. In consequence, things will actually go down more and more; and if we permit this losing of ground to make us still more discouraged, we lose still more power, to be followed by still more adversity and loss. It is therefore evident that the way we go in mind everything in our world will go also, and that if we change our minds and stay changed, everything else will change and stay changed. If we continue to go up in mind, never permitting retrogression for a moment, everything in our world will continue to go up, and there will not even be signs of reverse, much less the loss of anything which we wish to retain.

When things seem to go wrong we should stay right and continue to stay right, and things will soon decide to come and be right also. This is a law that works and never fails to work. When we permit ourselves to go wrong because things seem to go wrong, we produce what may be termed the letting go attitude of mind, and when we cease to hold on to things, things will begin to slip away. We must hold on to things ourselves, if we wish to retain them for ourselves; and the secret of holding on to things is to continue positively in that attitude of mind that is perpetually going up into the larger and the greater. The laws of life will continue perpetually to give to those who have placed themselves in the receiving attitude, and those same laws will take away from those who have placed themselves in the losing attitude. When you create a turn in yourself you will feel that things are also taking a turn to a degree; and if you continue persistently in this feeling, everything in your life will positively take the turn that you have taken. As you go everything in your world will go, providing you continue to go; the law of action and reaction explains why. In the last analysis, however, everything depends upon whether consciousness determines how every force, element, power of faculty is to act, because they are all controlled by consciousness. When your consciousness does not have the proper hold on things, the power of your being will fail to gain the proper hold on things; but when your consciousness does possess this holding power, all the powers of your being will gain the same firm grip upon everything with which they may have to deal.

To establish the accumulative consciousness, that is, that consciousness that has complete hold on things, train yourself to inwardly feel that you have full possession of everything in your own being. Feel that you possess yourself. Affirm that you possess yourself. Think constantly of yourself as possessing yourself—everything that is in yourself, and you will soon be conscious of absolute self-possession. Some have this conscious feeling naturally, and they invariably gain vast possessions, either in tangible goods or in wisdom and higher spiritual powers. But every one can develop this state of conscious possession of his whole self by remaining firm in the conviction that "All that I am is mine." When you begin to feel that you possess yourself you actually *have* something in consciousness, and according to the laws of gain and possessions you will gain more and more without end. You are in the same consciousness with those who have, and to you will be given. You have established the inner cause of possession through the conscious possession of your entire inner life, and the effect of this cause, that is, the perpetual increase of external possession, must invariably follow. In brief, you have applied the great law—To Him That Hath Himself All Other Things Shall Be Given.

CHAPTER XIV

THE LIFE THAT IS WORTH LIVING

To the average person life means but little, because he has not discovered the greater possibilities or his real existence. He has been taught to think that to make a fortune or to make a name for himself are the only things worth while, and if he does not happen to have the necessary talent for these accomplishments there is nothing much else for him to do but to merely exist. However, if he has been touched with the force of ambition, or if he has had a glimpse of the ideal, mere existence does not satisfy, and the result is a life of unhappiness and dissatisfaction. But such a person must learn that there are other openings and opportunities in life besides mere existence, regardless of what the mental capacity of the individual may be. These other opportunities, when taken advantage of, will give just as much happiness, if not more, than what is secured by those who have won the admiration of the world; besides, when one learns to live for these other things real living becomes a fine art, and he begins to live a life that is really worth while.

There is many a person whose present position in life depends almost wholly upon his financial returns, and if these are small, with no indications of immediate increase, his life seems to be almost, if not wholly, a barren waste; not because it is a barren waste, but because he has not found the real riches of existence. The trouble with this person is the point of view; he is depending upon things instead of depending upon himself. He must learn that there is something more to live for besides his salary and what his salary can buy. The value of the individual life is not measured by the quantity of possessions, but by the quality of existence. The value of life comes not from having much, but from being much; and happiness is invariably a state of mind coming, not from what a person has, but from what he is. We must remember, however, that he who is much will finally gain much, providing the powers in his possession are practically applied; and his gains will have high quality whether they be gains in the world of things or in the world of mind, consciousness and soul.

The problem for the average person to solve is what he actually can do with himself in his present position. He may not be earning much now, and his opportunities for earning more may not be clearly in evidence, but he is nevertheless living in a great sea of opportunities, many of which may be taken advantage of at once. The first of these is the opportunity to make of himself a great personality, and in taking advantage of this opportunity he should remember that to do great things in the world is not the only thing worth while. To be great in the world is of equal if not greater worth, and he who is now becoming great in his own life will, without fail, do great things in years to come. The majority of those who have practical capacity are making strenuous efforts to do something great, something startling, that will arrest the attention of the world; while those who do not possess this practical capacity are not satisfied because they are not similarly favored. In the meantime neither class gains happiness, and the best forces of life are employed in the making of things, most of which are valueless, while the making of great personalities is postponed to some future time.

The capacity to make great things is not the only capacity of value in the possession of man; but all minds do not possess this capacity; all minds, however, do possess the power to remake themselves in the exact likeness of all that is great and beautiful and ideal. Begin now to rebuild your own personality and proceed in the realization of the fact that you have the power to produce an edition DeLuxe out of your own present personal self. You could hardly find a purpose of greater interest and of greater possibility than this, and results will be secured from the very beginning. To find your own personality passing through a transformation process, bringing out into expression the finest and the best that you can picture in your ideals, is something that will add immensely to the joy and the worth of living. In fact, this alone would make life not only worth living, but so rich that every moment would become a source of unbounded satisfaction in itself.

The average person usually asks himself how much money he can make during the next ten years, but why should he not ask himself how much happiness he can enjoy during those same years, or how much brilliancy he can develop in his mind, or how much more beautiful he may become in body, character and soul? He would find that by living for these latter things he would not only perpetually enrich his life and live a life that is thoroughly worth living, but he would find that the earning of money would become much easier than if he simply lived for material gain alone. The ambition of the average person is to do something great in the world of things; but why is he not ambitious to do something great in the perfecting of his own being, the most wonderful world in the universe? Such ambitions are truly worth living for and working for, but our attention has not been called to their extraordinary possibilities; therefore, we have neglected the greater while wasting most of our energies on the lesser.

There are a number of ambitions outside of the usual ones that could engage our attention with the greatest of profit, because they not only have worth in themselves, but they lead to so many other things that have worth. The desire to secure as much out of life as life can possibly give will not only make living intensely interesting, but the more life a person can live the more power he will get. Live a great life and you gain great power. The increase of your power will enable you to carry out a number of other ambitions, thus adding to the richness of your life from almost every imaginable source. When a person declares that his greatest ambition is to live he is taking the most interesting, the most satisfying, the most profitable and the most complete course in life that can possibly be selected. Living, itself, when made a fine art, is one continuous feast, and the fact that all increase of power comes from the increase of life makes the ambition to live not only the greatest ambition of all, but the means through which all other ambitions may be realized.

If your present life does not hold as much as you would wish, do not think of it as an empty state of existence. Do not depend upon those few things that you are receiving from the external world; but begin to draw upon the limitless life and power that exists in the vastness of your interior world. Then you will find something to live for. Then you will begin to live a life that is thoroughly worth while. Then you will find the real riches of existence, and you will also find that these riches will so increase your personal power and worth that you will become able to take advantage of those opportunities that lead to things of tangible worth.

When the world of things does not seem to hold any new opportunities for you resolve to grow more and more beautiful in body, character and soul with the passing of the years. Make this your ambition, and if you do your utmost to carry out this ambition, you will gain far more satisfaction from its realization than if you had amassed an immense fortune. Live to express in body, mind and soul all that is high and beautiful and ideal in your sublime nature, and you will not only give yourself unbounded joy, but you will become a great inspiration to the entire world. The life that is not expressed through the beautiful nor surrounded by the beautiful is not worth a great deal to the mind of man; but there is practically no end to the joy and richness that man may gain through that which is actually beautiful. The beautiful not only gives happiness, but it opens the mind of man to those higher realms from which proceeds all that is worthy or great or ideal. To look upon the beautiful is to gain glimpses of that vast transcendent world where supreme life is working out the marvelous destiny of man. Therefore, there can be no greater ambition than to live for the purpose of giving higher and more ideal expression to the life of that sublime world.

To give expression in personal life to the great riches of the interior world is worth far more, both to yourself and to the race, than it is to gain possession of any number of things in the external world. The man who simply gains wealth never gains happiness; besides, he is soon forgotten. But the man who will live for the purpose of giving expression to mental and spiritual wealth will gain unlimited happiness, and his life will be so illustrious that his name will never be forgotten. And remember that no matter how insignificant your position in life may be to-day, or how small your income, or how limited your opportunities, you can begin this moment to give expression to the vast riches of your interior life; and before you take your departure from this sphere you may become such a great light in the world of higher illumined attainment that your accomplishments in this unique sphere of action will continue to inspire the world for ages yet to come.

To live for the purpose of developing the gold mines of the mind and the diamond fields of the soul, are ambitions that might engage the attention of millions who have found no satisfaction in the world of things; and to those who will make these their leading ambitions a rich future is certainly in store; and, in addition, the present will be filled to overflowing with almost everything that can give interest and happiness to life. To develop a charming personality, to live a long life, to live a happy life, and to retain your health, your youth and your vigor as long as you live, these are ambitions that anyone can work for with the greatest interest and profit; and to him who will accomplish these things the world will give more honor than it has given to its greatest musicians, its most brilliant orators or its most illustrious statesmen.

To live for the purpose of unfolding the latent powers of your being is a work that will not only prove interesting to an exceptional degree, but will prove exceedingly rich in future possibilities. That there is practically no end to the possibilities that are latent in man is now the firm conviction of all real psychologists. Therefore, we need not weep because there are no more worlds to conquer. We are on the borderland of greater worlds than were ever dreamed of by the most illumined seers that the world has ever known. We need not feel discouraged because our position in life seems uninteresting or insignificant. We have opportunities at our very door that are so great and so numerous that it will require an eternity to take advantage of them all. Though the external world may not as yet have given us much to live for, the internal world stands ready to lavish upon us so much that is rich and marvelous that not a single moment need be otherwise than a feast fit for the gods. The doors of this internal world are open, and he who will walk in will begin to live a life that is great, indeed.

When we look into life as life really is there is so much to live for and there is so much to accomplish and attain that even eternity seems too short. The problem to solve is to know the greatest thing we can do now; and the solution may be found by resolving to live for that which is nearest at hand, whatever that may be. Accept the greatest opportunity that you can take advantage of now, and then begin to live for the working out of everything that that opportunity may contain. Do not long for opportunities that are out of reach. The majority do this and thus waste their time. Do not wait for opportunities to do great things. The opportunity to make of yourself a great soul, a marvelous mind and a higher developed personality is at hand, and by taking advantage of this opportunity you will awaken within yourself those powers that can do great things. You will thus cause your present to become all that you may wish it to be; you will build for a future that which will be nothing less than extraordinary; and you will be living a life that is thoroughly worth living in the great eternal now. You will be making the ideal real at every step of the way, but every moment will lead you into worlds that are richer and realms that are fairer than you ever dreamed of before. It is therefore evident that when we learn to live the life that is really worth living, there is no reason whatever why a single moment should be empty, dull or uninteresting in the life of any person, because there is so much to live for that has real worth, so much to enjoy that holds real enjoyment, so much to do that is thoroughly worth doing; besides, the whole of life, when actually lived, is eternally alive with interest, ever revealing the splendor of its vast transcendent domains. And he who aims to live for the purpose of gaining the realization of, and the possession of, as many spheres of this life as possible will find full expression for every ambition and every aspiration that he can possibly arouse in his mind. Life to him will be a continuous feast and existence will become an endless advancement into the highest attainments and the greater achievements than even the most illustrious mind can picture as its goal.

CHAPTER XV

WHEN ALL THINGS BECOME POSSIBLE

When the mind is placed in conscious contact with the limitless powers of universal life all things become possible, and faith is the secret. To have faith is to possess that interior insight through which we can discern the marvelous possibilities that are latent in the great within, and to possess the power to enter into the very life of the great within. To most minds there seems to be a veil in consciousness between the spheres of present understanding and the spheres of the higher wisdom, and though there are many who feel distinctly that there is something greater within them, yet it seems hidden, and they cannot discern it. Faith, however, has the power to perceive those greater things within that previously seemed hidden, and this is the reason why faith is the evidence of things not seen. Faith does not simply believe. It knows; it knows through higher insight, because faith is this higher insight. Faith is not blind, objective belief, but a higher development of consciousness through which the mind transcends the circumscribed and enters into the life of the boundless.

When faith is active, consciousness is expanded so much that it breaks all bounds and penetrates even those realms that objective man has never heard of before. In this way new truth and discoveries are brought to light, and this is how man gains the understanding of what previously seemed to be beyond his comprehension. When we define faith as that power in mind through which consciousness can penetrate into the larger sphere of life we perceive readily why almost anything can be accomplished through faith, and we also understand why no one can afford to work without faith. When consciousness enters a larger sphere of action its capacity is naturally increased, and the greater power that can be drawn upon in performing any kind of work increases in proportion; likewise, the knowing how to work will be promoted in the same manner. To do anything successfully one must know how to do it and have the power to do what one knows should be done, and both these essentials are increased in proportion to the enlargement of consciousness. One of the principal metaphysical laws declares that whatever you become conscious of you express through your personality; therefore, according to this law more life, more power and more wisdom will come into actual possession in the personal life as we become conscious of more and more of these things in the mental life; in other words, the ideal is made real.

The art of extending consciousness into the realms of unlimited life and power and wisdom is the secret through which all great attainments and great achievements become possible; but without faith this enlargement of consciousness cannot take place, because faith is that power that perceives and enters into the greater things that are still before us. Faith looks into the beyond of every faculty, talent or power and perceives that there is much more of these same talents and powers further on. In fact, there is no visible limit to anything when viewed through the eyes of faith. Consciousness does not extend itself in any direction until it feels that there will be tangible grounds upon which to proceed. You can become conscious only of those things that seem real; therefore, to extend your consciousness in any direction you must secure evidence of the fact that there is more reality in that direction; and here we find the great mission of faith. Faith supplies this evidence. Faith looks further on into the beyond and sees real reality at every step, and proves to consciousness that things not seen are thoroughly substantial. Faith discerns that there is no danger in going on and on because there is solid ground all the way, no matter how far into the limitless we may wish to go; there is no danger of being lost in an empty void by following faith. Instead, faith gives us a positive assurance of finding more life, more power, more wisdom and a fairer state of existence than we ever knew before.

The practical value of faith is therefore to be found in its power to enlarge all the faculties and spheres of action in the mind of man, and as this enlargement can go on indefinitely, as there is no end to the visible, we conclude that anything can be accomplished by following faith. No matter how much wisdom or power we may require to reach the goal we have in view we can finally secure the required amount through the perpetual enlargement of consciousness. This is evident, and since faith is that something in mind that leads consciousness on and on into larger fields of action it becomes indispensable to all growth, to all great achievements, to all high attainments and to the realization of all true ideals. The man who has no faith in himself can neither improve himself nor his work. When nothing is added to his ability, capacity or skill there can be nothing added to the quality or the quantity of what he is doing. The effect will not improve until we have improved the cause; and man himself is the cause of everything that appears in his life.

Modern psychology, however, has discovered and conclusively demonstrated that no faculty can be improved until the conscious sphere of action of that faculty is enlarged and thoroughly developed. Therefore, to promote the efficiency of any faculty the conscious action of that faculty must become larger and imbued with more life. This is the fundamental principle in all advancement, but consciousness will not enlarge its sphere of action until it perceives that there is reality beyond its present sphere, and it is only through the interior insight of faith that the greater reality existing beyond present limitations is discovered to be real. The lack of this interior insight among the great majority is the principal obstacle that prevents them from becoming more than they are. Their minds have not the power to see the potential side of their larger nature. They are aware of the objective only and can do only as much as the limited power of the objective will permit. But they are not aware of the fact that there is limitless power within, nor do they realize that they can draw upon this great interior power and thus accomplish not only more and more, but everything that they may now have in view. Not having the power to look beyond present attainment, the little world in which they live is all that is real to them. Occasionally there is a dream or a vision of greatness, but it soon fades away, and in those rare instances when the high vision continues for some time the knowledge of how to make real the ideal is usually not at hand.

The human race is divided into three classes; first, those who live in the limited world and never see anything beyond the limited; second, those who live in the limited world but have occasional glimpses of greater things, though having neither the knowledge nor the power to make their dreams come true; and third, those who are constantly passing from the lesser to the greater, making real every ideal as soon as it comes within the world of their conscious comprehension. The last group is small, but there are millions to-day who are on the verge of a larger sphere of existence, and for this reason we should usher into the world at once a greater movement for the promotion of faith than has ever been known before. It is more faith that these millions need in order to enter into the beautiful life they can see before them. It is more faith they must have before they can become as much as they desire to be. It is faith, and faith alone, that can give them the power to do what this great sphere of existence may require.

To make real the ideal in any life faith must be combined with work, and no work should be undertaken unless it can be animated thoroughly with the power of faith. The reason why is found in the fact that all practical action is weak or strong, depending upon the capacity of that part of the mind which directly controls that action; and the capacity of the mind increases in proportion to the attainment of faith. To accomplish what we have in view, it is not only necessary to know how to go about our work, but it is necessary to have sufficient power, and faith is the open door to more and more power. The very moment you obtain more faith you feel stronger; you are then certain of results and the very best results; and the reason why is found in the fact that faith always connects the mind with the larger, the greater and the inexhaustible. On the other hand, you may have an abundance of energy, but do not see clearly how to apply that energy in such a way that results will be as desired; again the remedy is more faith. Faith elevates the mind and lifts consciousness up above doubt, uncertainty and confusion. When you go up into faith you enter the light and can see clearly how to proceed; but in this connection we must avoid a very common mistake. When we discover the remarkable power of faith there is a tendency to depend upon faith exclusively and ignore other faculties. We sometimes come to the conclusion that it matters little how we work or think or act so long as we have an abundance of faith, because faith will cause everything to come right. The fact, however, that we sometimes come to this conclusion proves that we have not found real faith, because when we have an abundance of real faith we can see clearly the great truth that all thought and action must be right to secure results, and that all faculties and powers must be employed in their highest states of efficiency if we wish to make real the ideal. Though it is absolutely necessary to have the vision, still the vision is not sufficient in itself. After the vision has been discovered in the ideal it must be made real; the principle must be applied; the new discovery must be worked out in practical action; but these things require both fine intelligence and practical skill.

Faith without works is dead, because it does nothing, uses nothing, creates nothing; it is as if it were not; and works without faith are so insignificant and ordinary that they are usually very little better than nothing. But when work and faith are combined then everything becomes possible. The power of faith is placed in action; work becomes greater and greater, and whatever our purpose may be we shall positively scale the heights. The great principle is to combine unlimited faith with skillful work. Work with all the skill that you can possibly cultivate, but inspire all your efforts with the mighty soul of a limitless faith. Become as learned, as intellectual and as highly developed in mind as possible, but animate your prodigious intellect with the supreme spirit of faith. Faith does not come to take the place of art, skill or intellect. Faith comes to give real soul to art, skill and intellect. Faith comes to fill all physical and mental action with renewed life and power. It comes to open that door through which all our efforts may pass to higher and greater things. Faith is not simply for the moral and spiritual life; it is not simply for what is sometimes called higher endeavor. It is for all endeavor, and it has the power to push all endeavor with such energy and force that we simply must succeed, no matter what our work may be. The man who has faith in his work, faith in himself, faith in the human race and faith in the Supreme—that man simply cannot fail, if he gives the full power of his faith to everything that he undertakes to do.

We must eliminate the idea that faith is something apart from every-day life, and that it is something for the future salvation of the soul only. We have held to that belief so long that real faith has actually been separated from human existence, and we find very few people to-day who really know what faith actually is. The fact is that if you are not giving your faith to everything you do, be it physical, mental or spiritual, you have not as yet obtained any faith. When faith comes it never comes to give greater power to a part of your life. It comes to give supreme power to all your life, and it comes to push all your work toward higher efficiency and greater results. When you have real faith you never undertake anything without first placing your entire being in the very highest attitude of faith. Even the most trivial things you do are done invariably in the spirit of faith. This is very important, because by training yourself to be at your best in little things it soon becomes second nature for you to be your best in all things, and when you are called upon to do something of exceptional importance, something that may seem very difficult, you do not fall down; you are fully equal to the occasion. The more we exercise faith the more it develops; it is therefore profitable to use faith at all times and in everything that we do.

When we know that faith is that something that takes mind into the superior side of life and thus places in action superior powers it is not difficult to understand how to proceed when we place ourselves in faith. As we think more and more of this higher side of our nature, this better side, this wonderful side, we gradually become conscious of its remarkable possibilities and soon we can feel the power of superiority becoming stronger and stronger in everything that we do in mind or body. To develop the power of faith the first thing to do is to train the mind to hold attention constantly upon the limitless side of life; that is, to live in the upper story of being and to think as much as possible about the true idea of faith, as well as the interior essence of faith itself. When you begin to see clearly that faith is this higher development of mind, this insight that leads to higher wisdom, greater power and more abundant life, you actually find yourself entering into the realization of those greater things whenever you think of faith. By concentrating your attention upon the inner meaning of faith your mind becomes clearer, your faculties become stronger and your entire being feels the presence of more life; and that you can do much better work while in this condition is too evident to require any more elucidation. While in the attitude of faith you cannot only do your present work better, but you will steadily develop the ability and the capacity to do more difficult work— work that will prove more useful to the community and more remunerative to yourself. The world wants everything well done and is more than willing to pay for good work. We are all seeking the best and the majority aim consciously or unconsciously to give their best, but without faith it is not possible for anyone to be his best, give his best, or do his best.

Do your best and the best will come to you in return. The universe is founded upon justice, and justice will positively be done to you if you have faith in justice. Everything in life is moving toward greater worth, and since justice is universal, the greater the worth of a man the greater the value of those things that he will receive in life. The worthy soul is always rich in those things that have real worth; and when we learn to harmonize our-selves more fully with all the laws of existence we shall place ourselves in that condition where we not only can give more that has worth but will also receive everything of worth that actually is our own. Whether you are working in the commercial world, the professional world, the artistic world, the intellectual world; in brief, whatever your work may be, to have the best results you must have faith, and it is practical results in practical everyday life that determines how rapidly and how perfectly the ideal shall be made real in your own world. Whoever will do his present work as well as he possibly can, and continue to work in the highest attitude of faith will positively advance and perpetually continue to advance. He may not have accomplished much thus far; but if he takes this course, combining efficient work with supreme faith, he certainly has a splendid future before him.

If your present work is not to your liking do not plan to change at once.

First proceed with your present work in this higher attitude of faith. You may thus find your present work to be the very work you want; or your present work, if it is not what is intended for you, will become the open door through which you will reach that field of action that will be to your liking, providing you animate your present work with all the faith that you can possibly realize. Make yourself the best of your kind whatever your sphere of action may be, because by so doing you are not only increasing the number of great minds in the world, but you are adding immeasurably to the world's welfare and joy; and he who combines his work with limitless faith will become the greatest and the best in his sphere. In the application of faith, however, the whole of attention must not be directed upon the improvement of your work, but more especially upon the improvement of yourself. The more you improve the better work you can do, but while you are improving yourself your improvement will be incomplete and insufficient unless you each day practically employ in your work what you have developed in yourself. Give the power of every moment to greater attainment in yourself and to greater achievement in your present occupation, and you will fulfill that dual purpose in life that invariably leads to the heights. Develop more power, more ability and more faith and combine these in everything that you do. Through the power of faith you will not only discern higher and higher ideals, but you will also give greater capacity to your practical ability. In other words, you will not only gain the power to see the ideal, but you will gain the power to practically apply what you have seen; you will make tangible in real life what the visions of the soul have revealed in the ideal life; and as you grow in faith, so great will this power become that there is no ideal you cannot make real. You will have placed yourself in touch with limitless power—the power of the Supreme, and therefore to you, all things will become possible.

CHAPTER XVI

THE ART OF GETTING
WHAT IS WANTED

We frequently hear the statement "I never received what I wanted until the time came when I did not care for it and did not need it." This statement may in most instances be based upon an unguided imagination, though this is not always the case, because there are thousands of people who actually have this very experience. They never get what they want until the desire for it, as well as the need of it, have disappeared. There may be occasional exceptions, but the rule is that what we persistently desire we shall sooner or later receive. Too often it is later, the reason being that most desires are purely personal and are not inspired by those real needs that may exist in the great eternal now. Mere personal desires are usually out of harmony with the present process of soul-growth, and therefore there is no supply in our immediate mental vicinity for what those desires naturally need. This is the reason why more time is required for the fulfilling of these desires, and frequently the time required is so long that when the desire is fulfilled we do not need it any more. When we desire only those things that are best for us now, that is, those things that are necessary to a full and complete life in the present, we shall receive what we desire at the very time when those things are needed. What is best for us now is ready in the mental world to be expressed through us. Every demand has its own supply in the immediate vicinity, and every demand will find or attract its own supply without any delay whatever, but the demand must be natural, not artificial.

The average person is full of artificial desires—desires that have been suggested by what other people possess or require. But the question is not what we need now to compete with other people so as to make more extravagant external appearances than other people. The question is, what do we need now to make our present life as full, as complete and as perfect as it possibly can be made now. Ask yourself this question and your artificial desires will disappear. In the first place, you will try to ascertain what you are living for, and what may be required to promote that purpose of life that may seem true to your deeper thought on the subject. In the second place, you will realize that since it is the present and the present only for which you are living you will concentrate your attention upon the living of life now. This will bring the whole power of desire down upon the present moment and engage all the forces of life to work for the perfection of the present moment. The result will be the elimination of nearly everything that is foreign to your present state of existence.

To know what to desire and what to ignore in the present may seem to be a problem, but it is easily solved by depending upon the demands of the soul instead of the demands of the person. The desires of the average person are almost constantly colored or modified by suggestions from the artificial life of the world; they are therefore not normal and are not true to real life. The desires of the soul, however, are always true and are always in harmony with the greatest good and the highest welfare of the entire being of man in his present sphere. It is the soul that lives; therefore the soul can feel truly what is necessary to fulness and completeness in present life. Real life never lives for the past or for the future. Real life lives now, and therefore knows the needs of life now. It is the soul that grows and develops; therefore the soul can feel what is required to promote present development. For these reasons it is perfectly safe to follow the desires of the soul and those desires only; it will mean the best of everything for body, mind and spirit, and the right things will appear in the right places at the right time.

We live not to acquire things nor to provide for an extravagant personal appearance. We live to become more than we are. We live to live a larger and a greater life perpetually; therefore every desire must desire only those things that are conducive to growth, advancement, attainment and superior states of existence. The expression of desire, however, must not confound cause with effect, but must so place every desire that the power of cause invariably precedes the appearance of effect. To promote advancement in life we must advance in our own conscious beings before true advancement in the external world can follow. Forced advancement is artificial, and is detrimental to the permanent welfare of the soul. Do not push the person forward. Live to give greater expression to the soul and you will develop all the power that is necessary to push the person forward toward any lofty goal you may have in view. Become more than you are from the within, and external environments, demands and opportunities will ask you to come forward. Thus you promote true advancement.

There are a number of people who believe that to follow the desires of the soul is to be led into poverty, and hardships in general, but those who have this belief know practically nothing about the real nature of the soul. He who follows the desires of the soul will be led away from sickness, trouble and poverty and will enter into the possession of the best of everything, physical, mental and spiritual. This is natural, because the ruling desire of the soul is to promote the attainment of greater power, greater ability, a larger life, superior qualities and greater capacity so that things may be done that are really worth while. The soul lives to unfold the limitless possibilities that are latent in the within. Therefore, to live the life of the soul and follow the desires of the soul is to become greater, more able, more competent and more worthy every day. By developing greater power in yourself you overcome sickness and trouble; and by constantly increasing your ability, your talent and your genius you pass from poverty to abundance, no matter where you may live or what your work may be.

The man who lives to perfect his entire being will naturally desire only those things that are conducive to the growth and the development that he is trying to promote, and such desires will be supplied without delay, because they are natural, and they are in harmony with real life. What life may require now that life *can* receive now. This is the law. But every artificial desire that we may hold in mind interferes with the workings of this law, and since the average person is full of artificial desires he usually fails to receive what is needed to promote the welfare of real life. Every desire that is held in mind uses up energy; therefore, if the desire is artificial, all that energy is thrown away, or it may be employed in creating something that we have no use for when it does come. It has been very wisely stated that a strong mind should weigh matters with the greatest of care before uttering a single prayer, because most of the prayers of such a mind are answered; and should he pray for something that he cares nothing for when it does come he will have a burden instead of a blessing.

The majority are entirely too reckless about their desires; they desire things because they want them at the time, but do not stop to think whether the things desired will prove satisfactory or not when they are received; and since we usually get, sooner or later, what we persistently desire, the art of knowing what to desire is an art, the development of which becomes extremely important. It is not an act of wisdom to pray for future blessings or to entertain desires that will not be fulfilled until some future time. When the future comes you may have advanced so far, or changed so much, that the needs of your life will be entirely different from what they are in the present. Let every desire be just for to-day, and let that desire be prompted by the ruling desire of your life; that is, the desire to become a more powerful personality, a stronger character, a more brilliant mind and a greater soul. Live perpetually in the desire that you will receive the best that life can give to-day, that all things will work together for good to you now, and that everything necessary to the promotion of your highest welfare will come in abundance during the great eternal now. Make this desire so strong that your heart and soul are in it with all the power of life, and let every present moment be deeply inspired by the very spirit of this desire. The result will be that the best of everything will constantly be coming into your world, and everything that may be necessary to make your life full and complete now will be added in an ever increasing abundance.

In this connection we must remember that it is not best for anyone to pass through sickness, trouble and misfortune. When people have misfortune they sometimes console themselves with the belief that it is all for the best, but this is not the truth; though we can and should turn every adverse circumstance to good account. When you come into trouble you have not been living for the best. You have made mistakes or entertained artificial desires, and that is why trouble came. Had you lived in the faith that all things are working together for good, nothing but good would have come; and had you lived in the strong desire for the best and the best only, you would have received the very best that you could appreciate and enjoy now. The belief that we have to pass through trouble to reach peace and comfort is an illusion that we have inherited from the dark ages, and the belief that we are purified through the fires of adversity is another illusion coming from the same source. We are purified by passing through a perpetual refining process, and this process is the result of consciousness gaining a deeper, a higher, a truer and a more beautiful conception of that divinity in man that is created in the image and likeness of the Supreme; and it is well to remember that this refining process can live and act only where there is peace of mind, harmony of life and the joy of the spirit.

Higher states of life do not come by passing through adversity but by living the soul-life so completely that you are never affected by adversity. The peace that passeth understanding does not come from the act of overcoming trouble, but is the product of that state of mind that is so high and so strong that it is never moved by trouble. The greatest victory does not come through successful warfare, but through a life that is so high and in such perfect harmony with all things that it wars against nothing, resists nothing, antagonizes nothing, pursues nothing, overcomes nothing. The life that is above things does not have to overcome things, and it is such a life that brings real peace, true joy and sublime harmony. The belief that we have to fight for our rights is another illusion; likewise, the belief that wrongs have to be overcome. The higher law declares, *be* right in all things and you will have your rights in all things. Be above all things and you will not have to overcome anything. Live in the spirit of the limitless supply and you will not have to demand anything from any source, because you will be in the life of abundance.

There is value in the silent demand, but it is not the highest thought. The highest thought is to desire with heart and soul whatever we may need now, and live in the absolute conviction that all natural demands are supplied now; then we shall not have to make any demands whatever, silent or audible. A mental demand usually becomes a forced mental process, and such a process, though it may succeed temporarily, as all forced actions do, will finally fail; and when it does fail the mind will not be as high in the scale as it was before. The highest state is pure realization, a state where we realize that everything is at hand for us now and will be expressed the very moment we desire its tangible possession. Here we must remember never to turn our desires into mental demands, but to make every desire an inward soul feeling united perfectly with faith. The highest desire is always transformed into a whole-souled gratitude, even before the desire has been outwardly fulfilled, because when the desire is high in the spirit of faith it knows at once the prayer will be answered, and consequently gives thanks from the very depths of the heart.

The prayer that is uttered through the spirit of faith and through the soul of thanksgiving—the two united in one, is always answered, whether it be uttered silently or audibly. The desires that are felt in such a prayer are inspired by the divinity that dwells within and are therefore true to real life. They are soul desires. They belong to the present and will be fulfilled in the present at the very time when we want them and need them. When we fail to get what is wanted, our wants are either artificial or so full of false and perverted wants that the law of supply is prevented from doing its proper work for us. Under such conditions it is necessary to ask the great question, "What am I living for?" Then eliminate those desires that are suggested by the world, and retain only those that desire the highest state of perfection for the whole man. It is the truth that when man seeks first the kingdom of the true life, the perfect life, all other things needful to such a life will be added. He who desires more life will receive more life, and with the greater life comes the greater power—that power with which man may create his own destiny and make everything in his life as he wishes it to be. In order to get what is wanted or what is needed the usual process of desire must be reversed. Instead of desiring things, desire that greater life and that greater power that can produce things. First, desire life, power, ability, greatness, superiority, high personal worth, and exceptional spiritual attainments. Never desire definite environments, special things or certain fixed conditions. Leave those things to Higher Power, because when Higher Power begins to act you will receive the very best environments, the richest things and the most perfect conditions that you can possibly enjoy. Desire real life first, and all that is beautiful and perfect in the living of such a life in body, mind and soul, will invariably be added. Follow the desires of the soul and you will receive everything that is necessary, not only for the life of the soul but for the life of mind and body as well. Seek the Source of all good things and you will receive all good things.

CHAPTER XVII

PATHS TO HAPPINESS

To be happy is the privilege of everybody, and everybody may be happy at all times and under all circumstances through the knowing and living of a few simple principles. The reason why happiness is not as universal and as abundant as it might be is because the majority seek happiness for itself alone. Happiness is an effect. It comes from a definite cause. Therefore, if we would obtain happiness we must not seek happiness for itself, but seek that something that produces happiness. He who seeks happiness directly, who desires happiness for the sake of gaining happiness or who works directly for the attainment of happiness will find but little real joy in his life. To seek happiness is to fail to find it, but to seek the cause of happiness is to find it in an ever increasing measure. Happiness, however, is not the result of any one single cause. It is the result of many ideal states of being grouped together into one harmonious whole. In brief, happiness is the result of true being perfectly lived upon all planes of consciousness.

Happiness does not come from having much, but from being much; therefore, anything that will tend to bring forth into tangible expression more and more of the real being of man will add to his joy. To promote the larger and larger expression of the real being of man; in other words, to promote the living in the real of more and more of the ideal, a number of methods may be presented; but as happiness is based upon simplicity, methods for producing the cause of happiness must also be based upon simplicity, therefore only those principles that are purely fundamental need be employed. These principles however must not be applied singly. It is necessary to combine them all in practical everyday living, and when this is done, more and more happiness will invariably follow. The principles necessary to the perpetual increase of happiness are as follows:

1. **Live the simple life.** The complex life is not only a burden to exis-

tence, but is invariably an obstacle to the highest attainments and welfare of man; and the majority, even among those whose tangible possessions are very insignificant, are living a complex life; but when the average person is told to remove complexity from his world and adopt simplicity he almost invariably destroys the beauty of life. The art of living a life that is both simple and beautiful is an art that few have mastered, though it is by no means difficult. Most of the life that is called simple is positively devoid of beauty and has nothing whatever that is attractive about it. In fact, it is positively a detriment both to happiness and advancement. To live the simple life is not to return to primitive conditions nor to decide to be satisfied with nothing, or next to nothing. It is possible to live the simple life in the midst of all the luxuries that wealth can buy, because simplicity does not spring from the quantity of possession but from the arrangement of possession. The central idea in the living of a simple life is to eliminate non-essentials. The question should be, "Which of the things that are about me do I need to promote the greatest welfare of my life?" To answer this question will not be difficult, because almost anyone can determine at first thought what is needed and what is not needed to a complete life. When the decision is made, non-essentials should be removed as quickly as possible. True, we must avoid extremes, and whatever we do we must do nothing to decrease the beauty or the harmony of life.

There are a great many things in the world of the average person that he simply thinks he needs, though he knows that those things never did anything but retard his progress. It it therefore necessary to remove non-essentials from the mind before we attempt to simplify our immediate surroundings. The simple life is a beautiful life, with all burdens removed, and it is only the unnecessary that is burdensome. To live the simple life, surround yourself only with those things that are directly conducive to your welfare, but do not consider it necessary to limit the quantity of those things. Surround yourself with *everything* that is necessary to promote your welfare, no matter how much it may be, although do not place in your world a single thing that is not a direct power for good in your world. You thus establish the harmony of simplicity without placing any limitations whatever upon your possessions, your welfare or your highest need. You thus eliminate everything that may act as a burden; and we can readily understand that when all burdens are removed from life the happiness of life will be increased to a very great degree.

2. **Live the serene life.** Be calm, peaceful, quiet and undisturbed in all things and at all times. Confusion and hurry waste energy, and it is a

well-known fact that depression and gloom are produced, in most instances, simply by the energy of the system running low. The serene life, if lived in poise, will keep the system brimful of energy at all times, and so long as you are filled through and through with life and energy you will be full of spirit and joy. Our saddest moments are usually the direct results of reactions from turbulent thinking and living; therefore, such moments will be eliminated completely when thinking and living are made peaceful and serene. It is not necessary to live the strenuous life in order to accomplish a great deal, although on the other hand it is not quantity but quality that we seek. Our object should not be to do many things, but to do good things. If we can do many things that are good, very well, but we must have quality first in the mind; the quantity will increase as we grow in capacity, and there is nothing that promotes the increase of mental and physical capacity more than calm, serene living. The sweetest joys that the mind can feel usually come from those deep peaceful realizations of the soul when all is quiet and serene. Therefore, to cultivate the habit of living always in this beautiful calm will invariably add happiness to happiness every day of continued existence.

3. **Be in love with the world.** He who loves much will be loved much in return, and there is nothing in the world that can give more joy and higher joy than an abundance of real love. The selfish love, that is only personal, and that *must* be gratified to be enjoyed, gives but a passing pleasure, the reaction of which is always pain. When we love with such a love we are always unhappy when not directly loved in return, and the purely selfish love never brings real love in return. When we love everybody with the pure love of the soul, that love that does not ask to be loved in return but loves because it *is* loved, we shall positively be loved in return; and not simply by a few here and there, but by great numbers. To feel that you are loved unselfishly, that you are loved not because anything is expected in return, but because the love is there and *must* come—to feel this love is a source of joy which cannot be measured, and this joy everybody can receive in abundance now. The simple secret is to love the whole world at all times and under every circumstance; love everybody with heart and soul and *mean* it, and everything that happens to you will add both to the pleasure of the mind and to the more lofty joys of the soul.

4. **Be useful.** "Give to the world the best that you have and the best will come to you." Hold nothing back. If you have something that you can share with the world, let everybody have it to-day. Do all that you can for

everybody, not because you expect reward, but because it is a part of your nature. Be all that you can be and do all that you can do. Never say, "I will do only as much as I am paid for." Such an attitude has kept many a person in poverty for life. Reward is an effect, not a cause. Do not place the reward first, and the service second. Increase your service and the reward will increase in proportion; you will thus not only place yourself in a position where you can secure more and more of the good things of life, but you will live in that position where you are bringing into expression more and more of the good things that exist in your own life. And we must remember that the greatest joy does not come from gaining good things from the without, but from the expression of good things from the within; and when both of these are combined harmoniously we shall secure all the joys of life—the joys that come from the outer world and the joys that come from the beauty and the splendor of the inner world. To combine these in your life, be useful; express your best; be your best; do your best. You thus bring forth riches from within and attract riches from without. Give richly of the best you have and good things in an ever increasing number will constantly flow into your life. That deep soul-satisfaction that comes to mind when we have rendered valuable service to man is entirely too good to be ignored; it is one of the deepest and highest joys that man can know. Those people who are the most valuable wherever they go are always the happiest, and we all can be of service in a thousand ways; therefore, we may add to our happiness in just as many ways, if we will always remember to be and do the best we can wherever we may go in the world.

5.   **Think and speak the beautiful only.** Every word or thought that you express will return to you. Never say anything to make others discouraged or unhappy; it will come back to yourself. He who gives unhappiness to others is giving unhappiness to himself. He who adds to the joys of others is perpetually adding to his own joy. You can say something good about everybody. Then say it. It will give joy to everybody concerned, yourself included. Think only of the beautiful side of everybody. Everybody has a beautiful side. Find it and think of that only. You will thus live in the world of the beautiful, and he who lives in the world of the beautiful is always happy. Speak kindly and pleasantly to everybody; think kindly and pleasantly of everybody, and your days of gloom will be gone. When every word is animated with the spirit of kindness and joy, you will not only increase the power of joy in your own life, but you will be sowing the seeds of joy in the garden of the universal life; and one of these days you will reap

abundantly from what you have sown. Let this sowing time be continuous and the harvest will be continuous; thus you will be reaping a harvest of boundless joy every day of your endless existence.

6. **Forgive and forget everything that seems wrong.** We have spent many a weary day simply because we persisted in remembering something that was unpleasant. Forget the wrong and it will disturb you no more. Forgive others for what they have done and you will have no unpleasant memories to cloud the sky of your mental world. When people speak unkindly of you, never mind. Let them say what they like, if they must. Nothing can harm you but your own wrong thinking and living. If people do not treat you right remember they would act differently if they knew better, and you know better than to become offended. So therefore forgive it all and resolve to be happy. Forgive everybody for what is not right and forget everything that is not conducive to the right. You have no time to brood over ills and troubles that exist only in your memory. Your memory is created for a better purpose. Remember the good, the true and the beautiful; this is one of the greatest secrets of perpetual happiness. When you forgive those who have wronged you, you usually come to a place where you think more of those very persons than you ever did before, and when you come to that place you will realize a joy that is far too sweet and beautiful for pen to ever describe. It seems to be a blessing coming direct from heaven and it does not go away. This fact proves that he who learns to forgive rises in the scale of life. He who can forget and forgive the wrongs of the lowlands of undeveloped life, invariably ascends to the heights, and it is upon the heights that we find real happiness. Such is the reward of forgiveness. It will therefore not be difficult to forgive when we know that the results are so rich and so beautiful; indeed, to forgive and forget everything that seems wrong will thus become a coveted pleasure.

7. **Be perfectly contented with the present.** We have heard a great deal about the value of divine discontent, but discontent is never divine any more than indignation is ever righteous. Perfect contentment is one of the highest states of the soul and is one of those attainments that invariably follows ideal living. Discontent, however, in any of its shapes or forms, always indicates that we are not on the true path. So long as there is discontent there is something wrong in our living, but the moment this wrong is righted perpetual contentment will be realized. If your present lot is not what you wish it to be, discontent will not make it better. Be perfectly content with the present and create more lofty mansions for the future; thus

you will not only improve your condition every year, but you will be supremely happy every day. The more perfect your present contentment the more power you will have to create for yourself a greater future, and the more mental light you will have to build wisely for days to come. The more contentment you realize in your mind the more brightness and strength there will be in your mind.

Find the good that you already possess, then enjoy it. Better things are even now on the way and through the harmony of contentment you will be prepared to receive them. You will also be in that higher state of mental discernment where you can know good things when you see them. Many people are so much disturbed by the discord of discontent that they are unable to recognize the good things already in their world; thus they add doubly to the cause of discontent. Contentment, however, does not mean to be so satisfied with present conditions that we do not care to change them. True contentment not only appreciates the full value of the present, but also appreciates those greater powers in life that can perpetually add to the value of the present; therefore, the contented mind gains everything that life can give in the great eternal now, while at the same time perpetually increasing the richness, the worth and the beauty of the great eternal now. To be contented, find fault with nothing. Those things that are not quite right can be made better. Proceed to make them better, and one of the greatest joys of life comes directly from that action of life that is causing things to become better. The process of growth and advancement is invariably conducive to joy; therefore, if we cease finding fault, and use all our time in promoting improvement, we will find sources of happiness in every imperfection that we may meet in life. In other words, when we aim to improve everything that we meet, we bring out all the good that is latent in our world, and to increase the expression of the good in our world is to increase our own measure of joy.

8. **Seek the ideal.** Look for the ideal everywhere; live in ideal environments when possible; but if not possible in an external sense create for yourself an ideal environment in the internal sense. Live in ideal mental worlds no matter what external worlds may be. Associate as much as possible with ideal people, and if you are living an ideal life in your own mental and spiritual life, you will attract ideal people wherever you go. And one of the greatest joys of life is to associate with those who are living in lofty realms. We have no time to give to the common and the ordinary. We want the best. We deserve the best, and we can secure the best by seeking the

best and the best only. Live your own ideal life. Seek the ideal both in the within and in the without, and aim to make the ideal real in every thought, word and deed; you will thus cause every moment to add to your joy.

9.   **Develop the whole man.** To promote an orderly growth through-out your entire being is highly important, and to establish perfect harmony of action among all the various members of mind and body is indispensable to happiness. Develop everything in your nature and place all the elements in your being in perfect harmony. You will thus ascend perpetually to higher states of being and greater realms of joy. Much of the discord and unhappiness that comes into life is the direct result of one-sidedness and undevelopment, and these can be permanently removed only through the orderly development of the whole man. Body, mind and soul must be per-fectly balanced in every sense of that term. The more perfectly you are balanced the greater will be your joy, because a balanced nature is conducive to harmony, and harmony is conducive to happiness.

10.   **Open the mind to beautiful thoughts only.** The world is full of thoughts, all kinds of thoughts, but only those that are invited will come to you. There is nothing that affects life more than the thoughts we think; and the thoughts we are to think will depend almost entirely upon our mental attitude toward that which we meet in life. When we resolve to receive only beautiful thoughts from everything with which we come in contact the change for the better in life will be simply remarkable. All things will become new. We will actually enter a new heaven and a new earth, and the joys of existence will multiply many times.

11.   **Be in touch with the harmony of life.** The universe is full of music, and happy is the soul that can hear the symphonies of heaven; he can find no greater joy. Every soul that has been in tune with higher things is familiar with that deep pleasure that comes to mind when the sensations of sublime harmony sweetly thrill every fiber of being; and we can all so live that we can be in tune with the music of the spheres. When you learn how to place yourself in harmony with the music of life you may for hours at a time remain within the gates of everlasting joy, and you may enter into the very life of that sublime something which eye has not seen nor ear heard. It is then that you understand why the kingdom of heaven is within and why all souls that have found that inner life are radiant with joy. Here is happiness without measure, happiness that you may enjoy anywhere and at any time. No matter what your environments may be, enter into these lofty realms and you will be the happiest soul in the world.

12.   **Consecrate every moment to the higher life.** The mind that is

ever ascending can never be sad. Perpetual ascension means perpetual joy. The happiest moments that come to you are those moments that come when you see yourself rising in the scale of sublime existence. You are then as-cending to the heights. You are entering into the cosmic realms—those realms where joy is supreme; and one single moment in that lofty realm gives more happiness than we can imagine were a million heavens united in one. It is in these realms that we enter the secret places of the Most High, and to enter into that sublime state is to gain all the happiness that life can give and have that happiness while eternity shall continue to be.

CHAPTER XVIII

CREATING IDEAL SURROUNDINGS

We all believed, not so very long ago, that the circumstances in which each individual was placed were produced by inevitable fate, and that the individual himself could not change them, but would have to remain where he was until something in his favor happened from external sources. What was to cause that something to happen we did not know, nor did we give the matter much thought. We believed more or less in chance and luck, and had no definite conception of the underlying laws of things. But now many of us have changed our minds, as we have received a great deal of new light on this most important subject. The many, however, are still in the old belief; they are ignorant of the fact that man can create his own destiny, and that fate, circumstances and environments are but the products of man himself, acting alone, or in association with others. But this is the fact, and it can be scientifically demonstrated by anyone under any circumstance.

This new idea that man can change his surroundings or transport himself to more agreeable environments through the use of psychological and metaphysical laws may seem unthinkable and far-fetched to a great degree; but when we study the subject with care we find that the principles, laws and methods involved are not only natural but thoroughly substantial and can be applied in tangible every-day affairs. If the surroundings in which you live are not what you wish them to be, know that you can change them. You can make those surroundings ideal. You can make those surroundings better and better at every step in your advancement, thus making real higher and higher ideals in your life. This is a positive truth and should be impressed so deeply upon every mind that no former belief on the subject can cause us to doubt our possession of this power for a moment. The importance of thus impressing this fact upon the mind becomes very evident when we understand that no matter how much we may know, we will have no results so long as we are in doubt as to whether what we have undertaken is really possible or not. There are thousands of people who believe, in a measure, that they can better their own conditions and they understand fully all the principles involved, but they have no satisfactory results because one moment they believe that the change is possible while at the next moment they entertain doubts. To have real results in any undertaking, especially in the changing of one's surroundings, one must believe with his whole heart that he can, and he must constantly employ all the necessary principles in that conviction. No undertaking ever succeeded that was not animated through and through with the positive faith that it could be done, and such a faith is simply indispensable if you wish to create ideal surroundings for yourself, because the process depends directly upon the way you think. You must think that you can so as to fully annihilate the belief that you cannot. Know that you can, and in that attitude continue to apply the necessary methods. Let nothing disturb your faith in the possibility of what you have undertaken to do in this respect, and you will positively succeed.

To create ideal surroundings, the first essential is to gain a clear understanding of what actually constitutes your surroundings. The world in which you live is a state of many elements, factors, forces and activities. The physical environment with all its various phases and conditions has been considered the most important, but this is not necessarily true, because the mental environment is just as much a part of the world in which you live as the physical. The term "world" is not confined simply to visible things; it also includes states of mind, mental tendencies, thoughts, desires, motives and all the different phases of consciousness. The place in which you live physically, the place in which you live mentally, the place in which you live morally and spiritually, these places combined constitute the world in which you live. All of these states and conditions are necessary parts of your surroundings, and it is your purpose to make these necessary parts as beautiful, as perfect and as ideal as possible.

The place where you work with your hands and with your brain is a part of your world, but the same is true of the place where you work in your dreams, in your aspirations and in your ideals. The circumstances and events of your life, physically and mentally; the opportunities that are constantly passing your way; the people you meet in your work; the people you think of in your thoughts; the people you associate with and friends that are near; the various elements of nature, both visible and invisible; the many groups of things in all their various phases that you come in contact with in your daily living; all of these belong in your world. To enter into details it would be possible to mention many hundreds of different elements or factors that compose the world in which the average person lives; but to be brief we can say that your world is composed of everything that enters your life, your home, your experience, your thought and your dreams of the ideal. All of these play their part in bringing to you the good that you may desire or the ills that you may receive. Consequently, since the world in which you live is so very complex and since so much of it belongs to the mental side of life, the process of change must necessarily involve mental laws, as well as physical laws; but here the majority have made their mistake.

Many great reformers and human benefactors have tried to emancipate the race through the change of exterior laws and external conditions alone, forgetting that most of the troubles of man and nearly all of his failures have their origin in the misuse of the mind. We all know that mind is the most prominent factor in the life of man, and yet this factor has been almost entirely overlooked in our former efforts to change the conditions of the race. Everything that man does begins in his mind; therefore, every change that is to take place in the life of man must begin in his mind. This being true, we understand readily why modern metaphysics and the new psychology can provide the long looked for essentials to human emancipation and advancement. When we examine all the various things that go to make up the world in which we live we may find it difficult to discover the real source of them all. How they were produced; who produced them; why they happened to come to us, or why we went to them; these are problems that we are called upon to solve before we can begin to create ideal surroundings.

To solve these problems the first great fact to realize is that we are the creators of our own environments; but at first sight this fact may not be readily accepted, because there are so many things that seem to be the creation of others. There are two kinds of creation, however, the direct and the indirect. In direct creation you create with the forces of your own life, your own thought and your own actions, and your own creations are patterned after the ideas in your own mind; but in what is termed indirect creation some one else creates what you desire. It is your creation, however, in a certain sense, because it was your desire that called it forth. To state the fact in another manner, the world in which you live may be your own direct creation or it may be the creation of another, but you went into that other one's world to live. In the majority of cases, the world in which the individual lives is produced partly by his own efforts and partly by the efforts of others, though there is nothing in his world that he has not desired or called forth in some manner and at some time during his existence. There are a number of people who are living in worlds created almost entirely by others; in fact, the world of the average person is three-fourths the creation of the race mind; but the question is, why does a person enter into a world that is created by others; why does he not live exclusively in a world created by himself?

There are many fine minds who are living in the world of the submerged tenth, but they did not create that world. That inferior state existed long before the birth of its present inhabitants; but why have those gone to live there who were not born there, and why have those who were born there not gone away to some better world of their own superior creation? Why do the people who live in that inferior world continue to perpetuate all its conditions? No world can continue to exist unless the people who live in that world continue to create those conditions that make up that world. Then why do not those people who live in the world of the submerged tenth cease the creating of that inferior world and begin the creation of the superior world when we know they have the power to do so? These are great questions, but they all have very simple answers. To answer these questions the first great fact to be realized is that the mind of man is the most important factor in everything that he does, and since no person can change his environments until he changes his actions we realize that the first step to be taken is the change of mind. Learn to change your mind for the better, and you will soon learn how to change your surroundings for the better. Before you proceed, however, there is another important condition to be considered; it is the fact that a portion of what is found in our world is created by ourselves, while the rest is the product of those minds with which we work or live. In the home each individual contributes to the qualities of the world which all the members of that home have in common, but each individual lives in a mental world distinctly his own, unless he is so negative that he has not a single individual purpose or thought. When the mental world of each individual is developed to a high degree it will become so strong that the fate of that individual will not be affected by the adverse conditions that may exist in the home.

The same is true of the environments that we meet in our places of work. No man need be affected very long by adverse surroundings or obstacles that he may meet in his work. He will finally become so strong that he can overcome every adversity that may exist in his physical world and thus gain entrance to better surroundings. However, we can readily see how a great deal of discord can be produced in a home or in our place of work where the different members are not in harmony with each other, and we can also understand how the events, circumstances and conditions of all those members, as well as each individual member, will be affected more or less by that inharmony; providing, however, that each individual is not developing that power of his mental world that can finally overcome all adversity. We can also understand how harmony and co-operation in a home or in a place of work would become a powerful force for good in the life of each individual concerned. Where a few are gathered in the right attitude there immense power will be developed; in fact, sufficient power to do almost anything that those few may wish to have done. This has been fully demonstrated a number of times; therefore, where many minds are associated in the creation of a world in which all will live, more or less, these higher mental laws should be fully understood and most thoroughly applied.

To enter a world that does not correspond with yourself and to go in and live where you do not naturally belong is to go astray, and such an action will not only cause all the forces and elements of your life to be misdirected, but you will place yourself in that position where nothing that is your own can come to you. There are vast multitudes, however, who have gone astray in this manner, and that is the reason why we find so many people who are misplaced, who do not realize their ideals, and who have not the privilege to enjoy their own. But we may ask, why do people go astray in this manner; why do we associate with people that do not belong in our world; why do we enter environments that do not correspond to our nature; why do we enter vocations for which we are not adapted, and why do we pursue plans, ideas and ambitions that lead us directly away from the very thing that our state of development requires? These are questions that we must answer, because no one can get the greatest good out of life or make the most of himself unless he lives in a world where he truly belongs. It is only when you live in a world created by yourself or in a world that others have created in harmony with you that you can be your real self, and since one must be truly himself to be wholly free and to promote his own advancement naturally and completely the subject is of great importance.

There are two reasons why we stray from our own true world and enter worlds where we do not belong; first, because we frequently permit the inferior side of our nature to predominate; and second, because we permit the senses to guide us in almost everything that we do. No person who has qualifications for the living of life in a superior world will ever enter an inferior world if he does not permit inferior desires to lead him into destructive paths; and no person, no matter what his work may be, will go down the scale so long as he follows the highest mental and spiritual light that he can possibly see during his most lofty moments. Follow the highest and the best that is in you, and you will constantly ascend into higher and better worlds; all your creative forces will thus build for you better and better surroundings, because so long as you are rising in the scale everything in your life in the external as well as in the internal must necessarily improve continuously. There is no need whatever of any person ever entering an inferior world. No one need pass into environments and surroundings that are less desirable than the ones in which he is living now. In fact, a person may take the opposite course. Endeavor constantly to attain superiority and you will steadily work yourself up into superiority, and as you become superior you will find an entrance into those worlds, those environments and those surroundings that are superior. There is a higher light, a better understanding within yourself that will guide you correctly in all your associations with people and environments. Do not follow physical desires or physical senses; let these be servants in the hands of higher wisdom. Follow this higher wisdom and you will make few mistakes, if any. You will constantly pass into better and better surroundings, because you will constantly pass into a higher, a better and a superior life. To follow the highest and the best that is within you under all circumstances does not constitute supernaturalism. It is simply good sense enlarged, and those who take this course will continue to make real the ideal in everything that may exist in the world in which they live. In consequence, both the mental world and the physical world in which we live will perpetually change for the better; and all our surroundings will improve accordingly, becoming more and more ideal until everything that exists about us is as beautiful as the visions of the soul.

CHAPTER XIX

CHANGING YOUR OWN FATE

When you discover that you are living in a world that you did not create and that does not correspond with your ideals, there is a tendency to break loose from external conditions at the earliest possible moment; but this tendency must be checked. Nothing is gained through an attempt to change from one world of effect to another world of effect without first changing the cause. The majority believe that when things are wrong in the outer world the only remedy is to change external conditions; but the fact is that external conditions are simply effects from internal causes, and so long as those internal causes remain the same, no attempt to change external conditions will prove of permanent value. So long as there are adverse causes in your inner life there will be adverse effects in your outer life, no matter how many times you may change from one condition to another or from one place to another.

When you begin to seek emancipation from the false world in which you are living now; in other words, when you begin to take positive measures to change your own fate, the first thing to do is to resolve not to make any forceful effort to change external conditions without first changing the inner cause of those conditions. Let outer things be as they are for the time being and continue to remain where you are until you can open a door to better things; but while you are waiting for this door to open do not be idle in any manner whatever. Although you are letting things be as they are in the external sense, and although you are not forcing yourself into different places or circumstances, still your purpose must be to entirely remake yourself. You came into this false state of life because you were misled by your own judgment, and if you should break loose, this same judgment will mislead you again; you will thus pass from one world that is not your own into some other world that is not your own, and there will be no improvement in the change. If you have not improved yourself in any manner whatever, your judgment will be just as inferior and unreliable as it was before, and no attempt to follow this judgment into different conditions will help matters in the least. Your object is not to set yourself free from the false world in which you are living now and then enter some other world that is not your own. You are not ready to move, neither physically nor mentally, until you have created a world of your own just as you would have it in your present state of development. Therefore, all thought of change will but divert your attention from the real purpose in view. So long as you are constantly thinking about external changes your mind cannot concentrate upon internal changes. So long as you are trying to change external conditions you cannot change yourself, and as you, yourself, are the cause of the new world which you are trying to create, you must recreate yourself before you can create the external world as desired.

To change your fate begin with yourself. If the environments in which you live are beneath your ideal, nothing can be gained by leaving those environments until the way is opened naturally to better things. If you simply get up and leave, you will gravitate into something elsewhere that will be just as uncongenial as those conditions you left behind. First, find the reason why you are living in your present adverse environments, then proceed to remove that cause. There may be many reasons, but in most cases the principal reason is a lack of ability or the lack of power to apply the ability you possess. In such a case you must remove inability by becoming more proficient, and as soon as you are competent to render better service you will readily find a better place. This means larger remuneration, and you will thus be able to secure more desirable surroundings. The many, however, will think that to promote sufficient improvement so as to command greater recompense, and do so in a short time, is practically impossible under the average conditions; but all difficulties that may be met in this connection may be readily removed through the principles of modern metaphysics.

Continuous improvement in everything pertaining to the life, the power, the capacity or the mentality of the individual can be readily promoted by anyone and decided results secured in a very short time. Therefore, no person need remain in adverse or limited conditions. He can, through the awakening and the expression of the best that is in himself, become competent to take advantage of greater opportunities and thus change his fate, his future and his destiny. If you wish to improve your physical environments, remain content where you are while you develop the power to earn and create better environments. Contentment with things as they are and harmony with everything about you are indispensable essentials if you wish to increase your ability, your capacity and your worth. To continue to kick against the pricks is to remain where pricks are abundant; but when we cease this mode of action and begin to polish off all the rough corners of our nature and improve ourselves in ever manner possible, things will take a turn. We will leave the world of pricks and enter a smoother path. The polished man is admitted to the polished world where there are no rough places and where adverse conditions are few, if existing at all.

When circumstances are against you, do not contend with circumstances. So long as we contend with things, things will contend with us. Do not resist present conditions; you prolong their existence by so doing. Whatever comes, meet all things in the attitude of perfect harmony and you will find that all things, even the most adverse, can be readily handled and turned to good account. We all know the marvelous power of the man who can harmonize contending factions, be they in his own life or in his circumstances. He not only gains good from everything that he meets, but he becomes a most highly respected personage, and is sought wherever opportunities are great and where great things are to be accomplished. Learn to harmonize the contending factions in your own life and experience, and you will find yourself entering new worlds where circumstances are more congenial and opportunities far greater. You will thus meet more desirable events, more desirable people, and superior advantages of every description will appear in your pathway. If your present friends are not to your liking admire them nevertheless for every good quality that they may possess. Emphasize their good qualities and ignore everything in their nature that seems inferior. This will help you to develop superior qualities in yourself; and this is extremely important, because as you develop superiority you prepare yourself for places higher up in the scale.

Make yourself over, so to speak, in your own friendship; increase your personal worth; polish your own character; refine your mind, and make real more and more of the ideal; double and treble your love and your kindness and constantly increase your admiration for everything that has real quality and high worth. Continue thus until you have results, whether those results begin to come at once or not; they will positively come ere long, and the things that you develop in yourself you will meet in your external world. Change yourself for the better in every shape and manner, and you change your fate for the better, but the change that you produce in yourself must not simply be negative in its action. It is the positive character, the positive mind, the positive personality that meets in the external world what has been developed in the internal world. The fact that a change in yourself can produce a similar change in your fate, your environments, your circumstances, in brief, everything in your outer world, may not seem clear at first; but it is easily demonstrated to be the truth when we analyze the relationship that exists between man and the world in which he lives. Everything that exists in your outer world has a correspondent in your inner world. This inner correspondent is the cause that has either created or attracted its external counterpart, and the process is easily understood.

To state it briefly, environment corresponds with ability. Circumstances are the aggregation of events brought about by your own actions and associations and friends, which follow the law of like attracting like. That environment is the direct effect of ability may not seem true when we observe that there are many people living in luxury that have practically no ability, but we must first demonstrate that these people have no ability. We shall find that those who have actually accumulated their own wealth have ability, in fact, exceptional ability, though they may not always have employed it according to the exact principles of justice. On the other hand, when we understand the process of creation we shall find that ability employed according to principle will produce far greater results than when it is employed unjustly. Therefore, the law underlying the power of ability to create its own environment acts wholly in the favor of him who lives according to the highest ideals of life.

This fact becomes more evident when we discern that success is not measured simply by the accumulation of things, but also by the accumulation of those elements in life that pertain to quality and worth in man's interior nature. It is wealth in the mental and the spiritual worlds that has the greatest value or the greatest power in promoting the welfare and the happiness of man, and this higher wealth can be accumulated only by those who are living according to their ideals. However, the accumulation of mental and spiritual wealth will have a direct tendency to increase the power and the capacity of practical ability, and practical ability when scientifically applied will tend to increase tangible wealth; that is, to improve the value and the worth of external environments. When we consider this subject from the universal view-point we shall find a perfect correspondent existing between the size of a man's possessions, physical, mental and spiritual, and the size of his brains, taking the term "brains" to signify ability, capacity and worth in the largest sense; but the size of brains can be increased perpetually. We therefore conclude that possessions in the larger sense can be increased perpetually, and he who is perpetually increasing his possessions on all the planes of his life is constantly changing his fate for the better. We shall also find that when a person increases the power of his own life he will bring about, through his own actions, new events, and these new events will produce new circumstances.

To change circumstances is to change fate; and whatever the change may be in fate, circumstances or events it will be a change for the better, if the increase of power is applied according to the principles of ideals. Again, when a person develops quality and superiority in himself he will, through the law of attraction, meet friends and associations that are after his own heart. In other words, he will enter a world where his ideals, both as to persons and as to things, are constantly being made real in every sphere of his present state of existence. He is thus creating for himself a better fate in every sense of the term and opening doors and pathways to a larger and a more beautiful future than he has ever realized before; but the beginning is in himself; in fact, every change for the better must begin within the life of man himself, and whoever will begin to change for the better in the within will positively realize greater and greater changes for the better in the without.

CHAPTER XX

BUILDING YOUR OWN
IDEAL WORLD

To build your own ideal world, the first essential is to begin to build in the real everything that you can discern in the ideal; and the second essential is to continue to rebuild your ideal world according to higher and higher ideals. However congenial or desirable or perfect our world may be, we should continue to improve upon it constantly. When we cease to promote progression we return to the ways of retrogression. One of the principal causes of undesirable environments or unexpected reverses among the more capable is found in the tendency to "stop, rest and enjoy" what we have gained whenever conditions are fairly satisfactory. It is the mind that is ever creating the new and ever recreating everything according to higher ideals that is always free and that is always enjoying the best. No one can be in bondage to the lesser who is constantly rising out of the lesser, and he who is ever growing into the best is constantly enjoying the best. In the last analysis, retrogression is the only cause of bondage, while constant progression is the only cause of perfect freedom; and constant progression is promoted by the continuous recreation of everything in your world according to higher and higher ideals.

To begin, your entire mentality must be changed and constantly changed so as to correspond perfectly with your newest thoughts on every subject and your highest ideals of everything that you can discern in your life. The mind is the cause and is the source of every force that can act as a cause of whatever may be developed, expressed or worked out through yourself into your external world. Therefore, begin with the mind and with all the elements of the mind. All desires, motives and ambitions must be concentrated upon the larger and the perfect in their various spheres of action. All the mental states must be in harmony with each other, and with the outer as well as the inner conditions of life. All mental qualities must be expanded

and enlarged constantly, and consciousness must be trained to act perpetually upon the verge of the limitless. The entire world of thought must be
perpetually renewed, enlarged and perfected, and every step taken in the
mental world must be practically expressed and applied in the outer world.
In order to bring all the creative forces of mind into harmony with the goal
in view the ideal wished to be realized must be thoroughly established in
consciousness, and the goal in view must be constantly held before the
mental vision.

In the rebuilding of your own world one of the principal causes of failure will be found in a tendency to change in your plans, motives or desires;
therefore, do not permit yourself to entertain one group of desires to-day,
and a different group to-morrow, and do not permit your faith to fall into
periodical states of doubt. Decide upon what you wish to do, accomplish, promote and attain, and proceed to live, think and work for those
things, regardless of may happen. The powers within you follow the
predominating states of mind, and when these states are constantly changing, the creative forces will be employed simply in taking initial steps, but
never in completing anything. On the other hand, when your mental states,
desires, motives, plans, etc., continue to concentrate upon the one supreme
goal in view your creative forces will perpetually build toward that goal,
and you will be daily rebuilding your entire world according to the higher,
the better and the greater that you have in view. There are thousands of fine
minds that are down in the scale to-day and cannot get up, because they are
constantly changing their plans, motives and desires. To create a new world
you must fix in your mind what you wish to create, and then continue to
build until the complete structure is finished. Recreate your present world,
then constantly make it better, larger and more beautiful. All the elements
of your mind, both conscious and subconscious, must be constantly inspired
with your highest thought of the larger, the better and the more beautiful.
Not a single thought should enter your mind that is inferior or in the least
beneath your ideal of life, and not a single moment of discouragement or
doubt should ever be permitted. Fix your mind on the soul's vision and hold
it there through all sorts of circumstances or conditions. Do not waver for
a moment. Keep the eye single upon the heights and all the powers of your
being will build that great world that you can see in your mental vision as
you concentrate attention upon the heights.

The mind must be clean, strong and high. It is the mind that does things.
It is the mind that originates things. Therefore, if you wish to build for
yourself an ideal world, the mind must be ideal in every sense of the term,

and every element of the mind must always be its best and act at its best. To promote the right use of mind the imagination must be guided with the greatest of care. The imagination is one of the most important powers in the mind. The imagination when misdirected can produce more ills than any other faculty, and when properly directed can produce greater good than any other faculty. In fact, the imagination when scientifically applied becomes a marvelous power in the great creative process of the vast mental domain. Train the imagination to picture, not only the goal you have in view but all the highest ideals that you can possibly imagine as might exist within the realms of that goal. Train the imaging faculty to impress upon the mind only those superior qualities that you wish to incorporate in your new world, and whatever you impress upon the mind will be created in your mental world. To create superior qualities in the mental world means that you will create, as well as attract, the superior in your outer world, and you thus promote the building of an ideal world.

To build your own ideal world, the more opportunities that you can take advantage of the better, but opportunities come only to those who have demonstrated their worth. Prove to the world that you have worth, and you can have your choice of almost any opportunity that the world can offer. There is nothing that is in greater demand than great men and women— minds of ability and power, people who can do things. The great mind is constantly in the presence of opportunities to change his environment and his field of action; therefore, he may enter into a new world almost any time. Those opportunities, however, do not come of themselves; they come be- cause he has made himself equal to those opportunities. Make yourself equal to the best and you will meet the best. This is a law that is universal and is never known to fail. Make yourself a great power in your present sphere of action. Learn to do things better than they have ever been done before. Produce something for the world that the world wants and the gates to new and greater opportunities will open for you. Henceforth, you may secure almost anything that you may wish, and all the elements that may be neces- sary for you to employ in order to build the ideal world you have in mind may be readily obtained because you have placed yourself in touch with the limitless supply of the best that life can give.

Those who are in search for new and greater opportunities should elim- inate the belief that the best things have been said, that all great things have been done and that all remarkable discoveries have been made. The fact is we are just in the A B C of literature, invention, art, music, industrial achievements and extraordinary human attainments. The human race is now on the verge of hundreds of undeveloped fields that have just been discovered, and they have more possibilities in store than we have ever dreamed. Many of these possibilities when developed will supply the world with the very things that the present development of the race is demanding in every expression of thought and desire. It is therefore easier to attain greatness, and do something of exceptional value at the present time than it ever was before. The opportunities of this age are very numerous, and some of them hold possibilities that are actually marvelous. Those who will prepare themselves to meet the requirements of this age will therefore find a number of rich fields already at hand, and all minds can prepare themselves as required. Every person of moderate intelligence can, in a short time, place himself in the path of some of these new opportunities, and all minds can find better opportunities in their present spheres if they will proceed to become more than they are.

Train all the elements of your being to work toward a higher goal and you will bring forth into expression those greater powers that will make for you a mentality that the world will demand for its highest places of action and achievement. When you proceed to build in yourself an ideal mental world—a mental world of power, ability, capacity and high worth you will find it necessary to adapt this mental world to the external world in such a way as to promote harmony of action. The added power of your new mental world must work in harmony with your external world if practical results are to be secured. Circumstances come from personal actions; therefore, to change circumstances, personal actions must be changed, and to change personal actions your ideal mental life must be expressed in your personal life, and to this end the development of a high degree of harmony becomes necessary. Harmony, however, will not only promote the united action of the inner world with the outer world, but will also tend to eliminate mistakes from personal actions, and when we eliminate mistakes from personal actions we will cease to produce adverse circumstances. When you are in perfect harmony with yourself and everything you eliminate mental confusion. You thus place your mind in that position where you can think clearly, reason logically and judge wisely. The result is, you will do the right thing at the right time. The elements of your life will be properly blended, and this is necessary in order to create an ideal world.

Another essential in the practical application of your ideals to real life is the development of what may be termed interior insight. This faculty will guide you perfectly in your expression of the finer things of life through the tangible things of life; in other words, you will see clearly how to combine the ideal with those actions that are promoted for the purpose of rebuilding the real. To combine the ideal with the real and make the two one, we must come into the closest possible relationship with the finer things in life and learn to use that phase of mind that is always in a cleared-up condition. The lower story of the mind is often darkened with false conclusions about things, and is frequently more or less filled with ideas that have been impressed through the senses; but in the upper story we can see things as they are; we can think clearly, and invariably come to the right conclusions. The power to think in the upper story of the mind, the cleared-up side of consciousness where the sun is always shining and where there are no clouds, is called interior insight. This interior insight not only discerns the ideal, but can discern the practical possibilities that every ideal may contain, and we make the ideal real when we proceed to develop and apply in actual life those practical possibilities that our ideals may contain. Interior insight will also elevate all our mental faculties and cause those faculties to function with far greater efficiency. In fact, the entire mind will be lifted up into a state of greater power, greater brilliancy and greater ability for high and efficient mental expression.

To develop interior insight aim to use consciousness in the discernment of what may be termed the spirit of all things. Do not simply think of things as they appear on the surface, but try to think of things as they are in the spirit of their interior existence. The mere effort to do this will develop the power to look through things or to look into things; and the growth of this power promotes interior insight. You may thus discern clearly the real worth and the real possibilities that exist in the lofty goal that you have in view, and by keeping the eye single upon that lofty goal, never wavering for a moment, all the powers of your being will work together and build for those greater things that you can see upon the heights of that goal. Thus your entire world in the within as well as in the without will constantly be re-created and rebuilt according to the likeness of your supreme ideals; in consequence, you will not only build for yourself an ideal world, but you will be building for yourself a world that is ever becoming more and more ideal, and to live in such a world is ideal living indeed. The world that is ever becoming more and more ideal is *the* world in which to live, and the power to create such a world is now at hand in every human mind.

JUST BE
GLAD

All things respond to the call of rejoicing; all things gather where life is a song.

This is the message of the new order, the new life and the new time. It is the golden text of the great gospel of human sunshine. It is the central truth of that sublime philosophy of existence, which declares that the greatest good is happiness, and that heaven is here and now.

To live in the spirit of this wonderful message; to be a living example of this great gospel, to work out in everyday life the principle of this inspiring philosophy, the first and most important thing to do, is to lay aside our sorrows and glooms, and just be glad.

Wherever you are, or whatever has happened, just be gald. Be glad because you are here. You are here in a beautiful world; and all that is beautiful may be found in this world. It is a world wherein all that is rich in life may be enjoyed beyond measure; a world wherein happiness may overflow eternally in every human heart; a world wherein all the dreams of life may be realized, and all the visions of the soul made true. Then why should we not be glad; first of all, that we are here; that we are in this world; that we may stay here for a long time if we so desire, and enjoy every minute to the full.

The real truth is that this world is nothing less than a limitless sea of happiness, the vastness and glory of which we are just beginning to know. And life itself is a song, while time is one eternal symphony. To be in tune with life, therefore, and to be in harmony with the endless music of time, we must of necessity be glad. But after we have learned to be glad, under every circumstance, it is no longer a necessity; it is a privilege, and has become a part of our active, living, thinking self.

Just be glad, and you always will be glad. You will have better reason to be glad. You will have more and more things to make you glad. For great is the power of sunshine, especially human sunshine. It can change anything, transform anything, re-make anything, and cause anything to become as fair and beautiful as itself.

Just be glad and your fate will change; a new life will begin and a new future will dawn for you. All things that are good and desirable will begin to come into your world in greater measure, and you will be enriched far beyond your expectations, both from the without and from the within. And the cause of the change is this, that **all things respond to the call of rejoicing; all things gather where life is a song.**

When you are tempted to feel discouraged or disappointed, be glad instead. Know that you can, say that you will, and stand uncompromisingly upon your resolve. Be strong and be glad. For when strength and rejoicing combine in your soul, every trace of gloom or despair must disappear; because such conditions can exist only where weakness is the rule and mastery the exception.

Combine strength with rejoicing and you will exercise a magic power— you will possess a secret that will serve you royally no matter what your difficulties or obstacles may be. All joy is light; and it is the light that dispels the darkness.

When things are not to your liking, be glad nevertheless, for the glad heart can cause all things to be as we wish them to be. When things do not give you pleasure, proceed instead to create pleasure in your own heart and soul. And you can if you will always be glad. Besides, things will soon change for the better if you continue in the spirit of rejoicing. It is the law that all good things will sooner or later come and be, where the greatest happiness is to be found. Therefore, be happiness in yourself, regardless of times, seasons or circumstances.

When things do not please you, resolve to please yourself by being glad, and you can add immeasurably to your happiness in this simple manner. Then you must remember that the fountain of joy within your own soul is infinitely greater than all external sources of joy combined. But as far as we can, we should add the joys from without to the joys from within, and in all things be glad.

Rejoice in your strength, rejoice in your talents and powers, rejoice in the wonders of your own nature. For there is far more in you than you ever dreamed. So whatever may come, you are greater than it all, richer than it all. And knowing this, why should you not be glad.

When evil befalls you, consider the fact that the good that is yet in your possession is many times as great as all the evil you could ever know. Consider this stupendous fact and be glad. Then remember, with rejoicing, that neither evil nor wrong can exist very long in the radiant sunshine of a glad triumphant soul.

If you have lost anything, have no regrets. Be glad and begin again. Be glad that you can begin again. Be glad to know that the future is always richer and better than the past if we only try to make it so. Then forget the loss, and rejoice in the fact that you have the power to secure something far better in return. You know that you have this power; then you can never be otherwise than glad.

Whatever comes or not, sing again and again the song of "the soul victorious"; and mean it with your whole heart. Enter into this song with all the power of mind and spirit, for it is always that which we know and sincerely believe that contains the greater worth and power.

When you resolve to be glad at all times and under every circumstance, resolve also to give your whole heart and soul to the spirit of your rejoicing. Give power to your gladness, and give life to your song. Open the way for all the sunshine of your soul; and see that every sunbeam from within be one of power as well as one of joy.

It is the full joy of the soul that makes the heart young and the mind great. For as it is in nature, so it is also in man. It is the full glory of the noonday sun that quickens the earth, that makes the fields green, that causes the flowers to bloom. Where the sun is strong all growth is luxurious and all nature bountiful. It is the same when the sunshine of the soul is full, strong and constant in the daily life of man. So therefore rejoice with great joy. Rejoice always and give life and power to your joy.

There is magic in the sunshine of the soul; there is a charmed power in the radiant splendor of a beaming countenance. Such a countenance can dispel anything that may threaten to give disappointment or dismay. So remember to be glad and mean it. It is the greatest remedy in the world, and the greatest protector in the world. It can harm nothing for it turns all wrong into right. It is the sunshine from within that causes all darkness to cease to be. It therefore brings good to everybody, and he who is always glad is always adding to the welfare of every member of the race.

When fate seems unkind, do not be unkind to yourself by becoming disheartened or dismayed. Instead, rejoice in the great fact that you are greater and stronger than any fate; that you have the power to master your whole life, and determine your destiny according to your own invincible will. Then resolve that you will begin at once to prove that strength, and cause all the elements of fate to come with you, and work with you, in building for that greater future which you have so often longed for in your visions and dreams.

Therefore, whatever your fate may be, just be glad. You can change it all. And as you proceed to exercise this divine right, the darkness of today will become the sunshine of tomorrow, and the disappointments of the present will become the pastures green of the future.

When calamities or catastrophes have overtaken your life, do not think that fate or Providence has ordered it so. Do not think that it has to be. Instead, forget the sorrow and the loss, and congratulate yourself over the fact that you now have the privilege to build for greater things than you ever knew before. Do not weep over loss; but rejoice to think that now you are called upon to prove the greater wisdom and power within you. You have been taken out into a new world. Before you lie vast fields of undeveloped and unexplored opportunities—fields that you would not have known had not this seeming misfortune come upon you. So count it all joy. All things are working together for a greater good. Now it is for you to come forward in joy and accept the greater good. A richer life and a greater future are in store. Therefore, rejoice and be glad, and give strength to your rejoicing. Let your soul repeat again and again that sweet re-assuring refrain—just be glad. In that refrain there is comfort and peace; it lifts the burdens, removes the clouds, dispels the gloom; it takes away the sadness and the loss, and all is well again. And naturally so, for all things respond to the call of rejoicing; all things gather where life is a song.

There is more to live for than you ever imagined. Thus far most of us have only touched the merest surface of human existence; we are only on the verge of the splendor of life as it is; we are standing on the outside, so to speak, of the real mansion of mind and soul; and one reason is we live too much in the limitations of our disappointments, our lost opportunities, our blasted hopes, our vanquished dreams. We remain in that small world, deploring fate, when, if we would only permit mind and soul to take wings and go out upon the vastness of real existence, we would find, not only freedom, but a life infinitely richer than we had ever dreamed.

But if mind and soul are to take wings in this fashion, we must learn to be glad. The heart that lives in disappointments is heavy. It will sink into the lowlands, and remain among the marshes and the bogs. But the glad heart ascends to the mountain tops. Therefore it is when we have such a heart that we can go out in search of new worlds, new opportunities, new possibilities, new joys. And the glad heart always finds that for which it goes in search. The reason is simple; **for all things respond to the call of rejoicing; all things gather where life is a song.**

The great soul is always in search of ways and means for adding to the welfare of others. But no way is better, greater or more far-reaching than this—just be glad.

Life becomes worth the living only when the living of life makes living more worth while for an ever increasing number. It is only the joys we share that give happiness; it is only the thoughts we express that enrich our own minds; it is only the strength we use in actual helpfulness that makes our own souls strong. Therefore, to add to the pleasures of others, is to add to our own pleasure; to add to the wealth and comfort of others is to add in like manner to our own. This the great soul knows; and every soul is great that has learned to be glad regardless of what may come or go in the world.

To be glad at all times is to be of greater service to mankind than any other thing that we can do. If we have not the power or ability to apply ourselves more tangibly in behalf of others, we can instead be glad. We can always give sunshine. And we shall find that just being glad is frequently sufficient, even when needs seem great and circumstances extreme. In most instances it is all the world wants; but it does want human sunshine so much, that those who can give it at all times need not do anything else to reap immortal fame.

Surround us with an abundance of human sunshine, and the day's work will easily be done; we shall, with far less effort, overcome our obstacles; our troubles will largely be removed, and our burdens entirely laid aside. Give us the privilege to work to the music of rejoicing and our work will become a pleasure; every duty will become a privilege, and all we do will be well done. This is the way the world thinks and feels. So therefore be glad. Give an abundance of human sunshine everywhere and always, and you will please the world immensely.

Then turn to the home. Can we picture anything more beautiful than a home where every soul therein is a sunbeam; where every countenance is ever lit up with the light of rejoicing; where every word spoken rings with the music of love; and where every thought, uttered or unexpressed, is inspired by the spirit of joy.

It is in such a home that the beautiful, the great and the wonderful in human nature will grow; it is in such a home that our highest ideals will be realized and the divine within find full and resplendent expression. But it is not necessary to describe the pleasures and privileges of such a home; only to say that if you want such a home, just be glad.

Then consider again the worker, and where the workers must gather; what a power for good human sunshine would be in such a place. Consider how all things change when the glad soul arrives, and how all work lightens when the spirit of joy is abroad. And every man has the power to dispense the spirit of joy wherever he may work or live. Every man can ease the ways of others in this remarkable manner; and the secret is simple—just be glad.

The work you do, be it with mind or muscle, invariably conveys the spirit of your own soul. Therefore work in the spirit of joy and your work will be the product of joy—a rare product—the best of its kind.

It is the man who blends rejoicing with his work who does the best work; it is the man who deeply and sincerely enjoys his work who gives the greatest worth to his work; and the more worth we give to our work the more of the rich and the worthy our work will bring to us.

We realize therefore that it is profitable in every way to learn to be glad. But it is not only profitable to ourselves; also to all others that we may reach through word or deed. Then the profit that comes from the art of being glad is never the result of selfishness. The glad heart is never selfish. The sunbeam does not dance and sing to please its own restricted desire; it does what it does because it is what it is—a happy, carefree sunbeam. It is the same with the glad heart, it sings because it has become the spirit of song; and all are charmed with the song.

No selfish heart can really be glad. No soul that acts solely for personal gain can enter the spirit of joy; and no man who seeks only his own pleasure and comfort can ever take part in the music of rejoicing. And yet, the glad heart receives far more of everything of worth in life than does the one who forgets gladness in pursuit of gain for self alone. And again the answer is simple. For all things respond to the call of rejoicing; all things gather where life is a song.

BE glad for the things you have, and you will find you have far more than you thought. Then you will not miss, in the least, the things you have not. Besides, the happier you are over what has come to you, the more and the more will come to you in the future. This is indeed a great secret, and if universally applied would cause want to disappear from the face of the whole earth.

Be glad, for nothing is as serious as it seems to be. Then remember that sunshine can banish any gloom; and you can create in yourself all the sunshine you need; so just be glad.

When trouble and misfortunes surround you, just be glad. The glad heart and the cheerful soul always make things better. It is the happy heart that has the most courage; it is the joyous soul that has the greatest power; and it is the presence of sunshine that keeps darkness and gloom away.

When things go wrong, do not become disheartened; it is much easier to set them right when your soul is full of sunshine; so just be glad. It is the best way out.

When all seems lost, remember that it requires strength to regain everything; and it is the glad heart that remains strong. When the heart saddens, weakness will overtake you, and it will not be possible to regain your position. So therefore be glad regardless of what may transpire. It is one of the royal paths to everything that life holds dear.

But sadness does not merely bring weakness, it also brings illness, and age, and it shortens the length of our days. In gladness, however, there is health and youth, strength and longevity. The glad heart will not grow old, nor can illness ever enter where the spirit of joy is supreme.

When in pain, be glad; and you can. Be glad that you are greater than pain. Be glad that pain has come to prevent you from going wrong. Be glad that you can prevent all pain in the future. And be glad that it is wholly impossible for pain to come any more after gladness has become the rule of your life.

For your own advancement, be glad. The spirit of joy is the spirit that makes the heart kind, the soul strong and the mind brilliant. It is this spirit that makes for greatness, for nobleness, for excellence, for worth. We repeat it, therefore, just be glad.

Would you be a pleasure and a delight to others, then be glad always. And would you add to the measure of your own joy, then give all the joy you can to the largest possible number. This you can do by living more and more in the spirit of that joy that is in itself the essence of real joy. And it is better to become the living incarnation of this spirit than to possess all the wealth in the world. It is better to have attained to perpetual gladness than to have become the crowned monarch of an entire solar system. The reason is simple. The glad heart is the sunshine of all life, a benediction to every man, a perpetual blessing to everything in creation.

Inspire every atom in your own being to thrill with the spirit of joy; not the joy of sentiment, but the joy of strength, of triumph, of victory—the joy that inwardly feels its power sublime as the soul ascends in masterful mien to the splendor of empyrean heights. It is such a joy that makes life a power, a blessing, an inspiration. And it is such a joy that comes perpetually to him who causes his soul to repeat again and again, that sweet reassuring refrain—just be glad.

Sing ever the song of triumph, of victory, of freedom—the song that declares the supremacy of the spirit over all that may be temporal or wrong. Sing the song of the soul rising above adversity or loss, proclaiming its freedom over all that is or is to be. When the soul continues to sing in this triumphant manner, all the elements of life follow the music of that which is always well; and in such a spirit everything must be always well.

Be glad, and smile with the smile that is sincere, the smile that shines just as sweetly and as naturally as the sunbeam. It is such a smile that is a smile indeed; it is such a smile that comes from the soul—from the soul that is ever singing—just be glad. And how soon such a smile can change the world.

Meet adversity with such a smile; charm away tribulation with such a smile bursting forth into song; and let the music of the soul restore peace, love and harmony where these might have been absent. Then be stronger than adversity; rise superior to tribulation, and know that you are infinitely greater than all that is unfortunate or wrong.

In the midst of adversity combine strength with rejoicing, and fate must change. Before that music of the soul that is so high and so strong that it stirs the depth of every soul, all the world pays homage on a bended knee. And wisely, because such a power can change anything, transform anything, elevate anything, emancipate anything.

Go forth therefore into life with strength in your soul and music in your soul, and the future shall steadily and surely shape itself to comply with your dearest wishes and your highest aspirations. Array yourself in the strength of truth, conviction, courage, faith, resolution, victory and triumph; and add to these another raiment—the music of gladness—and yours will be a life filled with glory, power and light.

The spirit of gladness when combined with the spirit of strength, will enlarge the mind, expand the soul, and enrich all thought and life; it is the moving mystery from within that makes everything good in human nature grow; that makes man noble and great; that makes human existence a world of immeasurable richness and sublime worth. It is the same spirit that makes life "a thing of beauty and a joy forever"; that makes the lovely and the true become the tangible and the real; that causes all things we have loved so much come forth into our world in abundance. Therefore be glad when you feel strong, and be strong when you feel glad; and always know that you can.

Whatever your present position may be, there is a way from where you now stand that leads to better things and greater things for you than you ever knew. So whatever happens, just be glad. Live in the spirit of gladness; think in the spirit of joy; thus you will be able to see the royal path, for the mind that is illumined with gladness is never in the dark, never under the clouds of doubt or dismay.

When overtaken with calamity or tribulation, come forth undaunted and undismayed. Inspire the soul to reach for the high realms of victory and joy; and hold fast to that lofty position even though the whole world seem to disappear beneath your feet. With such a victory for your strong inspiration, your own soul will prove more than sufficient for all that life may demand of you.

Then remember that mankind stands ready to welcome and exalt every soul whose strength is greater than any circumstance, whose joy is greater than any tribulation, and whose faith is greater than all doubts and failures in the world.

When your plans cannot be carried through at present, do not feel downcast or discouraged. Just be glad. Give gladness to your mind and you give clearness to your mind; and a clear mind can see how to evolve better plans.

When your dreams do not come true and your ideals do not become real, refuse to be sad or disconsolate. Instead, rejoice with great joy to know that you are greater than your dreams, and wholly sufficient unto yourself regardless of what may transpire in the real or the ideal. Thus you will give expression to that greater power within you which surely can make your ideals real and make all your dreams come true.

Prove that your cherished dreams are not necessary to your happiness, and all of those dreams will come true. Prove that you do not need the things you want, and you will get them, provided of course that you give all that is in you to the life you live. Prove that you already are sufficient in yourself, and have sufficient in the richness of your own world, and more and more will gather for you, both in the within and in the without. It is much gathering more; much in the within gathering more everywhere; it is your own strength inspiring all things to come with strength; it is the spirit of the great life aroused in yourself causing all things of greatness and worth to come and gather in the entire world of your own life. And it is in this spirit that we live and move and have our being, when the soul continues to sing that sweet reassuring refrain—just be glad.

Whatever may be, therefore, or come to pass, continue in the spirit of this refrain. For to live in the music of such a refrain is to enjoy life infinitely more than it was ever enjoyed before. And that in itself is much indeed. Besides, be glad whatever happens, and something better will happen. When the good happens, let the soul sing with rejoicing; then greater good will happen, and there will be cause for greater rejoicing. When that which is not good happens, let the soul sing in the same triumphant spirit, and the power of that spirit will cause all ills to vanish as darkness before the glory of the morn.

Remove the cause of sadness by giving all the elements of life to the spirit of joy. Smile away the darkness and the gloom; sing away the discord and the pain; banish tribulation with rejoicing; then you may in truth be joyous and be glad; and every hour of your long and triumphant life will add new evidence to that great inspiring statement—all things respond to the call of rejoicing; all things gather where life is a song.

WHETHER we believe that life was made for happiness or that happiness was made for life, matters not. The fact remains that he alone can live the most and enjoy the best who takes for his motto—just be glad. Whatever comes, or whatever may fail to come, this one thing he will always remember—just be glad. Though every mind in the world may give darkness, his will continue to give light; and though all may be lost, so there seems nothing more to give, he will not forget to give happiness.

The one great thing to do under every circumstance and in the midst of every event is this—just be glad. Wherever you may be, add sunshine. Whatever your position may be, be also a human sunbeam. What a difference when the sunbeam comes in; then why should the sunbeam remain without?

There is a sunbeam in every heart. Why hide it at any time? Does not the world need your smiles? Is not everybody made happier and better when in the presence of a radiant countenance? Do we ever forget the face that shines as the sun? And does not such a memory continue to give us strength and inspiration all through the turnings and complexities of life? We are not here to give sadness, but joy. We were not made to hide our souls in a dark thunder cloud, but to let the spirit shine in all its splendor and beauty. We are made to make life an endless song, and the sweet refrain of that beautiful song is—just be glad.

When things go wrong, just be glad. It is sunshine that brings forth the flowers from the cold and soggy earth. It is light-heartedness that puts to flight the burdens of life. It is the smile of human sweetness that dispels the chilly night of isolation and brings friendship and love to the bosom of the yearning soul. Then why be sad when gladness can do so much? Why be sad for a single moment when the smile of a single moment has the power even to change the course of human destiny. We all remember how soon a smile of God can change the world. Why not always live in that magical smile and just be glad? **Then we should remember that all things respond to the song of rejoicing; all things gather where life is a song.**

Do you think that life is too difficult for smiles, and that you have too much to pass through to ever have happiness? Then remember that the glad heart knows no difficulty. The sunbeam even smiles at darkness, and converts the blackness of the storm into a brilliant rainbow. Just be glad, and your tears shall also become a bow of promise; yes, and more, for in that promise you shall discern the unmistakable signs of a brighter day upon the coming morn.

Do not think that happiness must keep its distance so long as you have so much to pass through. The more you have to pass through, the more you need happiness. It is the shining countenance that never turns back; it is the glad heart that finds strength to go on; it is the mind with the most sunshine that can see the most clearly where to go and how to act that the goal in view may be gained.

Just be glad, and half the burden is gone. Just be glad, and your work becomes mostly pleasure. Just be glad, and you take the keenest delight in meeting even the greatest of obstacles and the most difficult of problems.

When you meet reverses, just be glad; for do we not again remember how soon a smile of God can change the world? It is not gloom that dispels darkness; it is not disconsolance that makes the mind brilliant and the soul strong. But if we would turn the tide of ill fortune we need all our brilliancy and all our strength. To master fate, to conquer destiny, to make life our own, we must be all there is in us to be. Then we must remember that it is sunshine that makes the flowers grow, and that transforms the acorn into a great and massive oak. Everything in nature, and in man, the crowning glory of nature, responds with pleasure to the magic touch of the smiling sunbeam. **For again we must remember that all things respond to the call of rejoicing; all things gather where life is a song.**

Promise yourself that whatever may come you will always remember—just be glad. When good things come into life, gladness will make them better. When things come that should not have come, gladness will so brighten your mind that you can see clearly how to turn everything to good account. Whatever happens or not, just be glad, and it will be much better than it possibly could have been otherwise. Therefore, gladness is not a mere sentiment. It pays. It is not a luxury for the favored few alone. It is a necessity that all should secure in abundance.

If it is your belief that there is nothing in your life for which you can justly be glad, stop and count your blessings. You will surprise yourself; and you will then and there resolve never to depreciate yourself again. Henceforth, you will find it easier to be glad; and you will also find that the more things you are glad for, the more things you will have to be glad for. Gladness is a magnet and it draws more and more of everything that can increase gladness. Just be glad—always and under every circumstance, and nothing shall be withheld from you that can add to your welfare and happiness.

Should you find it easy to be glad when things go right, and difficult to be glad when things go wrong, you are not creating your own sunshine; and it is only the sunshine that we create ourselves, in our own world, that makes things grow in our own world. Be glad because you want to be glad, regardless of events, and you will have found that fountain of joy within that is ever ready to overflow. Be glad at all times because it is best to be glad at all times; and be glad in the presence of everything because gladness makes it better for everything.

Just be glad, and the world will be kind to you. The sunbeam has no occasion for regrets. It is always welcome; it is always loved. Just be glad, and you will have friends without number; and it is he who has many friends—friends that are good and true, who finds everything that is rich and beautiful in human existence. Just be glad, and you will be sought for, far and wide. The world is not looking for gloom and depression; it is looking for sunshine and joy.

Just be glad, even though the whole world be against you, and all the elements of nature be in a conspiracy to place you in the hands of destruction. Even at such a time, just be glad. Thus you prove your strength. And he who can prove that he is stronger than any adversary, will win the respect—yes, and the friendship, of every adversary. What was against you will be for you. And this was your secret—you refused to be downcast, you refused to weaken, you refused to be less than your greatest self—even when everything seemed lost, you were strong enough to be true to all that you knew to be true, and you tuned your life to the music of that sweetest of all refrains—just be glad. Because you were glad, even when there was nothing to make you glad, you proved that you deserved everything that has the power to make you glad. And that which we truly deserve must come to remain as our own.

Just be glad. Whether there is anything to be glad for or not, just be glad. It is the royal path to happiness. It is the royal path to all that is worthy and beautiful in life. Above all things, possess gladness, and you will soon possess those things that produce gladness. Be your own sunbeam, and you will attract a million sunbeams. Be your own source of your own joy, and you will attract everything and everybody that can add to your joy. To him that hath shall be given. And he already hath who has found the riches of his own nature. To find those riches is the first step. All else must follow. All other things will be added. And to find those riches, use well every talent you possess. Then whatever comes, just be glad. **For all things respond to the call of rejoicing; all things gather where life is a song.**

ABOUT THE AUTHOR

Christian D. Larson (1874–1962) was born in Iowa, the third of seven children to Norwegian immigrants. Raised in the American heartland, Larson was headed for a career in the ministry. In 1894, he enrolled in a Lutheran seminary but left within a year after he embraced a more ecumenical and mystical worldview. In 1901, at age twenty-seven, Larson launched one of the first metaphysical journals devoted to positive-thinking, *Eternal Progress*. He moved to California and grew into a popular New Thought and inspirational writer and speaker, admired throughout the United States for his more than forty books. Also an editor of *Science of Mind* magazine, Larson was an influence on motivational figures such as Ernest Holmes and Norman Vincent Peale. Larson's most enduring work is the meditation called "The Optimist Creed," which he originally published in 1910 as "Promise Yourself." In 1922, it was officially adopted as the manifesto of Optimist International and today is quoted around the world. His other notable works include *The Pathway of Roses, Your Forces and How to Use Them, Just Be Glad, The Ideal Made Real*, and *Mastery of Self*, all featured in this volume.

Printed in the United States
by Baker & Taylor Publisher Services